Adolf Grünbaum

Thinking Clearly about Psychology
Volume 2: Personality and Psychopathology

Thinking Clearly about Psychology

Thinking Clearly about Psychology

Volume 2: Personality and Psychopathology

Edited by William M. Grove and Dante Cicchetti

Essays in honor of Paul E. Meehl

University of Minnesota Press
Minneapolis   Oxford

Published by the University of Minnesota Press
2037 University Avenue Southeast, Minneapolis, MN 55414
Printed in the United States of America on acid-free paper

Library of Congress Cataloging-in-Publication Data

Thinking clearly about psychology : essays in honor of Paul E. Meehl / edited
by Dante Cicchetti and William M. Grove.
p.   cm.
Includes bibliographical references and index.
Contents: v. 2. Personality and psychopathology.
ISBN 0-8166-1892-5 (hc : v. 2)
ISBN 0-8166-1918-2 (hc : set)
1. Psychology, Clinical.   2. Psychology.   I. Meehl, Paul E. (Paul Everett),
1920-   .   II. Cicchetti, Dante.   III. Grove, William M.
RC467.T43   1991
150—dc20   90-15474
                                                 CIP

A CIP catalog record for this book is available from the British Library

Contents

Contents of Volume 1

Matters of Public Interest

Personality and Abilities

The Originating Self
B. F. Skinner

Is there a place in a scientific analysis of behavior for an initiating, originating, creative self? Having dispensed with God as a creator, must science also dispense with that image of God called Man? We feel the need for a creative god because we see the world but very little of the process through which it came into existence, a product but not the production. Perhaps it is because we see human behavior but very little of the process through which it comes into existence that we feel the need for a creative self. With behavior, however, we have other evidence: We can see or introspectively observe our own bodies as we behave, and it is possible that what we see is the process of creation. Call it mind or will. Is it only retrospectively that we have attributed the creation of the world to a greater Mind or Will—to a god in the image of man?

It does not matter, because science has changed all that. Astronomers may have no explanation of the big bang, but they are giving an increasingly plausible account of the formation of the chemical elements and of their distribution in space. Chemistry suggests ways in which living things could have emerged from nonliving, and biologists explain the origin of species, including *homo sapiens*, through natural selection. There is less for a creator to do.

Behavior has also come within the scope of a scientific analysis. It is the product of three kinds of selection, the first of which, natural selection, is the field of ethology. The second, operant conditioning, is the field of behavior analysis. The third, the evolution of the social contingencies of reinforcement we call cultures, explains the large repertoires of behavior characteristic of the human species.

The terms we use to designate a behaving individual depend upon the type of selection. Natural selection gives us *organism*, operant conditioning gives us *person*, and, it will be argued here, the evolution of cultures gives us *self*. An organism is more than a body; it is a body that does things; both "organ" and "organism" are etymologically related to "work." The organism is the executor.

3

Person is derived from the word for the masks through which actors spoke their lines in the Greek and Roman theater. A mask identified the role the actor was playing; it marked him as a character. By wearing different masks, he could play different roles. Contingencies of operant reinforcement have rather similar effects. Starting with the organism that has evolved through natural selection, they build the behavioral repertoires called persons. Different contingencies build different persons, possibly within the same skin, as the classical examples of multiple personalities show.

In a long chapter called "Self-Control" in *Science and Human Behavior* I used "self" very much as I would now use "person." I reviewed techniques through which a person manipulated the environmental variables of which his behavior was a function and distinguished between controlling and controlled selves, defining them as repertoires of behavior. But that was thirty years ago, and behavioristic theory has advanced. A clearer distinction can now be made between person and self: a person, as a repertoire of behavior, can be observed by others; the self, as a set of accompanying internal states, is observed only through feeling or introspection.

Several problems of usage need to be mentioned. We need the reflexive pronoun self because there are other people in the world. It is only when there are others in the world that we need to distinguish a self. The self I see in a mirror or video recording is the person others see. "I made it myself" means little more than that I was the one who made it. In Webster's *Third New International Dictionary* there are about 500 entries beginning with "self-," and in most of them the word is merely reflexive.

That is not the self we are considering here, however. Only under special kinds of verbal contingencies do we respond to certain features of our body. Looking back at an unusual occasion, I may report that "I was a different person," but others could say the same thing. "I was not myself," however, suggests that I *felt* like a different person. The self is what a person *feels like*. It is the self we know when we follow the advice of the Delphic oracle, "Know thyself," and it is the self we change when, in response to the injunction "Behave yourself!" we do more than "behave differently."

There is another problem of usage. The English language evolved when it was generally believed that behavior started within the individual. One sensed the environment and acted upon it. In a behavioral analysis the environment acts first, in either of two ways. As a consequence it reinforces behavior and an operant comes into existence. As a setting it elicits or evokes behavior. Very few English words, certainly not "person" or "self," are at home in such a behavioral version. We are more readily understood when we ask why people observe certain conditions of their bodies than when we ask why the conditions evoke self-observation. The traditional version can scarcely be avoided in practical use, or in paraphrasing technical expressions, even though the self then remains the very initiator whose existence we are questioning.

In what follows, however, we shall look at a different interpretation of several common examples.

Self-Observation

Under what verbal contingencies of reinforcement, for example, do we observe our self and report that we are doing so? An organism seldom behaves effectively without responding to its own body. The contingencies responsible for the behavior itself explain that kind of self-stimulation. Very different contingencies account for self-observation. The first to evolve may have been associated with modeling. To model is to behave in ways which are easily observed and imitated, first by others but possibly also by the modelers themselves. Operant modeling, and the self-observation it facilitates, appears to be exclusively human; reinforcement from the behavior of an imitator is apparently too long delayed to reinforce modeling in other species. (Deferred consequences raise no problem for the modeling due to natural selection, because the survival of the species is necessarily a deferred consequence.)

Contingencies promoting self-observation must have multiplied rapidly with the advent of vocal verbal behavior. (Modeling is verbal, although not necessarily vocal, in the sense that the reinforcement is mediated by other persons: We cannot imitate unless there is a model, and we are not modeling unless our behavior has been imitated.) When the vocal musculature of the human species came under operant control, people could tell others what to do as well as show them, and it must then have been much easier to see and to talk about what they themselves were doing. (Doing includes sensing, of course. We not only observe that we do things, we observe that we see things.)

Many verbal contingencies promoting self-observation are more explicit. People are asked to report what they are doing or why they are doing it, and when they reply they may tell themselves as well as others. Psychotherapy is often an effort to improve self-observation, to bring more of what is done and why it is done "into consciousness." In both psychotherapy and literature, character analysis is often called a "search for the self." More often, it is a search for the "real self," a self that must be searched for presumably because it has been hidden. Behavior is most often hidden, from oneself as well as from others, when it has been punished, and that may explain why the real self is so often badly behaved. Witness the self that is said to have been exposed by de Sade. (In such a case "real" could mean "primitive," because what is felt is due either to natural selection or to reinforcing consequences—food, sex, and aggressive damage—similar to consequences which must have played a predominant role in natural selection.)

Self-Esteem

A culture commends and rewards those of its members who do useful or interesting things, in part by calling them and the things they do good or right. In the process, behavior is positively reinforced, and bodily conditions are generated that may be observed and valued by the person whose self it is. It is a self that is especially vulnerable to scientific analysis. I have pointed to a parallel in natural selection.[1] A woman has a baby. It is her baby and we give her credit for her achievement. However, geneticists tell us that she is not responsible for any of its features. She gave it half its genes, but she got them from her own father and mother. She has sheltered and nourished the growing fetus, but she has made no other contribution. In saying so, however, we seem to rob her of the credit she has received for having the baby and hence destroy a sense of worth.

An operant parallel is not as simple. A poet "has" a poem in the sense of writing it. It is his poem. Critics will reveal "influences," however, and if we knew enough about what he had read and done, we could presumably explain the whole poem. That seems to invalidate any commendation the poet has received from others and destroys his own sense of worth.

The Responsible Self

The self one esteems appears to be a product of the positively reinforcing practices of a social environment, but cultures more often control their members with aversive stimuli, either as negative reinforcers that strengthen wanted behavior or as punishments that suppress unwanted behavior. Cultures thus hold their members *responsible* for what they have done, and members "feel responsible."

They seldom protest, however, when a behavioral analysis shifts the responsibility to the environment. (The juvenile delinquent readily agrees that his early environment is responsible for his delinquency.) Instead, the usual response to a behavioral analysis is to protest the control it demonstrates, whether positive or negative. Thus, withholding food from a prisoner so that it can be used as a positive reinforcer is protested as a violation of the right to freedom from want, and the use of aversive stimuli, either as negative reinforcers or punishment, is protested as a violation of the right to freedom from fear.

Self-Confidence

Even though we are not actually in control of our behavior, is it not important that we *believe* that we are? Is it not true that it is only when we believe in ourselves that we do our best? But the self in which we have faith may be a product of doing well rather than the cause. When I have at last got the top off the child-proof aspirin bottle and exclaim, "I've done it!" I report an instance of behavior. If someone asks me whether I can get the top off and I say, "I believe I can," I am either making a prediction based upon past successes or reporting a bodily condition resulting from them. People who are not successful in what they do may lose faith in themselves, but a counselor may restore faith by reminding them of overlooked successes, thus restoring something of the bodily state they once felt. A more effective way of restoring belief in oneself, of course, is to restore successes, perhaps by simplifying contingencies of reinforcement.

A more immediate effect of success is often called self-confidence. The tennis player who makes a series of bad shots "loses confidence" and is often said to make other bad shots because he has lost it. A brilliant shot "restores his confidence," and he plays better. To put it another way, however, bad shots extinguish behavior in the sense of reducing its probability of occurrence, and good shots recondition it. One who has played badly may be on the point of giving up tennis altogether until a very successful day "changes his mind" in the sense of changing the probability of his playing. If the self-confidence gained from one fine play extends to a whole repertoire, better play is more likely to be due to what sportscasters call improved "concentration." The more strongly inclined one is to play, the less likely one is to be distracted.

The Rational Self

A different self seems to be felt when engaging in rule-governed behavior. That must have been the case when "person" meant the mask through which an actor spoke, because actors do not speak their own lines. They say and do what they are told to say and do. That is also true of those who take advice, observe rules, and obey laws. If that is all they do, they are not "being themselves." The bodily conditions they feel are not the products of contingencies to which they themselves have been exposed; they are indirect products of the contingencies which have affected those who gave the advice or formulated the rules. It is only when advice has been taken, rules observed, or laws obeyed, and reinforcing consequences have followed, that "the real self" can be felt.

Actors "know what they are saying," however, in the sense that they know their lines before they say them, and something of the sort may be said of those who take advice, observe rules, and obey laws. They "know what they are doing" in the sense that it has already been put into words. People who formulate descriptions of contingencies for their own use "know what they are doing" in that way and are said to act rationally. In reply to the question "Why did you do that?" one may simply mention a felt or introspectively observed state ("I wanted to do it" or "I felt like doing it"), or one may "give a reason" by alluding to a controlling variable. ("I intended to get a drink" or "I was afraid the rope would break.") Reasons are not consequences, however; they are the names of consequences.

We are said to have acted rationally when we can give reasons for our behavior, but most of our behavior is not rational in that sense. Contingencies of selection affect our behavior whether or not we recognize them. Freud is perhaps responsible for the fact that "rationalizing" suggests giving the *wrong* reasons. These are issues, however, which more directly concern the mind rather than the self.

The Mind and the Self

As the word for a felt or introspectively observed state that accompanies behavior, "self" is obviously close to "mind." Whenever the mind is said to do something, it is usually possible to substitute "organism" or "person."[2] The "vast resources of the human mind," for example, are the vast resources of the human species. Something of the sort can also be said of the self, but a useful distinction can still be made. Like the distinction between thinking and doing, it concerns the order of events. "I changed my mind" is not far from "I changed what I was *on the point of* doing." Mind seems to be something "farther back inside" than self and is therefore even more likely to be mistaken for an originator. A further step back would, of course, reach the environmental contingencies.

Summary

We have looked at several selves of which people often speak. They include: (1) a self observed (a bodily condition that accompanies behavior), (2) a self esteemed (a bodily condition resulting from commendation by others or self-commendation learned from others), (3) a confident self (the accompaniment of positively reinforced behavior), (4) a responsible self (an accompaniment of the product of aversive contingencies), and (5) a rational self (an accompaniment of behavior governed by rules, including rules made by the behaving person). We have traced them to contingencies of reinforcement responsible for both the behavior and the bodily conditions accompanying it, and the necessarily verbal contingencies responsible for observing, esteeming, and feeling confident, responsible, and rational.

Shall we ever be able to say more about what is felt? Almost certainly not through introspection. We do not have sensory nerves going to relevant parts of the body or any chance of agreeing upon words which refer to private events of any kind. Eventually, the body will be more accurately observed in a different way by physiology, especially neurology, but it will then be observed as the product of specifiable contingencies of variation and selection, rather than as what was less accurately seen through introspection.

Almost every field of science has two languages, one for the things observed casually in daily life and one for presumably the same things observed with the instruments and methods of science. The field of human behavior has had a third, referring to things within the observer felt or introspectively observed. The reflexive "self" is part of the first language, and the "selves" we have been discussing are part of the third. Both the first and the third have many practical uses, the third because when people tell us how they feel, they report the effect of what has happened to them, from which we often infer something of what happened. The *use* of the word self is verbal behavior, and as such is a referent of the second language, but to answer the question with which we began, the *word* self itself is not part of that language.

Notes

1. A lecture on "having a poem." In B. F. Skinner, *Cumulative record* (3rd Ed.). New York: Appleton-Century-Crofts, 1972, pp. 345–355.

2. Whatever happened to psychology as a science of behavior? *American Psychologist, 42*, 8, 780–786.

Personality Traits: Issues of Definition, Evidence, and Assessment

Auke Tellegen

From his writings and teaching it is evident that Paul Meehl is a trait psychologist who has long been sympathetic to and intrigued with the ideas of such classical trait theorists as Allport, Murray, Thurstone, and Cattell. Meehl considers Murray's (1938) classification of needs and press a major systematic contribution, admires Thurstone's pioneering *The Vectors of Mind* (1933), and shares Allport's (1937) view that personality traits are real and have biological underpinnings.

Meehl's assessment of Cattell's work appears more mixed. He does not share Cattell's faith in factor-analytic methods, particularly not his faith in rotation to versions of Thurstonian simple structure as the royal road from observable behaviors to underlying causes (e.g., Catell, 1966). Nor has Meehl adopted the ambitious classification of human personality traits Cattell developed with this approach (though it seems that one of Cattell's constructs, Surgency, has struck a responsive cord with Meehl [1975] and others).

Meehl definitely shares Cattell's conviction (especially as presented in Cattell, 1946) that *covariation* is the one essential justification for claiming the existence of trait entities. Meehl himself points to the primacy of the "fact of covariation" as "the rock bottom basis" for *any* scientific view, citing as examples within psychology the diverse ideas of Skinner, Freud, Allport, Murray, and Thurstone (Meehl, 1986, pp. 328–329). Accordingly, Meehl provides a general characterization of traits (e.g., pp. 317, 322) as families of covarying responses. He distinguishes (amending Cattell's well-known dichotomy) between "surface traits" (the members of the response family are similar in content) and "source traits" (the members of the response family can be quite dissimilar and an inferred internal entity is invoked to explain their covariation).

The trait-relevant facts of covariation have been hotly debated: what are the real facts and what are their implications for the existence and importance of personality traits? Skeptical questions about traits are not new; the generality of traits was disputed at the beginning of this century (Epstein, 1979). The current "trait debate" was instigated primarily by Mischel's (1968) well-known anti-trait critique. Having commanded a great deal of attention for some 20 years, this latest debate now appears to have run its course. Two of the participants have taken stock: Kenrick and Funder (1988) review succinctly the main issues that were raised, in what manner they were resolved, and what lessons were learned. I will try to convey the gist of Kenrick and Funder's analysis, and will use it as a starting point for my own observations concerning the nature and status of traits, which will be defined here essentially as source traits in Meehl's sense.

Kenrick and Funder consider a number of skeptical alternatives to the idea that traits are real and important. They order these alternatives cogently as seven nested hypotheses from most to least inclusive. They conclude that none of these negative hypotheses is supported by the data, and their appraisal of each may be summarized and paraphrased somewhat as follows:

(1) Contrary to the first skeptical hypothesis, personality is not "in the eyes of the beholder," i.e., personality traits are not merely subjective and idiosyncratic constructs about self and others. The evidence indicates that observers who know their targets well tend to arrive at converging ratings that sometimes show substantial agreement. (2) This agreement among observers, unlike what skeptics have claimed, is not solely attributable to "semantic generalization," i.e., to observers' shared expectations about what goes with what. Take the case of two observers agreeing that A is "gregarious" and solely on that basis also agreeing that A is "altruistic" because they share a network of semantic similarities (or, more interestingly, an explanatory trait conception) linking these two different characteristics. This does not call into question A's gregariousness as an actual and independently observed attribute, only the reality of his altruism. In addition, Kenrick and Funder might agree that even the inference of altruism could be a valid generalization from previous observations. (3) Agreement that cannot be attributed to shared preconceptions cannot automatically be dismissed as merely a "Barnum effect," i.e., a high concordance rate for high base-rate characteristics (for example, agreement between two raters that someone "wants to succeed in life"). High base rates can only explain concordance of ratings by raters who fail to differentiate among the persons they rate, not the *covariation* of ratings when raters do differentiate. (4) Covarying ratings in turn are not solely the result of raters sharing stereotypes that are based on obvious but erroneous cues (e.g., "overweight people are sociable, thin people are not"), since ratings are known to correlate with actual behavioral measures. (5) Covariation is also not dependent on communication among observers, since independent observers have been shown to agree as well. (6) Neither can covariation always be explained away as the result of raters observing their targets in the same situation, in view of the evidence of covariation among ratings made in diverse settings. (7) Finally, again

contrary to the hypothesis, behavioral covariation attributable to traits is often substantial and the contribution of traits to behavior makes a difference in life.

The dismissal of these trait-dismissive hypotheses does not leave us empty-handed: it leaves us with traits. But according to Kenrick and Funder we have "not simply come full circle to an acceptance of traits as they were understood 20 years ago" (p. 23). They reject the notion that the debate was mostly about straw men that no one took seriously: the straw man "pure trait" position "that people show powerful unmodulated consistencies in their behavior across time and diverse situations" (pp. 23–24) or its straw-man antagonists (p. 31). They characterize the debate as replete with useful lessons, such as: to achieve predictive power, use multiple raters who know the rated person well rather than superficially (or not at all); use trait measures that are derived from multiple behavioral observations rather than from single behavioral instances; select behaviors relevant to these dimensions; and do not expect predictive accuracy in situations in which behavioral norms markedly restrict individual variation.

These and other lessons were perhaps especially meant for experimentalists who, possibly heeding Cronbach's (1957) advice, became interested in individual differences. Reflecting on their own training as experimental social psychologists, Kenrick and Funder recount how radical versions of the anti-trait view were passed on uncritically to a generation of psychology students, and how someone undergoing clinical training might also encounter exponents of something close to a "pure trait" position, clinicians "overconfidently making grand predictions from minuscule samples of behavior of highly questionable reliability and validity" (p. 31). It appears from these remarks that Kenrick and Funder could not ignore what they thought were "straw-man" concepts after all, because in reality too many took these concepts seriously. Beyond the practical lessons now learned, Kenrick and Funder point also to significant developments taking place at the interface of social and personality psychology (pp. 31–32).

Remarkably, from the perspective taken in the present article, the trait debate did not deal directly with one core issue: the nature of personality traits, that is, the nature and viability of a strong, rather than straw-man, trait position. Kenrick and Funder (p. 31) point out that the final truth emerging from the debate appears to be neither the white of a "pure" trait position or the extreme black of its anti-trait alternatives, but to be "somewhere in the less striking gray area." Before leaving the debate behind us it may be helpful to examine the nature and current status of a non-straw-man trait position. In the following such an attempt is made. A number of questions will be posed not unlike Kenrick and Funder's skeptical hypotheses. In answer I will start out with a source trait type of definition and will then consider issues that arose in the trait debate that are relevant to personality-trait constructs: the concept of disposition, features peculiar to dispositions of personality (such as trait-situation matching which entails, as we will see, the "behavioral tendency" of traits and "unconditional" trait assessment), the significance of situational effects, of findings resulting from aggregation, of situation x person and situation x trait interactions, and of variations in "traitedness." The hoped-for result is a fuller picture of what plausible trait constructs do and do not mean or imply.

Questions and Answers about Traits

What Are Traits?

Q. Are trait constructs not patent fictions meant to satisfy our need for order and simplicity in areas that are unimaginably complicated?

A. Yes, and some of these are stated clearly enough to be evaluated empirically, and may then appear close enough to the truth to be worth efforts to improve them.

Q. In that case, how can ideas about traits be stated clearly?

A. The phrase was "clearly enough." Meehl (1978) has given reasons why especially in the social sciences theoretical ideas are extremely difficult to refute or corroborate compellingly. Like other scientific constructs, social science constructs, rather than being explicitly ("operationally") defined, are "open" concepts, concepts that are linked to observable facts via a list of indicators that is indefinitely extensible, and whose meaning also depends on the theoretical structure as a whole. But Meehl points out that in the social sciences, including psychology, the openness is more pervasive because of the marked fallibility of its probabilistic indicators and the extreme sketchiness of the embedding theoretical context (one might say, the concepts here are not just open but wide open). This state of affairs reflects the complexity of the subject matter, it goes with the territory. Meehl warns that the problems this creates cannot be sidestepped by "false operationism" or "fuzzy verbalism" (p. 815). Hogan and Nicholson (1988) bring this point of view specifically to bear on the nature and validation of personality constructs. In the same spirit it does not seem an idle exercise to make more explicit than has been done in recent years what can plausibly be meant by "personality trait" as a term referring to characterizations and explanations of behavior.

We can begin by defining a *trait* as an inferred relatively enduring organismic (psychological, psychobiological) *structure* underlying an extended family of behavioral dispositions. In the case of personality traits it is expected that the manifestations of these dispositions can substantially affect a person's life. A trait as defined here can be inferred from particular behaviors and on the basis of that inference additional behavioral and other phenomena can be predicted. The positive affective character and vigor of a person's expressive movements might lead us to infer a high level of Positive Emotionality (roughly the same as "extroversion") and to predict on the basis of that construct assertive social behavior and achievement strivings; someone who emotionally overreacts to minor mishaps is probably high on Negative Emotionality ("neuroticism") and is for that reason also likely to experience unaccountable feelings of guilt and anxiety; someone who is prudish and believes in conventional good manners is probably high on Traditionalism and therefore probably and understandably endorses strict and punitive disciplinary methods.

In cases such as these, trait T is inferred from behavior B_1, and from the inference follows in turn the prediction of additional behavior(s) B_2. This B_1-T-B_2 sequence requires, of course, a construct about trait structure T, specifying the two steps, B_1-to-T and T-to-B_2. However, some constructs are no more than suggestive labels for scales (like "aggression" or "sociability"). A well-constructed scale may lead one to go beyond a label and formulate a descriptive construct that includes the item-content, item-covariation, and nontest correlates of that scale. Even then, if the construct goes no further, it merely postulates on empirical grounds a cluster, C1. From an explanatory viewpoint the construct is vacuous. The inferential B_1-to-T step of the B_1-T-B_2 sequence is merely a low-level generalization from previously observed covariation ("if I observe behavior B_1 then I expect also to observe the other behaviors belonging to empirical cluster C1"), and step T-to-B_2 is not a true theoretical derivation but a tautological statement ("if I can consider C1 as given, then by the same token I can consider behavior B_2 as given, since C1 includes B_2"), so that no causal explanations are provided.

Other trait constructs do have explanatory content. Their "surplus" meaning provides causal accounts based on inferred structures and processes, and can entail predictions that go well beyond the test behaviors, including predictions of novel phenomena under experimentally manipulated conditions. By linking Positive Emotionality to a psychobiological behavioral activation system (Depue, Krauss, & Spoont, 1987; Fowles, 1980; Gray, 1982; Tellegen, 1985), or Negative Emotionality to a tendency to construe everyday life occurrences as catastrophic events (Tellegen, 1985; Watson & Clark, 1984)—perhaps reflecting a limited psychophysiological capacity for attenuating the cumulative impact of life's expectable stresses—or Traditionalism to a generalized need for a highly structured social environment (one that issues unambiguous marching orders), these constructs begin to acquire surplus meaning which leads to explanations and testable hypotheses about additional phenomena.

Explanations involving a trait construct usually concern correlations between the trait measure and some target variable. In experimental studies correlations of trait with target may differ systematically across different experimental conditions. For example, correlations of a trait with a task-performance measure may be expected to differ for different levels of induced arousal, or task difficulty, or response feedback. In other words, traits and treatments may be expected to interact. Constructs that predict trait x treatment interactions are likely to postulate certain underlying processes involved in these interactive trait manifestations, and would then have true surplus meaning. The significance of systematic interactions in developing and testing explanatory trait concepts is further considered and illustrated in the section dealing specifically with interactions.

Positive Emotionality, Negative Emotionality, and Traditionalism (for more detail about these traits, see Tellegen, 1982; 1985) are just three examples of the large class of (lower- and higher-order) *dimensional traits*. The dimensional approach treats data on individuals collectively, but accommodates individual differences by recognizing quantitative individual variations in location or level on a trait dimension. Obviously, the more closely certain behavioral measures reflect individual trait-level differences on one and the same dimension, the more these measures should covary across individuals and the less discrepant they should be within individuals. Variables believed to mirror individual differences on a given trait dimension particularly well are called trait (or trait-level) indicators. If their use is convenient, trait indicators may find their way into a psychological test. Observed covariation among measures of this sort may be the first occasion for inferring a trait dimension and an underlying structure. In any case, "the fact of covariation" is the one justification without which the inference of an underlying dimensional trait is not defensible.

A trait dimension is clearly not itself an individual organismic structure, but a population concept representing an orderly statistical structure of covariation. One can view a trait dimension from an organismic perspective as reflecting quantitative psychological variations (in trait level) among persons who are qualitatively (structurally) the same or very similar with respect to the trait in question. A dimensional trait, then, is an organismic structure that recurs in a population, albeit with quantitative individual variations. A dimensional trait is called nomothetic if it is considered quasi-universal.

It is timely to consider briefly at this point a proposed "subjectivist" alternative to the realist view, adopted here, of traits as underlying structures. This alternative seems to reduce the study of personality structures to an analysis of categorical lay constructions or "prototypes" of personality (Cantor & Mischel, 1977; Cantor 1981). Each prototypal concept or image is made up of features commonly associated with a particular personality category (like "extrovert" or "bully"). The same approach has been taken to psychiatric classification (Cantor, Smith, & Mezzich, 1980). Here the prototypal features are those commonly associated by diagnosticians with particular nosological categories. One finding coming out of this approach is that the prototypes for middle-level categories ("public relations type," "schizophrenic") have features that are richer and more distinctive than those for less inclusive ("door-to-door salesman," "paranoid schizophrenic") and more inclusive ("extrovert," "psychotic") ones. It has been suggested that this kind of information can guide the choice of psychodiagnostic and personality descriptive category levels. What is one to think of this approach?

An individual's representations of self and others are undoubtedly important psychological processes. Furthermore, the cognitive-psychological analysis of the structure of everyday personality descriptions and diagnostic thought is valuable because, for one thing, personality assessments and psychiatric diagnoses depend heavily on human judgments. These judgments may reflect language-embedded "folk concepts" (such as the "Big Five" personality factors), and their covariation may reflect actual underlying trait structures. On the other hand, it is necessary, as Kenrick and Funder (1988) point out, to recognize the common judgmental errors and biases that not only cognitive experimental psychologists (e.g., Nisbett & Ross, 1980) but also psychometrically oriented psychologists (e.g., Guilford, 1954; Chapman & Chapman, 1967; 1969) have amply demonstrated.

What is more, the study of personality and personality disorders cannot simply be reduced to an analysis of how lay persons or even experts process information about people. To psychologize to that degree is to turn serious inquiry into trivial pursuits. Nineteenth-century astronomers formulated and developed the "personal equation" to capture and correct for observers' systematic errors in timing stellar transits (Boring, 1950). These developments did not reduce stellar events to mere perceptual-judgmental phenomena or turn astronomy into a branch of experimental psychology. Likewise, awareness and investigation of prototypes is no reason for viewing the structure of traits and disorders of personality as merely person-perceptual and labeling phenomena, or for turning all of personality assessment and psychodiagnostics over to social-cognition theorists.

Traits and Dispositions

Q. Returning to traits as structures underlying behavioral dispositions, is the idea of disposition not open to the criticism that it lacks reference to situations? Don't trait conceptions ignore situational determinants?

A. It seems that the concept of disposition is often viewed as synonymous with "action tendency," without reference to circumstances. This, at least, would explain why "dispositional" trait concepts have been criticized for being "situation-free." Yet, 50 years ago Murray coordinated his motivational trait constructs or needs to distinctive classes of releasing stimulus conditions or "press" (Murray, 1938, ch. 4). Murray speaks in addition of the time-place-mode-object (tpmo) formulas that societal organization imposes on the expression of our needs: "A child is allowed to play during the day but not at night (time). He may defecate in the toilet but not on the floor (place). He may push other children but not hit them with a mallet (mode). He may ask his father but not a stranger in the street for money (object)'' (Murray, 1938, p. 136). (Interestingly, because of his psychodynamic orientation, Murray's emphasis was not on showing how tpmo formulas prevent indiscriminate [situation-free] need expression, but how they circumvent indiscriminate inhibition under presumably ordinary conditions of acculturation.) More recently, commenting on the trait debate, Rorer and Widiger (1983, p. 446) made the same point: ''It is clear that one does not go to a restaurant to get one's hair cut. One does not have sexual intercourse in the church during church services.'' And though viewing traits as indeed highly generalized, Allport, too, conceived of traits as intrinsically linked to arousing stimuli (Allport, 1937, pp. 290–295; see also Allport, 1961, pp. 345–347).

This view implies that any disposition subsumed by a trait concept is to be explicated as a ''disposition to exhibit reaction R under condition S.'' Trait constructs therefore should (and often explicitly or implicitly do) delineate the particular circumstances in which the behavioral trait manifestations are likely to take place. This does not rule out the possibility that some temperamental dispositions, those governing a person's prevailing mood or level of ''engagement,'' are situationally so broad that their manifestations are practically contingent only on the person ''being in the world,'' awake or just alive. These are interesting limiting cases.

The situational reference of traits does not simply imply passive waiting for a trait-relevant situation to come along. It has been pointed out (e.g., Rorer & Widiger, 1983; Snyder, 1981; Wachtel, 1973) that trait dispositions inherently include a tendency to search for situations that enable trait expression. Not only selection, but creation of trait-appropriate situations is involved. A dominant person may make career decisions that raise the probability of coming into a leadership position, but the same person is also likely to structure open-ended situations into ones in which he or she is in charge.

Often the transformation that creates a trait-congruent situation is largely the result of perceptions and interpretations generated by the individual's characteristic cognitive schemata. Perceptions that mediate trait expression may be consensual but can also be highly subjective. They are more or less consensual and ''accommodative'' insofar as they are attuned to socially recognized realities and possibilities. They are subjective and ''assimilative'' insofar as the cognitive trait schemata create and maintain a nonconsensual but trait-congruent environment. Highly assimilative trait manifestations can be adaptive: a person high on Positive Emotionality may interpret to good effect hostile criticism as constructive, or major setbacks as bracing challenges. Sometimes assimilative responses transcend seemingly overwhelming circumstances. Victor Frankl (1959) recounts several episodes from his days in Auschwitz, including the freezing pre-dawn winter morning, when cold and weak, as he and fellow inmates slipped and stumbled on their way to a work site outside the camp, driven by shouts and rifle butts, he summoned up and contemplated the image of his young bride and conversed with her and felt sustained.

Assimilative trait expression can also be merely unrealistic. Frankl describes how upon arrival in Auschwitz he and others clung to "shreds of hope," and compares this to clinical "delusions of reprieve" which he attributes in his own case to his "inborn optimism." Although his high level of Positive Emotionality under those circumstances may have been quite adaptive after all, other personality trait expressions, in minor and major ways, are not: an affiliative person responding with a lengthy personal story to a perfunctory "How are you?"; a ceremonious person delivering a thunderous oration at a bag luncheon; a happy extrovert's imperviousness to someone's obvious distress; a suspicious person reading maliciousness into a casual remark. Murray's distinction between alpha press and beta press (Murray, 1938) allows for marked discrepancies between objective and consensual reality ("alpha press") and personal interpretation ("beta press"), with beta press covering the whole spectrum of pragmatic discernment, transcendence, and maladaptive blindness or delusion.

Trait-Situation Matching and the Behavioral Tendency of Traits, Unconditional and Situation-Blind Assessments

Q. What started out as a hopeful search with clearcut if-S-then-R signposts now seems mired in subjectivity. How can one assess personality dispositions when the appropriate situations cannot be objectively identified?

A. The problem of subjectivity should not be exaggerated. The disposition to socialize, be aggressive, respect authority, etc., often manifests itself in consensually recognizable trait-relevant situations. More important, both subjective and consensual construals of situations are part of the more general process, described earlier, of selecting, seizing, and creating trait-congruent situations. This process, which is characteristic of traits we know, amounts to a matching of trait levels and situations. This "trait-situation matching" leads to trait expression, in other words, to "trait-behavior matching," a matching of trait levels and levels of behavioral expression. Trait-behavior matching gives rise to "trait-behavior covariation," the covariation over people between strength of trait disposition (trait level) and amount of behavioral trait expression. This tendency toward trait expression and toward trait-behavior covariation can be called the "behavioral tendency of traits."

The behavioral tendency of traits makes it possible to assess trait levels by aggregating behavioral trait manifestations over a period of time (extended enough for the behavioral tendency to manifest itself reliably). The trait-level estimates should be "unconditional" rather than conditional on first placing, as in an experiment, the person to be assessed in a specific situation. Strictly situation-conditional estimates would be misleading here. They would obscure the contribution a person's trait disposition makes to the behavior record and to individual differences in behavior by virtue of generating trait-appropriate circumstances (i.e., trait-situation matching).

Ideally, trait-level estimates, conditional and unconditional, are based on behaviors that are interpreted in the context of their beta press (the situation as experienced by the actor). Situational appraisals present problems, however, when beta presses are nonconsensual and hard for others to identify. In such cases one may resort to interpreting behavior "site unseen," without the aid of independent situational clues. For this kind of "situation-blind" assessment to be valid the behaviors in question must be inherently recognizable as taking place in a particular kind of psychological situation, and thus as expressing a particular trait disposition. Fortunately, behavioral trait manifestations seem often indeed to be identifiable as such (as affiliative, aggressive, conscientious, etc.) even if independent information about the psychological situation is not available. Expressive-affective behavioral features in particular often disclose to the observer what kind of situation the actor is experiencing.

Unconditional trait estimates that are in part based on situation-blind assessments, though seemingly an easy target of situationist criticism, emphatically do not assume that behavioral trait manifestations are "situation-free." On the contrary, unconditional estimates assume, as do other trait estimates, that traits manifest themselves through the activation of if-S-then-R tendencies (dispositions), which implies that these manifestations are "situated." So when an unconditional estimate relies in part on situation-blind behavioral assessments, the behaviors in question must as such be "situation-diagnostic" so that they are linkable to if-S-then-R tendencies indicative of particular traits.

Various methods are available for unconditional assessments: aggregate measures based on behavioral sampling procedures, "act frequency" reports (Buss & Craik, 1983), global behavior ratings by self or knowledgeable others. These known modern and traditional methods, explicitly or implicitly, take into account the frequency and intensity of trait-indicative behaviors over a period of time. Their use for assessing trait levels is justified by the behavioral tendency of traits, the tendency of trait dispositions to be reflected in actual behaviors.

The concepts of trait-situation matching and the behavioral tendency of traits are related to others that have been formulated in recent years. They are related to the genotype-environment (GE) correlation discussed by behavior geneticists (Plomin, DeFries, & Loehlin, 1977; Scarr & McCartney, 1983). Plomin et al. (1977) distinguish between three types of GE correlation: passive, reactive, and active. A passive GE correlation comes about when parents in different families not only provide their children with different genes but also with different rearing environments such that certain genetic and environmental characteristics covary (as would be true if, because of partially genetic factors, parents who are more talkative compared to other parents not only tend to have children who are more talkative but also tend to expose these children to more talk, irrespective of how naturally talkative these children happen to be). A reactive GE correlation arises when children, because of their genetic differences, evoke different responses from the environment (as when children's genetically influenced differences in talkativeness elicit systematically differing degrees of verbal response from their environment). An active GE correlation comes about when children, because of their genetic differences, differ in the extent to which they actively seek and procure opportunities for conversation, etc.

Scarr and McCartney (1983) have made the three GE correlations the basis of a developmental model of individuality. They believe that the influence of passive GE effects declines from infancy to adolescence, that the evoked effects persist throughout life, and that active GE covariation effects become increasingly important. As the active GE effect becomes more influential with development, the overall importance of GE covariation increases. The authors suggest that, barring severely restricted environmental opportunities, personality, motivational, and intellectual differences between people mostly reflect genetically determined differences in the kind of experiences they elicit and actively seek out, particularly the latter.

GE covariation and the trait-situation matching process are closely linked. Depending on the mix of genetic and environmental antecedents of a trait, the trait-situation covariation that arises from trait-situation matching represents in part GE covariation and in part covariation of early E and late E. In other words, trait processes mediate GE and EE covariation. Buss (1984) has cast personality traits in just this mediating role. In a study presented under the banner of the GE correlation model, he demonstrates assortative mating for a variety of personality characteristics. Buss points out that these findings are evidence of person-environment correlation (i.e., trait-situation matching and trait-situation covariation) in an important area of adult development.

The Role of Situational Constraints

Q. Is not the idea that we seek or fashion situations to suit our individual personalities plausible only up to a point? Don't people often find themselves out of necessity in situations that exercise a strong "pull" and leave very little room for individual variation, let alone trait-based covariation? Transcendence of very strong press is by definition an uncommon occurence. Depending on the situation, one may feel compelled to be helpful or just stand there, to be vindictive or nonpunitive. Doesn't the sway of situational variations belie the importance of personality variation stressed by trait psychologists?

A. Situational constraints are as much a fact of life as personal choices of situations, and are not only recognized by social psychologists and other social setting scientists, but are also, one could claim, part and parcel of the formal trait model. Even the oldest intelligence tests contain items varying widely in difficulty. These difficulty differences are the psychometric analogue of situational differences.

Modern Item Response Theory or IRT (e.g., Hambleton & Swaminathan, 1985) incorporates item difficulty formally as one of its parameters. Although originally developed for the assessment of cognitive functions, IRT methods have recently been applied successfully to a series of dimensional personality scales (Reise & Waller, in press). In the assessment of personality through self-report True-False items, the "easy" and "difficult" items are, respectively, those answered often and rarely in the keyed direction. The importance of difficulty is especially evident in the so-called information curve, which shows us whether a given scale measures trait levels reliably over a sufficiently broad range of individual differences. For this to be the case, binary items must span a wide range of difficulty levels. Whether we are dealing with cognitive or other personality scales, very easy and difficult items represent psychometric situations extreme and compelling enough that they are variables bordering, so to say, on being constants. The exceptional persons who pass the most difficult personality items or fail the easiest are among the most interesting representatives of a trait dimension.

Psychometricians are generally not interested in recreating real-life situational differences in their tests. Instead they create artificial but trait-relevant item hurdles of varying difficulties that will enhance, for testing purposes, the discriminability of individual trait-level differences. How visible these individual differences are in real life depends on how trait-relevant, abundant, and varied in difficulty the hurdles are in real life.

The Issue of Aggregation

Q. Although allowing for "situation main effects" (discussed in the previous section), the trait model, of course, places special emphasis on "Person main effects" which reflect the covariation attributed to traits. But is it not true that the degree of covariation typically attributable to traits is low? Is it not the case that single-response indicators of the same trait rarely intercorrelate more than about .30 to .40 and often .20 and less, reflecting marked specificity and instability (the latter resulting from the influence of fluctuating psychological states)? Doesn't this eliminate traits as important explanatory factors?

A. Trait psychologists agree that correlations among single-response indicators tend to be low, but dispute the conclusion that traits are unimportant. Psychometricians, in particular, have always been aware of the weak covariation among single-response measures. Low item correlations are common even in measures of intellectual functions (Green, 1978; Tryon, 1973), whose trait-like consistency specifists apparently do not dispute (Mischel, 1968, 1973), perhaps in part because psychometricians have been able to develop internally consistent and stable trait measures by aggregating noisy items. The same observations apply to other data domains as well. Although Hartshorne and May (1928, 1929) interpreted the low correlations among their separate behavioral measures of honesty as evidence against a general underlying honesty trait, they also acknowledged, as Epstein and O'Brien (1985) point out, that the internal consistency reliability of an aggregate consisting of just nine behavioral honesty items was .73. Because of the ubiquitous specificity and instability of single behavioral measures, Epstein and others have argued that only the internal consistency and stability of appropriately assembled aggregates, and their intercorrelations, can tell us something about the existence and cross-situational generality of personality traits (e.g., Epstein, 1979; Epstein & O'Brien, 1985; Rushton, Brainerd, & Pressley, 1983).

Q. The case for aggregation seems on the face of it reasonable and pragmatic. But the importance of the results achieved by aggregation has been disputed. Mischel and Peake (1982) consider the demonstrations of increased reliability following aggregation a trivial psychometric exercise, and the presumably more relevant evidence of covariation between situationally distinctive aggregates (representing different facets of the same trait) unimpressive. What then do aggregation findings tell us about the existence and importance of traits?

A. Results of aggregation are unquestionably relevant to inferences about traits, but the meaning of aggregation seems still in need of clarification. Let us first consider what significance, if any, should be attached to the increase in reliability often achieved by aggregation. As we saw, some consider it a trivial finding that does not help settle issues concerning traits. Epstein (1979) himself points out that the phenomenon is a familiar one and has found it to conform rather closely to the classical Spearman-Brown prophecy formula. But he insists that aggregation findings can provide crucial evidence for the existence of meaningful personality traits (e.g., Epstein & O'Brien, 1985). To evaluate this claim it is helpful to imagine an ideal version of the "classical" studies reviewed by Epstein and O'Brien.

We start with a large set of basic response measures (referred to in the following as "responses"), representing diverse behaviors observed in diverse situations. The difficult problem of deciding what constitutes a basic response or basic unit of behavior, and how to quantify it, need not concern us here: the present issue is not how to define basic units but how to evaluate aggregates made up of basic units, however defined. In an ideal case the response measures would show a pattern of correlations suggesting an underlying dimension, one that is psychologically meaningful in view of both its stronger and its weaker response correlates (convergent and discriminant validity). Epstein is correct in that a coherent correlational pattern can in principle strongly suggest a meaningful underlying trait. In this connection it seems that the *relative* sizes of the correlations, linking certain responses more strongly than others to the dimension, can be more important than their absolute sizes. The same differential pattern of correlations at a lower absolute level might suggest an equally meaningful, though behaviorally weaker, underlying trait.

In the preceding paragraph a distinction is made between responses and an underlying or (in path-analytic language) "latent" variable which can only be inferred and estimated from the responses. This distinction is crucial in discussing aggregation. It makes it possible to state in so many words that a psychologically meaningful latent variable, such as a trait dimension, can be suggested by and be inferred from the response data, but that the latent variable may account for much or very little response covariation; and that in either case aggregation of enough responses can boost reliability to a statisfactory level and produce a "powerful measure of the overall construct" (Epstein & O'Brien, 1985, p. 522). The distinction between responses and latent variables makes it plain that the resolving power (reliability) of an aggregate trait *measure* is not to be confused with the behavioral power ("response penetration," or influence on response covariation) of the *trait*.

Where reliable aggregates have been found, both trait psychologists and specifists have been especially interested in correlations between aggregates that presumably represent the same underlying trait but that are based on behaviors in different situations. These correlations are interesting because they permit a direct test of cross-situational trait generality. Mischel and Peake (1982) obtained low correlations, suggesting a lack of trait generality. Jackson and Paunonen's (1985) reanalysis, on the other hand, disclosed that Mischel and Peake's a priori trait constructs were not optimal for their data and that situationally distinctive aggregates representing the same factor-analytic dimension intercorrelated substantially.

To evaluate the significance of these cross-situational correlations between aggregates, the distinction between responses and latent variables in again relevant. In the reported analyses aggregates clearly function as measures of latent variables, explicitly so when correlations between aggregates are corrected for attenuation (e.g., Epstein & O'Brien, 1985; Mischel & Peake, 1982), which changes them into estimated latent correlations. A high latent correlation, especially between very distinctive aggregates (such as only a higher-order source trait construct would link), could be theoretically interesting, and some of the reported correlations are. To take an extreme hypothetical case, no investigator would walk away from a disattenuated (latent) correlation of .90 between two behavioral aggregates, one measuring "vitality" and based on measures of expressive movement (Allport & Vernon, 1933), the other measuring "social dominance," derived from behavioral observations made 10 years later. Yet, the *response* correlations (which could also be obtained) across time and across the two behavioral domains could equally well be very weak or very strong. They are a joint function of the correlation between the two latent variables (assumed to be high in this hypothetical case) and the response penetration of both (which could be weak or strong).

Summing up, correlational findings must be evaluated in the context of a theoretical model, as Ozer (1985) has shown with cogent examples. The correlational results obtained with aggregates are a clear case in point and require a distinction between responses and latent variables. This distinction makes it possible to interpret results of recent analyses of aggregates (e.g., Epstein & O'Brien, 1985; Rushton et al., 1983) as consistent with, and even corroborating, the existence of a number of meaningful dimensional personality traits (such as honesty and conscientiousness) and as documenting some strong relations between situationally distinctive latent variables representing the same broad latent trait. But these analyses do not as such permit us to reach conclusions about the response penetration of these latent traits, i.e., about the magnitude of their contributions to the covariation of basic response variables. Now, if response variables were to be defined narrowly as measures of single responses (so that their intercorrelations are only to be corrected for observational or instrument error), response penetration of latent traits as judged by customary correlational standards would be found slight. There is probably little disagreement on this point. Therefore, had the distinction between responses and latent traits explicitly been observed from the beginning, much of the dispute over aggregation, and much of the confusion that surrounds it according to Epstein (1983), might have been avoided.

When behavioral aggregates are used to estimate latent trait scores, they serve in effect as tests; Epstein and O'Brien (1985) in fact consistently use the term "items" for what I have called "responses." Among trait measures, aggregates based on behaviors monitored in real life admittedly occupy a special place. Their internal structure reveals to what extent the true or latent orderliness of personality exists as an element of orderliness in people's daily actions.

Irrespective of how personality traits are measured, to evaluate the *significance in life* of traits, i.e., the cumulative impact of their behavioral manifestations, we need to know the relations between trait measures and important life outcomes or "track record." Cattell (1957) refers to these outcomes as life-record or L-data. Researchers have included a variety of occurrences and conditions in this category: number of organizations joined, job promotions, awards, number of traffic citations accumulated over a certain time period, drug abuse, friendship network, etc. Other outcomes are more subjective, such as one's sense of accomplishment, frustration, or stagnation, qualities that reflect a mixture of life experiences and emotional temperament. Block's (1971) *Lives through Time* exemplifies how biographical data can be exploited to show connections of major personality dimensions to major life outcomes.

Interactions between Situations and Persons

Q. Given that the trait model allows for situation main effects and emphasizes trait main effects, with the latter representing the covariation attributable to traits, how well does it actually fit the facts of covariation? Is it not true that in certain supposed trait domains, like "anxiety" and "hostility," even test items specially selected to tap these traits reveal sizable situation x person interactions rather than primarily the anticipated main effects?

A. "Interactions" and "interactionism" have become popular terms for conveying sensitivity to the interrelatedness of organism and environment (some noteworthy essays presenting differing perspectives on interactions and interactionism: Bowers, 1973; Golding, 1975; Olweus, 1977). The term "interaction" is suggestive in part because it can mean very different things (Olweus, 1977), and its use has sometimes been confused. Much of the data-oriented debate has focused on analysis-of-variance interactions, particularly the person x situation interactions referred to in the question. Person x situation interactions indicate that the rank-ordering of individuals on the basis of their measured responses (say, their self-reported fears) differs for different situations (fear of "being interviewed for an important job" may not be highly correlated with fear of "being alone in the woods at night").

Sizable interactions of this sort, which reflect inconsistency and clear multidimensionality, have been found in inventories that supposedly measure one trait (such as anxiety or hostility). These findings have been interpreted not only as evidence that the particular trait concepts invoked are inadequate, but that trait concepts generally are questionable and must give way to a supposedly competing interactionist conception. This conclusion is mistaken for several reasons.

First of all, reported interactions have been obtained on inventories representing *unexamined* trait constructs. Given these a priori constructs, the interactions are not surprising, and prove nothing about trait constructs in general. The following case is representative.

The well-known S-R Inventory of Anxiousness (Endler, McV. Hunt, & Rosenstein, 1962) was constructed entirely on the basis of its authors' rational-intuitive ideas about what sorts of responses indicate "anxiousness" and what sorts of situations provoke it (the authors include the two just mentioned as examples). The authors' own factor analyses of the inventory indicated multidimensionality of a kind and degree that one can only interpret as disconfirming the original anxiousness construct. Particularly striking are the findings on the "mode-of-response" variables (these include such responses as "become immobilized," "perspire," "enjoy the challenge," and were aggregated over situations for these mode-of-response analyses). Factor analyses of these variables showed, in addition to a large "distress" factor (essentially Negative Emotionality), a smaller but still substantial "exhilaration" factor (essentially, Positive

Emotionality). In other words, this a priori measure of anxiousness in fact includes what I think are the two major dimensions of emotional temperament (Tellegen, 1985). Companion factor analyses of the situation variables (aggregated over response modes) showed two additional meaningful dimensions: an interpersonal and a physical threat dimension. The results of these analyses are not surprising: the surest way to obtain multidimensional results that disconfirm a trait construct is to give an a priori and overinclusive trait construct its first empirical trial.

The multidimensionality of the S-R Inventory of Anxiousness is reflected in its substantial situation x person and response-mode x person interactions (since individuals are expected to be rank-ordered differently on variables that tap different dimensions). The multidimensionality and the interactions are the predictable result of using an unexamined trait construct. Findings of this sort are hardly grounds for also abandoning examined constructs, some of which (like the two Emotionality dimensions) are as broad as some unexamined ones but have been developed empirically through an iterative sequence of construct (re)formulation and corrective empirical trials.

Second, multidimensionality is not invariably incompatible with the idea of a general trait dimension. The distinction between lower- and higher-order traits is relevant here. The idea of higher-order trait implies not only a positive manifold, i.e., generally positive correlations among the recognized trait markers, but also stronger covariation among markers of the same lower-order dimension than among markers of different ones. These covariation differences within the same general trait domain are particularly likely in the case of broad source traits, and are reflected in systematic item (read: situation) x person interactions. Although the Full Scale Wechsler score measures a familiar general factor, Wechsler item responses not only reflect this highest-order factor but necessarily also the systematic item x person interactions attributable to the existence of several lower-order factors. Even the S-R Inventory of Anxiousness might have shown interactions consistent with a higher-order superfactor, although the results in this case are not convincing.

Finally, note that in the preceding examples of situation x person interactions, situational variation was introduced by using different test stimuli (sometimes representing different lower-order dimensions), and person variation was introduced by simply treating each individual as a separate ''level.'' An alternative is to create situational differences through experimental manipulation, and to represent person differences as individual variations on some trait dimension which we treat as an independent variable. This makes it possible to examine behavioral correlates of individual trait-level differences under different experimental circumstances. In this way, systematic situation x trait interactions may be encountered that substantially support *or* disconfirm a trait construct, or begin to fill in one that is still quite open. These interactions demonstrate the inherently inter-active character of the trait constructs in question.

Example 1: An unstructured but potentially relaxing setting facilitates relax-ation of subjects scoring high on a measure of "absorption," but not of low-absorption subjects; a performance-oriented biofeedback relaxation task has the reverse effect: it increases the relaxation of low- but not of high-absorption subjects (Qualls & Sheehan, 1981). This suggests, in conjunction with the con-tent of the absorption scale and some of its correlates, that with respect to relax-ation the absorption dimension is one of readiness to function in an "experiential-respondent" mode (as contrasted to an "instrumental-operant" mode) (Tellegen, 1981).

Example 2: Caffeine (in the morning), compared to a placebo, reliably en-hances task performance of subjects scoring high on an impulsiveness measure, and has the opposite effect on low impulsives (Revelle, Humphreys, Simon, & Gilliland, 1980). Combined with other data, this finding suggests a nomological network in which impulsiveness is associated (in the morning) with low arousal, while arousal itself, in accordance with the well-known Yerkes-Dodson in-verted-U function, is curvilinearly related to performance; that is, caffeine is be-lieved to raise the arousal level of impulsives, who tend to be insufficiently aroused, closer to the optimum, and the level of the nonimpulsives, who are more highly aroused to begin with, beyond the optimum (the inverted-U relation may itself be the joint effect of arousal enhancing sustained task attention but impairing short-term memory, as explained by Humphreys, Revelle, Simon, & Gilliland, 1980; see also Humphreys & Revelle, 1984).

These interactive findings aid the elaboration of a trait construct: they provide a differentiated dispositional or if-S-then-R characterization that may suggest specific underlying processes and structures. Both sets of studies combine Cronbach's two disciplines of scientific psychology, experimental and correla-tional, to demonstrate replicable treatment x trait interactions (both were pub-lished, as it happens, in an experimental journal). In spite of Cronbach's later pessimism (because of the ever-present possibility of new interactions) about the half-life of new insights in our discipline (Cronbach, 1975), complementing Meehl's about their birth rate (Meehl, 1978), findings from investigations of this sort illustrate growth of systematic knowledge and understanding of traits.

The two examples also nicely demonstrate that situation-blind assessment has its limits. Although a more or less situation-blind approach is often a justified expediency, some potentially trait-indicative responses can obviously not be in-terpreted correctly unless the specific situation is independently identified. In the first example, the relaxation response indicates either high or low absorption, de-pending on whether the situation is structured as experiential or instrumental; in the second, good task performance in the morning is in effect an indicator of either high or low impulsiveness, depending on whether the internal milieu is altered by a stimulant or not.

In sum, some situation x person and situation x response-mode interactions may force one to modify or abandon a construct; in the case of unexamined trait constructs, such disconfirmatory interactions are quite likely. Other interactions are entirely consistent with higher-order dimensional constructs. Still other interactions, the most interesting ones, are inherent in the nature of the dispositions specified by well-articulated trait constructs. And no interaction has implications for trait constructs in general.

The Traitedness Puzzle

Q. Granted that aggregation findings, life record data, and systematic interactions seem to confirm the reality and importance of certain traits and to clarify underlying processes and structures, are these findings not limited to certain groups of persons? How often do we encounter *nomothetic* traits? Should we not expect correlational patterns to differ in different populations (females, males, different cultures, etc.)? Has it not even been suggested that no trait construct applies to more than a possibly small section of any population? Using a distinction made earlier, should one not take seriously the possibility that groups of people differ not only quantitatively but structurally, i.e., in basic personality organization? Didn't Allport (1937; 1955; 1961) go further in claiming all along that each individual personality is distinctive in this basic way and can be truly understood only through idiographic assessment? Shouldn't we at least relinquish traditional nomothetic trait psychology and limit our predictive efforts to only those subgroups of people for whom a given trait construct is demonstrably appropriate and who alone behave trait-consistently and predictably in the domain in question?

A. Profound individual and group differences in trait structure, if they exist, can obviously not be ignored. Bem and Allen's (1974) ideas along these lines, focusing on group differences, have received a great deal of attention. Baumeister and Tice (1988) recently expanded on these ideas and introduced the idea of "metatrait" as "the trait of having or not having a trait," that is, of being "traited" or "untraited." One can also think quantitatively of "traitedness," namely, as the degree to which a particular trait structure is approximated in a given person. In their study Bem and Allen assessed traitedness with measures of response consistency. They undertook to show that more consistent individuals are more predictable from trait measures than less consistent individuals are. But their results, although reported positive, in reality amounted to two replication failures (as later explained by Chaplin and Goldberg, 1985).

It appears that response consistency is a very weak indicator of traitedness, although variations in consistency are the cardinal consequence of variations in traitedness. The explanation is that consistency measures also reflect factors other than traitedness, such as the variability of probabilistic trait indicators and the occurrence of extrinsic measurement error or "faultiness" (Tellegen, 1988). In other words, measures of consistency rather straightforwardly reflect uneven covariation, and presumably for that reason were at one time attractive indices of traitedness (Bem & Allen, 1974), but now, in view of their other determinants, appear far from optimal.

Other efforts to demonstrate individual variation in cross-situational trait predictability have had mixed results. Two of the better studies (Chaplin & Goldberg, 1985; Paunonen & Jackson, 1985) yielded thoroughly negative outcomes. However, by combining several such studies in a comprehensive meta-analysis, Zuckerman, Bernieri, Koestner, and Rosenthal (1989) showed that in the aggregate, across a variety of traits, direct self-ratings of consistency tend to moderate the correlations between self-ratings and ratings by others. That is, the correlations for these traits tend to be higher among the more consistent subjects than among less consistent ones. Zuckerman et al. (1989) demonstrated similar moderator effects for ratings of trait "relevance" and "observability." Still, studies in this area have not led to conclusive findings of important individual differences in predictability for specific traits, let alone to a systematic psychology of individual differences in traitedness.

Pragmatically speaking, additional trait indicators may make a greater contribution to prediction than the moderators that have so far been investigated. Bem and Allen, using single measures as predictors, obtained substantial average correlations with target variables in their "predictable" subsample only. But in their re-analysis of Bem and Allen's results, Tellegen, Kamp, and Watson (1982, pp. 101–102), by merely using the unweighted sums of two measures as predictors, achieved comparable results in Bem and Allen's *full* sample.

From a theoretical viewpoint, true traitedness variations remain a fascinating topic and a challenge. In the first volume of this work, Lykken convincingly argues and illustrates the importance of recognizing individual differences in structure, which is what traitedness differences are. Meehl (1978), who assumes that people do differ in how their dispositions are organized, considers such differences one reason why psychology is such a slow-moving discipline. If encountered, marked traitedness differences will undoubtedly force us to rethink certain nomothetic trait constructs and current personality assessment practices.

On the other hand, one should not overlook the possibility that certain patterns of low and high traitedness are interpretable from a nomothetic perspective. Loevinger's sweeping nomothetic source trait construct of Ego Development (Loevinger & Wessler, 1970; Loevinger, 1976) could be explicated as one that links individual differences in developmental stage to systematic individual differences in traitedness for certain behavioral traits (conformity, conscientiousness, etc.). Each developmental stage may be characterized by a high degree of traitedness for (and salience of) one or more stage-appropriate traits and a lower degree of traitedness for other traits, those that are salient in an earlier or later stage (Tellegen, 1988). In other words, it may be possible to make allowances for individual differences in personality *structure* in a systematic *nomothetic* framework. Certainly, structural differences are not the exclusive province of unconnected idiographic or typological analyses. Possibilities of this sort involve specific hypotheses and suggest focused measures rather than global empirical searches and all-purpose measures of trait relevance or consistency.

Stepping Back

The trait debate and its ramifications are not the only significant development of the last 20 years. Methodologically, a construct-guided approach to scale development has been shown capable of producing strong results (Jackson, 1971). Scale construction clearly can be more than an ad hoc procedure or a mechanical routine. In its most interesting applications it is a method for comparing ideas of covariation with the facts. Used in that way it is one of the best methods for testing trait constructs (Loevinger, 1957), and the best for shaping them (Tellegen, 1982; 1985, pp. 685-688).

Substantively, a number of trait concepts have become increasingly accepted, including the earlier mentioned set of folk concepts, the Big Five (e.g., Digman & Takemoto-Chock, 1981; Goldberg, 1980; McCrae & Costa, 1987; Norman, 1963), although the psychological nature of these five, their relation to other personality constructs, and their place in the larger personality sphere need to be further clarified.[1] New personality scales have been constructed that are coherent in content and structure and embody important new or updated conceptions (to name just two examples: scales for assessing Ego Development [Loevinger & Wessler, 1970] and for assessing the updated "interpersonal circumplex" [e.g., Wiggins, Trapnell, & Phillips, 1988]).

Important longitudinal studies, completed or underway during this same period, permit or will permit evaluation of the stability and change of personality traits, and their contributions to personal environments and life outcomes. Behavior-genetic studies clarify the genetic and environmental underpinnings of basic personality traits, and explore new models (e.g., Lykken, 1982; Scarr & McCartney, 1983). The two disciplines of psychology continue to be combined in experimental studies designed to elucidate the dispositional and related interactional specifics of personality traits and corresponding underlying processes and structures.

With few objecting, it is possible today not only to echo Meehl and say that traits are real, but to add that methodological, conceptual, and empirical advances in personality trait psychology, though slow for the many reasons he has cited, are also real.

Summary

In this article the nature of personality traits and their assessment are considered in the context of the "trait debate" of the last 20 years. A trait was defined as an inferred organismic structure underlying an extended family of consequential behavioral dispositions, a dimensional trait as one whose qualitative structure recurs with quantitative individual variations, and a nomothetic dimensional trait as one that is quasi-universal. A current alternative to this realist view, namely the view that traits are prototypal cognitive constructions, if adopted as the basic trait model, would distract theory and research from much of the substance of personality psychology and psychopathology.

A salient feature peculiar to personality dispositions (related to their "if-S-then-R" character) is the selection and creation, behaviorally and through cognitive structuring, of trait-congruent situations. This trait-situation matching gives rise to trait-behavior matching (a matching of trait levels and levels of behavioral trait expression) and trait-behavior covariation, in other words, to the "behavioral tendency of traits." The behavioral tendency of traits justifies and calls for an "unconditional" approach to trait assessment with traditional and newer methods. Because of the trait-situation matching, dimensional traits mediate genotype-environment and early environment-late environment covariation.

Situational effects and constraints ("difficulty" effects) are discussed, as is the use of aggregation for demonstrating trait effects. To evaluate the correlation-boosting results of aggregation it is necessary to distinguish between responses and latent variables. It is then possible to recognize that aggregation findings confirm the reality and stability of broad latent traits, and within certain trait domains indicate substantial correlations among cross-situational latent variables, but cannot as such demonstrate a high degree of response penetration or of life importance of the latent traits.

Among reported situation x person interaction effects, some represent marked multidimensionality disconfirming unexamined trait constructs. Others are consistent with higher-order dimensional constructs. Still other interactions, the most interesting ones, are situation x trait interactions inherent in the dispositions implied by trait constructs. These interactions are specified by well-explicated and testable constructs which postulate underlying processes and structures.

Marked variations in covariation suggesting differences in "traitedness" are of great interest but have not been convincingly demonstrated. Although such variations would obviously complicate dimensional structures, they could still fit an overarching nomothetic (e.g., ego-developmental) scheme.

In view of the most recent trait debate and other developments in personality trait psychology, it is reasonable to conclude that not only are certain quasi-nomothetic personality traits real, but that progress in identifying, understanding, and measuring basic personality traits, and documenting their significance in life, though predictably slow, is also real.

Note

1. In a forthcoming paper (Tellegen & Waller, in preparation) we will report an analysis of data based on a new set of 400 adjectival trait descriptors sampled from the dictionary. Our results reveal seven, and no more than seven, major dimensions which include what appear to be a substantially clarified Big Five.

References

Allport, G. W. (1937). *Personality: A psychological interpretation.* New York: Holt.

Allport, G. W. (1955). *Becoming: Basic considerations for a psychology of personality.* New Haven, CT: Yale University Press.

Allport, G. W. (1961). *Pattern and growth in personality.* New York: Holt.

Allport, G. W., & Vernon, P. E. (1933). *Studies in expressive movement.* New York: Macmillan.

Baumeister, R. F., & Tice, D. M. (1988). Metatraits. *Journal of Personality, 56,* 571–598.

Bem, D. J., & Allen, A. (1974). On predicting some of the people some of the time: The search for cross-situational consistencies in behavior. *Psychological Review, 85,* 485–501.

Block, J. (1971). *Lives through time.* Berkeley, CA: Bankcroft.

Boring, E. G. (1950). *A history of experimental psychology* (2nd ed.). New York: Appleton-Century-Crofts.

Bowers, K. S. (1973). Situationism in psychology: An analysis and a critique. *Psychological Review, 80,* 307–336.

Buss, D. M. (1984). Toward a psychology of Person-Environment (PE) correlation: The role of spouse selection. *Journal of Personality and Social Psychology, 47,* 361–377.

Buss, D. M., & Craik, K. H. (1983). The act frequency approach to personality. *Psychological Review, 90,* 105–126.

Cantor, N. (1981). A cognitive-social approach to personality. In N. Cantor & J. F. Kihlstrom (Eds.), *Personality, cognition, and social interaction* (pp. 23–44). Hillsdale, NJ: Erlbaum.

Cantor, N., & Mischel, W. (1977). Traits as prototypes: Effects on recognition memory. *Journal of Personality and Social Psychology, 35,* 38–48.

Cantor, N., Smith, E. E., & Mezzich, J. (1980). Psychiatric diagnosis as prototype categorization. *Journal of Abnormal Psychology, 89* (2), 181–193.

Cattell, R. B. (1946). *Description and measurement of personality.* Yonkers-on-Hudson, NY: World Book Company.

Cattell, R. B. (1957). *Personality and motivation structure and measurement.* Yonkers-on-Hudson, NY: World Book Company.

Cattell, R. B. (1965). *The scientific analysis of personality.* Baltimore: Penguin Books.

Cattell, R. B. (1966). The meaning and strategic use of factor analysis. In R. B. Cattell (Ed.), *Handbook of multivariate experimental psychology* (pp. 174–243). Chicago: Rand-McNally.

Chaplin, W. F., & Goldberg, L. R. (1985). A failure to replicate the Bem and Allen study of individual differences in cross-situational consistency. *Journal of Personality and Social Psychology, 47,* 1075–1090.

Chapman, L. J., & Chapman, J. P. (1967). Genesis of popular but erroneous diagnostic observations. *Journal of Abnormal Psychology, 72* 193–204.

Chapman, L. J., & Chapman, J. P. (1969). Illusory correlation as an obstacle to the use of valid psychodiagnostic signs. *Journal of Abnormal Psychology, 74,* 271–280.

Cronbach, L. J. (1957). The two disciplines of scientific psychology. *American Psychologist, 12* 671–684.

Cronbach, L. J. (1975). Beyond the two disciplines of scientific psychology. *American Psychologist, 30,* 116–127.

Depue, R. A., Krauss, S. P., & Spoont, M. R. (1987). A two-dimensional threshold model of seasonal bipolar affective disorder. In D. Magnusson and A. Ohman (Eds.), *Psychopathology: An interactional perspective* (pp. 95–123). New York: Academic Press.

Digman, J. M., & Takemoto-Chock, N. K. (1981). Factors in the natural language of personality: Re-analysis, comparison, and interpretation of six major studies. *Multivariate Behavioral Research, 16,* 149–170.

Endler, N. S., Hunt, J. McV., & Rosenstein, A. J. (1962). An S–R inventory of anxiousness. *Psychological Monographs, 76* (17, Whole No. 536).

Epstein, S. (1979). The stability of behavior: I. On predicting most of the people much of the time. *Journal of Personality and Social Psychology, 37,* 1097–1126.

Epstein, S. (1983). The stability of confusion: A reply to Mischel and Peake. *Psychological Review, 90,* 179–184.

Epstein, S., & O'Brien, E. J. (1985). The person-situation debate in historical and current perspective. *Psychological Bulletin, 98,* 513–537.

Fowles, D. C. (1980). The three arousal model: Implications of Gray's two-factor learning theory for heart rate, electrodermal activity, and psychopathy. *Psychophysiology 17,* 87–104.

Frankl, V. E. (1959). *Man's search for meaning: An introduction to logotherapy.* Boston: Beacon Press.

Goldberg, L. R. (1980). Some ruminations about the structure of individual differences: Developing a common lexicon for the major characteristics of human personality. Unpublished manuscript.

Golding, S. L. (1975). Flies in the ointment: Methodological problems in the analysis of the percentage of variance due to persons and situations. *Psychological Bulletin, 82,* 278–288.

Gray, J. A. (1982). *The neuropsychology of anxiety: An enquiry into the function of the septo-hippocampal system.* Oxford: Oxford University Press.

Green, B. F. (1978). In defense of measurement. *American Psychologist, 33,* 664–679.

Guilford, J. P. (1954). *Psychometric methods* (2nd ed.). New York: McGraw-Hill.

Hambleton, R. K., & Swaminathan, H. (1985). *Item response theory: Principles and applications.* Boston: Kluwer-Nyhoff.

Hartshorne, H., & May, M. A. (1928). *Studies in the nature of character:* Vol. 1. *Studies in deceit.* New York: Macmillan.

Hartshorne, H., & May, M. A. (1924). *Studies in the nature of character.* Vol. 2. *Studies in service and self-control.* New York: Macmillan.

Hogan, R., & Nicholson, R. A. (1988). The meaning of personality test scores. *American Psychologist, 43,* 621–626.

Humphreys, M. S., & Revelle, W. (1984). Personality, motivation, and performance: A theory of the relationship between individual differences and information processing. *Psychological Review, 91,* 153–184.

Humphreys, M. S., Revelle, W., Simon, L., & Gilliland, K. (1980). Individual differences in diurnal rhythms and multiple activation states: A reply to M. W. Eysenck and Folkard. *Journal of Experimental Psychology: General, 109,* 42–48.

Jackson, D. N. (1971). The dynamics of structured personality tests: 1971. *Psychological Review, 78* 229–248.

Jackson, D. N., & Paunonen, S. V. (1985). Construct validity and the predictability of behavior. *Journal of Personality and Social Psychology, 49,* 554–570.

Kenrick, D. T., & Funder, D. C. (1988). Profiting from controversy: Lessons from the person-situation debate. *American Psychologist, 43,* 23–34.

Loevinger, J. (1957). Objective tests as instruments of psychological theory. *Psychological Reports, 3*, 635–694.

Loevinger, J. (1976). *Ego development: Conceptions and theories*. San Francisco: Jossey-Bass.

Loevinger, J., & Wessler, R. (1970). *Measuring ego development: Vol. 1*. San Francisco: Jossey-Bass.

Lykken, D. T. (1982). Research with twins: The concept of emergenesis. *Psychophysiology, 19*, 361–373.

McCrae, R. R., & Costa, P. T., Jr. (1987). Validation of the five-factor model of personality across instruments and observers. *Journal of Personality and Social Psychology, 52*, 81–90.

Meehl, P. E. (1975). Hedonic capacity: Some conjectures. *Bulletin of the Menninger Clinic, 39*, 295–307.

Meehl, P. E. (1978). Theoretical risks and tabular asterisks: Sir Karl, Sir Ronald, and the slow progress of soft psychology. *Journal of Consulting and Clinical Psychology, 46*, 806–834.

Meehl, P. E. (1986). Trait language and behaviorese. In T. Thompson & M. D. Zeiler (Eds.), *Analysis and integration of behavioral units* (pp. 315–334). Hillsdale, NJ: Erlbaum.

Mischel, W. (1968). *Personality and assessment*. New York: Wiley.

Mischel, W. (1973). Toward a cognitive social learning reconceptualization of personality. *Psychological Review, 80*, 252–283.

Mischel, W., & Peake, P. K. (1982). Beyond déjà vu in the search for cross-situational consistency. *Psychological Review, 89*, 730–755.

Murray, H. A. (1938). *Explorations in personality*. New York: Oxford.

Nisbett, R., & Ross, L. (1980). *Human inference: Strategies and shortcomings of social judgment*. Englewood Cliffs, NJ: Prentice-Hall.

Norman, W. T. (1963). Toward an adequate taxonomy of personality attributes: Replicated factor structure in peer nomination personality ratings. *Journal of Abnormal and Social Psychology, 66*, 574–583.

Olweus, D. (1977). A critical analysis of the "modern" interactionist position. In D. Magnusson & N. S. Endler (Eds.), *Personality at the crossroads: Current issues in interactional psychology* (pp. 221–233). Hillsdale, NJ: Erlbaum.

Ozer, D. J. (1985). Correlation and the coefficient of determination. *Psychological Bulletin, 97*, 307–315.

Paunonen, S. V. (1988). Trait relevance and the differential predictability of behavior. *Journal of Personality, 56*, 599–619.

Paunonen, S. V., & Jackson, D. N. (1985). Idiographic measurement strategies for personality and prediction: Some unredeemed promissory notes. *Psychological Review, 92*, 486–511.

Plomin, R., DeFries, J. C., & Loehlin, J. C. (1977). Genotype-environment interaction and correlation in the analysis of human behavior. *Psychological Bulletin, 84*, 309–322.

Qualls, P. J., & Sheehan, P. W. (1981). Role of the feedback signal in electromyographic biofeedback: The relevance of attention. *Journal of Experimental Psychology: General, 110*, 204–216.

Reise, S., & Waller, N. G. (in press). Fitting the two-parameter model to personality data: The parameterization of the Multidimensional Personality Questionnaire. *Applied Psychological Measurement*.

Revelle, W., Humphreys, H. S., Simon, L., & Gilliland, K. (1980). The interactive effect of personality, time of day, and caffeine: A test of the arousal model. *Journal of Experimental Psychology: General, 109*, 1–31.

Rorer, L. G., & Widiger, T. A. (1983). Personality structure and assessment. In M. R. Rosenzweig & L. W. Porter (Eds.), *Annual Review of Psychology, 34*, 431–463.

Rushton, J. P., Brainerd, C. J., & Pressley, M. (1983). Behavioral development and construct validity: The principle of aggregation. *Psychological Bulletin, 94*, 18–38.

Scarr, S., & McCartney, K. (1983). How people make their own environments: A theory of geno-type-environment effects. *Child Development, 54*, 424–435.

Snyder, M. (1981). On the influence of individuals on situations. In N. Cantor & J. F Kihlstrom (Eds.), *Personality, cognition, and social interaction* (pp. 309–329). Hillsdale, NJ: Erlbaum.

Tellegen, A. (1981). Practicing the two disciplines for relaxation and enlightenment: Comment on Qualls and Sheehan. *Journal of Experimental Psychology: General, 110*, 217–226.

Tellegen, A. (1982). Brief manual of the Multidimensional Personality Questionnaire. Unpublished manuscript.

Tellegen, A. (1985). Structure of mood and personality and their relevance to assessing anxiety, with an emphasis on self-report. In A. H. Tuma & J. D. Maser (Eds.), *Anxiety and the anxiety disorders* (pp. 681–706). Hillsdale, NJ: Erlbaum.

Tellegen, A. (1988). The analysis of consistency in personality assessment. *Journal of Personality, 56*, 621–663.

Tellegen, A., Kamp, J., & Watson, D. (1982). Recognizing individual differences in predictive structure. *Psychological Review, 89*, 95–105.

Tellegen, A., & Waller, N. G. (in preparation). Re-examining dimensions of natural language trait descriptors.

Thurstone, L. L. (1933). *The vectors of mind.* Chicago: University of Chicago Press.

Tryon, R. C. (1973). Basic unpredictability of individual responses to discrete stimulus presentations. *Multivariate Behavioral Research, 8*, 275–295.

Wachtel, P. (1973). Psychodynamics, behavior therapy and the implacable experimenter: An inquiry into the consistency of personality. *Journal of Abnormal Psychology, 82*, 324–334.

Watson, D., & Clark, L. A. (1984). Negative affectivity: The disposition to experience negative emotional states. *Psychological Bulletin, 96*, 465–490.

Wiggins, J. S., Trapnell, P., & Phillips, N. (1988). Psychometric and geometric characteristics of the revised Interpersonal Adjective Scales (IAS-R). *Multivariate Behavioral Research, 23*, 517–530.

Zuckerman, M., Bernieri, F., Koestner, R., & Rosenthal, R. (1989). To predict some of the people some of the time: In search of moderators. *Journal of Personality and Social Psychology, 57* 279–293.

Personality Structure and the Trait-Situation Controversy: On the Uses of Low Correlations

Jane Loevinger

Personality theory has been preoccupied with two challenges: On the one hand, behavior is attributed mostly to situations rather than to enduring predispositions; low correlations between personality tests and behavioral items are cited as evidence. A frequent reply is that appropriate aggregation of tests and behaviors yields reasonably high predictions. The challenge and the reply share the assumption that high correlations are a good thing, the higher the better. On the other hand, Piagetian theorists argue for logically necessary relationships as the basis for constituting measures of stage-types. Allowing for various error factors, which they call décalage, they also expect very high correlations among the elements or components of a stage sequence, the high correlations being the attenuated consequence of the logical necessity. As an alternative to both positions, the present argument is that high correlations rarely reveal new discoveries, whereas patterns of relatively high correlations in universes characterized by generally low correlations are fields where discoveries about personality potentially can be made.

Probabilistic Functionalism

Edward C. Tolman (1932) challenged the Watsonian behaviorist account of learn-

Earlier versions of this paper, "Less is more: The value of low correlations," were presented as the Robert C. Tryon Memorial Lecture at the University of California, Berkeley, January, 1983, and as the Presidential address to Division 24, Theoretical and Philosophical Psychology, of the American Psychological Association, Anaheim, CA, August, 1983.

Research reported here was supported in part by Grants M-1213 and MH-05115 and by Research Scientist Award MH-00657, all from the National Institute of Mental Health, Public Health Service, and by a grant from the Spencer Foundation.

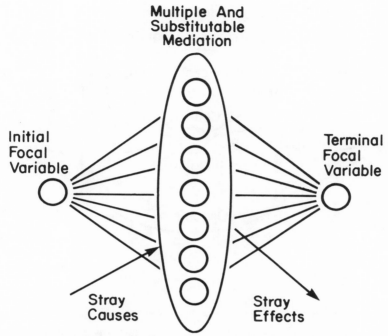

Figure 1. The lens model. Adapted from "The conceptual framework of psychology," by E. Brunswik. In O. Neurath, R. Carnap, & C. Morris (Eds.), *International Encyclopedia of Unified Science*, Vol. 1, Pt. 2. Copyright 1952 by the University of Chicago. Reprinted by permission.

ing, based on experiments he and his students had been doing. The animals had not learned specific movements, as the early behaviorists had thought, but, rather, said Tolman, a cognitive map of the maze. At the same time, Egon Brunswik (1943, 1952; Tolman & Brunswik, 1935) and others at the University of Vienna were looking for the one essential cue for distance perception in humans. No single cue was essential, they found. Perception uses whatever is available; the cues are potentially interchangeable and mutually substitutable (Brunswik, 1952; Hammond, 1966a).

Tolman and Brunswik (1935) grasped the abstract similarity in their programs and findings; Brunswik called the common element the "lens model" (Figure 1). Crudely rendered, the lens model states that there is a specific initial cause (problem, stimulus, etc.), a specific final result (achievement, perception, etc.), but many alternative, mutually substitutable means for going from one to the other. For Tolman, the lens is the family of alternative behaviors by which an organism achieves its purposes. For Brunswik the lens is the family of alternative perceptual clues by which an organism reconstructs the objective world. Putting these

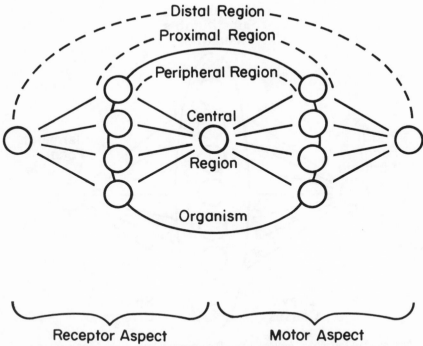

Figure 2. The functional unit of behavior. Adapted from "The conceptual framework of psychology," by E. Brunswik. In O. Neurath, R. Carnap, & C. Morris (Eds.), *International Encyclopedia of Unified Science*, Vol. 1, Pt. 2. Copyright 1952 by the University of Chicago. Reprinted by permission.

two applications of the model together produces a model of the behavioral act (Figure 2).

The cues that impinge on the organism are "local representatives" of distal and hence life-important objects, events, and situations. Just because there are many interchangeable cues that function vicariously for each other, each cue by itself is necessarily equivocal in its meaning. Similarly, specific actions, represented in Figure 2 as "peripheral behavior" or "proximal effects," are generally equivocal in whether they achieve the organism's purposes. The task of the organism is to make the best possible inferences about the actual nature of the environment on the basis of those cues or local representatives available and then to make the best possible choice of peripheral actions as local representatives of goals and aspirations. Perception and behavior are always a series of wagers. Brunswik advocated that psychology concentrate its main efforts on the distal objects, both the initial situations and the achievements, as being focal points of the lens of behavior. At this point the Tolman-Brunswik psychological metatheory, which Brunswik called "probabilistic functionalism," came into conflict with the views of mainstream psychologists who aim to be scientifically rigorous. The rigorists believe that the only way to be really scientific is to study exclusively the proximal-peripheral rather than the distal layers of environment and achievement. But for Tolman and Brunswik "vicarious functioning" (Hunter, 1932), i.e., the lens model, is the very definition of behavior as the subject matter of psychology.

The essence of the lens model is that relatively high correlations can be obtained between events at the two foci of the lens, even when all correlations between events at the foci and mediational events within the lens are very low. That is, a given cause may lead to a given effect with some assurance even when the means of getting from cause to effect is highly variable. Thus there is a kind of paradoxical prediction-at-a-distance or correlation-at-a-distance.

Brunswik and Tolman did not dispute the regularity of the universe with respect to physical laws; the probabilistic character of the environment was not the result of abrogation of the laws of physics. Rather, the environment has the character or texture of a set of probabilities because of the way a living organism interacts with the environment in pursuit of its goals. The higher the organism, the more it depends on distal rather than proximal aspects of the environment, hence the more important the lens model becomes for it. The most important part of the environment for a person is the social environment, the environment as constituted by other people. In that case, probabilities are piled on probabilities, and the possibilities for exact prediction and control are further limited.

What Brunswik presented was an outline for a theory, or metatheory, of the nature of persons, of their environments, and of person-environment interaction, and hence of the appropriate methodology for psychology as a science (Hammond, 1966a). What follows is an application of this theoretical and methodological orientation in the field of personality measurement.

Application to Personality Measurement

The low correlations typical for attempts to predict from personality tests were pointed out by Guilford (1949) on the basis of experience in World War II:

> One general conclusion that was brought home to us by repeated experience is that we should have greater respect for low correlations. Tradition had taught us that unless coefficients of correlation are substantial, for example .40 or above, there is too little relationship to bother with. We must face the fact, unpleasant though it may be, that in human behavior, complex as it is, low intercorrelations of utilizable variables is the rule and not the exception. Highly valid predictions must ordinarily be based on multiple indicators. Although each may add a trifle to the total variance of the thing predicted, by summation the

aggregate prediction can mean a very substantial degree of correlation. Predictions based upon relationships represented by correlations that are very small, even between .10 and .20, may be practically useful when the conditions are right, and when large numbers of individuals are involved. If we are to place dependence upon low correlations, however, it must be remembered that very large samples are required to establish the fact of any correlation at all. (p. 5)

Twenty years later, in an often quoted review of the literature on personality measurement, Mischel (1968) set an upper limit of about .3 on predictions from personality tests. The exact value of that upper limit is ambiguous, because it depends on what counts as a unit to be predicted. If the to-be-predicted behavior is another test performance, higher correlations may be obtained. If the to-be-predicted behavior is something radically different from a personality test, say, success in a pilot-training course, then a prediction even as high as .3 or .4 is hard to come by. That fact itself is predictable from Brunswik's model. No single measurable trait totally determines any performance. Real-life performances have many complex causes. That necessarily implies that the correlation between one cause or set of causes and the performance cannot be high (cf. Meehl & Hathaway, 1946).

Disappointment in those low correlations is reacted to by different psychologists in different ways. Fiske (1978) reacts by retreating to more and more fragmentary acts, which Brunswik would call micromediational research. That is the opposite of what Brunswik recommended. Mischel, on the other hand, has stressed the importance of the situation in determining behavior. Superficially, that would appear to be consistent with Brunswik's (1943) stress on environmental determinants and the ecology of behavior. However, social learning theorists have rarely studied the natural ecology of behavior, at least until recently (Cantor, 1980). That has been the work of Roger Barker (1966), whose frame of reference was similar to that of Brunswik. Although Mischel (1984) has yielded considerable ground to the temporal and cross-situational stability of personality indicators and acknowledges the necessarily probabilistic texture of behavior and environment, he continues to denigrate low correlations. Apparently he does not yet fully appreciate their special value in context of discovery.

Among psychologists who have disputed Mischel's position recently, one argument is that low correlations can be overcome by cumulation of sufficient instances to generate more reliable measures (Block, 1977, 1981; Epstein, 1979, 1986; Rushton, Brainerd, & Pressley, 1983). Another argument is that what personality testers are seeking as traits does not correspond to the idiosyncratic organization of traits in their subjects (Bem & Allen, 1974); another makes reference to the fit of the trait of the subject to the nature of the situation (Bem & Funder, 1978). Mischel and Peake (1982) have answered some of these and other arguments, and there have been several rejoinders and ripostes. (See especially Jackson & Paunonen, 1985.) What I propose, however, takes the discussion in a radically different direction. Of the rejoinders to Mischel and Peake, only that of Conley (1984), criticizing the situationists for their molecular rather than molar approach, hints at the direction taken here.

The import of this essay and of the research cited here is that relationships between test responses, though small and even statistically nonsignificant, can under appropriate circumstances be made to yield insights into personality not available by other empirical methods. Search for universes yielding high correlations is the wrong direction; the method is to search for patterns of *relatively* high correlations in a universe of low correlations. A set of test responses which have only low correlations with each other can be thought of as a lens of the lens model (Figure 3). If there is a lens, it must have some initial focus which can be inferred to be the central focus, i.e., a trait or personality structure (Loevinger, 1966b). Traits and personality structures are not available to direct observation. Thus their reconstruction by the lens model is a truly creative project, rather than the last refuge of despair.

An Objective Test, the Family Problems Scale

An example of constructive use of correlations between items of an objective personality test can be found in a study of mothers' attitudes toward problems of family life (Loevinger, Sweet, Ossorio, & LaPerriere, 1962). The pool of items was intentionally drawn broadly enough to permit testing many alternative hypotheses (Loevinger, 1957); many initial theories about trait and attitude structure did not survive the data (Loevinger et al., 1962).

The statistical method used, homogeneous keying, involved in principle correlating every item with every other item. (Limitations of computers then available and the large pool of items required this to be accomplished in stages.) The method of homogeneous keying (Loevinger, Gleser, & DuBois, 1953) was used because it makes no assumption about the hypothetical structure of underlying factors or traits but merely sorts items into groups or clusters according to their statistical coherence. In the matrices of covariances between items, a high relation between two items was represented by a covariance between .07 and .09, corresponding to a correlation between items of no more than .36. With the 202 cases in the first major sample, a few of the highest correlations were statistically significant, though disappointingly low. Only the redundancy in patterns of items permitted the project to continue in the face of such low correlations (Loevinger, 1957).

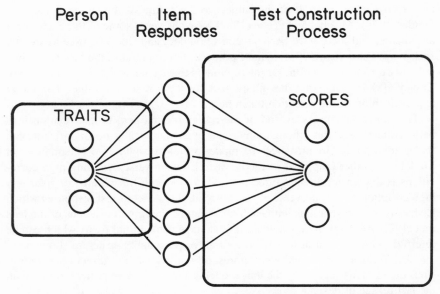

Person   Item Responses   Test Construction Process

Figure 3. Test construction as a receptor process. From J. Loevinger, ''Psychological tests in the conceptual framework of psychology.'' In K. R. Hammond (Ed.), *The psychology of Egon Brunswik.* Copyright 1966 by Holt, Rinehart & Winston. Reprinted by permission.

On the basis of a sympathetic (although even then dated) reading of psychoanalytic theory, a cluster or set of clusters was sought corresponding to psychosexual stages. There was no statistical trace, direct or indirect, of such unities. Items referring to toilet training correlated just as highly with items referring to thumb sucking as with other toilet training items (Loevinger & Sweet, 1961). Thus, there being no lens, no focal trait or syndrome needed to be postulated.

The most salient cluster in the pool of items resembled a prominent factor in many other studies of parental attitudes (Schaefer & Bell, 1958; Sears, Maccoby, & Levin, 1957; Shoben, 1949), usually called something like punitiveness-permissiveness. Results showed that the title is a misnomer. Some items referring directly to punishment of children were uncorrelated with this cluster, whereas some statistically central items referred to entirely different topics. Had the traditional test-construction method of internal consistency been used, the a priori characterization of the supposed trait as punitiveness-permissiveness would not have been questioned, for as originally constituted the entire pool of items displayed high internal consistency. The inclusion of the punitive and permissive items in a pool of items drawn more broadly plus rigorously empirical cluster search led to a change in the conception of personality structure.

The salient cluster of items proved to be best described as Authoritarian Family Ideology. In general, this trait resembles authoritarianism as defined in the Berkeley studies of the authoritarian personality (Adorno, Frenkel-Brunswik, Levinson, & Sanford, 1950), even though their study began with a research focus primarily political and a sample predominantly male, whereas the focus here was entirely small-scale domestic concerns and the sample entirely female. Convergence in the findings of two such different researches vividly demonstrates cross-situational generality.

The Berkeley group originally denied developmental implications of authoritarianism. Variance analysis of a later study of Authoritarian Family Ideology found, however, that it decreased with age, with parity (i.e., first versus second or third child), and with educational level. Relation of Authoritarian Family Ideology to parity and education held up with age covaried out. When education and experience in childrearing were held constant, Catholics, Protestants, and Jews did not differ with respect to the variable (LaPerriere, 1962). Together, these and other findings led to a developmental interpretation of the variable (Loevinger et al., 1962). Because of the broad character of the variable at issue, it was called *ego development*, although that term had other accepted usages (Loevinger, 1966a, 1976). Subsequent studies confirmed the salience and robustness of Authoritarian Family Ideology (Ernhart & Loevinger, 1969).

The Sentence Completion Test of Ego Development

To verify the ego developmental interpretation, Elizabeth Nettles began a study using a sentence completion test (hereafter, SCT) as a validational instrument. Because there was no scoring manual for it, one had to be created (Loevinger & Wessler, 1970).

The first task in manual construction was selecting or constructing a tentative scale: What is the test supposed to measure? Based on the objective test of mothers' attitudes, a generalization of Authoritarian Family Ideology was sought, conceived in the broader terms of ego development. The first scale used was adapted from that of C. Sullivan, M. Q. Grant, and J. D. Grant (1957), who had been studying delinquency in young men. The adaptability of their scale to use with normal women is another demonstration of cross-situational generality. Four points of their scale, corresponding to the stages now called Impulsive, Conformist, Conscientious, and Autonomous (see Table 1 in Loevinger, 1966a or 1976), covered the cases studied.

The first, tentative scoring manual was constructed as follows. For a small pilot sample, all responses to a given sentence stem were sorted into the above four stages; then all the responses within one stage were sorted into a few content categories. Those categories served three purposes. First, they guided the raters of the next sample, showing which features of the response governed the rating; that was the original intention in making categories. Second, by means of the categories, results from one sample could be summarized and used to improve the manual for use with later samples. Third, when the scoring manuals for many items had undergone such successive revisions, the conception of the stages was revised in light of the collated results.

To speak with any assurance from such a data base requires an immense amount of data. Data on over 1,700 cases, most of them completing a 36-item SCT, were used before the scoring manual was published (Loevinger & Wessler, 1970; Loevinger, Wessler, & Redmore, 1970).

The basic process in constructing the published SCT scoring manual was as follows: For some representative sample of cases, all responses to one item were typed together. Each response was assigned to some stage on the scale of ego development, when possible to a particular content category within the stage. When all item responses had been scored, raters scored each protocol as a whole, so that each was given a single total protocol score. Those total protocol scores were used to correct category placement. Every category at every level for each of the 36 stems was evaluated, shifted up or down, split in two, or altered as called for by the data. The method was complicated, however, because base rates (Meehl & Rosen, 1955) of the several levels in the given sample had to be taken into account (Loevinger & Wessler, 1970, pp. 24–25). Suppose a sample has five cases at the Impulsive Stage and 500 cases at the Conformist Stage. A category of response occurs on two of the Impulsive cases and on 20 of the Conformist. That means that 40% of the Impulsive cases have given responses in this category, whereas only 4% of the Conformists have done so. Obviously, the two Impulsive cases make a slim reed to hang conclusions on; therefore, one must take account of experience with similar responses to other stems and of theory, which presumably encodes much experience. In many such cases the category will be called Impulsive, though because of the small number of crucial cases there is no stringent rule. That, at any rate, is the kind of reasoning one must use in creating the manual.

If the decision is made to put this category at the Impulsive Stage, then a small percentage of the Conformist cases in the next similar sample can be expected to have at least one Impulsive level item rating. The method builds in such "errors" (Funder, 1987); it works so long as it is not always the same Conformists who get low ratings. The method of assigning total protocol ratings must take account of such built-in errors. The rules for assigning total protocol ratings based on the cumulative frequency distribution of item ratings do so (Loevinger & Wessler, 1970, p. 129).

The most conspicuous result of manual construction has been delineation of an about eight-point scale of ego development, giving detailed portraits of the attitudes and frame of reference of persons at each level, including many unexpected but plausible details. Further, it has helped to adjudicate differences between alternative versions of similar scales (Loevinger, 1984), for many psychologists have had insight into this major aspect of personality development (Loevinger, 1976, Chapter 5). Following are a few examples of substantive findings revealed in the course of manual construction.

Putative signs of early psychosexual stages were originally interpreted as signs of early stages of ego development; this seemed invariably to lead to erroneous inferences. Thus, as with the Family Problems Scale, the psychoanalytic theory of psychosexual stages provides no useful guidance to ego stage.

The raters insisted that it was necessary to interpolate a stage between the Impulsive and the Conformist Stage. This stage was at first called Opportunistic. One of its surprisingly frequent signs was hostile humor. (W. C. Fields is a classic example.)

Those at the highest ego levels often give the impression of being particularly well-balanced and well-adjusted individuals. However, when category titles for use in the next sample were written on that basis, raters in the next cycle picked up responses by persons whose total protocols clearly put them in the Conformist range. Thus Conformists, not those at the highest levels, are likely to describe themselves as well balanced and well adjusted. Those at the highest stages display a conscious and forthright coping with conflict and paradox, which may give the impression of poor adjustment when an item is taken out of context. (Indeed, that is how such responses are scored in some sentence completion tests; see Rotter & Rafferty, 1950.) What marks the Autonomous and Integrated subjects as better-adjusted than others (if indeed they are so) is their acceptance of conflict and paradox as inevitable to the human condition rather than as an outrage directed at them personally. That is an example of how the method can lead to unexpected and counter-intuitive findings.

Certain responses expressing not self-criticism of a selective sort but total self-rejection turn out to be characteristic of the lowest ego levels. Examples are: "The thing I like about myself is—nothing" and "Sometimes she wished that—I was dead" or "she was dead." Such responses obviously can be made by depressed persons, even perhaps by teen-agers in a bad mood. The scoring method allows for a few low-level responses being made by persons who have on the whole achieved a higher stage. That is part of its probabilistic format. However, the ego level that is most over-represented among persons giving such responses is the lowest, or Impulsive, stage.

Independent confirmation of this finding appears in *The Impulsive Personality* (Wishnie, 1977). Wishnie treated drug addicts and other male delinquents in an inpatient setting over a long period of time. The men, as he described them, fit the Impulsive Stage. One of the hazards of treatment that he describes is that there is a deep depressive tendency just below the surface that may erupt at any time. Thus the finding of certain depressive-sounding responses as characteristic of low ego levels is confirmed by his clinical experience. Similarly, in a study of factors predictive of suicide in young people, Robins (1989) found that depression frequently coexists with impulsive behavior or conduct disorder. This finding, she points out, is contrary to a formerly received opinion in the field that impulsivity is a defense against depression. It is consonant with the conclusions arrived at in the course of manual development.

When the SCT scoring manual was essentially completed, two experienced raters (Augusto Blasi and the writer) independently scanned all the category titles from all the items, taking one stage or transitional level at a time. On this basis each wrote new characterizations of what appeared to be the common elements at that level. We discovered that the earlier characterization of the Opportunistic Stage was not justified in terms of the themes that appeared frequently in responses of normal women at that level; rather, the most evident signs were of self-protectiveness. The stage name was changed accordingly. Also, some hypotheses about the transition from the Conformist to the Conscientious Stage had to be changed. At one time this transition was referred to as "Self-Conscious"; although responses of that sort appear, they are not prototypic enough to justify naming the level so. The name was changed to Self-Aware, then Conscientious-Conformist, emphasizing that it is basically a conformist level. Self-Aware is now the accepted usage. Any implication that it might be a particularly unstable or maladjusted level has found no support in research in our laboratory or any other. Thus, with a progressively deeper understanding of each stage, the conception of ego development took shape. That illustrates the use of the scoring categories to aid theory.

What is at issue is not the value of the SCT as a psychological test. If that were being argued, questions such as the discriminative validity of the test would need to be addressed — in particular, the differentiation of ego development from correlated variables such as verbal fluency, intelligence, age, and socioeconomic status. However much the measure of ego level may be confounded with those variables, no reading or contemplation of those variables could have yielded the detailed dialectic of ego growth that has come from study of the SCT. Those insights into personality structure are the topic of the present paper.

Empirical Stages versus "Hard" Stages

The foregoing method of manual construction uses patterns of response to define the characteristics of each stage. Because each person gives only one response to each stem, and there are many possible responses to each stem at each stage, each category of response has only a low probability of occurring on the protocol of any given person at the corresponding stage, and it occurs on protocols of adjacent stages with probability only slightly lower. Thus what the scoring manual records is the lens of the lens model. The scoring manual has frequently been criticized on this account, i.e., because there is not a simple, compelling logic tying each response unequivocally to a particular scoring stage (Kohlberg, 1981; Broughton & Zahaykevich, 1977).

In a recent review of cognitive stage theories, Fischer and Silvern (1985) state that the invariant sequence that is one criterion for a stage theory "holds only when performance and assessment conditions are described in highly abstract terms, not when particular behaviors, tasks, or procedures are specified (p. 632)." To make a scoring manual, however, requires exactly that particular instances be specified, the more specific, the more useful the manual.

In modern logic, mathematics, and taxonomy, such classifications are often called "fuzzy sets" (Wickelgren, 1981). Scholnick (1984) argues that Piagetian stages cannot be fuzzy sets; the implication that stages could be described empirically and probabilistically is unacceptable to her. Stage descriptions like those found in the SCT scoring manual are also called "prototypes" (Cantor, 1980; Cantor & Mischel, 1979; Evans, 1967) and "family resemblances" (Wittgenstein, 1953).

Thus from a strict, Piagetian point of view (which may not have been Piaget's view), aiming for what Kohlberg has called "hard stages," the levels of ego development as embodied in the SCT manual do not qualify as a stage sequence, despite the fact that claims to some correspondence have been made in the past (e.g., Loevinger, 1976). Once one steps out of the Piagetian framework, however, and accepts the use of empirical and probabilistic methods, results are impervious to the criticism that the ego development stage descriptions are not strictly logically coherent.

The method by which the SCT scoring manual was created would seem to be a much less powerful technique than using as categories of response only ones that are tied to the stage by a strict logic and hence are highly probable to occur at that stage and improbable at adjacent stages. That is the prescription that Kohlberg and his colleagues (Colby & Kohlberg, 1987) have been following for many years. But methods which use only highly probable responses cannot, in principle, yield new discoveries in the process of manual construction. By contrast, the method described, precisely because it uses low probabilities, is uniquely suited to making new discoveries about the several stages.

Structural Analysis as Method

The research with the Family Problems Scale can be seen as an outgrowth of earlier work in psychometrics where the relations of tests or test items revealed something about the structure of the mind. (The reasons for choosing homogeneous keying rather than factor analysis to find the structure underlying responses to the Family Problems Scale are given elsewhere [Loevinger, Gleser, & DuBois, 1953; Loevinger et al., 1962]. They are not germane to the present thesis.) The first and most famous example was Spearman's (1904) discovery of a hierarchy in the correlations of a wide variety of mental tests, and his demonstration that a single general factor, which he called g, could account for the finding. However flawed the conception of general intelligence may be, most psychologists and other people still find some version of it indispensable.

Many further uses of factor analysis, begun with large promises of discovering at last the structure of abilities and personality, have become predominantly methodological discussions, generating few substantial, generally accepted insights into either abilities or personality. There may be some substantial discoveries, but there is no way to identify which of the many alternative and even contradictory findings deserve to be so labeled. Early in the factor-analysis movement, the hope was cherished that rotation of the factors to "simple structure" would produce factors substantially independent of the particular tests and particular samples chosen, hence replicable from study to study. Such a demonstration would have persuaded many psychologists of the importance of those recurrent factors of ability or personality. That independence of specific circumstances did not materialize.

There is one splendid exception, Meehl's (1945; Meehl & Hathaway, 1946) discovery of the K factor in the MMPI (Minnesota Multiphasic Personality Inventory). It is one of the clearest examples of the use of the lens model. Meehl and Hathaway (1946) pointed out that there are no personality test items that are even approximately pure with respect to any trait; all personality items are multiphasic, in the sense that they have many possible meanings. Reasonably valid scales are formed by adding scores on items which, despite the equivocality of each one, together correlate with some criterion. (This effect depends on having different error factors in each item.) Because of the equivocality of the items, however, those scales are far from perfectly univocal. In the circumstance that led to their study that fact is shown by the presence of false positive and false negative cases in the diagnostic use of the MMPI. That is, for each of the scales designed to diagnose a psychiatric syndrome, there were some cases having that syndrome not diagnosed by the test and some normals diagnosed as having the syndrome. Their research, which involved several factor analyses and other techniques, culminated in the K scale, used as a correction to the diagnostic scales, resulting in fewer errors of both kinds. Because of the low communality of the items, the K scale was also equivocal, so they built in a correction factor to it. Even so, with a correction factor and a correction for the correction factor, discrimination could not be made anywhere near perfect.

So far their work would seem to be just test technology, improving the discriminating power of fallible clinical scales, and perhaps that was all they originally intended. What marked this work as an original and significant discovery was the fact that many correction scales were worked out for several clinical scales and for the test in general using several different methods, but a scale evolved by one method or for one diagnosis could be interchanged with a scale worked out by another method or for another clinical scale with little loss. This kind of interchangeability is, in effect, a "lens"; there must be some initial focus, or factor. They chose to call it the K factor, but they recognized that it could not be merely a technical correction factor. There had to be some corresponding psychological reality. As they foresaw, the K factor has proved to be an interesting personality variable in its own right, even though by itself it has negligible clinical significance. At one extreme, it measures a general tendency to be defensive, denying symptoms; at the other, a tendency to self-denigration, claiming symptoms on a minimal basis.

In principle, factor analysis or any other factorial technique could be used to determine the structure of personality, but probably the method that in intent and potential application is closest to the methods described here is the multitrait-multimethod matrix (Campbell & Fiske, 1959).

Although the Campbell and Fiske article showed instances in which the results of a large factor analysis could have been found directly and rapidly by examination of an appropriately arranged matrix of simple correlations, this technique has been neglected as a factorial method. (It is, however, used effectively in conjunction with factor analysis. See Widaman, 1985.) The chief application of their method has been to reveal the heavy weighting of method variance in many psychological tests. They advocated, however, that the method be used primarily as a means for simultaneously improving tests and developing the corresponding trait constructs, as has been done in the studies described above. In light of the frequently low correlations in the universes they are concerned with and the small differences between correlations whose magnitude is being compared, test construction and refinement of constructs by their methods would be similar to the projects sketched above. They certainly recognize that the universe of tests whose intercorrelations they sampled is characteristically equivocal; they do not mention that that is a manifestation of the lens model; and they seem not to recognize that it may be a favorable circumstance for discovering the structure of personality.

Summary and Conclusion

It has long been known, on purely statistical grounds, that the sum of a group of moderate or even low reliability items could under certain circumstances generate a more valid test than an equal number of extremely reliable items. This has been called the Attenuation Paradox (Loevinger, 1954). An example of extremely reliable items would be a perfect Guttman scale. Despite the apparent precision of tests so constituted, the only sets of items that have turned out to be Guttman-scalable have been almost completely redundant in content. No insights into personality structure have ever come that route. This paper presents a parallel point, based on substantive rather than statistical considerations.

The low correlations that lead some psychologists to denigrate personality measurement are the stock in trade of the methods described here. That leads some neo-Piagetians to disdain the methods as being merely statistical and empirical rather than rigorously logical; their accusations are correct. In Brunswik's terms, the multiple, minimally correlated, mutually substitutable signs of a given ego level become the lens of the lens model. In discovering the focus of the lens, something is learned about the structure of personality.

Although many applications of Brunswik's metatheory of psychology have been published (Hammond, 1966b), the implications for the trait-situation controversy presented here have not been noted previously. The prejudice of psychologists against low correlations has probably prevented them from appreciating their unique value in the context of discovery.

As distant as the present methods are from the Piagetian tracing of logical stage sequences, they are more distant from the a priori collection of items to constitute a scoring key, which, prior to the MMPI, was the standard method for constructing tests. The use of undergraduate students or other amateurs to guess what items go together to form a structure of personality or character (cf. Mischel, 1984) is no improvement on psychologists' inability to fathom structure prior to data.

In their classic article on construct validity Cronbach and Meehl (1955) pointed out that genuine discoveries inevitably are manifest in evidence beyond that which gave rise to the inference in the first place. The major insights arising from the foregoing studies, studies primarily of women and originally concerned with problems of family life, confirm and are confirmed by studies done elsewhere mainly using men and originating in concerns of delinquency or of political orientation. This convergence of results on some major concepts demonstrates the power of the techniques and the cross-situational generality of the insights obtained.

References

Adorno, T. W., Frenkel-Brunswik, E., Levinson, D. J., & Sanford, R. N. (1950). *The authoritarian personality*. New York: Harper & Row.

Barker, R. G. (1966). The nature of the environment. In K. R. Hammond (Ed.), *The psychology of Egon Brunswik* (pp. 317– 339). New York: Holt, Rinehart & Winston.

Bem, D. J., & Allen, A. (1974). On predicting some of the people some of the time: The search for cross-situational consistencies in behavior. *Psychological Review, 81*, 506–520.

Bem, D. J., & Funder, D. C. (1978). Predicting more of the people more of the time: Assessing the personality of situations. *Psychological Review, 85*, 485–501.

Block, J. (1977). Advancing the psychology of personality: Paradigmatic shift or improving the quality of research? In D. Magnusson & N. S. Endler (Eds.), *Personality at the crossroads* (pp. 37–63). Hillsdale, NJ: Erlbaum.

Block, J. (1981). Some enduring and consequential structures of personality. In A. J. Rabin, J. Aronoff, A. M. Barclay, & R. A. Zucker (Eds.). *Further explorations in personality* (pp. 27–43). New York: Wiley.

Broughton, J., & Zahaykevich, M. (1977). Review of J. Loevinger's *Ego development: Conceptions and theories. Telos, 32*, 246–253.

Brunswik, E. (1943). Organismic achievement and environmental probability. *Psychological Review, 50*, 255–272.

Brunswik, E. (1952). The conceptual framework of psychology. In *International Encyclopedia of Unified Science* (Vol. 1, pp. 655–760). Chicago: University of Chicago Press.

Campbell, D. T., & Fiske, D. W. (1959). Convergent and discriminant validation by the multitrait-multimethod matrix. *Psychological Bulletin, 56*, 81–105.

Cantor, N. (1980). Perceptions of situations: Situation prototypes and person-situation prototypes. In D. Magnusson (Ed.), *Toward a psychology of situations: An interactional perspective* (pp. 229–244). Hillsdale, NJ: Erlbaum.

Cantor, N., & Mischel, W. (1979). Prototypes in person perception. In L. Berkowitz (Ed.), *Advances in experimental social psychology*, Vol. 12 (pp. 4–53). New York: Academic Press.

Colby, A., & Kohlberg, L. (1987). The measurement of moral judgment. Cambridge: Cambridge University Press.

Conley, J. J. (1984). Relation of temporal stability and cross-situational stability in personality measurement: Comment on the Mischel-Epstein debate. *Psychological Review, 91*, 491– 496.

Cronbach, L. J., & Meehl, P. E. (1955). Construct validity in psychological tests. *Psychological Bulletin, 52*, 281–302.

Epstein, S. (1979). The stability of behavior. I. On predicting most of the people much of the time. *Journal of Personality and Social Psychology, 37*, 1097–1126.

Epstein, S. (1986). Does aggregation produce spuriously high estimates of behavioral stability? *Journal of Personality and Social Psychology, 50*, 1199–1210.

Ernhart, C. B., & Loevinger, J. (1969). Authoritarian family ideology: A measure, its correlates, and its robustness. *Multivariate Behavioral Research Monographs*, no. 69–1.

Evans, S. H. (1967). A brief statement of schema theory. *Psychonomic Science, 8*, 87–88.

Fischer, K. W., & Silvern, L. (1985). Stages and individual differences in cognitive development. *Annual Review of Psychology, 36*, 613–648.

Fiske, D. W. (1978). *Strategies for personality research*. San Francisco: Jossey-Bass.

Funder, D. C. (1987). Errors and mistakes: Evaluating the accuracy of social judgment. *Psychological Bulletin, 101*, 75–90.

Guilford, J. P. (1949). Some lessons from aviation psychology. *American Psychologist, 3*, 3–11.

Hammond, K. R. (1966). Probabilistic functionalism: Egon Brunswik's integration of the history, theory, and method of psychology. In K. R. Hammond (Ed.), *The psychology of Egon Brunswik* (pp. 15–80). New York: Holt, Rinehart & Winston. (a)

Hammond, K. R. (Ed.). (1966). *The psychology of Egon Brunswik*. New York: Holt, Rinehart & Winston. (b)

Hunter, W. S. (1932). The psychological study of behavior. *Psychological Review, 39*, 1–24.

Jackson, D. N., & Paunonen, S. V. (1985). Construct validity and the predictability of behavior. *Journal of Personality and Social Psychology, 49*, 554–570.

Kohlberg, L. (1981). *The meaning and measurement of moral development*. Worcester, MA: Clark University Press.

LaPerriere, K. (1962). Maternal attitudes in different subcultural groups. Unpublished doctoral dissertation, Washington University, St. Louis.

Loevinger, J. (1954) The attenuation paradox in test theory. *Psychological Bulletin, 51*, 493–504.

Loevinger, J. (1957). Objective tests as instruments of psychological theory. *Psychological Reports, 3*, 635–694.

Loevinger, J. (1966). The meaning and measurement of ego development. *American Psychologist*, *21*, 195–206. (a)

Loevinger, J. (1966). Psychological tests in the conceptual framework of psychology. In K. R. Hammond (Ed.), *The psychology of Egon Brunswik* (pp. 107–148). New York: Holt, Rinehart & Winston. (b)

Loevinger, J. (1976). *Ego development: Conceptions and theories*. San Francisco: Jossey-Bass.

Loevinger, J. (1984). On the self and predicting behavior. In R. A. Zucker, J. Aronoff, & A. I. Rabin (Eds.), *Personality and the prediction of behavior* (pp. 43–68). Orlando, FL: Academic Press.

Loevinger, J., Gleser, G. C., & DuBois, P. H. (1953). Maximizing the discriminating power of a multiple-score test. *Psychometrika*, *18*, 309–317.

Loevinger, J., & Sweet, B. (1961). Construction of a test of mothers' attitudes. In J. Glidewell (Ed.), *Parental attitudes and child behavior* (pp. 110–123). Springfield, IL: Charles C Thomas.

Loevinger, J., Sweet, B., Ossorio, A., & LaPerriere, K. (1962). Measuring personality patterns of women. *Genetic Psychology Monographs*, *65*, 53–136.

Loevinger, J., & Wessler, R. (1970). *Measuring ego development 1. Construction and use of a sentence completion test*. San Francisco: Jossey-Bass.

Loevinger, J., Wessler, R., & Redmore, C. D. (1970). *Measuring ego development 2. Scoring manual for women and girls*. San Francisco: Jossey-Bass.

Meehl, P. E. (1945). The dynamics of "structured" personality tests. *Journal of Clinical Psychology*, *1*, 296–303.

Meehl, P. E., & Hathaway, S. R. (1946). The *K* factor as a suppressor variable in the Minnesota Multiphasic Personality Inventory. *Journal of Applied Psychology*, *30*, 525–564.

Meehl, P. E., & Rosen, E. (1955). Antecedent probability and the efficiency of psychometric signs, patterns, or cutting scores. *Psychological Bulletin*, *52*, 194–216.

Mischel, W. (1968). *Personality and assessment*. New York: Wiley.

Mischel, W. (1984). On the predictability of behavior and the structure of personality. In R. A. Zucker, J. Aronoff, & A. I. Rabin (Eds.), *Personality and the prediction of behavior* (pp. 269–305). Orlando, FL: Academic Press.

Mischel, W., & Peake, P. K. (1982). Beyond déjà vu in the search for cross-situational consistency. *Psychological Review*, *89*, 730–755.

Robins, L. N. (1989). *Suicide attempts in teen-aged medical patients. Alcohol, drug abuse, & mental health administration, report of Secretary's Task Force on Youth Suicide. Vol. 4. Strategies for prevention of youth suicide*. DHHS Publ. No. ADM 89-1624. Wash. DC. Supt. of Docs., U.S. Govt. Printing Office. Pp. 94–114.

Rotter, J. B., & Rafferty, J. E. (1950). *Manual, The Rotter Incomplete Sentences Blank, College Form*. New York: Psychological Corporation.

Rushton, J. P., Brainerd, C. J., & Pressley, M. (1983). Behavioral development and construct validity: The principle of aggregation. *Psychological Bulletin*, *94*, 18–38.

Schaefer, E. S., & Bell, R. Q. (1958). Development of a parental attitude research instrument. *Child Development*, *29*, 339–361.

Scholnick, E. K. (1984). Are stages "fuzzy sets"? *Genetic Epistemologist*, *12*, 1–5.

Sears, R. R., Maccoby, E. E., & Levin, H. (1957). *Patterns of child rearing*. Evanston, IL: Row, Peterson.

Shoben, E. J., Jr. (1949). The assessment of parental attitudes in relation to child adjustment. *Genetic Psychology Monographs*, *39*, 101–148.

Spearman, C. (1904). "General intelligence" objectively determined and measured. *American Journal of Psychology*, *15*, 201–292.

Sullivan, C., Grant, M. Q., & Grant, J. D. (1957). The development of interpersonal maturity: Applications to delinquency. *Psychiatry*, *20*, 373–385.

Tolman, E. C. (1932). *Purposive behavior in animals and men*. New York: Appleton-Century-Croft.

Tolman, E. C., & Brunswik, E. (1935). The organism and the causal texture of the environment. *Psychological Review*, *42*, 43–77.

Wickelgren, W. A. (1981). Human learning and memory. *Annual Review of Psychology*, *32*, 21–52.

Widaman, K. F. (1985). Hierarchically nested covariance structure models for multitrait-multimethod data. *Applied Psychological Measurement*, *9*, 1–26.

Wishnie, H. (1977). *The impulsive personality*. New York: Plenum.

Wittgenstein, L. (1953). *Philosophical investigations*. New York: Macmillan.

Not Personality Scales, Personality Items
Paul H. Blaney

This essay arises out of my profound dismay regarding the current state of the field of objective personality assessment in terms of self-report. In my view, the major problems are not those inherent in the use of self-report, nor are they specific to any particular instrument or to the approach of any one group of researchers or clinicians. Rather, they are pervasive and fundamental; they reflect prevailing folkways of personality assessment in both clinical and research contexts. When there is as much intense scholarly and clinical inquiry — by as many highly trained, intelligent individuals — as there is in this field, one should be able to identify clear progress. Instead, even the uncynical among us often experience our field in terms of the rise and fall of fads and fancies.

In my view, the most salient aspect of the personality assessment landscape today is the huge number of instruments available. I suspect that even the well-read scholar, in examining a current issue of the *Journal of Consulting and Clinical Psychology* or the *Journal of Personality and Social Psychology*, would come upon a half dozen inventory scales s/he did not recognize, even though none of the constructs being measured was novel.

While to an extent the proliferation of instruments is a reflection of the theoretical pluralism of our field, I do not believe pluralism to be the major culprit. Arcane nuances aside, the number of basic assessment questions that all reasonable students of human nature might wish to pose is, I believe, large but not unmanageably so. In contrast to this finite number of possible items, the number of possible *scales* is virtually infinite, for three reasons: (a) languages are essentially open-ended systems; (b) items can be grouped and packaged in diverse combinations and permutations, and (c) many classes of psychologically relevant events have large arrays of instances, each of which can form an item that differs, if only superficially, from the others. The number of questions we wish to ask is,

I suspect, now exceeded by the number of scales we have devised for asking them.

This proliferation of scales probably arises in part from the fact that rewards—in citations and in dollars—may accrue from developing a scale or test which takes hold. (At the very least, writing a new scale may spare one from having to pay royalties to someone else.) Conversely, there are few disincentives facing the individual whose dreams run in the direction of new scale development, and there are few incentives that would induce him/her to explore fully what prior instrument development had been carried out. And the barriers to carrying out such an exploration are formidable: the large number of published scales, the fact that scale names tell so little about scale contents, the expense of obtaining even examination copies of commercially published instruments, and the difficulty of locating copies of unpublished ones. Pity the scholar who *does* take it upon him/herself to know about all existing published and unpublished instruments relevant to his/her own area.

In our field, the only strong tradition of critical evaluation of new scales is with respect to rather limited psychometric characteristics. For instance, when an author submits a journal manuscript presenting a new scale, the editorial process may address reliability and validity, but it does not typically include a systematic examination of the extent to which the scale overlaps in content with existing scales; whether such overlap is detected depends upon which existing tests the editorial reviewers happen to be intimately familiar with. Our *Standards for Education and Psychological Testing* (1985) may, if anything, contribute indirectly to the problem by legitimizing scale development that meets specified procedural standards. Those *Standards* don't even mention that, before embarking on scale development, the author might be obliged to become familiar with what already exists in the domain s/he wishes to assess. And, as noted above, if such an obligation were specified, it would entail an effort which usually ranged from heroic to epic, if undertaken by a single researcher or small research team.

In my view, a major aspect of the problem is the fact that our field operates on the scale level rather than the item level. Because our traditions allow for scales with diverse item content[1] and because there are no rules governing the naming of scales, the relation between the scale name and scale content is often loose. Nonetheless, we tend to think of two scales as similar if they have similar names. If two scales have dissimilar names, we assume that they are dissimilar scales; if their items were very similar, it might faze us if we noticed it, but we probably wouldn't. If two differently named scales had similar items, it probably would not occur to us to generalize our findings on the one to the other. If we found the two to be empirically related, we might decide it was theoretically interesting and publish our findings, still without noticing the item similarity (Nicholls, Licht, & Pearl, 1982). Once a scale is a scale, apart from the ritual performance of factor analyses, we tend to pay as little attention to its items as possible. Even factor analysis often occurs so late in the scale-development process that its limited use-fulness is compromised (Briggs & Cheek, 1986).

I believe that my grim appraisal of the field of personality assessment is likely to meet with ready assent by persons who have much contact with it. I believe that the chaos can be ignored but not denied. Because of this, and because it is not clear what would constitute satisfactory documentation of my grim assessment, I do not choose to offer much documentation. For possible doubters, I offer an example (elaborated from Monroe & Steiner, 1986, and from Nicholls et al., 1982) regarding items involving social reticence. Such items appear in one form or another on scales labeled alienation, anhedonia, anxiety, dominance, introversion, loneliness, need for affiliation, neuroticism, masculinity, shyness, social support, and support-seeking coping. (See Nicholls et al. [1982] for other examples.)

It is just as well that there is no person or group who can place absolute limits on the use and development of scales. But we have something approaching the opposite extreme—an absence of even the flexible constraints that strong critical traditions provide. The key word in understanding the negative impact upon progress in our field is *fragmentation*. When, blinded by the name of the scale one is using, a researcher fails to note commonalities between one's research and other studies using scales with similar or overlapping item content but dissimilar names, an opportunity for the cumulative building of a common knowledge base is lost.[2]

We are in much the same position that chemistry would be in if, any time a chemist formulated a compound which seemed novel to him, s/he were free to give it whatever name s/he chose, and publish studies on it under that name, without checking if anybody else had done research on that compound. The problem, of course, would lie not in the use of multiple names to identify variables per se, but in the lack of a universal indexing, referencing, and notation system which would allow—and oblige—researchers who had opted for different nick-names to acknowledge their common ground. Chemistry has one, personality assessment doesn't. Or, to use an example closer to home, the fragmentation of personality scales impedes progress in the same way that progress would be impeded in psychopathology research if there were many, overlapping diagnostic taxonomies jostling for a piece of the action, none of which was a standard point of departure, and if they were too numerous for anyone to keep track of all of them, much less of their similarities and differences. Psychopathology has a point-of-departure nosology, the domain of self-report personality items does not.

Nicholls et al. (1982) have suggested that problems such as I (and they) have put forward "should not occur if, instead of starting with single constructs, we started with a comprehensive, theoretically justified, and perhaps hierarchically related set of constructs" (pp. 578–579) and "if we focus on personal and social action construed at a lower level of abstraction'' (p. 579). They also ''suggest that journal reviewers scrutinize scales referred to in submitted manuscripts'' (p. 579), to consider on an item-content level what might account for obtained empirical relations. I concur strongly with these recommendations, though I am less concerned that what emerges be ''theoretically justified'' than that it be usable by scholars of all persuasions. While it would be nice to have a great conceptual leap forward, what we need most is a universal tool.

Specifically, from my vantage what is needed is a taxonomy of items — a taxonomy of the domain of personally relevant, objectively scored self-statements and descriptors.[3] The goal would be to provide a framework in which *all* existing personality, psychopathology, interest, coping, cognitive, and behavioral self-report test items could be identified. The need for theoretical neutrality imposes a strong bias in favor of item groupings based on ostensive characteristics, groupings that can be given labels which accurately summarize the form and content of the items included in them.[4]

The Structure of the Taxonomy

One can group items in *columns*, in cells within a *matrix*, and *hierarchically*. The columnar approach merely lists those deemed to be alike.[5] The defining characteristic of a matrix approach is that some ''columns'' crosscut each other; that is, items are cross-filed. The key to a hierarchical approach is that some items are subsidiary to others.

Most psychological tests have used the columnar approach. The most familiar instance of the *matrix* approach is Guilford's (1967) intelligence model; in personality, I can think only of the Alienation Test (Maddi, Kobasa, & Hoover, 1979), and the Endler, Hunt, and Rosenstein (1962) S-R test and its derivatives. Apart from the use of higher- and lower-order factor scales, if a personality test were to be structured *hierarchically*, it would probably be done by a flowchart approach. For instance, one could ask if the subject has been experiencing unpleasant emotions; then, only if the response is yes, ask: Depression? Anger? Anxiety? etc. This would correspond to a hierarchical taxonomy in which depression, anger, and anxiety are all found in subcategories under the heading of unpleasant emotions. I know of no instance of this in a self-report inventory, though it is implicit in unstructured clinical interviews and has long been a part of structured diagnostic interviews (e.g., Spitzer, Burdock, & Hardesty, 1964).

In the context of item taxonomy development, sole reliance on the columnar approach would be hopelessly inefficient. The matrix approach is more efficient and can be used to show the diverse ways items are similar to one another and to suggest kinds of items that might not otherwise come to mind. The main shortcoming of the matrix approach is that it can suggest cells for which no reasonable instance can be found or created; one must be willing to tolerate empty cells or cells which can be filled only by trivial or ponderously worded items.

The compelling logic behind the use of a hierarchical approach is that the purpose of a taxonomy is to group similar elements together, and similarity can lie at various levels of abstraction. One source of information regarding hierarchical levels might be the results of higher- vs. lower-order factor analysis. In this vein, Goldberg (1981) has offered the fact that personality information is hierarchically structured as a major reason that orthogonal factor analysis cannot provide totally satisfactory accounts of personality test item variance.

Fortunately, given the fact that they both have clear advantages in the taxonomy context, matrix and hierarchical approaches can be merged. Doing so requires merely that the matrix be organized hierarchically, that is, that it incorporate sub- and superordinate categories.

Ultimately, one would like to have a taxonomy that is useful cross-culturally and cross-linguistically. Goldberg (1981) has offered a few relevant comments that merit repeating: "that languages differ from each other not so much in what they *can* convey, but rather in what they can *easily* convey" (p. 151), and that cross-linguistic comparability is most likely to be evident at hierarchical levels that are neither too specific nor too general and abstract.

Classes of Items

Here, for purposes of discourse, and with apologies for its lack of true novelty (cf. Angleitner, John, & Lohr, 1986), is my first-iteration attempt at a content-free list of kinds of items:

(a) *characterological statements*; i.e., trait statements that are tied to covert or overt behavioral referents only by some theoretical or inferential link (e.g., "I have an anal personality").

(b) *typical behavior statements*; i.e., trait statements having clear behavioral referents; also known as dispositions. Included here are everything from pathological symptoms to coping mechanisms.

(c) *situation-specific behavior statements*; i.e., trait statements (such as above), but having clear situational referents, e.g., traumatic stressors, cultural opportunities. Some items may deserve inclusion here even though they lack explicit mention of a situation; the reason is that an eliciting situation is implied by some response-oriented wordings (e.g., "I've been grieving recently").

(d) *situation-specific imaginary behavior statements*; i.e., statements like (c) above but having hypothetical situational referents. Here the question is "How would you respond to . . . ?" rather than "How have you responded to . . . ?" Examples of existing instruments organized around such items are the Defense Mechanisms Inventory (Gleser & Ihilevich, 1969), the Cognitive Bias Questionnaire (Krantz & Hammen, 1979), and tests employing the S-R format (see Endler et al., 1962).

(e) *state statements*; i.e., statements regarding how the individual is feeling or acting at the moment. When the assessor can specify the effective stimulus context prevailing during the examination, state items may be viewed as providing situation-specific response information in a way that is more direct than with (c) or (d) above. There are probably no state-descriptors that cannot also be viewed as descriptors of responses to noncurrent or hypothetical stimuli. Many affective words in our language are used to describe both states and traits (see Clore, Ortony, & Foss, 1987), such that items using those words must include clarifying language if ambiguity is to be avoided.

(f) *personal history and life situation statements*; e.g., significant childhood events, recent stressful experiences, current social resources.

(g) *attitudinal statements*; i.e., items having to do with one's views regarding the world and one's prospects in it. The domain of such items is perhaps infinite, but our primary interest in attitudes toward the self, other people, and relationships narrows the range considerably. A given attitudinal statement may have much in common with a particular situation-specific response item—classed as (c) or (d) above. For instance, the items "Mechanics magazines are fun" and "I like mechanics magazines" may be on some level equivalent to "For me, looking at mechanics magazines results (or would result) in a positive affective state." It may be that the crux of the distinction between attitudinal (g) and situation-specific response items (c and d) lies in the extent to which the first-person aspect of the item is implicit or explicit in its phrasing, an aspect that was included in the item characterization system offered by Angleitner et al. (1986).

Content Classes and Instances

The above list is content free. Even the most cursory attempt to flesh it out with content would make apparent the parallels across these noncontent categories. For instance, the particular situations and behaviors appropriate for *situation-specific behavior statements*, and for *situation-specific imaginary behavior statements*, would be similar to one another, and the behaviors from both would mirror the structure of *typical behavior statements*. Indeed, it appears likely that one would be well along the path of developing an all-purpose content system if one had taxonomies of situations and of responses, crossed in matrix fashion with the noncontent categories in the prior section; only *characterological statements* would be unincorporated since, at least as I have used the term, these statements refer to descriptors that lack self-evident behavioral or experiential referents.

We have strong traditions in psychology to tell us what traits and responses might be included (or at least sampled from) in the development of a truly "adequate taxonomy" (Norman, 1963). And there have been major systematizing efforts, for instance the work of Goldberg (1982) and Wiggins (1979) in the domain of traits, the recent work of Clore et al. (1987) and of Storm and Storm (1987) for affects, and the earlier work of Meehl et al. (1959) covering a broad domain. Our field is not well developed with respect to situations (Fiske, 1986), though it appears there has been some progress in this area (see Block & Block, 1981; Cantor, Mischel, & Schwartz, 1982; Schlundt & McFall, 1987).

Some research on situations has taken the approach of classifying them on the basis of shared responses (Dore & Kirouac, 1985; Magnusson & Ekehammar, 1975). While this is a reasonable approach, it relies upon normative situation-response linkages (see also Harrison, 1986), and we are commonly at least as interested in the non-normative as in the normative. As Buss and Craik (1983, p. 117) noted, "displaying little emotion when meeting an old friend at the airport constitutes an aloof act, but displaying little emotion . . . while reading the newspaper probably does not." More generally, what often makes a response nontrivial and psychologically interesting is the situation in which it occurs.

Indeed, I suspect that any interest in an act-frequency approach to traits/dispositions is tied in with our assumption that if the individual engages in the behavior a lot, some of the situations in which s/he does so represent nontrivial (deviant, diagnostic) occurrences. We would probably be wiser, for instance, to use the label "aggressive" for the person whose aggressive behavior was infrequent but always unprovoked than for the one whose aggressive behavior was frequent but always in response to a veridical, unsolicited external threat.

There is at least one situational class for which no satisfactory universal instance exists, the class of "novel experiences." While there are other situational classes that *can* be individualized (e.g., fun things to do), their use entails defining situations in terms of the responses to them. We really should do our best to avoid the circularity of the law of effect. The abundance in our language of response terms that tend to imply situation-response linkages (e.g., "grieving") is problematic, in that such terms confound the response with the inference regarding its eliciting context. Another source of conceptual difficulty is the fact that one's experience of a situation is, in part, a function of cognitive/perceptual responses (see Block & Block, 1981).

There are at least four overlapping reasons why, in some cases, broad situation and response category labels, though available, are best avoided, that is, in which the purposes of testing are best served by the use of highly specific instances, even seemingly trivial ones, rather than items that articulate the class for which they stand. First, there are classes the very name of which may entail heavy evaluative baggage; such classes may have instances that are less obviously evaluative, and thus more likely to generate an unbiased response. Second, the use of superordinate class names may elicit more variability in interpretation than do instances, in which case intraindividual differences in item responses may reflect differences among individuals in the instances that the superordinate category name conjures up—and to which they thus respond; for example, the item "Every now and then I like to do something that's just a bit outrageous" may elicit images of *skydiving naked* for some persons, images of *staying up past ten-thirty* for others. Third, superordinate categories may place a greater reliance upon the subjects' inferential processes and abilities. Finally, the nonspecificity of superordinate categories can entail item ambiguity that may interfere with test-taker comfort and cooperativeness and with response reliability.

In any case, the developers of a taxonomy need not, and should not, determine how specific versus general actual test items should be. The taxonomy need only provide a framework in which items of various degrees of specificity can be described and compared. Given that not every specific instance can be listed in a taxonomy, research that suggests particularly good instances for categories (e.g., Buss & Craik, 1983) can help a taxonomy come to life.

Factor Analysis

I suggested above that prevailing practice involves an inattention to items in scales. The major exception to this—and the context in which researchers do note cross-instrument item similarity—is when factor analyses are carried out. Commonly, in naming and describing a factor, researchers look at the items that load on the factor, and note commonalities between items in the factors at hand and items characterizing factors reported in the literature. Recently, some scholars have gone a step farther and, noting cross-study commonalities, argued that we now have consensual ways of looking at personally descriptive items (McCrae & Costa, 1986; Watson & Tellegen, 1985). Such efforts are welcome for their potential focusing and organizing value. However, I think it very important that we be aware of their limitations, and I would object to heavy reliance upon such strategies in the development of a comprehensive item taxonomy. There are three such shortcomings, the latter two pertaining to reliance on factor analysis more generally.

First, whenever one relies heavily upon consensus across studies, one tends to select for replicability (which is good), but, regrettably, one tends also to ignore variables that, for any number of trivial reasons, emerge only part of the time. Cross-sample consensus tends to favor a lowest common denominator standard of acceptability.

Second, factor-analytic techniques rely wholly upon linear correlational logic, and any conclusion based on factor analysis incorporates the limitations of correlational research. As we all know from Psychology 101, if A correlates with B, it may be because A causes B, because B causes A, or because C causes both A and B. With test items, it may also be because A and B have considerable semantic overlap. When a factor analysis is carried out, item A can thus load together with items representing what item A causes, with items representing what

A is caused by, with items representing outcomes that have the same cause that item A does, and with items that are somewhat synonymous with item A. While most psychologists who employ factor-analytic techniques probably once taught Psychology 101, one would not suspect it from their research reports, which commonly evidence a systematic inattention to the question of why subjects give the responses they do.

Just as correlational approaches can group together items that have important differences, they can also *fail* to group items that deserve to be together. There are at least five reasons for this: (a) the fact that two items have markedly different endorsement frequencies constrains the magnitude of their correlation with each other; (b) two items may represent complementary outcomes having a common cause, as when they represent alternative expressions of the same underlying tendency, with the one expression *reducing* the need (or opportunity) for the other (as in a hydraulic model of motivational states); (c) two items may represent alternative independent causes for a common outcome;[6] (d) their relation may be markedly nonlinear; and (e) the close relation they have may be found only in a minority of subjects. Just as every large correlation should lead us to ask *Why?*, many small correlations should also be the occasion for asking *Why?*

Third, as typically implemented, the goal of factor analysis is to minimize the number of variables. I wish to take issue with this prevalent reductionism. We should be glad that chemists and physicists are not still trying to account for all matter in terms of, say, ten elements that combine into 100 compounds. If there is an *a priori* reason to believe that personal attributes can be portrayed using a scheme simpler than the periodic table of elements, I am unaware of it. Statements verbalizing this viewpoint are not easy to find in the published literature, but here is one, albeit a bit dated: "There are perhaps 200 words in English designating color experience. By tetrachoric correlations this list might be greatly reduced, but what an inadequate vocabulary would result for the profusion of distinguishable color sensations, estimated to exceed 2,000,000 in number! From the point of view of the trait-hypothesis it seems equally unreasonable to factor out a handful of independent units in the excessively complex equations of human nature" (Allport & Odbert, 1936, p. 34). (See also Dahlstrom, 1972.)

The most likely justification for minimizing the number of variables is the difficulty of getting subjects to discriminate between similar stimuli. This is a legitimate concern. As Wiggins has noted, "the thinness with which we slice the . . . pie is limited by the reliability with which respondents can distinguish between closely synonymous words or phrases" (1979, p. 400). The crucial point, however, is that factor analysis is ill-suited to be an arbiter of item discriminability. If two items fall on different factors they are probably discriminable, but the fact that two items load heavily on the same factor may be for reasons other than that subjects cannot reliably distinguish one from the other!

Moreover, factor analysis can be aimed at deriving the largest possible roster of distinguishable factors, each at the lowest order possible; the major impediment to such an effort with a broad-based item pool is the large sample size needed to foster replicability. Indeed, there are factor-analytic results which support the view that subjects are able to make discriminations more fine-grained than is implied by the 2–16 factors that typically emerge in large-scale factor analyses of diverse item pools. First, when focused item sets are submitted to factor analysis, several factors commonly appear; examples are self-esteem (e.g., Briggs & Cheek, 1986), sensation-seeking (e.g., Eysenck, 1983) and locus of control (e.g., Levenson, 1974). Second, there is at least one factor analysis that yielded 40 factors (Meehl, Lykken, Schofield, & Tellegen, 1971); granted that the data were clinician ratings rather than self-reports, the evidence from this research was that items loading on most of the factors were easily seen as belonging with each other and not with other groupings.

I suspect that the reductionism that pervades the field of personality assessment really arises in large part from what might be referred to as data overload syndrome. Who is there among us who has never, following an arduous data collection effort, found oneself looking with terror at, say, a 10 X 10 correlation matrix, based on 150 subjects? At such a time, one asks oneself: *Can I make sense of these data? If so, should I? Of the 45 correlations, which are the two or three that are significant by chance? What will the journal's editor say?* Faced with such anguish, few among us can remain strong. We welcome any defensible strategy that reduces the number of variables, regardless of how psychologically arbitrary that strategy may be. The antidote should be large sample sizes, but we use the palliative of factor analysis instead.

When all is said and done, perhaps the clearest indictments of factor-analytic approaches continue, two decades after they were written, to be Meehl et al.'s (1971) observations regarding the fact that constructs which originated solely from factor analysis just do not make it into widespread professional discourse and Lykken's (1971) dramatic empirical demonstration of how poorly factor analysis matches reality within a well-understood domain. My conclusion: methods such as factor analysis are tools and sources of information rather than ultimate arbiters. If they are to be useful, one must be mindful of their limitations. They should be contributors rather than arbiters in the development of an item taxonomy.

Response Determinants

As Meehl (1945) noted, objective items often have a projective quality to them. Self-report items, even when printed very neatly on clean paper, are commonly ambiguous stimuli. While the classic viewpoint of empirical test development was that between-individual differences in possible meanings of items are to be ignored (Meehl, 1945), we generally do not take the projective aspect of self-report items to be one of their major virtues. When we want ambiguous stimuli, we tend to use projective tests, and we relish the relative freedom from ambiguity that objective inventories provide. In fact, though, both idiosyncratic and normative response determinants of commonly used personality test approaches are remarkably underresearched. From a broad scientific perspective, Fiske's (1986) statement that we need "to achieve a better understanding of the way people go about making their decisions in responding to self-report items" (p. 43) may appear obvious, but it is a call that few make and fewer heed.

The research effort that a serious response to this call implies is enormous, but it is one which, in my view, is much more likely to result in real progress than are the numerous studies devoted to the correlates of multi-item scales. Notwithstanding possible contextual influences and interitem dependencies, subjects usually respond to items one at a time, and if we are to know the determinants of their responses, we are going to have to start at the level of items and classes of items. There are several approaches that can be taken.

First, we can ponder the probable consensual meaning of various statements; as members of the linguistic community our own introspections are likely to be informative. This we routinely do in initial steps of item-pool derivation but not subsequently, and the results of these ponderings are not usually viewed as meriting mention as part of the public record of a scale's derivation, in spite of the central role they may play in that process. There are empirical data which suggest that, unfortunately, membership in the psychological community may be associated with having semantic judgments which differ systematically from those found in the broader population (Kastner, 1986).

Second, we can ask subjects why they gave the response they did to a given item (Kastner, 1986; Kuncel, 1973). Subjects' reports are likely to be informative if not definitive.

Third, correlational analyses can, after all, be very informative regarding the determinants of a response.

Fourth, item research can pursue a psychophysical strategy, as when psychophysical methods are used to place descriptor series (many, some, few) on an interval scale (e.g., Newstead, Pollard, & Riezebos, 1987). Such methods can also be useful in detecting large intraindividual variation in word meanings. Loehlin (1967) has developed an approach that allows some assessment of the extent to which individual differences in self-referent responding are due to (a) intrapersonal inconsistency of word meanings and (b) individual differences in word meanings, as opposed to (c) meanings that are consistent across persons and within persons across time. The impact of minor variations in wording can be examined from this viewpoint.[7]

Even when consistency of meaning has been maximized by the use of clearly phrased items, there remain six classes of determinants to self-report items (see also Paulhus, 1986; Shrauger & Osberg, 1981):

(a) reality; the totally accurate, consensually understood answer to our inquiry; our mythic goal.

(b) prior experience. Subjects' responses, particularly to situation-specific items, depend in part upon the particulars of their real-life exposure to the situation. Similarly, when items involve an implicit or explicit comparison between self and others, the response is determined in part by the characteristics of the "others" in one's life space.

(c) information-processing abilities. Many items require that one observe and remember aspects of one's experience, that one average across times and contexts, and that one make comparisons within self and between self and others. Individuals presumably differ in cognitive skills relevant to these abilities.

(d) affective bias. There is reason to believe that the emotional state of the respondent may influence a variety of information-processing tasks, many of which are involved in self-report responses (see Blaney, 1986).

(e) self-perception needs. Individuals may bias their beliefs regarding themselves and the world in ways that maximize self-esteem, minimize anxiety, promote consistency, etc.

(f) self-presentational needs. Individuals may modify their self-reports in the service of creating a desired impression on the examiner.

Corresponding to the fact that they have diverse determinants, item responses can be viewed as informative in at least three ways: as the *report* of objective reality, as a *reflection* of the subject's perception of reality, and as an *instance* of the subject's interpersonal communications. For example, if a subject endorses the statement "I have severe aches in most of my muscles most of the time" (even putting aside individual differences in the calculation of "most"), this can be taken as a report of private pain events, or as a reflection of somatic preoccupation, or as an instance of pervasive complaining behavior. The item could have empirical validity *vis-à-vis* chronic inflammatory conditions and, simultaneously, content validity *vis-à-vis* both severe hypochondriasis and malingering, with its imperfect validity in each context due to the presence of the other two.

The specific role a given response determinant plays, of course, is not discernible from a given response by a particular subject. Assuming it is reality we're after, this can be a problem. While some self-report data can be checked against data from other sources, as Buchwald (1961) has noted "for the events for which we most need verbal utterances as evidence, the relationship [between the utterance and that which it describes] is apt to be least unequivocal" (p. 465); or, in Loevinger's (1957) words, "many of the personality traits and attitudes which psychologists are eager to assess are just those which people feel they must defend or disguise" (p. 4). We can make inferences regarding what kinds of items lend themselves to these kinds of deception and regarding what kinds of persons are likely to engage in them (e.g., Linden, Paulhus, & Dobson, 1986), but still our skills at doing so are not very advanced, and there are probably aspects of persons that we should never rely solely on self-report to assess.

I believe that the greatest progress in understanding what inferences can and should be drawn from item responses will result from a focus upon research on the determinants of particular kinds of items. It should be possible to develop a knowledge base regarding the relationships between these various classes of determinants and the various item classes outlined above. Some relationships are apparent. For instance, the *typical behavior statement* "I laugh often" requires more information processing than does the statelike "I'm laughing now." And above, in the discussion of relations between items phrased in terms of classes of events vs. instances of those classes, I suggested that using instances may minimize individual differences in the interpretation of events (because responses to classes are more dependent upon subjects' prior experience). These propositions, and others which are perhaps less self-evident, are in any case subject to empirical evaluation.

I am under no illusion that this discussion of response determinants is profound or subtle; given that these points are pretty fundamental, the most striking thing about them is how rarely they are made. If test-developers are mindful of such considerations, they apparently do not see them as central enough to report how they have dealt with them. Painstaking consideration of the determinants of item responses is not viewed as part of what a scale is judged by, nor is it assumed to be of interest to the community of scholars. This appears to be tied to our lack of interest in items and kinds of items, and our fixation on scales.

A Specific Proposal

Psychologists from time to time bemoan the fact that the American Psychiatric Association has effective control of psychopathological taxonomics. The domain of self-report statements is every bit as important, and it is available to psychologists for the organizing, but we have not done it.[8] In 1950 the American Psychological Association (APA) undertook to establish standards for psychological tests. I believe it is time for the APA (or its research-oriented successor) to establish a new committee whose role it is to generate a taxonomy of items, subject to periodic revision, and for the association to lend its moral force to the establishment of a professional ethic which obliges authors to relate their research involving personality inventories to that taxonomy.

As part of the promulgation of the taxonomy, two lists would be compiled and made available (on computer disk) to the profession: (a) one in which the item numbers of all tests and scales in current use were listed, each item coded in terms of its taxonomic designation, and (b) one which listed all taxonomic categories, each accompanied by a list of all existing items (by scale name and item number) which were instances of that category. At that point, the scholar wishing to employ an existing scale could readily understand and describe its contents in terms of the taxonomy; and, if s/he didn't, a journal reviewer could conveniently look it up. The scholar reporting results on a scale could relate his/her findings to other research using similar items, irrespective of scale name. And the scholar wishing to offer a new measuring instrument would either (a) package items (or kinds of items) already in the taxonomy, thus incurring a responsibility to note explicitly their relation to existing scales and to justify the new package, or (b) create new kinds of items, in so doing bearing the burden of showing that there is a domain of self-report statements that had not been noticed by those developing the taxonomy and that should thus be added to it.

Development of the taxonomy, with associated item indexes, is a task probably on the order of magnitude of compiling a couple of issues of *Psychological Abstracts*. That is, it is the kind of specialized task that is commonly carried out without great hoopla, albeit at considerable expense. I believe that if such a task were well executed by a broadly based group of collaborators, and under APA's aegis, it would stand a chance of gaining the kind of acceptance the work of the original test standards committee and its successors have.

Although I have suggested various taxonomic strategies, I am less concerned about those specifics than (a) that the taxonomy be as complete as possible, i.e., that it be possible to classify virtually all plausible self-report items in terms of it, (b) that it be neutral with respect to competing test, theoretical, and disciplinary subcultures, and (c) that desires for taxonomic simplicity defer to the need for items classed together to be as homogeneous as possible (even if this necessitated a taxonomy as complex as APA's *Thesaurus of Psychological Index Terms*, and I seriously doubt it would).

While, if done well, the taxonomy might constitute a cafeteria of consensual assessment instruments (item groups or flowchart segments), its avowed purpose would not be to do so. Rather, it would be to provide a common reference arena for the description of existing and proposed tests, thus increasing the cross-scale generality of research on item characteristics. Ultimately, the endeavor could be judged a success if interest in the taxonomy were accompanied by a rise in the standards that scholars felt they had to meet in justifying their choices among existing scales and their decisions to create new ones, and by a more questioning attitude regarding what our scales really measure.

Notes

1. Actually, I believe our traditions may, perversely, *encourage* a troublesome diversity of item content within scales. Specifically, our understanding of measurement theory fosters long scales in the service of reliability, and so we commonly bypass the opportunity to have highly focused scales, and instead increase scale length by including items of arguable relevance. See Burisch (1984a, 1984b) and Carver (1989) for revealing discussions of related issues.

2. I believe there to be a like situation regarding laboratory manipulations in experimental personality and social psychology. Similar manipulations are, over the decades, employed by diverse researchers, without note of their commonalities. For instance, failure manipulations are sometimes viewed as addressing frustration, stress, helplessness, expectancies, self-esteem, reinforcement, and evaluation anxiety. The problem is not that there are alternative conceptualizations, but that the presence of divergent labels for the same manipulations reduces the chances that information from similar studies will have a cumulative impact on our understanding of the phenomena under study. Conversely, wildly diverse manipulations are often given the same name. An example is the term "stress." Indeed, what some stress researchers refer to as a "stress induction," others consider a *control* condition, useful only as a baseline against which to compare *their* stress induction. The potential for confusion is obvious.

3. In using terms such as category and taxonomy, I am *not* arguing or assuming that items are best viewed in terms of discrete, discontinuous classes. My focus is on the need for a comprehensive and consensual system—typological or dimensionalized—for organizing, labeling, and coding items. Even when underlying conceptions are continuous, we often prefer to carry on our discourse categorically, in prototypes, though the preferability of doing so may be more illusory than real (see Meehl, 1979).

4. It is possible that the taxonomy could also incorporate (a) items by which persons rate other persons, (b) semi-structured incomplete sentences, and (c) open-ended interrogatories.

5. I count circumplex approaches as columnar. A circumplex model is one in which the columns have specified relations with one another. A matrix is an alternative way of specifying such relations.

6. Actually, when two items represent independently occurring, alternative causes for a single outcome, it is possible to obtain a large negative correlation between them. This can be expected when subjects are selected for the outcome for which the two items reflect alternate causes; most such subjects will manifest the one cause or the other, but not both, hence the negative correlation. This might mislead one to treat them as polar opposites, even though they really belong together by virtue of their functional interchangeability. Any study of an exclusively deviant sample risks this possibility. See Golden and Meehl (1978) for a related discussion.

7. While our usual inclination, when faced with individual differences in item interpretation, is to view them as nuisance variance, an alternative is to treat the differences as important information. This notion is given substance in some research inspired by Kelly's (1955) personal construct theory (e.g., McPherson & Gray, 1976), and by Osgood, Suci, and Tannenbaum's (1957) semantic differential approach (e.g., Marks, 1966).

8. That is, the most extensive efforts (e.g., Angleitner et al., 1986; Meehl et al., 1959) are not as comprehensive as I believe is necessary, nor are they official (which seems to make a difference).

References

Allport, G. W., & Odbert, H. S. (1936). Trait-names: A psycho-lexical study. *Psychological Monographs, 47* (1, Whole No. 211).

Angleitner, A., John, O. P., & Lohr, F.-J. (1986). It's *what* you ask and *how* you ask it: An itemmetric analysis of personality questionnaires. In A. Angleitner & J. S. Wiggins (Eds.), *Personality assessment via questionnaires: Current issues in theory and measurement* (pp. 61–108). Berlin: Springer-Verlag.

Blaney, P. H. (1986). Affect and memory: A review. *Psychological Bulletin, 99,* 229–246.

Block, J., & Block, J. H. (1981). Studying situational dimensions: A grand perspective and some limited empiricism. In D. Magnusson (Ed.), *Toward a psychology of situations: An interactional perspective.* Hillsdale, NJ: Erlbaum.

Briggs, S. R., & Cheek, J. M. (1986). The role of factor analysis in the development and evaluation of personality scales. *Journal of Personality, 54,* 106–148.

Buchwald, A. M. (1961). Verbal utterances as data. In H. Feigl & G. Maxwell (Eds.), *Current issues in the philosophy of science.* New York: Holt, Rinehart & Winston.

Burisch, M. (1984a). Approaches to personality inventory construction: A comparison of merits. *American Psychologist, 39,* 214–227.

Burisch, M. (1984b). You don't always get what you pay for: Measuring depression with short and simple versus long and sophisticated scales. *Journal of Research in Personality, 18,* 81–98.

Buss, D. M., & Craik, K. H. (1983). The act frequency approach to personality. *Psychological Review, 90,* 105–126.

Cantor, N., Mischel, W., & Schwartz, J. C. (1982). A prototype analysis of psychological situations. *Cognitive Psychology, 14,* 45–77.

Carver, C. S. (1989). How should multifaceted personality constructs be tested? Issues illustrated by self-monitoring, attributional style, and hardiness. *Journal of Personality and Social Psychology, 56,* 577–585.

Clore, G. L., Ortony, A., & Foss, M. A. (1987). The psychological foundations of the affective lexicon. *Journal of Personality and Social Psychology, 53,* 751–766.

Dahlstrom, W. G. (1972). *Personality systematics and the problem of types.* Morristown, NJ: General Learning Press.

Dore, F. Y., & Kirouac, G. (1985). Identifying the eliciting situations of six fundamental emotions. *Journal of Psychology, 119,* 423–440.

Endler, N. S., Hunt, J. McV., & Rosenstein, A. J. (1962). An S-R inventory of anxiousness. *Psychological Monographs, 76* (Whole No. 17).

Eysenck, H. J. (1983). A biometrical-genetical analysis of impulsive and sensation seeking behavior. In M. Zuckerman (Ed.), *Biological bases of sensation seeking, impulsivity, and anxiety.* Hillsdale, NJ: Erlbaum.

Fiske, D. W. (1986). The trait concept and the personality questionnaire. In A. Angleitner & J. S. Wiggins (Eds.), *Personality assessment via questionnaires; Current issues in theory and measurement* (pp. 35–46). Berlin: Springer-Verlag.

Gleser, G. C., & Ihilevich, D. (1969). An objective instrument for measuring defense mechanisms. *Journal of Consulting and Clinical Psychology, 33,* 51–60.

Goldberg, L. R. (1981). Language and individual differences: The search for universals in personality lexicons. In L. Wheeler (Ed.), *Review of personality and social psychology,* Vol. 2 (pp. 141–168). Beverly Hills: Sage.

Goldberg, L. R. (1982). From ace to zombie: Some explorations in the language of personality. In C. D. Spielberger & J. N. Butcher (Eds.), *Advances in personality assessment* (Vol. 1). Hillsdale, NJ: Erlbaum.

Golden, R. R., & Meehl, P. E. (1978). Testing a dominant gene theory without an acceptable criterion variable. *Annals of Human Genetics (London), 41,* 507–514.

Guilford, J. P. (1967). *The nature of human intelligence.* New York: McGraw-Hill.

Harrison, R. H. (1986). The grouping of affect terms according to the situations that elicit them: A test of a cognitive theory of emotion. *Journal of Research in Personality, 20,* 252– 266.

Kastner, M. (1986). Pragmatic validity to be considered for the construction and application of psychological questionnaires. In A. Angleitner & J. S. Wiggins (Eds.), *Personality assessment via questionnaires: Current issues in theory and measurement* (pp. 35–46). Berlin: Springer-Verlag.

Kelly, G. A. (1955). *The psychology of personal constructs, Vol. 1: A theory of personality.* New York: Norton.

Krantz, S., & Hammen, C. (1979). Assessment of cognitive bias in depression. *Journal of Abnormal Psychology, 88,* 611–619.

Kuncel, R. B. (1973) Response processes and relative location of subject and item. *Educational and Psychological Measurement, 33,* 545–563.

Levenson, H. (1974). Activism and powerful others: Distinctions within the concept of internal-external control. *Journal of Personality Assessment, 38*, 377–383.

Linden, W., Paulhus, D. L., & Dobson, K. S. (1986). The effects of response styles on the report of psychological and somatic distress. *Journal of Consulting and Clinical Psychology, 54*, 309–313.

Loehlin, J. C. (1967). Word meanings and self-descriptions: A replication and extension. *Journal of Personality and Social Psychology, 5*, 107–110.

Loevinger, J. (1957). Some principles of personality measurement. *Educational and Psychological Measurement, 27*, 3–17.

Lykken, D. T. (1971). Multiple factor analysis and personality research. *Journal of Experimental Research in Personality, 5*, 161–170.

Maddi, S. R., Kobasa, S. C., & Hoover, M. (1979). An alienation test. *Journal of Humanistic Psychology, 19*, 73–76.

Magnusson, D., & Ekehammar, B. (1975). Perceptions of and reactions to stressful situations. *Journal of Personality and Social Psychology, 31*, 1147–1154.

Marks, I. M. (1966). Semantic differential uses in psychiatric patients. *British Journal of Psychiatry, 112*, 945–951.

McCrae, R. R., & Costa, P. T. (1986). Clinical assessment can benefit from recent advances in personality psychology. *American Psychologist, 41*, 1001–1002.

McPherson, F. M., & Gray, A. (1976). Psychological construing and psychological symptoms. *British Journal of Medical Psychology, 49*, 73–79.

Meehl, P. E. (1945). The dynamics of "structured" personality tests. *Journal of Clinical Psychology, 1*, 296–303.

Meehl, P. E., et al. (1959). *Minnesota-Ford pool of phenotypic personality items* (August, 1962 Edition). Minneapolis: University of Minnesota.

Meehl, P. E. (1979). A funny thing happened to us on the way to the latent entities. *Journal of Personality Assessment, 43*, 564–577.

Meehl, P. E., Lykken, D. T., Schofield, W., & Tellegen, A. (1971). Recaptured-item technique (RIT): A method for reducing somewhat the subjective element in factor naming. *Journal of Experimental Research in Personality, 5*, 171–190.

Monroe S. M., & Steiner, S. C. (1986). Social support and psychopathology: Interrelations with preexisting disorder, stress, and personality. *Journal of Abnormal Psychology, 95*, 29–39.

Newstead, S. E., Pollard, P., & Riezebos, D. (1987). The effect of set size on the interpretation of quantifiers used in rating scales. *Applied Ergonomics, 18*, 178–182.

Nicholls, J. G., Licht, B. G., & Pearl, R. A. (1982). Some dangers of using personality questionnaires to study personality. *Psychological Bulletin, 92*, 572–580.

Norman, W. T. (1963). Toward an adequate taxonomy of personality attributes: Replicated factor structure in peer nomination personality ratings. *Journal of Abnormal and Social Psychology, 66*, 574–583.

Osgood. C. E., Suci, G. J., & Tannenbaum, P. H. (1957). *The measurement of meaning*. Urbana: University of Illinois Press.

Paulhus, D. L. (1986). Self-deception and impression management in test responses. In A. Angleitner & J. S. Wiggins (Eds.), *Personality assessment via questionnaires: Current issues in theory and measurement* (pp. 143–165). Berlin: Springer-Verlag.

Schlundt, D. G., & McFall, R. M. (1987). Classifying social situations: A comparison of five methods. *Behavioral Assessment, 9*, 21–42.

Shrauger, J. S., & Osberg, T. M. (1981). The relative accuracy of self-predictions and judgments by others in psychological assessment. *Psychological Bulletin, 90*, 322-351.

Spitzer, R. L., Burdock, E. I., & Hardesty, A. S. (1964). *Mental Status Schedule*. New York: Biometrics Research, N.Y. State Department of Mental Hygiene.

Standards for educational and psychological testing, (1985). Washington, DC: American Psychological Association.

Storm, C., & Storm, T. (1987). A taxonomic study of the vocabulary of emotions. *Journal of Personality and Social Psychology, 53*, 805–816.

Watson, D., & Tellegen, A. (1985). Toward a consensual structure of mood. *Psychological Bulletin, 98*, 219–235.

Wiggins, J. S. (1979). A psychological taxonomy of trait descriptive terms: The interpersonal domain. *Journal of Personality and Social Psychology, 37*, 395–412.

Deception, Rational Man, and Other Rocks on the Road to a Personality Psychology of Real People

Brendan A. Maher

No contemporary surveyor of the terrain of the psychology of personality can draw much delight from the landscape that meets the eye.[1] The truth of the matter is that the small real increment in our knowledge during recent years stands in humble contrast to our failure to solve major questions that have been around for one century or more. The list of these is long, too long for enumeration here, but the now venerable trait-situation debate is a good example. We still have no adequate operational definition of a trait, hence no assurance that the study of traits is a productive path to the goal of predicting individual human behavior. We have no independent metric for defining and quantifying situational variables (except by citing what most people actually do in them). *All* of this, though we have lived through nearly two decades of debate about the relative contribution of traits and situations to our understanding of the bases of human behavior. Perhaps most important of all, we have no agreed upon map of the boundaries of personality psychology itself, particularly at the frontier that separates it from social psychology.

In response to this, various solutions have been proposed. One time-honored approach is to assert that individual behavior cannot be predicted, but only "understood" after it occurs. This solution puts the study of personality firmly into the arena of hermeneutics, i.e., the humane study of texts — the texts being the lives of individual people. It treats the consistency of personality as a given, the task of the personality psychologist being not to test for its presence but to discern it behind the complex and often chaotic set of empirical observations of which such texts are composed. Close examination shows us clearly that this approach is indistinguishable from that of the biographer writing as a contributor to nonfiction literature. It has a long and honorable history in the humanities; its best practitioners combine a felicitous way with words and as keen an eye for patterns in human behavior as any psychologist can bring to bear — sometimes keener, given that the biographer may be unblinkered by a prior belief that the pattern to be found has been pre-discovered by a specific psychological theory.

A second solution has been to propose that individual behavior at any one point of observation is simply the end result of an accumulation of learning experiences—thereby placing personality psychology firmly in the bailiwick of the general psychology of learning. From this vantage point, accurate prediction of the behavior of an individual requires that we know what elements in the current environment have been made pertinent to that individual by past learning. Just as we might safely predict the behavior of a laboratory pigeon if we are told what past responses have been reinforced in the presence of the environment in which we watch it, so we might do likewise in the case of a human being, given that we have the same kind of information. From which follows the sobering conclusion that there is no important fundamental respect in which the psychology of persons differs from the psychology of pigeons—other than the minor modifications that have to be introduced because humans speak and write.

Both of these strategies have value. Nonetheless, neither of them has yet produced a wholly satisfying answer to the major question of personality psychology. This may be a matter of time, of course, but personality psychology is not an infant discipline—it has been a focus of study for more than two thousand years. Enough time has passed to warrant looking at some of the fundamentals of the way in which we have been doing things to see if the problem might lie there.

It is possible that some part of our difficulty stems from our own methodological practices and the conception of human behavior that underlies them. These concepts and their associated methodologies have, I shall argue, led us to invent artificial problems to solve. In doing so we have missed the point of our basic mandate, which is to solve real problems, namely the identification of the processes that govern the behavior of man in the natural habitat. At the heart of the matter is our misunderstanding of the limits of the laboratory study of man, and our mistaken belief that the rational man of our theories would survive in the real world.

Journals devoted to laboratory studies of the problems of human personality give us a clear picture. It is that here are two kinds of people. One consists of real people living their lives in a real world—in short, the people that we meet every day, the people among whom we are numbered, and whose behavior we wish to understand. The other consists of a set of hypothetical ideal human beings created in the minds of psychologists, and with whom real people tend to compare quite unfavorably. The prototypical ideal person is a formal rational person, begotten by social cognitive psychology out of old-fashioned economics.

Real people are distressingly often less intelligent and perceptive than these ideal rational men and women. Their cognitions reveal an inadequate understanding of statistical principles, they exhibit biases in their judgments of others, they are ethnocentric, they do not realize that religion has been replaced by science as a basis for the conduct of life, they misattribute effects to causes, they distort reality to reduce dissonance, they fail to recognize that altruism is selfishness, that terms such as freedom and dignity are gross self-deceptions, they are "mindless" when they should be "mindful"—the list goes on.

Astonishingly enough, these real people survive in a world in which one would think that natural selection would have solved their population problem aeons ago. They stand in sharp contrast to the psychologist's rational person, a creature whose cognitions are unfailingly congruent with stimulus input, who lives in constant awareness of the effects of sample size, observer bias, experimenter influence, etc., who is perpetually and mindfully on the alert for the very best solution to each immediate problem presented by the environment, who perceives and interprets simulated nonverbal cues with facility, and whose interpersonal relations are marked by a mature understanding of all the factors that might influence anything that anybody ever says or does in relation to somebody else. A striking exception to this unflattering contrast between real people and rational people is provided by psychologists themselves, whose reports imply that they survive the comparison with their own creations quite nicely, although years of informal observation of the rationality of the decisions that psychologists make in their own lives, and in the conduct of their professional concerns, leaves room for some doubt about this.

To put some flesh on the bare bones of the provocative assertion that psychologists have failed to distinguish between the real world and the looking-glass world of laboratory artifact, an anecdote may help. Some years ago the writer happened to be a member of a search committee seeking to make a junior faculty appointment in a university psychology department. One candidate presented an account of a research project in which, among other things, a group of subjects had been taught the principle of regression to the mean. Later, they had been given a pencil-and-paper multiple-choice test to see how well they could apply this knowledge to concrete situations. Included in the test were many items like this. "John Doe is a salesman who travels all over the country. He enjoys good food, and whenever he happens across a restaurant in which he has a particularly fine meal he recommends it to his friends in that town. To his disappointment he finds that those of his friends who take his advice generally tell him that when they went to the restaurant they had a rather mediocre meal, not at all as good as he had led them to expect."

The respondent is then asked to choose the most likely reason for this:

(a) the chef had an off day, (b) his friends had different tastes in food than his, (c) they had gone to the wrong restaurant, (d) very good meals are statistically infrequent exceptions to the mean, and tend to fail to recur because of regression to the mean."

Apparently, the subjects of this research tended to "fail" this item, and indeed did not do too well on the test as a whole. Unsurprisingly, these real people had failed to live up to the standards of the hypothetical ideal created by the experiment. During the oral presentation of this research, one questioner asked whether or not the creation of that particular item had been guided by prior empirical evidence that good meals in restaurants actually are most often examples of chance combinations of favorable factors. The speaker dismissed the question as irrelevant to the important theoretical point that had guided the research, which seemed to be that people make judgments about things in a much less sophisticated way than psychologists think that they should, and that they do so even when the psychologists have shown them the right way to do it.

One member of the search committee, who supported this response, and was favorably disposed to the strategy of this research, then remarked to the members of the committee who were to go to dinner with the candidate, "I suggest that we go to Blank's Restaurant. The food there is always excellent." That is where we went, and the food was good. Nobody seemed to be unduly concerned about the discrepancy between the real world in which we all lived (in which good restaurants are good and bad restaurants are bad) and the hypothetical world of the researcher in which the candidate's subjects had failed so signally to make the correct response. What the subjects had done, of course, was to respond to what they — and the search committee — knew to be true about the real world, which is that there are good restaurants and bad restaurants; the *Guide Michelin* has done quite well for itself and its publishers by assessing and reporting this difference quite reliably for decades.

For another example of this kind, we can turn to a study in which subjects asked to imagine that having won the lottery they are now entitled to receive $100 are asked to state a preference for one of two alternatives to the receipt of the hypothetical $100. One is to receive a single payment of $120 one week later, the other is to get $1,300,000 one year later. At a discounted interest rate of 20% per week, the latter alternative is of slightly lower magnitude than the former, equaling $99.20 at the beginning of the year. The preference of most subjects for the latter is then interpreted as a failure of rationality in decision-making. It was, in fact, a failure at an ambiguously defined problem in mental arithmetic, and one that requires at least a calculator handy if one is to solve the relative discounted values at short notice. It was only a problem in arithmetic because the subjects were not actually going to get any money as a result of this decision. But in the real world of investments and banks, the opportunity of getting a bank to pay out a rate of interest of 20% weekly (which compounds to an astronomically high annual percentage rate) for each of 52 weeks, is very rare indeed, one so rare and so valuable that it is worth taking the risk that the bank that would make such a deal will go bankrupt before the year is out. In the latter event the loss of the initial $100, or the proffered $120 after one week, may be judged trifling against the folly of rejecting such an opportunity merely to make a 20% interest rate for one week. We may put the wisdom of the subjects' choice succinctly by asking the experimenters whether they would have preferred to pay out $120 after one week, or $1,300,000 after one year, in return for an initial deposit of $100! Oddly enough, investigators concerned with the irrational nature of human decision-making appear to have few qualms about accepting as valid self-reports by their subjects on the matter of what they would *do* under hypothetical circumstances, but have no confidence in their self-report of *why* they would do it. It is more than probable that both classes of data need independent validation.

The point of these two illustrations is that people live in a world of restaurants that serve good meals, banks that do not normally compound interest at 20% weekly, and the like. If they are to survive, people's choices must be adaptive, which means they must be guided by the real variables that control outcomes, not by the trivial variables of deception and hypothetical choices that are available in the laboratory.[2]

These examples might be dismissed as insignificant instances of research that could have been done better, with prior testing of the items for content bias and the like. It is the purpose of this essay to suggest that it reflects something much more serious than technical methodological inadequacy; it reflects, I shall argue, some fundamental failures in our collective appreciation of the nature of the phenomena that we study.

The Two Realities of Psychological Research

Psychological research of a certain kind deals with two quite different realities. One is the reality of the situation as it might be seen by an omniscient outside observer; the other is the reality as the psychologist has found it convenient to define and arrange. Sometimes the two realities converge; sometimes they do not. Here are some examples. These examples are drawn from the research literature, but have been modified and abbreviated to serve as prototypes. All of the originals upon which these modified versions are based were conducted by rightly respected investigators and appeared for the most part in major journals. They are described here by way of example, not as targets for criticism.

An investigator studying nonverbal communication presented subjects with an actor who has been instructed to act out certain emotional states. Subjects were required to judge the emotional states allegedly experienced by the actor. On the basis of the concordance between the subject's judgment and the state that the actor was instructed to portray, subjects were classified as good or poor interpreters of nonverbal cues to other people's emotional states. At a later point in time, the subjects were contacted by telephone by another confederate of the experimenter claiming to be a graduate student in desperate need of volunteer subjects for dissertation research. This was a pose. No actual research was intended. It turned out that the "poor" receivers refused to volunteer to serve, while the "good" receivers were willing to do so. From this it was concluded that the definition of ability or inability to read nonverbal cues in the first part of the study had been cross-validated in the second part of the study.

There are, however, two realities in this kind of study. From the point of view of the experimenter, subjects were presented with opportunities to respond to nonverbal cues and either succeeded or failed to do so. The experimental conditions, as the investigator had defined them, constituted the reality; it was a definition of reality that was theoretically convenient to the experimenter. From this imagined reality generalizations were then to be offered about the world outside the experiment.

Our omniscient outside observer can see a different reality, one in which the "poor" receivers behaved much more adaptively than the "good" receivers. They did not judge that an actor was experiencing an emotional state that he was, in fact, merely simulating. We are not told what emotion the actor was actually experiencing; perhaps it was some modest anxiety about doing well at the task in which he was engaged. As we do not know this, and as we do not know what options the poor receivers selected in their judgments of the actor's emotion, we cannot really assert that the poor receivers perceived the true state of the actor accurately. But we do know that the good receivers were deceived by the act and that the poor receivers weren't. In cruder terms, the poor receiver is perhaps better at detecting deception than is the good receiver, and on that basis is likely to behave more adaptively in the real world. Poor receivers may have behaved in terms of the objective reality of the situation and not in terms of the reality that was convenient to the psychologist. But we, as psychologists doing this kind of research, do not criticize the good receivers for being gullible, we applaud their superior sensitivity!

In the field of the psychology of bias in judgment we find another kind of example. A confederate of an investigator, in various guises, contacts a series of individuals who are the real subjects of the study. They are of several kinds: personnel officers approached by the confederate ostensibly as a candidate for employment; physicians approached by the confederate presenting as a medical patient in need of treatment; admissions officers approached by the confederate as a candidate for entry into a selective program of education. To half the subjects the confederate presents a normal personal history; to the other half the confederate presents a false history of prior mental illness. In each case the respondent subject has an implicit opportunity to exhibit bias against former psychiatric patients, by rejecting the employment application, giving inadequate medical treatment, etc. Bias is judged to be present to the extent that the quality of the response to the confederate is systematically related to the kind of personal history that was presented. If no bias is detected, it is concluded that bias against former psychiatric patients is much less than had been suspected. If bias is detected (either positively or negatively), it is interpreted as either sympathy for or rejection of former psychiatric patients.

Here again, there are two realities. The facts are that the confederate does not actually want the job, or the medical care, or the education that he or she claims to be seeking, and does not have the history of mental illness that is recounted to some subjects. An adaptive response of a subject to this reality is to treat the confederate in the same way regardless of the presence or absence of the psychiatric patient script. In these experiments, this is what actually happened. When this happened, the parsimonious interpretation is that the subjects had responded to what was objectively true about the confederate, namely that he or she was actually medically and mentally healthy. The subjects have not been deceived into accepting the psychologist's theoretically convenient definition of reality, hence their behavior in the experiment is an unreliable guide to their probable behavior in the presence of a real psychiatric patient. In fact, the experimenters interpreted the lack of effect of the deception as evidence that there really was no bias against former psychiatric patients on the part of the respondents, not that their subjects had behaved as if undeceived.[3]

Deception as deception, and deception as reality

The problem of interpretation created by the dual reality of experiments that employ experimental deception is brought into sharp relief by the fact that the psychologist feels at liberty to decide arbitrarily whether or not the deception is deception and should have been detected by the subject, or is a sample of reality to which the subject should respond as if it were reality. We can illustrate this by looking first at the well-known and controversial study of Rosenhan (1973). One way to look at it is the way in which Rosenhan intended. The capacity of normal people to deceive psychiatrists into thinking that they are suffering from symptoms that they falsely present, and their willingness to remain hospitalized rather than seek discharge, reflects unfavorably upon the sagacity of the clinicians in failing to recognize deception when they see it. In this case deception is deception, and should have been recognized as such. Their alleged failure to recognize it is assumed to tell us something about the validity of what psychiatrists do. Now let us suppose that we are really interested in the kind of diagnosis that certain symptoms will elicit when they are presented to a psychiatrist. Being unwilling or unable to wait until patients with these symptoms appear in the normal course of events, the investigator decides to ask confederates to simulate them. They do so. Diagnoses are obtained, and conclusions drawn about the relationship of symptom to diagnosis. That the psychiatrists were deceived would not be seen as a finding at all. The two experiments would be identical in all respects, and presumably the variables that were actually operating would be the same in all respects. But the conclusions that are drawn would be dependent upon the arbitrary decision of the experimenter that in one case the results reflect the invalidity of psychiatric judgment and in the other that they reflect the reliable operation of symptoms upon a reliable diagnostic process. Indeed, in the second version, had the deception arranged by the investigators failed, it would have constituted a methodological frustration, not a testimony to the perspicacity of the clinicians. Deception is deception (and as such ought to be detected) when the experimenter wants it to be so defined—as Rosenhan did; it is not a deception but a defensible "sample" of the real thing, when it is too difficult, too much trouble, or too dangerous to present the real thing, and when the experimenter wants it to be so defined, and does not want it to be detected.

What is disturbing about this state of affairs is that we all accept in principle the scientific canon that the outcome of any situation is determined by a set of variables that are actually operating in that situation. The nature, power, and consequences of these variables do not change when we decide to classify them in a different way. If the Rosenhan study, for example, tells us only that psychiatrists cannot tell when they are being deceived by an investigator's confederate, then the classic study of Milgram (1974) on obedience to authority, surely tells us the same thing about the normal population. Ironically, there is reason to think that psychiatrists have few *a priori* grounds to suppose that people coming to seek admission to a psychiatric hospital and describing hallucinatory symptoms are confederates in a psychological investigation and are really free from psychiatric disorder—the base rate for such appearances must be very low indeed; hence the decision that the symptoms were real was very much in line with the probabilities. On the other hand, to most normal subjects serving in an experiment such as Milgram's the *a priori* probability that a professor in a major American university would demand the administration of a genuinely life-threatening shock to a subject who is begging to be released, and who seems to be having a heart attack, must also seem to be very low. The reaction of the subjects indicated that either, counter to the probabilities, they took the deception for reality, thereby demonstrating to us all the depths of viciousness to which decent humans can be induced to descend in such circumstances, or they went with the probabilities, assumed (correctly) that nothing terrible could really be happening, and followed the experimenter's instructions. But in the former case we do not interpret the results to demonstrate the gullibility of normal persons. We think that it tells us something about the power of that kind of situation, and—by extension—why Auschwitz happened. And so, when the psychiatrists go with the actuarial probabilities, we think that it tells us something about them, and when Milgram's subjects do not go with the actuarial probabilties, we think that it tells us something not about them, but about the situation!

There is a practical implication to all of this. One hypothesis that should always be advanced in experiments of this kind is that all or some of the subjects are responding to the real variables present in the experiment, and not to the simulated ones that the experimenter hopes are present. The failure of results to conform to the pattern that is predicted from the assumed reality of deceptions should be seen not as a simple failure to reject the null hypothesis, but as a possible confirmation of the hypothesis that it was the real variables that determined the outcome.

Sometimes the data are consistent with both hypotheses. Returning to the nonverbal communication study described earlier in this chapter, we find that the individual differences between good and poor receivers could be interpreted as consistent with the notion that there is a key individual difference in sensitivity to nonverbal cues. It could equally well be consistent with the notion that there is a key individual difference in responding adaptively to the real motives and intentions of an actor or experimenter versus the simulated versions that they wish to manipulate in the experiment. Other things being equal, there would seem to be reason to prefer a science based upon data consistent with the operation of real variables rather than upon the assumption of the reality of simulated variables.

We do not develop psychology along these lines, however, perhaps because we have permitted ourselves to believe that human subjects coming into the laboratory are naïve in the way that laboratory pigeons and rats are said to be naïve. That is to say, we assume that the independent variables that we have chosen to control are indeed the variables that are operative in our research and, more important than that, that the pattern of responses that we will see from our subjects will be determined by the magnitudes of the independent variables as we have applied them in the experimental setting. In certain kinds of experiments that manipulate physical variables, as is the case in psychophysics, studies of the magnitude and timing of reinforcements, and the like, we are safe in making that assumption. For experiments in personality and social psychology this is doubtless sometimes the case, but it is a crucially vulnerable assumption and should always be compared for explanatory power with the hypothesis that real-world extra-experimental factors have played the dominant role.

The Disappearance of George Zipf

If the problems of personality psychology lay only in the methodological limitations of deceptive experiments employing imaginary variables applied in hypothetical scenarios, the solution might be nearer at hand than it seems to be. But the very creation of these kinds of experiments, and the constructs that guide their design, stems from a failure to consider closely the nature of the habitat in which real people live. Paradoxically, one aspect of this failure is highlighted by the perceptive application of our understanding of environmental probabilities to the behavior of animals and our parallel failure to do the same thing with human behavior. It consists essentially of a failure to take seriously those determinants of organismic behavior that came into prominence with Darwin and others who came after. Many discoveries in psychology arise, and make the reputations of their discoverers, because the generation that discovered them was unaware that the same things had been discovered one or more times in previous generations. The rise, fall, and resurrection of such figures as Kraepelin, Bleuler, and Hughlings Jackson, and the contemporary rediscovery of Charles Darwin, remind us that knowledge more often progresses in spirals than in straight lines.[4] But, in the case of Darwin at least, the revival of interest in the adaptive aspects of behavior has been more evident in the work of animal behaviorists than in that of personality psychologists. Perhaps we can go some part of the way to rectifying this state of affairs by remembering the seemingly forgotten work of George Zipf and trying in some measure to revive it.

George Zipf presented a theory of human behavior in two major works (1935, 1949). For our purposes, his *Human Behavior and the Principle of Least Effort: An Introduction to Human Ecology* (1949) provides the most complete summary of his theoretical proposals and the arguments that he used to sustain them. By way of introduction it is helpful to note that Zipf was primarily a mathematical linguist, but had made substantial efforts to integrate the quantitative aspects of language usage into a comprehensive theory of human behavior.

The central thesis of Zipf's work was that behavior develops in ways that routinize the solution of recurring problems and the performance of recurring tasks, so that the average amount of work expended in their performance is minimized. In the calculation of work expenditure he included the effort spent in developing solutions in the first place. What Zipf referred to as *mentation*, i.e., the cognitive processes involved in working out an optimal average solution to recurring problems, is a cost. It is included with other costs such as the motor energy employed in performing the solution to the task, the resources used in implementing the solution and so forth. All of this is laid out in his Principle of Least Effort. Zipf put it this way.

> In simple terms, the Principle of Least Effort means, for example, that a person in solving his immediate problems will view these against the background of his probable future problems, *as estimated by himself*. Moreover, he will strive to solve his problems in such a way as to minimize the *total work* that he must expend in solving both his immediate problems and his probable future problems. That in turn means that the person will strive to minimize the *probable average rate of his work-expenditure* (over time). And in so doing he will be minimizing his *effort*. (1949, p. 1, italics in the original)

In actual application, the principle is more complex than this brief quotation suggests. As behavior in one situation affects the possible solutions available in another, the probable average of work expenditure has to take into account not only the impact of a given solution upon the problem to which it is directed, but also its impact upon the solutions that might be feasible for other problems.

The effect of the operation of this principle is that on a given occasion, the solution that we see somebody apply to a specific instance of a problem may appear to us unintelligent in relation to the concrete details of that problem, until we know the base rate for the occurrence of this problem for the individual concerned. Another way of putting this is that the effort spent in producing the best solution to each instance of a problem may not be worth the increment of gain; hence to spend such effort is maladaptive. If we wish to assess the intelligent deployment of effort, we must assess the effectiveness of the given problem solution on repeated occasions, not just because repeated samples have higher reliability, but because the adequacy of the average solution cannot be assessed from a single case.

Zipf cited the development of the Morse Code for telegraphy as a good example of the least effort principle in practice. Letters of the alphabet with the highest frequency of use in English were assigned the shortest transmission signal. Thus E is a single short ".", A is .-, T is a single -, while infrequently used letters such as Q and X are – -.-, and -..- respectively. Although some messages that have an atypically high frequency of Q, X, Y and other low-frequency letters create significant costs in time and effort to transmit, over many messages the code ensures that the average transmission cost will be optimally minimal.[5]

Zipf proposed that what had been developed systematically in the case of the Morse code, develops naturally and inevitably in the human being, on the basis of experience. Thus his observation that the frequency of the use of a word in a language is inversely related to its length, and that when a previously low-frequency word comes into wide use, it is promptly shortened, as when "television," owned by few people, became "TV" (or "Telly" in the U.K.) when owned by many.

Because carefully thought through decision-making is a needless expense when applied each time to repeated recurrences of a standard problem, it is natural that decision rules develop at the folk level. These are, of course, the real function of proverbs. Thus the metaphorical meanings of "Take care of the pence and the pounds will take care of themselves," or of "Who sups with the Devil must have a long spoon" are not valid in every case, but perhaps often enough to provide a decision guide that will prove optimally efficient over the long haul. Children are taught in this way and thus acquire optimal-average solutions without having to evolve them exclusively through costly experience.

Experiments of the kind that were described in the opening paragraphs of this chapter suffer from the fact that they expect that the subject will provide the best possible solution to the specific single problem that is presented. This is so, even when the experimenter's correct solution would be a correct solution to that specific problem when it occurs in the natural habitat. What is lacking, however, is the analysis of the subject's behavior in terms of what would be the optimal solution to the *class of problems* averaged out over a variety of common situations.

A good example of this can be found in investigations reported by Tversky and Kahneman, as cited in a recent paper by Herrnstein and Mazur (1987). People were presented with a hypothetical problem, worded as follows:

"Imagine that you are about to purchase a jacket for $125 and a calculator for $15. The calculator salesman informs you that the calculator is on sale for $10 at the other branch of the store, located twenty minutes drive away. Would you make the trip to the other store?" They reported that 68% of their subjects said they would drive to the other store. A second group of subjects was presented with another version of the same problem, except that now the jacket costs $15 and the calculator $125, with the latter being available for $120 on sale at the branch store. Now only 29% of the respondents state they would make the drive. Given that the actual savings in these hypothetical situations was the same, i.e., $5.00, and the total bill for the same goods would be the same at $140, why would not rational people make the same choice in both cases? We will pass over the fact that the entire problem was verbal and that the investigators did not actually observe what people would do. We will also pass over the possibility that the person who seriously goes into a store to buy a $15 jacket and a $125 calculator may be a little different from the person who goes in to buy a $15 calculator and a $125 jacket. What is important is that the investigators solved the problem of the "irrationality" of their subjects by concluding that their responses are determined by the way the question was framed, namely by the 33% discount that $5 bears to $15 in one case and the 4% that it bears to $125 in the other.

From the vantage of the Principle of Least Effort none of this is new or surprising. On the average, an individual will save resources by going with the percentages over many cases of savings opportunities, rather than working out the absolute dollar cost in each case. The higher the percentage discount, the rarer the opportunity is likely to be. Going for the rare benefit may be foolish on occasion (as in this case) but wise on the average over many cases. The irrationality of the subjects can only be gauged by looking at the empirical consequences of applying the percentage criterion over many cases of actual sales discounts, i.e., over a class of problems rather than specific single instances.

Zipf emphasized, as pointed out above, that the mentation that is required to work out solutions to problems is itself a cost, and could be substantial. Complex cognitive activity costs. It must be amortized over the anticipation of the frequent recurrence of the problem to which it has provided a solution.

On this basis, Rosenhan's clinicians, for whom the diagnosis of incoming patients is a repetitive task with a high base rate of real patients and a negligible base rate of pseudo-patients, would have been ill-advised to develop detailed examination strategies for deciding with each new patient whether or not this is a pseudo-patient engaged in deceptive research. Milgram's subjects had a comparable situation. If they entered the experiment with any prior strategy for their behavior in a psychological experiment it was probably simply to follow the experimenter's instructions. They almost certainly did not come with previous experience in participating in experiments that required them to deliver painful shocks to sick people on a recurring basis; they may have come with prior experience that psychological experiments in laboratories are often not what they seem to be. Whatever their expectations, they did not have the background of past experience or the expectation of future repetitions of it to meet Zipf's criterion for developing a strategy for solving future anticipated repetitions of the problem that they faced. One is tempted to wonder what their subsequent response was to invitations to take part in other psychological experiments. Judging by their reported distress at being debriefed about the purposes of the experiment, it seems unlikely that they would volunteer for the role of subject for any psychologist again, let alone for a repeat performance in the Milgram experiment—surely a requirement if the analogy to Auschwitz is to be pressed.

The Principle of Least Effort clearly antedated and encompassed the phenomena now included in contemporary formulations of optimized rationality. It provided a rationale for studies of foraging behavior, culturally generated evolutionary changes in language, the basic rationality of economy of effort (including mental effort), the natural preference for actuarial decision rules when these have sufficient predictive accuracy—all of these well before their reappearance in modern forms.

It is obvious that there are strong similarities in this to the argument advanced by Paul Meehl (1954) at about the same time, that the best strategy of the clinician is to apply probability tables to predictions in such a way that the batting average of success is optimized. To appreciate the congruence of views, a quotation from Meehl may be helpful. In this passage he is explaining that his promotion of the actuarial approach was not intended to render the clinician totally nonfunctional. He explained:

> I did want to influence clinical practice towards a more optimal
> utilization of skilled time, by removing the clinical judge from loci in
> the decision process where he functions ineffectively, thereby both (a)
> improving predictive accuracy and (b) freeing the clinician's time for
> other activities, whether cognitive or manipulative, in which he is
> efficient or unique. (Meehl, 1967, reprinted in Meehl, 1977, p. 166)

The lesson is clear: actuarial methods provide "optimal utilization" of a resource, i.e., skilled time. Optimal utilization of resources leaves time and energy for other pursuits. We should not leave this particular topic, however, without recognizing that Meehl had an additional, and perhaps more provocative, argument to add in favor of actuarial prediction. Actuarial predictions were not only less costly of effort; they were much more accurate on the average than predictions based upon "mindful" analysis of each individual case.

The superior economy and efficiency of actuarial prediction, and its use in ordinary life by people in general, requires us to consider carefully what we have in mind when we study "bias" in human judgment. At one extreme we might concede that if we predict future behavior on the basis of a sign that is perfectly correlated with the criterion, we would not be judged guilty of bias, even if the sign had no intuitively obvious functional relationship with the criterion. At the other extreme, we would be guilty not only of bias but of self-injurious bias if we persisted in making important predictions on the basis of a sign that was perfectly orthogonal to the criterion. We might perhaps quantify bias in terms of the reliance placed upon predictive signs of varying degrees of imperfection in their correlations with a relevant criterion. So long as other people are not involved, substantial bias affects only the person displaying it, as he or she will bear the consequences of invalid predictions.

When we get into the matter of judgments made by one person about another, the matter becomes more complex. For example, the judgment that bias has occurred in the selection of candidates for a rewarding position requires that we know not only the correlations between various predictor variables and the criterion, but also the ratio of candidates to openings. Now more or less forgotten, the Taylor-Russell Tables factored this in to provide a basis for deciding when a given predictor would add to, or leave unchanged, the base rate for successful selection. The purpose of these tables was to save time and money in selection, as well as the costs involved in mistakes in selection. Economic, least-effort values dictated the logic of the tables, and of the selection process generally.

Psychological studies of bias are, inevitably, confounded by two conflicting sets of values, one adaptive, the other moral. When a job applicant is rejected for a position, or is deprived in any other way on the basis of a predictor with less than perfect predictive validity, the process may be effective economically — in "batting average" terms — but unjust when considered in terms of an individual's right not to suffer deprivation. The selector's actuarial efficiency is the rejectee's discrimination. If the rejected candidate is indeed one of the false negatives associated with the predictor, the discrimination is real. When we consider the matter in these terms, we feel, quite rightly, that it is essential to conduct our selection in ways that are consonant with our views about justice, and this leads us to prefer more expensive methods of selection, even if the marginal increase in accuracy that they produce violates the least-effort principle. When the effect of a selection procedure is to protect the false negative, the same principle of justice prompts us to regard it not as biased, but as prudently cautious. Consider Meehl's cautionary tale of the student clinician who permitted a patient to go home because his depression had lifted (Meehl, 1977). The patient committed suicide. Meehl pointed out to the unfortunate clinician that the actuarial probability of such an event had been established as from 3–5% in patients who had been discharged and followed up in a two-year period, and that the clinician had acted incompetently and irresponsibly in permitting the patient to leave the hospital. We endorse Meehl's judgment, even though it means that the threshold for the discharge of the 95 false negatives will be higher than it might otherwise be because of the need to protect the other five who will kill themselves. This, then, is not defined as bias in action, but competent caution properly applied.

In essence then, the confusion of prediction error with the violation of individual rights means that the term "bias" has lost its scientific meaning. It can only retain a claim to describe maladaptive cognitions about other people and things if we define adaptive behavior as that allegedly displayed by the nonexistent population of "rational" persons.

Turning now from the issue of bias, we note that it follows that any routinized decision rules that save cognitive effort but do so by producing wrong solutions more often than right ones, would ultimately lead to the elimination of the organism that persisted with them. What Meehl pointed out as the advantages of formal, conscious application of actuarial principles to clinical prediction parallel exactly the advantages that accrue to any organism, animal or human, through the evolution in its own life time of rules that embody the Principle of Least Effort.

Why, we might ask, do many psychologists fail to appreciate the functional efficiency of least-effort solutions, and fail to understand why these are hard to detect in the laboratory? The answers to these questions are undoubtedly complex, but some possibilities come to mind. The first of these is the nature of the scientific enterprise in general, and in which psychologists are personally engaged. Scientific work, by and large, consists of trying to solve as comprehensively as possible yet unsolved problems. When a problem has been more or less solved, or at least solved as well as seems possible with the methods and data available, the task of the scientist is completed. He or she can now move on to another problem or can decide to devote more time and thought to developing ways in which the previous solution might be bettered. In neither event can the task be handled by the simple application of an existing solution—this being the role of the technician, to whom the systematic application of validated procedures to the solution of routine problems has been assigned. But most people in the world are not employed in finding unsolved problems to solve; they are mainly engaged in other things, one of which is the development of behavioral practices that save effort and time in dealing with normal tasks of life. Their lives are generally quite unlike those of scientists. New problems are nuisances, or even threats, and their solution is necessary if one is to get on with other matters, the other matters being the real business of living. Real people quite reasonably apply time-tested solutions to such repeated problems as they encounter, unless the effort demanded in applying these solutions is great enough to justify the investment of effort in finding a new solution. Then, briefly, they become scientists. Except for these occasions their daily working life is not like that of the professional scientist; the work of the latter is the exception, that of the former is the rule. Ignoring this, psychologist-scientists are prone to the error of assuming that their subjects should be like them, and finding that they are not, they write about them in patronizing tones and contemplate training programs that might improve them.

A second variable of interest is the status-significance of the concept of "false consciousness." Scientists in the natural sciences have achieved the status and respect that they now enjoy because they have discovered things that the non-scientist did not know. In so doing they have created the base of an effective (albeit sometimes double-edged) technology. Because of the natural scientists, the world looks different to us from the way that it did to our forefathers. To put the matter more crudely, the layman's explanations of why things happen as they do often proved to be inferior to the scientist's explanation of the same events.

Psychologists, and social scientists in general, are in a much more difficult position. Because we all have our own explanations for our behavior, and tend to be perfectly satisfied with them, psychological scientists cannot easily do what natural scientists do without the beginning assertion that individual conscious-ness is an inadequate source for explanations of individual behavior. Instead, it is necessary to postulate that much of human consciousness is false and misleading, especially when explanations of one's own behavior are involved. If it were not so, there would be no need of much of the apparatus of behavioral research, for we could simply ask our subjects why they do what they do. Both Marx and Freud depended upon the notion of false consciousness as an essential rebuttal to the fact that the motives that they ascribed to people were not at all the same as the motives that people ascribed to themselves. Skinner solved the problem to much the same effect by simply abolishing the study of consciousness from the bailiwick of behavioral psychology.

Now there are good reasons to doubt the validity of self-report as data, but the reasons have to do with the sometimes demonstrably superior explanations of be-havior that are developed in spite of self-report data that would contradict them, not with some dogmatic proposition that self-report is *ipso facto* misleading. However, self-report might always be a good place to begin the development of explanations for subjects' behavior. It might also bring our creature, the psycho-logical ideal man, into closer correspondence with the people that we are sup-posed to be studying.

Rather than study personality through a framework in which people are com-pared with a hypothetical ideal created by the psychologist, it will surely be more profitable to study the behavior of people with the *a priori* premise that behavior is overwhelmingly often adaptive—and then seek to discover what aspects of the environment are responsible for the particular adaptation that we see. It is a strat-egy that has paid off handsomely in contemporary attempts to understand animal behavior. Perhaps personality psychology may profit from a like attempt.

Notes

1. I am greatly indebted to my wife and colleague, W. Barbara Maher, for her incisive comments on preliminary drafts of this chapter, as I am for discussions with her over some years on the problems with which the chapter deals.

2. In none of the experiments described here does there seem to have been any attempt to ask the subjects why they made the choices that they did. Presumably the power of the notion of false consciousness was sufficient to make that step appear irrelevant.

3. There are other problems with this kind of study, of course, especially with the lack of representative design in the provision of stimulus persons (Maher, 1978).

4. It also hints to the cynical that if one wishes to be an innovator at what is called the "cutting edge" of the field, one can do worse than study some of the older journals!

5. Darwin believed that evolutionary principles could be applied fruitfully to the study of language, quoting with approval a passage from Max Müller: "A struggle for life is constantly going on amongst the words and grammatical forms in each language. The better, the shorter, the easier forms are constantly gaining the upper hand" (Darwin, 1871, p. 466).

References

Darwin, C. (1871). *The descent of man*. In *The origin of species and the descent of man*. New York: Modern Library.

Herrnstein, R. J., & Mazur, J. E. (1987). Making up our minds. *The Sciences, 27*, 40–47.

Maher, B. A. (1978). Stimulus sampling in clinical research: Representative design reviewed. *Journal of Consulting and Clinical Psychology, 46*, 643–647.

Meehl, P. E. (1954). *Clinical versus statistical prediction: A theoretical analysis and a review of the evidence*. Minneapolis: University of Minnesota Press.

Meehl, P. E. (1967). What can the clinician do well? In D. N. Jackson & S. Messick (Eds.), *Problems in human assessment*. New York: McGraw-Hill.

Meehl, P. E. (1977). *Psychodiagnosis: Selected papers*. New York: Norton.

Milgram, S. (1974). *Obedience to authority*. New York: Harper & Row.

Rosenhan, D. L. (1973). On being sane in insane places. *Science 179*, 250–258.

Zipf, G. K. (1935). *The psychobiology of language*. Boston: Houghton-Mifflin.

Zipf, G. K. (1949). *Human behavior and the principle of least effort*, Cambridge, MA: Addison-Wesley.

Agency and Communion as Conceptual Coordinates for the Understanding and Measurement of Interpersonal Behavior
Jerry S. Wiggins

Not like the brazen giant of Greek fame,
With conquering limbs astride from land to land . . .
Mother of Exiles . . . cries she
With silent lips. "Give me your tired, your poor,
Your huddled masses yearning to breathe free,
The wretched refuse of your teeming shore.
Send these, the homeless tempest-tossed to me"

This inscription at the base of the Statue of Liberty (1886) expressly contrasts Liberty with another famous bronze giant, the Colossus of Rhodes (circa 280 A.D.), one of the Seven Wonders of the Ancient World. The latter statue depicted Helios the sun god, the principal deity of the Rhodians, who was honored annually by flinging four horses and a chariot into the sea for his personal use (Durant, 1939, p. 177). The images of Helios driving his flaming chariot across heavens and of Liberty nurturing her wretched masses vividly symbolize two fundamental modalities of human experience. Following Bakan (1966), I will refer to these modalities as *agency* and *communion*. Agency refers to the condition of being a differentiated individual, and it is manifest in strivings for mastery and power which enhance and protect that differentiation. Communion refers to the condition of being part of a larger social or spiritual entity, and it is manifested in strivings for intimacy, union, and solidarity with that larger entity. Figure 2 provides a preliminary schematic representation of agency (A+) and communion (C+) and their conceptual opposites of passivity (A-) and dissociation (C-), respectively.

In this essay, I shall present selected examples from the extensive literature that attests to the pivotal nature of the concepts of agency and communion in the social sciences and humanities, beginning on a highly abstract and philosophical

Figure 1. Statue of Liberty and Colossus of Rhodes.

level, and concluding on the much more concrete level of personality measurement. My purpose in doing so is to offer a somewhat broader context than is usually provided for the argument that agency and communion should serve as conceptual coordinates for the measurement of interpersonal behavior. The general topics that will be treated are world views, persons, language, and men and women. The concepts to be discussed and the writers who proposed them within each of the topical areas are listed in Table 1. This overview, together with Figure 2, may serve to clarify the exposition that follows.

World Views

Confucius

The concepts of agency (A) and communion (C) have often appeared as dualistic processes that are integrated within a larger totality. Consider, to take an early example, the cosmology attributed to Confucius (circa 551–479 B.C.) and his disciples. As interpreted by Hackett (1979, pp. 25–29), the Confucian cosmology conceived of heaven, earth, and man as being in dynamic interaction within a Great Whole governed by objective moral principles. Because the principles that

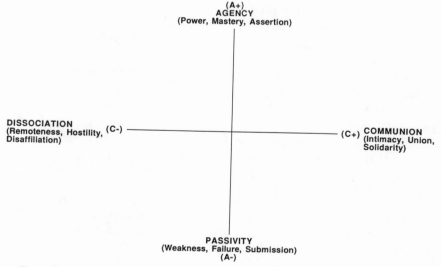

Figure 2. Structural representation of agency and communion.

govern the natural order and the moral order are essentially the same, the former provides a guide for individual and social life, the ultimate purpose of which is the achievement of oneness with the Great Whole. In achieving the ultimate oneness, a person passes through a series of levels or "spheres" of ethical existence (Hackett, 1979, pp. 27–28). Those who lead the unreflective life and are governed only by instincts and emotions exist in the natural sphere. However, when one is guided by self-seeking, egoistic motives, one has entered the *utilitarian sphere* (A). When one comes to recognize one's place in the larger social order and one's moral obligations to that order, one has entered the *moral sphere* (C). And finally, the recognition that the social order is part of the Great Whole signals entry into the transcendent sphere which is governed by the principle of maximizing the good of all reality.

Angyal

A modern version of the manner in which agency and communion are integrated within a larger totality can be found in the personality theory of Andras Angyal (1941). The larger totality in this theory is the biosphere, the realm in which life takes place. The biosphere is a holistic unit comprising both person (subject) and environment (object). Tensions exist within the biosphere because of the opposing directional tendencies of subject and object. The organism is motivated by a trend toward increased *autonomy* (A)—the desire to master and assimilate the environment by striving for individuality and superiority. The environment (so-

Table 1. Conceptions of Agency and Communion

	Agency	Communion
World Views		
Confucius	utilitarian sphere	moral sphere
Angyal (1941)	autonomy	homonomy
Bakan (1966)	agency	communion
Persons		
Freud	able to work	able to love
Adler (1912, 1964)	striving for superiority	social interest
Horney (1937)	moving against others	moving toward others
Fromm (1941)	separate entity	oneness with world
Sullivan (1953b)	need for power	need for tenderness
Erikson (1950)	autonomy	basic trust
Hogan (1983)	achieving status	maintaining peer popularity
McAdams (1985b)	power motivation	intimacy motivation
Language		
Brown (1965)	pronouns of power	pronouns of solidarity
White (1980)	dominance/submission	solidarity/conflict
Benjafield & Carson (1985)	assured-dominant words	warm-friendly words
Men and Women		
Constantinople (1973)	masculinity?	femininity?
Bem (1974)	masculinity	femininity
Spence (1985)	self-assertion	expressiveness
Measurement of Interpersonal Behavior		
Freedman et al. (1951)	dominance/submission	affiliation/hostility
Foa & Foa (1974)	status	love
Norman (1963)	surgency	agreeableness

cial, natural, spiritual) exerts pressure on the organism to become assimilated, to surrender itself to and become part of a larger entity. Angyal calls this pressure a trend toward *homonomy* (C). The opposing tendencies of autonomy and homonomy are integrated within a larger totality by the superordinate biospheric tendency toward "self-expansion." The organism grows and expands by assimilating and mastering the environment, and the environment is enriched and expanded by the creative contributions of the organism.

Bakan

Maddi (1976) has called attention to the high degree of similarity between the formulations of Angyal and the more recent ones of Bakan (1966), which appear to have been developed independently. Bakan's essay deals with a broad range of topics including: "social organization, science, ideology, myth, sexuality, death, disease, and man's psychological life. These are relevant to man's ultimate concern, to being and not-being" (p. 2). In Bakan's view, *agency* (A) manifests itself in: "self-protection, self-assertion, and self-expansion . . . in the formation of separations . . . [and] in isolation, alienation, and aloneness" (p. 15). *Communion* (C) manifests itself: "in the sense of being at one with other organisms . . . in the lack of separations . . . [and] in contact, openness, and union." Bakan's concern with the integration of these two opposing tendencies is expressed primarily in the context of interpersonal relations, particularly between men and women: "The ideal marriage which one may conceive of is the one in which, through the integration of agency and communion which takes place between marriage partners, a corresponding integration takes place within each of the partners" (p. 153).

Bakan's formulation of the integrative roles of agency and communion in the dynamics of interpersonal relations provides us with a modern version of a theme that may be traced from the early days of what is now known as "personality theory" to the present time. The contexts in which this theme has been expressed and the forms that it has assumed are diverse, but the substance of concern is clearly evident.

Persons

Freud

Within the voluminous writings of Freud, it would no doubt be possible to find concepts that are related to agency and communion. Bakan (1966), for example, has argued that in his later years Freud's concepts of Thanatos and Eros bore some resemblance to those of agency and communion, respectively. However, Bakan's argument is complex and is based primarily on a psychohistorical analysis of Freud and on the assumption of an association between agency and cancer. It is true, of course, that Freud emphasized the importance of being able to work (A) and to love (C) for psychological well-being. But Freud's contribution to the advancement of agency and communion to the center stage of personality theory may very well have been a negative one, for it was mainly on issues related to communion that the neo-Freudians parted company with Freud.

Adler

Before his formal break with Freud in 1911, and increasingly thereafter, Alfred Adler (1912) argued that the most basic human drive is a *striving for superiority* (A) through mastery of one's biological, physical, and social environments. This concept evolved over a period of years from the rather narrowly defined notion of "organ inferiority" to the more encompassing concept of striving for perfection, each subsequent stage revealing a somewhat different facet of agency. In his later writings, Adler introduced the concept of *social interest* (C) which, together with the notion of striving for individual perfection, provided a larger integrated totality. Social interest means:

> *feeling with the whole, sub specie aeternitatis*, under the aspect of eternity. It means a striving for a form of community which must be thought of as everlasting . . . the ultimate fulfillment of evolution. (Adler, 1964, pp. 34–35)

Horney

Karen Horney (1937) felt strongly that "Freud's disregard of cultural factors not only leads to false generalizations, but to a large extent blocks an understanding of the real forces which motivate our attitudes and actions" (pp. 20–21). Both normal and neurotic development can best be understood in terms of interactions between individual conflicts and cultural difficulties. Contemporary Western culture contains inherent contradictions such as that between "competition and success on the one hand [A], and brotherly love and humility on the other [C]." Faced with such a contradiction, the individual may place a one-sided emphasis on one modality to the exclusion of the other, or the individual may attempt to avoid the conflict by withdrawing. These three general classes of attempted solutions were called "moving against" (A), "moving toward" (C), and "moving away" (C-) from others.

Fromm

Given his background in history, sociology, and political science, and his deep respect for the theories of Marx, it is not surprising that Erich Fromm was among the most outspoken critics of Freud's neglect of communion: "*The understanding of the unconscious of the individual presupposes and necessitates the critical analysis of his society*" (Fromm, 1959, p. 110). Fromm's (1941) critical historical analysis of society stressed the gradual emergence of man from a state of oneness with his natural and social worlds (C) to a state of awareness of himself as a separate entity (A). This process of individuation was accelerated after the Middle Ages by religious and industrial developments that emphasized independence and personal achievement, but that also led to increased feelings of loneliness and isolation. Reactions to the dilemma posed by this basic contradiction in human life can be either constructive or destructive, and the bulk of Fromm's writings were dedicated to the identification of constructive solutions. His final formulation sought a resolution in the distinction between "being" and "having": "being is life, activity, birth, renewal, outpouring, flowing out, productivity. In this sense being is the opposite of having ego boundedness and egotism" (Fromm, 1976, p. 65).

Sullivan

The radical interpersonalism of Harry Stack Sullivan placed such a heavy emphasis on "communal existence" (Sullivan, 1972) that the notion of individuality was regarded as an illusion (Sullivan, 1950), or, at best, as "invariably much less significant in the person's living than he has been taught to believe" (Sullivan, 1953a, p. xii). Personality, or individuality, for Sullivan was *"the relatively enduring pattern of recurrent interpersonal situations which characterize a human life"* (Sullivan, 1953b, p. xi). Interpersonal situations involve two or more persons, and it does not make sense to describe individuals apart from such situations. Sullivan's ideas were not easily accessible because of the difficulty of expressing them in "individualistic" language (Sullivan, 1953a). Nonetheless, Sullivan has unquestionably become the major theoretical influence on contemporary interpersonal psychology (Anchin & Kiesler, 1982; Carson, 1969; Leary, 1957). A fundamental assumption of interpersonal psychology is that interpersonal transactions and integrations are best understood when viewed within the coordinates of a need for power (A) and a need for tenderness (C) (Sullivan, 1953b). Although Sullivan's formulations are among the most recondite to be found in theories of personality, they have inspired the development of measurement procedures that have shown considerable empirical promise (Wiggins, 1982).

Erikson

More than any other writer in the psychoanalytic tradition, Erik Erikson (1950) expanded and elaborated Freudian theory to include an account of the manner in which social and institutional forces influence the development of individuals throughout the life cycle. Freud's theory of psychosexual development was viewed by Erikson as the biological component of an epigenetic ground plan in which each stage of maturation creates a succession of potentialities for significant interaction with other members of society. The manner in which the child, and those around the child, solve the successive psychosocial crises associated with each phase of development determines the subsequent personality development of the child. Successful resolution of a crisis at one stage of development equips the child for coping with the next stage.

As did Freud, Erikson emphasized the importance for adult development of resolving the conflicts of early childhood. Erikson's first stage of development corresponds to Freud's oral stage, and the psychosocial crisis provided by the infant feeding situation involves the development of an attitude of *basic trust* (versus mistrust) in one's mother and in one's self. The establishment of an attitude of trust is the foundation for "hope" which serves to maintain the individual's belief in the trustworthiness of the society in which he or she develops (C). The second stage of psychosocial development corresponds to Freud's anal stage, and the crisis provided by the toilet-training situation involves the acquiring of a sense of *autonomy* (versus shame and doubt) with respect to one's own capacity for independent action. The establishment of a sense of autonomy gives rise to "will" which is: "*the unbroken determination to exercise free choice as well as self-restraint* [A]" (Erikson, 1964, p. 119; italics in original). Although Erikson does not view these crises as permanently resolvable during the first two years of life, the attitude of basic trust (C) and the sense of personal autonomy (A) are clearly the cornerstones of adult personality development.

Hogan

The concepts of agency and communion have continued to be central tenets in contemporary theories of personality. They are clearly implicated, for example, in the two metatheoretical assumptions that form the basis of Robert Hogan's (1983) socioanalytic theory of personality: "(a) people always live in groups, and (b) every group is organized in terms of a status hierarchy" (p. 56). Socioanalytic theory is a synthesis of psychoanalysis and symbolic interactionism in which a heavy emphasis is placed on biological evolution:

> The problems of achieving status [A] and maintaining peer popularity [C] are biologically mandated. The importance of status is obvious; it provides the opportunity for preferential breeding and reproductive success. The importance of popularity may seem puzzling until one realizes that homicide rates among hunter-gatherers are high even by modern urban standards. In these circumstances, popularity has substantial survival value. A moment's reflection also suggests that status and popularity exist in a state of tension. As Oscar Wilde once noted, people can forgive you anything but your success—that is, success breeds resentment in others. Conversely, popularity is sometimes bought at the price of individual achievement. (Hogan, 1983, pp. 56–57)

McAdams

An excellent example of the heuristic power of the concepts of agency and communion in clarifying psychological constructs, generating measurement procedures, and guiding empirical research is found in the work of Dan McAdams. On the level of measurement, McAdams has employed the TAT content-analytic procedures developed by McClelland and his associates (1953) to score the needs for power (Winter, 1973) and intimacy (McAdams, 1980), which he postulates to be the two basic tendencies in human lives. This has proven to be an especially fruitful approach to empirical research (e.g., McAdams, 1982, 1984, 1985a, 1985b). In his conceptualization of these constructs, McAdams (1985b) evinces a deep appreciation of their subordinate relation to the meta-constructs of agency and communion:

> This is not to say, however, that intimacy motivation *is* communion or that power motivation *is* agency. Bakan's constructs are much broader, encompassing a host of personality variables at a number of different levels of analysis. Thus, communion and agency are highly general thematic clusterings in lives which may be mirrored in conscious values, specific attitudes, particular interests, stylistic traits, characteristic self-schemata and social motives such as intimacy and power. (p. 89)

From the time of the neo-Freudians to the present, the concepts of agency and communion have occupied an increasingly explicit role in theories of personality, particularly since the appearance of Bakan's (1966) essay. This increasing emphasis on the cultural matrix in which personality is embedded has suggested the possible universality of agency and communion as organizing concepts for social life. An additional source of evidence bearing on the pancultural nature of these concepts is found in the study of language. Psycholinguistic studies of twentieth-century languages have illuminated the nature of contemporary social institutions. Historico-developmental studies of languages have shed light on the origins and evolution of these institutions.

Language

Pronouns of Power and Solidarity

Roger Brown and his colleagues (Brown, 1965, ch. 2; Brown & Ford, 1961; Brown & Gilman, 1960) have provided a fascinating account of the manner in which forms of address in different languages mirror the structure of societies with respect to the underlying dimensions of power (A) and solidarity (C). The most familiar example of two singular forms of address is to be found in the contemporary French language distinction between *tu* and *vous*. This evolved from the Latin *tu* and *vos*, as did the early Italian *tu* and *voi*, the early Spanish *tu* and *vos*, the early German *du* and *Ihr*, and the early English "thou" and "ye" (later "you"). Brown and Gilman used the symbols *T* and *V* to denote this distinction in any language in which it occurs.

In tracing the semantic evolution of T and V from ancient times to the present, Brown and Gilman identified a set of norms, which appear to have emerged between the twelfth and fourteenth centuries, that they call the "nonreciprocal power semantic" (p. 255). Personages addressed their subordinates as T and were in turn addressed as V. This principle governed the relationships between ruler and ruled, master and slave, and nobility and common people. Powerful, high-status persons addressed each other as V, and less powerful, low-status persons exchanged Ts.

Although there was originally no clear-cut rule for the differential use of T and V among persons of equal status, there gradually emerged a distinction between the T of intimacy and the V of formality which Brown and Gilman identified as the "solidarity semantic" (p. 257). The solidarity semantic is reciprocal and is based on similarities "that make for like-mindedness or similar behavior dispositions. These will ordinarily be such things as political membership, family, religion, profession, sex, and birthplace" (p. 258). Under this principle, persons of equal status, be it high or low, may address each other as T if they are like-minded and have similar interests and background, or as V if they do not. To the extent that reciprocal T address is confined to persons of *equal* status, the power semantic and the solidarity semantic provide a clear-cut and consistent set of rules for social transactions. However, to the extent that solidarity is perceived between persons of *unequal* status, a potential conflict exists. For example, how does an officer address a soldier who is from the same home town and who graduated from the same high school? Brown and Gilman observed that during the past century the solidarity semantic has been increasingly emphasized and that potential conflicts now tend to be resolved in the direction of reciprocal solidarity.

In reflecting upon the wide-ranging linguistic studies that he and his colleagues conducted, Brown (1965) concluded that: "the forms of address in all the languages we have studied operate in identical fashion. There is an invariant, a universal norm in our materials" (p. 92). It is not surprising that linguistic conventions reflect the institutions of a society. What is impressive is the apparent universality of power (A) and solidarity (C) as coordinates for the understanding of social transactions (Hook, 1984; Slobin, Miller, & Porter, 1968).

Conceptual Universals in Interpersonal Language

The universal norm governing forms of address found by Brown and his associates may be but one instance of a more general psycholinguistic phenomenon: conceptual universals in interpersonal language based on the meta-concepts of agency and communion. The small, but impressive, body of evidence that supports this contention has been reviewed by Geoffrey White (1980).

Shweder (1972), for example, studied the meaning-similarity of 81 personality descriptors in the Oriya language of the state of Orissa in India. Twenty-five adult male informants were asked to sort those terms that were similar in meaning into any number of piles and then to merge them into successively smaller piles. Multidimensional scaling of these data produced a clear two-dimensional solution based on two bipolar orthogonal axes. The personality descriptors were distributed in a continuous circular configuration around the larger values of these axes (circumplex).

White (1978) studied the meaning-similarity of 37 personality descriptors in the A'ara language of Santa Isabel in the Solomon Islands. Informants were asked to select for each term the five other terms that most closely matched it in meaning. Multidimensional scaling of these data again produced a clear bipolar two-dimensional solution in which the personality descriptors were arrayed in a continuous circular fashion around the two coordinates.

White (1980) called attention to the striking structural similarities between the solutions obtained in the Oriya and A'ara languages, and interpreted the coordinates of both solutions as dominance/submission (A) and solidarity/conflict (C). This substantive interpretation was based, in part, on the extensive body of literature that documents the ubiquitousness of circumplex solutions in the English language, specifically, those based on dimensions of dominance/submission and affiliation/hostility (Wiggins, 1982). These English-language solutions obtain under conditions of meaning-similiarity ratings (e.g., Conte & Plutchik, 1981), self-report (e.g., Wiggins, 1979), and other-ratings (e.g., Lorr & McNair, 1965). A representative circumplex of interpersonal variables (Kiesler, 1983) may be seen in Figure 3.

The appearance of the two-dimensional circumplex structure of personality descriptors in languages as different as Oriya, A'ara, and English led White (1980) to speculate that:

these dimensions represent a universal conceptual schema produced by the interaction of innate psycholinguistic structures and fundamental conditions of human social life, for example, the potential for concord or discord in the goals and actions of multiple actors (solidarity/conflict), and for the asymmetrical influence of one actor upon another (dominance/submission). (p. 759)

Origins of Interpersonal Language

As just noted, White has argued that schemas for conceptualizing interpersonal behavior, such as the one illustrated in Figure 3, are organized around the *basic dimensions* of dominance/submission (A) and solidarity/conflict (C). A number of interpersonal theorists (e.g., Foa & Foa, 1974; Leary, 1957; Wiggins, 1979) have made the same argument, and have suggested that all interpersonal behaviors may be thought of as "blends" of these two basic dimensions whose nodal points are dominance, submission, solidarity, and conflict. Unfortunately, it is

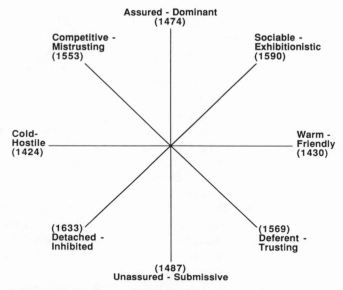

Figure 3. Circumplex of interpersonal variables. (After Kiesler, 1983)

not readily apparent how one might establish that any two directions in two-dimensional space are more "basic" than any other two directions. For example, with reference to Figure 3, it is being argued that the "basic" coordinates are assured-dominant *vs.* unassured-submissive and warm-friendly *vs.* cold-hostile. But what if one were to argue that the "basic" coordinates are really sociable-exhibitionistic *vs.* detached-inhibited and deferent-trusting *vs.* competitive-mistrusting? (See McCrae & Costa, 1989.)

The issue of "basic" coordinates cannot be resolved with traditional methods of multivariate analysis: For circumplex solutions, unlike those of simple structure, every rotation in two dimensions is as good as every other rotation, hence any solution is arbitrary. One can in effect appeal to scholarly authority, as I am doing in this paper, by emphasizing the diversity of conceptual analyses that appear to converge on the "basicness" of agency and communion. But a lingering sense of arbitrariness remains. In this context, the results of a recent study by Benjafield and Carson (1985) provide a small, but most welcome, ray of hope.

Benjafield and Carson (1985) emphasized that the trait-descriptive terms of interpersonal circumplex models are part of ordinary language and that this language has developed over time. From a historico-developmental perspective, language evolves from a relatively global and undifferentiated structure to a more differentiated and articulated structure. This implies that: "In the present context, the words which label the essential dimensions should be older than the words which label less central dimensions" (p. 340). With reference to Figure 3, this means that words classified as falling at the nodal points of assured-dominant, warm-friendly, unassured-submissive, and cold-hostile should have earlier dates of entry into the language than words classified as falling in the four off-quadrants.

From a list provided by Kiesler (1982), 225 words were selected that had been classified as falling in one of the eight categories shown in Figure 3. The date of entry of each word into the English language was obtained from the Oxford English Dictionary, the definitive source for that purpose. The average date of entry of words within each of the eight categories is provided under the labels in Figure 3, where it can be seen, for example, that the mean date of entry for words in the cold-hostile category was 1424 A.D. and that of words in the detached-inhibited category was 1633 A.D.

It is immediately evident from Figure 3 that words from the nodal points of the presumably "basic" dimensions entered the language much earlier than did those from the presumably "less basic" dimensions. Analysis of variance revealed that there were reliable differences between octants ($p < .001$) and when comparisons were made between octant means, 13 of the 16 predicted differences were statistically significant. There was also no comparison in which the four "basic" categories differed significantly from one another and no comparison in which the four "less basic" categories differed from one another (Benjafield & Carson, 1985, pp. 341–343). From the perspective provided by a historico-developmental analysis, there is nothing "arbitrary" involved in designating agency and communion as fundamental coordinates of trait-descriptive language.

Men and Women

Since ancient times the concepts of agency and communion have been assumed to be associated with the male and the female of the species, respectively. From a *sociological* perspective, this association arises from the need for a division of labor within a society to ensure its efficient functioning and ultimate survival. Broadly speaking, the common goals of members of a society are those of getting a living [A] and of living together [C] (Redfield, 1960). Since males are typically larger and stronger than females, it may appear "natural" that their specialized roles would include hunting, protecting, and leadership functions. Since females are uniquely equipped to breed and suckle their young, it may seem equally "natural" that their specialized roles would include child-rearing, preparation of food, and household maintenance.

Since at least the 1930s, cultural anthropologists have identified societies that are exceptions to this arrangement (e.g., Mead, 1935), and sociologists have called attention to the inherent psychological conflicts generated by such sex-role differentiations (e.g., Kirkpatrick, 1936). But despite exceptions and potential difficulties, males have enacted agentic roles and females have enacted communal roles in most societies, up to and largely including the present era. The fact that this pattern of sex-role differentiation is normative does not establish that it arises from natural origins. Alternative patterns of division of labor may also ensure the efficient functioning and ultimate survival of a society. This division of labor assigns "instrumental" (A) roles to males (getting things done in the outside world) and "expressive" (C) roles to females (maintaining harmony within the family) (Parsons & Bales, 1955).

From an *evolutionary* perspective, sex differences in agency and communion may be evaluated in terms of their differential survival or reproductive value in the course of natural selection. Contemporary evolutionary biology focuses on natural selection at the levels of individuals and genes rather than at the levels of societies and species (Williams, 1966). Genes survive in healthy offspring, and the circumstances that foster successful gene propagation may differ for males and females.

Darwin's (1871) theory of *sexual selection* posited competition among members of one sex for opportunities to mate with reproductively valuable members of the opposite sex. Trivers's (1972) concept of *parental investment* was put forth to explain the greater degree of competition among males for this purpose. Females' parental investment in their offspring includes extended periods of gestation and lactation, which limit the number of potential offspring they can produce. Although males have less parental investment, they are limited in reproductive success by the availability of multiple mates, especially reproductively valuable or fertile mates. Since some males gain access to multiple mates, others are left with none. Consequently, males exhibit a much greater variance in the number of offspring they can potentially produce. Under these circumstances, the characteristics that ensure successful reproduction will be different for males and females.

For males, access to reproductively valuable females is often increased by general aggressiveness and by competition with other males for status on a dominance hierarchy. Because this aggressiveness poses a potential threat to females and their offspring, their best strategy is to foster cooperation, reciprocity, and low levels of aggressiveness within the group. The agentic characteristics of males and the communal characteristics of females are thus interpreted as different proximate tactics (e.g., competing with other males for status) that are associated with ultimate outcomes of evolutionary significance (e.g., success in passing genes to succeeding generations).

Neither sociological nor evolutionary accounts of the linkage of males to agentic roles and females to communal roles have been accepted uncritically or with equanimity. Feminist writers in particular have characterized both sociological (e.g., Bem, 1985) and evolutionary (e.g., Bleier, 1984) accounts as lacking firm scientific evidence and as spuriously justifying the favored position of males in modern society. It has been within this context of controversy and uncertainty that the psychological concepts of "masculinity" and "femininity" have been reexamined in recent years.

Constantinople

The dimension of masculinity-femininity (M-F) has figured prominently in the psychological assessment of adults for the last 50 years. Although dissatisfaction with various aspects of M-F measurement were expressed periodically, the essential murkiness of this concept did not become completely apparent until the incisive review of Constantinople (1973). Constantinople reviewed some of the major tests of M-F which were based on highly heterogeneous domains of content, including attitudes, interests, personality characteristics, sexual preferences, and adjustment. She concluded that none of these tests was based on a coherent theoretical rationale that would justify the various measurement procedures. Moreover: "there is no . . . body of data which indicates that M-F, or M or F alone, consistently is related to other variables in predictive ways (except whether or not the subject is male or female!)" (p. 389).

Constantinople also directed critical attention to three untested assumptions that appear to underlie many M-F instruments: (1) M-F is best defined in terms of sex differences in item endorsements, (2) M-F is a bipolar construct, and (3) M-F is a unidimensional construct. She concluded that: (1) differences in item endorsement are a vague and insufficient criterion for item selection, (2) M-F is not necessarily best represented by a single score in which the opposite of a feminine response can be assumed to indicate masculinity, and (3) the possibility exists that M and F are independent dimensions in their own right and should be measured *separately*. The last conclusion had been drawn by earlier writers on both conceptual (e.g., Carlson, 1971, 1972) and empirical (e.g., Gonen & Lansky, 1968) grounds. It was destined to have an extraordinary effect on subsequent research on M-F.

The take-home message from Constantinople's analysis was that the concept of M-F might be better construed as independent concepts of M and F. In structural terms this is clear enough: M and F form two orthogonal factors rather than a single bipolar factor. But note that "masculinity" and "femininity," bipolar or orthogonal, have still not been clearly defined. The main issue here is substantive rather than structural. What is "masculinity" and what is "femininity"?

Bem

In the early 1970s, several writers more or less independently explicated the notion that M and F are separate dimensions relevant to the understanding of both men and women (Bem, 1974; Block, 1973; Spence, Helmreich, & Stapp, 1974). Bem, for example, asked judges to rate the desirability of 200 personality characteristics for men and women in American society. Items judged to be more desirable for men than for women were assembled into a Masculinity scale and items judged to be more desirable for women than for men were assembled into a separate Femininity scale in the Bem Sex-Role Inventory (BSRI). Bem's Masculinity and Femininity scales were indeed found to be independent and, equally important, to enter into interesting empirical relations with a variety of trait variables and experimental manipulations.

The items in the BSRI Masculinity scale (e.g., "dominant," "forceful," "individualistic") and in the Femininity scale (e.g., "warm," "sympathetic," "compassionate") for the most part index two substantively homogeneous and clear-cut dimensions. Subsequent factor analyses of the total item pool (e.g., Gaudreau, 1977) revealed that a few items had insufficient loadings on one or the other of these two dimensions to justify their inclusion in one or the other of the scales. In particular the item "masculine" does not belong in the BSRI Masculinity scale and the item "feminine" does not belong in the BSRI Femininity scale. This apparent paradox arises from exactly the same set of considerations that earlier led me to characterize Constantinople's conclusions as problematic: The structural issue of whether M-F is better construed as two independent dimensions of M and F cannot be answered in the absence of definitions of M and F.

Although originally proposed as measures of M and F, Bem's Masculinity and Femininity scales, in fact, measure the interpersonal *dispositions* of dominance (A) and nurturance (C), coordinates known for some time to be orthogonal (LaForge et al., 1954). Moreover, when items such as "masculinity" and "femininity" are deleted, Bem's scales are not only psychometrically and substantively equivalent to standard measures of interpersonal dominance and nurturance (Wiggins & Holzmuller, 1981), they are among the best available markers of these two orthogonal dimensions (Wiggins & Broughton, 1985).

Spence

The orthogonality of dominance and nurturance might shed some light on the relation between M and F if it could be demonstrated that dominance and nurturance are related to self-perceptions of "masculinity" and "femininity" or to the tendency to identify with the traditional sex role of one's biological sex. Thus, for example, it could be the case that women who are highly nurturant perceive themselves as highly "feminine" and identify strongly with roles such as "housewife." However, as Janet Spence (1985) has forcefully pointed out, empirical evidence suggesting such associations is decidedly lacking:

> The journals are littered with dozens of BSRI . . . studies testing hypotheses derived from the assumption that these instruments measure the abstract concepts of masculinity and femininity or sex-role identification that failed to be confirmed. (p. 76)

It would appear that dominant (A) and nurturant (C) dispositions do not differentially predispose men and women toward the acceptance of or identification with the traditional sex-role differentiations of society. Nor does it appear that the orthogonal dimensions of dominance and nurturance shed much light on the still largely unanalyzed dimensions of M and F. Although the meta-concepts of agency and communion may still be in the wings here, their precise application to the concepts of masculinity and femininity has yet to be realized.

Structural Considerations

A by-product of the research on masculinity and femininity just described was an emphasis on the importance of structural considerations in the conceptualization of concepts such as agency and communion. In our earlier schematic representation of these concepts, agency and communion were depicted as being at right angles to one another (see Figure 2, p. 91). This orthogonal representation implies that the amount of A present in the universe, a society, or an individual is independent of, or uncorrelated with, the amount of C and vice versa. Although this may appear to be a relatively noncommittal assumption, it in fact obviates the issue of a possible conflict or opposition between A and C. The representation in Figure 2 suggests that all combinations of A and C are possible in a society or in an individual: for example, an individual may be agentic but not communal, communal but not agentic, or strongly agentic *and* strongly communal. Development in one modality does not restrict development in the other; there is no inherent conflict between the two.

The depiction in Figure 2 also suggests that agency and communion have logical opposites or poles. Passivity is the opposite of agency (A-) and dissociation is the opposite of communion (C-). This assumption may also have relatively strong implications. One could infer, for example, that a society characterized by institutions which emphasize disaffiliation, or an individual with a pronounced disposition to be hostile, would be unlikely or even unable to express communion (cf. Paulhus & Martin, 1987). In this sense, the negative poles of passivity and dissociation not only restrict development of agency and communion, respectively, they are in conflict with, or opposition to, their polar opposites.

Because agency and communion are viewed as the essential ingredients of a well-ordered and harmonious society and of a psychologically fulfilled and well-integrated individual, virtually all writers view them to be virtuous or good. From the bipolar representations of Figure 2, it could easily be concluded that passivity and dissociation are evil or bad, or more euphemistically, "socially undesirable." It is difficult to think of society, as we know it, being governed exclusively by principles of passivity and dissociation. It is also difficult to think of passivity and dissociation as healthy or normal dimensions of personality. Psychiatrist Andras Angyal (1965) explicitly equated agency and communion with psychological health, and passivity and dissociation with neuroticism. Some recent writers appear to equate passivity with neuroticism and dissociation with psychoticism (Eysenck & Eysenck, 1985). However, from an interpersonal perspective, problems of living would be expected to occur in *all* regions of the space defined by the coordinates of agency and communion (Horowitz, 1979).

On a very basic level, Figure 2 can be interpreted as representing agency and communion as continua; societies and individuals can be more or less agentic and more or less communal. Conjoined with the notion of goodness, this could mean the more the better, as far as the expression of these two modalities is concerned. Bakan (1966), however, emphasized the importance of a *balance* between these two modalities and described the manner in which each modality served to mitigate the potentially excessive effects of the other. Unmitigated agency may lead to isolation, alienation, and hostility (C-) (Bakan, 1966; Borkenau, 1986; Buss & Craik, 1986). Unmitigated community may lead to total submission, loss of self, and masochism (A-) (Bakan, 1966; Borkenau, 1986; Buss, 1990; Spence, Helmreich, & Holahan, 1979). Agentic strivings mitigated by a concern for others and communal feelings mitigated by a sense of self are the much preferred expressions of these two modalities.

Figure 2 should not be construed as a static model that fails to take *interaction* into account. Neither individuals nor institutions exist in isolation. Unmitigated agency is likely to evoke negative reactions that, in turn, increase isolation. Unmitigated communion is likely to be taken advantage of in ways that increase submission and powerlessness. A framework for viewing the interactions between individuals in terms of agency and communion is presented in the next section.

It should be clear by now that the meta-concepts of agency and communion underlie, in fundamental and complex ways, our world views, our understanding of persons, our language that describes social relations, and our view of the relations between men and women. The reason that these, and no doubt many other, aspects of social existence are so well captured by agency and communion is that these meta-concepts express the common challenges provided by all societies: getting a living and living together (Redfield, 1960). The universal and inescapable motifs of group living are getting ahead and getting along (Hogan, Jones, & Cheek, 1985). Measurement procedures for the quantification of interpersonal behavior must be cast within the framework of the common challenges presented by a society and the principal themes that characterize interpersonal transactions within that society.

The Measurement of Interpersonal Behavior

The Interpersonal Circumplex

The meta-concepts of agency and communion have guided efforts to quantify significant aspects of interpersonal behavior for almost 40 years (Wiggins, 1982). During the early stages of this tradition, members of the Kaiser Foundation research group attempted to objectify and systematize the insights of Harry Stack Sullivan in the context of their own work involving direct observations of patients in group psychotherapy (Freedman, Leary, Ossorio, & Coffey, 1951). Patients' behaviors were rated in terms of what they appeared to be doing to others, using transitive verbs (e.g., dominate) to characterize *interpersonal mechanisms*. A set of interpersonal mechanisms was arranged on a circular continuum whose nodal points were dominance (A +) vs. submission (A-) and affiliation (C +) vs. hostility (C-). All interpersonal mechanisms were considered to be blends of the orthogonal coordinates whose nodes defined the circular system.

The originators of this coding system regarded interpersonal mechanisms as process variables, or "personality in action," and *interpersonal traits* as structural variables that reflected enduring tendencies of personality (Freedman et al., 1951, p. 156). Interpersonal traits were indexed by adjectives corresponding to the verbs of interpersonal mechanisms (e.g., dominant) and they were employed in scales which assessed perceptions of self and significant others within the same circular arrangement of variables, organized around agency and communion (LaForge & Suczek, 1955).

Throughout the last four decades, and particularly since the appearance of Leary's (1957) seminal work, many variations on the system just described have been proposed by different authors, all of which were guided by the concepts of agency and communion, and most of which were based on the circular order that came to be known as a circumplex (Wiggins, 1982, pp. 184–200). The system proposed by Kiesler (1983), illustrated in Figure 3, is representative of recent formulations on this topic. I will not attempt to summarize this extensive literature, except to note that circumplex models derived from the meta-concepts of agency and communion have proven fruitful in the conceptualization and measurement of interpersonal acts, traits, affects, interpersonal problems, and personality disorders.

Societal Structures of the Mind

On a conceptual level, the most comprehensive framework for relating the meta-concepts of agency and communion to the measurement of interpersonal behavior is found in Foa and Foa's (1974) *Societal Structures of the Mind*. In the Foas' view, the interdependence between persons in society emanates from the need to exchange resources that are essential to the well-being of individuals, social institutions, and the larger society in which both are embedded. In the course of the development of individuals within societies, these social exchanges become "meaningful" through the acquisition of cognitive schemas organized around the facets of directionality (giving vs. taking away), object (self vs. other), and the critically important facet of resource. Although there are a number of classes of resources whose exchange among individuals is important for effective social life, the two resources that are most important for understanding interpersonal behavior, and that in effect *define* interpersonal behavior, are *status* (A) and *love* (C).

Foa (1961) has demonstrated that a facet analysis (Guttman, 1958) of the postulated cognitive dimensions of directionality, object, and the resources of status and love yields a structure that is isomorphic with the empirical structure of the interpersonal circumplex. Conceptually, this suggests that interpersonal behavior may be construed, by lay persons and psychologists, as the granting or denial of status (A) and love (C) between two or more persons. Thus, for example, the assured-dominant octant of the interpersonal circumplex (Figure 3) may be understood as the granting of love and status to self and the granting of love but *not* status to others. This and many other features of the Foas' conceptual analyses provide a useful framework for understanding the roles of agency and communion in the measurement of interpersonal behavior.

Dimensions of Human Characteristics

The necessity of agency and communion as conceptual coordinates for the measurement of interpersonal behavior is so self-evident that one is led to the question of the sufficiency of these concepts for that purpose. The answer to such a question depends very much on how it is interpreted. How well do the bipolar coordinates of agency and communion encompass the universe of content of interpersonal behavior? If one defines interpersonal behavior as *"dyadic interactions that have relatively clear-cut social (status) and emotional (love) consequences for both participants (self and other)"* (Wiggins, 1979, p. 398) and if one assumes that the interpersonal circumplex may be sectored into 'an infinite number of units, then it would appear that agency and communion are sufficient coordinates, admittedly by definition. How well do these coordinates capture the full range of individual differences in human characteristics? The answer to this question is more complicated and it must be given within the context of a taxonomy of the major dimensions of human characteristics.

Within the field of personality assessment there is reasonably widespread agreement (for a field that is not noted for consensus) that the full range of individual differences in human characteristics is well captured by five orthogonal factors, which are known informally as the "Big Five" factors of personality research (Goldberg, 1981). When scales are employed that are representative of trait-descriptive terms in the English language (Allport & Odbert, 1936), the Big Five factors emerge with regularity across diverse samples and situations (Norman, 1963). These factors are usually labeled: I. Surgency, II. Agreeableness, III. Conscientiousness, IV. Emotional Stability, and V. Culture.

The first two Big Five factors of Surgency and Agreeableness are collinear with the two factors of Dominance (A) and Love (C) of the interpersonal circumplex (e.g., McCrae & Costa, 1989). Because the factors of Surgency and Agreeableness have tended to account for the lion's share of the variance in Big Five studies (Peabody & Goldberg, 1989), it could be said, to return to our question, that the coordinates of agency and communion capture a substantial portion of variance of the full range of human characteristics. Moreover, when subjects are allowed to spontaneously generate their own self-descriptions, the dimensions of Surgency and Agreeableness are of much more concern to them than are the other Big Five dimensions (John, 1990, p. 267).

It is important to bear in mind that Surgency (A) and Agreeableness (C) are relatively *orthogonal* to Conscientiousness, Emotional Stability, and Culture; these three domains, and doubtless many others, tap something "different" from agency and communion. It follows that a full characterization of persons must be made with reference to these additional dimensions, as well. For example, the clearly agentic quality of *leadership* can be expressed in ways that are conscientious (Ralph Nader) or non-conscientious (Ferdinand Marcos); stable (Winston Churchill) or unstable (Captain Queeg); and cultured (Pierre Trudeau) or uncultured (Attila the Hun).

Clearly, the concepts of agency and communion, by themselves, do not fully capture the broad spectrum of important individual differences that characterize human transactions. In terms of the Big Five factors, dominant (I) and nurturant (II) dispositions interact with characterological (III), emotional (IV), and cognitive (V) dispositions, and doubtless with many other factors as well. Nevertheless, as I have suggested in this essay, agency and communion are propaedeutic to the study of these additional determinants of interpersonal behavior.

Author note

I would like to acknowledge my personal indebtedness to Paul Meehl—not for the contents of this particular essay, but for providing inspiration over the last thirty years that has resulted in an essay of this kind. As a graduate student, my interests were strongly shaped by a total and joyful immersion in Meehl's early and classic writings (1945–1956). Later, these interests were more clearly expressed in my attempt to survey the field of personality assessment (Wiggins, 1973), in a book which would have been more of a monograph had it not been for the contributions of Meehl described therein. As I continue to read Meehl, I am still impressed by the manner in which he draws upon his formidable erudition to cast problems in a broader perspective than those held by his contemporaries. In honor, but not emulation, of this approach, I have used this occasion to "stretch" the topic of interpersonal assessment a bit beyond its usual boundaries.

Preparation of this essay was greatly facilitated by Social Sciences and Humanities Research Council of Canada Grant 410–87–1322. I would like to thank David M. Buss, Lewis R. Goldberg,

Stewart Grant, Robert Hogan, Donald J. Kiesler, Delroy Paulhus, Aaron Pincus, Paul Trapnell, Candace Taylor Wiggins, Tannis MacBeth Williams, and Roderick Wong for their help and suggestions.

References

Adler, A. [1912]. The neurotic character. In H. L. Ansbacher & R. R. Ansbacher (Eds) (1956), *The individual psychology of Alfred Adler*. New York: Harper.

Adler, A. (1964). *Social interest: A challenge to mankind*. New York: Putnam.

Allport, G. W., & Odbert, H. S. (1936). Trait names: A psycho-lexical study. *Psychological Monographs, 47* (1, Whole No. 211).

Anchin, J. C., & Kiesler, D. J. (Eds.). (1982). *Handbook of interpersonal psychotherapy*. New York: Pergamon.

Angyal, A. (1941). *Foundations for a science of personality*. New York: Commonwealth Fund.

Angyal, A. (1965). *Neurosis and treatment: A holistic theory*. New York: Wiley.

Bakan, D. (1966). *The duality of human existence: Isolation and communion in Western man*. Boston: Beacon.

Bem, S. L. (1974). The measurement of psychological androgyny. *Journal of Consulting and Clinical Psychology, 42*, 155–162.

Bem, S. L. (1985). Androgyny and gender schema theory: A conceptualization and empirical integration. In T. B. Sonderegger (Ed.), *Nebraska Symposium on Motivation, 1984, 32*, 179–226. Lincoln: University of Nebraska Press.

Benjafield, J., & Carson, E. (1985). An historicodevelopmental analysis of the circumplex model of trait descriptive terms. *Canadian Journal of Behavioural Science, 4*, 339–345.

Bleier, R. (1984). *Science and gender: A critique of biology and its theories on women*. New York: Pergamon Press.

Block, J. (1973). Conceptions of sex role: Some cross-cultural and longitudinal perspectives. *American Psychologist, 28*, 512–526.

Borkenau, P. (1986). Toward an understanding of trait interrelations: Acts as instances for several traits. *Journal of Personality and Social Psychology, 51*, 371–381.

Brown, R. (1965). *Social psychology*. New York: Free Press.

Brown, R., & Ford, M. (1961). Address in American English. *Journal of Abnormal and Social Psychology, 62*, 375–385.

Brown, R., & Gilman, A. (1960). The pronouns of power and solidarity. In T. A. Sebeok (Ed.), *Style in language*. Cambridge: Technology Press.

Buss, D. M. (1990). Unmitigated agency and unmitigated communion: An analysis of the negative components of masculinity and femininity. *Sex Roles, 22*, 555–568.

Buss, D. M., & Craik, K. H. (1986). The act frequency approach and the construction of personality. In A. Angleitner, A. Furnham, & G. van Heck (Eds.), *Personality psychology in Europe, Vol. 2: Current trends and controversies*. Berwyn: Swets North America, Inc.

Carlson, R. (1971). Sex differences in ego functioning: Exploratory studies of agency and communion. *Journal of Consulting and Clinical Psychology, 37*, 267–277.

Carlson, R. (1972). Understanding women: Implications for personality theory and research. *Journal of Social Issues, 28*, 17–32.

Carson, R. C. (1969). *Interaction concepts of personality*. Chicago: Aldine.

Constantinople, A. (1973). Masculinity-Femininity: An exception to a famous dictum? *Psychological Bulletin, 80*, 389–407.

Conte, H. R., & Plutchik, R. (1981). A circumplex model for interpersonal personality traits. *Journal of Personality and Social Psychology, 40*, 701–711.

Darwin, C. (1871). *The descent of man and selection in relation to sex*. London: Murray.

Durant, W. (1939). *The story of civilization*: Part II. *The life of Greece*. New York: Simon and Schuster.

Erikson, E. H. (1950). *Childhood and society*. New York: Norton.

Erikson, E. H. (1964). *Insight and responsibility*. New York: Norton.

Eysenck, H. J., & Eysenck, M. W. (1985). *Personality and individual differences: A natural science approach*. New York: Plenum.

Foa, U. G. (1961). Convergences in the analysis of the structure of interpersonal behavior. *Psychological Review, 68*, 341–353.

Foa, U. G., & Foa, E. B. (1974). *Societal structures of the mind*. Springfield, IL: Charles C Thomas.

Freedman, M. B., Leary, T. F., Ossorio, A. G., & Coffey, H. S. (1951). The interpersonal dimension of personality. *Journal of Personality, 20*, 143–161.

Fromm, E. (1941). *Escape from freedom*. New York: Avon Books.

Fromm, E. (1959). *Sigmund Freud's mission: An analysis of his personality and influence*. New York: Simon and Schuster.

Fromm, E. (1976). *To have or to be?* New York: Harper and Row.

Gaudreau, P. (1977). Factor analysis of the Bem Sex Role Inventory. *Journal of Consulting and Clinical Psychology, 45*, 299–302.

Goldberg, L. R. (1981). Language and individual differences: The search for universals in personality lexicons. In L. Wheeler (Ed.), *Review of personality and social psychology*, Vol. 2 (pp. 141–165). Beverly Hills, CA: Sage.

Gonen, J. Y., & Lansky, L. (1968). Masculinity, femininity, and masculinity-femininity: A phenomenological study of the *Mf* scale of the MMPI. *Psychological Reports, 23*, 183–194.

Guttman, L. (1958). Introduction to facet design and analysis. In *Proceedings of the 15th International Congress of Psychology*, Brussels, 1957. Amsterdam: North Holland.

Hackett, S. C. (1979). *Oriental philosophy*. Madison: The University of Wisconsin Press.

Hogan, R. (1983). A socioanalytic theory of personality. In M. M. Page (Ed.), *Nebraska Symposium on Motivation, 1982*, 55–89. Lincoln: University of Nebraska Press.

Hogan, R., Jones, W., & Cheek, J. M. (1985). Socioanalytic theory: An alternative to armadillo psychology. In B. R. Schlenker (Ed.), *The self and social life* (pp. 175–198). New York: McGraw-Hill.

Hook, D. D. (1984). First names and titles as solidarity and power semantics in English. *International Review of Applied Linguistics in Language Teaching, 22*, 183–189.

Horney, K. (1937). *The neurotic personality of our time*. New York: Norton.

Horowitz, L. M. (1979). On the cognitive structure of interpersonal problems in psychotherapy. *Journal of Consulting and Clinical Psychology, 47*, 5–15.

John, O. P. (1990). Towards a taxonomy of personality descriptors. In D. M. Buss & N. Cantor (Eds.), *Personality psychology: Recent trends and emerging directions* (pp. 261–271). New York: Springer-Verlag.

Kiesler, D. J. (1982). *The 1982 interpersonal circle: A taxonomy for complementarity in human transactions*. Richmond: Virginia Commonwealth University.

Kiesler, D. J. (1983). The 1982 interpersonal circle: A taxonomy for complementarity in human transactions. *Psychological Review, 90*, 185–214.

Kirkpatrick, C. (1936). Inconsistencies in marriage roles and marriage conflict. *International Journal of Ethics, 46*, 444–460.

LaForge, R., Leary, T. F., Naboisek, H., Coffey, H. S., & Freedman, M. B. (1954). The interpersonal dimension of personality: II. An objective study of repression. *Journal of Personality, 23*, 129–153.

LaForge, R., & Suczek, R. F. (1955). The interpersonal dimension of personality: II. An interpersonal check list. *Journal of Personality, 24*, 94–112.

Leary, T. (1957). *Interpersonal diagnosis of personality*. New York: Ronald.

Lorr, M., & McNair, D. M. (1965). Expansion of the interpersonal behavior circle. *Journal of Personality and Social Psychology, 2,* 823–830.

Maddi, S. R. (1976). *Personality theories: A comparative analysis.* Homewood, IL: Dorsey.

McAdams, D. P. (1980). A thematic coding system for the intimacy motive. *Journal of Research in Personality, 14,* 413–432.

McAdams, D. P. (1982). Experiences of intimacy and power: Relationships between social motives and autobiographical memory. *Journal of Personality and Social Psychology, 42,* 292–302.

McAdams, D. P. (1984). Love, power, and images of the self. In C. Malatesta & C. Izard (Eds.), *Emotion in adult development.* Beverly Hills, CA: Sage.

McAdams, D. P. (1985a). Motivation and friendship. In S. Duck & D. Perlman (Eds.), *Understanding personal relationships: An interdisciplinary approach.* Beverly Hills, CA: Sage.

McAdams, D. P. (1985b). *Power, intimacy and the life story: Personological inquiries into identity.* Homewood, IL: Dow Jones-Irwin.

McClelland, D. C., Atkinson, J. W., Clark, R. A., & Lowell, E. L. (1953). *The achievement motive.* New York: Appleton-Century-Crofts.

McCrae, R. R., & Costa, P. T., Jr. (1989). The structure of interpersonal traits: Wiggins' circumplex and the five-factor model. *Journal of Personality and Social Psychology, 56,* 586–595.

Mead, M. (1935). *Sex and temperament in three primitive societies.* New York: Norton.

Norman, W. T. (1963). Toward an adequate taxonomy of personality attributes. *Journal of Abnormal and Social Psychology, 66,* 574–583.

Parsons, T., & Bales, R. F. (1955). *Family, socialization and interaction process.* New York: Free Press.

Paulhus, D. L., & Martin, C. L. (1987). The structure of personality capabilities. *Journal of Personality and Social Psychology, 52,* 354–365.

Peabody, D., & Goldberg, L. R. (1989). Some determinants of factor structures from personality trait-descriptors. *Journal of Personality and Social Psychology, 57,* 552–567.

Redfield, R. (1960). How society operates. In H. L. Shapiro (Ed.), *Man, culture, and society* (pp. 345–368). New York: Oxford University Press.

Shweder, R. A. (1972). *Semantic structure and personality assessment.* Unpublished Ph.D. dissertation, Harvard University, Cambridge, MA.

Slobin, D. L., Miller, S. H., & Porter, L. W. (1968). Forms of address and social relations in a business organization. *Journal of Personality and Social Psychology, 8,* 289–293.

Spence, J. T. (1985). Gender identity and its implications for the concepts of masculinity and femininity. In T. B. Sonderegger (Ed.), *Nebraska Symposium on Motivation, 1984, 32,* 59–95. Lincoln: University of Nebraska Press.

Spence, J. T., Helmreich, R. L., & Holahan, C. K. (1979). Negative and positive components of psychological masculinity and femininity and their relationships to self-reports of neurotic and acting out behaviors. *Journal of Personality and Social Psychology, 37,* 1673–1682.

Spence, J. T., Helmreich, R. L., & Stapp, J. (1974). The Personal Attributes Questionnaire: A measure of sex-role stereotypes and masculinity-femininity. *JSAS Catalog of Selected Documents in Psychology, 4,* 43–44, MS 617.

Sullivan, H. S. (1950). The illusion of personal individuality. *Psychiatry, 13,* 317–332.

Sullivan, H. S. (1953a). *Conceptions of modern psychiatry.* New York: Norton.

Sullivan, H. S. (1953b). *The interpersonal theory of psychiatry.* New York: Norton.

Sullivan, H. S. (1972). *Personal psychopathology.* New York: Norton.

Trivers, R. (1972). Parental investment and sexual selection. In B. Campbell (Ed.), *Sexual selection and the descent of man: 1871–1971.* Chicago: Aldine.

White, G. (1978). Ambiguity and ambivalence in A'ara personality descriptors. *American Ethnologist, 5,* 334–360.

White, G. M. (1980). Conceptual universals in interpersonal language. *American Anthropologist, 82,* 759–781.

Wiggins, J. S. (1973). *Personality and prediction: Principles of personality assessment.* Reading, MA: Addison-Wesley.

Wiggins, J. S. (1979). A psychological taxonomy of trait-descriptive terms: The interpersonal domain. *Journal of Personality and Social Psychology, 37,* 395–412.

Wiggins, J. S. (1982). Circumplex models of interpersonal behavior in clinical psychology. In P. C. Kendall & J. N. Butcher (Eds.), *Handbook of research methods in clinical psychology* (pp. 183–221). New York: Wiley.

Wiggins, J. S., & Broughton, R. (1985). The Interpersonal Circle: A structural model for the integration of personality research. In R. Hogan & W. H. Jones (Eds.), *Perspectives in personality* (Vol. 1, pp. 1–47). Greenwich, CT: JAI Press.

Wiggins, J. S., & Holzmuller, A. (1981). Further evidence on androgyny and interpersonal flexibility. *Journal of Research in Personality, 15,* 67–80.

Williams, G. C. (1966). *Adaptation and natural selection: A critique of some current evolutionary thought.* Princeton, NJ: Princeton University Press.

Winter, D. G. (1973). *The power motive.* New York: The Free Press.

Some Unfinished Business
Harrison G. Gough

People react in different ways to things that are incomplete, partial, or unfinished. For instance, some individuals would probably prefer to have an artist's preliminary, inchoate sketch of a later masterwork than the finished version, or the writer's notes for a story rather than the published version. In 1949, when the initial staff at the Institute of Personality Assessment and Research (IPAR) in Berkeley was preparing for its first assessment, one of the things done was to create a library of 1,000 self-descriptive items that seemed to be relevant in one way or another to the realization of intellectual and creative potential. This pool of items included the statement "The unfinished and the imperfect often have greater appeal for me than the completed and polished."

Knowing that this chapter would be dealing with incomplete and unfinished business, I got interested in the fate of this item and what diagnostic or other properties it had subsequently revealed. How do people respond to the statement, and are there consequential differences between those who agree or answer true, and those who disagree or answer false? Presumably those who answer true will tend to be sympathetic to what is reported in this chapter, whereas those who answer false may find its account unpersuasive and of little merit.

A number of personality scales were developed in whole or in part from the IPAR collection of 1,000 items. A first review (itself partial and incomplete) was to see if the item appeared on any of these measures. This search found survival of the item in at least two scales, both developed by Frank Barron. The first was his measure of personal complexity (Barron, 1953a), and the second was his scale for independence of judgment (Barron, 1953b); in both cases the scored response was "true." Although the item did not appear on Barron's (1957) scale for originality, a "true" response is nonetheless positively correlated with the score on this measure. So a first finding is that expressing a liking for the unfinished and imperfect is, among other things, somewhat diagnostic of one's degree

114

of psychological differentiation, of one's capacity to resist or stand apart from an incorrect social consensus, and of one's creative potential.

From 1950 through 1981, all incoming graduate students in psychology at Berkeley were asked to participate in an eight-hour experimental testing battery, including several self-report devices, one of which contained the item on the unfinished. Among 623 males who took these tests, 54.4% answered "true" to the item, and among 405 females 52.8% did the same. Among University of California undergraduates tested in more recent years, 43.4% of males and 38.4% of females responded "true." Apparently a liking for the incomplete and imperfect is somewhat stronger among psychologists than among students-in-general. Are psychologists or psychologists-in-training more intraceptive and empathic than students-in-general? If so, then this implication can be added to what is tentatively inferrable from a positive response to the item.

There is a Jungian flavor to the discussion above (specifically, the concept of differentiation or internal individuation), which raises the question of more explicit examination of Jungian themes. A sample of 198 college students (99 of each sex) took the Myers-Briggs Type Indicator (MBTI; Myers & McCaulley, 1985), and also the experimental item. The MBTI is scored for introversion versus extraversion, intuition versus sensing, feeling versus thinking, and perceiving versus judging. Dummy weights on the item of "1" for true and "0" for false were correlated with the four MBTI continuous scales, and these coefficients obtained: introversion, $r = .13$; intuition, $r = .12$; feeling, $r = .02$; and perceiving, $r = .17$. Correlations of .14 and above are statistically significant at or beyond the .05 level of probability for this sample.

The direction of the rather modest correlations just cited suggests that persons answering the item "true" tend to be higher on perceiving than judging, probably more introverted than extraverted, and possibly more intuitional than sensing in viewing the world and others. There was no trend on the thinking versus feeling scale, on which higher scores indicate feeling as the preferred basis for evaluating experience.

The 198 students also took the California Psychological Inventory (CPI; Gough, 1987). Instead of citing all of the correlations between the item and the CPI scales, only those with statistically significant ($p < .05$) coefficients will be mentioned. The largest was with Achievement via Conformance (Gough, 1953), with a value of -.21 (-.17 for males alone, -.24 for females alone). Persons with higher scores on Ac tend to prefer and do best in structured, articulated, and rule-governed environments; persons with lower scores, assuming good intellectual and other talents, tend to perform below level in strongly regulated settings.

The second largest CPI correlation was on the Socialization or So scale (Gough, 1960), with a coefficient of -.18 in the total sample (-.16 for males, -.20 for females). Persons with high scores on So tend to have strongly internalized superego systems, rebel little if at all against constraints and societally imposed limitations, and tend to behave in prudent, moderate, and socially responsible ways. It should also be mentioned that among very talented persons, high So scores are negatively related to the creative expression of that talent (Gough, 1965).

Related to the finding for the So scale were the correlations for Responsibility (Re) and Self-control (Sc). For Re, the coefficient in the total sample was -.15, and for Sc it was -.16. The finding for Re is understandable from the comments on So. The Sc scale, in addition to the rule-observing inclinations already mentioned, carries implications of over-control or undue dampening of impulse.

From the files, information was gathered concerning Scholastic Aptitude Test (SAT) scores and college academic performance among these students. College grade point average correlated .12 with the 1-0 dummy weights for the item in the total sample, with coefficients of .08 for males alone and .17 for females. For SAT-Verbal the correlation was .07 in the total sample, and for SAT-Mathematical the coefficient was -.03. No trend is discernible here, but at least the students answering "true" are not falling behind those who answer "false" on either academic aptitude or performance.

To this point I have cited findings from other self-report sources, or from the academic record. What about "O" or observational data? That is, how do observers react to persons who reply "true" or "false" to the item? In the study of the 198 students, each was rated after a full day of assessment on a list of 19 personal attributes or dispositions by panels of from 15 to 20 staff observers. Interjudge reliabilities on the ratings ranged from a low of approximately .75 to a high of .99. These staff ratings were correlated with the 1–0 dummy weights on the item, with three of the 19 coefficients turning out to be significant ($p < .05$).

The largest was a correlation of -.22 in the total sample (-.13 for males, -.28 for females) with the rating on need for order. The next largest was a coefficient of -.18 (-.11 for males, -.25 for females) on sense of responsibility. The third was a coefficient of .16 (.11 for males, .20 for females) on sensation-seeking (wanting and seeking out stimulating, excitement-inducing experiences). These three relationships are in agreement with trends already discerned in the "S-data" or self-report measures.

Each of the 198 assessees was also described on the Adjective Check List (Gough & Heilbrun, 1983) by a panel of 10 staff observers. By tallying the number of observers who checked each of the 300 adjectives about a subject, a score going from 0 to 10 was defined which could then be correlated with the 1-0 dummy weights. By chance, three of the 300 items would correlate at or beyond the .01 level of probability; in fact, 23 items reached this level in the total sample. To avoid information overload, only the five largest positive and five largest negative correlations will be listed. The five adjectives with largest positive correlations (hence associated with replying "true" to the item) were: adventurous (r = .24), daring (r = .24), progressive (r = .22), restless (r = .26), and unconventional (r = .22). The five largest negative correlations (descriptions more often given to those who replied "false") were: methodical (r = -.18), planful (r = -.18), prudish (r = -.18), responsible (r = .18), and thorough (r = -.18).

The students were also described by the staff on the 100-item California Q-set (Block, 1961). Consensual descriptions were derived for the panels of five or six observers reporting on each assessee, and then the ratings of each Q-set item were correlated with the 1-0 dummy weights for the self-report item. By chance, only one item would be significantly correlated at the .01 level of confidence; in fact, six items appeared at this level. Three of these were sorted as more characteristic of those who had expressed a liking for the incomplete and imperfect: "Various needs tend toward relatively direct and uncontrolled gratification; unable to delay gratification" (r = .18); "Enjoys sensuous experiences (including touch, taste, smell, physical contact)" (r = .19); and "Tends to be rebellious and nonconforming" (r = .25).

The three Q-sort items most descriptive of those not liking the unfinished and incomplete were: "Is fastidious" (r = -.22); "Favors conservative values in a variety of areas" (r = -.18); and "Judges self and others in conventional terms like 'popularity,' 'the correct thing to do,' social pressures etc." (r = -.20).

The O-data correlates are all rather low, as one would expect for a single self-report item, but *in toto* they begin to paint a clear picture of the kind of person who takes pleasure in the unfinished and imperfect and of the kind of person who does not. The former appears to be imaginative, venturesome, rule-doubting, and somewhat undercontrolled. The latter appears to be orderly, prudent, dutiful, and somewhat overcontrolled.

What does all of this mean in regard to the report of unfinished business to be given in the following section? First, among psychologically minded readers, about half will respond to the presentation with favorable anticipations and about half will be dubious. Among other readers, perhaps four of ten will think it a good idea to write about a study which was only partly completed whereas the other six will be skeptical at best. For those bemused by the incomplete, I hope the material below will be sufficiently unorthodox and provocative to sustain their interest; for those not so bemused, I hope the occasional inclusion of demonstrable findings will diminish their doubts.

The PAR Project

In the mid-1940s at the University of Minnesota, Herbert McClosky, Paul Meehl, and I joined forces to launch a study of political participation. McClosky, a political scientist, had some very interesting ideas about why people do or do not take part in the political process, drawn from his own thinking as well as from classical studies of political involvement such as those of Gosnell (1930), Lasswell (1930, 1935), Lazarsfeld, Berelson, and Gaudet (1944), and Rice (1928).

With a certain degree of logical lenience, political participation can be arrayed on a continuum going from never voting or paying attention to the process, to voting in major but not minor elections, to voting in most elections, to doing these things plus giving time, money, or other support to causes and candidates, to doing these things plus entering into committee and caucus assignments, and so on up to very large investments of effort and running for elected offices. Many factors — demographic, economic, educational, ethnic, geographic, historical, and psychological — may be aligned with this continuum. Our interest was primarily in its psychological covariants and in the development of methods for their assessment.

McClosky and I were both members of the newly established Laboratory for Research in Social Relations, where I was attracted by McClosky's thinking and offered to contribute whatever I could to the psychological aspects of a study. McClosky was a close personal friend of Meehl, and I was then writing my doctoral dissertation under Meehl's supervision, which meant that Meehl knew about the project from its inception, and at McClosky's invitation agreed to take part. Later, in 1948, Kenneth E. Clark, also a member of the Laboratory, became affiliated with the project.

In the academic year 1946–47, and particularly during the summer of 1947, we had innumerable meetings, and several memorable near-marathon sessions at a cabin the McCloskys had rented at Lake Owassa, just north of St. Paul (and in Lake Wobegon country). The project very early took on the name "PAR," standing for participation, awareness, and responsibility. A basic hypothesis was that entering into the political process by way of consistent voting, giving of one's time and money, and trying to reach intelligent positions on current issues, depended on an awareness of the essential obligations of the citizen in a democratic society, and in addition on an evolved personal sense of responsibility which would prompt one to do what ought to be done.

Folk as well as professional notions of American democracy encompass components such as popular sovereignty, representative government, and the accountability of those who govern to those who are governed; this accountability, of course, is most tangibly registered in the voting process. The vast rise in technology, urbanization, population, and the complexity of political and social life, already apparent in those early postwar years, suggested the timeliness of an inquiry into these factors of participation, awareness, and responsibility. To do this we proposed a series of studies, including questionnaire surveys of objectively defined criterion groups such as nonregistered nonvoters, occasional voters, regular or consistent voters, active members of political parties, members of political associations (for example, the League of Women Voters), office-holders, graduate students in political science, and others. In addition to this broad survey, intensive individual assessments were to be carried out on perhaps 300 to 500 persons, selected from various regions along the "PAR" continuum, and to involve several personal interviews, examination by means of clinical devices such as the MMPI, and laboratory procedures.

The questionnaire was intended to include a wide range of variables conceptualized as relevant to PAR, and also internal scales from which the actual level of political participation could be estimated. In the early planning sessions mentioned above, one of our activities, perhaps the major activity, was an attempt to develop a taxonomy of these directly or indirectly implicated factors. As things moved along, the work became more and more an emergent, spontaneous attempt to delineate a theoretical model of the trait structures from which political as well as other kinds of participation could be forecast. For each element or theme within the model, we either borrowed self-report questionnaire items from prior instruments, or wrote new items that we hypothesized to be psychodynamically associated with the component.

By the time this work was finished we had a list of 84 categories, and almost 2,000 self-report items for their assessment. Our hope was to administer and analyze this huge set, looking for linkages to criterion classifications along the axis of political participation, and also for internally homogeneous clusters for as many of the 84 concepts as would yield separable scales. The first analysis we carried through to completion was for the concept of prosocial interpersonal dominance (Gough, McClosky, & Meehl, 1951), and the second was for the concept of social responsibility (Gough, McClosky, & Meehl, 1952). The scale for dominance contained 60 items and that for responsibility contained 56 items. Every item had been shown to possess classificatory validity when pitted against subsamples nominated by peers as being either distinctly high or distinctly low on each attribute. These two scales in somewhat shortened versions were later included among the 18 folk concepts incorporated in the first edition of the California Psychological Inventory (CPI) (Gough, 1957).

The next paper to be published on scales within the context of the 84 concepts was McClosky's (1958) analysis of conservativism as a dispositional variable. By this time, I had left Minnesota for a position at the University of California, Berkeley, and in the early 1960s McClosky also moved to Berkeley. In 1961, Kenneth E. Clark was appointed Dean of the College of Arts and Sciences at the University of Colorado, Boulder.

McClosky kept active in the use of PAR materials and their derivatives (see McClosky, 1957, 1964, 1969; McClosky & Brill, 1983; McClosky & Chong, 1985; McClosky, Chong, & Zaller, 1982; McClosky & diPalma, 1970; McClosky & Schaar, 1965; and McClosky & Zaller, 1985), but the efforts of the other members of the group were largely expended in different ways. I, for example, was deeply engaged in the scaling and validational studies for the new CPI (see Gough, 1952, 1960, 1965), and Meehl was preparing his classic treatise (Meehl, 1954) on clinical versus statistical prediction. So for various reasons, certain of the initial aims of the PAR project, in particular the systematic consideration of the 84 proposed concepts and their measures, were never carried through to completion. This is the "unfinished business" referred to in the title of this chapter. A note, however, should be recorded that McClosky and Meehl have come together once more, and are currently preparing a report on the ideological nature of and conflicts between liberalism and conservatism.

The PAR Categories

To my knowledge, the complete set of 84 dispositional concepts embodied in the PAR categories has never been reported in full in any publication. This volume in honor of Paul Meehl would seem to be an excellent occasion for presenting the list. The complete library of items is too large to permit citation in full in this chapter, but the inclusion of illustrative items for each concept should help to illuminate meanings and also to give the flavor of the total pool.

Category 1. Claimed political knowledge
Representative items: "I have read the Constitution of the United States at least once," "I really don't know very much about politics," "I can name both of the senators from my state," and "I can name most of the members of the President's cabinet."

Category 2. Claimed political participation
Representative items: "I never pay any attention to political news," "I vote at practically every election," "I would not sign a political petition even if I agreed with it," "I have sometimes sent my friends and relatives letters or cards in support of political candidates," and "I have been a delegate to state or county conventions of my political party."

Category 3. Political cynicism
Representative items: "There's no such thing as an honest government," "The best way to get elected to public office is to put on a good show," "No really decent person would go into politics," "Voting is just a matter of choosing the lesser of two evils," and "The politician who is against something gets more votes than the one who is for something."

Category 4. Political indifference
Representative items: "Politics is for other people: I don't really have time for it," "It is too much trouble to vote," "I think political campaigns are just boring," and "I don't care who holds public office as long as things go all right in business and everyday affairs."

Category 5. Feelings of political impotence
Representative items: "There isn't much anyone can do to change the way politicians act," "Political parties are so big that the average member hasn't got much to say about what goes on," "In a country as big as ours, one person's vote means nothing," and "Once a law has been passed, there isn't much anyone can do about it."

Category 6. Equalitarian attitudes
Representative items: "There is far too much special privilege in the world," "We should see to it that people are treated the same, no matter what race or religion they have," "I am afraid too many Americans have sort of forgotten that all people are created equal," and "A poor person ought to have just as much right to a private hospital room as someone who can pay for it."

Category 7. Anterograde algamnesia (uneasy anticipation of the future)
Representative items: "More and more things about the world seem uncertain to me," "I sometimes feel that I won't be able to take care of myself in the years to come," "The future is too uncertain for a person to make serious plans," and "Life is very uncertain for most of us."

Category 8. Faith in government
Representative items: "Very few ever get cheated by the government," "The government tells us only what it wants us to know," "I feel sorry for anyone who has to have dealings with the government," "The less government we have, the better off we are," "I usually have confidence that the government will do what is right," and "A government worker is the best person to go to for advice."

Category 9. Faith in people
Representative items: "There are very few people in the world who are really bad," "There are a lot of crooks and cheapskates in the world," "Most voters are terribly stupid," "In the long run, the people can be depended on to act wisely," and "Most people try hard to do what is right."

Category 10. Egoistic assertions
Representative items: "I would rather have people dislike me than look down on me," "When I disagree with people it generally turns out later that I was right," "Most people have learned to have a healthy respect for me and my views," "I often lend things to people even when I don't want to," "I sometimes feel that people who let others take advantage of them deserve what they get," and "I can't stand people who are meek and humble in the presence of their so-called 'superiors.' "

Category 11. Stoicism
Representative items: "People ought to be satisfied with what they have," "Even if people have troubles, there is no reason why they cannot keep up a cheerful front," "We should bear our troubles bravely, and not complain about them," and "I think people are getting soft and weak from too much coddling and babying."

Category 12. Feelings of bewilderment, confusion, and helplessness
Representative items: "Nothing seems right nowadays," "It makes me nervous to think about all the people in the world," "The government is getting too big," "All the experts disagree, so how can a person decide

what is right?'' ''The world is too complicated now to be understood by anyone but experts,'' and ''I sometimes feel like a tiny cog in a huge machine.''

Category 13. Elitist tendencies

Representative items: ''I sometimes wish we had a royal family in this country,'' ''We might as well frankly admit that some are born to lead, others to follow,'' ''All over the world, the common people are on the march,'' ''All great movements begin among the common people,'' ''The great mass of people are too ignorant and worthless to deserve much power,'' and ''It might not be popular to say this, but most people would be better off if the upper classes in our country would run the government.''

Category 14. Caste and status factors

Representative items: ''I would be disappointed if I had a child who did not marry into a good family,'' ''I respect and admire people who have been able to earn a great deal of money,'' ''I prefer to be with people of wealth and good breeding,'' and ''Things would be better today if the laboring man had more say in politics.''

Category 15. Babbitt syndrome (exaggerated middle-class ideology)

Representative items: ''Free enterprise and democracy mean about the same thing,'' ''The sales tax is the fairest kind of tax,'' ''After all, it is the people with money who get things done in this country,'' ''The government costs too much money,'' and ''You can't have democracy unless you have the profit system.''

Category 16. Political suspiciousness

Representative items: ''Many politicians are bought off by some private interest,'' ''Politicians are mostly interested in getting rich at the public's expense,'' ''My political leaders are smarter than I am,'' ''All public officials should be treated with respect,'' and ''Most politicians will do anything for votes.''

Category 17. Motives for voting

Representative items: ''I feel it is a duty to vote at election time,'' ''I don't vote unless they are trying to increase the taxes,'' ''I really don't know why I bother to vote,'' and ''I am more likely to vote if the election seems close.''

Category 18. Sense of responsibility

Representative items: ''Every citizen should take the time to find out about national affairs, even if it means giving up some personal pleasure,'' ''A person who doesn't vote is not a good citizen,'' ''If I get too much change in a store I always give it back,'' ''I wouldn't sneak into a movie even if I could do it without being caught,'' and ''People have a real duty to take care of their aged parents, even if it means making some pretty big sacrifices.''

Category 19. Chauvinism

Representative items: "Our country is the greatest and best in the world," "Any government as good as ours ought not to be criticized by foreigners," "I think it is thrilling to sing the Star Spangled Banner and watch the flag go up," "We ought not to let any other country push us around, even if it means war," and "I'm for my country, right or wrong."

Category 20. Paranoid ideas

Representative items: "It is very bad for others to know how much money you make," "I wouldn't think of leaving the house for more than five minutes without locking the door," "It is safer to trust nobody," "I often feel that the really important matters are decided behind the scenes by people we never even hear about," and "Anyone who cashes a personal check without knowing the person very well is just foolish."

Category 21. Taking the initiative in politics

Representative items: "I subscribe to one or more political magazines," "I generally read the editorial page and political columns in my newspaper," "I do not like to be around people who are talking politics," "I find political discussions very interesting," and "I dislike people who have strong views on politics."

Category 22. Conventionality

Representative items: "I like my men manly and my women womanly," "I would be terribly embarrassed to be seen quarreling in public," "Women and children first is a good principle," "I dislike people who try to be different," "I feel that 'good manners' are not really very important," and "It is wrong ever to break a law."

Category 23. Dominance

Representative items: "I have very little sympathy for people who are too timid to look after their own interests," "I want to be an important person in the community," "I'm not the type to be a political leader," "When people ask me to do things I find it very hard to say no," "I have a natural talent for influencing people," and "I like to give orders and get things moving."

Category 24. Dependence-independence

Representative items: "I value being independent of other people," "I almost never ask anyone for advice," "I often need someone to help me," "If I had to choose between liberty and security I'd take security," "I get all the sympathy I deserve," and "I have always prided myself on my ability to look after my own affairs."

Category 25. Insistence on own rights

Representative items: "I would fight if anyone tried to take my rights away," "I regard the right to speak my mind when I want to as very important," "The right to criticize the government is very important," and "Nobody has the right to tell another person what to read or not to read."

Category 26. Hostility and need:rejection

Representative items: "There are some people I really hate," "It is hard to be nice to people when you are busy," "I like to poke fun at people," "I like to see a good fight once in a while," "I think most people are kind and honest at heart," and "Few people measure up to my standards."

Category 27. Subjective rewards for participation

Representative items: "When you are interested in politics you meet a lot of interesting people," "I like the excitement of politics," "Most of my friends would think less of me if I did not vote," "It gives me a good feeling to cast my vote," and "I vote because I feel I stand to gain if my candidate wins."

Category 28. Self-confidence

Representative items: "I enjoy competing with other people," "I worry a lot about my ability to do my job," "I have a certain knack for winning arguments," "I am quick to see a mistake in someone's poor reasoning," and "My judgment is better than that of the average person."

Category 29. Pessimism-optimism

Representative items: "The country is going to the dogs," "The future looks bright to me," "The old and young will never understand each other," "I'm afraid that democracy is on the way out," and "Although there are setbacks now and then, on the average the world keeps getting better and better."

Category 30. Calvinism

Representative items: "It is our duty to work hard and save for the future," "Duties are more important than rights," "I believe we are made better by the trials and hardships of life," "I sometimes feel that laziness is almost like a sin," "There is something wrong with a person who is not willing to work hard," and "Financial success is a sort of proof of a person's merit."

Category 31. Irritability

Representative items: "Hot weather often makes me cross," "I can't stand people who make noises when they eat," "Daily life seems to be full of little petty annoyances," "There ought to be a law against unnecessary noise," and "I wish I could be as calm about little irritations as others seem to be."

Category 32. Religiosity

Representative items: "I have complete faith in God," "I am quite certain the Bible is the word of God," "I do not see how religion can be of much practical use in solving the problems of the world today," "I must admit that religion doesn't play much of a part in my life," and "I prefer being with religious people."

Category 33. Puritanism
Representative items: "Women are doing too much drinking these days," "There ought to be strict laws about sex," "There ought to be very severe punishments for people who do something sexual with a child," and "There is too much fast living going on today."

Category 34. Enthusiasm and zest
Representative items: "I don't seem to get as tired at night as some people do," "I do not seem to need as much sleep as most people do," "I talk a lot," "I like excitement," "It makes me restless to sit still for very long," "It is hard for me to keep from driving faster than I should," and "I like the excitement of crowds and lots of people."

Category 35. Material aspirations
Representative items: "Most people think too much about making money," "I would do a lot to have a million dollars," "Any job is all right with me so long as it pays well," and "People who claim they are not interested in money are just kidding themselves."

Category 36. Attitudes toward family
Representative items: "My father and I have had about the same political opinions," "My parents always made me solve my own problems," "I have always been a little afraid of my father," "I think my mother was a very intelligent woman," "I don't think my mother understood me." "My father was too strict with me," "I had my own way as a child," "My mother liked to read," "My childhood was very happy," "I don't think my father understood me," and "When I was a child, what my parents said was the law."

Category 37. Need:inviolacy
Representative items: "The best policy is to keep things to one's self," "It is not a good idea to tell anyone all about yourself," "Nowadays more and more people are prying into things that ought to remain personal and private," "Compared to your own self-respect, the respect of others means very little," and "I must admit I get very stubborn when people try to find out about my personal affairs."

Category 38. Life satisfaction
Representative items: "I wish I had more friends than I do," "I feel content about my religious beliefs," "I have good health," "I have been pretty lucky in life so far," "It bothers me that I am not better looking," "My work is very interesting to me," "Life is simply a daily grind with no future in it," and "My daily life is full of things that keep me interested."

Category 39. Sense of justice
Representative items: "People get just about what they deserve in this world, no more, no less," "No person is rightfully entitled to enjoy privileges that others don't have," "If I were on a jury, I would be inclined to

vote against the side which could more easily stand the loss,'' and ''You can't really have a strong and efficient society if you have to run back all the time to help the stragglers.''

Category 40. Fatalism

Representative items: ''I do not believe much in free will,'' ''I believe in Fate,'' ''What happens to a person is mostly a matter of getting the 'breaks','' ''Some day we will find out that astrology (reading the stars) can explain a lot of things,'' and ''We are all helpless against the big forces.''

Category 41. Tolerance

Representative items: ''Most of the great ideas that we now accept were once unpopular,'' ''Parents should expect their children to disagree with them on some things,'' ''People who hate our way of life should still have a chance to talk and be heard,'' ''Nothing about communism is any good,'' ''Nothing about fascism is any good,'' and ''We shouldn't be tolerant of ideas that are morally wrong.''

Category 42. Hypomania (MMPI Ma scale)

Representative items: ''At times I have fits of laughing or crying that I cannot control,'' ''I have had periods in which I carried on activities without knowing later what I had been doing,'' ''I have never done anything dangerous for the thrill of it,'' and ''Something exciting will almost always pull me out of it when I am feeling low.''

Category 43. Managerialism

Representative items: ''I'd sacrifice the right to vote if I thought more efficient government would be the result,'' ''What we need are more strong leaders who can tell us what to do,'' ''Most people know as much about politics as the so-called 'experts','' and ''We'd be better off if we let the experts handle more things instead of trying to figure them out ourselves.''

Category 44. Atypical or uncommon opinions (MMPI F scale)

Representative items: ''There is something wrong with my mind,'' ''My soul sometimes leaves my body,'' ''I believe in law enforcement,'' ''I believe my sins are unpardonable,'' ''I believe I am being followed,'' and ''Everything tastes the same.''

Category 45. Depression (MMPI D scale)

Representative items: ''I brood a great deal,'' ''I cry easily,'' ''I don't seem to care what happens to me,'' and ''My sleep is fitful and disturbed.''

Category 46. Teamwork

Representative items: ''People who talk about teamwork are usually people who can't get things done by themselves,'' ''I get a thrill out of working in a group or toward a common goal,'' ''I would much rather work with others on a project or problem than by myself,'' and ''The spirit of teamwork is what has made this country great.''

Category 47. YMCA syndrome

Representative items: "Every child should belong to a youth group like the Boy Scouts or Girl Scouts," "People should take a lot more exercise than they do," "You will find that a boy who is active in sports is the one who stays out of trouble," "I would enjoy being director or counselor at a summer camp for young people," and "A candidate for office should give us hope, and a vision of the great things ahead."

Category 48. Intellectuality

Representative items: "Clever people frighten me," "A little experience will give you more understanding about the world than a library full of books," "I must admit that I feel I have superior intelligence," "I would rather write a great book than inherit a million dollars," "The president of the United States ought to be someone of great learning," and "Bright children are usually sickly and nervous."

Category 49. Vertical mobility

Representative items: "Ambition is a terrible curse," "I do not mind a lot of work and trouble if it means advancing myself in the world," "I would give a lot to become really famous," and "Everyone should try to amount to more than his or her parents did."

Category 50. Horizontal mobility

Representative items: "I prefer to be among the same people year after year," "It gets tiresome to stay in one place all the time," "I like the idea of a job that keeps me moving from place to place," and "A person who keeps the same job for more than five years is in a rut."

Category 51. Folksiness

Representative items: "I am usually on pretty close terms with my nearest neighbors," "The feeling of 'knowing everyone' that you get in a small town apeals to me," "I must admit that a great many people bore me," "The best kind of politician is the one who is just like the rest of us," and "I like people I can call by their first names almost as soon as I meet them."

Category 52. Need:exhibition

Representative items: "I must admit that I imagine myself to look rather 'interesting' to others," "A person needs to 'show off' a little now and then," "I feel embarrassed if attention is called to me in a group," "I must admit I like to be the center of attention," and "Beauty contests are really very silly things."

Category 53. Community identification

Representative items: "I have a strong sense of belonging to my community," "Every person ought to be a booster for his or her home town," "I feel a sense of pride in my community," and "I don't care what goes on in my community so long as I am left alone."

Category 54. Reform drive and sense of mission
Representative items: "It is usually dangerous to change things much," "I feel we ought to make some drastic changes in the prison system," "I feel very strongly that many things about the world need to be changed," "The trouble with most reformers is that they take themselves too seriously," and "People who think they can improve the world seem a little silly to me."

Category 55. Political and moral indulgence
Representative items: "Politicians have to cut a few corners if they are going to get anywhere," "It is never fair to fool or trick another person," "In politics you have to expect some corruption," "A person wouldn't get very far in this world if he or she always told the truth," and "The political machine is necessary in American politics."

Category 56. Faith in democracy
Representative items: "The main trouble with democracy is that most people don't really know what's best for them," "Our country is great because it is the people who rule," "I sometimes think we would be about as well off even if we didn't have the right to vote," and "A good dictator might solve our problems better than we do as a democracy."

Category 57. Rigidity
Representative items: "I would be pretty easy going if I were a judge or police officer," "I set a high standard for myself and feel others should do the same," "I like to have a place for everything and everything in its place," and "I don't like to talk to people whose political views are different from mine."

Category 58. Psychopathy (MMPI Pd scale)
Representative items: "At times I very much wanted to leave home," "I have never been in trouble with the law," "During one period when I was a youngster, I engaged in petty thievery," "My hardest battles are with myself," and "I find it hard to make talk when I meet new people."

Category 59. Party loyalty
Representative items: "I generally vote for the candidates of a particular party, rather than for certain candidates or issues," "I think it is more important to vote for the person than for the party," and "I must admit it doesn't bother me very much when my party's candidates fail to get elected."

Category 60. Political "lie" items
Representative items: "I read most of the speeches of my representatives," "I never make any statements about politics that I cannot prove," "I have never been fooled yet on anything connected with politics," "I never get the least bit angry when I talk about politics," and "I would sacrifice personal gain in order to vote every time."

Category 61. Guilt

Representative items: "People today have forgotten how to feel properly ashamed of themselves," "Life is a constant struggle against temptation," "I have often failed to do what I really should," "I often feel ashamed of myself," "I am an unworthy person," and "There is no such thing as being too strict where conscience and morals are concerned."

Category 62. Humor

Representative items: "I try to remember good jokes so I can tell them to people," "I must admit it is pretty hard to make me laugh," "I become irritated when someone breaks into a serious discussion just to tell a joke," and "I admire people who can always find a joke to tell."

Category 63. Sympathy and kindness

Representative items: "I dislike old people," "It is not good to be too softhearted," "I must admit I am a poor one from whom to get sympathy," "I honestly feel that I am kinder and more sympathetic than most people," and "When other people suffer some pain or misfortune, I feel as though it were happening to me."

Category 64. Gletkin syndrome (totalitarian ideology)

Representative items: "The unhappiness of a few people simply doesn't matter when it is a question of a step forward for the majority of the people," "A book or a work of art is good only if it carries a great message," "Members of a political movement must learn to obey orders without question," "Almost any unfairness or cruelty may have to be justified when some great purpose is being carried out," and "I do not think we should allow books to be printed which are written from a viewpoint that is dangerous to society."

Category 65. Sentimentality

Representative items: "I make a point of never giving way to my emotions," "Sentimental people are usually weak," "Everyone is really sentimental at heart, but some are just afraid to admit it," "I treasure deeply some of the gifts my parents gave me when I was a child," and "Warm, personal feelings should be felt and acted on, but not talked about."

Category 66. Perseverance

Representative items: "Once I start a job I feel I have to finish it," "I am known as a hard and steady worker," "I am easily defeated," "I often start things I never finish," and "I must admit that if I find something hard to do, I don't stick at it very long."

Category 67. Need for publicity and celebration

Representative items: "It embarrasses me to have someone praise me in front of others," "People who take a back seat never get anywhere," "It annoys me if someone else gets the credit for something I have done," "I must admit I like to have people talk about me, even if it is only gossip,"

"I am one person who doesn't care whether my name ever gets in the papers or not," and "You can't expect people to do things unless they get credit for them."

Category 68. Sense of history

Representative items: "I often think of our present day activities as just a tiny moment in the great stretch of history," "I could stand a lot of abuse and criticism now, if the next 100 years proved that I was right," "One of our main duties is to make the world a better place to live in for future generations," and "I often wonder what the people 100 years from now will think about us."

Category 69. Love of spectacle

Representative items: "The bigger the show, the more likely I am to enjoy it," "I don't see much sense in parades and celebrations," "I feel I could do almost anything when I am in a big crowd with a band playing and everyone feeling excited," and "Big crowds make me feel gay and excited."

Category 70. Realism versus utopianism

Representative items: "Some day in the future there will be real 'peace on earth'," "We might as well face the fact that there will always be a lot of bad and worthless people in the world," and "We could all be happy if we would just realize that our world troubles are only the result of greed and selfishness."

Category 71. Suggestibility

Representative items: "I often seek the advice of other people and follow it," "When in a group I usually do what the others want," "I give praise rather freely when I have a chance," "I make up my mind myself, regardless of how others try to influence me," and "There are certain people whom I admire very much and whose opinions influence me greatly."

Category 72. Curiosity

Representative items: "I must admit I have no great desire to learn new things," "I ask more questions than most people do," "I am more curious than most people," "I hate to miss out on the first news of a big event," and "I like to learn about a great many things even if they're not useful."

Category 73. Courage versus timidity

Representative items: "I hardly know the meaning of the word 'fear'," "A sudden loud noise can easily frighten me," "I am afraid of angry, barking dogs," "When I'm home alone at night I hate to answer a knock on the door," and "It isn't safe to be out on the streets late at night."

Category 74. Belongingness versus isolation

Representative items: "I must admit I have sometimes thought about suicide," "Most people's lives seem to be more meaningful than mine," "Even when I am with people I often feel somewhat alone," "People pretend to care more about one another than they really do,'' and ''I am really pretty lonely.''

Category 75. Envy
Representative items: ''I am content with what I have,'' ''I wouldn't want an expensive car even if I could afford to buy one,'' ''I do not honestly care much whether I am a 'success' in the eyes of others,'' and ''It is human nature always to want more than you have.''

Category 76. Self-presentational style (MMPI K scale)
Representative items: ''I think nearly anyone would tell a lie to keep out of trouble,'' ''What others think of me does not bother me,'' ''I like to let people know where I stand on things,'' and ''I certainly feel useless at times.''

Category 77. Stability versus disorganization
Representative items: ''It often seems that my mind wanders,'' ''I am a carefree person,'' ''It is often hard for me to make up my mind,'' ''I am often in low spirits,'' and ''I guess I am not very well adjusted to life.''

Category 78. Neurasthenia versus vigorous determination
Representative items: ''When I finish one job I can hardly wait to get started on the next one,'' ''I am able to concentrate better than most people,'' ''It is hard for me to relax,'' ''People who are afraid of hard work annoy me,'' and ''I very seldom do things impulsively, on the spur of the moment.''

Category 79. Social extraversion
Representative items: ''I have a hard time making friends,'' ''I like to be alone as much as possible,'' ''I am a better talker than listener,'' ''I often chat with clerks when they are waiting on me,'' ''I make a point of introducing myself to strangers at a party,'' and ''It is hard for me to work when other people are watching me.''

Category 80. Masculinity/femininity
Representative items: ''I like to go to parties and other affairs where there's lots of loud fun,'' ''I think I would like the kind of work a forest ranger does,'' ''I would like to be a florist,'' ''I used to keep a diary,'' ''If I were an artist I would like to draw flowers,'' and ''I very much like hunting.''

Category 81. Self-misrepresentation (MMPI L scale)
Representative items: ''I do not always tell the truth,'' ''I get angry sometimes,'' ''Once in a while I put off until tomorrow what I ought to do today,'' and ''I gossip a little at times.''

Category 82. Prejudice
Representative items: ''Most people are honest chiefly through fear of being caught,'' ''Most people inwardly dislike putting themselves out to help other people,'' ''I think most people would lie to get ahead,'' and ''Most people make friends because friends are likely to be useful to them.''

Category 83. Liberal versus conservative opinions
Representative items: "It is never wise to introduce changes rapidly, in government or in the economic system," "If all people were equally well off, we would have no progress," "Many of my ideas are pretty radical," "The old ways of doing things are usually the best," "The right to own private property is as sacred as the right of free speech," "We experiment in science; we should do the same thing in politics and economics," and "I am really a quite conservative person in my beliefs."

Category 84. Miscellaneous
Representative items: "I never exaggerate when I talk about things," "I can control my feelings so well that very few can tell my true reaction by just watching my face," "I would never let another person take the blame for something I did," "I think most people like me," "I do not like cottage cheese," "People often come to me with their problems." "Nature intended us to look out for ourselves first," "I can usually tell what another person is thinking," and "On several important social topics I feel differently now from the way I did five or ten years ago."*

Subsequent Uses of the PAR Materials

As mentioned above, items from the PAR library were incorporated in the subsequent work of all three initial investigators. For the California Psychological Inventory the project was of particular importance. First, the Dominance and Responsibility scales of the CPI were originally developed in the PAR program, although it should be noted that in the current version of the inventory (Gough, 1987), the scales have been shortened from 60 to 36 items for Dominance, and from 56 to 36 items for Responsibility.

Second, PAR items were liberally employed in the development of the other scales of the CPI. The present version of the inventory contains 462 items, of which 194 came from the original MMPI (Hathaway and McKinley, 1943); of these 194 items, 175 were retained in the new edition of the MMPI (MMPI-2; see Butcher, Dahlstrom, Graham, Tellegen, and Kaemmer, 1989). Approximately 50 more CPI items came from the PAR collection, and about 40 from an experimental questionnaire created in 1949–50 by the staff of the Institute of Personality Assessment and Research in Berkeley (see Gough, 1988). The remaining 178 items were written explicitly for the scales of the CPI as they were being developed.

---

*MMPI items in Categories 42, 44, 45, 58, 76, and 81 are quoted by permission. Minnesota Multiphasic Personality Inventory (MMPI) copyright © The University of Minnesota 1943, renewed 1970. Reproduced by permission of the publisher.

Some examples of the use of PAR items in the CPI may be of interest. From the need:exhibition Category (No. 52), the item "A person needs to 'show off' a little now and then" is included in the CPI, where it is scored for "true" on three scales (Sociability, Social Presence, and Empathy), and "false" on two others (Self-control and the internality vector). From PAR Category 57 (Rigidity), the item "I set a high standard for myself and feel others should do the same" now appears on four CPI scales, where it is scored for "true" on Self-acceptance, Achievement via Conformance, and the v.2 (vector) measure for norm-favoring dispositions, and "false" on Flexibility. The item "People today have forgotten how to feel properly ashamed of themselves," from PAR Category 61 (Guilt), is scored for "false" on four CPI scales: Social Presence, Empathy, Achievement via Independence, and the v.3 vector scale for ego integration.

There are also PAR items in the CPI that are scored on only one scale. From Category 23 (Dominance), the item "I want to be an important person in the community" is in fact not scored on Dominance, but rather on the bipolar measure of Femininity/Masculinity, where a false response is coded for femininity. From Category 25 (Insistence on Own Rights), the item "I regard the right to speak my mind when I want to as very important" appears in slightly modified form on the CPI scale for Communality, scored for "true." In the CPI norm samples of 1,000 of each sex, 85% of the males and also 85% of the females expressed agreement with this statement. From Category 35 (Material aspirations), the item "Any job is all right with me so long as it pays well" is scored for "false" on the Intellectual Efficiency scale.

The PAR items and categories were also used by Meehl himself in his work with colleagues on the Minnesota-Hartford Personality Assay (Meehl, Schofield, Glueck, Studdiford, Hastings, Hathaway, & Clyde, 1962; also, Glueck, Meehl, Schofield, & Clyde, 1964). In generating this list of phenotypic attributes 1,222 items were classified under 13 major and 17 subordinate categories. The 1,222 items were selected from an initial set of 6,682 items drawn from 73 different sources, in one of which the Minnesota Political Behavior Study or PAR project was included.

Later (Meehl, Lykken, Schofield, & Tellegen, 1971), a shortened form of 329 phenotypic descriptors was applied to a sample of 791 psychiatric patients by their therapists, and the interitem matrix of correlations computed and factored. Each description was rated on an 11-step scale, with a total of 248 therapists taking part in the study.

Forty factors were extracted and rotated, with the strongest (Cognitive Slippage) accounting for 8.3% of the variance, and the weakest (Effeminacy) accounting for 0.7%. Among the other factors were included Surgency, Manifest Hostility, Altruism, Accomplishment Motivation, Heterosexual Drive, and Dominance-submission. The full set of 40 factors constitututes one of the broadest and most systematic collection of themes for describing personality that has been proposed to date. From the 84 PAR categories, factor analyses might well produce a similarly large number of discrete dimensions.

The question of how best and most economically to describe personality is attracting considerable attention from contemporary researchers. For instance, from the observational side, evidence now suggests that five or six major themes may be specified (see Tupes & Christal, 1961; Norman, 1963; Digman, 1990; Digman & Takemoto-Chock, 1981; Goldberg, 1981, 1990; Hogan, 1983; McCrae & Costa, 1987), including extraversion, agreeableness, conscientiousness, emotional stability, culture or intelligence, and openness to experience. There is also some evidence (McCrae, 1982) that these same themes can be identified in the self-report domain. But before the case is closed, and perspectives limited to only these five dimensions, additional study of large, diverse, and heterogeneous item pools should be carried out. Good starting points would be compilations such as the Minnesota-Hartford Personality Assay on the observational side and the PAR items in the self-report domain. It is for this reason, among others, that more than 400 individual PAR items have been cited in this chapter. Readers drawn to the study of self-report data may wish to undertake new experimentation with these items, or to generate new descriptors on the basis of the category labels. Any and all such work is to be encouraged, to provide linkage to past endeavor and to open up new pathways for the future. Should this occur (and I hope that it will), an important part of the "unfinished business" of the PAR project can even now be carried through to completion.

References

Barron, F. (1953a). Complexity-simplicity as a personality dimension. *Journal of Abnormal and Social Psychology, 68,* 163–172.

Barron, F. (1953b). Some personality correlates of independence of judgment. *Journal of Personality, 20,* 385–401.

Barron, F. (1957). Originality in relation to personality and intellect. *Journal of Personality, 25,* 730–742.

Block, J. (1961). *The Q-sort method in personality assessment and psychiatric research.* Springfield, IL: Charles C Thomas. (Reprinted, 1978, Palo Alto, CA: Consulting Psychologists Press.)

Butcher, J. N., Dahlstrom, W. G., Graham, J. R., Tellegen, A., & Kaemmer, B. (1989). *Manual for the restandardized Minnesota Multiphasic Personality Inventory: MMPI-2. An administrative and interpretive guide.* Minneapolis, MN: University of Minnesota Press.

Digman, J. M. (1990). Personality structure: Emergence of the five-factor model. In M. R. Rosenzweig & L. W. Porter (Eds.), *Annual review of psychology* (Vol. 41, pp. 417-440). Palo Alto, CA: Annual Reviews.

Digman, J. M., & Takemoto-Chock, N. K. (1981). Factors in the natural language of personality: Reanalysis, comparison, and interpretation of six major studies. *Multivariate Behavioral Research, 16,* 149–170.

Glueck, B. C., Meehl, P. E., Schofield, W., & Clyde, D. J. (1964). The quantitative assessment of personality. *Comprehensive Psychiatry, 5,* 15–23.

Goldberg, L. R. (1981). Language and individual differences: The search for universals in personality lexicons. In L. Wheeler (Ed.), *Review of personality and social psychology* (Vol. 2, pp. 141–165). Beverly Hills, CA: Sage.

Goldberg, L. R. (1990). An alternative "description of personality": The big-five factor structure. *Journal of Personality and Social Psychology, 59*, 1216–1229.

Gosnell, H. F. (1930). *Why Europe votes.* Chicago, IL: University of Chicago Press.

Gough, H. G. (1952). Predicting social participation. *Journal of Social Psychology, 35*, 221–233.

Gough, H. G. (1953). What determines the academic achievement of high school students? *Journal of Educational Research, 46*, 321–331.

Gough, H. G. (1957). *Manual for the California Psychological Inventory.* Palo Alto, CA: Consulting Psychologists Press.

Gough, H. G. (1960). Theory and measurement of socialization. *Journal of Consulting Psychology, 24*, 23–30.

Gough, H. G. (1965). The conceptual analysis of psychological test scores and other diagnostic variables. *Journal of Abnormal Psychology, 70*, 294–302.

Gough, H. G. (1987). *The California Psychological Inventory administrator's guide.* Palo Alto, CA: Consulting Psychologists Press.

Gough, H. G. (1988). Along the way: Recollections of some major contributors to personality assessment. *Journal of Personality Assessment, 52*, 5–29.

Gough, H. G., & Heilbrun, A. B., Jr. (1983). *The Addictive Check List manual—1983 edition.* Palo Alto, CA: Consulting Psychologists Press.

Gough, H. G., McClosky, H., & Meehl, P. E. (1951). A personality scale for dominance. *Journal of Abnormal and Social Psychology, 46*, 360–366.

Gough, H. G., McClosky, H., & Meehl, P. E. (1952). A personality scale for social responsibility. *Journal of Abnormal and Social Psychology, 46*, 360–366.

Hathaway, S. R., & McKinley, J. C. (1942). *The Minnesota Multiphasic Personality Schedule.* Minneapolis: University of Minnesota Press.

Hogan, R. (1983). Socioanalytic theory of personality. In M. M. Page (Ed.), *1982 Nebraska Symposium on Motivation: Personality—current theory and research* (pp. 55–89). Lincoln, NE: University of Nebraska Press.

Lasswell, H. D. (1930). *Psychopathology and politics.* Chicago, IL: University of Chicago Press.

Lasswell, H. D. (1935). *World politics and personal insecurity.* New York: McGraw-Hill.

Lazarsfeld, P. E., Berelson, B., & Gaudet, H. (1944). *The people's choice.* New York: Duel, Sloan and Pearce.

McClosky, H. (1957). Attitude and personality correlates of foreign policy orientation. In J. Rosanau (Ed.), *Domestic sources of foreign policy* (pp. 51–109). New York: Free Press.

McClosky, H. (1959). Conservatism and personality. *American Political Science Review, 42*, 27–45.

McClosky, H. (1964). Consensus and ideology in American politics. *American Political Science Review, 48*, 361–382.

McClosky, H. (1969). *Political inquiry.* New York: Macmillan.

McClosky, H., & Brill, A. (1983). *Dimensions of tolerance: What Americans believe about civil liberties.* New York: Basic Books.

McClosky, H., & Chong, D. (1985). Similarities and differences between left-wing and right-wing radicals. *British Journal of Political Science, 15*, 329–363.

McClosky, H., Chong, D., & Zaller, J. (1982). Patterns of support for democratic and capitalist values in the United States. *British Journal of Political Science, 13*, 401–440.

McClosky, H., & diPalma, G. (1970). Personality and conformity: The learning of political attitudes. *American Political Science Review, 54*, 1054–1073.

McClosky, H., & Schaar, J. (1965). Psychological dimensions of anomy. *American Sociological Review, 30*, 14–40.

McClosky, H., & Zaller, J. (1985). *The American ethos: Public attitudes toward capitalism and democracy*. Cambridge, MA: Harvard University Press.

McCrae, R. R. (1982). Consensual validation of personality traits: Evidence from self-reports and ratings. *Journal of Personality and Social Psychology, 43*, 293–303.

McCrae, R. R., & Costa, P. T., Jr. (1987). Validation of the five-factor model of personality across instruments and observers. *Journal of Personality and Social Psychology, 52*, 81–90.

Meehl, P. E. (1954). *Clinical versus statistical prediction: A theoretical analysis and a review of the evidence*. Minneapolis, MN: University of Minnesota Press.

Meehl, P. E., Lykken, D. T., Schofield, W., & Tellegen, A. (1971). Recaptured-item technique (RIT): A method for reducing somewhat the subjective element in factor naming. *Journal of Experimental Research in Personality, 5*, 171–190.

Meehl, P. E. Schofield, W., Glueck, B. C., Jr., Studdiford, W. B., Hastings, D. W., Hathaway, S. R., & Clyde, D. J. (1962). *Minnesota-Ford pool of phentotypic personality items* (August 1962 edition). Minneapolis: University of Minnesota Press.

Myers, I. B., & McCaulley, M. H. (1985). *Manual: A guide to the development and use of the Myers-Briggs Type Indicator*. Palo Alto, CA: Consulting Psychologists Press.

Norman, W. T. (1963). Toward an adequate taxonomy of personality attributes: Replicated factor structure in peer nomination personality ratings. *Journal of Abnormal and Social Psychology, 66*, 574–583.

Rice, S. A. (1928). *Quantitative methods in politics*. New York: Knopf.

Tupes, E. C., & Christal, R. E. (1961). Recurrent personality factors based on trait ratings. *USAF ASD Technical Report* (No. 61–97).

Are Intelligence Tests the Only Way to Assess Intelligence?

George S. Welsh

"It is doubtful that there exists any best approach to studying intelligence" admit the authors (Sternberg & Slater, 1982, p. 25) of the introductory chapter in the huge *Handbook of human intelligence* (Sternberg, 1982). Yet all of the 23 contributors seem to favor a cognitive conceptualization (now called the "information-processing" viewpoint) that requires subjects to find a "correct" answer to problems on the basis of their own knowledge or the information given. Although the term *personality* does appear in the index — an advance over an earlier monumental volume, *The nature of human intelligence* (Guilford, 1967) — the entries are scant. Indeed, anyone interested in personality would look in vain for references to familiar assessment devices like the Minnesota Multiphasic Personality Inventory (MMPI) or the California Psychological Inventory (CPI). Few in the cognitive camp seem to have heeded the decades-old admonition that "it is not only unrealistic but misleading to think of man's intellectual gifts and capabilities purely in cognitive terms" (Wiseman, 1967, p. 7).

There are, however, some early examples demonstrating the value of a noncognitive approach to intelligence testing. Many years ago in factor-analytic studies R. B. Cattell found that the second largest source of variance in peer-group description could be interpreted as a bipolar factor contrasting "general intelligence" and "mental defect" (Cattell, 1946). Particularly worth noting is the early work of H. G. Gough in a paper entitled "A nonintellectual intelligence test" (Gough, 1953); from this approach evolved three different personality scales for assessing intellective performance (Gough, 1957).

The present study follows this personality tradition and utilizes two broad but clearly specified dimensions of personality, "origence" and "intellectence." These dimensions can be related to the work of traditional theorists such as Jung and Freud as well as to the concepts of contemporary psychologists like Carl Rogers and John Holland. This two-dimensional model has the advantage that it is closely tied to an objective metric but is not dependent on any particular test; counterpart scales have been developed for many of the most widely used personality assessment devices.

Two standard, but quite different, tests of intelligence were employed to demonstrate the importance of the differential relationship between them and personality variables. It is unfortunate that many researchers report merely that "subjects were matched for IQ" without indicating how the matching was accomplished or, worse, without even specifying which intelligence test was used. It will be shown that the use of different intelligence tests can have important implications for personality assessment, a matter that may be investigated only if careful psychometric reporting of procedures is followed.

Subjects

Data were obtained from two different groups of subjects. The first group comprises gifted and talented adolescents attending a selective summer program, the Governor's School of North Carolina, for special study in academic and arts areas. Subjects in the second group were students in an advanced psychology course, tests and measurements, which included personality assessment.

The gifted adolescents (GA) were given a battery of tests similar to that used at Berkeley's Institute of Personality Assessment and Research (IPAR) (MacKinnon, 1962) in their study of creative adults. There were approximately 400 GAs tested for each of three summers with a total N of 1,163. These subjects were rising juniors and rising seniors from public and private high schools throughout North Carolina with a modal age of 16 (M = 16.22, SD = .77). A description of the school and the selection procedures as well as a statistical summary of the major tests included in the research battery is available (Welsh, 1969).

The psychology students (PS) took a series of various tests for didactic purposes as part of regular class procedure. Some of the tests were the same ones given to the GAs in the research project at the Governor's School. Thirty-two successive classes were tested, although not all the classes had exactly the same tests, over a period of two decades. The mean class size was 31.7 (SD = 12.8) with a total N of 1,026. Most of the students were senior undergraduates majoring in psychology although there were some undergraduates and a few graduate students from other departments. They were not required to report their age but most were probably from 19 to 21 years old.

Intelligence

Intelligence was assessed by two standard, but quite different, tests: a typical verbal one dependent on knowledge of vocabulary and specific information, the other nonverbal and free from those requirements.

The first is the Concept Mastery Test (CMT) developed by L. M. Terman for use in follow-up studies of the gifted children he had identified in the 1920s (Terman, 1954). The CMT comprises 190 items in two parts, 115 word pairs in Part I and 75 analogies in Part II. The word pairs in Part I, Synonyms and Antonyms, are to be answered by the subject as to whether "the two words mean the same or nearly the same" or whether they are opposite in meaning. Although there are a few relatively easy items to begin with, the vocabulary becomes fairly unusual or specialized, e.g., glabrous — hispid.[1] Likewise, the analogies in Part II are at first rather obvious but soon become difficult, deltiology : psephology :: collection : (a. cognition b. adumbration c. sortition). A summary of the development of the CMT and evidence for its validity and reliability are given in Welsh (1975a, pp. 27–38). The CMT is significantly correlated with tests like the Scholastic Aptitude Test (SAT) and the Miller Analogies Test as well as other tests similar in format (Terman, 1956).

The nonverbal test used is the D-48, which was originally developed in Europe but has been modified and adapted in the United States by Black (1963). There are 44 test items and four explanatory examples in the form of sets of dominoes in which the last domino is blank and the subject has to work out the sequence or the analogy which will lead to a solution. Thus, no specific knowledge or verbal skills are required, the subject has merely to be able to see and to count dots in order to discern the patterned relationships. Although the D-48 is significantly correlated with verbal intelligence tests, the magnitude of such coefficients is usually lower than for those with other verbal tests. The American adaptor has interpreted the D-48 as a relatively pure measure of the "g" or general factor of intelligence without any loading on visual perception (Black, 1963). But Boyd and Ward (1966) factored 10 tests and reported that the D-48 loaded on "convergent thinking" and "cognitive ability" although not on "perceptual speed." In an analysis of a 14-test battery Horn and Bramble (1967) found the D-48 to be loaded primarily on "fluid intelligence" with secondary loadings on "crystallized intelligence" and "general visualization" although without any loading on "general fluency."

The relationship between the CMT and the D-48 is shown in Table 1, which gives statistical summaries for the two groups of subjects in the present study. It may be seen that although the verbal and the nonverbal intelligence tests are significantly correlated for the two subject groups, there is a marked drop in magnitude of the correlation in the student group. Nonetheless, the relation between the two parts of the CMT is equivalent to parts correlation reported in the *Manual* (Terman, 1956). There are differences in the means of the GAs and the PSs, although standard deviations are about the same. It is of interest to note that the students score proportionately higher on the CMT vocabulary than on the other means. The difference between the PS and the GA means, 18.05 (42.82 − 24.77), divided by the average of the two standard deviations gives a ratio of

Table 1. Raw Score Statistical Summary for Intelligence Tests

Test	Gifted Adolescents (N = 1163)		Psychology Students (N = 413)	
	M	SD	M	SD
CMT				
Part I: Vocabulary	24.77	18.20	42.82	19.18
Part II: Analogies	32.25	12.67	40.22	11.62
Total score	57.02	28.87	83.04	28.73
	(N = 770[a])		(N = 413)	
D-48	29.55	6.07	30.84	5.93
Intercorrelations				
CMT and D-48	.44		.26	
Vocabulary and Analogies	.72		.72	
Vocabulary and D-48	.33		.20	
Analogies and D-48	.49		.31	

[a]The CMT was given for three summers at the Governor's School; the D-48 was not given the first summer.

.97; for analogies the value is .66, while for the D-48 it is only .23. This implies that increase in age and education[2] may be related to the kind of knowledge required for performance on verbal tests but may be less important for nonverbal tests like the D-48. One other point of interest is that for both groups the D-48 is more highly correlated with CMT analogies than with vocabulary. Some of the implications of this differential association have been explored by Welsh (1971, 1977).

Personality

Many of the basic analyses to be reported are based on a two-dimensional model originally developed in a study of the relationship of creativity and intelligence from a personality standpoint. Included in the test battery given to the GAs at the Governor's School was the Welsh Figure Preference Test (WFPT), a test that was originally developed as a nonverbal analogue to the MMPI.[3] The items consist of figures, drawn initially on 3 x 5 cards, ranging in appearance from ruled line, simple geometric figures to complex freehand drawings. The subject responds to each item with either "Like" or "Don't Like." Thus, neither the items nor the response requires any verbal ability and the test can be used with children as well as adults, with aphasics or other patients with language disability, with illiterates, and can be administered in foreign countries without the need for translation except for the simple instructions. Indeed, it has been given to many disparate groups including illiterate nomadic Bedouins tested in the Negev desert (Amos Goor, personal communication) and has been used with mental retardates in this country (Krop, 1970; Mitchell, 1971a, 1971b; Watson, 1964).

An outgrowth of a factor analysis using a series of preliminary scales, some of which were based on Rorschach scoring categories such as "movement" and "shading," was the development of an art scale. The original Barron-Welsh Art Scale (BW) (Barron & Welsh, 1952) or the Revised Art Scale (RA) (Welsh, 1959) have been widely used in studies of creativity. The scale has consistently differentiated between creative and noncreative groups and within groups has distinguished between the more and the less creative (Welsh, 1975a, Chap. 3 and Appendix A).

The question of the relationship between creativity and intelligence can be studied psychometrically by correlating scores on RA with tests of intelligence. For the Governor's School subjects RA and the CMT were uncorrelated. Subsequently, RA was found to be uncorrelated with other intelligence tests in other groups of subjects (Welsh, 1975a, pp. 73–75). Using RA as an index of creativity and the CMT as an index of intelligence, it was possible to form four groups of GAs on the basis of either high or low scores on both RA and the CMT considered conjointly: 1. high RA, low CMT; 2. high RA, high CMT; 3. low RA, low CMT; 4. low RA, high CMT.

Differences in personality characteristics of these four groups were studied by using three tests from the battery given: Gough's Adjective Check List (ACL), the MMPI, and the Strong Vocational Interest Blank (SVIB).[4] The pools of items for each test were searched for items that differentiated each group from the other three groups. For example, suppose that on the ACL 92% of subjects in group 1 had checked *adventurous* as self-descriptive while the percentages for the remaining groups were 70, 65, and 67. It is clear that the item is characteristic of group 1 but does not distinguish among the other groups. Thus it would be a useful item in identifying persons who might be like the high RA, low CMT type. Or, in the logic of objective personality tests (Meehl, 1945), a subject who checks *adventurous* is more likely to be correctly classified as falling into group 1 than one of the other groups. The greater the number of items a subject answers in the same direction as a given group, the greater the probability of correct identification in terms of group membership.

For each of the four sets of items on the three tests a summary psychological description was made, then from features common across tests two personality dimensions were inferred. From the types high on RA which had been plotted on the vertical axis, a dimension entitled "origence" was construed; for the horizontal dimension of the CMT a personality dimension of "intellectence" was

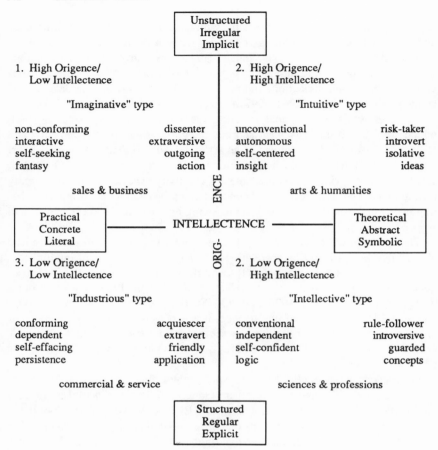

Table 2. Summary of Characteristics Associated with Origence/Intellectence Typology

nominated. Details of these procedures are given in Welsh (1975a, Chaps. 6 and 7). A summary of the typology and the two dimensions is shown in Table 2 where the four types have, for convenience, been labeled alliteratively as 1. "imaginative," 2. "intuitive," 3. "industrious," and 4. "intellective."

Origence contrasts those at the lower pole who prefer and are more at home in a regular, structured environment where problems can be solved by the application of rules and regulations with those at the upper pole who find congenial an open and unstructured situation where they can deal with matters in a more personal and unconventional way. At the left pole of intellectence preference is found for practical and pragmatic problems of the everyday world while the right pole favors the application of general principles and abstract formulations. A more extensive account of the implications for personality of these dimensions is given in Welsh (1975a, Chap. 6).

The items characteristic of each of the four types can be used as scales on the three tests; lists of items and T scores for the ACL, MMPI, and SVIB are given in Welsh (1975a, Appendixes C and D). A four-scale profile can then be used to describe a subject, as has been done for the ACL (Gough & Heilbrun, 1980). Instead of a profile interpretation based on fourfold data, however, it is possible to translate these into two-dimensional scores. T scores for the two low origence scales, 3 and 4, are subtracted from the sum of the two high origence scales, 1 and 2, to give a single value for the dimension of origence. Intellectence is found by subtracting the two low intellectence scales, 1 and 3, from the two high scales, 2 and 4. For the norm group these values will have a mean of zero and a standard deviation of 20. The procedure is illustrated in Table 3 using data for two American presidents reported originally in Welsh and Munger (1974) which have been recalculated using norms from the more recent ACL *Manual* (Gough & Heilbrun, 1980).

It can be seen that although both men got the same raw score and T score on the scale for type 1, they differ on the other three types and fall in opposite directions on the origence/intellectence array. It may be noted parenthetically that not only do most ordinary persons fall in the low origence/low intellectence corner, as does Ford, but also that when subjects are asked to describe their ideal self in addition to self-description, the tendency is for the *ideal* to fall away from other positions and toward the low/low type.

By way of comparison, the locations of Freud and Jung (Welsh, 1975b) have been recalculated on the newer ACL norms; Freud has a difference score of + 29 on origence and + 59 on intellectence; the location of Jung is quite similar, + 20 and + 58. A contrast of creative and representative architects on the MMPI (Welsh, 1980b) shows the former to have difference scores of + 21 and + 31, while the latter are lower on both dimensions, with -2 and + 20. This is consistent with the hypothesis that persons falling relatively higher than their peers on both dimensions will be judged as more original and creative than those falling lower.

Counterpart scales for the CPI have been developed utilizing the same methodology with psychology students as was done with the gifted adolescents. The four scores can be converted to dimensional scores as well. However, for the WFPT dimensional scores are given directly by two new scales, WOR and WIN (Welsh, 1980a). It may be noted that any one of these tests may be used to obtain scores for origence and intellectence, or composite scores may be derived by combining scores from two or more tests. The latter has the advantage of reducing methods variance and of providing more stable psychometrics (Welsh, 1981).

Table 3. Calculation of Origence and Intellectence Dimensional Scores

	Nixon	
Raw Scores	T Scores	

A-1	A-2
6	9

A-3	A-4
2	8

A-1	A-2
55	58

A-3	A-4
26	41

113 ⌉
      ⎬ + 46 Origence
67 ⌋

81   99
⌊_____⌋
   + 18

Intellectence

	Ford	
Raw Scores	T Scores	

A-1	A-2
6	1

A-3	A-4
12	11

A-1	A-2
55	32

A-3	A-4
63	50

87 ⌉
      ⎬ -26 Origence
113 ⌋

118   82
⌊_____⌋
   -36

Intellectence

A-1, high origence/low intellectence; A-2, high origence/high intellectence; A-3, low origence/low intellectence; A-4, low origence/high intellectence. Origence = (A-1 + A-2)−(A-3 + A-4). Intellectence = (A-2 + A-4)−(A-1 + A-3).

Results

Dimensional scores for origence and intellectence can be used for correlational studies relating personality and intelligence. It is also feasible to develop a typological classification based on these scores; since they were uncorrelated, two orthogonal axes—vertical for origence and horizontal for intellectence—were used to plot the location of each of the GAs. If a normal distribution is cut approximately one-half standard deviation below and above the mean, it will divide

Table 4. Raw Score CMT Statistics for Gifted Adolescents Grouped
by Origence/Intellectence Types with Analysis of Variance Summary

	(1)	(1-2)	(2)	High Origence
N	129	100	124	353
M	32.26	56.16	85.60	57.77
SD	21.00	24.07	29.62	33.82
	(1-3)	(0)	(2-4)	Medium Origence
N	127	148	124	399
M	35.75	59.50	81.19	58.68
SD	20.52	18.19	24.36	27.68
	(3)	(3-4)	(4)	Low Origence
N	133	153	103	389
M	36.41	57.32	75.43	54.96
SD	18.53	17.11	22.07	24.34
	Low Intellectence	Medium Intellectence	High Intellectence	Total
N	389	401	351	1141
M	34.82	57.84	81.06	57.13
SD	20.11	19.50	26.06	28.75

Analysis of Variance Summary

Source	df	MS	F	p
Origence	2	1464.65	11.64	<.0001
Intellectence	2	197,405.12	1568.20	<.0001
Interaction	4	100,662.76	799.67	<.0001
Error	1132	125.88		

the distribution into thirds. With a plot of two independent distributions there will be, then, a division into nine parts or "novants"[5] and not only the extreme scoring groups, but also the medium groups, can be examined.

The correlations for 1,141 GAs on whom complete test results were obtained for the personality dimensions and the CMT are: intellectence .73 and origence .05. The value for intellectence is much higher than might be obtained if another verbal intelligence test had been correlated with the CMT. No doubt this is a consequence of using the method of extreme groups in developing the personality scales. Extreme scoring GAs totaled 240, 10 boys and 10 girls each from the three summers for the four subgroups, comprising about 20% of all the subjects.

Table 4 gives a somewhat unanticipated picture of the relationship between personality and intelligence scores when the novant classification is used. Marginal totals for intellectence show a very nice, and expected, increase from low, through medium, to high: 34.82, 57.84, 81.06. Each of the three levels of origence gives the same kind of increase along intellectence, but the marginal totals indicate a different relationship. By looking at the novant means it can be seen that there is an inverse ordering for the CMT and origence for the three low intellectence subgroups, but the relationship is positive for those at the high intellectence end.

Thus, type 1 scores the lowest, 32.26, and type 2 the highest, 85.60, of all the subgroups. It may be noted that for the three medium intellectence novants, it is the medium origence novant, (O), that obtains the highest CMT score. So maximum performance for each level of intellectence is associated with a similar level of origence.

Although the correlational relationship of intellectence and the CMT was perhaps inevitable, a question may be raised of whether this finding will cross-validate with another, different intelligence test. Since the D-48 correlated .44 with the CMT, as seen in Table 1, it seemed likely that the correlation with intellectence would be positive but lower than that reported above. In fact, for 762 GAs the correlation is only .37, but the correlation with origence is not zero but negative, -.16 (p < .0001).

Table 5 shows the novant results and a summary of the analysis of variance. In addition to a clearcut increase in means for intellectence, there is a decrease along origence that is consistent with the negative correlation. These relationships hold both for rows and columns of the novants. Thus type 1 subjects score lowest on the D-48, as they did with the CMT. But in contrast to type 2, which scored highest on the CMT, it is type 4 that obtains the highest score on a nonverbal intelligence test.

A similar typological approach was used with the psychology students to see if these findings would hold up. Composite scores for origence and intellectence were calculated from four of the tests given in class: ACL, SVIB, CPI, and WFPT. The same two intelligence tests, CMT and D-48, were used. Since this study requires each subject to have taken all six tests, there were not enough subjects to justify a novant classification and a quadrant method was followed. Results for the CMT are shown in Table 6, for the D-48 in Table 7. Note that the scores are expressed in T-score form rather than in raw scores as was shown for the GAs. There are the expected differences along intellectence, but the relation to origence is nonsignificant. Nonetheless, type 2 subjects score highest on the CMT while type 4s score highest on the D-48. In contrast with the gifted adolescents, however, it is the type 3 psychology students who score lowest on both intelligence tests.

Table 5. Raw Score D-48 Statistics for Gifted Adolescents Grouped by Origence/
Intellectence Type with Analysis of Variance Summary

	(1)	(1-2)	(2)	High Origence
N	79	68	86	233
M	25.58	29.24	30.31	28.39
SD	6.66	5.36	5.14	6.12
	(1-3)	(0)	(2-4)	Medium Origence
N	84	104	75	263
M	26.12	30.49	32.27	29.60
SD	6.82	5.30	4.56	6.17
	(3)	(3-4)	(4)	Low Origence
N	93	111	62	266
M	28.37	31.33	32.47	30.56
SD	6.51	4.89	5.15	5.81
	Low Intellectence	Medium Intellectence	High Intellectence	Total
N	256	283	223	762
M	26.77	30.52	31.57	29.57
SD	6.77	5.22	5.06	6.09

Analysis of Variance Summary

Source	df	MS	F	p
Origence	2	291.40	10.64	<.0001
Intellectence	2	1577.18	57.60	<.0001
Interaction	4	986.49	36.03	<.0001
Error	753	27.38		

We may point out that with a group of ordinary high school students using a different intelligence test, the Otis Test of Mental Ability, a novant analysis based on WOR and WIN scales of the WFPT supported the results of the gifted adolescents found for the D-48. That is, there was a systematic increase with intellectence and a decrease with origence so that type 1 scored the highest and type 4 lowest (Welsh, 1986). The Otis is a spiral omnibus type of test and does not depend on verbal knowledge and skills to the extent that the CMT does. Perhaps for that reason it follows the D-48 in its pattern of relationship.

Earlier it was shown that groups of GAs selected in terms of differential performance on the CMT and the D-48 showed differences in interests as measured

Table 6. Score CMT Statistics for Psychology Students Grouped by Origence/
Intellectence Types, with Analysis of Variance Summary

	(1)	(2)	High Origence
N	83	83	166
M	42.36	51.82	47.09
SD	7.67	11.23	10.71
	(3)	(4)	Low Origence
N	83	84	167
M	40.98	50.96	46.00
SD	8.10	11.46	11.12

	Low Intellectence	High Intellectence	Total
N	166	167	333
M	41.67	51.39	46.54
SD	7.92	11.35	10.93

Analysis of Variance Summary

Source	df	MS	F	p
Origence	1	99.35	1.37	ns
Intellectence	1	7866.51	108.47	<.0001
Interaction	1	7976.69	109.99	<.0001
Error	329	72.52		

by the SVIB (Welsh, 1967, 1971). For example, three groups were matched in terms of summed standard scores on the two tests, but one group scored higher on the CMT, one higher on the D-48, and one did equally well on both. The high CMT group was significantly higher, the D-48 group lower, on three "verbal-linguistic" scales (Darley & Haganah, 1955), Advertising Man, Lawyer, and Author-Journalist.

This intelligence test pattern was explored further with the psychology students. As before, the CMT and the D-48 T scores were summed so that students could be matched for overall ability, but to sharpen the verbal/nonverbal distinction a difference score of the CMT vocabulary in T score minus the D-48 T score was used. The relation of this verbal/nonverbal difference score to the origence/intellectence typology is shown in Table 8. Here the high intellectence groups are more verbal than the low, and there is also a slight difference in favor of origence. Thus, type 2 is the most verbal and type 3 the most nonverbal.

It must be interjected that even type 2 has a slight negative score, indicating

Table 7. T Score D-48 Statistics for Psychology Students Grouped by Origence/ Intellectence Types, with Analysis of Variance Summary

	(1)	(2)	High Origence
N	83	83	166
M	50.75	53.05	51.90
SD	8.93	9.88	9.49
	(3)	(4)	Low Origence
N	83	84	167
M	50.67	54.57	52.63
SD	9.89	8.42	9.38
	Low Intellectence	High Intellectence	Total
N	166	167	333
M	50.71	53.81	52.27
SD	9.42	9.20	9.44

Analysis of Variance Summary

Source	df	MS	F	p
Origence	1	45.23	.53	ns
Intellectence	1	801.83	9.44	<.005
Interaction	1	898.91	10.58	<.001
Error	329	84.93		

that these subjects averaged almost a T score point higher on the D-48. By way of explanation it may be noted that the T-score conversions for the CMT and the D-48 were developed during the first decade of the psychology class while the data reported here came from more recent classes. In Table 6 it can be seen that the total CMT mean is only 46.54, about three and a half T-score points below the original norm; Table 7 shows the total D-48 mean to be 52.27, two and a quarter points above the norm. The decline in CMT scores parallels the notorious drop in SAT scores during the same time period. Thus, if level of intelligence is inferred from the CMT, the psychology students are losing ground, but if D-48 scores are used they are becoming "brighter."

A second kind of analysis could be carried out by grouping the subjects in terms of the intelligence test pattern and then looking at the personality variables. The overall index of performance and the difference score described above were used to make a high versus low sum and a verbal or nonverbal classification. It was possible to cut each distribution at its median and get four approximately

Table 8. Verbal/Nonverbal Difference Score (CMT Vocabulary—D-48)
Statistics for Psychology Students Grouped by Origence/Intellectence Types,
with Analysis of Variance Summary

	(1)	(2)	High Origence
N	83	83	166
M	-7.59	-.71	-4.15
SD	10.38	12.97	12.24
	(3)	(4)	Low Origence
N	83	83	167
M	-8.51	-3.55	-6.01
SD	11.51	13.67	12.88
	Low Intellectence	High Intellectence	Total
N	166	167	333
M	-8.04	-2.14	-5.08
SD	10.97	13.40	12.60

Analysis of Variance Summary

Source	df	MS	F	p
Origence	1	288.43	2.05	ns
Intellectence	1	2908.20	20.63	<.0001
Interaction	1	3278.96	23.26	<.0001
Error	329	141.00		

equal groups as shown in Table 9 where the data for origence are reported. The verbal groups are much higher on origence, but there is only a modest difference for the high and low groups. Even so, the high verbal group obtains the highest origence mean while the high nonverbal has the lowest.

The intellectence results in Table 10 show that the high verbal group also has the highest mean but that the lowest mean falls to the low nonverbal group. It may be noted that the values are more extreme than those found for origence. This suggested an evaluation of the conjoint distribution by origence and intellectence; the 16-cell array is shown in Table 11.

It can be seen that the types are unevenly distributed across the intelligence test classes as might have been expected from the analyses previously discussed. Particularly striking is the difference between the two high-scoring groups. Those doing relatively better on the nonverbal D-48, N+, tend to be type 4s; 31

Table 9. Origence Statistics for Psychology Students Grouped by Intelligence Test Pattern, with Analysis of Variance Summary

	High Nonverbal	High Verbal	High Sum CMT + D-48	
N	82	84	166	
M	-1.31	+ 5.25	+ 2.01	
SD	13.61	16.17	15.32	
	Low Nonverbal	Low Verbal	Low Sum CMT + D-48	
N	87	80	167	
M	+ .91	+ 2.25	+ 1.55	
SD	14.24	15.10	14.66	
	Nonverbal	Verbal	Total	
N	169	164	333	
M	-.17	+ 3.79	+ 1.78	
SD	13.98	15.72	14.99	

Analysis of Variance Summary				
Source	df	MS	F	p
High/Low	1	17.47	.08	ns
Verbal/Nonverbal	1	1302.02	5.98	<.025
Interaction	1	1880.00	8.63	<.005
Error	329	217.86		

of 82, 37.8%, are low origence/high intellectence. The other high-scoring group, V + , performing relatively better on the CMT vocabulary, comprises high/high types with 38 of 84, 45.2% falling in the type 2 category.

The two low-scoring groups, N- and V-, do not show as much difference along origence and the 1s and 3s are almost equal in distribution, 30 to 32 for N-, and 23 to 24 for V-. N-, however, has relatively more of these low intellectence types.

It is of interest to note that the high- and low-scoring groups do not differ along origence, as can be seen by marginal totals; the splits are 82/84 for the high group and 84/83 for the low. However, there is a clear association with intellectence, so that 109 of 166 (65.7%) of the high scorers are also high intellectence types. For the low scorers the figures are reversed, 109 are low intellectence types.

Marginal totals for the nonverbal and verbal groups show differences for origence as well as for intellectence. The verbal groups have 92 (56.1%) in high

Table 10. Intellectence Statistics for Psychology Students Grouped by
Intelligence Test Pattern, with Analysis of Variance Summary

	High Nonverbal	High Verbal	High Sum CMT + D-48
N	82	84	166
M	+ 1.86	+ 10.63	+ 6.29
SD	13.80	14.45	14.80
	Low Nonverbal	Low Verbal	Low Sum CMT + D-48
N	87	80	167
M	-8.08	-3.65	-5.96
SD	12.05	13.95	13.18
	Nonverbal	Verbal	Total
N	169	164	333
M	-3.26	+ 3.66	+ .15
SD	13.85	15.90	15.29

Analysis of Variance Summary

Source	df	MS	F	p
High/Low	1	12,493.12	73.26	<.0001
Verbal/Nonverbal	1	3,987.93	23.39	<.0001
Interaction	1	16,502.53	96.78	<.0001
Error	329	170.52		

origence while there are only 74 (43.8%) for the nonverbal groups. The latter
also has relatively fewer in high intellectence as well, 70, as contrasted with 97 in
the verbal groups.

Discussion

The results reported above are consonant with other studies utilizing the personality dimensions of origence and intellectence in conjunction with tests of intelligence. At the Johns Hopkins University young adolescents (13–14 years of age) in a research project for the verbally gifted took the ACL and the CMT in a test battery (Mary C. Vierstein, personal communication). For 120 subjects origence was uncorrelated with the CMT, but for intellectence the r of .43 is highly significant.

With subjects at the other end of the age scale systematic relations between

Table 11. Frequency Distribution of Origence/Intellectence Types by Classification on Intelligence Test Pattern for Psychology Students

	N+			V+			High CMT & D-48		
(1)	(2)		(1)	(2)		(1)	(2)		
18	14	32	12	38	50	30	52	82	
(3)	(4)		(3)	(4)		(3)	(4)		
19	31	50	8	26	34	27	57	84	
37	45	82	20	64	84	57	109	166	
	N-			V-			Low CMT & D-48		
(1)	(2)		(1)	(2)		(1)	(2)		
30	12	42	23	19	42	53	31	84	
(3)	(4)		(3)	(4)		(3)	(4)		
32	13	45	24	14	38	56	27	83	
62	25	87	47	33	80	109	58	167	
	Nonverbal			Verbal			Total		
(1)	(2)		(1)	(2)		(1)	(2)		
48	26	74	35	57	92	83	83	166	
(3)	(4)		(3)	(4)		(3)	(4)		
51	44	95	32	40	72	83	84	167	
99	70	169	67	97	164	166	167	333	

(1) High Origence/Low Intellectence, (2) High Origence/High Intellectence
(3) Low Origence/Low Intellectence, (4) Low Origence/High Intellectence

personality and intelligence test scores can be demonstrated. Research on aging was conducted in public institutions of North Carolina using subjects from 35 to 70 years old (Fogelman, 1975). Included in the test battery was a nonverbal intelligence test, Raven's Progressive Matrices, and a completely verbal test, the Mill Hill Vocabulary Test. Intellectence and origence were scored from a modified form of the ACL. For 329 women intellectence correlated .53 with vocabulary and .30 with the Raven; for 128 men the values are .41 and .34. Both tests were essentially uncorrelated with origence. Education, as might be expected, correlated .36 and .30 with intellectence. It is interesting to find in this study that age itself was negatively correlated with origence, -.25 and -.29. It might be pointed out that two-thirds of the women and half of the men fell into the type 3, low origence/low intellectence, category; this is consistent with the observation made above that most ordinary persons are of this type.

One other example (Freedy, 1984) may be cited in which students from the same department as in the present study were subjects. A sample of 201 students in beginning and advanced psychology courses was obtained. Differences on the ACL between "psychometric" intelligence as measured by the SAT and "academic" intelligence as measured by grade point average (GPA) were examined. These two measures were significantly correlated, r = .44, as is generally found. Scores on the SAT for 173 students correlated .31 with intellectence and -.02 with origence. The GPA subsample comprised only 86 students since four semesters of grades were required for this measure; again intellectence showed a significant positive correlation, .29, but origence was negatively related, -.28. Regression analysis predicting GPA from SAT-V and SAT-M showed a marked improvement when ACL origence was included; in fact, origence by itself was almost as good (F = 7.075) as when SAT scores were used alone (F = 7.984). The negative relation of origence to academic performance is not unexpected. Although origence is positively related to measures of originality and creativity, many undergraduate courses stress rote memory of facts and figures. Often punctuality, neatness, and attendance are considered in assigning grades; indeed, "some success may also accrue because of stylistic features related to persistence and planfulness as well as to personal characteristics of deference to authority and self-effacement" (Welsh, 1975a, p. 128). A contrast of adjectives checked by persons high on origence—confused, quarrelsome, disorderly, forgetful, outspoken, rebellious—with those at the low pole—appreciative, organized, clearthinking, methodical, logical—clearly illustrates the stylistic differences.

These results support the findings in the body of this paper. Different measures of the personality dimension of intellectence correlate with cognitive intelligence tests in many cases about as well as the usual kinds of intelligence tests correlate with each other. Origence adds a new dimension, since it relates not only to creative characteristics but in studies of intellectual performance it also contributes to comprehending verbal/nonverbal distinctions.

From a pragmatic point of view there are, in many instances, important advantages to be gained from employing personality scales.

On any test that requires specific kinds of knowledge—word meanings or items of information—a person who lacks this background is at a disadvantage. He cannot answer items of this nature and will get a low score on such a cognitively-based measure whether it is called a test of creativity, divergent thinking, or even general intelligence. Thus, a subject may be classified as "uncreative" or "unintelligent" merely because he lacks some particular bits of knowledge required by such a test.

However, on personality scales that do not require the subject to give a response to cognitive items that are scored as "correct" or "incorrect", but rather to describe his own attitudes and personality traits, it is entirely possible for the subject to be recognized as having characteristics associated with intelligent behavior or creativity as manifested outside of a test situation. That is, he will not be handicapped *per se* because his background or education has deprived him of specific content required by conventional tests. (Welsh, 1975a, p. 3)

It can be seen that in addition to assessment of intelligence, the scales of origence and intellectence yield interesting information about other aspects of personality that are not covered by the conventionally constrained cognitive requirements of customary intelligence tests. This additional information gained by personality assessment ranges all the way from aesthetics (Welsh, 1970) to subjective reaction to drugs (Ionescu-Pioggia, Welsh, & Cole, 1987).

The answer to the question posed in the title of this paper, then, is that there *are* other ways to assess intelligence and that easily scored scales from widely used personality tests can be a helpful addition for research in understanding the nature of human intelligence.

Notes

1. The examples given are not actual items from the test but they are similar in nature.

2. A group of 32 GAs came back to the Governor's School the following summer as "returnees." Although the test/retest correlation on the CMT of .89 implies stability of scores, there was in fact a marked shift upward in mean from 60.75 (SD 30.52) to 74.81 (SD 34.30). Some of the GAs were later in the author's tests and measurements class after four or five years and showed increases of as much as 54 points.

3. The WFPT was developed from a doctoral dissertation (Welsh, 1949) directed by Paul E. Meehl.

4. The Men's form of the SVIB (Strong, 1959) was given to the girls as well as the boys. The SVIB is construed as a personality test by Holland (1966); "Attempts to differentiate interest tests sharply from other types of personality tests are probably not worthwhile" (Horst, 1968, p. 22).

5. This term is now used descriptively and not in the special sense in which it was first employed (Welsh, 1965).

References

Barron, F., & Welsh, G. S. (1952). Artistic perception as a possible factor in personality style: Its measurement by a figure preference test. *Journal of Psychology, 33*, 199–203.

Black, J. D. (1963). *Preliminary Manual, the D-48 Test*. Palo Alto, CA: Consulting Psychologists Press.

Boyd, M. E., & Ward, G. (1966). A factor analysis of the D-48. *Proceedings of the West Virginia Academy of Science, 38*, 201–204.

Cattell, R. B. (1946) *Description and measurement of personality*. New York: World Book.

Darley, J. G., & Hagenah, T. (1955). *Vocational interest measurement*. Minneapolis: University of Minnesota Press.

Fogelman, D. (1975). *Psychological assessment of ageing in relation to geographic regions of high and low mortality rates*. Unpublished doctoral dissertation, University of North Carolina, Chapel Hill.

Freedy, J. R. (1984). *A personality approach to academic intelligence*. Unpublished honors thesis, University of North Carolina, Chapel Hill.

Gough, H. G. (1953). A nonintellectual intelligence test. *Journal of Consulting Psychology, 17*, 242–246.

Gough, H. G. (1957). *Manual for the California Psychological Inventory*. Palo Alto, CA: Consulting Psychologists Press.

Gough, H. G., & Heilbrun, A. B., Jr. (1980). *The Adjective Check List Manual: 1980 Edition*. Palo Alto, CA: Consulting Psychologists Press.

Guilford, J. P. (1967). *The nature of human intelligence*. New York: McGraw-Hill.

Holland, J. L. (1966). *The psychology of vocational choice: A theory of personality types and model environments*. Waltham, MA: Blaisdell.

Horn, J. L., & Bramble, W. J. (1967). Second-order ability structure revealed in rights and wrongs scores. *Journal of Educational Psychology, 58*, 115–122.

Horst, P. (1968). *Personality: Measure of dimensions*. San Francisco: Jossey-Bass.

Ionescu-Pioggia, M., Welsh, G. S., & Cole, J. O. (1987). Contribution of personality variables to the subjective effects produced by Methaqualone and D-Amphetamine. *Proceedings of the 48th Annual Scientific Meeting, the Committee on Problems of Drug Dependence*. NIDA Research Monograph 76, 80.

Krop, H. (1970). Perceptual preferences of the mentally retarded. *Training School Bulletin* (American Institute for Mental Studies), *66*, 188–190.

MacKinnon, D. W. (1962). The nature and nurture of creative talent. *American Psychologist, 17*, 484–495.

Meehl, P. E. (1945). The dynamics of "structured" personality tests. *Journal of Clinical Psychology, 1*, 296–303.

Mitchell, M. M. (1971a). Analysis of Welsh Figure Preference Test scores of educable mentally handicapped children. *Training School Bulletin* (American Institute for Mental Studies), *67*, 214–219.

Mitchell, M. M. (1971b). Personality assessment of retarded children. *Training School Bulletin* (American Institute for Mental Studies), *68*, 186–191.

Sternberg, R. J. (Ed.). (1982). *Handbook of human intelligence*. New York: Cambridge University Press.

Sternberg, R. J., & Salter, W. (1982). Conceptions of intelligence. In R. J. Sternberg (Ed.), *Handbook of human intelligence* (pp. 3–28). New York: Cambridge University Press.

Strong, E. K., Jr. (1959). *Manual for the Strong Vocational Interest Blanks for men and women, revised blanks (Forms M and W)*. Palo Alto, CA: Consulting Psychologists Press.

Terman, L. M. (1954). The discovery and encouragement of exceptional talent. *American Psychologist, 9*, 221–230.

Terman, L. M. (1956). *Manual, the Concept Mastery Test*. New York: The Psychological Corporation.

Watson, W. G. (1964). *An analysis of responses to the Welsh Figure Preference Test to evaluate its effectiveness as a measure of mental ability*. Unpublished doctoral dissertation, University of North Carolina, Chapel Hill.

Welsh, G. S. (1949). *A projective figure-preference test for diagnosis of psychopathology: 1. A preliminary investigation*. Unpublished doctoral dissertation, University of Minnesota.

Welsh, G. S. (1959). *Preliminary manual, the Welsh Figure Preference Test (research ed.)*. Palo Alto, CA: Consulting Psychologists Press.

Welsh, G. S. (1965). MMPI profiles and factor scales A and R. *Journal of Clinical Psychology, 21*, 43–47.

Welsh, G. S. (1967). Verbal interest and intelligence: Comparison of Strong VIB, Terman CMT, and D-48 scores of gifted adolescents. *Educational and Psychological Measurement, 27*, 349–352.

Welsh, G. S. (1969). *Gifted adolescents: A handbook of test results*. Greensboro, NC: Prediction Press (distributed by Consulting Psychologists Press).

Welsh, G. S. (1970). Color preferences of gifted adolescents. *Sciences de l'Art—Scientific Aesthetics, 7*, 55–61.

Welsh, G. S. (1971). Vocational interests and intelligence in gifted adolescents. *Educational and Psychological Measurement, 31*, 155–164.

Welsh, G. S. (1975a). *Creativity and intelligence: A personality approach*. Chapel Hill, NC: Institute for Research in Social Science.

Welsh, G. S. (1975b). Adjective Check List descriptions of Freud and Jung. *Journal of Personality Assessment, 39*, 160–168.

Welsh, G. S. (1977). Personality correlates of intelligence and creativity in gifted adolescents. In J. C. Stanley, W. C. George, & C. H. Solano (Eds.), *The gifted and the creative: A fifty-year perspective* (pp. 197–221). Baltimore: Johns Hopkins University Press.

Welsh, G. S. (1980a). *Manual for the Welsh Figure Preference Test (rev.ed.)*. Palo Alto, CA: Consulting Psychologists Press.

Welsh, G. S. (1980b). Relationship of creativity/intelligence scales to MMPI profiles of gifted adolescents. In W. G. Dahlstrom & L. E. Dahlstrom (Eds.), *Basic readings on the MMPI: A new selection on personality measurement* (pp. 328–341). Minneapolis: University of Minnesota Press.

Welsh, G. S. (1981). Personality assessment with Origence/Intellectence scales. *Academic Psychology Bulletin, 3*, 299–306.

Welsh, G. S. (1986). Positive exceptionality: The academically gifted and the creative. In R. T. Brown & G. R. Reynolds (Eds.), *Psychological perspectives on childhood exceptionality* (pp. 311–343). New York: Wiley.

Welsh, G. S., & Munger, F. J. (1974). Personality traits of Nixon and Ford as seen by political science students. *Research Previews: Institute for Research in Social Science, 21*, 1–10.

Wiseman, S. (Ed.). (1967). *Intelligence and ability*. Baltimore: Penguin.

Some Unconventional Analyses of Resemblance Coefficients for Male and Female Monozygotic and Dizygotic Twins

Lloyd G. Humphreys

Several years ago I published analyses of cross-twin and within-twin correlations among 40 tests for male and female monozygotic and dizygotic twins in the Project Talent national sample (Humphreys, 1974). My analyses were based on adaptations of a method of genetic analysis that had been in the literature for a number of years (Lerner, 1950), but had been little used by behavioral geneticists. A description of the methodology starts with the score matrix. Given N pairs of twins and n test scores, the score matrix is formed by selecting one member of each twin pair at random and recording the n scores across the N rows for what I shall call the Twin A matrix. This is followed by recording the n scores across N rows for the remaining members of the twin pairs to form the Twin B matrix. Now the latter matrix is duplicated and moved to a position opposite the Twin A matrix so that the scores of both members of the twin pair appear in the same row. The Twin A matrix is also duplicated and placed in position opposite the Twin B matrix. The score matrix now has $2n$ columns and $2N$ rows.

The $2n \times 2n$ R-matrix computed from the preceding score matrix can be divided into four $n \times n$ symmetric matrices. The ones in the upper-left and lower-right quarters of the master R-matrix are identical and contain within-twin correlations. The ones in the lower-left and upper-right quarters are also identical and contain cross-twin correlations. The diagonal of a cross-twin matrix contains the correlations ordinarily used by behavioral geneticists in estimating heritabilities in twin data; that is, the vocabulary score of one member of the twin pair is

---

I am indebted to the following graduate students who worked with me on various aspects of these data over a period of many years: Thomas Taber and John Long in the earlier analyses, and Randolph Park and Mary Roznowski in the later ones. It is difficult to single out any one student for special mention, but Dr. Park's collaboration was particularly important in demonstrating what factor analysis could and could not accomplish in these data.

correlated with the vocabulary score of the other member of the twin pair, and so on for the remaining n tests. These are cross-twin, same-test correlations. However, with high frequency, the $n-1$ cross-twin, different-test correlations with a given test are neglected.

Assuming the simplest genetic model and absence of assortative mating, if the cross-twin, same-test correlations for monozygotic and dizygotic twins are 1.00 and .50, respectively, heritability of the total score variance is estimated to be 1.00. Given the same assumptions, if the ratio of a given cross-twin, different-test correlation to its within-twin counterpart for the same two types of twins is 1.00 and .50, respectively, heritability of the common variance is estimated to be 1.00.

In 40 x 40 matrices of within-twin and cross-twin correlations, respectively, there are 39 ratios of cross-twin, different-test to within-twin correlations for each of the 40 tests. My adaptations involved grouping tests in several different ways as a means of reducing sampling error "noise" in the data. A second source of error present in all within-twin and cross-twin correlations considered singly is measurement error, but this is controlled by the use of ratios. The same reliability coefficients needed to correct for attenuation would be used for the cross-twin correlation in the numerator and for the within-twin correlation in the denominator.

My conclusion, based on the published analyses, was that there were no differences in the degree of heritability of a test's common variance as a function of type of test. That is, the factors determining covariation among the 40 tests appeared to be no more heavily genetic in origin for narrow information than for so-called aptitude tests. The correlations involving information about the Bible, mechanics, farming, domestic science, etc. are no less and no more genetically determined than those involving word knowledge or abstract reasoning.

This conclusion followed from the results of three different methods of analysis. In one approach tests were categorized in various ways, and means within categories of the mean cross-to within-twin ratios were computed without finding anything but trivial differences as a function of type of test. Item types that might be found in a standard test of intelligence, for example, cannot be distinguished from other categories. Differences were observed, however, with respect to sex. Female dizygotic twins tended to have appreciably higher ratios than their male counterparts. A selection of data based on this approach is presented in Table 1.

In a second approach correlations were computed in which the ratios for each test in one sample of twins were plotted against the ratios of the same tests in another sample. For both types of twins the correlations of male and female ratios were essentially zero, indicating that the observed variation among the 40 ratios carried no information about differential heritability.

Finally, linear weights that maximized the cross-twin correlation (a canonical problem) in one sample of monozygotic twins were used to obtain a composite

Table 1. Ratios of Cross-Twin to Within-Twin Correlations for Four Groupings of
the Tests

Measure	Males		Females	
	Mono	Di	Mono	Di
40 tests	.869	.602	.900	.718
18 information tests	.861	.619	.912	.717
11 intelligence tests	.872	.580	.885	.719
4 spatial visualization tests	.887	.512	.887	.744

score in the sample of the other sex. This composite was then compared with one
based on unit weights. In both of the cross-validation comparisons the weights
that maximized the similarity of monozygotic twins produced a smaller cross-
twin composite correlation than the unit weights.

The cross-twin correlations based on unit weights are of interest in their own
right and are shown in Table 2. Although the magnitude of the numbers in each
of the four categories is similar to the values in Table 1, the latter are means of
ratios of cross-to within-twin correlations of different tests. Table 2 contains the
cross-twin correlations for the same test, the unit weighted composite. These correlations are comparable to those commonly reported for tests of general intelligence. Monozygotic twins are substantially more similar to each other than are
dizygotic twins; and female twins, especially the dizygotes, are more similar to
each other than are the males. The latter finding is in conflict with the standard
genetic model, but Kamin (1987) has found several sets of data in which similar
sex differences were found.

These analyses supported a hypothesis that the variance of the general factor
in intelligence is the best bet to contain a substantial genetic contribution. This
hypothesis is only superficially contrary to data such as that discussed by Plomin
et al. (1980) which show different heritability estimates of measures of so-called
primary mental abilities. The general factor in intelligence is not held constant in
studies of family resemblance in separate abilities.

In the present report I shall, at the outset, present and discuss some heritability
estimates for Project Talent tests and combinations of tests. Then, in an effort to
avoid some of the problems associated with the usual heritability analyses, I shall
examine factor analyses of the eight correlation matrices defined by type of twin,
sex, and type of correlation (within vs. cross). The amount of attention being
paid to sex differences has actually increased in recent years, with interest in spatial visualization still being prominent. For this reason I shall discuss the spatial
factor in more detail than others. In conclusion I shall resort to an analysis of
intercorrelations of nine linear composites formed from tests suggested by the

Table 2. Cross-Twin Correlations of Unit-Weighted Composites of 40 Tests

Males		Females	
Mono	Di	Mono	Di
.849	.588	.875	.700

factor analyses and by educational-social criteria. Unit-weighted composites do not capitalize on chance, they reduce the number of variables to a perceptually and cognitively manageable set, and they allow tests of hypotheses concerning differences associated with sex and type of twin that make fewer assumptions than more complex multivariate methodologies.

The Data

Samples

Project Talent has been described by Flanagan et al. (1962). For present purposes only the essentials are needed. High school students in grades 9 through 12 were tested in 1960 on a large battery of cognitive and self-report tests. More than 900 high schools were selected in a stratified random design. Students tested in these schools numbered almost 100,000 in each grade. A subsample of potential twins who responded appropriately to a single item on a questionnaire were sent a follow-up questionnaire that explored in considerable detail degrees of physical similarity with the twin. Items on the questionnaire were validated in small samples diagnosed by blood criteria. The questionnaire was then ''scored'' by computer.

The sizes of the twin samples obtained were as follows: 360 male monozygotes, 130 male dizygotes, 475 female monozygotes, and 250 female dizygotes. It is disconcerting to find that the ratio of identical to fraternal twins is larger than expected, as is the ratio of females to males. There is also an interaction between sex and zygosity in that the sample of male dizygotes is disproportionately small. The selection that produced the shortage of dizygotic twins is seemingly not a serious matter for the research previously reported and now to be reported. My interest is not in estimates of degree of heritability, but in differences in heritability of the functions measured by the various tests. The selection that produced the shortage of males is more worrisome, because I am looking at sex differences. However, to explain the smaller cross-twin to within-twin ratios for dizygotic males found in the earlier research selection against high similarity in test scores would be required. This seems highly improbable.

Tests

The 40 tests analyzed in these studies are listed in Table 3. Included are tests

Table 3. Identification of Tests in Twin Analyses

1. Vocabulary	21. Memory for Words
2. Literature[a]	22. Disguised Words
3. Music	23. Spelling
4. Social Studies	24. Capitalization
5. Mathematics	25. Punctuation
6. Physical Science	26. English Usage
7. Biological Science	27. English Expression
8. Aero-Space	28. Word Functions in Sentences
9. Electricity	29. Reading Comprehension
10. Mechanics	30. Creativity
11. Farming	31. Mechanical Reasoning
12. Home Economics	32. Spatial Visualization—Two Dimensions
13. Sports	33. Spatial Visualization—Three Dimensions
14. Art	34. Abstract Reasoning
15. Health	35. Arithmetic Reasoning
16. Business	36. Intermediate Mathematics
17. Bible	37. Arithmetic Computations
18. Outdoors	38. Table Reading
19. Theater	39. Clerical Checking
20. Memory for Sentences	40. Object Inspection

[a]Starting with Literature and running through Theater, the tests measure quite specific information.

that would ordinarily be labeled aptitude, academic achievement, and information. It is also possible to categorize the information tests as largely academic and largely nonacademic. The so-called aptitude tests measure factors that would be labeled perceptual speed, verbal memory, spatial visualization, verbal comprehension, numerical facility, and quantitative reasoning. Information concerning the reliabilities of these tests has been published by the Project Talent staff (Flanagan et al., 1964). Most have fairly modest reliabilities resulting from a decision to measure as many constructs as possible within the limited amount of testing time that the schools were able to provide. Confidence can be placed in the reliabilities reported except, as made clear by the authors cited, for a small number of tests, mainly those that were speeded.

As a matter of incidental interest, the tests in Table 1 do not include all of the cognitive tests administered in Project Talent. Some 15–20 additional information tests that had been administered in a separate test booklet were not included in the R-matrix. There are also numerous composite scores available in the data bank which, if included, would have introduced spurious part-whole correlations.

Methodology

Computation of Intercorrelations

The score matrix involved separating members of each twin pair arbitrarily into an "A" set and a "B" set. The left half of the score matrix was composed of 40 test scores defining the columns and N (number of twin pairs) "A" twins followed by N "B" twins defining the rows. To form the right half of the matrix, the 40 scores of the "B" twins were moved up to the same N rows occupied on the left by the co-twin in the "A" set. Similarly, the 40 scores of the "A" twins were moved down to occupy the lower N rows. Product-moment correlations were then computed for the full score matrix defined by 80 columns and 2N rows.

Intercorrelations of the first 40 columns are within-twin correlations. From the sampling point of view these correlations are less stable than a sample size of 2N, more stable than a sample size of N, would indicate. The second member of the twin pair is not independent of the first, but the information furnished is not completely redundant. Correlations of the first 40 columns with the second 40 are cross-twin correlations. The correlations on the principal diagonal of the cross-twin matrix are classical intraclass correlations that are the univariate measures of twin resemblance. These are only trivially more stable than ordinary product-moment correlations based on N observations. Correlations off the principal diagonal in this matrix, however, have sampling characteristics similar to those in the within-twin matrix. They are more stable than the sampling error based on N, but by an unknown amount.

Factor Analyses

Principal factors were extracted from each of the 8 R-matrices after inserting squared multiple correlations as communality estimates in the principal diagonal. Over the course of time various numbers of factors were selected for rotation. Orthogonal rotations used the Varimax program and oblique rotations were accomplished with both BINORMAMIN and DAPPFR. Because the tests are complex and rather highly intercorrelated, none of these rotations was satisfactory. The two oblique programs frequently provided quite different correlations among the oblique factors, thus defining a second-order general factor differently. The Varimax program frequently produced factors with similar test content but widely different contributions to total variance. Inspection revealed, however, that the solutions were not well determined. A rotation of two factors that would produce greater similarity among analyses could be accomplished without harm to the approximation to simple structure.

One solution to the rotational problem is to fit a model developed from the less than adequate rotations. The high level of intercorrelations indicated the importance of including a general factor. Given the model, an orthogonal PROCRUSTES program can be used to provide a least squares fit. LISREL would be considered the only choice by many methodologists today, but the sampling characteristics of the within- and cross-correlations make that choice problematic. It is also noteworthy that the chi square from LISREL is frequently used descriptively rather than for more typical hypothesis testing.

Following the factoring, nine linear unit-weighted composites were formed based more or less on factors that appeared in one or more analyses. To some extent also, considerations of "ecological" validity were employed. Although the sampling stability of these composites cannot be precisely determined, one can use z-transformations to look for differences between twin types and sexes. However, as described earlier, the N to be used for the standard errors of the z-transforms is uncertain. The number of twin pairs is conservative.

The Problem of Heritability Estimates

In none of the earlier analyses were heritabilities as such presented, even though the necessary cross-twin, same-test correlations were available. These correlations have now been inserted in the Falconer formula (Plomin et al., 1980) without correcting for attenuation. The formula assumes a linear combination of genetic and environmental variances with the latter assumed to be equal for the two types of twins. Correcting for measurement error would increase all estimates of heritability. Because the vast majority of the reported reliabilities vary within a fairly narrow range (.6–.8), a correction would have little effect on the rank-ordering.

For males the highest heritabilities are found for Disguised Words (.82), Theater (.81), Mechanics (.80), and Bible (.70). For females a similar set of four includes Numerical Operations (.64), Bible (.54), Social Studies (.52), and Farming (.46). If one combines data from both sexes, information about the Bible has the single highest heritability (.62) of the 40 tests. The correlation between male and female heritabilities computed over those 40 tests is .06.

Just as the highest heritabilities for males are well above the female distribution, the mean heritabilities differ in the same direction. The mean for males is .374, for females .270. Although these means are based on observed correlations, there is little difference on average in the reliabilities of the tests for the two sexes. (Small differences in reliability that vary as a function of subject matter could have increased the correlation of .06 previously reported by only a small amount.) Correcting for the modest reliabilties of the Talent tests would increase the mean heritabilities, but would also increase the difference between the sexes. Thus when the same formula is used on the correlations between the more reliable composites in Table 2, the estimate of male heritability is .52, of female .35.

The examples of high heritability in the male and female samples are contrary to any reasonable expectation. These tests should simply not have higher heritabilities than Vocabulary, Reading Comprehension, Abstract Reasoning, and Arithmetic Reasoning. Was it proper to apply the Falconer formula to these tests? It is not easy to say.

Plomin et al. specify that the data should fit the model, but their one example is whether the estimate of h^2 is greater than 1.00. Use of reasonable estimates of reliabilities for analyses of the Mechanics and Theater tests do push the heritabilities above 1.00, but this is not true for Bible or Disguised Words. The same authors also note, however, that heritabilities of individual traits and of covariances among traits have sampling errors. Thus one must inquire into how much higher than 1.00 a sample h^2 might be without being so much above as to negate the use of the methodology. Although a precise answer cannot be given, it is informative to look more closely at sampling errors.

Let us start with samples of monozygotic and dizygotic twins of 400 and 200 pairs, respectively. These Ns are representative of the sample sizes of the Project Talent twins. Because we are dealing with cross-twin correlations involving the same test, sampling errors of intraclass correlations are only trivially more stable than ordinary product-moment correlations. The standard errors of the z-transformations of the observed correlations are approximately .05 and .071, respectively. The 95% confidence intervals around the sample z's are the observed values $\pm$ .14 and $\pm$ .20 for the two kinds of twins, respectively. Because heritabilities are estimated from correlations and not from z's, and because the observed correlations for monozygotes are considerably higher than the ones for dizygotes, translating the confidence intervals from z to r reveals a narrow band of possible population correlations for the monozygotic twins. Especially for a high heritability estimate, the observed correlation for the latter twins is expected to be close to 1.00, so one of the two correlations in the Falconer formula can be quite stable in samples of 400. Even if the sample size for the fraternal twins were also 400, the cross-twin correlation for that group would be a good deal less stable.

It is also essential to correct for the attenuation caused by measurement error before estimating h^2. Dividing each correlation by a number less than 1.00 increases each, but the larger of the two more than the smaller. Thus error is increased by the correction, and the lower the reliability the larger the error. Kelly (1924) developed standard errors for the corrected correlations, but there is nothing available for the z-transformation of r. It is conservative to correct the upper and lower bounds of each confidence interval, as well as the observed correlation, with the available reliability coefficient. This may result at times in upper-bound correlations becoming greater than 1.00, but this does not invalidate the procedure. It merely indicates the amount of error in the process.

The corrected intervals provide an infinite number of possible combinations of population values for the cross-twin, same-test correlations of the two types of twins, with many being surprisingly large, many surprisingly small. Because the samples of twins are independent of each other, a positive sampling error in one is as likely to be accompanied by a negative error in the other as by a positive error. The amount of error revealed, however, is only one-half the error in the estimate of h^2, which is double the difference between the two correlations. Estimates of heritability that are either zero or greater than 1.00 from samples the size of those in the present research may well be sampling deviations from population values more in keeping with the genetic model.

Without regard to the problems of h^2 estimation arising from sampling error, it is clear that males and females should not be combined in these samples. The correlation of .06 between male and female estimates requires separation of the sexes. Pooling as a method of compensating for sampling errors could be reconciled with a correlation of moderate size, but a trivial correlation is a different matter. The examples of tests having the highest estimates are dramatic because of their content, but it is the .06 that is more convincing. That only one of the four highest estimates for each sex is common to the set of four is, of course, in line with that correlation.

Factor Analyses

Number of Factors

Eigenvalues for the first 10 factors for both males and females are presented in Table 4. Also included are the estimated Eigenvalues for random data matrices based on the same number of variables as in the real data and for sample sizes of both N and 2N (Montanelli & Humphreys, 1976). The parallel analysis criterion for the number of factors was developed for typical product-moment correlations, not for these atypical ones that are more stable than the number of twin pairs would indicate but less stable than the number of individuals would indicate. We also gave consideration to breaks in the curve of the latent roots, but there are typically several breaks.

By either of the preceding criteria the cross-twin correlations for fraternal twins do not appear to define as many factors as the within-twin correlations. The Eigenvalues of the cross-twin matrices for identical twins are a little smaller than the corresponding values for within-twin correlations so that it might be difficult to define small factors in these matrices as well.

Because these criteria for the number of factors are fallible at best and particularly fallible for the correlations in these matrices, we gave consideration to the

Table 4. Eigenvalues of Eight R-Matrixes Compared with
Those from Random Data Matrixes

	Mono-Males				Di-Males			
	Within	Random(N)	Random(2N)	Cross	Within	Random(N)	Random(2N)	Cross
1.	15.40	.82	.54	13.38	15.15	1.53	1.00	9.52
2.	1.99	.78	.51	1.70	2.70	1.45	.95	2.11
3.	1.62	.70	.46	1.28	1.70	1.31	.86	1.45
4.	1.09	.63	.41	.66	1.64	1.20	.78	.89
5.	.59	.58	.38	.48	.82	1.10	.71	.77
6.	.53	.53	.34	.47	.77	1.02	.62	.62
7.	.42	.49	.32	.37	.64	.94	.60	.56
8.	.34	.45	.29	.35	.62	.87	.56	.53
9.	.28	.42	.27	.29	.54	.81	.52	.49
10.	.25	.39	.25	.25	.45	.75	.48	.42
	Mono-Females				Di-Females			
1.	14.71	.71	.47	13.22	16.03	1.04	.68	11.68
2.	1.93	.67	.44	1.50	1.63	.98	.64	1.20
3.	1.15	.60	.40	1.06	1.60	.88	.58	.84
4.	.97	.55	.36	.75	.99	.80	.52	.68
5.	.74	.50	.32	.63	.88	.74	.48	.47
6.	.59	.46	.30	.53	.59	.68	.44	.42
7.	.40	.42	.27	.34	.51	.62	.40	.38
8.	.39	.39	.25	.32	.46	.58	.37	.34
9.	.36	.36	.23	.27	.39	.54	.34	.28
10.	.28	.33	.21	.21	.33	.50	.32	.23

following additional criteria: (1) There is no expectation that the number of factors within twins of the same sex should differ because of zygosity; (2) The number of factors decision should not alone determine a sex difference; (3) A seemingly prominent factor in one matrix should not be overlooked in another by making a conservative decision concerning the number of factors.

The first rotated factors to be presented are those that are most reasonable in the light of our criteria, even to the extent of defining two factors somewhat differently in the hierarchical models for the two sexes. Four factors seemed to be eminently sound for males except in the cross-twin correlations of the fraternal twins, but we used five in all groups. This allowed a factor defined consistently in the female data an opportunity to appear in the male data. This also allowed for possible weak factors, comparable to the other male factors, to appear in the fra-

Table 5. Mean Squared Loadings of Markers and Cross- to Within-Twin Ratios in the Hierarchical Models for Males and Females

Factor	Sex	Markers	Monozygotic Twins			Dizygotic Twins		
			Within	Cross	Ratio	Within	Cross	Ratio
General	Male	1-40	.281	.246	.87	.279	.174	.62
	Female	1-40	.313	.279	.89	.338	.243	.72
I	Male	1-8, 14-19, 29, 36	.166	.144	.87	.201	.122	.61
	Female	1-8, 14, 19, 29	.159	.139	.87	.167	.112	.67
II	Male	22-29, 5, 35-37	.172	.142	.83	.189	.098	.52
	Female	22-29	.126	.112	.89	.168	.071	.43
III	Male	31-34	.150	.122	.82	.195	.135	.69
	Female	31-34	.152	.132	.87	.145	.032	.22
IV	Male	38-40	.300	.157	.53	.340	.247	.73
	Female	38-40	.377	.260	.69	.320	.170	.53
V	Male	11-12	.025	.010	.40	.025	.080	3.20
	Female	11-12	.100	.090	.90	.090	.105	1.17
VI	Female	20-21	.145	.110	.77	.165		

ternal twins cross-twin correlations. When five factors are rotated to the hierarchical model one general and five group factors are automatically defined.

In contrast, six factors for females seem sound in the identical twin data and marginal for the within-twin fraternals. For the cross-twin correlations for the fraternals, however, we had discovered that neither orthogonal nor oblique rotations could produce sensible factors in that number. Even four was marginal, but we added a fifth to make possible a spatial visualization factor if it could be defined in the data. Again, the hierarchical model added a general factor.

The Rotated Factors and Cross to Within Ratios

Table 5 includes the mean squared factor loadings of the defining tests for the eight analyses. The numerical designations under "Markers" refer to the tests in Table 3. Also included are the cross-twin to within-twin ratios of the contributions to variance of the marker tests. Factor loadings on orthogonal factors are correlations with a hypothetical true score so that a squared factor loading is comparable to a correlation unsquared within or across twins. Thus the ratios in Table 5 can be directly compared with those in Table 1.

Independence of measurement error is not the only useful property of these ratios. They are partially independent of the sampling errors in the identical and fraternal twins matrices. This is not a small matter because sampling errors of correlations among correlated variables are themselves correlated. The absolute levels of correlations can differ for the two types of twins because the samples are independent of each other. This affects differences between cross-twin correlations of identicals and fraternals, but this source of error is controlled in the ratios. Finally, by forming the ratios from all of the marker tests for the factor, additional sampling error is wrung out of the data.

On the other hand, the ratios provide no information about the possible proportion of genetic variance to the total variance of the test. This information is found in the size of the squared loadings. Factor loadings are attenuated by measurement error, and a substantial portion of total variance of the Talent tests is measurement error variance. This was the result of the decision to keep individual tests short in order to obtain as much information as possible within the necessarily limited time for test administration. The ratios also treat nonerror specific variance as if it were measurement error. Specifics are generally small in the Talent tests so that only small contributions to variance are missing. More important, one can quite properly be skeptical whether neglecting the specific in one of the information tests in Table 3 also neglects a source of genetic variance. Thus I shall assume that the putative genetic variance in the covariances among tests or with one or more common factors represents virtually all of the genetic variance in these tests.

If the additive genetic model is congruent with the data for a given factor, the expected value of the ratio of cross-twin to within-twin squared factor loadings for identical twins in these data should approach 1.00. The Talent "ability" tests typically have cross-twin correlations for these twins that are only slightly lower than the published reliabilities. Thus when measurement errors are excluded, within-family variance (also called random or independent) tends to be quite small. (This constitutes an important difference from the findings with most personality tests.) The true score variance of the within-twin correlations is presumably the same combination of genetic and between-family variance (also called correlated) as in the cross-twin correlations. When all of the tests in a cross-twin correlation matrix contain little within-family true score variance, the cross-twin, different test correlations will also be almost as large as the corresponding within-twin correlations.

The separation of genetic from between-family variance depends on the cross-twin correlation for dizygotic twins. For high heritability this correlation should be close to .50. It requires both high heritability and unusually large (for ability tests) within-family variance for this correlation to drop much below .50. Correlations greater than that value can arise as a result of assortative mating, for which the degree presumably varies for each of the 40 tests, and from between-family environmental variance. Using these properties I shall discuss whether the results of the factoring are reasonably congruent with the additive model. I shall also compare the factors with each other.

Interpretation of the Factors

The general factor at the top of the hierarchy is indeed general. The highly speeded tests 38–40 consistently have small loadings. Tests with high loadings are vocabulary and reading comprehension, but information tests that are the most academic also have high loadings. The loadings on the general factor are substantially higher across 40 different tests than are group factor loadings based on the many fewer marker tests. The one exception is Factor IV defined by the three highly speeded tests having very simple items. The latter factor is almost orthogonal to other first-order factors. Controlling general factor variance has little effect on speed of performance.

The ratios of cross- to within-twin contributions to the variance of the factor by the marker tests for the general factor parallel quite closely the ratios in Table 1 obtained from observed correlations. The similarities are in no sense artifactual. Independent methodologies produced similar outcomes. Dizygotic female twins are appreciably more similar to monozygotic females with respect to the size of general factor loadings than to their male counterparts. Female twins of both types also have, on average, higher general factor loadings than the males in spite of the fact that we placed in the model one additional factor for three of the four female matrices.

There is no ready interpretation of the larger ratios for female fraternals. The original screening of the samples missed more males than females. Would not the fraternal twins least like each other be the ones most likely to be overlooked? Assortative mating would affect both sexes equally. Female ratios suggest higher environmental similarity. Whatever the explanation may be, if the ratios of the squared group factor loadings differ markedly in pattern from the ones for general factor loadings, the contributions of genetic and environmental factors presumably differ.

Factor I is quite heterogeneous in content. The markers with the highest loadings are information tests that tap, by and large, the most academic information. All markers are verbal, but this is also true for Factor II. Individual loadings are substantially smaller than those on the general factor, but this finding is expected when the hierarchical model is applied in a wide range of talent. The ratios, being based on 16 different tests for males, 11 for females, should be quite stable. They are also highly similar to those for the general factor. Thus the evidence is congruent with similar genetic and environmental contributions to variance for both this group factor and the general factor.

Factor II is defined by English and mathematics tests in the males and entirely by the English markers for the females. Again, because of the number of markers, the ratios should be quite stable. The ratio for dizygotic females has now dropped substantially below values for the general factor and for Factor I. Seemingly, the group factor is highly heritable in this sex. It is noteworthy that this factor is defined by tests that show a sizable sex difference in favor of females. The ratios for male twins have also dropped relative to results for the general factor and Factor I, but this result is confounded by the absence of appreciable loadings of the mathematics tests on the factor for dizygotic males.

Factor III is defined by three tests that are well known as markers for a spatial visualization factor plus a test of reasoning having figural content. The factor could have modest heritability in males, but the loadings for females do not fit the standard genetic model. Given the property of PROCRUSTES rotations to capitalize on chance, the loadings for female dizygotic twins are little if any larger than zero. This virtual disappearance of the visualization factor in the cross-twin fraternal female matrix is also not the expected outcome for the now discredited sex linkage hypothesis.

Factor IV represents speed of performance in which there is no penalty for wrong answers. It is the only factor that appeared virtually unchanged in terms of defining tests in every previous analysis as long as at least three factors were extracted. The ratios, however, suggest little genetic contribution to individual differences in this factor. The Project Talent retest of 9th graders in the 12th grade (Shaycoft, 1967) showed that there was little stability in individual differences on these tests over that time span. This factor may represent temporary motivational dispositions more than a presumed ability of cognitive speed.

Factor V has small but seemingly significant loadings in the female sample, but Procrustes rotations were even less successful for males for this factor than they had been for female fraternal twins for spatial visualization. It is interesting that test 10 had a higher loading than the markers in the male samples and was at least as high as the markers for females. The male ratios are essentially meaningless, being based on such small loadings, and the female ratios clearly do not fit the genetic model.

Factor VI, which appears in only three of the female samples, was small but defined in earlier orthogonal and oblique rotations in the same samples. The markers are short-term memory tests, but in the identical twin matrices mathematics tests 5 and 36 have higher loadings than the markers. There is no obvious explanation why the loadings of the two mathematics tests drop essentially to zero in the within-twin matrices for the dizygotes. The size of the ratio for female identicals suggests a low degree of heritability of this factor.

Accuracy of the Factor Models

We missed in all samples a large loading of mechanical information on Factor V. We also missed in the female monozygotic twins large loadings of two mathematics tests on Factor VI. For the remaining factors we missed no tests with

Table 6. Mean Squared General Factor Loadings of the
Group Factor Markers and the Cross- to Within-Twin Ratios in the
Hierarchical Models for Males and Females

Factor	Sex	Markers	Monozygotic Twins			Dizygotic Twins		
			Within	Cross	Ratio	Within	Cross	Ratio
I	Male	1-8, 14-19, 29, 36	.355	.307	.87	.318	.201	.63
	Female	1-8, 14, 19, 29	.392	.352	.90	.418	.300	.72
II	Male	22-29, 5, 35-37	.317	.279	.88	.311	.173	.55
	Female	22-29	.348	.312	.90	.373	.274	.74
III	Male	31-34	.293	.267	.91	.254	.112	.44
	Female	31-34	.259	.231	.89	.337	.252	.75
IV	Male	38-40	.084	.068	.80	.148	.112	.76
	Female	38-40	.088	.063	.72	.073	.044	.61
V	Male	11-12	.186	.139	.75	.148	.112	.76
	Female	11-12	.360	.325	.90	.372	.256	.69
VI	Male	20-21	.047	.064	1.36	.140	.104	.74
	Female	20-21	.183	.162	.88	.204	.135	.66

substantial loadings, but there was a small amount of overlap between tests that were expected to have secondary loadings on a particular factor and some that had been targeted at zero. For example, the mathematics tests targeted on Factor II for males had relatively low loadings for dizygotic twins. For monozygotic twins generally hits and misses were essentially identical in within and cross matrices. The high degree of similarity between cross- and within-matrix factors for monozygotic twins was always true in the preliminary factoring as well. Whatever the mix of determinants may be for the intercorrelations of these 40 tests, monozygotic twins are generally highly similar whether two factors or ten are extracted.

General Factor Loadings of Group Test Markers

The loadings of the 40 tests on the general factor showed essentially the same degree of resemblance between types of twins and sexes that the raw score cross and within correlations had, but this finding might be true only for the set of 40 tests considered as a whole. Table 6 contains mean general factor loadings for the group factors markers, factor by factor, as well as the cross to within ratios.

The general factor loadings of the markers for Factor I for both sexes have ratios that are almost identical with the ratios for the group factor. This supports more directly the conclusion reached in the discussion of the ratios of the marker tests for the group factors that the relative contributions of genetic and environmental determinants for the general and for this group factor could be the same.

For Factor II the female ratios are essentially the same as for Factor I, but the similarity of male dizygotics is somewhat less. Overall, however, the English tests show the same general factor-loading pattern as the 40 tests as a whole.

For Factor III, the spatial visualization factor, the ratio based on the general factor loadings has a pattern that approaches the expectation for a sex-linked trait, but these are for the general factor loadings. The ratios based on the raw-score correlations that appeared in Table 1 were determined primarily by the pattern of general factor loadings, not the pattern for the group factor. Identical twins of both sexes have ratios that are congruent with a substantial degree of heritability, but fraternal twins show a large sex difference.

Even the general factor loadings of the speed of performance factor, Factor IV, show evidence of low heritability. This finding reinforces the conclusion reached earlier that these tests do not measure an ability as usually conceived.

The ratios of general factor loadings of Factor V markers indicate no heritability component in the males while the ratios for females do not differ appreciably from the typical female pattern. Not only was Factor V essentially undefined in the male samples, the tests that defined the factor in the female samples are less adequate measures of the general factor for males. The rural information tests have very different functional characteristics for the two sexes.

Factor VI, the short-term memory factor, also shows ratios congruent with a substantial genetic component of variance for females. The ratios for monozygotic males are based on very small loadings so are not reliable. These tests did not measure individual differences in short-term memory adequately for these males.

In summary, with the exception of the general factor loadings of the highly speeded tests, female identical twins show a substantial degree of similarity of general factor loadings of the markers. The variation in ratios is only from .88 to .90. Variation of the ratios for fraternal females is somewhat larger, but it is only from .66 to .75, which brackets the trend in the 40 tests as a whole. Male identicals have ratios congruent with a high degree of heritability for only three of the six group factors. Similarity for male fraternals for the visualization markers drops well below the general trend of the data in the 40 tests as a whole.

Correlations among Composites

The factor analyses were not highly satisfactory. Perhaps the most important finding in light of discussions in the literature is the inability to define a separate factor of spatial visualization in dizygotic females. We decided, therefore, to pursue a somewhat different strategy as our next step. We formed composites that more or less reflected the factors. To the extent that the composites departed from the factors, the modification was designed to be meaningful educationally.

Table 7. Names of the Composites, Their Abbreviations,
and the Tests Used to Form Them

1. Spatial Visualization	(Vis)	31, 32, 33, 34
2. Mathematics	(Math)	5, 35, 36, 37
3. Rural Information	(Rural)	10, 11, 12
4. English	(Engl)	23, 24, 25, 26, 27, 28
5. Memory	(Mem)	20, 21
6. Technical Information	(Tech)	6, 7, 8, 9
7. Verbal	(Verb)	1, 29
8. Aesthetic Information	(Aesth)	2, 3, 14, 19
9. Performance Speed	(Speed)	38, 39, 40

Methods

We decided to use precisely the same tests in each composite and to provide unit variance for each test. The second of these decisions allowed the actual weights of tests to vary somewhat as a function of differences in the level of covariances among the tests in a composite. Unit weights do not give undue weight to a test that is somewhat peripheral to the function measured by the remaining components. For example, test 32 was too highly speeded to be highly valid for the function common to tests 31, 33 and 34. Thus #32 did not receive one-quarter of the weight.

Table 7 lists the names of the composites, their abbreviations, and the tests selected for each. Referring back to Table 5 the liberties taken with the factor findings can be determined. The tests defining composites 6 and 8, for example, appeared on Factor I, but they are so different in content that we wished to see how they would perform separately. In contrast the inclusion of mechanical information in the rural information tests was based directly on the factor analyses. Tests 1 and 29 did not define a separate verbal factor for the very good reason that verbal tests were split between factors I and II, but a verbal factor is defined so commonly that a separate composite was indicated for reference purposes.

We also estimated reliabilities of each composite by using the cross-twin same-test correlation for identical twins of a given sex as the reliability estimate for each component. There is no question but that the latter are lower-bound estimates, but the error resulting from this choice may not be very substantial. We also computed composite reliabilities using the internal consistency estimates published by the Project Talent staff (Flanagan et al., 1964). For composites 2, 3, 4, 6, 8, and 9 there was little difference and the differences were almost as often negative as positive. There were no published reliabilities for the highly speeded tests for obvious reasons. The reliability of the spatial visualization composite was appreciably smaller when the cross-twin correlations were used as estimates, but the inflation of the internal consistency reliability of test 32 by speeding accounts for most of the difference. The largest discrepancy is for the memory composite, but the published reliabilities were discounted by the Project Talent staff because the internal consistency methodology was not adequate.

Reliabilities of composites are also not highly sensitive to the reliabilities of the components. The level of intercorrelations is a critical factor. Thus it follows that the greater the number of components, the less sensitive is the reliability of the composite to errors in individual reliabilities. Also, if the tests in a composite hang together well, there is less sensitivity to errors in individual reliabilties.

Macro Analyses, the General Factor

Tables 8 to 11 contain the intercorrelation of the nine composites for the sex and twin-type samples. The first 9 x 9 matrix in a given table contains within-twin correlations, the second cross-twin correlations. The diagonal entries in the within matrix are reliability estimates; those in the cross matrix are the same-test, cross-twin correlations used in standard heritability estimation.

It requires little more than visual inspection of these tables to reveal several interesting properties of the correlations. In the first place, there are relatively few correlations that are trivially different from zero and only one of these is negative. Furthermore, the one negative occurs in dizygotic twin cross-correlations that are expected to be smaller than the rest. The composites do measure a large general factor.

Most of the correlations of trivial size involve Speed. In the earlier analyses there was little basis for considering the tests in this composite to be measuring an ability as usually conceived, but that conclusion can now be made a bit more precise. The composite correlations avoid the uncertainties associated with a decision about number of factors or method of rotation. A general factor loading for speed of performance can only be a small positive value.

Other small correlations are associated with Mem, especially in the male monozygotic matrices. In the latter sample the two memory tests have only a within-twin correlation of .21 with each other, which does not drop in size in the cross-twin matrix. The small amount of variance common to the two memory tests provides an inadequate basis for a composite. Common variance in the remaining three sets of twins is substantially higher and provides better justification for the composites.

A number of other relatively small correlations appear in the male dizygotic cross-twin matrix relating Vis to the remaining composites. The spatial visualization factor is well defined in male dizygotes because it has less overlap with other factors. The largest amount of overlap is actually with speed of performance. This appears to be the result of including too much speed of performance

Table 8. Within and Cross Correlations of Nine Composites
for Male Monozygotic Twins

Within-Twin[a]

		1	2	3	4	5	6	7	8	9
Vis	1	(810)								
Math	2	520	(894)							
Rural	3	474	461	(766)						
Engl	4	530	799	431	(850)					
Mem	5	284	299	134	327	(472)				
Tech	6	578	603	627	562	229	(867)			
Verb	7	560	762	613	754	303	741	(842)		
Aesth	8	473	717	539	701	297	664	816	(907)	
Speed	9	226	153	056	128	123	050	115	169	(759)

Cross-Twin[a]

		1	2	3	4	5	6	7	8	9
Vis	1	(748)								
Math	2	444	(800)							
Rural	3	423	395	(660)						
Engl	4	456	711	383	(737)					
Mem	5	237	235	132	253	(472)				
Tech	6	506	518	598	479	163	(774)			
Verb	7	506	672	492	672	261	632	(776)		
Aesth	8	444	666	444	631	289	595	772	(818)	
Speed	9	232	114	062	142	127	080	115	149	(576)

[a]Decimals are omitted throughout.

variance in the measures of Vis rather than the reverse. This is especially applicable to test 32 in the Vis composite.

Macro Analyses, the Number of Factors

The number of group factors our nine composites actually measure can be determined by comparing the diagonal entries in a given matrix with the remaining correlations in the row and column. If the correlation of a given composite with another composite or combination of composites is as high as the correlation of the composite with itself, within or cross as the case may be, the first composite cannot define a separate factor. There must also be a separate factor in the cross-

Table 9. Within and Cross Correlations of Nine Composites
for Male Dizygotic Twins

		Within-Twin[a]								
		1	2	3	4	5	6	7	8	9
Vis	1	(804)								
Math	2	439	(887)							
Rural	3	453	579	(765)						
Engl	4	404	731	515	(861)					
Mem	5	333	488	421	460	(515)				
Tech	6	469	602	602	586	446	(868)			
Verb	7	454	759	712	750	496	749	(840)		
Aesth	8	328	703	673	625	455	645	818	(864)	
Speed	9	387	179	186	055	161	042	151	188	(784)

		Cross-Twin[a]								
		1	2	3	4	5	6	7	8	9
Vis	1	(443)								
Math	2	169	(550)							
Rural	3	230	402	(426)						
Engl	4	187	456	334	(496)					
Mem	5	190	243	232	154	(208)				
Tech	6	307	483	391	431	260	(675)			
Verb	7	227	512	376	499	226	511	(581)		
Aesth	8	176	431	369	387	161	442	491	(496)	
Speed	9	247	087	062	053	098	-009	064	118	(602)

[a]Decimals are omitted throughout.

twin correlations for dizygotic twins to support some degree of genetic determination of that factor when it appears in within-twin correlations or in cross-
correlations of monozygotic twins.

Looking first at the within-twin correlations, it appears that the separation of
Verb and Aesth is generally trivially small. In some instances, as a matter of fact,
differences between their correlations with other composites suggest more separation of the two than their correlation with each other would make possible.
There is some uniqueness for Mem in the male monozygotes, but this is hardly
uniqueness in a common factor. As described earlier, there is little justification
for the composite in this sample. The same composite in male dizygotes has better psychometric properties, but there is zero uniqueness in the within-twin cor-

Table 10. Within and Cross Correlations of Nine Composites
for Female Monozygotic Twins

		1	2	3	4	5	6	7	8	9
					Within-Twin[a]					
		1	2	3	4	5	6	7	8	9
Vis	1	(778)								
Math	2	631	(862)							
Rural	3	495	538	(782)						
Engl	4	556	715	518	(857)					
Mem	5	361	509	336	443	(597)				
Tech	6	478	603	578	540	363	(791)			
Verb	7	583	709	621	789	469	702	(859)		
Aesth	8	480	617	556	687	396	687	826	(883)	
Speed	9	304	267	076	214	101	078	173	144	(796)
					Cross-Twin[a]					
		1	2	3	4	5	6	7	8	9
Vis	1	(716)								
Math	2	553	(786)							
Rural	3	442	481	(721)						
Engl	4	491	643	478	(797)					
Mem	5	297	444	323	365	(506)				
Tech	6	420	524	513	475	347	(721)			
Verb	7	500	621	569	704	360	629	(813)		
Aesth	8	446	577	510	649	342	602	771	(847)	
Speed	9	239	194	044	196	073	042	144	120	(662)

[a]Decimals are omitted throughout.

relations. In contrast, the within-twin correlations in the female samples support separate Mem factors.

The pattern of correlations in the monozygotic cross-twin data for both sexes is virtually identical to the within-twin correlations. Cross-twin correlations are, in the main, merely a little smaller than the within, and one reaches the same conclusions about the factors represented. A separate Mem factor is abandoned for males, and there is only a slight basis for maintaining the distinction between Verb and Aesth. There is a reasonable basis in the remaining composites for independent group factors.

The cross-twin correlations of the dizygotic twins present quite a different picture. For males the combination of Verb and Tech can account for the variance of

Table 11. Within and Cross Correlations of Nine Composites
for Female Dizygotic Twins

					Within-Twin[a]					
		1	2	3	4	5	6	7	8	9
Vis	1	(794)								
Math	2	660	(872)							
Rural	3	543	532	(782)						
Engl	4	512	738	537	(875)					
Mem	5	355	452	354	511	(612)				
Tech	6	571	657	648	533	356	(793)			
Verb	7	645	772	672	757	510	729	(859)		
Aesth	8	483	720	603	679	382	677	854	(887)	
Speed	9	271	098	146	131	137	084	149	188	(778)

					Cross-Twin[a]					
		1	2	3	4	5	6	7	8	9
Vis	1	(476)								
Math	2	427	(594)							
Rural	3	457	371	(631)						
Engl	4	393	518	378	(573)					
Mem	5	283	303	227	324	(318)				
Tech	6	427	447	439	372	176	(545)			
Verb	7	485	561	485	571	343	490	(667)		
Aesth	8	491	552	456	542	269	473	658	(703)	
Speed	9	250	111	115	074	033	085	094	125	(486)

[a]Decimals are omitted throughout.

Math, Rural, Engl, and Aesth, and the earlier exclusion of Mem is reinforced. This leaves Vis, Tech, Verb, and Speed with sufficient unique variance in this matrix to support group factors.

The cross-twin matrices for female dizygotic twins provide appreciable support for only three distinct group factors. Any difference between Verb and Aesth appears to be trivial at best. A Verb composite of six tests can readily be justified. This combined Verb factor accounts for the communalities of Vis, Math, Engl, and Mem. The addition of Rural to the combined Verb does the same for Tech. The third group factor in this matrix is, of course, Speed, which stands apart.

The explanation of why factors are defined by the cross-twin correlations of monozygotic twins, but not in dizygotic twins, starts with a reminder concerning the methodology. The formation of composites has held constant the variance of the general factor of intelligence. The group factors account for only a small portion of the total covariances of the tests. It is not unreasonable that this variance should be determined by between-family variance that is larger for monozygotic twins in these tests. Thus a basic assumption of the Falconer estimate of heritability is violated in these instances.

Micro Analyses, Differences in Correlations

Differences among factors are determined by differences among correlations, but the latter differences do not have to be statistically significant to determine the former. In these data there are a number of correlations that do differ significantly, using the number of twin pairs as N. Holding N constant, it seems reasonable to attend to p-values somewhat larger than the traditional .05.

There is no satisfactory *a priori* reason why within-twin correlations of monozygotic and dizygotic twins of the same sex should differ. When female monozygotic and dizygotic twins are compared correlation by correlation, this expectation appears to hold. Out of 36 correlations among nine variables there are only two comparisons for which the critical ratio is larger than 2.00 and none beyond 2.50. In contrast, there are a large number of significant differences in the same male comparisons. Accumulative distribution shows one greater than 3.00, five greater than 2.00, and 14 greater than 1.50. Given that the number of twin pairs provides a conservative estimate of the sampling stability of these correlations, the total is quite impressive. It is also noteworthy that there is more power for the female than for the male comparisons.

Of course, a series of critical ratios for differences between correlations when all correlations are computed in the same two independent samples cannot be expected to follow a binomial distribution. Sampling errors are themselves correlated. Thus the largest critical ratio and three others greater than 2.00 for males involve correlations with the Mem composite. In each case the correlation is higher in the fraternal twin sample. The larger correlations for fraternal twins involving Rural and, successively, Math, Verb, and Aesth are significant at .10, .10, and .05, respectively. Four differences involving the Vis composite are either close to p-value of .10 or smaller. Finally, the problem with the inclusion of the mathematics tests as targets along with English tests for Factor II in males is documented here by a p of .10 for the difference between Math and Engl for which the identical twins had the higher correlation.

Sex differences can be evaluated most powerfully in the monozygotic twin samples, and there are a moderately large number of statistically significant differences. Accumulating as before, there are two >3.00, five >2.50, eight >2.00, and 13 >1.50. The comparison of fraternal twins involves less power, so the number of large critical ratios is expected to be smaller. Unfortunately, how-

Table 12. Cross-Twin Same-Test Correlations of Estimated True Scores
and the Estimated Heritabilities

	Males			Females		
	Monozygotic	Dizygotic	h^2	Monozygotic	Dizygotic	h^2
1	.923	.551	.744	.920	.599	.641
2	.895	.620	.550	.912	.681	.462
3	.862	.557	.610	.922	.807	.230
4	.867	.576	.582	.930	.655	.550
5	1.000	.404	1.192	.848	.520	.656
6	.893	.778	.230	.912	.687	.450
7	.922	.692	.460	.946	.776	.340
8	.902	.574	.656	.959	.793	.332
9	.759	.768	0	.832	.625	.414

ever, all too few differences are in the same direction. Given the differences between the male twins, this is not unexpected.

The largest sex differences for identical twins involve the Mem composite, but the male twins also differ most for correlations involving this variable. The difference between Vis and Math is significant in both sets of twins. Math and Vis are more highly related in females, but the size of the difference is smaller in unselected samples of high school students. Math is more closely related to Eng, Verb, and Aesth for male identical twins, but these same differences are trivial in size and different in sign for fraternals. The higher correlations for female identical twins of Rural with Math and Engl are of borderline significance. There are also three comparisons involving dizygotic twins in which borderline or significant differences are accompanied by differences of the same sign in identical twins. These are the larger correlations for females for Vis with Engl, Verb, and Aesth.

Micro Analyses, Heritability Estimates

The composites entering Tables 8–11 have increased the reliability of the variables and reduced the number from 40 to 9. We also have estimates of reliabilities for each, based on the present samples, that are undoubtedly a little low, but probably not by very much. The correction of correlations for measurement error contains less error when reliabilities are relatively high, and the formation of composites allows trends in the data to be seen more clearly. It now seems appropriate, therefore, to estimate heritabilities of these variables in the standard manner. Note that the true score variance contains general and group factors with the latter contained in the uniqueness of the composite. Table 12 contains the cross-twin correlations for both types of twins and both sexes corrected for attenuation and the resulting estimates of heritability.

I shall first discuss the heritability estimates of the composites that correspond, more or less, to the group factors in the hierarchical analysis and follow with those for which there is no corresponding factor. After the discussion of the heritabilities, there will be a discussion of approximations to genetic variances. Approximations are required because the twin data tape did not include distribution statistics, requiring the discussion of variances to be based on data from other Project Talent samples.

The Vis composite in the male twins has the highest heritability estimate other than Mem. Spatial visualization stands out as a separate factor in all analyses of male cross-twin correlations, so this estimate represents both general and group factor variance. Data in Tables 5 and 6 also indicate, however, that it is the general factor content that largely determines the high heritability.

The same composite has the second highest estimate for females as well (Mem is again higher), but the high heritability of Vis in females is due entirely to the general factor content of the tests in the composite. A group factor cannot be defined in the cross-twin correlations in Table 11 and is essentially a null factor in the hierarchical analysis as shown in Table 5.

The heritability estimate for the Mem composite in males should be disregarded. The large differences in the correlations of memory with other tests in identical and fraternal twins precludes any interpretation. The heritability estimate is high for females, but the evidence in Table 11 indicates that this finding depends entirely on the general factor.

The Engl composite for females omitted two other marker tests from the factor analysis, but the problem posed by the results for the English tests is not explained by the difference in composition. Reasoning from the data in Tables 5 and 6, the heritability estimate for this composite should depend primarily on the group factor content, but the cross correlations of the English composite in the dizygotic female twins can account entirely for the common variance in the cross-twin same-test correlations. Thus the two methods of analysis do not furnish congruent results. Is there heritable nonerror specific variance in the English tests that define the composite? The cross-twin correlations for the tests in the composite for female dizygotics reveal essentially zero unique variance in each of the six separate tests.

Table 12 shows a substantial heritability component in Speed for females. The results in Tables 5 and 6 suggested small heritabilities for both the group and the general factor, while the data in Tables 10 and 11 appear to be at odds with the conclusion from Table 12. The corresponding data for males hang together better and indicate little heritability.

In males the Rural composite has no common variance that cannot be accounted for by the general factor. The relatively high heritability of that factor would differ sharply from the data in Tables 5 and 6 were it not for the addition of mechanical information to the marker tests in forming the composite. Test 10, as a function of its covariances, has more than one-third the weight in the variance of the composite. It also has one of the highest heritability estimates for males when analyzed in isolation.

The Rural composite is one of the three factors defined by the intercorrelations of the composites in female dizygotics. The low estimate of heritability applies, therefore, to the combination of general and group factor content of the tests. The data in Table 5 indicate low heritability of the group factor while in Table 6 the same tests show high heritability of the general factor content. The addition of mechanical information to the composite is again responsible for the discrepancy. It had zero heritability for females when used in isolation.

The remaining four composites have no factor counterparts. All were represented to some degree in Factor I, which was defined primarily by a wide variety of information tests. Also included, however, were vocabulary, reading comprehension, and introductory mathematics. For both sexes there appeared to be a genetic component in Factor I in addition to the genetic component in those tests deriving from their general factor loadings, but the data in Table 12 indicate that Factor I was not homogeneous with respect to estimates of h^2.

There are higher heritability estimates for males for three of the four composites. The relatively low h^2 is for Tech, on which the male mean is substantially higher than the female. The relatively high h^2 is for Aesth, on which the difference in means is reversed. These findings suggest the hypothesis that there is more between-family environmental variance in measures of achievement in areas where family pressures are strongest, but this explanation is not tenable for Math.

It is possible, however, that total genetic variance in the two sexes could be equal in spite of widely different heritabilities. The latter are computed in a metric having unit variance. Equality of genetic variance in spite of a difference in h^2 requires a difference of appropriate size in raw-score variance, but to test this hypothesis requires more than knowledge of the variances. The units of measurement for the test must be equal in all parts of the distribution. The importance of this assumption also increases as the separation in means of the distributions for the two sexes increases. Project Talent tests are short, which makes approximate equality of units suspect on *a priori* grounds, but there is also in the vast majority of the Talent tests a large positive correlation between means and variances (Humphreys, Lin, & Fleishman, 1976). In the absence of information for the present samples, the relative sizes of sex differences in means and variances are estimated from the distribution statistics obtained by Humphreys, Davey, and Kashima (1986) and are presented in Table 13.

The transformation used by Humphreys, Lin, and Fleishman to minimize the correlation between means and variances would reduce the sex difference in vari-

Table 13. Ratios of Female to Male Means and Variances Estimated
from Other Talent Samples

				Composite					
	Vis	Math	Rural	Engl	Mem	Tech	Verb	Aesth	Speed
Ratio of									
Means	.84	.93	.99	1.09	1.12	.68	.95	1.05	1.04
Ratio of									
Variances	.88	.92	1.06	.88	1.12	.64	.79	1.04	.85

ability most for the Tech composite and to a lesser extent for Verb, Vis, Math, Mem, and Aesth. The same transformation would increase the sex difference in variance of composites where the mean difference is in the opposite direction from the variance difference. The largest effect would be for Engl. Even without the transformation, the variance difference for Tech is not sufficient to equate genetic variance in raw scores. The size of genetic contributions to total variance would be larger than the differences in h^2 for Vis, Math, Verb, and Engl. The large sex difference for Aesth in h^2 would become only slightly smaller in terms of genetic contribution to total variance. Sex differences in estimates of h^2 extend to genetic contributions to total variance.

Conclusions

The data analyzed in this paper constituted the basis for an earlier report but have now been analyzed in different ways. We started with traditional estimates of heritability of the 40 different tests.

1. Tests that have the highest h^2 estimates do not conform in either sex with *a priori* expectations.

2. These traditional estimates have large sampling errors when based on observed correlations but sampling errors become huge when the correlations are corrected for attenuation, as they must be.

3. There is an essentially zero relationship between h^2 values in males and females across the 40 tests that even large sampling errors cannot explain.

In order to reduce the number of variables to be comprehended and to investigate one method of holding constant the variance of the general factor in the variance of the tests, we conducted hierarchical factor analyses.

1. Three group factors are common to all matrices defined by sex, twin type, and both within and cross correlations. These are a broad information factor, an English factor, and a speed of performance factor.

2. A fourth factor, spatial visualization, is common to all matrices other than the cross-twin matrix of female dizygotic twins.

3. A rural information factor and a memory factor could only be defined in the female correlations and then not in the cross-twin dizygotic matrix.

4. Cross-twin to within-twin ratios for the tests defining factors common to any given set of matrices were congruent to a modest degree with similar ratios obtained for the raw scores of the 40 tests reported previously and reproduced here. The rural information and speed of performance factors were exceptions to this finding.

5. In the same matrices and with the same exceptions the ratios for the general factor loadings of the tests defining the group factors are substantially more congruent with the ratios for the entire set of 40 tests.

To check on the factor analyses by a more objective methodology, we formed unit-weighted composites from tests defining hypothetical factors and educationally meaningful clusters. A global look at these correlations supported several conclusions.

1. The importance of the general factor is clearly evident in all matrices. One negative correlation of trivial size is found in the cross-twin matrix of male dizygotic twins.

2. When cross-twin different-test correlations are compared to the cross-twin same-test correlation for each composite in turn, there is sufficient unique variance to allow only four group factors in male dizygotic twins. These are spatial visualization, technical information, verbal comprehension, and speed of performance.

3. The same analysis in female dizygotic twins provides for only three group factors. These are verbal comprehension, rural information, and speed of performance.

The next step involved looking at the differences between twin type and sex samples for the composite correlations considered pair by pair.

1. The search for sex differences is complicated by an unreasonably large number of significant differences between within-twin correlations for the two types of male twins. There is no *a priori* genetic or environmental basis for these differences.

2. One cluster of these differences for male twins centers on the memory composite, but it is the male monozygotes who differ most from other twins of both sexes. There is concern about possible bias in the selection of dizygotic twins in these samples, but this concern is irrelevant in this instance.

3. Relatively few significant sex differences in correlations of the composites were independent of twin type. One consistent difference was the higher correlation between spatial visualization and mathematics in females, but this difference is smaller in larger samples of unselected high school students.

4. Not unexpectedly there are many differences between cross-twin and within-twin correlations for the two types of twins.

As a final step, traditional heritabilities were estimated for the nine composites with the help of lower-bound estimates of reliabilities.

1. Two different estimates of the reliabilities of the tests entering the composites were available for eight of the nine composites. A comparison of composite reliabilities in which both estimates were used indicated that the ones we selected were not seriously in error.

2. There is only modest agreement between inferences about the heritabilities of the general and group factors drawn from this analysis and from the factor-analytic findings.

3. Males have higher estimates of h^2 for all composites other than technical information and speed of performance.

4. Sex differences in the contribution of genetic variance to total variance are, in the main, equally large. There are actually more instances in which estimates of raw-score variances increase rather than decrease the differences in presumptive genetic variance.

Looking back over all analyses there appear to be two findings that stand out from the rest. One is the independence of heritability estimates in the two sexes and the generally lower level of those estimates in the female twins. The second is the inability to find evidence for a group factor of spatial visualization in the cross correlations of female dizygotic twins when the variance of the general factor is controlled. These data do support the ubiquitous findings that monozygotic twins are a good deal more similar than dizygotic twins, but to my knowledge there is not presently a genetic model that can explain the two major findings.

References

Flanagan, J. C., Daily, J. T., Shaycoft, M. F., Gorham, W. A., Orr, D. B., & Goldberg, I. (1962). *Design for a study of American youth.* Boston: Houghton-Mifflin.

Flanagan, J. C., Davis, F. B., Daily, J. T., Shaycoft, M. F., Orr, D. B., Goldberg, I., & Neuman, C. A. (1964). The American high school student. Final report for cooperative research project #635, U.S. Office of Education, Department of Health, Education, and Welfare. Pittsburgh: American Institutes for Research and University of Pittsburgh.

Humphreys, L. G. (1974). The misleading distinction between aptitude and achievement tests. In D. R. Green (Ed.), *The aptitude-achievement distinction.* Monterey: CTB/McGraw-Hill.

Humphreys, L. G., Davey, T. C., & Kashima, E. S. (1986). Experimental measures of cognitive privilege deprivation and some of their correlates. *Intelligence, 10,* 355–576.

Humphreys, L. G., Lin, Pang-Chie, & Fleishman, A. (1976). The sex by race interaction in cognitive measures. *Journal of Research in Personality, 10,* 42–58.

Kamin, L. J. (1987). Personal communication.

Kelley, T. L. (1924). *Statistical method.* New York: Macmillan.

Lerner, I. M. (1950). *Population genetics and animal improvement.* London: Cambridge University Press.

Montanelli, R. G., and Humphreys, L. G. (1976). Latent roots of random data correlation matrices with squared multiples on the diagnonal: A Monte Carlo study. *Psychometrika, 41,* 314–348.

Plomin, R., DeFries, J. C., & McClearn, G. E. (1980). *Behavioral genetics*. San Francisco: W. H. Freeman.

Shaycoft, M. F. (1967). The high school years: Growth in cognitive skills. Interim report #3, Project #3051, Contract # E-6-10-065. Pittsburgh: American Institutes for Research and University of Pittsburgh.

A Twice-Told Tale: Twins Reared Apart
Thomas J. Bouchard, Jr.

Langmuir (1943), in a paper dealing with the limits and applicability of ''scientific knowledge,'' introduced an important distinction between two types of natural phenomena: convergent phenomena and divergent phenomena.

> First, those in which the behavior of the system can be determined from the average behavior of its component parts and second, those in which a single discontinuous event (which may depend upon a single quantum change) becomes magnified in its effect so that the behavior of the whole aggregate does depend upon something that started from a small beginning. The first class of phenomena I want to call convergent phenomena, because all the fluctuating details of the individual atoms average out giving a result that converges to a definite state. The second class we may call divergent phenomena, where from a small beginning increasingly large effects are produced. (p. 3)

London (1946), building from Langmuir's conceptualization, has convincingly shown that historical phenomena, by their very nature, are divergent in origin. Any interpretation of history is, consequently, a matter of studying retrospective causation. Retrospective causation involves a backward tracing between events in a fashion that is ''satisfying'' or ''consistent'' with a predefined point of view. This approach to a subject may be informative and useful, but according

Portions of this chapter have appeared in Bouchard (1987b), McGue and Bouchard (1990), Tellegen et al. (1988), Arvey et al. (1989), and have been presented in public talks by Bouchard. The formal discussions of convergent and divergent phenomena were brought to my attention by Meehl (1978). All research on twins reared apart was supported by grants to the Minnesota Center for Twin and Adoption Research (MICTAR) from The Pioneer Fund, The Seaver Institute, The Koch Charitable Foundation, The Spencer Foundation, Harcourt Brace Jovanovich, Inc., the National Science Foundation (BNS-7926654), and The Graduate School of the University of Minnesota. I would like to London is "not science." London then generalizes his argument to the study of the events of one person: "Is he amenable to the scientific reduction, or will he present the same difficulties to the psychologist as history to the historian?" (p. 179).

The answer is that,

> Divergence of phenomena prevents much of psychology and psychiatry from being exact sciences in the sense that it is always possible to set up the invariable relationship: if A then B; and gives them more of the aspect of an art than a science. (p. 180)

The view that psychological aspects of human development are largely the result of a random walk (divergent path) through time is widely held even by theorists of remarkably different persuasions. This view is complemented by a strong belief in the influence of common family environmental factors, that is, family rearing styles, common schools, socioeconomic status, material possessions, etc., factors that are seen as making family members similar to one another.

Social learning theorists, for example, view personality development as the acquisition of a wide array of different responses as a function of idiosyncratic and systematic environmental encounters. The systematic factors are common family environmental factors and the idiosyncratic factors are largely random. I believe that the following quotation taken from Mischel (1981) conveys the view of many personologists:

> Genes and glands are obviously important, but social learning also has a dramatic role. Imagine the enormous differences that would be found in the personalities of twins with identical genetic endowments if they were raised apart in two different families—or, even more striking, in two totally different cultures. Through social learning vast differences develop among people in their reactions to most of the stimuli they face in daily life. (p. 311)

I am often asked, "Given your experience with identical twins reared apart, what is your feeling about determinism and free will?" This is an interesting question. Observation of similarity between twins reared apart constantly stimulates me to ponder the problem of genetic determinism. I am not prepared to even attempt to try to answer the question. However, the distinction between con-

to thank Nancy L. Segal for a critical reading of this manuscript and Greg Carey for suggesting the inclusion of Figure 2. I am indebted to my colleagues and collaborators on the twin project, David Lykken, Nancy L. Segal, Auke Tellegen, Elke Eckert, Leonard Heston, and Matthew McGue, for help and advice. A large number of individuals have been involved in testing participants in the project. We would especially like to thank Dale Feuer, Joy Fisher, Margaret Keyes, Susan Resnick, Nancy L. Segal, Kimerly Wilcox, Mary Moster, Jeffery McHenry, and Daniel Moloney and Ellen Rubin.

vergent and divergent phenomena sheds some light on the question of free will vs. biological determinism. There is a parallelism between the concepts of divergence/free will and convergence/determinism, and each point of view predicts different outcomes for monozygotic twins reared apart (MZA twins).

According to London:

> The divergence of psychological events must lend confidence to the feeling that the individual is not quite subservient to the years that went before, nor is he the invariable expression of his childhood down to the last detail; that in a certain sense his future always represents a semi-break with his past, "lawful" continuity being maintained by the converging aspects of those events for which he was both machine and repository; that a man, by taking advantage of the appearance of favoring divergencies, within and without, can help fashion his own future and semidirect his fate. For so doing, every moment presents its opportunity and renders him his own circumscribed free-agent.
>
> According to this view, then, free will may be looked upon as a function of divergence, operating within the limits imposed by the internally and externally convergent. (p. 181)

The most recent application of the divergence model for fostering the image that we control our development (free will?) is described by Bandura (1982) in "The Psychology of Chance Encounters and Lifepaths." Bandura argues that "chance encounters play a *predominant* (my emphasis) role in shaping the course of human lives" (p. 748). However, virtually all the evidence presented by Bandura rests on retrospective causation. The important point is not that Bandura is entirely wrong (he probably is not); it is, rather, that the evidentiary basis of his arguments is methodologically very weak. The course of a life path is ascribed to environmental events on the basis of retrospective analysis, but as London has argued: It is "not science." A much more powerful method is needed for estimating the relative roles played by chance and systematic converging factors. Only behavior genetic studies, especially those that include twins, can shed light on this question.

The belief that personality structure is determined by unpredictable and idiosyncratic events, and follows divergent pathways, has also led many thoughtful theorists to argue that the trait (or individual difference) approach to personality is fundamentally inadequate and should be replaced by an idiographic model (Holt, 1962; Lamiell, 1981). Evidence from twin research, however, leads to exactly the opposite conclusion. Inspection of a series of photographs of a pair of identical twins, taken across their life span, is an insightful exercise.

These photographs illustrate the important phenomenon of *genetically programed change*. The pace and direction of morphological change is highly syn-

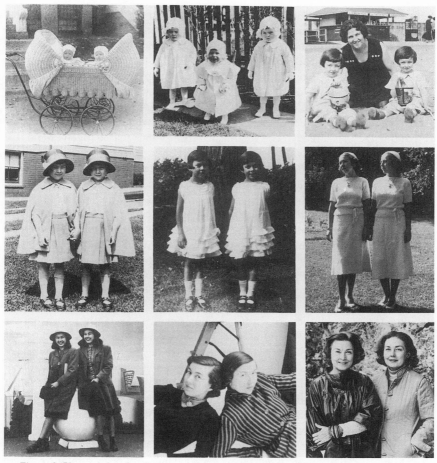

Figure 1. Photographs of a single pair of monozygotic twins reared together across various stages of life. From life to right: ages 7 months, 2 years, 4 years, 7 years, 9 years, 17 years, 19 years, 30 years, and 54 years. All photographs copyright (c) 1981 by Kathryn McLaughlin Abbe and Frances McLaughlin Gill, except for the last, lower-right, copyright (c) 1981 Greta Mitchell. Reproduced with permission.

chronized, that is, it is to a considerable extent a convergent phenomenon. These women are currently morphologically quite different than they were when they were children, but they are still remarkably alike.

This remarkable morphological similarity between identical twins which is clear in the photographs (and which everyone accepts as largely genetic in origin), as well as the striking behavioral similarities one observes when working with twins, has led many psychologists to ask: To what extent might complex human behavioral and mental traits—for example, mental abilities and personality—also, in part, reflect genetic influences?

An overwhelming body of evidence now demonstrates that much of human behavior is influenced by genes (Loehlin, 1989; Plomin, 1990; Rowe, 1987). The evidence that I will discuss in this chapter is drawn primarily from monozygotic and dizygotic twins reared apart (MZA and DZA twins), and monozygotic and dizygotic twins reared together (MZT and DZT twins). What I hope to show is that this fact has already been established using twins reared together and that the data gathered with twins reared apart is largely confirmatory. Data on twins reared apart is useful evidence, however, because a) it closes the door on a variety of widely accepted challenges to the validity of conclusions based on just one type of twin design and b) it extends findings based mostly on young people to a sample largely composed of mature adults.

When using the twins reared together design we assume that monozygotic (MZ) and dizygotic twins (DZ) experience approximately similar trait-relevant environments and that the differences between the two types of twins reflect one-half the genetic effect. Put another way, the excess similarity found for the MZ twins, relative to the DZ twins, is ascribed to the influence of heredity.

Unfortunately, it *appears* that monozygotic twins are treated more alike than dizygotic twins, such that critics of behavior genetics constantly assert that the greater similarity usually found in monozygotic twins is due to such treatment.

Notice, for example, that in the first seven frames of Figure 1 the twins are wearing the same clothes and have identical haircuts. Unlike morphological similarity, these features of their appearance are environmental in origin. Their mother dressed and groomed them alike from the time they were infants. When identical twins are reared together, the causes of behavioral similarities are ambiguous. If adult identical twins support the same political party, add the same amount of sugar to their coffee, and have similar IQs we do not know to what extent these similarities are due to their genetic similarity or to similar treatment while they were growing up. Similar photographs of dizygotic twins would on average demonstrate that they do not experience similar influences to the same degree.

The evidence is overwhelming that similar treatments, of the type under discussion, are *not* the cause of greater MZ twins similarity, but the proof is highly complex (Bouchard, 1984; Loehlin & Nichols, 1976; Scarr & Carter-Saltzman, 1979). Consequently, it is desirable to surmount the problem directly.

The most direct way to circumvent the problem is to study twins who have been reared apart from infancy, and who have had little or no contact during their formative years. Such twins might show some similarity owing to placement in similar homes (e.g., same social class level), but there is little doubt that their home experiences are much more different than those of twins who have been reared together. If these twins were randomly placed with respect to trait-relevant environmental factors, then the only reason they should show any similarity would be because they share genes. If there is selective placement, it can be examined and evaluated quantitatively.

EEGs

It is important to demonstrate that monozygotic twins reared apart are alike on traits that are known to be influenced by genetic processes. Because brain waves reflect processes that underlie behavior in a more direct way than any other physical characteristic, they constitute an important test case. Lykken (1982) showed that with respect to resemblance in the four classic EEG bands (Delta, Theta, Alpha, and Beta), MZA twins did not differ from MZT twins. The mean intraclass correlation across the bands was .80 for MZA twins (N = 25 pair) and .81 for MZT twins (N = 89 pair). EEG data based on a somewhat larger sample, which included MZT, MZA, DZT, and DZA twins, have now been analyzed using more sophisticated methods (Stassen, Lykken, & Bomben, 1988; Stassen, Lykken, Propping, & Bomben, 1988).

Paraphrasing their conclusion Stassen et al. find that: (1) the individual characteristics of the resting EEG are primarily determined by genetic factors; (2) monozygotic twins are only slightly less like each other (if there is any difference at all) than an individual is to him/herself over time; (3) dizygotic twins are more similar to each other than are pairs of unrelated individuals, a finding that is true for both DZA and DZT twins; (4) the EEGs of monozygotic twins reared apart are as similar to each other as are the EEGs of the same individual over time; and (5) there is no statistically significant difference in MZA and MZT twin pair resemblance for resting EEG.

While these data require a great deal more analysis before they are thoroughly understood, the results render a genetic interpretation of the psychological data to be discussed subsequently much more plausible than it would have been had the EEG data not demonstrated a substantial genetic influence.

Intelligence and Specific Cognitive Abilities

IQ has been at the center of the nature-nurture debate since the widespread introduction of intelligence tests in the United States in the years before World War I. The IQ data on MZA twins have been heavily cited by supporters of the nature side of the debate and heavily attacked by supporters of the nurture side of the debate (Kamin, 1974; Snyderman & Rothman, 1988, Table 3.1, p. 93; Taylor, 1980). In our study we have gathered three different measures of IQ: the Wechsler Adult Intelligence Scale (WAIS), the First Principal Component of two ability batteries (discussed below), and a composite score based on the Raven and

Table 1. Sample Sizes and Intraclass Correlations for All IQ Measures and Weighted Averages for Four Studies of MZA Twins

Study and Test Used (Primary/Secondary/ Tertiary)	N for Each Test	Primary Test	Secondary Test	Tertiary Test	Mean of Multiple Test
Newman et al. (1937) (Stanford-Binet/Otis)	19/19	.68 ± .12	.74 ± .10	–	.71
Juel-Nielsen (1965) (Wechsler-Bellevue/ Raven)	12/12	.64 ± .17	.73 ± .13	–	.69
Shields (1962) (Mill-Hill/ Dominoes)	38/37	.74 ± .07	.76 ± .07	–	.75
Bouchard et al. (1990) (WAIS/Raven-Mill-Hill/First Principal Component)	48/42/43	.69 ± .07	.78 ± .07	.78 ± .07	.75

Source: Bouchard, Lykken, McGue, Segal, & Tellegen (1990).

Mill-Hill vocabulary test. Our clinical measure, the individually administered WAIS, is administered by two different psychometrists hired specifically for the task to avoid any charge of biased test administration (see Bouchard, Lykken, McGue, Segal, & Tellegen, 1990). Table 1 shows the similarity in IQ of our MZA twins on all measures in comparison with the results of the three previous studies.

The consistency of the MZA correlations across country of origin, tests, and time periods is striking. These data strongly suggest that the broad heritability of IQ is in the range .64-.74. This range is a bit higher than recent estimates by others (cf. Chipuer, Rovine, & Plomin, 1990; Loehlin, 1989), but it should be kept in mind that virtually the entire literature on IQ similarity between relatives is based on children and adolescents. There is reason to believe that a careful analysis based on adult data only would yield a higher figure (Bouchard, in press).

Special mental abilities were assessed with a modified version of the Hawaii Battery, a battery of specific cognitive ability tests used in the large Hawaii Family study (DeFries, Johnson, Kuse, McClearn, Polovina, Vandenberg, & Wilson, 1979). We added three subtests from the Kit of Factor-Referenced Cognitive Tests

Table 2. Loadings of the Four Special Mental Ability Factors on the Fifteen Special Mental Ability Measures

	Factor			
Variable	Verbal	Spatial	Perceptual Speed and Accuracy	Memory
Vocabulary	**.79**	.16	.04	-.04
Word beg. and end.	**.78**	.17	-.02	.12
Pedigrees	**.68**	.32	.24	.21
Subt. and mult.	**.60**	-.15	.37	.08
Things	**.46**	.22	.28	.09
Card rotations	.04	**.78**	.24	.02
Cubes	.23	**.71**	.15	.02
Mental rotations	.02	**.69**	.04	-.05
Paper form board	.21	**.65**	.34	.19
Paper folding	.20	**.62**	.02	.22
Hidden patterns	.32	**.58**	.39	.12
Lines and dots	.05	.30	**.42**	.07
Identical pictures	.40	.30	**.63**	.06
Delayed visual memory	.18	.06	-.09	**.85**
Immediate visual memory	.02	.07	.19	**.52**
% total variance accounted for	10.9	33.9	6.5	3.8

Source: Bouchard & McGue, 1989.
Note: Highest factor loading for each variable is indicated in boldface. Cluster identification determined by highest loading.

(the Identical Pictures, Cubes, and Paper Folding subtests [Ekstrom, French, & Harman, 1976]) to the battery. The 15 cognitive subtests were selected to represent four broad areas or clusters (as identified by factor analysis) of cognitive performance: Verbal Reasoning (5 tests), Spatial Ability (6), Perceptual Speed and Accuracy (2), and Visual Memory (2). We also administered the Comprehensive Ability Battery (CAB) developed by Hakstian and Cattell (1978). A full description of all these tests, their administration time and reliabilities, can be found in Bouchard, Segal, and Lykken (1990). Table 2 shows the factor structure of the Hawaii Battery.

Table 3 shows the mean squares, intraclass correlations, and results of a genetical model analysis of the 15 scales and 5 factor scores. Note that our models are fit to mean squares, not intraclass correlations. The correlations are presented for purposes of interpretability. Parameter estimates are reported only when the general model statistically fitted the mean squares. Our model assumes: i) all resemblance between reared apart relatives is due to genetic factors; ii) there is no assortative mating; iii) all genetic effects are additive (i.e., there is no dominance or epistasis); iv) genetic and environmental effects are independent (i.e., there is no genotype-environment covariance) and combine additively in the determination of the phenotype (i.e., there is no genotype by environment interaction). See McGue and Bouchard (1989) for a defense of these assumptions and see the discussion of placement effects below. The statistical test associated with the general model tests the adequacy of fit of the general model to the twin data and is primarily sensitive to the two constraints imposed by that model: the total variance for the two types of individuals is equal, and the DZA correlation is half the MZA correlation. Comparison of the restricted model with the general model is used to test the significance of genetic factors. A model specifying no genetic effect was rejected for all factors except visual memory. On average, the proportion of the variance associated with genetic factors appears to be largest for the Spatial Ability tests, next for the Verbal Reasoning and Perceptual Speed and Accuracy measures, and least for Visual Memory. It is worth noting that, for the Verbal Reasoning Factor, while the MZA and DZA correlations are comparable, significant genetic effects were observed. This reflects the relatively small size of the DZA sample so that the DZA correlation does not significantly deviate from one-half the MZA correlation as implied by the general model.

Table 4 shows the results of the same genetic model analysis of the CAB. The findings clearly replicate those for the Hawaii Battery.

Finally, Nichols (1978) has reported a meta-analysis of the results of a large number of twin studies of mental abilities. Applying Falconer's (1960) formula $[h^2 = 2(R_{MZ} - R_{DZ})]$ his data estimate heritabilities of .38, .48, .46, and .32 for the Verbal, Spatial, Perceptual Speed and Accuracy, and Memory factors, respectively. There is a suggestion that the memory factor shows less heritability than do the other specific cognitive abilities (see DeFries et al. 1979). The remaining abilities appear to have heritabilities in the .40 to .50 range. Correction for unreliability would most likely increase these figures by approximately .05 to .07.

Taken all together, then, the results suggest that the three major special mental abilities have heritabilities in the neighborhood of .50 and visual memory has a somewhat lower heritability. Our small study appears to slightly overestimate the heritability of the Verbal, Spatial, and Perceptual Speed and Accuracy factors and underestimate the heritability for Visual Memory.

Table 3. Mean Squares, Intraclass Correlations, and Results of Genetical Model Analysis for Hawaii Battery

Variable	MZA			DZA			Parameter Estimates			p value for test of	
	MSB	MSW	r	MSB	MSW	r	G	E	h^2	General Model	No Genetic Effect
Scales											
Vocabulary	1.65	.61	.46	1.16	.64	.29	.45	.55	.45	.64	<.001
Word beg. and end.	2.14	.45	.65	.84	.14	.71	–	–	–	.006	–
Pedigrees	1.30	.50	.44	1.74	.61	.48	.56	.49	.53	.28	<.001
Things	1.32	.67	.32	1.43	.59	.41	.38	.64	.37	.48	.01
Subt. and mult.	1.50	.72	.34	1.48	.40	.57	.38	.62	.38	.13	.01
Card rotations	1.62	.31	.67	1.56	.78	.34	.74	.32	.69	.76	<.001
Cubes	1.33	.56	.41	1.25	1.12	.06	.42	.65	.39	.40	.03
Mental rotations	1.42	.46	.51	1.42	.88	.23	.55	.48	.53	.69	.001
Paper form board	1.81	.57	.52	.83	.62	.15	.53	.54	.50	.25	<.001
Paper folding	1.61	.55	.48	1.34	.51	.45	.51	.52	.49	.47	<.001
Hidden patterns	1.76	.56	.51	1.01	.45	.38	.54	.48	.53	.22	<.001
Lines and dots	1.35	.66	.34	1.49	.92	.24	.38	.62	.38	.76	.01
Identical pictures	1.78	.47	.58	1.11	.52	.36	.58	.44	.57	.43	<.001
Delayed visual memory	1.15	.43	.45	1.72	1.13	.21	.67	.50	.53	.08	.01
Immediate visual memory	1.10	.86	.12	1.28	.82	.22	.17	.84	.17	.73	.25
Mean			.45			.34			.47		
Factors											
Verbal	1.75	.47	.57	1.33	.44	.51	.60	.45	.57	.33	<.001
Spatial	1.76	.30	.71	1.47	.64	.40	.74	.30	.71	.98	<.001
Perceptual speed	1.74	.52	.53	1.26	.38	.54	.56	.49	.53	.18	<.001
Visual memory	1.04	.43	.42	1.64	1.42	.07	–	–	–	.006	–

Source: McGue & Bouchard, 1989.
Note: Degrees of freedom vary between 42-47 for dfb MZA; 45-50 for dfw MZA; 22-24 for dfb DZA; and 23-25 for dfw DZA.

Table 4. Mean Squares, Intraclass Correlations, and Results of Genetical Model Analysis for Comprehensive Ability Battery

Variable	MZA			DZA			Parameter Estimates			p value for test of	
	MSB	MSW	r	MSB	MSW	r	G	E	h²	General Model	No Genetic Effect
Verbal	1.63	.32	.67	1.41	.46	.51	.65	.30	.68	.59	<.001
Number	2.01	.41	.66	0.97	.63	.21	.69	.39	.64	.36	<.001
Space	1.62	.42	.59	1.60	.45	.56	.64	.40	.61	.31	<.001
Speed of closure	1.07	.57	.31	1.49	.65	.40	.39	.56	.41	.33	.033
Perceptual speed	1.23	.53	.40	1.27	.40	.52	.39	.50	.44	.24	<.001
Induction	1.21	.49	.42	1.69	.84	.34	.55	.51	.52	.30	<.001
Flexibility of closure	1.31	.66	.33	1.32	.91	.18	.36	.68	.35	.88	.135
Associative memory	1.79	.58	.51	0.84	.77	.04	.51	.56	.48	.34	<.001
Meaningful memory	1.22	.71	.26	1.39	.71	.32	.32	.69	.32	.64	.156
Memory span	1.41	.60	.40	1.70	.99	.26	.54	.63	.46	.52	.032
Spelling	1.59	.34	.64	1.49	.51	.49	.65	.33	.66	.64	<.001
Mechanical ability	1.02	.35	.49	2.33	1.89	.10	–	–	–	.00	<.001
Word fluency	1.51	.39	.59	1.78	.33	.68	.68	.37	.65	.07	.104
Mean			.48			.35			.52		

Source: Bouchard, Segal, & Lykken, 1990.

Note: Degree of freedom vary between 39-46 for dfb MZA; 41-48 for dfw MZA; 24-26 for dfb DZA; and 25-27 for dfw DZA. In the original publication the data for Meaningful memory and Memory span were transposed.

Does Placement Bias Explain the Similarity between Reared Apart Twins?

This is an excellent place to discuss one of the major criticisms of adoption studies. It is often asserted that findings like the one reported to this point can, in large part, be explained by placement factors. That is, the twins are similar largely because they have been raised in similar adoptive homes. More specifically, the rearing parents are of similar socioeconomic and educational levels. I have, for example, heard a distinguished scholar assert that it should not be unexpected that our first pair of twins, the "Jim Twins," were similar because "they grew up about 100 miles apart in central Ohio" and "were probably raised in similar family environments." This sort of question can be dealt with quantitatively. In the domain of mental abilities it is often asserted that family socioeconomic background, educational level, and material resources are the major determinants of mental ability. The implication is that if there is selective placement, twins are placed in homes that are similar on these factors, then placement explains the correlation. It is important to realize that, taken alone, this inference is incorrect. It is absolutely necessary to demonstrate that the "environmental factors" on which placement occurs are a) trait-relevant and that b) the magnitude of the "causal effect" is sufficient to influence the twin correlation. Furthermore, the demonstration of a causal effect must occur in the context of an adoption design; it cannot depend on data gathered on biological families in which genetic and environmental influences are confounded (Bouchard & Segal, 1985).

For purposes of detecting environmental effects directly, as well as for assessing placement bias, a number of presumably important environmental characteristics were assessed in the Minnesota Study of Twins Reared Apart (MISTRA) project. Specific measures included; a) adoptive parents' years of education, b) maximum occupational status attained by adoptive mother or father [occupational status was coded using the Duncan SEI system according to the procedures outlined by Mueller and Parcell (1981)] and, c) *yes* or *no* responses to the availability of 41 different physical facilities in the adoptive home. The 41-item physical facilities questionnaire was further summarized through factor analysis. Principal-axes factor analysis of the dichotomous responses identified four interpretable varimax rotated factors that accounted for 34.6% of the total variance. The first factor accounted for 22% of the total variance and loaded highest on tape recorder, hi-fi or stereo set, and power tools. The factor also correlated substantially and significantly with age, indicating that it partly reflected secular trends in the availability of these items. The first factor was interpreted as a Material Possessions factor. The second factor accounted for 5% of the total variance and loaded highest on chemical and laboratory equipment, photographic darkroom, and telescope. The second factor was interpreted as a Scientific/Technical factor.

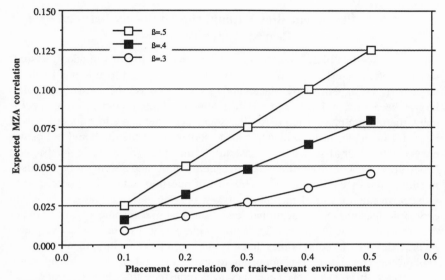

Figure 2. Effect of selective placement on MZA correlations on the assumption of no heritability.

The third factor accounted for 4.2% of the total variance and loaded highest on world atlas, reproductions of famous paintings, collection of classical records, samples of original art work, and art supplies or equipment. The third factor was interpreted as a Cultural factor. The fourth factor accounted for 3.4% of the variance and loaded highest on fishing or hunting equipment, automotive tools, and carpentry tools. Factor four was interpreted as a Mechanical factor. Factor scores for the four physical facilities factors were estimated using least squares.

On the assumption that the actual heritability equals zero, to what extent can placement explain our results? Figure 2 shows the effects of selective placement on MZA data under a number of plausible conditions. The beta coefficient represents the correlation between the trait-relevant environmental factor and the trait (e.g., correlation between Parental Education and Offspring's IQ) as demonstrated in an adoption study.

Note the severe limits on the possible effects of placement. The highest MZA correlation under a placement coefficient of .5 with a trait-relevant environmental effect of .5 is .125. That is, if the placement coefficient is .5 and the environmental measure correlated .5 with the trait in an adoption study (we are ignoring the possibility of biased placement in the study itself, i.e., matching characteristics of adoptive and biological families), then the twin correlation will be .125.

Table 5 shows the placement coefficient for the environmental factors discussed previously, the trait relevance of the factors, and the joint contribution of

Table 5. Placement Coefficients for Environmental Variables, Correlations
between IQ and the Environmental Variables, and Estimates of
the Contribution of Placement to Twin Similarity in WAIS IQ

Placement Variable	MZA Similarity (R_{ff})	Correlation between IQ and Placement Variable (r_{ft})	Contribution of Placement to the MZA Correlation $(R_{ff}*r^2_{ft})$
SES indictors			
Father's Education	.134	.100	.001
Mother's Education	.412	-.001	.000
Father's SES	.267	.174	.008
Physical facilities			
Material possessions	.402	.279*	.032
Scientific/technical	.151	-.090	.001
Cultural	-.085	-.279*	-.007
Mechanical	.303	.077	.002
Relevant Moos scales			
Achievement	.11	-.103	.001
Intellectual orientation	.27	.106	.003

Source: Bouchard, Lykken, McGue, Segal, & Tellegen, 1990.
*r_{ft} significantly different from zero at $p < .01$.

both to the MZA WAIS IQ correlations in our study. Table 5 shows that while significant placement occurred on some of these factors for the MZA twins in our study, the factors simply do not have sufficient causal power (i.e., do not correlate with mental abilities at a meaningful level) to explain more than a small fraction of the twin similarity.

It should be very clear that while we have not excluded all the important variables that may influence our twin correlations (considerable work remains to be done in this domain), it is necessary for a critic of these findings to demonstrate (using an adoption sample) that the purported placement variable that "explains" the results is trait-relevant. The demonstration of significant trait-relevant environmental influences in the domain of mental abilities is very difficult (Bouchard & Segal, 1985). Results similar to these, demonstrating minimum placement effects on MZA similarity, have also been reported for the Hawaii Battery (McGue & Bouchard, 1989).

The conclusion that it is difficult to identify potent environmental factors that influence mental abilities is not unique to this study. Bouchard (1982, 1983,

Table 6. Intraclass Correlations and Results of Genetical Model Analysis for
Information-Processing Factors

Variable	Intraclass r		Parameter Estimates			p value for test of	
						General	No Genetic
	MZA	DZA	G	E	h^2	Model	Effect
Basic Speed	.56	.24	.55	.47	.54	.09	<.001
Acquisition Speed	.20	.10	.31	.82	.27	.51	.24
Spatial Speed	.36	.53	.39	.68	.58	.67	<.001

Source: McGue and Bouchard, 1989.

1987a, in press) responding to serious misinterpretations of previous work with twins reared apart (Farber, 1981; Kamin, 1974; Taylor, 1980), has shown that the environmental factors purported to explain the similarity in IQ of MZA twins studies prior to the MISTRA project, do not do so when subjected to careful scrutiny. Misinterpretations of that work are still prevalent as illustrated by a recent citation of Taylor (1980) in support of an environmental explanation of the MZA IQ correlations by Bronfenbrenner (1986).

Information-Processing Abilities

As part of our assessment battery we also include a number of measures of information processing. There are three principal tasks: the Posner letter identification (Posner, Boies, Eichelman, & Taylor, 1969), the Sternberg memory search (Sternberg, 1969), and the Shepard-Metzler cube rotation (Shepard & Metzler, 1971).

A factor analysis of the eight reaction-time measures yielded three factors with eigen values greater than 1.0 which accounted for a total of 51% of the total variance. The first factor accounted for 25% of the total variance and loaded highest on three measures that assess general speed of processing; this first factor was called Speed of Response. The second factor accounted for 15.8% of the total variance, loaded highest on acquisition speed measures; this factor was called Acquisition Speed. The final factor accounted for 10.2% of the total variance, loading highest on the two Shepard-Metzler measures; this factor was called Speed of Spatial Processing. Factor scores for the three factors were generated by least squares and used in subsequent genetical analysis.

The factor scores were subject to the same analysis as the specific mental ability data and the results for the three factors are shown in Table 6.

For the Basic Speed factor and the Spatial Speed factor we can reject the hypothesis of no genetic effect and we cannot reject the general model. The heritability estimates for these two factors are in the same range as those found for the Verbal, Spatial, and Perceptual Speed and Accuracy factors. For Aquisition Speed we are not able to reject the hypothesis of no genetic effect. Nor are we able to reject the general model. Both results are consistent with a modest genetic effect.

As in the case of special mental abilities, environmental factors were not able to account for a meaningful part of the twin correlations.

Personality

Almost all of our knowledge regarding environmental and genetic causal influences on stable personality traits has come from studies of twins reared together. The findings have been both remarkable and puzzling. On the genetic side, regardless of the trait studied, the intraclass correlation for fraternal or dizygotic (DZ) twins has approached .25, and that for identical or monozygotic (MZ) twins has approached .50 (Goldsmith, 1983; Nichols, 1978). Application of the simplest genetic model, the Falconer (1960) formula for heritability, to those results yields a heritability of about .50.

Another striking phenomenon in the personality domain is the apparent lack of differences in heritability among personality variables. Loehlin and Nichols's (1976) findings are a case in point. Their twin personality data involved a well-known instrument, the California Psychological Inventory (CPI: Megargee, 1972), and revealed that the scales of this multimeasure instrument have very similar heritabilities. The differential heritability of personality variables (or the lack thereof) has, subsequently, become a subject of substantial controversy (Carey, Goldsmith, Tellegen, & Gottesman, 1978; Carey & Rice, 1983; Loehlin, 1982; Zonderman, 1982). What on the surface may appear to be lack of differential heritability among psychologically diverse scales may, in reality, reflect substantial content (and item) overlap and high correlations between scales in inventories such as the CPI (Carey et al., 1978).

To test the hypothesis of differential heritability of personality variables, it is necessary to use an instrument composed of relatively independent scales. The Multidimensional Personality Questionnaire (MPQ) was developed using a factor-analytic strategy (Tellegen, 1978/1982). Its scales, compared to those in other multiscale inventories, are relatively independent, but can still be meaningfully combined into higher-order factor measures. The latter correspond rather closely to the superfactor scales developed by Eysenck and Eysenck (1975), and analyzed by Eaves, Eysenck, and Martin (1989) and others. Thus, the MPQ permits us to assess differential heritability on lower- as well as higher-order factor levels.

Table 7 gives the correlations between four types of twin pairs on the 11 major personality traits measured by the Multidimensional Personality Questionnaire

Table 7. Intraclass Correlations for Eleven Primary Scales for the Multidimensional Personality Questionnaire for Four Kinship Groups

MPQ Scale	MZA	DZA	MZT	DZT
1. Well-Being	.48	.18	.58	.23
2. Social Potency	.56	.27	.65	.08
3. Achievement	.36	.07	.51	.13
4. Social Closeness	.29	.30	.57	.24
5. Stress Reaction	.61	.27	.52	.24
6. Alienation	.48	.18	.55	.38
7. Aggression	.46	.06	.43	.14
8. Control	.50	.03	.41	-.06
9. Harm Avoidance	.49	.24	.55	.17
10. Traditionalism	.53	.39	.50	.47
11. Absorption	.61	.21	.49	.41
Number of twin pairs	44	27	217	114

Source: Tellegen, Lykken, Bouchard, Wilcox, Segal, & Rich, 1988.

(Tellegen, Lykken, Bouchard, Wilcox, Segal, & Rich, 1988). Table 8 gives estimates of genetic and environmental variance components from a biometric model applied to the variances (analysis of variances can, under some circumstances, yield different results from the analysis of intraclass correlations).

These results, both from an examination of the intraclass correlations and the model-fitting, confirm and extend earlier findings and have several implications for current thinking and future research concerning determinants of variation in personality. First, our analyses indicate that, on average, about 50% of measured personality diversity can be attributed to genetic diversity. This result confirms previous findings and represents an extension to a rather wide range of distinctive personality characteristics. The remaining 50% is technically classified as all environmental and includes the unshared environmental effect which in turn includes measurement error and nontrait score fluctuations that reflect the influence of transient states on self-report trait measures. If one considers both the internal consistency and stability of personality scales (see Conley, 1984), it is not unreasonable to guess that not more than about 70 to 85% of the observed variance represents trait variance. Since the 15 to 30% nontrait variance is presumably confined to the environmental 50% of the observed variance, the environmentally based trait variance might not amount to more than 20 to 35%, compared to the roughly 50% that is genetic in origin. Improving the consistency and stability of a trait scale should increase its measured genetic and trait-relevant environmental components, but not their relative magnitude. It seems reason-

Table 8. Estimates of Genetic and Environmental Variance Components from a Biometric Model Applied to MPQ Data of Twins Reared Apart and Together

MPQ Scale	Variance Component (Std. Error)			
	Genetic	C-parameter	Shared Familial	Unshared
1. Well-being	.48* (.08)	.29 (.16)	.13 (.09)	.40* (.04)
2. Social potency	.54* (.07)	.05* (.21)	.10 (.08)	.36* (.04)
3. Achievement	.39* (.10)	.13 (.27)	.11 (.11)	.51* (.05)
4. Social closeness	.40* (.08)	.19 (.22)	.19* (.09)	.41* (.05)
5. Stress reaction	.53* (.04)	.49 (.17)	.00†	.47* (.04)
6. Alienation	.45* (.13)	.50†	.11 (.12)	.44* (.04)
7. Aggression	.44* (.05)	.27 (.19)	.00†	.56* (.05)
8. Control	.44* (.05)	.00*†	.00†	.56* (.05)
9. Harm avoidance	.55* (.04)	.31 (.15)	.00†	.45* (.04)
10. Traditionalism	.45* (.10)	.50†	.12 (.10)	.43* (.04)
11. Absorption	.50* (.10)	.50†	.03 (.10)	.47* (.04)

Source: Tellegen, Lykken, Bouchard, Wilcox, Segal, & Rich, 1988.
    *Significantly different from null value.
    †Boundary solution; therefore, no standard error computed.

able, therefore, to conclude that personality differences are more influenced by genetic diversity than they are by environmental diversity.

To illustrate the generality of these conclusions Table 9 shows the results of our analysis of the CPI based on the MZA and DZA data (Bouchard & McGue, 1990) in comparison with the results from an adult twin sample enrolled in a study of personality factors as predictors of coronary problems (Horn, Plomin, & Rosenman, 1976). The results hardly differ from the MPQ data shown above. It is worth noting that the results of these studies also hardly differ from the National Merit Scholarship study by Loehlin and Nichols (1976). Consequently, heritability of personality does not appear to change with age. This conclusion is consistent with the longitudinal work of Costa and McCrae (1987), who conclude that there is a "remarkable consistency of personality over intervals of up to 30 years, despite biological aging, the acquisition and loss of social roles, and the occurrence of major life events" (p. 23).

What about environmental influences on personality? Loehlin and Nichols (1976) carried out an extensive analysis of the environmental difference correlates of the MZ twin differences. The MZ twin differences in personality must be entirely environmental in origin. They found median correlations of .06 for MZ and .07 for DZ twins, and were forced to conclude that treatment differences in early childhood were not highly predictive of differences in personality observed

Table 9. Intraclass Correlations and Heritabilities for MZA and DZA Twins, and MZT and DZT Twins for California Psychological Inventory Scales

Scale	Bouchard & McGue, 1990			Horn, Plomin, & Rosenman, 1976		
	r_{MZA} (n = 45)	r_{DZA} (n = 26)	$h^2 \pm$ (s.e.) (model fitting)	r_{MZT} (n = 99)	r_{DZT} (n = 99)	$h^2 \pm$ (s.e.) (Falconer)
Dominance	.53	.24	.541	.53	.28	.50
Capacity for status	.60	.39	.652	.54	.25	.58
Sociability	.39	.40	.479	.54	.18	.66
Social presence	.47	.53	.562	.54	.21	.66
Self-acceptance	.62	.11	.616	.47	.23	.48
Well-being	.59	.17	.583	.43	.13	.60
Responsibility	.48	.34	.626	.44	.33	.22
Socialization	.53	.39	.577	.43	.25	.36
Self-control	.64	-.28	.612	.45	.12	.66
Tolerance	.55	.22	.602	.47	.17	.60
Good impression	.53	-.19	.464	.42	.13	.58
Communality	.17	-.18	.104	.22	.06	.32
Ach. via conformance	.44	.02	.414	.41	.01	.80
Ach. via independence	.62	.25	.665	.49	.25	.48
Intellectual efficiency	.49	.37	.621	.49	.30	.38
Psychological mindedness	.20	.28	.289	.36	.18	.36
Flexibility	.10	-.02	.051	.49	.10	.78
Femininity	.27	.16	.280	.27	.15	.24
Mean	.46	.18	.49	.44	.19	.51

Source: Bouchard & McGue, 1990.

in adolescence. It is worth noting that the twin difference method has been utilized in the study of schizophrenia as well and has not revealed systematic environmental influences (Gottesman & Shields, 1972; Wahl, 1976).

We carried out a similar analysis in our study of the CPI (Bouchard & McGue, 1990). We correlated MZA twin differences on self-report measures of child-rearing practices, gathered with the Family Environment Scale (FES) (FES; Moos & Moos, 1986) with MZA twin differences on the CPI. Since most of our twins, both MZA and DZA, were adopted, we were also able, as in our previous environmental analyses, to directly correlate the FES scores with the twin CPI scores. We concluded that "the generally modest adoptive environment–adult personality correlations and the generally small MZA difference correlations are both consistent with the argument that common family environmental factors are of limited importance in the determination of similarity between twins and perhaps all first-degree relatives" (pp. 288–89).

Social Attitudes and Values

Allport (1935) declared that attitude is social psychology's "most indispensable concept." While interest in attitudes as psychological constructs has waxed and waned, it continues to be a central construct in modern cognitive social psychology. For example, Greenwald (1989) concludes a recent chapter with the following remark: "Attitude is thus the central theoretical construct for describing the motivation significance of mental objects" (p. 439). There has, however, been very little research on the transmission of attitudes within families and almost no behavior genetic studies. Indeed, it is widely believed that attitudes and values are largely immune from genetic influence. In a recent review Plomin (1989) concluded that "Religiosity and certain political beliefs . . . show no genetic influence" (p. 107). One of the most provocative early behavior genetic studies of attitudes was that of Scarr and Weinberg (1981). They included the California F-scale, a measure of authoritarianism, in their adoption project as a control measure to demonstrate pure social transmission. To their surprise they found a significant genetic influence on this measure. It was possible to explain most of the genetic variance in the F-scale through its correlation with Verbal IQ, and this was their preferred explanation. This explanation may be only partly correct. The traditionalism scale on the MPQ is a personality measure of authoritarianism and as seen in Table 8 it shows a heritability of .45. Martin, Eaves, Heath, Jardine, Feingold, and Eysenck (1986) examined the influence of genetic and environmental factors on attitudes (conservatism, radicalism, and toughmindedness), using cross-national samples of twins (England and Australia). The most striking finding was that models that set genetic effects at zero give a very poor fit, and when allowance is made for assortative mating, models that include genetic effects and leave out cultural inheritance give an extremely good fit. Heritabilities were in the range of about .60.

In response to the Martin et al. (1986) study, we explored the role of genetic and environmental factors in the expression of religious interests, attitudes, and values, using the MZA and DZA data bases as well as relevant data from the Minnesota Twin Registry (Lykken, Bouchard, McGue, & Tellegen, 1990). Religiosity was chosen because it was one of the few attitudinal type of constructs that we had measured. Fortuitously the construct was represented in a number of different instruments and thus we had multiple measures. In addition, the heritability of all four religiously oriented items in the Martin et al. (1986) study showed a significant heritability (Divine law, .22; Moral training, .29; Church authority, .29; Bible truth, .25). We thought these were striking results given that they were based on *items* and wondered what the findings might be if measures based on scales were used. Our measures consisted of a Religious Leisure Time Interest scale, a Religious Occupational Interest Scale (both constructed earlier for the Minnesota Twin Registry and included retroactively in the MISTRA project), the Wiggins Religious Fundamentalism scale of the *MMPI*, the Religious Interests scale of the Strong-Campbell Vocational Interests Inventory, and the Religious Values scale of the Allport-Vernon-Lindzey Study of Values. Table 10 shows our results.

The average heritability across the five measures is .47, a figure quite comparable to that found in the personality and ability domains. We were able to show that our measures had sufficiently modest correlations with Verbal, Performance, and Full Scale IQ that the findings could not be explained away. Taken together these three studies make it clear that social scientists will have to discard the a priori assumption that individual differences in religiosity and other social attitudes are free of genetic influence. Serious causal modeling will require data gathered on twins and adoptees as well as on nuclear families.

Job Satisfaction

Personal experience informs us that some coworkers or friends seem dissatisfied across a variety of job circumstances, while other individuals appear satisfied regardless of past and present job histories. Consequently, there is a reasonable possibility that job satisfaction, a variable widely studied by industrial and organizational psychologists, and presumed by default to be environmental in origin, is significantly influenced by genetic factors. To explore this question a measure of job satisfaction was added to the MISTRA project. Since this instrument was added later and was not completed by our younger twins, our sample size is much smaller for these variables than for those previously discussed. The DZA sample was too small to use in this analysis.

Table 10. Intraclass Correlations, Numbers of Pairs of Twins, and Estimated Genetic and Environmental Sources of Variance for Five Measures of Religious Interests, Attitudes, and Values

	Intraclass Correlation		Sources of Variance	
Scale	MZ Twins	DZ Twins	Genetic	Environmental
Reared Together				
Religious Leisure	.60	.30		
Time Interests	(458)	(363)		
Religious Occupational	.41	.19		
Interests	(458)	(363)		
Reared Apart				
Religious Leisure	.39	.04	.47	.53
Time Interests	(32)	(24)		
Religious Occupational	.59	.20	.41	.59
Interests	(31)	(25)		
Wiggins Religious	.55	-.22	.46	.54
Fundamentalism	(50)	(30)		
Strong-Campbell Vocational	.49	.15	.48	.52
Interests Inventory:	(52)	(31)		
Religious Interests				
Allport-Vernon-Lindzey	.55	-.08	.52	.48
Religious Values	(38)	(21)		

Source: Waller, Kojetin, Bouchard, Lykken, & Tellegen, 1990.
Note: Estimates of genetic and environmental influence on the first two variables based on all four groups (MZA, MZT, DZA, & DZT).

We used the short form of the Minnesota Job Satisfaction Questionnaire (MSQ) developed by Weiss, Dawis, England, and Lofquist (1967). Respondents were asked to respond to the job they had held for the longest period of their lives and/or the job that they considered to be their "major job." Housewife was considered a major job and respondents were asked to respond as such (Arvey & Gross, 1977). The number and type of jobs respondents targeted as their major job were wide and diverse, ranging from research chemist to coal miner.

Because it is traditional to measure both intrinsic and extrinsic aspects of job satisfaction, scales for extrinsic, intrinsic, and general satisfaction were formed

Table 11. Intraclass Correlations for Age- and Sex-Adjusted Job Satisfaction and
Job Characteristic Variables (N = 34 MZA Pairs)

Variables	Intraclass Correlation for Age- and Sex-Adjusted Scores
Job Satisfaction	
Intrinsic	**.315**
Extrinsic	.109
General	**.309**
Job Characteristics	
Complexity	**.443**
Motor skill requirements	**.356**
Physical demands	**.338**
Working conditions	-

Source: Arvey, Bouchard, Segal, & Abraham, 1989.
Note: Correlations significant at $p < .05$ are indicated in bold face; intraclass correlations less than zero are not reported.

for each respondent using the MSQ manual as the guide to which items were scored on each scale. On the basis of common sense we predicted that genetic influences would be stronger for intrinsic job satisfaction indicators than for extrinsic job satisfaction variables (Arvey, Bouchard, Segal, & Abraham, 1989). The results for the job satisfaction variables are shown in the top part of Table 11.

The results demonstrate a significant correlation for intrinsic and general satisfaction but not for extrinsic satisfaction. However, the difference between the correlations for intrinsic and extrinsic satisfaction are not significant.

A possible artifact that may have influenced these results is that MZA twins seek out similar jobs, and it is this fact that causes the observed levels of similarity in job satisfaction. To test this hypothesis, each job was assigned several scores derived from the 4th edition of the *Dictionary of Occupational Titles* (U.S. Department of Labor, 1977) by Roos and Treiman (1980). These scores have been used by Gerhart (1987) in developing relatively objective non-self-report based indices of job characteristics.

To explore the issue of active genotype-environment covariance, we first calculated the intraclass correlations using the DOT-derived scores as dependent variables. If there is a genetically based propensity to seek out similar jobs, the heritabilities for these scores should be significant. The results are shown in the bottom part of Table 11. Of the four variables only the intraclass correlation for working conditions was not significant. These results represent evidence that the twins held jobs that were similar in complexity level, motor-skill requirements, and physical demands. These results are also compatible with the hypothesis that there is a genetic component in the seeking out and holding of jobs by individuals.

To assess the question concerning whether the heritabilities obtained for the job satisfaction variables were due, in part, to the propensities of the twins to hold similar jobs, job complexity, motor skills, and physical demand scores were partialed out of the various job satisfaction measures and the intraclass correlations for satisfaction recalculated. Only slight changes in the intraclass correlations were observed. The statistically significant correlations remain significant.

These results suggest that genetic factors may be important for certain facets of job attitudes, and they extend our general findings that genetic factors have a pervasive influence on behavior into a domain not previously explored by behavior geneticists.

Conclusions

The results of our work and that of many others are in good agreement in assigning approximately 50% of the variance in personality, special mental abilities to genetic influences. While our conclusion must be phrased more cautiously because of the small number of studies, our work and that of others suggests that genetic factors will prove to be nearly as important with respect to a very wide range of psychological traits (information-processing skills, social attitudes, job satisfaction, etc.).

We have been able to show that widely accepted environmental explanations of these results fail to provide an explanation of even modest amounts of the individual difference variance. Such findings have profound implications for research on the origins of psychological traits. Genes and environment are regularly confounded in research on individual differences, with genetic effects treated as irrelevant. In their analysis of the mental ability and information-processing data gathered from the twins reared apart, McGue and Bouchard (1989) argued:

> The failure to find non-zero correlations between the socioeconomic characteristics of the parents and the cognitive test performance of their adopted children assessed as adults indicates that, whatever the relevant environmental contributors to a child's cognitive development may be, these factors are unrelated to the educational and socioeconomic status of that child's parents. A corollary conclusion is that non-zero correlations between SES characteristics of a parent and the cognitive abilities of the biological child of that parent (e.g., White, 1982) must reflect a common genetic and not environmental influence.
> *Environmental influences cannot be reliably studied in intact nuclear*

*families where both genetic and environmental factors are contributing
to familial resemblance.*

This is not a new message (Bouchard, 1987a, 1987b; Meehl, 1973, 1978; Plomin & Daniels, 1987; Wilson, 1983; Scarr & McCartney, 1983; Rushton, Fulker, Neale, et al., 1986). Its corollary, however, that most of the literature on socialization and parental antecedents of personality and mental ability development is completely uninterpretable, is widely ignored. Social scientists continue to report and cite correlational data gathered within ordinary families as though it could be interpreted as supporting or refuting substantive environmental theories without even considering the possibility of genetic transmission. In general such studies can only set the groundwork for further more powerful designs. That is, they only demonstrate familiality or the existence of a relationship.

Twin and adoption studies will have to be widely applied in psychological research before psychologists can claim to be generating powerful cumulative knowledge. For the social scientist, these designs are the only methods that allow one to resolve the genetic and environmental sources of familial resemblance. Naïve application of nuclear-family designs will only deter identification of the genetic and environmental factors influencing psychological traits and other important human performances.

References

Allport, G. W. (1935). Attitudes. In C. A. Murchison (Ed.), *A handbook of social psychology* (Vol. 2). New York: Russell & Russell.

Arvey, R. D., Bouchard, T. J., Jr., Segal, N. L., & Abraham, L. M. (1989). Job satisfaction: Environmental and genetic components. *Journal of Applied Psychology, 74*, 187–192.

Arvey, R. D., & Gross, R. H. (1977). Satisfaction levels and correlates of satisfaction in the homemaker job. *Journal of Vocational Behavior, 10*, 13–24.

Bandura, A. (1982). The psychology of chance encounters and lifepaths. *American Psychologist, 36*, 747–755.

Bouchard, T. J., Jr. (1982). [Review of *The intelligence controversy*]. In *American Journal of Psychology, 95*, 346–349.

Bouchard, T. J., Jr. (1983). Do environmental similarities explain the similarity in intelligence of identical twins reared apart? *Intelligence, 7*, 175–184.

Bouchard, T. J., Jr. (1984). Twins reared apart and together: What they tell us about human diversity. In S. Fox (Ed.), *The chemical and biological bases of individuality*. New York: Plenum.

Bouchard, T. J., Jr. (1987a). The hereditarian research program: Triumphs and tribulations. In S. Modgil & C. Modgil (Eds.), *Arthur Jensen: Consensus and controversy*. London: Falmer International.

Bouchard, T. J., Jr. (1987b). Diversity, development and determinism: A report on identical twins reared apart. In M. Amelang (Ed.), *Proceedings of the meetings of the German Psychological Association – 1986*. Heidelberg, Germany.

Bouchard, T. J., Jr. The genetic architecture of human intelligence. (in press). In P. E. Vernon (Ed.), *Biological approaches in the study of human intelligence*. New York: Plenum Publishing Co.

Bouchard, T. J., Jr., Lykken, D. T., McGue, M., Segal, N. L., & Tellegen, A. (1990). Sources of human psychological differences: The Minnesota study of twins reared apart. *Science, 250*, 223–228.

Bouchard, T. J., Jr., & McGue, M. (1990). Genetic and rearing environmental influences on adult personality: An analysis of adopted twins reared apart. *Journal of Personality, 58*, 263–292.

Bouchard, T. J., Jr., & Segal, N. (1985). Environment and IQ. In Wolman, B. J. (Ed.), *Handbook of intelligence: Theories, measurements, and applications* (pp. 391–464). New York: Wiley.

Bouchard, T. J., Jr., Segal, N. L., & Lykken, D. T. (1990). Genetic and environmental influences on special mental abilities in a sample of twins reared apart. *Twin Research, 39*, 193–206.

Bronfenbrenner, U. (1986). Ecology of the family as a context for human development: Research perspectives. *Developmental Psychology, 22*, 723–742.

Carey, G., Goldsmith, H. H., Tellegen, A., & Gottesman, I. I. (1978). Genetics and personality inventories: The limits of replication with twin data. *Behavior Genetics, 8*, 299–313.

Carey, G., & Rice, J. (1983). Genetics and personality temperament: Simplicity or complexity? *Behavior Genetics, 13*, 43–63.

Chipuer, H. M., Rovine, M. J., & Plomin, R. (1990). LISREL modeling: Genetic and environmental influences on IQ revisited. *Intelligence, 14*, 11–29.

Conley, J. J. (1984). The hierarchy of consistency: A review and model of longitudinal findings on adult individual differences in intelligence, personality and self-opinion. *Personality and Individual Differences, 5*, 11–25.

Costa, P. T., & McCrae, R. R. (1987). On the need for longitudinal studies and multiple measures in behavior-genetic studies of adult personality. *Behavioral and Brain Sciences, 10*, 22–23.

DeFries, J. C., Johnson, R. C., Kuse, A. R., McClearn, G. E., Polovina, J., Vandenberg, S. G., & Wilson, J. R. (1979). Familial resemblance for specific cognitive abilities. *Behavior Genetics, 9*, 23–43.

Eaves, L. J., Eysenck, H. J., & Martin, N. G. (1989). *Genes, culture and personality: An empirical approach.* New York: Academic Press.

Ekstrom, R. B., French, J. W., & Harman, H. H. (1976). *Manual for kit of factor-referenced cognitive tests.* Princeton, NJ: Educational Testing Service.

Eysenck, H. J., & Eysenck, S. B. G. (1975). *Manual of the Eysenck Personality Questionnaire.* San Diego, CA: Edits.

Falconer, D. S. (1960). *Introduction to quantitative genetics.* New York: Ronald Press.

Farber, S. (1981). *Identical twins reared apart: A reanalysis.* New York: Basic Books.

Gerhart, B. (1987). How important are dispositional factors as determinants of job satisfaction? Implications for job design and other personnel programs. *Journal of Applied Psychology, 72*, 366–373.

Goldsmith, H. H. (1983). Genetic influences on personality from infancy to adulthood. *Child Development, 54*, 331–335.

Gottesman, I. I., & Shields, J. (1972). *Schizophrenia and genetics: A twin study vantage point.* New York: Academic Press.

Greenwald, A. G. (1989). Why attitudes are important: Defining attitude and attitude theory 20 years later. In A. R. Pratkanis, S. J. Breckler, & A. G. Greenwald (Eds.), *Attitude structure and function.* Hillsdale, NJ: Erlbaum.

Hakstian, A. R., & Cattell, R. B. (1978). Higher-stratum ability structures on a basis of twenty primary mental abilities. *Journal of Educational Psychology, 70*, 657–669.

Holt, R. (1962). Individuality and generalization in the psychology of personality. *Journal of Personality, 30*, 377–404.

Horn, J. M., Plomin, R., & Rosenman, R. (1976). Heritability of personality traits in adult male twins. *Behavior Genetics, 6*, 17–30.

Kamin, L. (1974). *The science and politics of IQ.* New York: Halstead Press.

Lamiell, J. T. (1981). Toward an idiothetic psychology of personality. *American Psychologist, 36*, 276–289.

Langmuir, I. (1943). Science, common sense and decency. *Science, 97*, 1–7.

214   THOMAS J. BOUCHARD, JR.

Loehlin, J. C. (1982). Are personality traits differentially heritable? *Behavior Genetics, 12*, 417–428.
Loehlin, J. C. (1989). Partitioning environmental and genetic contributions to behavioral development. *American Psychologist, 44*, 1285–1292.
Loehlin, J. C., & Nichols, R. C. (1976). *Heredity, environment and personality: A study of 850 sets of twins.* Austin: University of Texas Press.
London, I. D. (1946). Some consequences for history and psychology of Langmuir's concept of convergence and divergence of phenomena. *Psychological Review, 53*, 170–188.
Lykken, D. T. (1982). Research with twins: The concept of emergenesis. *Psychophysiology, 19*, 361–373.
Lykken, D. T., Bouchard, T. J., Jr., McGue, M., & Tellegen, A. (1990). The Minnesota Twin Family Registry: Some initial findings. *Acta Geneticae Medicae et Gemellologiae, 39*, 35–70.
Martin, N. G., Eaves, L. J., Heath, A. C., Jardine, R., Feingold, L. M., & Eysenck, H. J. (1986). Transmission of social attitudes. *Proceedings of the National Academy of Sciences, USA, 83*, 4364–4368.
McGue, M., & Bouchard, T. J., Jr. (1989). Genetic and environmental determinants of information processing and special mental abilities: A twin analysis. In R. J. Sternberg (Ed.), *Advances in the psychology of human intelligence (Vol. 5).*
Meehl, P. E. (1973). *High school yearbooks: A reply to Schwarz.* In P. E. Meehl, *Psychodiagnosis: Selected papers.* Minneapolis: University of Minnesota Press, 1973. (Originally published 1971.)
Meehl, P. E. (1978). Theoretical risks and tabular asterisks: Sir Karl, Sir Ronald, and the slow progress of soft psychology. *Journal of Consulting and Clinical Psychology, 46*, 806–834.
Megargee, E. I. (1972). *The California Psychological Inventory handbook.* San Francisco: Jossey-Bass.
Mischel, W. (1981). *Introduction to personality.* (3rd ed.) New York: Holt, Rinehart and Winston.
Moos, R. H., & Moos, B. S. (1986). *Manual: Family Environment Scale.* Palo Alto: Consulting Psychologists Press.
Mueller, C. W., & Parcell, T. L. (1981). Measures of socioeconomic status: Alternatives and recommendations. *Child Development, 52*, 13–20.
Nichols, R. C. (1978). Twin studies of ability, personality, and interests. *Homo, 29*, 158–173.
Plomin, R. (1989). Environment and genes: Determinants of behavior. *American Psychologist, 44*, 105–111.
Plomin, R. (1990). The role of inheritance in behavior. *Science, 248*, 183–188.
Plomin, R., & Daniels, D. (1987). Why are children in the same family so different from one another? *Behavioral and Brain Sciences, 10*, 1–16.
Posner, M., Boies, S., Eichelman, W., & Taylor, R. (1969). Retention of visual and name codes of single letters. *Journal of Experimental Psychology, 79*, 1–16.
Roos, P. A., & Treiman, D. J. (1980). Worker functions and worker traits for the 1970 U.S. census classification. In A. R. Miller, D. J. Treiman, P. S. Cain, & P. S. Roos (Eds.), *Work, jobs and occupations: A critical review of the Dictionary of Occupational Titles.* (Appendix F), Washington DC: National Academy Press.
Rowe, D. C. (1987). Resolving the person-situation debate: Invitation to an interdisciplinary dialogue. *American Psychologist, 42*, 218–227.
Rushton, J. P., Fulker, D. W., Neale, M. C., Nias, D. K. B., & Eysenck, H. J. (1986). Altruism and aggression: To what extent are individual differences inherited? *Journal of Personality and Social Psychology, 50*, 1192–1198.
Scarr, S., & Carter-Saltzman, L. (1979). Twin method: Defense of a critical assumption. *Behavior Genetics, 9*, 527–542.
Scarr, S., & McCartney, K. (1983). How people make their own environments: A theory of genotype-environment effects. *Child Development, 54*, 424–435.

Scarr, S., & Weinberg, R. A. (1981). The transmission of authoritarianism in families: Genetic resemblance in socio-political attitudes. In S. Scarr (Ed.), *Race, social class, and individual differences*. Hillsdale, NJ: Erlbaum.

Shepard R., & Metzler, J. (1971). Mental rotation of three dimensional objects. *Science, 171*, 701–703.

Snyderman, M., & Rothman, S. (1988). *The IQ controversy: The media and public policy*. New Brunswick, NJ: Transaction Books.

Stassen, H. H., Lykken, D. T., & Bomben, G. (1988). The within-pair EEG similarity of twins reared apart. *European Archives of Psychiatry and Neurological Science, 237*, 244-252.

Stassen, H. H., Lykken, D. T., Propping, P., & Bomben, G. (1988). Genetic determination of the human EEG: Survey of recent results on twins reared together and apart. *Human Genetics, 80*, 165–176.

Sternberg, S. (1969). The discovery of processing stages: Extension of Donders' method. *Acta Psychologica, 30*, 276–315.

Taylor, H. F. (1980). *The IQ game: A methodological inquiry into the heredity-environment controversy*. New Brunwick, NJ: Rutgers University Press.

Tellegen, A. (1978/1982). *Brief manual for the Differential Personality Questionnaire*. Unpublished manuscript, University of Minnesota, Minneapolis.

Tellegen, A., Lykken, D. T., Bouchard, T. J., Jr., Wilcox, K. J., Segal, N. L., & Rich, S. (1988). Personality similarity in twins reared apart and together. *Journal of Personality and Social Psychology, 54*, 1031–1039.

U.S. Department of Labor (1977). *Dictionary of Occupational Titles*. (4th ed.) Washington, DC: U.S. Government Printing Office.

Wahl, O.F. (1976). Monozygotic twins discordant for schizophrenia. *Psychological Bulletin, 83*, 91–106.

Weiss, D. J., Dawis, R. V., England, G. W., & Lofquist, L. H. (1967). *Manual for the Minnesota Satisfaction Questionnaire*.

Weller, N. G., Kojetin, B. A., Bouchard, T. J., Jr., Lykken, D. T., & Tellegen, A. (1990). Genetic and environmental influence on religious interests, attitudes, and values: A study of twins reared apart and together. *Psychological* Science, *1*, 138–142.

White, K. R. (1982). The relation between socioeconomic status and academic achievement. *Psychological Bulletin, 91*, 461–481.

Wilson, R. S. (1983). The Louisville twin study: Developmental synchronies in behavior. *Child Development, 54*, 298–316.

Zonderman, A. B. (1982). Differential heritability and consistency: A reanalysis of the NMSQT CPI data. *Behavior Genetics, 12*, 193–208.

Methodology

Construct Validity: History and Application to Developmental Psychopathology

Judy Garber and Zvi Strassberg

Among Meehl's most important contributions to the field of psychology were his early works on defining and validating hypothetical constructs. The impact of this work is evident in the plethora of references in the literature to the now classic paper by Cronbach and Meehl (1955). In fact, the notion of construct validity has become so accepted that scores of additional articles exist that refer to construct validity without any longer citing the original references (American Psychological Association, 1954; Cronbach & Meehl, 1955).

Despite the current recognition of the importance of construct validity in psychology, it has undergone several modifications and has not been without controversy (see Bechtoldt, 1959). One purpose of this chapter is to briefly review the history of the development and evolution of construct validity. The second goal is to suggest how construct validity can contribute to progress in the field of developmental psychopathology. Developmental psychopathology is a relatively new field of inquiry that is concerned with the interface between developmental psychology and childhood and adult psychopathology (Cicchetti, in press; Sroufe & Rutter, 1984; Zigler & Glick, 1986). In particular, we propose here a general theoretical framework or "nomological network" (Cronbach & Meehl, 1955) for studying hypothetical constructs in the field of developmental psychopathology.

The History of Construct Validity

Definition of a Construct

In 1948 MacCorquodale and Meehl published an important paper in which they outlined the distinction between hypothetical constructs and intervening variables, suggesting that these concepts differed in their degree of abstraction from the data. Whereas intervening variables are directly observable and reducible to empirical laws (the authors cite Hull's notion of habit strength as an exemplar), hypothetical constructs refer to processes or entities that are not directly observed. Subsequently, Cronbach and Meehl (1955) defined a construct as: ''some postulated attribute of people, assumed to be reflected in test performance'' (p. 283).

Thus, constructs are basically unobservable and only indirectly measurable. Their existence is inferred through the relations between variables that can be observed and the performance on the tests that presumably measure the hypothesized entity. Examples of constructs are traits, attributes, disorders, or any quality that is not easily ''operationally defined.''

Construct Validity

The concept of construct validity (originally referred to as congruent validity in the preliminary report of APA, 1952) was first proposed by a subset (P. E. Meehl and R. C. Challman) of the larger committee that was formulating the Technical Recommendations for Psychological Tests and Diagnostic Techniques of the American Psychological Association (1954). Construct validity was developed further by two members of the committee in their now classic paper entitled: ''Construct validity in psychological tests'' (Cronbach & Meehl, 1955).

Meehl (1959) asserted that because hypothetical constructs are not easily defined operationally, and since there is no psychological analogue to the pathologist's report in medicine, the process of construct validation is the recommended strategy for studying the nature of a psychological construct. According to the Technical Report (APA, 1954):

> Construct validity is ordinarily studied when the tester has no definitive criterion measure of the quality with which he is concerned, and must use indirect measures to validate the theory. . . . The problem of construct validation becomes especially acute in the clinical field since for many of the constructs dealt with it is not a question of finding an imperfect criterion but of finding any criterion at all. (pp. 14–15)

Cronbach and Meehl (1955) stated that:

> *Construct validation* is involved whenever a test is to be interpreted as a measure of some attribute or quality which is not ''operationally defined.'' The problem faced by the investigator is, ''What constructs account for variance in test performance?'' Construct validity is not to be identified solely by particular investigative procedures, but by the orientation of the investigator. (p. 282)

Thus, construct validation is to be invoked whenever no criterion or universe of content is accepted as being entirely adequate to define the entity being measured.

Both the Technical Recommendations (1954) and Cronbach and Meehl (1955) asserted that construct validity was just one of four types of validity, with the other three being: content, concurrent, and predictive. Loevinger (1957), however, argued that: "Since predictive and content validities are all essentially *ad hoc*, construct validity is the whole of validity from a scientific point of view" (p. 636). Meehl himself (personal communication, February, 1988) agrees with Loevinger's assessment that the other types of validity really are part of the construct validation process, and he considers this point to be one of the major contributions of Loevinger's (1957) paper.

Despite the generally widespread acceptance of the importance of construct validity (e.g., Jessor & Hammond, 1957), it was not without its critics. Positivists (Gaylord & Stunkel, 1954; Spiker & McCandless, 1954) worried that constructs may be a refuge for the soft-headed or fuzzy-minded, rather than sufficiently relying upon data. Others expressed concern that construct validity would lead to the reification of test scores and traits (Bechtoldt, 1959; Campbell, 1960).

Bechtoldt (1959), one of the most outspoken critics of construct validity, argued that: "The 'constructs' of construct validity appear to be 'vague,' open, and 'not explicitly defined' as a matter of principle rather than as a matter of ignorance" (p. 622). Bechtoldt instead favored an empirically oriented methodology that used explicit operational definitions of variables.

In response to Bechtoldt, Campbell (1960) argued that construct validity did not in any way represent the abandonment of operationalism, and that "the general spirit of operationalism . . . is certainly compatible with construct validity" (pp. 550-551). According to Campbell, construct validity is necessary "where verifying operations against which to check tests are not automatically available" (p. 550).

In apparent anticipation of subsequent critiques such as the one by Bechtoldt (1959), Cronbach and Meehl (1955) stated, after outlining the fundamental principles of the nomological net, that:

> The preceding guide rules should reassure the "toughminded," who fear that allowing construct validation opens the door to nonconfirmable test claims. *The answer is that unless the network makes contact with observations, and exhibits explicit public steps of inference, construct validation cannot be claimed.* An admissible psychological construct must be behavior-relevant. (p. 290)

They clearly argued that although there may not always be one explicit criterion against which to validate a construct (particularly for those entities found in personality and psychopathology), it still was necessary that at least *some* of the critical components of the nomological net involve observables. Thus, Bechtoldt's primary concern was basically unfounded.

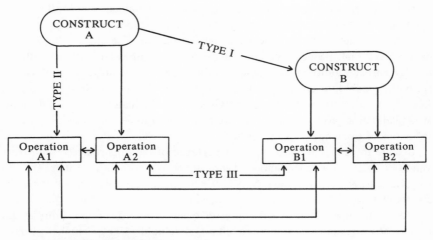

1. Relations within the nomological network.

The Logic of Construct Validity

There were at least three very important notions to come out of the paper by Cronbach and Meehl (1955) including: the nomological network, "bootstrapping," and the implications of negative evidence. Figure 1 presents the basic outline of the nomological network as described by Meehl in many graduate seminars, although not explicitly drawn in the original article.

According to Cronbach and Meehl (1955), a nomological network is an interlocking system of lawful relations that comprise a theory, and this network consists of both theoretical constructs and observable properties or operations. There are essentially two kinds of variables (constructs and operations) and three types of relations between them.

The Type I relations are between the theoretical constructs. This is the substantive component of the nomological net and is concerned with the question of how the construct of interest (A) is hypothesized to relate to another construct(s) (B). For example, according to the reformulated learned helplessness theory of depression (Abramson, Seligman, & Teasdale, 1978; Abramson, Garber, & Seligman, 1980), the construct of depression is hypothesized to be significantly associated with another construct known as attributional style.

Type II relations are between the theoretical construct and the operationalization of that construct. Here we are concerned with how to actually define and measure the entity of interest, and with the psychometric adequacy of the measure. Since, almost by definition, there is no *one* criterion measure, it becomes necessary to use multiple measures that will converge in order to approximate the underlying construct or trait of interest.

Hence, in the depression and attribution example noted above, we would want to use multiple measures of the construct (e.g., depression) including self-report, clinician ratings, and significant others' report. Similarly, multiple measures of the construct to which it is hypothesized to be associated (e.g., attributions) are also needed. This could include measures such as responses to hypothetical stories, attributions obtained in response to an actual event, and ratings of attributions of transcribed conversations.

Finally, Type III relations are concerned with the actual empirical associations found between the operations of the various constructs within the nomological net. The nature and degree of association between these operations comprise the test of the hypotheses represented by the Type III relations. Thus, following the earlier example, the learned helplessness model predicts (Abramson et al., 1978; 1980) that depression is associated with a particular attributional style, and thus, the measures (or operationalizations of the constructs) of depression and attributions should correlate significantly.

The nomological network for any particular construct, of course, can and should be elaborated to describe its hypothesized relation with multiple other constructs. The number of connections within the theoretical net expands as more knowledge is acquired about the construct. Moreover, the theory must grow to explain these newly observed relations. Thus, the enrichment of the network and the accompanying theory is justified if the hypothesized relations between the constructs is confirmed by observation of the Type III relations.

A second important concept to come out of the Cronbach and Meehl (1955) paper was "bootstrapping." Here the idea was that early in the validation process, it is necessary to begin with relatively fallible measures of the construct. By examining the empirical (Type III) relations among the measures, we may discover that the original fallible measure covaries with other indexes that possess better psychometric properties. It is then possible to abandon the less adequate initial measure for the newly discovered more adequate one. Cronbach and Meehl (1955) described this process as "lifting oneself up by one's bootstrap," and it is a partial answer to the frequently noted problem of not having a clear criterion against which to validate one's measure and construct.

The elegance of the bootstrapping notion is that it suggests an approach to studying some of the more difficult but also more interesting concepts in personality and psychopathology that could not be operationally defined. Bootstrapping provides a means to gradually develop an operationalized criterion through a series of successive approximations within the context of a larger theoretical framework.

Finally, the third very important contribution of Cronbach and Meehl (1955) was their suggestion for interpreting negative findings. They proposed that when one's predictions and data are discordant, this could be due to: (a) errors in the Type I relations, i.e., that the theory is incorrect; (b) errors in the Type II relations, i.e., that the measures are not adequate operationalizations of the construct; or (c) errors in the design and/or execution of the empirical tests of the Type III relations. Of course, any particular failure to support one's hypotheses empirically could be a function of any one or a combination of these factors.

Conceptual and Empirical Extensions of Construct Validity

Several important papers since the original article by Cronbach and Meehl (1955) have advanced the notion of construct validity even further. Two articles, for example, expanded on the role of theory in the construct validation process. Campbell (1960) suggested that construct validity could be divided into *trait validity* and *nomological validity*, the latter describing constructs that were embedded particularly in theory. Jessor and Hammond (1957) suggested that theory should play a role not only in the validation of a test, but also in the process of developing the test in the first place. More recently, Embretson (1983) presented the notion of construct modeling in which a distinction is made between construct representation and nomothetic span. The former is concerned with the theoretical mechanisms that underlie actual test responses, whereas the latter refers to the network of relations of the particular test to other measures.

As noted earlier, one of the most important conceptual extensions of construct validity was presented by Loevinger (1957), who proposed that the other types of validity (e.g., content and criterion) were really supporting evidence of construct validity. She also suggested three mutually exclusive, exhaustive, and mandatory components of construct validity: substantive, structural, and external. The substantive component expanded upon content validity; the structural component involved concepts such as homogeneity and functional unity of the construct itself; and the external component was concerned with nontest behavior and incorporated concurrent and predictive validity. Loevinger argued that for construct validation to be approximated, all of these components must be incorporated into the nomological net and resulting empirical tests.

Finally, the most important advance with respect to the actual methodologies used to validate a construct was the classic article by Campbell and Fiske (1959) entitled "Convergent and Discriminant Validation by the Multitrait-Multimethod Matrix." They proposed using a multitrait-multimethod matrix to examine the *true* relation between constructs in the presence of both method variance and random error. In addition, they described the pattern of correlations one would need to find between measures of the construct of interest as well as between measures of other constructs in order to demonstrate validity.

Whereas the Campbell and Fiske proposal for analysis of the multitrait-multimethod matrix has been quite influential, other researchers have noted problems with this approach. They include the necessity of making validity judgments that are qualitative, since Campbell and Fiske provided no method for quantifying the degree to which the criteria are met (Jackson, 1969), the desirability of separating method variance from random error due to potential unreliability of individual measures (Jackson, 1969), and the problem of intercorrelated trait and method factors (Althauser & Heberlein, 1970).

Recently, confirmatory factor analysis (Joreskog, 1974) has been suggested as a more interpretable alternative to the original multitrait-multimethod approach (e.g., Cole, 1987; Marsh & Hocevar, 1988; Schmitt & Stults, 1986). Confirmatory factor analysis (CFA) is particularly preferred to the qualitative judgments of the multitrait-multimethod approach because it allows for straightforward statistical tests of hypotheses and goodness-of-fit indexes that follow from most validation designs. In addition, explaining multitrait-multimethod matrixes on the basis of underlying factors solves the problem of differential reliability of measurement.

One problem not solved by the application of CFA to multitrait-multimethod matrixes is that of trait-method interactions. Marsh and Hocevar (1988) recommended the application of hierarchical confirmatory factor analysis to address this issue. This approach allows testing for increments in improvement of fit between data and hypothesized models of relations among variables as a function of inclusion of method effects (for further discussion, see Marsh & Hocevar, 1988; Widaman, 1985). Thus, the classic multitrait-multimethod matrix approach and the newer method of confirmatory factor analysis are important procedures that can be applied to validating constructs and their operations.

In sum, the concept of construct validity has exerted a substantial influence on the field of psychology. Despite some initial criticisms, construct validity continues to be an important perspective, particularly with regard to the more difficult to define constructs found in personality and psychopathology. The applicability of a construct validity approach to developmental psychopathology is discussed next.

Construct Validity and Developmental Psychopathology

Developmental psychopathology involves the integration of developmental psychology with the study of psychopathology across the life span. Its central focus is on the continuities and discontinuities of adaptation and maladaptation over the course of development, and between normality and deviation (Achenbach, 1978; Cicchetti, in press; Rutter & Garmezy, 1983; Sroufe & Rutter, 1984). A primary goal of the developmental perspective is to identify the mechanisms and processes underlying the various forms of psychopathology from childhood through adulthood. In addition, developmental psychopathology is concerned with how the study of atypical populations contributes to our understanding of normative development, and similarly how an understanding of normative development is central to the study of atypical outcomes.

The developmental perspective is not itself a theory; rather, it is a research strategy for addressing these various issues (Rutter, 1986, 1988). The purpose of the remainder of this chapter is to expand upon this developmental perspective by integrating it with a construct validation approach to developmental psychopathology. We suggest here a general framework that synthesizes psychopathological, psychometric, and developmental theories in order to study psychopathology over the course of development.

Dimensional versus Categorical Constructs

It should be emphasized from the beginning that a construct validation approach to developmental psychopathology does not necessarily restrict one to either dimensional or categorical constructs. Although traditionally the psychometric approach of construct validity has focused on dimensions or traits (e.g., egocentrism, neuroticism), whereas the classification approach to psychopathology has focused on discrete nosologic disorders (e.g., schizophrenia, autism), construct validity is not inherently dimensional, nor is classification necessarily categorical.

Most early (e.g., Hewitt & Jenkins, 1946; Peterson, 1961) as well as more recent studies of childhood psychopathology (e.g., Achenbach & Edelbrock, 1978, 1981; Quay, 1979) have used factor analysis to derive dimensions of psychopathology, in contrast to the current DSM-III-R system that emphasizes distinct nosologic disorders. Although there is no intrinsic contradiction between these approaches, there continues to be some question about whether childhood psychopathology is better characterized by dimensions or distinct categories (Achenbach, 1985; 1988). It is beyond the scope of this chapter to present all the various sides of this debate. We suggest, however, that this controversy does not need to constrain the process of construct validation. Rather, the question of whether a particular psychopathological construct falls along a continuum of severity or is a qualitatively distinct entity is a central issue for developmental psychopathologists that can be explored as part of the construct validation process.

Thus, the same general validation strategies can be used whether the construct is hypothesized to be dimensional or categorical. For example, Patterson (1986; Patterson & Bank, 1987) has used construct validation as a framework for studying the dimensions of aggression and antisocial behavior, and Garber (1987) has used construct validation to study the nosologic disorder of depression in children. Hence, whether the construct is derived according to a nosologic or a multivariate paradigm (Achenbach, 1988), the process of validation remains essentially the same. Construct validation involves investigating the Type I, Type II, and Type III relations within a nomological network. The components of this validation process with regard to developmental psychopathological constructs are outlined in the sections to follow.

The Framework for the Nomological Network

The basic framework for validating a psychopathological construct is derived from classic psychopathology theory (Kraepelin, 1883; Meehl, 1977; Rutter, 1965; Spitzer & Williams, 1985) and includes: manifest symptomatology, course, prognosis, response to treatment, and etiology. There really is no one "correct" or "natural" place to begin the construct validation process with respect to these various components of psychopathology. Whereas some have argued for beginning with treatment response (Andreasen, 1981; Fish, 1969; Gittleman-Klein, Spitzer, & Cantwell, 1978; Lehmann, 1977; Roth, 1978), the debate really has been between descriptive versus etiological approaches.

Although an ultimate goal of classification may be to incorporate etiologic information into the definition of a construct (Rutter, 1965), the identification of the clinical symptomatology is considered to be the "*logically necessary first step*" (Ni Bhrolchain, 1981; p. 161) in the process of validating a psychopathological construct. This perspective is consistent with Cattell's (1940) dictum that nosology necessarily precedes etiology, and Eysenck's (1953) view that classificatory knowledge precedes the identification of causes. Thus, precision in description is a prerequisite for studying the prevalence, course, prognosis, treatment, and etiology of a construct.

It is important to emphasize that the construct validation process is an iterative one in which the original fallible indicators that are based on a tentative theory are continually revised in response to new data and theory modification. For example, the construct of mental retardation, once thought to be a single diagnostic entity, was divided into a number of specific subtypes as a result of research demonstrating that there were several distinct biological abnormalities associated with it (Spitzer & Williams, 1985). Here, new data concerning etiology was informative for description and classification.

Meehl (1959, 1977) has suggested that despite the historical emphasis on syndrome description, "the reality of a diagnostic concept lies in its correspondence to an inner state, of which the symptoms or test scores are fallible indicators" (p. 115). Indeed, the identification of a specific etiology is the strongest validation of any nosological entity (Andreasen, 1981). Thus, the usual process of validating a psychopathological construct begins with the description of the clinical symptomatology and proceeds with the collection of data that support its internal validity (Loevinger, 1957; Skinner, 1981). Evidence is next gathered with regard to external validity, including biological, familial, and/or psychological factors, in order to identify the specific etiology underlying the construct. This continuous process of bootstrapping one's way to a more accurate measure, definition, and theory is the heart of construct validity.

Internal Validity

The essential steps in the process of validating a construct are: (a) the identification of a hypothetical construct of interest (e.g., aggression, anxiety, depression); (b) the formulation of a theory about the construct that defines the "nomological network"; (c) the development of methods or measures that serve as indexes of the construct; and (d) a "bootstrapping" methodology for test construction and validation (Cronbach & Meehl, 1955). This process can be subdivided further into internal and external validity.

The *internal validation* component of construct validity involves defining the construct, selecting the fallible indicators that serve as the operationalization of the construct, choosing the appropriate statistical techniques for deriving it, and evaluating its internal properties (e.g., reliability, homogeneity). Loevinger (1957) named the first part involving construct definition and item selection the substantive component, and the second part consisting of the statistical and evaluative portion of construct validity the structural component.

Thus, the internal validation phase includes defining, measuring, statistically analyzing, and evaluating the construct and its operations. We distinguish here between defining and measuring the construct. Whereas the definition is determined by one's theory about what symptoms and behaviors comprise the psychopathology, the measurement step is concerned with the operationalization of this definition. Spitzer and Williams (1985) similarly argued that we need to evaluate the validity of a diagnostic scheme separately from the validity of the assessment procedures used to arrive at a diagnosis. The remaining discussion outlines the steps in validating a psychopathological construct and highlights the developmental issues that arise at each phase of the process.

Defining the Construct

In attempting to define a psychopathological construct developmentally, we are guided by the "normative-developmental" perspective that is concerned with the changes in behavior over time and age-norms against which individual behaviors can be compared (Edelbrock, 1984). This perspective underscores the two central continuity questions that need to be addressed in the process of defining and validating a psychopathological construct from a developmental perspective: (a) To what extent is there continuity in the construct over the course of development? and (b) Where along the continuum from normality to pathology does the construct of interest fall?

The central issue with regard to temporal continuity for the definition of the construct is: To what extent do the symptoms that define the disorder change as a function of development? Which among the various multiple domains of functioning (e.g., biological, social, cognitive) are involved in defining the construct, and to what extent do the specific manifestations of symptoms within and across these domains change with development (Cicchetti & Sroufe, 1978)? Moreover, what is it that is continuous: the specific behaviors, general areas of functioning, or the even more general notion of patterns of adaptation to the salient developmental tasks of each age (Sroufe, 1979)?

The developmental perspective (e.g., Cicchetti & Schneider-Rosen, 1986; Rutter, 1986, 1988) suggests that it does not make sense to assume behavioral isomorphism across age or to simply rely on the same defining criteria from childhood to adulthood. Rather, we should expect age-related differences in the clinical manifestation of the symptoms because developmental advances in cognitive structures and functions especially will influence the manner in which children experience, interpret, and express emotions and other behavioral symptoms at different ages.

There are at least four ways to conceptualize the temporal continuity issue that incorporates the important distinction made in DSM-III-R (APA, 1987) between essential core versus associated symptoms: (a) the essential symptoms that define the construct are the same throughout childhood and adulthood; (b) the essential symptoms are the same, but the associated symptoms vary as a function of development; (c) the essential features are the same, although their specific manifestation varies with development; or (d) the essential features are somewhat different as a function of development.

The advantage of the first view is that it allows for direct comparisons between adult and child phenomena. The disadvantage of this approach is that it basically ignores the possible impact of development upon the clinical manifestations of the symptoms. Moreover, the demand for symptomatic isomorphism across ages may lead us to focus on the very small subset of children for whom this is true while missing a potentially larger group of children who display developmental variants of the symptomatology.

The second alternative is similar to the first except that it allows for age-specific variations in some of the associated symptoms that may covary with the syndrome at different ages (Cantwell, 1983). This is an important and interesting possibility that is relevant to the critical issue of comorbidity (e.g., Achenbach, 1988; Garber, 1987, Kovacs et al., 1984). According to this alternative, the original adult-oriented criteria would remain the same for children and adults, and, therefore, the same problems noted above are relevant here. In both instances, a lack of correspondence between the symptomatology of children and adults would cause one to question the assumption of either the continuity or the validity of the construct during childhood.

The third perspective, that the essential symptoms of the adult and child forms of the construct are the same although their clinical manifestation may vary as a function of development, is more compatible with the developmental perspective. Developmental psychopathologists (e.g., Cicchetti & Schneider-Rosen, 1986; Rutter, 1986) suggest that it is unrealistic to expect children to manifest the same core symptoms in precisely the same manner as adults since children are clearly at a different point with respect to their cognitive, linguistic, social, and affective development. They suggest, instead, that we should look for patterns of adaptation to the salient developmental tasks rather than looking for isomorphism in discrete symptoms and behaviors across development (Sroufe, 1979; Sroufe & Rutter, 1984).

This alternative requires that we broaden our definitions of the symptoms to reflect these developmental differences and that we begin to map the developmental course of symptoms over time. For example, if a young child is cognitively capable of experiencing low self-esteem, guilt, or hopelessness, what is the developmentally appropriate manner in which these symptoms are expressed? What does low self-esteem look like in a 4-year-old (see Vondra, Barnett, & Cicchetti, 1988 for a relevant discussion)? How would we know if a 6-year-old felt hopeless? Our definitions of the construct and the symptoms that comprise it should reflect these developmental differences in symptom manifestations. Moreover, these developmental considerations should be reflected in the assessment process as well.

It may be that the general areas of dysfunction that define a disorder (e.g., affective, cognitive, vegetative, and behavioral) are similar for children, adolescents, and adults, but the specific symptoms and behaviors that characterize these areas of dysfunction vary with age. Therefore, the definitions of the symptoms or domains of dysfunction should be broad enough to include age-appropriate variations. For instance, whereas anhedonia in adults typically is defined in terms of loss of interest in sex, in one's job, or in typical leisure activities, for children, anhedonia is more appropriately defined in terms of sustained periods of boredom, loss of interest in school, or decreased play with usual toys and games.

A second example is that the DSM-III-R criteria for depression now include nonverbal indications of sadness by children, rather than requiring that they explicitly verbalize the dysphoric mood. Both clinical experience and empirical data (e.g., Kazdin, Sherick, Esveldt-Dawson, & Rancurello, 1985; Poznanski, Mokros, Grossman, & Freeman, 1985) support the view that nonverbal expressions of sadness in young children are more common than are verbalizations of sad affect, and these nonverbal behaviors tend to be positively associated with other features of the syndrome. Thus, nonverbal expressions of sad affect are considered to be a developmentally appropriate manifestation of the symptom of dysphoria.

A potential problem for this view is how to decide when a symptom is a developmental equivalent of the adult criterion and when it is simply a different symptom altogether. Rutter (1986) warned that in our attempt to define the criteria in a more developmentally appropriate way, we run the risk of changing the meaning of the symptoms. He cites as an example the study by Chambers et al. (1985) in which they assessed the quality of depressive mood by asking about feelings of loneliness or of missing someone. Rutter asks with some skepticism to what extent are loneliness and depression really synonymous? Thus, although it makes sense from a developmental perspective that the actual displays of the defining symptomatology may vary with age, the equivalence of these different symptom manifestions across ages needs to be demonstrated empirically as part of the construct validation process.

The final view that the essential symptoms of adult and childhood forms of a disorder vary as a function of development is also compatible with the developmental perspective. According to this perspective, there may be additional symptoms that are age-specific manifestations of the core syndrome that are not included among the adult criteria, and there may be some adult criteria that are age-inappropriate given children's less well-developed cognitive and physiological systems.

Thus, for example, one may not expect to find among younger children symptoms of depression such as guilt or hopelessness that require a higher level of cognitive functioning, and therefore, these symptoms may need to be eliminated from the defining criteria for this age group. On the other hand, there may be other symptoms not typically associated with the adult syndrome that consistently covary with the symptoms in childhood, which, therefore, should be considered for inclusion among the essential symptoms for children. Ryan et al. (1987), for example, found that somatic complaints, social withdrawal, and hopelessness were very common among children and adolescents meeting the DSM-III-R criteria for Major Depressive Disorder (MDD), and, therefore, they proposed that these symptoms be considered for inclusion in the diagnostic criteria for MDD for this age group.

It would follow from this perspective that a more complex set of diagnostic rules may be needed to accommodate different base rates and different manifestations of symptoms over the course of development. Either a different combination of criteria may be needed (Carlson & Garber, 1986), or possibly a different minimum cutoff of symptoms for children and adolescents may be appropriate (Ryan et al., 1987).

An important question that this fourth perspective raises is how much overlap in manifest symptomatology is necessary to consider it the same construct? Although there is no clear answer to this question, the prototype view of categorization (Cantor, Smith, French, & Mezzich, 1980; Horowitz, Wright, Lowenstein, & Parad, 1981) or the "ideal types" in medicine (Blashfield, 1984; Kraepelin, 1883) may provide some direction. According to these views, a prototype or ideal type is "representative" of the construct. Features are neither necessary nor sufficient. Membership in the category is evaluated in terms of the overlap between the particular instance and the construct prototype. That is, the greater the number of representative features of the construct prototype presented by the individual, the greater the probability that the manifest symptomatology will be considered to be an instance of the construct.

The prototype or ideal type notion may be particularly useful for resolving the continuity question with regard to the description of psychopathological constructs over the course of development. Rather than there being a specific set of necessary and sufficient defining features that both children and adults must exhibit to be judged as manifesting the construct of interest, there could be a modal prototype from which there would be age-dependent variations. The degree of similarity between presenting features and the prototype could be judged in terms of the extent of overlap of those features with the category prototype.

Achenbach (1988) similarly has suggested that prototypes can be derived empirically through multivariate analysis (e.g., factor analysis) of features scored in a sample of children. Then the similarity between the individual case and the empirically derived prototype can be computed by examining the extent to which the prototype features are present. Such a prototypic approach could facilitate the recognition of developmental differences in the construct.

Thus, there are at least four different approaches to defining a psychopathological construct with regard to the temporal continuity issue. This continuity issue is relevant not only to differences between childhood and adult manifestations of symptoms, but also to changes in the symptoms over the course of the life span. We know, for example, that the topography of aggression tends to change with development despite the fact that aggression is known to be one of the more stable forms of behavior (Parke & Slaby, 1983). Other syndromes also are known to change with regard to which symptoms or combination of symptoms are most salient during a particular age period. For example, young children with Attention Deficit Hyperactivity Disorder are more likely to manifest problems of overactivity than are older children with ADHD, although the attentional problems seem to be continuous throughout the childhood and adolescent years (Gittelman, Mannuzza, Schenker, & Bonagura, 1985). These developmental differences in the topography, variety, and frequency of symptoms over the course of childhood are particularly relevant to the temporal continuity issue and the problem of construct definition.

The second continuity issue concerns the link between normality and pathology, and it too has implications for construct definition. Here, one needs to be concerned with such questions as: What are the parameters by which a particular behavior is judged to be deviant? What are the criteria for "caseness" (Beardslee, Klerman, Keller, Lavori, & Podorefsky, 1985; Eisenberg, 1986)? What are the base rates of symptoms and syndromes at various ages, and to what extent do these symptoms reflect age-appropriate reactions to the salient tasks of development? Given that all children at some time manifest some behaviors and attributes that are more or less abnormal, and that various problems are age-specific and dissipate over time (MacFarlane, Allen, & Honzik, 1954; Thomas,

Chess, & Birch, 1968), how do we decide that a particular symptom or set of symptoms should be included as part of the definition of a psychopathological construct?

The various parameters that typically are considered in differentiating normal variations in behavior from qualitatively distinct deviations include the intensity, duration, frequency, number, and particular combination of symptoms (Garber, 1984). To make judgments about these various parameters, it is, of course, first necessary to know about the normal course and development of the various symptoms of interest.

Although there is an increasing recognition of the need to consider these developmental parameters in definitions of childhood psychopathology (e.g., Edelbrock, 1984), the current DSM-III-R system is still rather limited in this regard. When an attempt is made to include developmental factors, the guidelines tend to be vague. For example, for Oppositional Defiant Disorder the oppositional and defiant behavior must be "*more common* than that seen in other people of the same mental age" (p. 56). For Conduct Disorder, a "*persistent pattern* of conduct in which the basic rights of others and major *age-appropriate* societal norms or rules are violated" (p. 53) is required. For Attention Deficit Hyperactivity Disorder, the defining behaviors must be "*considerably more frequent* than that of most people of the same mental age" (p. 52). Although DSM-III-R recognizes that the defining behaviors need to be more common, persistent, or frequent than among others of the same age, *how much* more common, persistent, or frequent is not articulated. Therefore, one of the goals of defining and validating constructs in developmental psychopathology is to more precisely specify these parameters based upon our knowledge of normal development.

Some of the best work in this area has been done by Achenbach and Edelbrock (1981), who have argued for, and produced age- and gender-specific norms for childhood behavior problems. They have demonstrated that there are important differences in the patterning of symptoms and clustering of children as a function of age and sex. Their work serves as an important model of a construct validity approach to developmental psychopathology.

Finally, there are at least two additional questions that should be addressed in attempting to define a psychopathological construct: To what extent is the child dysfunctional as a result of manifesting the particular pattern of symptoms? And, to what extent are the problem behaviors situation-specific versus cross-situational? The question of dysfunction requires that the definition of the construct include some description of the areas of functioning that are expected to be affected by the syndrome (e.g., academic, social, etc.), and specification of the extent to which dysfunction is a necessary part of the definition of the construct itself. For example, there is now some evidence that what really differentiates children with "normal" anxiety from children with an Overanxious Disorder is the extent to which the child is dysfunctional as a result of the anxiety-provoking concerns (Last, Hersen, Kazdin, Finkelstein, & Strauss, 1987). Thus, the concept of dysfunction may eventually need to be incorporated into the defining criteria of Overanxious Disorder as more such empirical evidence is gathered. In DSM-III-R, the concept of dysfunction currently is not explicitly included among the criteria for most disorders (see Schizophrenia and Phobias, for exceptions); instead, the notion of dysfunction is relegated to a separate axis (V) that is neither consistently used nor particularly well validated.

The question of situation-specificity versus cross-situational problems is important not only for defining a psychopathological construct, but also because it has implications for the kind of assessment strategy required. If one's theory about a construct is that the behaviors that characterize it are pervasive across situations, then it will be necessary to obtain information about the child in a variety of settings (e.g., home and school), and one would expect there to be at least a moderate degree of congruence between the child's behaviors across these diverse settings. Thus, for those constructs that are assumed to be cross-situational, it will be more important to find agreement among informants (e.g., parents and teachers) than it will be for those constructs defined as being more situation-specific.

In sum, the first phase of validating a psychopathological construct is the selection of the criteria that define it. The developmental perspective requires that questions of the continuity of symptoms over the course of development, the continuity between normal age-appropriate behavior and deviations from the norm, and issues of dysfunction and cross-situationality be addressed in the process of defining a psychopathological construct. Once these basic definitional issues are resolved, one can move to the phase of operationalizing the construct.

Operationalization of the Construct

The operationalization of the construct involves what was described earlier as the Type II relations and is essentially the development of the measurement operations. Although there has been some tendency in the literature to equate the process of test construction itself with construct validity, the original notion of construct validity was intended to address the validation of the theory and the construct underlying the measure (Cronbach & Meehl, 1955) and not simply the development and validation of the measure. Thus, although operationalization is critical, it should be done as part of the larger process of validating the construct and the theory that underlies it.

The developmental issues to consider at the measurement phase of construct validation include: What cognitive and linguistic limitations of children should be considered when developing a measure? Which of the various multiple methods and multiple informants should be used, and how is information from these various sources to be combined to yield the most reliable and valid representation of the underlying construct?

Only in the last decade or so has there been a recognition of the importance of talking directly to children (e.g., Puig-Antich, Chambers, & Tabrizi, 1983). Before this, it was generally assumed that although it may be possible to obtain intrapsychic and conflict-oriented information about children by observing their play, diagnostic data typically were obtained from parents (Cramer, 1980; Simmons, 1981). Recently, however, there has been a burgeoning of self-report measures and interviews with children to obtain their input (Edelbrock & Costello, 1988). With this recognition of the importance of children's own report has come the accompanying awareness of the limitations of children as informants.

Two central issues with respect to children's self-report are: (a) Are they willing to report? and (b) Are they able? There is some evidence that children may be more forthcoming when: (a) they feel comfortable in the assessment situation (Cramer, 1980; Pogul, 1980; Simmons, 1981), (b) there is some rapport with the examiner (Sattler, 1974), (c) the reason for the assessment has been explained to them (Palmer, 1970; Yarrow, 1960), (d) external motivators such as material or verbal rewards are provided (e.g., Gewirtz & Baer, 1958; Risley & Hart, 1968), and (e) they are reassured about the confidentiality of their responses (Nias, 1972). Also the method used to obtain the information from the child may be important. Whereas some children may self-disclose more in a face-to-face interview with an accepting adult, others may feel more comfortable reporting privately on a questionnaire (Brandt, 1958; Metzner & Mann, 1952) or directly into a computer. Finally, individual difference characteristics such as age (Ammons, 1950; Crandall, Crandall, & Katkovsky, 1965; Yarrow, 1960), gender (e.g., Castaneda, McCandless, & Palermo, 1956; Colman, MacKay, & Fidell, 1972), and culture (e.g., Ausubel, 1968; Crandall, et al., 1965; McCandless, 1967) have also been found to be associated differentially with children's willingness to self-disclose. Thus, children's willingness to respond can be affected by *who* does the asking, *how* the questions are asked, *where* the inquiry takes place, *why* they are asked, and their age and gender.

The second factor that affects the quality and validity of the information obtained from children is their *ability* to comprehend and respond to questions. Young children's more limited language comprehension, articulation abilities, and recall skills may reduce the accuracy and utility of the information they provide. In addition, when the questions and response alternatives are complex and ambiguous, the adequacy of the information is compromised even further. For example, children often have difficulty making the subtle distinctions between "never," "sometimes," and "always," or performing the "grammatical gymnastics" required to untangle double negatives (Rie, 1963).

Ambiguous or difficult to comprehend questions are more likely to lead to response sets such as Acquiescence (Eisenman & Townsend, 1970; Fisher, 1967), Extreme Responding (Light, Zax, & Gardiner, 1965; Zax, Gardiner, & Lowy, 1964), and Social Desirability (Crandall et al., 1965). Such response sets have been found to be a particular problem among younger children (Eisenman & Townsend, 1970; Light et al., 1965; White & Harvey, 1965). To circumvent some of these problems, clinicians and researchers (Biber & Lewis, 1949; Furman & Bierman, 1984; Klieger & Walsh, 1967; Yarrow, 1960) have suggested using more concrete stimuli such as pictures and dolls with young children, and to use structured rather than open-ended questions that place fewer demands on the children's cognitive and linguistic abilities.

One of the primary reasons for talking directly to children rather than relying solely on others' reports (e.g., parents, teachers, observers), of course, is to obtain children's own understanding and perception of themselves and their world. However, a variety of developing social-cognitive abilities are required for children to be able to adequately report their perceptions, beliefs, and experiences. These include skills relevant to person perception, social relationships, perspective-taking, and self-perception (Bierman, 1984), as well as the ability to monitor and understand one's inner experiences, to differentiate and label emotional states, and to comprehend the demands of the clinical situation (Kovacs, 1986).

Bierman (1984) further pointed out that it is unrealistic to expect children to be "accurate" in their report of objective information about themselves or their interpersonal relationships. The general trend, of course, is for children's understanding of others, themselves, and the clinical situation to gradually become more abstract, differentiated, and integrated. However, this does not necessarily mean that we should disregard young children's reports. It does mean that the utility and validity of children's reports will need to be evaluated with these limitations in mind.

Given these potential limitations of self-report, information should be obtained from other sources as well. Therefore, the operationalization of a construct from both the developmental and construct validation perspectives requires a multiaxial approach (Achenbach, McConaughy, & Howell, 1987) in which multiple methods and multiple measures are used. Since no single measurement operation defines a construct, a network of operations should be used (Cronbach & Meehl, 1955). The importance of multivariate assessment for construct validity has been outlined further by Campbell and Fiske (1959) and later in the various conceptual and methodological elaborations of the multitrait-multimethod approach that followed (e.g., confirmatory factor analysis, structural equation modeling).

There also are several recent books (e.g., Ollendick & Hersen, 1984; Rutter, Tuma, & Lann, 1988) and articles (e.g., Achenbach et al., 1987; Kazdin, 1987) that describe both the merits and problems of using multiple informants and multiple measures of child psychopathology. Although it is beyond the scope of this chapter to enumerate these issues in detail, at least three points should be emphasized here. The critical issues concern decisions about which measures to include in the nomological network and how to integrate the information once it is obtained (Patterson & Bank, 1987).

First, validation of a psychopathological construct requires using multiple methods and multiple measures. Multiple methods imply both several informants and various ways of obtaining information from these agents. The multiple informants could include: the children themselves, parents, teachers, peers, clinicians, and independent observers. The multiple methods could include questionnaires, interviews, projective measures, role-playing, sociometrics, and direct observation. Within each of these methods, there can be different types of measures such as written, oral, pictorial, or videotaped stimuli, structured versus open-ended questions, nominations versus rating techniques, and time- versus event-based coding of observations.

Selection of informants, methods, and measures is based primarily upon one's theory of the construct of interest and whatever reliability and validity data already exist about the measures being considered. Here, the previously noted issues of children's motivation and ability to provide valid information need to be considered in developing and selecting measurement strategies that include the children as informants.

There also exist extensive literatures concerning the general psychometric quality of a variety of assessment methods used with children such as projective techniques (e.g., Gittelman-Klein, 1978), sociometrics (e.g., Asher & Hymel, 1981), parent checklists (e.g., Achenbach & Edelbrock, 1981, Quay, 1979), and psychiatric interviews (e.g., Edelbrock & Costello, 1988). Although some of these methods have been found to have better validity than others, one cannot assume that a measure that has been found valid for one construct is necessarily valid for another. The validity of each measure needs to be reevaluated in the context of the theory about the specific construct being studied.

Of course, it is important to include informants who are in a position to observe the behaviors that define the construct. For example, in the case of aggression, this will most likely include peers and teachers; for Attention Deficit Hyperactivity Disorder this will likely include teachers, independent observers, and to a lesser extent parents; and for depression this will probably include parents and the children themselves. This does not mean that the other informants don't also have an important perspective to contribute, but some informants obviously will have more contact with the children in the context in which the target symptoms are more likely to occur, and therefore probably will be better informed about those specific behaviors.

Thus, there can be no single prescription of what are the best methods and measures, or who are the most reliable informants for all developmental psychopathological constructs. The main point is that no one method or perspective is necessary, nor is one method or informant ever really sufficient. If there were one perfectly reliable and valid measure of the construct, then the construct validation approach would not really be necessary. It is precisely because no single measurement operation defines the construct and the available measures are themselves imperfect that it is necessary to use a network of multiple measures and informants to bootstrap the way to the improved operationalization and validation of constructs in developmental psychopathology.

A second important issue with respect to the multivariate approach to construct operationalization concerns the extent to which there is concordance among the various measures and informants, and the manner by which lack of agreement is resolved methodologically and conceptually. According to the traditional notions of concurrent and convergent validity (Campbell & Fiske, 1959), two or more measures of the same construct should covary, for reasons more than simply that similar methods and informants were used, and these measures should correspond more with each other than they do with measures of other constructs (i.e., discriminant validity).

An important problem, however, is that the lack of concordance among informants about childhood symptoms and behaviors can be due to factors other than the unreliability of the observers or measures. Achenbach et al. (1987) recently reviewed the literature concerning cross-informant correlations and suggested that the generally low rates of concordance among various informants could be a function of actual cross-situational differences in the children's behaviors. Achenbach et al. (1987) further suggested that different informants may each contribute valid, although different, information because they differ in their opportunities for observing children, in their effects on the children, and in their standards of judgment of behavior.

Informants also may provide diverse information because of their different knowledge about children in general and about the target child in particular. For example, whereas teachers have a better sense of what is normal for children of a particular age because of their contact with large numbers of children, parents may have a better perspective on what is normal (typical) for a particular child because they have had greater contact with the child for a longer period of time. Moreover, different informants may have better access to some kinds of information than they do to other data. Whereas teachers are generally more knowledgeable about children's academic ability and classroom behaviors, peers may be better informants about social behavior, parents may have more information about sleep and appetite patterns, and the children themselves may be the best informants about their subjective experiences of distress. Thus, informants may not agree because of their different knowledge base and the variable contexts in which they typically interact with and observe children.

In addition to these various valid reasons for differences among reporting sources, biases held by informants can also influence the degree of concordance among them. For example, parental psychopathology such as depression has been found to be associated with a more negative reporting bias about noncompliant behavior (Forehand, Laughtenschlager, Faust, & Graziano, 1986; Griest, Wells, & Forehand, 1979; although see Conrad & Hammen, 1989 for a different perspective). Teachers may vary in their level of tolerance for particular behaviors in the classroom, and clinicians may have a propensity to diagnose some disorders more than they do others. For example, a clinician's particular interest in certain syndromes could lead him or her to ask more questions about the relevant symptoms, which could then result in either a more careful diagnosing or a biased overdiagnosing of the particular disorder(s). This may have been the case with regard to childhood depression, for example, which for many years was seemingly ignored, in contrast to the current trend to diagnose and in some cases possibly overdiagnose depression in clinical samples (e.g., Weinberg, Rutman, Sullivan, Penick, & Dietz, 1973).

A critical question with regard to the use of multiple measures and multiple informants is how best to combine the information into the most valid operationalization of the target construct. The goal is to create a composite measure that represents an aggregate across methods and informants. This can be done through both empirical and rational means. According to the principle of aggregation, the summing of a set of multiple measurements presumably will produce a more stable and less biased estimator of the underlying construct then will any single measure in the set (Rushton, Brainerd, & Pressley, 1983). Such empirical aggregation across methods of assessment will tend to average the errors and control for the biases/distortions associated with each individual measure, and thereby will produce a more generalizable estimate of the latent construct (Patterson & Bank, 1987). A possible exception to the preferred use of aggregated data from multiple informants would be when the construct is not hypothesized to be cross-situational, so that combining informants representing different contexts actually may distort the true nature of the construct.

There are also times when rational approaches to combining information from multiple informants are necessary. This is particularly true when trying to make clinical diagnoses on the basis of the newly developed structured (Costello, Dulcan, Kalas, & Klaric, 1984; Herjanic & Reich, 1982) and semi-structured (Puig-Antich & Chambers, 1978) clinical interviews. Based on these interviews, a clinician can generate dichotomous ratings of whether a symptom is present or absent, which can then be used to diagnose the child according to the DSM-III-R criteria. An important question when using such interviews is how to utilize information provided independently by parents and children, particularly when these informants do not agree.

There are at least five ways to combine information from different sources. The liberal solution is that if *either* informant says that a symptom is present, then it is scored as present. This approach always takes the higher score of the two informants and may lead to a high false positive rate. In contrast, the conservative approach requires that *both* informants report that a symptom is present for it to be rated as so. This would lead to a high false negative rate, since we already know that the average inter-informant agreement between parents and children is only about .22 (Achenbach et al., 1988), although this tends to vary with the age of the child and the nature of the symptoms being reported (Edelbrock, Costello, Dulcan, Kalas, & Conover, 1985).

A third approach would be to use "*clinical judgment*" to resolve the discrepancy between the parent's and child's report. This approach requires that the clinical interviewer decide who is the better informant regarding the symptoms over which there is some dispute. The reliability of such an approach would tend to be quite low, unless the clinician making the judgments could make his or her decision-making process more explicit and communicable to other clinicians.

A related approach would involve bringing the parent and child together with the clinician to discuss and resolve the discrepancy at the time of the interview. This is the approach recommended by the developers of the Kiddie-SADS (Chambers, Puig-Antich, Hirsch, Paez, et. al., 1985; Orvaschel, Puig-Antich, Chambers, Tabrizi, & Johnson, 1982). However, this may tend to be somewhat confrontational, since the clinician would essentially be suggesting that one or the other informant is inaccurate. Such an approach could lead to increased hostility toward the clinical interviewer and decreased cooperation in the future. On the other hand, such a confrontation could serve as an opening to the therapeutic process.

A final option for resolving the discrepancies between informants would be to use information from the source who is in the best position to know about the symptom in question. As noted earlier, whereas children may be the most appropriate informants about their subjective mood states or suicidal ideation, parents may be better informants about more objective behaviors such as attention span, level of activity, or conduct problems. Thus, the solution here would not be to necessarily favor one informant over another, but, rather, to use the information from the best source about particular symptoms. Although conclusive data do not exist regarding which sources provide the most valid information about which symptoms, the empirical literature is beginning to address this question (e.g., Edelbrock, et al., 1985; see also Reich & Earls, 1987 for a related discussion).

A final issue with respect to the multivariate assessment of child psychopathology is discriminant validity. Campbell and Fiske (1959) emphasized that it is necessary to demonstrate not only that different measures of the same construct covary with one another, but also that they do *not* covary with measures of other constructs with which they are not conceptually linked. This is particularly important given the increasing recognition of comorbidity among childhood disorders (Garber, 1987; Kovacs et al., 1984; Ryan et al., 1987). Although the finding of two distinct factors in childhood psychopathology (e.g., internalizing and externalizing) has been replicated frequently in the literature (Achenbach & Edelbrock, 1978; Lachar, Gdowski, & Snyder, 1982; Quay, 1979), it has also been found that certain clusters of children are high on both dimensions (Achenbach & Edelbrock, 1981). Thus, because of the problem of comorbidity and the question of whether childhood psychopathology is characterized by a continuum of severity rather than distinct nonoverlapping syndromes, it is critical to include in the nomological network constructs and measures that would not be expected to characterize children who manifested the main construct being studied, thereby affording judgments of discriminant validity.

In sum, the operationalization phase of validating a developmental psychopathological construct should employ multiple methods, measures, and informants that represent the child in multiple contexts. The contributions and limitations of the various potential informants (particularly the children themselves) should be considered. In addition, the question of how best to resolve the discrepancies between sources and to aggregate information needs to be addressed as well. Finally, additional discriminant constructs and measures that are expected not to be positively correlated with the construct of interest should also be included.

Statistical Techniques

The next question to address in the process of validating a psychopathological construct is how to utilize the information that was obtained from the various measures and informants in examining both its internal structure and its external validity with regard to other conceptually linked constructs. The goal here is to derive an index that can then be used to study the processes underlying the construct and to predict the association with other theoretical constructs and their operations.

Researchers must choose the multivariate statistical procedures that are most compatible with their theory about the target construct. The empirical methodology selected will depend upon whether the construct is conceptualized as being dimensional or categorical. The two main statistical procedures used to derive a construct empirically are factor analysis (Gorsuch, 1974) and cluster analysis (Anderberg, 1973; Everitt, 1977). Although both approaches may start with the same matrix of intercorrelations, they make very different assumptions about the nature of the construct being studied. Moreover, they typically yield different results because of their different treatment of the variance among the variables.

Factor analysis produces dimensions that are some linear combination of the observed variables that presumably represent the theoretical construct underlying the observed covariation among the items. In contrast, cluster analysis identifies discrete categories of objects or individuals who are more similar to each other than they are to other objects or individuals. A third empirical method known as latent class analysis (Lazarsfeld & Henry, 1968; Meehl & Golden, 1982) also produces distinct classes of individuals who are homogeneous with respect to the presumed underlying construct. Meehl (1979) has argued that this latter method is particularly appropriate for studying psychopathological constructs since a reasonably small set of fallible indicators can be generated without necessarily having in advance an independent criterion that is already known to be correct.

There really are few major developmental issues unique to any of these statistical techniques. One issue that should be addressed, however, is whether the factors or clusters that are derived vary as a function of age. Weiss and Weisz (1988), for example, recently found that the factor structure of the Children's Depression Inventory (Kovacs & Beck, 1977) changed from a unitary construct during middle childhood to a multifactorial structure during adolescence. Such a finding suggests that the nature of the construct underlying the responses to the CDI may change with development, and this has implications for the issue of the continuity of the construct, as discussed earlier. Achenbach and Edelbrock (1981) similarly have found that both their factor and cluster solutions varied as a function of the age and sex of the children.

Thus, the choice of which statistical procedure to use is determined by one's theory about the dimensional versus categorical nature of the construct. Regardless of which method is used, one should examine specifically the extent to which the solutions that are derived from these empirical procedures vary as a function of development.

Evaluation of Internal Properties

Once an empirical technique for deriving the construct has been selected, it is next necessary to evaluate the internal properties of the resulting solution. The results are subject to the same standards used to evaluate psychological tests (APA, 1954) and psychiatric classifications (Blashfield & Draguns, 1976). These include: reliability, coverage, homogeneity, robustness across samples (Skinner, 1981), and the content validity of the indicators that define the construct and its operationalization (Loevinger, 1957).

Loevinger (1957) also asserted that it is important to evaluate structural fidelity, which is concerned with the "extent to which the structural relations between the test items parallel the structural relations of other manifestations of the trait being measured" (p. 661). Basically, structural fidelity is concerned with how well the particular measurement model selected (e.g., continuous versus categorical) corresponds to the substantive domain being studied (Wiggins, 1973).

In addition, the incremental validity (Garb, 1984) of the multiple measures and multiple informants also should be evaluated. That is, to what extent does each individual method or measure add to the validity of the construct over and above the other measures. Finally, the other kinds of validity such as concurrent and predictive that are relevant to the question of external validity should be explored. External validity is addressed in the subsequent section.

Anastasi (1982) has presented an excellent description of most of the relevant types of reliability and validity. Again, the basic psychometric principles are applicable to both child and adult measures and constructs. One developmental issue worth noting, however, concerns test-retest reliability. The problem of evaluating retest reliability with children is that their behavior and their self-reporting ability change simply as a function of maturation. Thus, unless the retest is conducted over a relatively brief period of time during which the children would not be expected to naturally change simply because of maturation, test-retest reliability may be a less relevant psychometric property to evaluate. If the measures themselves can reflect these natural changes, then examining the relation between measures taken at two points in time makes sense. However, this does not so much reflect retest reliability as it does predictive validity.

The final step in the construct validation process is external validity. Once the construct has been operationally defined, statistically derived, and internally validated, the next question is whether it relates to other constructs as outlined in the nomological network.

External Validity

Cronbach and Meehl (1955) specified that validity must include some external relationships. External validity is concerned with the extent to which the construct is conceptually linked with other constructs (Type I relation) and the construct operations are associated with other nontest behaviors (Type III relations) in a manner consistent with the theory outlined in the nomological network. The nomological network generates testable predictions about the relation of the construct operation (e.g., test) to certain other variables. If the results are consistent with the hypotheses, then this supports the external validity of the construct.

Loevinger (1957) reiterated the view in A.P.A. *Technical Recommendations* (1954) that external validity includes concurrent and predictive validities, although she suggested it went beyond these. In addition, Loevinger noted that although the construct operation must show relevance to nontest behavior, "it need not be equivalent to non-test behavior" (p. 674). Thus, external validity is not simply concerned with finding other measures of the construct; rather, it is concerned with the association of the construct operation with theoretically relevant nontest variables.

H. A. Skinner (1981) suggested that the external validation of psychopathological constructs involves predictive validity regarding treatment outcome, descriptive validity, clinical utility, and generalization to other populations. We further suggest that once a psychopathological construct has been adequately defined and operationalized, it then should be examined with respect to the other significant aspects of psychopathology including course, prognosis, treatment response, and etiology. The developmental issues relevant to each of these components are discussed next.

Course

Both course and prognosis involve the prospective examination of the natural history and outcome of the construct over time in the absence of any intervention. Course is concerned with the onset, duration, chronicity, and remission of an episode of a disorder. The onset of a disorder can be acute or insidious; the duration can be short-lived and transient or stable and unchanging. The construct may show an episodic or cycling pattern with periods of remission, or it may be chronic and unremitting, with increasing deterioration. The study of the course of a disorder requires at least a short-term longitudinal research strategy.

Kraepelin (1883) considered information about the course and outcome of a disorder to be critical to its definition and classification. Various disorders in DSM-III-R are classified, in part, on the basis of their course. For example, Adjustment Disorders are by definition acute, transient, and remitting; schizophrenia can be acute or chronic with possible periods of remission; Major Affective Disorder must be present for at least two weeks and may be recurrent unipolar or episodically bipolar; Dysthymic Disorder by definition has a minimum two-year (1-year for children) duration. Thus, when the specific course is known, it can be used in defining the construct, thereby leading to more homogeneous groups. However, in the initial process of validating a psychopathological construct, course should be examined separately from the syndrome definition contained in the descriptive component of the network.

Several important developmental issues should be considered with regard to course and duration. First, rather than judging the duration of symptoms in children relative to what is typically seen in adults, we need to consider the duration of each symptom relative to how long other children who are not characterized by the psychopathological construct manifest the symptom. For example, if it typically takes most children 10 to 15 minutes to fall asleep (once they are ready to), and we learn that depressed children take about 45 to 60 minutes, as compared to adults who often report difficulties of up to 2 hours, then should we consider the 45–60 minutes of the "depressed" children deviant? The answer to this question depends upon information about the typical duration of the symptom among children who manifest and do not manifest the target construct. Thus, knowledge of the normal course and duration of symptoms and syndromes is necessary to determine when the duration of a particular symptom is deviant.

Moreover, in judging duration, the frequency with which the particular symptoms occur should also be considered. For example, very young children typically do not sustain a sad mood for long periods of time because they can often be distracted. However, despite the apparent transientness of their mood, young children may present a deviant affective pattern by their having frequent, albeit brief, periods of sadness over a sustained period of time. This suggests that one-time, cross-sectional observations of children may not be an adequate assessment strategy for some of these transient but recurrent symptoms. Thus, a more longitudinal assessment across situations and the inclusion of informants who have known the child over a longer period of time are necessary to accurately assess course and duration.

A related issue is how best to obtain accurate information about the onset and duration of symptoms. In general, children are not good informants about the timing and chronicity of symptoms. Children's cognitive limitations with regard to memory of events and their understanding of time (Kovacs, 1986) reduce the accuracy with which they can date the onset and duration of symptoms. Although parents may also have some difficulty recalling such information, they are generally more accurate than are children, especially the very young ones (Edelbrock et al., 1985).

Finally, Rutter (1988) has highlighted the potential significance of age of onset in classifying and understanding developmental psychopathology. For example, some disorders with an early age of onset have been found to be more chronic and to have a stronger association with family psychopathology than do the same disorders that occur at a later age (e.g., Loeber & Dishion, 1983; Strober & Carlson, 1982). Thus, age of onset may be informative about subtypes of a construct and their associated etiologic processes, and therefore should be considered in formulating one's theory about the target psychopathological construct.

Prognosis

Prognosis is concerned with the long-term outcome in the absence of treatment, the predictive validity of the construct to other constructs and outcomes over time, the relapse and recurrence of episodes of the disorder, and the central issue of the continuity between childhood and adult maladaptation. The questions most relevant to prognosis are: to what extent does the construct operation reliably predict future outcomes; and, most important from a developmental perspective, do certain forms of psychopathology or maladjustment during childhood predict particular outcomes in adulthood?

Evidence supporting the continuity between child and adult psychopathology has been inconsistent (Kohlberg, LaCrosse, & Ricks, 1972; Robins, 1966, 1978; Rutter, 1985). It depends upon the research strategy used (e.g., follow-up, follow-back, retrospective), sources of information (e.g., records, parent questionnaires, subject interviews), type of sample (e.g., general population, clinic-referred), type of disorder (e.g., conduct disorder, neurosis), outcome variable (e.g., global maladjustment, specific diagnoses), and the diagnostic criteria used. For example, the empirical literature concerning the relation between childhood and adult psychopathology suggests that there is more evidence of continuity for externalizing disorders than for internalizing disorders (Rutter, 1985).

What are the implications of continuity or lack of continuity for validating a psychopathological construct from a developmental perspective? The central questions here are whether or not it is necessary for a psychopathological construct occurring during childhood to continue to occur or recur (if left untreated) into adulthood, and whether adult psychopathology is necessarily preceded by childhood forms of the disorder. That is, is continuity of the construct a requirement of validity? We suggest that the answer to this question is not necessarily.

If a construct (X) is identified at Time 1 during childhood, but upon a second assessment at a later point (Time 2), there is no further evidence of the construct (X), or another construct (Y) has developed, does this mean that the original diagnosis of construct X at Time 1 was wrong or invalid? Possible explanations are that the constructs may have been misdiagnosed at either Time 1 or Time 2, that different criteria were used at the two assessments, or that not enough time had elapsed between the two assessments so that the subject had not yet reached the full risk period for the target disorder, particularly for episodic disorders such as depression.

Moreover, the change from one disorder at Time 1 to a different disorder at Time 2 (e.g., the association between childhood antisocial behavior and adult schizophrenia) may result from the constructs being independent and qualitatively distinct. That is, the earlier disorder may resolve, and a second one may emerge independently in response to new environmental demands or physiological changes. On the other hand, the disorders could have a different phenotype but a shared genotype. That is, although the manifest symptomatology may differ as a result of the child's level of cognitive, emotional, linguistic, and physiological functioning, the processes underlying the psychopathology could be similar.

Finally, a disorder assessed at Time 1 may simply be a transient developmental response to an environmental stressor (Lefkowitz & Burton, 1978), or it may be a disorder that will have only one or two episodes during childhood. It is also possible that the conditions that produce and maintain a disorder (e.g., biological vulnerability, environmental stress) change over time, or that the child matures cognitively or physiologically to a point where he or she either can cope with the precipitating conditions or grows out of them (Chess & Thomas, 1984).

Rutter's (1965) distinction between classifying disorders versus classifying children is relevant here. He suggested that it is possible for a child to have one kind of condition at age 5 and another at age 12. Therefore, rather than classifying the children themselves (e.g., as being a diabetic or a schizophrenic), it makes more sense to describe the children as having a particular disorder (e.g., diabetes, schizophrenia) at that one point in time. The continuity between child and adult disorders is a theoretically interesting and important issue that may have implications for etiology and treatment, but it should not be a necessary criterion for validating a psychopathological construct during childhood.

Thus, even though since the time of Kraepelin (1883) the natural history and outcome of psychopathological conditions have been regarded as important validating features of diagnostic classification, we suggest that the validity of a developmental psychopathological construct should be judged independently of its relation to adult psychopathology. It is not necessary for a construct to persist into adulthood for it to be considered a valid disorder in its own right during childhood (Garber, 1984). It also may not be necessary that childhood and adult phenotypes be similar for them to be considered essentially the same disorder. Thus, prognosis should be included in the nomological network about a psychopathological construct, although the continuity of the construct from childhood to adulthood should be explored as a hypothesis to be tested rather than being assumed or required for validity.

Intervention

The intervention component of the nomological network is concerned with what happens to the construct when there is an attempt to change it. Does the construct represent a homogeneous entity that responds in a predictable way to its manipulation? Can we predict on the basis of knowing whether an individual manifests that disorder or trait how he or she will respond to a particular intervention?

On the basis of one's theory about the reduction or prevention of the construct, it is possible to hypothesize that doing X will lower the probability of the onset of Y, or if Y is present, then doing Z will cause it to ameliorate. The validity of the construct is supported by evidence that a particular treatment significantly reduces the duration or severity of the homogeneously defined construct beyond what would have occurred without treatment.

A treatment that is effective for a particular syndrome in adults, which also is found to be effective with children manifesting the same or similar syndrome, provides evidence of the continuity and validity of a psychopathological construct during childhood. However, what are the implications for continuity and validity when the effective adult treatments do not appear to work for children manifesting the same construct?

First, it could be that there really is not continuity of the construct from childhood to adulthood. Thus, even if there is similarity in manifest symptomatology, the lack of continuity with regard to treatment may suggest that the childhood and adult forms of the syndrome really represent different underlying constructs.

A second possibility is that there is continuity, but the treatment needs to be modified for use with children. Since children typically are less motivated and less cognitively capable of participating in the therapeutic process, it may be necessary to alter the effective adult therapies to make them more developmentally appropriate for children. This can include anything from changing the dosage levels required for pharmacological therapies to modifying the verbal demands placed on the child in individual psychotherapy. Thus, the continuity of a developmental psychopathological construct with respect to intervention should not be judged until the adult treatment has been appropriately modified for use with children. If this modified intervention continues to be ineffective, then one can begin to question the continuity and/or validity of the construct during childhood.

A final possibility is that the adult intervention may work if it is combined with additional approaches that are responsive to the unique aspects of childhood. For example, cognitive therapy may be appropriate for treating depressive distortions in children as well as adults, but it is more likely to be effective if parents can be included in the therapeutic process. Whereas with adults it is often possible to treat only the patient (or sometimes to include the spouse), with children it is often important to include the parents, and sometimes the whole family or school personnel, at some point during treatment. An apparent lack of continuity between child and adult forms of treatment may not so much indicate a lack of continuity in the underlying construct as it may reflect not having supplemented the adult therapy with strategies that are responsive to the additional, unique issues that children face over the course of development.

Etiology

The final, and possibly the most important, component of the nomological network concerns the etiologic processes that underlie the construct. The strongest validation of a nosological construct is the identification of its specific etiology (Meehl, 1977).

Kenny (1979) has suggested that covariation is a necessary although not sufficient index of causality. The most common type of design used to examine covariation is correlational, in which the degree of association between the construct operation and its hypothesized correlates is calculated. The group differences methodology (Cronbach & Meehl, 1955) provides another kind of correlational evidence. On the basis of one's theory about the construct, it is predicted that two groups will differ with respect to some variable(s). If the group identified as manifesting the construct of interest behaves differently in the predicted direction than does the group not characterized by the target construct, then this provides further evidence of its validity.

Another interesting methodology for examining etiology involves identifying individuals who manifest the hypothesized etiologic variable (e.g., attributional style, genetic liability) and following them over time to observe whether significantly more of these "vulnerable" individuals develop the psychopathological construct of interest than do individuals who did not manifest that vulnerability (Abramson, et al., 1988).

Finally, although ethically questionable, the theoretically most interesting design for studying etiology involves the experimental manipulation of conditions

to actually produce the construct of interest. However, it is not ethically or practically possible to actually produce many of the conditions (e.g., abuse, loss of a
loved one, biochemical abnormalities) that are hypothesized to play a significant
etiologic role in the development of various forms of psychopathology. Therefore, human analog and animal studies are often used to produce a modified form
of the construct in the laboratory. Despite the problem of generalizability of results from these kinds of investigations, analog and animal studies provide an
ethically acceptable means of learning about the potential etiologic variables that
may contribute to the onset of psychopathological constructs in humans.

The developmental issues with respect to etiology are generally similar to the
A good example of both human and animal analog studies of psychopathology
is the work conducted by Seligman and colleagues (e.g., Seligman, 1975) on the
learned helplessness model of depression. According to this theory, organisms
exposed to uncontrollable aversive experiences develop a pattern of responses
that resembles the clinical phenomenon of depression (e.g., sad affect, response
initiation deficits, cognitive interference). In several laboratory analog studies
(e.g., Klein & Seligman, 1976; Miller & Seligman, 1975; Maier & Seligman,
1976), both humans and animals have been exposed to uncontrollable noise or
shock, respectively, and were subsequently observed to manifest the various
"depressive" patterns of affect and behavior. Although one could or would not
claim that these college student subjects or laboratory rats were clinically depressed, these studies demonstrated that exposure to uncontrollability was significantly more likely to produce "depressive" features than was exposure to either
controllable or no aversive stimulation. Such analog research is a powerful methodology for exploring the etiology of psychopathological constructs given the
ethical constraints that researchers face.

The developmental issues with respect to etiology are generally similar to the
various issues already discussed with regard to the other components of the nomological network. For example, as is the case with the definition and operationalization of the target psychopathological construct, the potential etiological
correlates need to be defined and measured in a developmentally appropriate
manner that is consistent with children's level of functioning within various domains.

A second developmental point with regard to etiology is that the same potential etiological variables may have a different impact depending upon the child's
developmental level. For example, considerable evidence exists that there are
differences in what children find to be stressful at different ages (Yamamoto,
1979; Yeaworth, York, Hussey, Ingle, & Goodwin, 1980), and in how children
react to the same life stressors such as separation or loss, failure, illness, war, and
natural disasters (Garmezy, 1986; Garmezy & Rutter, 1985). Studies of children's
responses to loss due to divorce, for instance, have found differences in children's abilities to cope with these experiences as a function of age (Hetherington,
Cox, & Cox, 1982; Wallerstein, 1983).

There is also evidence of developmental differences with regard to potential biological correlates of psychopathological constructs. The same biological processes may result in different symptoms for children and adults. For example, whereas adults tend to show the classic symptoms of depression in reaction to excessive blood levels of corticosteroids, children generally tend to become irritable and hyperactive (Eberlain & Winter, 1969).

Finally, certain etiological processes may not become evident or measurable until a certain age. Rutter (1986, 1988), for example, has pointed out the significant rise in the prevalence of depressive disorders after puberty and has suggested a variety of potential etiological factors that may contribute to this, such as the hormonal changes that accompany puberty, the increasing social, familial, and academic stressors associated with early adolescence, or the developing ability to make depressogenic attributions and expectancies. If there is continuity with respect to the etiological processes underlying the construct of depression, how do we account for such a marked change in the prevalence rate after puberty? What are the implications of this increasing prevalence rate for understanding the continuity and validity of depression before the onset of puberty? Answers to questions such as these are critical to validating psychopathological constructs from a developmental perspective.

In sum, the process of external validation of a psychopathological construct requires attention to its course, prognosis, treatment, and etiology. In response to new data generated by tests of the relations outlined in the nomological network, it is necessary to reevaluate and revise the construct definition, operationalization, and theory underlying it. Every change in the theory or measures requires "a fresh body of data" to test the new measure or altered hypotheses (Cronbach & Meehl, 1955). Thus, construct validation requires a flexible and open approach that is responsive to empirical data and alternative interpretations of these data.

General Conclusions

Meehl and colleagues have made a major contribution to the field of psychology by describing the process of construct validation. In the over 30 years since the notion of construct validity was formally introduced, it has served as a model for test construction, theory building, and hypothesis testing, particularly with regard to personality and psychopathology. The goal of this chapter was to further extend the influences of construct validity to the emerging field of developmental psychopathology. Several important developmental issues were outlined with respect to defining, operationalizing, and externally validating developmental psychopathological constructs. The issues of the continuity of psychopathology over the course of development, and between normal and abnormal functioning, are especially critical themes to address during the process of validating psychopathological constructs from a developmental perspective. The various developmental issues with regard to each of the descriptive, prognostic, etiologic, and treatment components of a psychopathological construct were outlined to provide a framework for future studies. The application of this proposed framework to such constructs in developmental psychopathology as childhood schizophrenia, childhood depression, attention deficit hyperactivity disorder, and/or conduct disorder should be the focus of future investigations.

References

Abramson, L. Y., Alloy, L. B., & Metalsky, G. I. (1988). The cognitive diathesis-stress theories of depression: Toward an adequate evaluation of the theories' validities. In L. B. Alloy (Ed.), *Cognitive processes in depression*. New York: Guilford Press.

Abramson, L. Y., Garber, J., & Seligman, M. E. P. (1980). Learned helplessness: An attributional analysis. In J. Garber & M. E. P. Seligman (Eds.), *Human helplessness: Theory and applications*. New York: Academic Press.

Abramson, L. Y., Seligman, M. E. P., & Teasdale, J. (1978). Learned helplessness in humans: Critique and reformulation. *Journal of Abnormal Psychology, 87*, 49–74.

Achenbach, T. M. (1978). The child behavior profile: I. Boys aged 6–11. *Journal of Consulting and Clinical Psychology, 46*, 478–488.

Achenbach, T. M. (1985). *Assessment and taxonomy of child and adolescent psychopathology*. California: Sage Publications.

Achenbach, T. M. (1988). Integrating assessment and taxonomy. In M. Rutter, A. H. Tuma, & I. S. Lann (Eds.), *Assessment and diagnosis in child psychopathology*. New York: Guilford Press.

Achenbach, T. M., & Edelbrock, C. S. (1978). The classification of child psychopathology: A review and analysis of empirical efforts. *Psychological Bulletin, 85*, 1275–1301.

Achenbach, T. M., & Edelbrock, C. S. (1981). Behavioral problems and competencies reported by parents of normal and disturbed children age four through sixteen. *Monographs of the Society for Research in Child Development, 46* (1, Serial No. 188).

Achenbach, T. M., McConaughy, S. H., & Howell, C. T. (1987). Child/adolescent behavioral and emotional problems: Implications of cross-informant correlations for situational specificity. *Psychological Bulletin, 101*, 213–232.

Althauser, R. P., & Heberlein, T. A. (1970). Validity and the multitrait-multimethod matrix. In E. F. Borgotta & W. Bohrnstedt (Eds.), *Sociological methodology 1970* (pp. 151–169). San Francisco: Jossey-Bass.

American Psychiatric Association. (1987). Diagnostic and statistical manual of mental disorders. (3rd ed., rev.) Washington, DC.

American Psychological Association. (1952). Technical recommendations for psychological tests and diagnostic techniques: Preliminary proposal. *American Psychologist, 7*, 461–476.

American Psychological Association. (1954). Technical recommendations for psychological tests and diagnostic techniques construct validity. *Psychological Bulletin*, Suppl. *51*, 1–38.

Ammons, R. B. (1950). Reactions in a projective doll-play interview of white males two to six years of age to different skin color and facial features. *Journal of General Psychology*, 323–341.

Anastasi, A. (1982). *Psychological testing*. 5th Edition. New York: Macmillan.

Anderberg, M. R. (1973). *Cluster analysis for applications*. New York: Academic Press.

Andreasen, N. C. (1981). *Affective disorders: Concept, classification, and diagnosis*. Unpublished manuscript, University of Iowa.

Asher, S. R., & Hymel, S. (1981). Children's social competence in peer relations: Sociometric and behavioral assessment. In J. D. Wine & M. D. Syme (Eds.), *Social competence* (pp. 125–157). New York: Guilford Press.

Ausubel, D. P. (1968). *Educational psychology: A cognitive view*. New York: Holt, Rinehart, & Winston.

Beardslee, W. R., Klerman, G. L., Keller, M. B., Lavori, P. W., & Podorefsky, D. L. (1985). But are the cases? Validity of DSM-III major depression in children identified in a family study. *American Journal of Psychiatry, 142,* 687–691.

Bechtoldt, H. P. (1959). Construct validity: A critique. *American Psychologist, 14,* 619–629.

Biber, B., & Lewis, C. (1949). An experimental study of what young children expect from their teachers. *General Psychology Monographs, 40,* 3–97.

Bierman, K. L. (1984). Cognitive development and clinical interviews with children. In B. Lahey & A. E. Kazdin (Eds.), *Advances in Clinical Child Psychology* (Vol. 6), (pp. 217–250). New York: Plenum Press.

Blashfield, R. K. (1984). *The classification of psychopathology*. New York: Plenum Press.

Blashfield, R. K., & Draguns, J. G. (1976). Evaluating criteria for psychiatric classification. *Journal of Abnormal Psychology, 85,* 574–583.

Brandt, R. M. (1958). The accuracy of self-estimate: A measure of self-concept reality. *Genetic Psychology Monographs, 58,* 55–99.

Campbell, D. T. (1960). Recommendations for APA test standards regarding construct, trait, or discriminant validity. *American Psychologist, 15,* 546–553.

Campbell, D. T., & Fiske, D. W. (1959). Convergent and discriminant validation by the multitrait-multimethod matrix. *Psychological Bulletin, 56,* 81–105.

Cantor, N., Smith, E. E., French, R., & Mezzich, J. (1980). Psychiatric diagnosis as prototype categorization. *Journal of Abnormal Psychology, 89,* 181–193.

Cantwell, D. P. (1983). Depression in childhood: Clinical picture and diagnostic criteria. In D. P. Cantwell & G. A. Carlson (Eds.), *Affective disorders in childhood and adolescence: An update* (pp. 19–38). New York: Spectrum Publications.

Carlson, G. A., & Garber, J. (1986). Developmental issues in the classification of depression in children. In M. Rutter, C. E. Izard, & P. B. Read (Eds.), *Depression in young people: Developmental and clinical perspectives* (pp. 399–434). New York: Guilford Press.

Castaneda, A., McCandless, B. R., & Palermo, D. S. (1956). The children's form of the Manifest Anxiety Scale. *Child Development, 27,* 317–326.

Cattell, R. B. (1940). The description of personality: I. Foundations of trait measurement. *Psychological Review, 50,* 559–594.

Chambers, W. J., Puig-Antich, J., Hirsch, M., Paez, P., Ambrosini, P. J., Tabrizi, M. A., & Davies, M. (1985). The assessment of affective disorders in children and adolescents by semi-structured interview. *Archives of General Psychiatry, 42,* 696–702.

Chess, S., & Thomas, A. (1984). *Origins and evolution of behavior disorders: From infancy to early adult life*. New York: Bruner/Mazel.

Cicchetti, D. (in press). An historical perspective on the discipline of developmental psychopathology. In J. Rolf, A Masten, D. Cicchetti, K. Neuchterlein, & S. Weintraub (Eds.), *Risk and protective factors in the development of psychopathology*. New York: Cambridge University Press.

Cicchetti, D., & Schneider-Rosen, J. (1986). An organizational approach to childhood depression. In M. Rutter, C. Izard, & P. B. Read (Eds.), *Depression in young people: Developmental and clinical perspectives* (pp. 71–134). New York: Guilford Press.

Cicchetti, D., & Sroufe, L. A. (1978). An organizational view of affect: Illustration from the study of Down's syndrome infants. In M. Lewis & L. Rosenblum (Eds.), *The development of affect* (pp. 309–350). New York: Plenum Press.

Cole, D. A. (1987). Utility of confirmatory factor analysis in test validation research. *Journal of Consulting and Clinical Psychology, 55*, 584–594.

Colman, S. W., MacKay, D., & Fidell, B. (1972). English normative data on the Children's Manifest Anxiety Scale. *British Journal of Sociological Psychology, 11*, 85–87.

Conrad, M., & Hammen, C. (1989). Role of maternal depression in perceptions of child maladjustment. *Journal of Consulting and Clinical Psychology, 57*, 663–667.

Costello, A. J., Dulcan, M. K., Kalas, R., & Klaric, S. H. (1984). *Development and testing of the NIMH Diagnostic Interview Schedule for Children in a Clinic Population.* (Final report, contract #RFP-DB-81-0027). Rockville, MD: Center for Epidemiologic Studies, NIMH.

Cramer, J. B. (1980). Psychiatric examination of the child. In H. I. Kaplan, A. M. Freedman, & B. J. Sadock (Eds.), *Comprehensive Textbook of Psychiatry/III* (3rd Ed., Vol. 3), (pp. 2435–2461). Baltimore: Williams & Wilkins.

Crandall, V. C., Crandell, V. J., & Katovosky, W. (1965). A children's social desirability questionnaire. *Journal of Consulting Psychology, 29*, 27–36.

Cronbach, L. J., & Meehl, P. (1955). Construct validity in psychological tests. *Psychological Bulletin, 52*, 281–302.

Eberlain, W. R., & Winter, J. G. (1969). Cushing's syndrome in childhood. In L. I. Gardner (Ed.), *Endocrine and genetic diseases of childhood* (pp. 428–436). New York: Harper & Row.

Edelbrock, C. (1984). Developmental considerations. In T. H. Ollendick & M. Herson (Eds.), *Child behavioral assessment*. New York: Pergamon Press.

Edelbrock, C., & Costello, A. J. (1988). Structured psychiatric interviews for children. In M. Rutter, A. Tuma, & I. S. Lann (Eds.), *Assessment and diagnosis in child psychopathology*. New York: Guilford Press.

Edelbrock, C., Costello, A. J., Dulcan, M. K., Kalas, R., & Conover, N. C. (1985). Age differences in the reliability of the psychiatric interview of the child. *Child Development, 56*, 265–275.

Eisenberg, L. (1986). When is a case a case? In M. Rutter, C. E. Izard, & P. B. Read (Eds.), *Depression in young people: Developmental and clinical perspectives* (pp. 469–478). New York: Guilford Press.

Eisenman, R., & Townsend, T. D. (1970). Studies in acquiescence: I. Social desirability; II. Self-esteem; III. Creativity; and IV. Prejudice. *Journal of Personality Assessment, 34*, 223–231.

Embretson, S. (1983). Construct validity: Construct representation versus nomothetic span. *Psychological Bulletin, 93*, 179–197.

Everitt, B. S. (1977). *Cluster analysis*. London: Heinemann Educational Books, Ltd.

Eysenck, H. J. (1953). *The structure of human personality*. London: Methuen.

Fish, B. (1969). Problems of diagnosis and definition of comparable groups: A neglected issue in drug research with children. *American Journal of Psychiatry, 125*, 900–908.

Fisher, R. M. (1967). Acquiescent response set, the Jesness Inventory and implications for the use of 'foreign' psychological tests. *British Journal of Social Clinical Psychology, 6*, 1–10.

Forehand, R., Laughtenschlager, G. J., Faust, J., & Graziano, W. G. (1986). Parent perceptions and parent-child interactions in clinic-referred children: A preliminary investigation of the effects of maternal depressive moods. *Behavior Research and Therapy, 24*, 73–75.

Furman, W., & Bierman, K. L. (1984). Children's conceptions of friendship: A multimethod study of developmental changes. *Developmental Psychology, 20*, 925–931.

Garb, H. (1984). The incremental validity of information used in personality assessment. *Clinical Psychology Review, 4*, 641–655.

Garber, J. (1984). Classification of childhood psychopathology: A developmental perspective. *Child Development, 55*, 30–48.

Garber, J. (1987). *Childhood depression: Validation of the construct*. Doctoral dissertation, University of Minnesota.

Garmezy, N. (1986). Developmental aspects of children's responses to the stress of separation and loss. In M. Rutter, C. E. Izard, & P. B. Read (Eds.), *Depression in young people: Developmental and clinical perspectives* (pp. 297–323). New York: Guilford Press.

Garmezy, N., & Rutter, M. (1985). Acute reaction to stress. In M. Rutter & L. Hersov (Eds.), *Child and adolescent psychiatry* (pp. 152–176). London: Blackwell.

Gaylord, R. N., & Stunkel, E. R. (1954). Validity and the criterion. *Education and Psychological Measurement, 14*, 294–300.

Gewirtz, J., & Baer, D. (1958). The effect of brief social deprivation on behaviors for a social reinforcer. *Journal of Abnormal and Social Psychology, 56*, 49–56.

Gittelman, R., Mannuzza, S., Schenker, R., & Bonagura, N. (1985). Hyperactive boys almost grown up. I. Psychiatric status. *Archives of General Psychiatry, 42*, 937–947.

Gittelman-Klein, R. (1978). Validity of projective tests for psychodiagnosis in children. In R. L. Spitzer & D. F. Klein (Eds.), *Critical issues in psychiatric diagnosis* (pp. 141–166). New York: Raven Press.

Gittelman-Klein, R., Spitzer, R. L., & Cantwell, D. (1978). Diagnostic classification and psychopharmacological indications. In J. S. Werry (Ed.), *Pediatric psychopharmacology*. New York: Bruner/Mazel.

Gorsuch, R. L. (1974). *Factor analysis*. Philadelphia: W. B. Saunders.

Griest, D. L., Wells, K. C., & Forehand, R. (1979). An examination of predictors of maternal perceptions of maladjustment in clinic-referred children. *Journal of Abnormal Psychology, 88*, 227–281.

Herjanic, B., & Reich, W. (1982). Development of a structured psychiatric interview for children: Agreement between child and parent on individual symptoms. *Journal of Abnormal Child Psychology, 10*, 307–324.

Hetherington, E. M., Cox, M., & Cox, S. (1982). Effects of divorce on parents and children. In M. Lamb (Ed.), *Non-traditional families* (pp. 233-288). Hillsdale, NJ: Lawrence Erlbaum.

Hewitt, L. E., & Jenkins, R. L. (1946). *Fundamental patterns of maladjustment; the dynamics of their origin; a statistical analysis based upon five hundred case records of children examined at the Michigan Child Guidance Institute*. Springfield, IL: State of Illinois.

Horowitz, L. M., Wright, J. C., Lowenstein, E., & Parad, H. W. (1981). The prototype as a construct in abnormal psychology: I. A method for deriving prototypes. *Journal of Abnormal Psychology, 90*, 575–585.

Jackson, D. N. (1969). Multimethod factor analysis in the evaluation of convergent and discriminant validity. *Psychological Bulletin, 72*, 30–49.

Jessor, R., & Hammond, K. R. (1957). Construct validity and the Taylor Anxiety Scale. *Psychological Bulletin, 54*, 161–170.

Joreskog, K. G. (1974). Analyzing psychological data by structural analysis of covariance matrices. In R. C. Atkinson, D. H. Krantz, R. D. Luce, & P. Suppes (Eds.), *Contemporary developments in mathematical psychology* (Vol. 2, pp. 1–56). San Francisco: W. H. Freeman.

Kazdin, A. E. (1987). Assessment of childhood depression: Current issues and strategies. *Behavioral Assessment, 9*,(3), 291–319.

Kazdin, A. E., Sherick, B. A., Esveldt-Dawson, K., & Rancurello, M. (1985). Nonverbal behavior and childhood depression. *Journal of the American Academy of Child Psychiatry, 24*, 303–309.

Kenny, D. A. (1979). *Correlation and causality*. New York: John Wiley and Sons.

Klein, D. C., & Seligman, M. E. P. (1976). Reversal of performance deficits and perceptual deficits in learned helplessness and depression. *Journal of Abnormal Psychology, 85*, 11–26.

Klieger, D. M., & Walsh, J. A. (1967). A pictorial rating technique for obtaining social desirability ratings from young children. *Psychological Reports, 20*, 295–304.

Kohlberg, L., LaCross, J., & Ricks, D. (1972). The predictability of adult mental health from childhood behavior. In B. A. Wolman (Ed.), *Manual of child psychopathology* (pp. 1217–1284). New York: McGraw Hill.

Kovacs, M. (1986). A developmental perspective on methods and measures in the assessment of depressive disorders: The clinical interview. In M. Rutter, C. Izard, & P. Read (Eds.), *Depression in young people: Developmental and clinical perspectives* (pp. 435–465). New York: Guilford Press.

Kovacs, M., & Beck, A. T. (1977). An empirical-clinical approach toward a definition of childhood depression. In J. Schulterbrandt & A. Raskin (Eds.), *Depression in childhood: Diagnosis, treatment, and conceptual models* (pp. 1–25). New York: Raven Press.

Kovacs, M., Feinberg, T. L., Crouse-Novak, M. A., Paulauskas, S. L., & Finkelstein, R. (1984). Depressive disorders in childhood. I. A longitudinal prospective study of characteristics and recovery. *Archives of General Psychiatry, 41*, 229–237.

Kraepelin, E. (1883). *Compendium der Psychiatric.* Leipzig: Barth.

Lachar, D., Gdowski, C. L., & Snyder, D. K. (1982). Broadband dimensions of psychopathology: Factor scales for The Personality Inventory for Children. *Journal of Consulting and Clinical Psychology, 50*, 634–642.

Last, C. G., Hersen, M., Kazdin, A. E., Finkelstein, R., & Strauss, C. C. (1987). Comparison of DSM-III separation anxiety and overanxious disorders: Demographic characteristics and patterns of comorbidity. *Journal of the American Academy of Child and Adolescent Psychiatry, 26*, 527–531.

Lazarsfeld, P. F., & Henry, N. W. (1968). *Latent structure analysis.* Boston: Houghton-Mifflin.

Lefkowitz, M. M., & Burton, N. (1978). Childhood depression: A critique of the concept. *Psychological Bulletin, 85*, 716–726.

Lehmann, H. E. (1977). Classification of depressive states. *Canadian Psychiatric Association Journal, 22*, 381–390.

Light, C. S., Zax, M., & Gardiner, D. H. (1965). Relationship of age, sex and intelligence level to extreme response style. *Journal of Personality and Social Psychology, 2*, 907–909.

Loeber, R., & Dishion, T. (1983). Early predictors of male delinquency: A review. *Psychological Bulletin, 94*, 68–99.

Loevinger, J. (1957). Objective tests as instruments of psychological theory. *Psychological Reports, 3*, 635–694.

MacCorquodale, K., & Meehl, P. E. (1948). On a distinction between hypothetical constructs and intervening variables. *Psychological Review, 55*, 95–107.

MacFarlane, J. W., Allen, L., & Honzik, M. P. (1954). *A developmental study of the behavioral problems of normal children between 21 months and 14 years.* Berkeley: University of California Press.

Maier, S. F., & Seligman, M. E. P. (1976). Learned helplessness: Theory and evidence. *Journal of Eperimental Psychology: General, 105*, 3–46.

Marsh, H. W., & Hocevar, D. (1988). A new, more powerful approach to multitrait-multimethod analyses: Application of second-order confirmatory factor analysis. *Journal of Applied Psychology, 73*, 107–117.

McCandless, B. (1967). *Children.* New York: Holt, Rinehart, & Winston.

Meehl, P. E. (1959). Some ruminations on the validation of clinical procedures. *Canadian Journal of Psychology, 13*, 102–138.

Meehl, P. E. (1977). Specific etiology and other forms of strong influence: Some quantitative meanings. *Journal of Medicine and Philosophy, 2*, 33–53.

Meehl, P. E. (1979). A funny thing happened to us on the way to the latent entities. *Journal of Personality Assessment, 43*, 564–581.

Meehl, P. E., & Golden, R. R. (1982). Taxometric methods. In P. C. Kendall & J. N. Butcher (Eds.), *Handbook of research methods in clinical psychology*. New York: John Wiley & Sons.

Metzner, H., & Mann, F. C. (1952). A limited comparison of two methods of data collection: The fixed alternative questionnaire and the open-ended interview. *American Sociological Review, 17*, 486–491.

Miller, W. R., & Seligman, M. F. P. (1975). Depression and the perception of reinforcement. *Journal of Abnormal Psychology, 82*, 62–73.

Ni Bhrolchain, M. (1981). Depressive illness: Clinically diverse? *British Journal of Psychiatry, 138*, 161–163.

Nias, D. K. B. (1972). The effects of providing a warning about the Lie Scale in a personality inventory. *British Journal of Educational Psychology, 42*, 308–312.

Ollendick, T. H., & Hersen, M. (Eds.). (1984). *Child behavioral assessment*. New York: Pergamon Press.

Orvaschel, H., Puig-Antich, J., Chambers, W., Tabrizi, M. A., & Johnson, R. (1982). Retrospective assessment of prepubertal major depression with the Kiddie-SADS-E. *Journal of the American Academy of Child Psychiatry, 21*, 392–397.

Palmer, J. O. (1970). *The psychological assessment of children*. New York: John Wiley & Sons.

Parke, R. D., & Slaby, R. (1983). The development of aggression. In P. H. Mussen (Ed.), *Handbook of child psychology*, Vol. IV. New York: Wiley.

Patterson, G. R. (1986). Performance models for antisocial boys. *American Psychologist, 41*, 432–444.

Patterson, G. R., & Bank, L. (1987). When is a nomological network a construct? In D. R. Peterson & D. B. Fishman (Eds.), *Assessment for decision* (pp. 249–279). New Brunswick, NJ: Rutgers University Press.

Peterson, D. R. (1961). Behavior problems of middle childhood. *Journal of Consulting Psychology, 25*, 205–209.

Pogul, L. J. (1980). Psychological testing in childhood. In J. R. Bemporad (Ed.), *Child development in normality and psychopathology* (pp. 477–508). New York: Brunner/Mazel, Inc.

Poznanski, E., Mokros, H. B., Grossman, J., & Freeman, L. N. (1985). Diagnostic criteria in childhood depression. *American Journal of Psychiatry, 142*, 1168–1173.

Puig-Antich, J., & Chambers, W. (1978). *The schedule for affective disorders and schizophrenia for school-age children (Kiddie-SADS)*. New York: Psychiatric Institute.

Puig-Antich, J., Chambers, W. J., & Tabrizi, M. A. (1983). The clinical assessment of current depressive episodes in children and adolescents: Interviews with parents and children. In D. P. Cantwell & G. A. Carlson (Eds.), *Affective disorders in childhood and adolescence: An update* (pp. 157–180). New York: Spectrum Publications, Inc.

Quay, H. C. (1979). Classification. In H. C. Quay & J. S. Werry (Eds.), *Psychopathological disorders of childhood* (2nd. Ed.). New York: John Wiley & Sons.

Reich, W., & Earls, F. (1987). Rules for making psychiatric diagnoses in children on the basis of multiple sources of information: Preliminary strategies. *Journal of Abnormal Child Psychology, 15*, 601–616.

Rie, H. E. (1963). An exploratory study of the CMAS/Lie Scale. *Child Development, 34*, 1003–1017.

Risley, T. R., & Hart, B. (1968). Developing correspondence between the non-verbal and verbal behavior of preschool children. *Journal of Applied Behavioral Analysis, 1*, 267–281.

Robins, L. (1966). *Deviant children grown up*. Baltimore: Williams & Wilkins.

Robins, L. (1978). Sturdy childhood predictors of adult outcomes: Replications from longitudinal studies. *Psychological Medicine, 8*, 611–622.

Roth, M. (1978). Psychiatric diagnosis in clinical and scientific settings. In *Psychiatric diagnosis: Exploration of biological predictors*. Spectrum Publications.

Rushton, J. P., Brainerd, C. J., & Pressley, M. (1983). Behavioral development and construct validity: The principle of aggregation. *Psychological Bulletin, 94*, 18–38.

Rutter, M. (1965). Classification and categorization in child psychiatry. *Journal of Psychology and Psychiatry, 6*, 71– 83.

Rutter, M. (1985). Psychopathology and development: Links between childhood and adult life. In M. Rutter and L. Hersov (Eds.), *Child and adolescent psychiatry: Modern approaches* (2nd Edition) (pp. 720–739). Oxford: Blackwell.

Rutter, M. (1986). The developmental psychopathology of depression. In M. Rutter, C. E. Izard, & P. B. Reed (Eds.), *Depression in young people: Developmental and clinical perspectives* (pp. 3–30). New York: Guilford Press.

Rutter, M. (1988). Epidemiological approaches to developmental psychology. *Archives of General Psychiatry, 45*, 486–495.

Rutter, M., & Garmezy, N. (1983). Developmental psychopathology. In E. M. Hetherington (Ed.), *Handbook of child psychology*. Vol 4. *Socialization, personality, and social development*. New York: Wiley.

Rutter, M., Tuma, A. H., & Lann, I. S. (Eds.). (1988). *Assessment and diagnosis in child psychopathology*. New York: Guilford Press.

Ryan, N. D., Puig-Antich, J., Ambrosini, P., Rabinovich, H., Robinson, D., Nelson, B., Iyengar, S., & Twomey, J. (1987). The clinical picture of major depression in children and adolescents. *Archives of General Psychiatry, 44*, 854–861.

Sattler, J. M. (1974). *Assessment of children's intelligence*. Philadelphia: W. B. Saunders.

Schmitt, N., & Stults, D. M. (1986). Methodology review: Analysis of multitrait-multimethod matrices. *Applied Psychological Measurement, 10*, 1–22.

Seligman, M. E. P. (1975). *Helplessness: On depression, development, and death*. San Francisco: W. H. Freeman.

Simmons, J. E. (1981). *Psychiatric examination of children*. Philadelphia: Lea & Febiger.

Skinner, H. A. (1981). Toward the integration of classification theory and methods. *Journal of Abnormal Psychology, 90*, 68–87.

Spiker, C. C., & McCandless, B. R. (1954). The concept of intelligence and the philosophy of science. *Psychological Review, 61*, 255–266.

Spitzer, R. L., & Williams, J. B. (1985). Classification of mental disorders. In H. I. Kaplan & B. J. Sadock (Eds.), *Comprehensive textbook of psychiatry* (Vol. IV) (pp. 591–612). Baltimore: Williams & Wilkins.

Sroufe, L. A. (1979). The coherence of individual development: Early care, attachment, and subsequent developmental issues. *American Psychologist, 34*, 834–841.

Sroufe, L. A., & Rutter, M. (1984). The domain of developmental psychopathology. *Child Development, 55*, 17–29.

Strober, M., & Carlson, G. (1982). Bipolar illness in adolescents with major depression. *Archives of General Psychiatry, 39*, 549–558.

Thomas, A., Chess, S., & Birch, H. G. (1968). *Temperament and behavior disorders in children*. New York: New York University Press.

Vondra, J., Barnett, D., & Cicchetti, D. (1988). *Perceived and actual competence among maltreated and comparison school children*. Unpublished manuscript. University of Rochester.

Wallerstein, J. S. (1983). Children of divorce: Stress and developmental tasks. In N. Garmezy & M. Rutter (Eds.), *Stress, coping and development in children* (pp. 265–302). New York: McGraw-Hill

Weinberg, W. A., Rutman, J., Sullivan, L., Penick, E. C., & Dietz, S. G. (1973). Depression in children referred to an educational diagnostic center: Diagnosis and treatment. Preliminary report. *Journal of Pediatrics, 83*, 1065–1072.

Weiss, B., & Weisz, J. R. (1988). Factor structure of self-reported depression: Clinic-referred children versus adolescents. *Journal of Abnormal Psychology, 97,* 492–495.

White, B. J., & Harvey, D. J. (1965). Effects of personality and our stand on judgement and production of statements about a central issue. *Journal of Experimental Social Psychology, 1,* 334–347.

Widaman, K. F. (1985). Hierarchically nested covariance structure models for multitrait-multimethod data. *Applied Psychological Measurement, 9,* 1–26.

Wiggins, J. S. (1973). *Personality and prediction: Principles of personality assessment.* Massachusetts: Addison-Wesley Publishing Company.

Yamamoto, K. (1979). Children's ratings of the stressfulness of experiences. *Developmental Psychology, 15,* 581–582.

Yarrow, L. J. (1960). Interviewing children. In P. H. Mussen (Ed.), *Handbook of research methods in child development.* New York: John Wiley and Sons.

Yeaworth, R. C., York, J., Hussey, M. A., Ingle, M. E., & Goodwin, T. (1980). The development of an adolescent life change event scale. *Adolescence, 15,* 91–97.

Zax, M., Gardiner, D. H., & Lowy, D. G. (1964). Extreme response tendency as a function of emotional adjustment. *Journal of Abnormal and Social Psychology, 69,* 654–657.

Zigler, E., & Glick, M. (1986). *A developmental approach to adult psychopathology.* New York: John Wiley & Sons.

Bootstrapsing Taxometrics:
On the Development of a Method for
Detection of a Single Major Gene
Robert R. Golden

The possibility of studying actual causal entities is especially appealing (if not a welcome relief) to that minority of psychometric researchers who are philosophical "realists," who are interested in psychiatric theories and constructs that refer to conjectural, if not established, *entities*. The significance of the methodology discussed herein does, of course, cut much deeper than mere talk about entities. In fact, we believe it fair to say that, with bootstrapsing taxometrics, it should be possible to start out with a small number of substantive and statistical conjectures (not really "knowing" anything) about a single major gene and its indicator-variables, and end up, solely on the basis of a statistical analysis of the associations of conjectural indicator-variables, with profound evidence that the conjectural gene exists or doesn't exist; and if it does, the approximate values of its base rate, the parameters of the latent distributions on the indicator-variables, and, for each individual, the probability of carrying the gene. That is, with bootstrapsing taxometrics, we start out knowing nothing and end up knowing just about everything we could ever hope to know! We will argue that it is even conceivable that a taxometrician not knowing anything about substantive issues in medical research, if given a set of ordinary variables selected for, say, epidemiological research, to play with, could make a profound contribution to the discovery of the specific etiological cause of schizophrenia or Alzheimer's disease. The researcher who is familiar with the results of traditional psychometric measurement must be warned emphatically that the intended purpose of bootstrapsing taxometrics (which is rigorous and convincing *detection* of conjectured entities)

I wish to thank Mary Mayer Golden for numerous substantive and analytical contributions which have helped bootstrap the content, style, and clarity not only of the present chapter, but also of my understanding of bootstrapsing taxometrics in general. I am grateful to Dr. Will Grove for many helpful comments on several drafts of this essay.

is in stark contrast to that of traditional psychometric *measurement* of personality and psychiatric traits, the results of which, in comparison, can often be characterized as arbitrary, unconvincing, and even fictional.

For over 25 years, one of Paul Meehl's major research interests has been the study of statistical detection of a "conjectural latent taxon." While a "taxon" can be generally defined as a causal-mathematical concept that cuts across all sciences, the term will be used here to mean a *"dichotomous specific etiological factor"* or *"strong causal influence"* (Meehl, 1978b) such as, say, a gene, a virus, or a biochemical threshold effect whose presence and absence results in a syndrome or statistical clustering of symptoms or traits. In this medical context, the "taxon" is composed of those individuals for whom the specific etiological factor is present. That is, the taxon consists of those individuals who have the full-blown disease plus those who are said to have a "latent," "subclinical" or "preclinical" form, that is, those who are symptomatic and those who are asymptomatic. Indeed, it would be preferable to have a term that designates individuals in such a taxon, but, evidently, in the field of medicine there is no such term that is generally accepted. Feinstein (1963) suggests that the term "lanthanic" would be preferable in some medical contexts to "latent," since it refers to both symptomatic and asymptomatic individuals with the disease.

A strong causal influence or specific etiological causal factor exists for a wide variety of diseases and syndromes. The general nature of such a factor or specific cause is probably most often that of a "basic lesion" (a derangement in some cell, tissue, or chemical) as described by Feinstein (1963). While the methodology we discuss in the present chapter is just as appropriate for the detection of taxa resulting from basic lesions and other etiological causal factors, we will be primarily concerned with a taxon that results from a single major gene acting in the role of a specific etiological cause. Restricting attention to the conceptually clear case of a single major gene simplifies, and, therefore, clarifies, discussion of some past misunderstandings and of recent developments in bootstrapsing taxometrics. The case of a single major gene is, of course, an important one, and there are many terribly complex issues involved in the application of genetics to the problems of discovery and confirmation of diseases and syndromes in psychiatry research, such as those described by Murphy (1964, 1987).

As one result of his research in taxometrics, Meehl (1973a, note 1) has proposed a novel and uniquely promising methodology that should make it possible to test the existence of a single major gene as a cause of a syndrome or disorder. A novel solution to this statistical problem, known as a "mixture" problem in the field of statistics, is required since there is no dependent or criterion variable (since the existence or not of such an etiological factor is the fundamental question to be answered)—*only the statistical associations between fallible, causally nonspecific, and conjectural indicators of the taxon are available.*

Meehl's interest in taxometrics began over a quarter-century ago when he published his theory of schizophrenia (Meehl, 1962), in which it was hypothesized that only a certain class of individuals—those who carry the "schizogene"—have any liability for schizophrenia. This hypothetical or conjectural class was referred to in subsequent publications as the "schizotypal taxon."

Later, Meehl (1973a) gave a comprehensive description of the general nature of the methodological and statistical problems encountered in testing this theory. A brief summary of this description is given in Golden and Meehl (1979): if, as Meehl proposes, the specific etiology of the schizotype personality is a single dominant gene, and the only indicators available are highly fallible phenotypic ones, how can the probability that a person carries this gene be estimated? Currently, there is no generally acceptable criterion variable and no definitive diagnostic touchstone, sign, symptom, or trait that can be measured reliably. Not all the correlates of schizotypy are sufficiently pathological to be called "symptoms" or valid enough to be called "signs" (hence, we will use the term "indicator"). Thought disorder or "cognitive slippage," which is viewed by Meehl (following Bleuler) as the primary indicator of schizotypy, is not sufficient by itself for taxonomic purposes. Meehl notes that clinical manifestations of cognitive slippage often seen during intensive psychotherapy of psychiatric patients can be used as inclusion tests for schizotypy, in that their presence is a quasi-infallible indication of the presence of this particular pathology. Unfortunately, these manifestations are too rare to be used successfully as exclusion tests; their absence does not necessarily imply absence of schizotypy.

No clearly valid psychometric test of cognitive slippage is available—an especially serious problem for researchers who would like to study schizotypy as a hypothetical taxon that includes both schizophrenics and schizotypes (many of whom never manifest diagnostically psychotic degrees of cognitive slippage). Therefore, we have a perfect example of a "bootstraps" problem, one in which we must start with a fallible set of indicators of unknown validities and hope to end up with accurate estimates of these validities on the basis of some internal statistical relationships among them.

More or less independent of such developments in taxometrics, there has been considerable renewed interest in a single major gene hypothesis regarding the etiology of schizophrenia. A recent linkage study noted in the November 1988 issue of *Nature* claims to have identified the approximate location of a gene for schizophrenia. The revival of interest in the conjectural schizogene is probably due, in most part, to recent laboratory research on smooth pursuit eye movement (SPEM) variables by Holzman and his colleagues (Holzman, Solomon, Levin, & Waternaux, 1984; Holzman, Kringlen, Matthysse, Flanagan, Lipton, Cramer, Levin, Lange, & Levy, 1988; Lipton, Levy, Holzman, & Levin, 1983) and by other teams of researchers who have repeatedly demonstrated the potential validity of these indicator-tests for the schizogene. With Meehl's taxometric methodology, it will evidently be possible to test this hypothesis by statistical analysis of, say, two or three smooth pursuit eye movement scores (obtained on different occasions) for a large sample (say 500) of first-degree relatives of diagnosed schizophrenics, such as the one being collected by Tsuang and his colleagues at Harvard. Lipton and I have recently found that a frequency distribution of SPEM scores for a sample of 101 first-degree relatives of schizophrenics is very similiar to that for a mixture of equal numbers of diagnosed schizophrenics and normals.

That Meehl's taxometric methodology is the most exciting development in psychiatric statistics is in part due to the fact that he has provided sophisticated, clear, and elegant philosophy-of-science explication and methodological clarification of important concepts of taxometrics such as "latent taxon," "syndrome," "specific etiological cause" and "disease" as well as many other methodological facets of the "latent taxon problem" (Meehl, 1972, 1973a, 1973b, 1978a, 1978b, 1979, 1986); also see Meehl and Golden, 1982, for a unified review of previous work up to that time. But for those of us intimately involved with the further development and application of this methodology, the excitement comes from the sense that we may soon see the validity of the methodology cleanly illustrated by empirical examples.

Origin of the Term "Bootstrap"

Meehl's publications in taxometrics began in 1965 with a very significant research report (Meehl, 1965)—the first of ten "yellow monsters," as they were called by colleagues (Meehl, 1968, 1982; Meehl et al., 1969; Golden & Meehl, 1973a, 1973b, 1974; Golden, Tyan, & Meehl, 1974a–c). In this initial report, he first described the precise nature of a solution to the interrelated statistical problems regarding covariance mixture analysis and consistency testing of auxiliary assumptions. This report also provided a number of significant preliminary theorems. The most notable of these was the "Super Bootstraps Theorem," which shows how taxometric analysis of a set of indicators of, say, a gene—all of which are conjectural and most of which are, in fact, highly fallible—can still result in the discovery of an infallible indicator, if one should exist.

Meehl's classic paper with Cronbach on construct validity (Cronbach & Meehl, 1955) formally introduced the term "bootstraps effect" to designate a paradoxical feature of the growth of knowledge concerning theoretical entities. They describe how the construct validity of an indicator of a conjectural entity, over the course of time, sometimes obtains a higher status than that accorded when the construct was initially identified and the indicator was originally validated. The classic example in psychology is the intelligence test, which was initially validated against such crude criteria as chronological age. They point out that this evidence, along with intra-test item analyses, has resulted in a bootstraps effect such that most teachers regard a combination of high IQ test score and poor school performance as indicative of academic underachievement.

Subsequently, the term "bootstrap" was also used in modern mathematical statistics to refer to a method developed by Efron (1979, 1982) for the study of the variability of parameter estimates. This method allows statisticians, in effect, to replace model assumptions with massive calculations (for a clear description of the method, see Diaconis and Efron, 1983, and Efron and Gong, 1983). The growth of knowledge (regarding estimation accuracy)—or the improvement in the reliability of scientific inference by means of this method—is also paradoxical, in that the data of only one random sample is used to estimate the variability of a parameter estimator that would obtain if a large number of such random samples were available. Efron's method is growing rapidly in popularity among statisticians so that now there are several types of bootstrap methods in statistics (for example, see Banks, 1988, for a comparison of some of these methods). The method is now used in most fields of science and was even recently described in the November 8, 1988, issue of the *New York Times*. As a result, use of the term "bootstraps"in the field of psychostatistics can cause confusion; in fact, a lecture with a title the same as this chapter, given in a department of psychiatry, attracted more statisticians than psychiatrists and social scientists. As but one example of the application of statistical bootstraps methods in psychological statistics, see Lunneborg (1985).

In the title of the present chapter, the meaning of the term is in the sense of Meehl and Cronbach's original usage. That is, we are interested in the use of conjectural indicators for the detection of a single major gene. If a single major gene were discovered (i.e., corroborated or confirmed), the "bootstrap effect" here would refer to the paradoxical feature of the growth of knowledge concerning that gene. We would then expect the construct validity of one or more indicators of the single major gene to obtain a higher status.

Bootstrapsing Taxometrics

Meehl has noted how much is conjectural and how little corroborated with respect to the "schizogene." We conjecture that there is such a taxon, but we do not "know it." If there is such a taxon, we do not know its base rate. We do not know whether the taxon complement is itself taxonically differentiated. We have tentative notions about some indicators of the taxon, but we lack numerical estimates of their validities. We do not know the valid and false positive rates achievable by the best cut score. We do not know what the indicator distributions within the taxon and within the complement are shaped like, and we are unwilling to conjecture that they are normal or equal in variance. We do not know whether the candidate indicators are appreciably correlated within the taxon (if it exists) or outside it. We are aware of the unpleasant possibility that a schizogene discriminator may also have some validity for some unidentified extra-taxon groups, in which case the indicators will necessarily be correlated in the complement. In short, we know essentially nothing, and about some of these quantitative questions we do not even have plausible conjectures. Such a knowledge situation is in our opinion a *classic case appropriate for bootstrapping taxometrics*.

Such considerations regarding our antecedent state of knowledge are mentioned solely to motivate the taxometric methodology. They should not be relied upon in the traditional statistician's sense of "necessary assumptions." We do not regard any of the conjectures, main or auxiliary, as "assumptions" in that strong sense. Everything that is said, whether in the formalism of the taxometric method or the interpretative text, is conjectural. Also, Meehl, following Popper (1962), points out the methodological advantage of a main conjecture that goes far beyond facts presently known: bold conjectures, if wrong, are easily refuted and, therefore, bold conjectures that survive strong tests are strongly confirmed.

However, it is sad but true that, almost 30 years after Meehl's initial insights, no gene, virus, or any other kind of such a dichotomous causal factor has been discovered by use of bootstrapsing taxometrics. And if Meehl is to receive full credit for his brilliant theoretical work and conceptual clarification, we must have one clear instance of success. I will argue in this chapter that the lack of a successful example does not result from a fatal flaw in basic methodology, but is in part due to assumptions previously used for the mathematical development of the method. That is, while I believe that bootstrapsing taxometrics is methodologically sound, it is evident that the mathematics of the methods still has some bugs in it.

In the present essay, I specifically discuss some of the lessons we have learned and pitfalls we have discovered, in attempting to use, test, and advance Meehl's taxometric methodology. For example, we analyze the underlying model assumptions we have commonly used in the past, such as independence of indicators within each taxonomic class. We show how the use of diagnostic or screening scales that sharply discriminate at one level of the underlying trait (described as "peaked" in the field of educational measurement) can easily result in a "pseudo taxon." Also, we discuss what is required of indicators in terms of "specificity" for the single major gene, level of measurement, and the homoscedasticity of measurement precision. Based on these considerations, a revised taxometric method is described and its application illustrated.

Since my own major research interests are in the field of "taxometrics" (or "numerical taxonomy" as it is called in the East), my intellectual debt to Meehl is even more enormous than one might expect for a student-cum-colleague. However, the reader should be aware that the present essay contains many of my own ideas about taxometrics—some of which Meehl has not heard and, therefore, may not fully endorse.

Past Taxometric Models

A wide variety of taxometric methods has been developed for different purposes by a number of researchers from various disciplines. These include, to name but a few, the popular cluster-analysis methods as described by Fleiss and Zubin (1969), Blashfield (1976, 1984), Blashfield and Aldenderfer (1978), Sneath and Sokal (1973), Mezzich and Solomon (1980), Hartigan (1975), Everitt (1980) and other prominent members of the Classification Society, the latent-class models developed by Lazarsfeld and Henry (1968), Clogg (1977), Goodman (1975), Young (1983), Young, Tanner, and Meltzer (1982), Haberman (1979), and Rindskopf and Rindskopf (1986) and the so-called normal "mixture models" described in Titterington, Smith, and Makov (1985) and in Everitt and Hand (1981) [also see Hasselblad (1968) and Day (1969)]. Application of mixture models to problems in psychiatry are described by Gibbons et al. (1984). A mathematically sophisticated treatment by Bartholomew (1987) shows how many of these latent variable models are formally related to each other and to the factor-analytic model.

Golden and Meehl (1978, 1979, 1980), Meehl and Golden (1982), and Golden (1982) have attempted to develop taxometric methods that would avoid the propensity for spurious taxon detection, an obvious shortcoming of the previous cluster methods, normal-mixture methods, and the latent-class methods. We have emphasized the necessity of developing strong (risk of refutation) tests of the assumptions underlying the model by making intra-model numerical point-estimations or other "risk-taking" predictions such as Sir Karl Popper, the philosopher of science, advocates. These tests were christened "consistency tests" by Meehl in the first yellow monster (Meehl, 1965). In this important way, the mathematics of our methods differs from the previous cluster, normal-mixture, and latent-class models.

Model validity checking by consistency tests is intended, of course, to help reassure us that our finding of a "taxon" is not "spurious" and that the parameter estimates are accurate. When a conjectured single major gene does not exist, the result of a taxometric analysis (even though it may have the appearance of cohesiveness and good content validity, and makes reasonably good intuitive sense) is what we will call a "pseudo-taxon."

An Example of a Psuedo-Taxon

I'll now describe how we discovered that it is quite possible to fool the consistency tests developed for one of these models. A pseudo-taxon was obtained in a recent application of a latent-class method, even though much work went into the development of rigorous consistency tests for the method.

Several researchers have proposed a single-gene theory of Alzheimer's disease that is similar in form to Meehl's theory of schizophrenia. In this theory it is also hypothesized that only a certain class of people—those with a particular genetic constitution—have any liability for Alzheimer's disease. If the specific etiology of Alzheimer's disease is a single dominant gene, and the only indicators available are highly fallible phenotypic ones, we again have the problem of estimating the probability that a person carries this gene without a generally acceptable criterion variable or a definitive diagnostic touchstone, sign, symptom, or trait that can be reliably measured. Memory impairment, currently viewed as the primary indicator of Alzheimer's disease, is not sufficient by itself for taxonomic purposes.

The latent-class model used for the present example required the use of dichotomous indicators. All indicators were coded 1 for positive and 0 for otherwise. This method has been described in detail in Golden (1982) and is based on the assumption that the latent within taxonomic class covariances are each zero; under this assumption we were able to derive estimates of the latent taxonomic class base rates and the latent valid and false positive rates for each of the indicators.

The method had been tested by several empirical trials. First was a study of nephrotic renal kidney disease in children (Freeman, 1981; Golden & Freeman, 1983), the results of which were very encouraging in that the estimates of the base rate and the indicator valid and false positive rates were always within two standard errors of the actual values. In another empirical trial, MMPI items (which were known to discriminate between the sexes and were on the masculinity-femininity scale) were used in a pseudo-problem in an attempt to detect a known underlying taxonomy of biological sex (Golden & Meehl, 1980).

Extensive Monte Carlo runs covering various latent parametric situations and a wide range of sample sizes were conducted, an important part of that procedure being to study how well the consistency tests detect sample results as untrustworthy—as giving the wrong answer. These Monte Carlo trials have shown that accurate parameter estimation requires at least five indicators with validities (valid positive rate less the false positive rate) of .40 or more, that for such a set of indicators and a sample size of 500 a taxon base rate of .10, or even .05, is not too low, that indicator correlations within taxonomic classes need only be less than .20 and, generally, that the consistency tests accurately warn us if parameter estimates are not sufficiently accurate.

In the present example, the mental-status item scores of a sample of 408 individuals (32 with a diagnosis of clinical dementia), age 80 and older and living in communities in New York City, were analyzed. The mental-status exam used was developed by Blessed, Tomlinson, and Roth (1968), and consists of simple questions testing knowledge of the year, month, day, name of the president and past presidents, and the name, age, address, and length of residence of the subject. The individual's responses are scored as either correct or incorrect, according to agreement with an accepted criterion source.

Starting with 28 mental-status items, the application of the method resulted in the selection of items for which the model estimates of the valid and false positive rates are given in Golden and Golden (in press). In this particular example, the estimates of the indicator valid and false positive rates and the taxon base rate were each within two standard errors of the corresponding observed values for the diagnostic classes for clinical dementia. Of the 408 individuals in the sample, 32 were clinically diagnosed (by a neurologist, on the basis of an interview and neuropsychiatric testing of the subject) as having clinical dementia (Alzheimer's disease, multiple infarct dementia, or other organic dementia). The diagnosis was made within a few months after the administration of the mental-status exam. For these 32 cases there was clear agreement (no near misses) with the taxometric method; the total mental-status score was always 8 or greater and the taxometrically estimated probability of misclassification was nearly always less than .10, usually less than .05. (A cut score of 8 is the one agreed on by clinicians for a diagnosis of clinical dementia.)

Of the 14 individuals who were classified by the taxometric method as in the dementia taxon but not diagnosed as having clinical dementia, 8 had mental-status scores of 10 and above with taxometric estimates of probabilities of misclassification less than .05. A review of the assessment records of mental-status testing revealed that 5 of these 8 individuals were most likely in the early stages of clinical dementia. In addition to these 5 individuals with preclinical dementia, the dementia status for 6 individuals could not be determined: 3 had died, 3 had dropped out of the study. Since reassessment of the remaining 3 individuals did not show any clear evidence of clinical dementia, we concluded that for the 402 individuals for whom data were available, the two methods of diagnosis were consistent for all but 3 to 8 individuals (depending on the true taxonomic status of the 5 individuals with eventual probable clinical dementia). Suffice it to say at this point that the small number of discordant cases can be easily explained by unreliability in each of the two methods of classification.

That this analysis resulted in very close to the same classification as did clinical diagnosis of a *manifest clinical syndrome*, i.e., clinical dementia, suggests that we should regard clinical dementia as taxonic (that is, owing to a single underlying dichotomous causal factor). As to the identity of this factor, it is evident that it is not a major Alzheimer gene, as we had hoped, for the estimated base rate is too low. Studies have consistently found that 20 to 30% or more of individuals aged 80 or older have clinical dementia, and it is believed most have Alzheimer's disease. Thus, we believe that for the present taxon to be a single major gene, the estimated base rate should have been between, say, .25 and .50, and should have included many more latent cases. Another reason that the factor is not a major Alzheimer gene is that most, if not all, of the members of the purported taxon were full-blown cases (or nearly so); that is, there were approximately 50 individuals who showed little or no abnormal responses to the present indicators (i.e., for each, the estimated probability of being in the taxon was less than .05), but were later (within the following six years) diagnosed with clinical dementia (mostly Alzheimer's disease).

The purported taxon does not bear directly on the question of testing the existence of a major gene having to do with a *latent vulnerability* or proneness for Alzheimer's disease. It does suggest that we should consider removing full-blown cases from the analyses or use indicators that are less likely to be as sensitive to manifestations of the disease as they are to the latent gene. We are currently pursuing the latter alternative. [We have accidently discovered a promising statistical model for the diagnosis of clinical dementia that should prove very useful in large sample epidemiological studies].

If the purported taxon is not as we conjectured it should be, then what should we make of it? It is well understood that clinical dementia is a syndrome for which there are many known etiological antecedents, and probably many more that are not known. Conjectural and/or known organic etiologies of clinical dementia include Alzheimer's disease, hereditary neurogenerative diseases such as Huntington's Chorea, intracranial tumors, meningitis, deficiency diseases, metabolic disorders, and brain damage owing to trauma, cerebrovascular accidents, enzyme deficit, or toxic substances. General cognitive impairment such as that usually associated with clinical dementia can also be due to functional disorders such as schizophrenia and depression, other organic brain disorders, drug toxicity, nutritional deficiencies, and general cognitive traits such as low intelligence and poor memory, as well as to environmental conditions resulting in lack of education, poor understanding of the language, and so on.

It is not generally agreed or even previously conjectured by my neurologist colleagues that there is a single underlying causal factor (sometimes called a "common neurological pathway") such as a threshold parameter concerning the number of functional (relative to dysfunctional) neurons for many or most of the above etiological factors. Since, among neurologists, the existence of such a threshold factor is certainly not an often-made conjecture, the present taxometric result has also raised some suspicion regarding the taxometric method.

To summarize, although we attempted to detect a latent major gene for Alzheimer's disease, the present taxometric method identified instead an easily recognized phenotypic clustering of the indicators—for the manifest or full-blown clinical dementia syndrome—which is known to have numerous etiologies, but for which there is no known or conjectural common neurological pathway threshold factor. The lack of conjectural expectation of the purported taxon brings us back to the question "How confident should we be that the result is not spurious—that is, for example, merely a reflection of certain psychometric properties of the indicators we used?"

In another application of the latent-class method, to the syndrome of tardive dyskinesia in autistic children (Golden, Campbell, & Perry, 1987), a phenotypic clustering that agreed very well with a diagnostic category was detected. Further application of the method to sets of indicators of neonatal brain dysfunction in a large sample of high-risk infants (Golden, Vaughan, Kurtzberg, & McCarton, 1988), and to sets of indicator-scales for 24 disorders such as depression, functional disability, fear of crime, and vision impairment in a large sample of older individuals living in the community (Golden, Teresi, & Gurland, 1984) has also resulted in detection of phenotypic clusterings that correspond closely to diagnostic categories. In the next section I discuss the reasons for my belief that each of these examples is very likely a pseudo-taxon.

"Peaked" Indicators

To understand these results, we consider a model where there are no taxonomic classes resulting from a dichotomous factor but where there is underlying or latent continuous or dimensional factor. The dimensional factor can be an actual etiological factor (such as a parameter regarding caloric intake for the disease of obesity) or the cumulative effect of numerous fungible etiological factors. Such a model of a nontaxonomic situation for dichotomous indicators known as the "latent-trait model" and also as "item-response theory" has already been developed for other purposes by Lord (1980), Lord and Novick (1968), Wright and Masters (1982), and Rasch (1960) (see Hambleton and Cook, 1977, for a brief overview). In this latent-dimension model, we assume that the probability of a positive response or "indicator characteristic curve" (icc) is a normal ogival or logistic function of the latent-dimensional variable F. The icc for item i is a function of two parameters denoted by a_i and b_i. The parameter a_i is proportional to the slope of the indicator characteristic curve at the point of inflection, which is the point of the icc where the ordinate (the probability of a positive response) is .50 and where the abscissa $F = b_i$. The latent variable F is defined, without loss of generality, to have a mean of 0 and a standard deviation of 1. The indicator b-value (which is usually between -3 and $+3$ units of F), is that point on the latent dimension F at which the slope of the icc is greatest, that is, where the indicator best discriminates higher from lower scores on F. The a-value, which is usually between 0 and 5, describes how discriminating the indicator is at the point of inflection as it is proportional to the slope of the icc at this point. The a-values and the b-values can be estimated by various maximum-likelihood methods, and, for each individual, the associated point on the dimension F and its standard error can be estimated. While the model rests mainly on the assumption of a single underlying dimension F, it is also assumed that at each point on the dimension F, the positive responses to the indicators are pairwise independent.

This latent-dimension model was applied to data samples of the above examples. In each case, most of the indicators were sharply discriminating at approximately the same point on the latent dimension. In other words, the set of items or the scale of items was "peaked," i.e., the scale had a much higher precision of measurement at a certain point on the underlying dimension (Lord, 1980). It should also be noted that it is easy to see from the latent-dimension model that if the items are discriminating sharply enough at the same point on the latent dimension, then there are two subsamples with low indicator correlations within each (and, therefore, viewed by the latent-class method as the "taxon" and the "complement") and the distribution for the total scale score will be bimodal and will give the appearance of taxonicity. Grayson (1987) believes that this phenomenon makes it difficult if not impossible to distinguish "categorical and dimensional views," and I believe he is absolutely correct. In any event, these analytical considerations and the above empirical results are sufficient to convince me, then, that the latent-class model—as it stands—is seriously prone to spurious detection. These spurious results were made possible by the analysis of items from a peaked scale with a model based on the assumption of independence of indicators within each taxonomic class. We have found this assumption is often approximately satisfied by a certain kind of peaked clustering that is *not caused by a single etiological factor*.

A peaked scale can be viewed as having a kind of psychometric (not causal) "threshold" which gives rise to a pseudo-taxonicity. A proper selection of items may produce a scale that has uniform measurement error variance over a wide range of scores, whereas another selection of items can maximize the discrimination power of the scale over a narrow range of scores. Eaves (1983) points out that such properties of a scale can usually be easily engineered by the psychometrician (especially one who has read Lord, 1980). To see this, imagine a dimensional syndrome such that the indicators have a multivariate normal distribution which has one common factor. Lord and Novick (1968) have proved that cut-scores for these indicators can be found such that the resulting dichotomous data perfectly fit the (normal-ogive) latent-trait model described above and that the items have the same b-value (discriminate at the same point of the latent-dimensional variable) and have a-values that are monotonic functions of the correlation of the indicator with the common factor. It follows that it is not at all difficult to select from a large set of dichotomous indicator-symptoms a subset that is sufficiently peaked to produce a pseudo-taxon.

Psychometric threshold effects can also be unwittingly built into the scale by the particular method of item selection used. Therefore, we conjecture that scales constructed for screening and diagnostic purposes tend to have such a threshold, and, therefore, should not be used to detect the kind of taxon we are interested in. We conclude that it is probably best not to use psychometric scales or tests as indicators for the present type of taxometric problem.

Such psychometric threshold effects are often created by selection of items of tests and scales, but they can also be influential in more general ways, such as when indicators (symptoms) selected are those perceived by patients as serious enough to seek medical care, or those that interfere substantially with effective daily living. I believe it is probably fair to say that many diagnostic categories in psychiatry and medicine have more to do with this sort of threshold—a pseudo-taxonicity. Why scales developed in psychiatric and medical research are often likely to be peaked is discussed in more detail in Golden and Golden (in press). In that same paper we propose a model of pseudo-taxonicity and a necessary condition for the existence of a taxon.

Reevaluation of Past Taxometric Results

The propensity of the latent-class model for spuriousness is of special interest with respect to the "Mendelian Latent Structure Analysis" model developed by Matthysee, Holzman, and Lange (1986) (also see Holzman et al., 1988); the Golden-Meehl pilot study where selected dichotomous MMPI items were used as indicators purportedly to detect a schizoid taxon (Golden & Meehl, 1979; Nichols & Jones, 1985; and Miller, Streiner, & Kahgee, 1982); and the study by Gangestad and Snyder (1985), who used versions of our methods and concluded that a certain personality variable, which they called "self-monitoring," was taxonomic. Also, a latent-class analysis of attentional and neuromotor indicator-tests for a sample of high-risk children (with one or more schizophrenic parent) produced a "taxon" that has various appropriate statistical properties (Erlenmeyer-Kimling, Golden, & Cornblatt, 1989), but also see Erlenmeyer-Kimling, Cornblatt, and Golden (1983) and Golden, Gallob, and Watt (1983). I suggest that it is now evident that these findings of taxonicity must be put to a more rigorous test. I will discuss below how this could be done with a new method.

In other taxometric analyses, it has often not been our intention to detect a single etiological factor. Much of my own recent research in taxometrics or numerical taxonomy has focused on classification or "diagnosis" (as opposed to "detection") based on phenotypic clustering of syndromes in psychopathology and medicine (e.g., Golden, 1982; Golden, Campbell, & Perry, 1987; Golden, Vaughan, Kurtzberg, & McCarton, 1988). Also, in the clinical dementia study previously described, we are using the excellent model fit and correspondence to the diagnostic category as a means of studying the cultural bias of various mental-status indicator items (Golden, Kawas, & Katzman, in preparation).

Formulation of a Taxometric Method

Because of our experience with dichotomous indicators as described above, we believe the use of quantitative, ordinal, or graded indicators to be essential for taxometric detection of a single major gene. (The problem encountered in the use of dichotomous indicators has been discussed above.) Supposing we do have such an indicator, the distributions of the taxon and of the taxon-complement are of unknown variance and distribution function, and we do not even know the base rate for the taxon. The "optimal" cut for discriminating between the taxon and the complement depends not only upon the character of the two distribution functions, but also upon the base rate of the taxon. For our purposes, the optimal cut is one that minimizes the misclassifications. Meehl (1965) has shown how this cut, which he has called the "hitmax" cut, is easily seen from geometry or can be shown by differentiating the expression for total hits, to be the abscissa value at which the ordinates of the frequency distributions are equal, i.e., the position on the indicator above which the two frequency functions intersect.

Let W, X, and Y be three continuous or, at least, graded or ordinal (or as we shall say, "dimensional") indicator variables such that W is the "input" indicator and X and Y are the "output" indicators for the conjectured taxon and let us use the following notation:

N	: compound sample size
w	: an arbitrary but fixed interval of indicator W
P	: base rate of the taxon
$Q = 1 - P$	: base rate of the complement
$p(w)$	: proportion of those in the w interval who are in the taxon
$q(w)$	: proportion of those in the w interval who are in the complement
$M(X)$	: compound mean for indicator X
$M_t(X)$	: taxon mean for indicator X
$M_c(X)$	: complement mean for indicator X
$V(X)$	: compound variance for indicator X
$V_t(X)$	: taxon variance for indicator X
$V_c(X)$	: complement variance for indicator X
$C(X,Y)$	: compound covariance for indicator X & Y
$C_t(X,Y)$	: taxon covariance for indicator X & Y
$C_c(X,Y)$	: complement covariance for indicator X & Y
$C(X,Y/w)$	: compound covariance for indicators X & Y where $W = w$
$C_t(X,Y/w)$	: taxon covariance for indicators X and Y where $W = w$
$C_c(X,Y/w)$	: complement covariance for indicators X and Y where $W = w$

The development of the present method is based on a general algebraic identity which states that if X and Y are two random variables defined for a population consisting of two mutually exclusive subpopulations, then the covariance between X and Y for the compound or mixed population is the sum of two terms representing weighted covariances between X and Y within each of the two subpopulations, and a third term owing to the separation between the two subpopulations' means on each X and Y. We apply the algebraic identity to the particular situation where one subpopulation is the taxon and the other is the complement. Since the identity applies to any two exclusive and exhaustive subpopulations, it applies to these two subpopulations even though they are latent and their properties are unknown.

Specifically, the covariance between X and Y for any interval w of indicator W is

$$C(X,Y/w) = p(w)C_t(X,Y/w) + q(w)C_c(X,Y/w) + p(w)q(w)d(X/w)d(Y/w), \qquad (1)$$

where $p(w)$ is the proportion of individuals in the w interval that are members of the taxon, $q(w)$ is the corresponding complement proportion such that $p(w) + q(w) = 1$, $C_t(X,Y/w)$ is the latent covariance between X and Y for the taxon in interval w, $C_c(X,Y/w)$ is the corresponding complement covariance, $d(X/w)$ is the mean of X for the taxon less that for the complement in interval w, and $d(Y/w)$ is the corresponding mean difference for Y.

Similarly, for the two compound conditional variances, we have

$$V(X/w) = p(w)V_t(X/w) + q(w)V_c(X/w) + p(w)q(w)d^2(X/w), \qquad (2)$$

and

$$V(Y/w) = p(w)V_t(Y/w) + q(w)V_c(Y/w) + p(w)q(w)d^2(Y/w). \qquad (3)$$

The present model will be based on these three fundamental identities in much the same way as the MAXCOV-HITMAX method can be shown to be based on Equation 1 (Meehl, 1973a).

The Independence Assumption and Indicator Specificity

If the indicators were correlated only because of their causal relationship to the underlying causal factor, then they would be uncorrelated within each taxonomic class. This would mean that the indicators were in a certain sense "specific" to the latent factor: within each taxonomic class, the residual sources of variance of such an indicator are uncorrelated with those of another indicator. For this context, I will say that an indicator is "taxon-specific" if it has a variance component owing to the hypothesized single major gene but no such variance components owing, say, to potentiator variables, variables correlated with decompensation owing to the onset of the clinical syndrome or disease or any other nuisance factors that cause indicators to be correlated within the taxon or within the complement. I never expect to be able to find such perfect indicators, since I believe there are always latent nuisance factors.

Probably, the best we can hope for as specific indicators of a major gene are what Iacono (1985), Zubin and Steinhauer (1981), and others engaged in genetically motivated research call "markers" or "marker-variables." But marker-variables should not always be a necessity for our purposes (the fish sex example, p. 286). In any event, most indicators, including marker-variables, are not perfectly specific by any means. For example, smooth pursuit eye-tracking scores are evidently influenced by the schizogene(s), but they are also affected by other disorders (e.g., manic depression treated with lithium), and various factors related to the eye-tracking trait. As one more example, the mental-status and memory-test scores are correlated not only because of a conjectural etiological factor for Alzheimer's Disease, but primarily because of the net effect of many other disorders and socioeconomic, educational, and cultural nuisance factors. It is safe to say that we can expect that indicators will not be correlated merely because of the conjectural causal variable. That is to say that the indicators are nearly always clearly nonspecific and under the causal influence of several, possibly a large number, of underlying traits, states, predispositions, and conditions. An improved taxometric method would be able to handle commonly available indicators that have discriminant validity but little taxon-specificity.

The assumption of independence within taxonomic classes was used for past models, not only because of the resulting mathematical tractability, but also because it follows from the causal assumption that the indicators have only the specific causal factor (the single major gene) in common. As we have seen, the problem with this assumption is that when the dichotomous item indicators are peaked, then evidently a different kind of taxon—one resulting from a phenotypic clustering resulting from a threshold rather than a single taxonomic causal variable—most frequently satisfies this assumption. Suffice it to say that we have at least empirically discovered that, with the kind of indicators we have been using, this assumption clearly just doesn't work for the problem of detecting a single major gene.

Auxiliary Assumptions about the Correlation of Indicators

We make the simplifying assumptions (denoted by A') that within the taxon and within the complement the conditional covariance of X and Y and the conditional variance of X and of Y are constant over w-intervals. We refer to these as the "homoscedasticity assumptions," and note that they refer to latent conditions within the two taxonomic classes. Under these assumptions, the first two terms in the above equations are constants.

By another assumption (denoted by A'') the validities $d_x = d(X/w)$ and $d_y = d(Y/w)$ are assumed to be constant for all values of w. Under these assumptions, the observed covariance (or variance) of such a mixed population is a function of

the within-interval within-taxonomic class covariance (or variance) and the indicator validities d_x and d_y and the fact of taxonomic mix.

The two assumptions just described are stated as:

$$A': \ C_t(X,Y/w) = C_c(X,Y/w) = C_{xy} \text{ for all } w, \tag{4}$$

$$V_t(X/w) = V_c(X/w) = V_x \text{ for all } w, \text{ and} \tag{5}$$

$$V_t(Y/w) = V_c(Y/w) = V_y \text{ for all } w. \tag{6}$$

$$A'': \ d(X/w) = d_x, \text{ a constant for all } w, \text{ and} \tag{7}$$

$$d(Y/w) = d_y, \text{ a constant for all } w. \tag{8}$$

If the regressions of X on W and Y on W within each of the taxonomic classes
are linear and parallel:

$$A''': \ M_t(X/w) = b_x w + a_{tx}, \tag{9}$$

$$M_c(X/w) = b_x w + a_{cx},$$

$$M_t(Y/w) = b_y w + a_{ty}, \text{ and} \tag{10}$$

$$M_c(Y/w) = b_y w + a_{cy}, \text{ then}$$

$$d(X/w) = a_{tx} - a_{cx} \text{ and} \tag{11}$$

$$d(Y/w) = a_{ty} - a_{cy}$$

are constant for all w, the condition required by A'. Thus, if we assume the taxonomic class regression functions of X and Y on W are linear and parallel, we
obtain A''.

These assumptions follow if the general single factor model holds within each
taxonomic class

$$Y_t = cF_t + dU_t + D$$

$$Y_c = cF_c + dU_c, \qquad \text{where}$$

F is a common dimensional factor within each taxonomic class, U is the unique
residual factor (uncorrelated with F) and D is the conjectured causal factor (uncorrelated with U and F) and c and d are constant coefficients. Thus, the assumptions of the model hold when the factor structure is the same for two taxonomic
classes or when the multi-indicator distributions for the taxon and for the complement are the same except that one is simply "shifted" from the other by an
additive constant.

It can be said that the model is compatible with the situation where, *within*
each taxonomic class, the disease or syndrome is "multifactorial" where the
causal effects of such multiple causes are usually thought of as approximately
additive and such that some or all of the variables are interchangeable or
fungible.

We do not make any further assumptions about what the indicator distributions are shaped like within the taxon or within the complement; we are unwilling to conjecture, for example, that they are normal in shape or equal in variance. We note that if we were to make the assumption of multivariate normality with each taxonomic class as is done in the normal-mixture model, then that model, when confronted with indicators violating this assumption because of skewness or (platy) kurtosis, would "think" that these violations were caused by normal components (it would have no other choice!) and this would lead to pseudo-taxa. We conclude our discussion of assumptions by noting that while we still know essentially nothing about the nature of acceptable assumptions, we now believe that we have some plausible conjectures.

Illustrative Pseudo-Real Trial: Biological Sex

The application of the method will be illustrated by one of our favorite empirical trials of past publications. In this example, MMPI masculinity-femininity interest scales are used in a "pseudo-real trial" to detect the existence of the two biological sexes (i.e., the presence or absence of the Y chromosome) for a mixed-sex sample of psychiatric patients. The MMPI items for these scales were selected by comparing two samples of males and females on each of the 550 MMPI items and using those items that best discriminated one sample from the other. The items were scored 1 for a "female" response and 0 for a "male" response. The "female" and "male" responses were determined by comparing the response proportions of these same male and female samples and by considering the item content (i.e., face validity); the two methods agreed perfectly. It was found that 49 items significantly discriminated between the two samples. These items were used to make the three scales. See Golden and Meehl (1980) for other details concerning these data and for pseudo-real trials of several cluster methods. The statistical properties of the scales for the males, females, and the mixed sample are described in Tables 1, 2, and 3.

The scales discriminate with a little less than two within-sex standard deviations and are moderately correlated within class (.27 to .53), thereby providing an interesting trial of the method. The interested reader will no doubt be objecting: What if these scales are peaked? Were they not constructed so that they very well might be? The reader is correct, and an analysis of, say, height, weight, and waist circumference for a sample of adult men and women would be better for this purpose. However, data such as these were not available. Suffice it to say that, fortunately, the statistics in Tables 1 and 2 show that these scales are not peaked within the sexes. We will proceed with this example even though we recognize that it is not as elegant as it could be or as we once thought it was. (We note here that it would be of extreme interest to study the effect of "peakedness" by use of empirical trials of various combinations of the Mf items. One question

Table 1. Descriptive Statistics for the Males for the Indicator-Scale **W**

w	freq	M(X/w)	SD(X/w)	M(Y/w)	SD(Y/w)	C(X, Y/w)
1	1	6.00	0.00	6.00	0.00	0.00
2	7	8.85	1.72	7.28	1.16	−0.05
3	13	8.53	3.02	7.17	2.33	4.26
4	33	7.78	2.68	6.60	2.10	3.52
5	48	8.79	2.59	8.08	2.69	3.76
6	63	9.27	2.47	7.88	2.37	3.28
7	67	9.71	2.15	8.97	2.35	2.45
8	62	10.08	2.40	8.64	2.40	2.85
9	59	10.18	2.28	9.23	2.44	1.80
10	36	10.55	2.02	9.97	2.16	1.57
11	22	9.45	2.23	9.68	2.26	1.37
12	11	10.90	3.05	10.54	3.05	6.23
13	6	11.83	3.53	10.50	1.25	0.75
14	1	8.00	0.00	4.00	0.00	0.00
15	0					
16	1	10.00	0.00	8.00	0.00	0.00
17	0					
18	0					
19	0					
Total	430	9.57	2.55	8.59	2.57	3.45

we could answer is "Do Mf items selected because they discriminate well at any arbitrarily given point on the masculinity-feminity trait always lead to a pseudo-taxon?")

Initial Tests of Taxonicity

If we apply the above assumptions to equations (1), (2), and (3), we see that for the compound sample, whereas the conditional mean for the output indicator must be a monotonically increasing function (ogival in shape) of the input variable, the conditional variances and covariance for the output indicators must be parabolic functions of the input variable—each having the same w-value for its maximum. These criteria serve as initial checks of the validity of the model. In our biological-sex example, we can see from Table 3, the conditional variance and covariance functions are parabolic in shape and have local maxima for the same w-interval, just as predicted by the taxometric model. It should be noted that, as can be seen from Tables 1 and 2, these criteria are dramatically failed, just as they should be, for each of the male and female samples.

Table 2. Descriptive Statistics for the Females for the Indicator-Scale W

w	freq	$M(X/w)$	$SD\ (X/w)$	$M(Y/w)$	$SD(Y/w)$	$C(X,Y/w)$
1	0					
2	0					
3	0					
4	3	11.33	1.70	8.33	2.62	2.55
5	3	9.60	2.49	8.66	3.30	6.22
6	13	11.84	3.30	10.84	2.76	4.28
7	17	12.35	2.11	12.11	1.74	2.01
8	27	12.44	2.52	11.29	2.03	2.86
9	59	13.59	2.65	11.88	2.30	2.93
10	87	13.66	2.23	12.18	2.18	2.02
11	110	13.70	2.29	12.61	2.54	2.90
12	97	14.45	2.41	12.74	2.27	2.25
13	91	14.69	2.49	14.03	2.35	3.61
14	83	14.72	2.41	13.30	2.34	2.27
15	51	15.39	1.91	14.15	2.50	1.42
16	26	14.88	2.24	13.80	2.03	3.24
17	5	15.20	0.74	14.60	1.74	0.68
18	2	15.50	0.50	17.00	1.00	−0.50
19	1	17.00	0.00	13.00	0.00	0.00
Total	675	14.10	2.52	12.84	2.52	3.37

It is of interest to note here that since the Mf scales were administered at the same point in time and are approximately parallel forms, the conditional variance referred to above is measurement error variance. The present model tells us that if we have homoscedastic measurement error variance within the taxonomic classes, then for the compound sample the measurement error variance should increase as the w-interval approaches the hitmax interval. It might be said that this model predicts that when two fuzzy things are mixed, the result should be fuzzier in proportion to the degree of mix! Also, it is of interest to note that in this situation, it is because the indicators *are unreliable* that they can be used with the present method.

Suppose we consider a w-interval between the means for the females and males of our example. If the model holds and regressions are linear within the taxonomic classes, then for the males in the w-interval, there should be regression toward the (lower) male mean on the output indicator, and for the females in the w-interval, there should be regression toward the (higher) female mean on the output indicator. *That is, there should be two simultaneous "regression toward the mean" processes, but in opposite directions!* Such a phenomenon results in

Table 3. Descriptive Statistics for the Mixed Sample for the Indicator-Scale W

w	freq	$M(X/w)$	$SD(X/w)$	$M(Y/w)$	$SD(Y/w)$	$C(X,Y/w)$
1	1	6.00	0.00	6.00	0.00	0.00
2	7	8.85	1.72	7.28	1.16	-0.53
3	13	8.53	3.02	7.07	2.33	4.26
4	36	8.08	2.79	6.75	2.20	3.91
5	51	8.84	2.60	8.11	2.73	3.94
6	76	9.71	2.80	8.39	2.69	4.53
7	84	10.25	2.39	9.60	2.57	3.70
8	89	10.79	2.67	9.44	2.60	4.18
9	118	11.89	3.00	10.55	2.71	4.62
10	123	12.75	2.59	11.53	2.40	3.31
11	132	13.00	2.78	12.12	2.72	4.38
12	108	14.09	2.71	12.51	2.45	3.36
13	97	14.51	2.66	13.81	2.45	4.02
14	84	14.64	2.51	13.19	2.53	2.98
15	51	15.39	1.91	14.15	2.50	1.42
16	27	14.70	2.38	13.59	2.28	4.13
17	5	15.20	0.74	14.60	1.74	0.68
18	2	15.50	0.50	17.00	1.00	-0.50
19	1	17.00	0.00	13.00	0.00	0.00

the increased variance for the w-interval and can sometimes be directly observed in a scatterplot for the compound sample.

Since the present method primarily analyzes various aspects of the statistical regression of one indicator on another, we refer to it as the "taxonic regression" method.

Estimation of the Parameters

The parameters V_x, V_y and C_{xy} are estimated from the tails of the compound distribution on W. The left tail used was those intervals with w less than or equal to 3 and the right tail those intervals with w greater than 16. The estimated parameter values for the biological sex example are: $V_x = 5.33$, $d_x = 3.860$, $V_y = 5.11$, $d_y = 3.523$, and $C_{xy} = 2.65$.

With these parameter estimates, we will obtain estimates of the intercepts (a's) and the common slope (b) of the latent linear regression functions of Y on W and X on W. It follows that $V(X/w)$ and $V(Y/w)$ each have a maximum at the hitmax interval (where the two latent frequency functions intersect) and from (2) and (3)

$$d_x^2 = 4\{\max[V(X/w] - V_x\} \text{ and} \tag{12}$$
$$d_y^2 = 4\{\max[V(Y/w] - V_y\}.$$

If we estimate a_{cx} and a_{cy} from the conditional means

$$\{a_{cx} = M(X/w = 1) \text{ and } a_{cy} = M(Y/w = 1)\}, \text{ then since}$$
$$a_{tx} = d_x + a_{cx} \qquad a_{ty} = d_y + a_{cy}, \tag{13}$$

we can obtain estimates of a_{tx} and a_{ty}.

Also, using statistics from the hitmax interval (which is where the conditional covariance [or variance] has a maximum value)

$$b_x = [M(X/w = h) - \{(a_{cx} + a_{tx})/2\}]/h \text{ and} \tag{14}$$
$$b_y = [M(Y/w = h) - \{(a_{cy} + a_{ty})/2\}]/h.$$

(Note: To avoid excessive sampling error in the conditional means in the hitmax interval, they are smoothed by least-squares fitting polynomials of W of the 3rd to 5th degree.)

The values for the example are $a_{cx} = 8.11$, $a_{tx} = 11.97$, $a_{cy} = 6.41$, and $a_{ty} = 9.94$. It follows that $b_x = .192$ and $b_y = .274$.

Next, we smooth the $V(X/w)$, $V(Y/w)$, and $C(X,Y/w)$ functions before using them to estimate the latent frequency distributions on W.

From (1) we can obtain

$$C(X,Y/w) = C_{xy} + \{M(X/w) - b_x w - a_{cx}\}\{- M(Y/w) + b_y w + a_{ty}\}, \tag{15}$$

which can be written as

$$C(X,Y/w) = C_{xy} + \{M(X/w)' - a_{cx}\}\{-M(Y/w)' + a_{ty}\} \tag{16}$$

where $M(X/w)' = M(X/w) - b_x w$ and $M(Y/w)' = M(Y/w) - b_y w$ are conditional means adjusted for correlation with W. Similar expressions can be obtained for $V(X/w)$ and $V(Y/w)$. These quadratic functions of the adjusted means are used with linear least-squares regression to predict and smooth the $V(X/w)$, $V(Y/w)$, and $C(X,Y/w)$ functions.

We have shown that if the model holds, then the conditional interval covariance (or variance) is a particular quadratic function of conditional interval means and the input interval value. This would seem to be a bold prediction that is easily observed to be true or not! It also follows that the coefficients of this quadratic function should satisfy certain constraints.

Finally, we use the smoothed $V(X/w)$, $V(Y/w)$, and $C(X,Y/w)$ functions to estimate the latent frequency distributions on W. This is done by solving equations (1), (2), and (3) each for $p(w)$. The results for the example are given in Table 4.

Table 4. Estimated and Observed Taxon (Female) Frequency Distribution on **W**

w	from $V(X/w)$	from $V(Y/w)$	from $C(X,Y/w)$	Observed
1	0.00	0.00	0.00	0
2	0.00	0.00	0.00	0
3	0.00	0.00	0.00	0
4	3.42	4.37	4.91	3
5	7.90	8.87	11.70	3
6	17.92	18.42	24.03	13
7	27.95	27.07	33.45	17
8	39.72	36.41	44.50	27
9	59.00	59.00	62.82	59
10	79.01	71.97	75.68	87
11	98.29	87.81	91.74	110
12	89.94	79.28	84.13	97
13	87.52	76.33	84.31	91
14	79.60	68.83	81.15	83
15	49.14	42.17	51.00	51
16	27.00	27.00	27.00	26
17	5.00	5.00	5.00	5
18	2.00	2.00	2.00	2
19	1.00	1.00	1.00	1
Total	674.42	615.52	684.43	675
Mean	11.44	11.34	11.28	11.68

The present method of estimation does not make use of statistical theories such as least-squares that yield estimators with optimal properties. Clearly, it should be a matter of highest priority to develop such an optimal estimation procedure. But if the estimated latent frequency distributions are quasi-normal or can be transformed to be quasi-normal and the corresponding latent variance and covariance estimates are approximately equal, then the maximum-likelihood solution for the normal-mixture model (e.g., see Everitt & Hand, 1981; Day, 1969; Titterington, Smith, & Makov, 1985; or Hasselblad, 1968) can be used for optimal estimation and to check the results of the present method. The estimates of the present method can be used as initial guesses for the iterative procedure for the maximum likelihood estimation. Existing maximum-likelihood solutions for mixture models of exponential, Poisson, binomial, and other forms of latent taxonomic-class density functions can, of course, be used in the same manner.

Consistency Tests

Optimal parameter estimates, by themselves, will not answer our most important question. We want to know if, upon application of the model, the assumptions of the model are approximately correct so that the inference regarding the existence of a dichotomous causal variable such as a single major gene is likely to be correct. This is not a matter to be decided by the magnitudes of the parameter estimates, but one for some sort of model goodness (or, badness) of fit tests or internal model validity checks (we have already referred to such tests above as "consistency tests"). These consistency tests will consist of numerical point-estimation or other "risk-taking" predictions, capable of providing useful checks of the auxiliary assumptions of the taxometric method for any application of the method. Rozeboom (1966) gives an articulate discussion of how to ask, but not answer, such questions for such a statistical method. We believe that the essential idea to remember here is that we are not operating in the "context of discovery," but in the "context of justification" (Reichenbach, 1938). That is, we want consistency tests that, when passed, allow us to be confident about the existence of a previously conjectured underlying causal factor such as a single major gene. These consistency tests should be such that the likelihood of an incorrect confirmation of a major gene hypothesis which is actually false can be reasonably inferred to be adequately small, say, less than 1 to 5%, even if this should result in a considerably higher risk of failing to confirm a major gene hypothesis which is actually true.

It should be possible to empirically calibrate the consistency test parameters such that the tests are passed for a variety of samples for diseases or syndromes known to be dichotomously taxonomic and failed for others known to have a dimensional structure. In our biological sex example, the fact that the conditional variance and covariance functions are parabolic in shape with local maxima for the same w-interval, and the fact that each can be accurately predicted from the smoothed conditional means are in agreement with the taxometric model. These criteria serve as initial checks of the validity of the model.

We have shown that if the model holds, then the conditional interval covariance (or variance) is a particular quadratic function of conditional interval means and the input interval value and that the coefficients of these quadratic functions should satisfy certain constraints. This set of results seems to be an excellent opportunity for consistency testing.

Other consistency tests of the model are possible. For example, if the model holds, then the conditional covariance and the two conditional variances are linear functions of one another. As before, we can use least-squares linear regression methods to test these relationships. These predicted relationships hold approximately for our example as we can see from Figures 1, 2, and 3. The

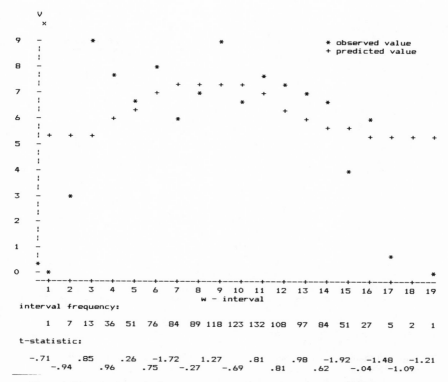

Figure 1. The mixed sample observed and conditional-mean-predicted values of the conditional variance of *X* as a function of interval for *W*. For each *W* interval, the t-statistic for comparison of these two values is given.

question is "How do we determine *how approximately* true such a relationship must be?" We are not interested in evaluating these relationships by significance testing (e.g., Student t-tests that compare observed and predicted values for each *w*-interval) in the traditional sense, as we never anticipate that any sample of data will result from a taxon for which the assumptions of the method are literally true. We understand that the old significance test controversy (e.g., see Morrison and Henkel, 1970; Meehl, 1970; Lykken, 1968; and Rozeboom, 1960) has, more or less, come and gone and those who know better don't rely very much, if at all, on such tests for evaluation of model fit.This is because we know in advance, for example, that the within taxonomic class regression functions will not be perfectly linear and parallel. Also, we know in advance, for example, that there is not just one specific etiological factor; we hope that the prevalence rates for all such factors other than the one of interest are sufficiently small. I discuss below

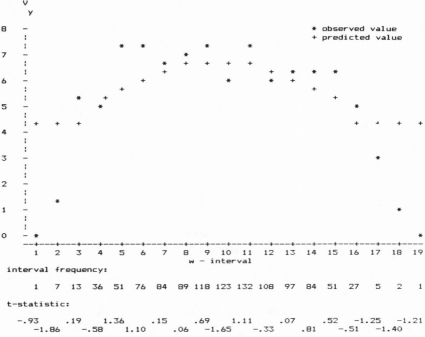

Figure 2. The mixed sample observed and conditional-mean-predicted values of the conditional variance of *Y* as a function of interval for *W*. For each *W* interval, the t-statistic for comparison of these two values is given.

how I believe the consistency tests can be empirically calibrated. Beyond this point, the development of the consistency tests is very incomplete and awaiting further research.

Steps in the Application of the Method

First, I believe that taxometrics or numerical taxonomy or cluster analysis should not be done without a sufficient "motivating text" (in terms of an explicit substantive theory or an underlying theoretical framework) that tells us what we are looking for with a taxonomic search method. Our philosophy is Bayesian in this sense—the prior probability of a taxon has to be high enough to make the analysis worth doing.

Second, if possible, the assumptions of linearity and parallel regression lines and homoscedasticity of variance and covariance within the taxonomic classes

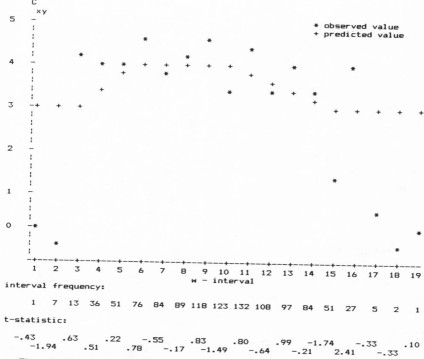

Figure 3. The mixed sample observed and conditional-mean-predicted values of the conditional variance of X and Y as a function of interval for W. For each W interval, the t-statistic for comparison of these two values is given.

should be checked in quasi-pure samples such as normals and those diagnosed to have the full-blown disease.

Third, the estimation procedures and consistency tests should be applied to the mixed sample. If the tests are passed, then the conjectural gene is "corroborated"; if the tests are failed, then either the conjectural gene is discorroborated or the auxiliary assumptions are not approximately valid or the indicators lack sufficient discriminant validity for the gene or something else is wrong with the data.

Fourth and last, the statistical bootstrap method developed by Efron can be used to obtain standard errors of each of the latent parameters estimated by the method. The consistency tests of taxonicity (which have dichotomous outcomes: pass or fail) can also be studied as to sampling variability with this method.

This will be a lot of work, but if statistical detection of a single major gene turns out to be possible, it should not be surprising that it required a major effort.

Pseudo-Real Trials

To many, the idea of using a statistical analysis of conjectural indicators for confirmatory detection or "discovery" of a conjectured major gene seems counterintuitive. One reason for skepticism is that the conjectural indicators proposed for use with this methodology are often ones developed as tests and scales for other purposes (such as clinical diagnosis or screening and epidemiological research). Experienced research psychologists are used to considering such tests and scales as measures of a trait, and often take pride in their ability to critically investigate what is 'in' a scale or a test in order to infer the nature of the trait being measured. But Meehl's methodology claims we might be able to use some of these same scales or tests not to measure a trait but to detect a gene! If some of us believe that attempts at trait measurement are often pretentious, then skeptics of the present methodology might believe that claiming to detect a gene by statistical analysis of conjectural indicators is probably absurd. The skeptic says: "How could eyetracking and thought disorder scales be used to detect a 'schizogene,' or intelligence and memory tests be used to detect an Alzheimer gene when these indicators are obviously under the influence of a very large number of causal variables and factors? We are asking the statistical method to somehow tell us if, among this large number of causal variables (undoubtedly many of which are totally unknown to us), there is one that has a comparatively profound causal influence on the indicators. Sounds impossible!"

While this may sound impossible to the skeptic, such questions are, in the final analysis, essentially empirical ones, and the answers have to be given in empirical terms. That is, it is necessary to provide examples of *known* etiological factors, nonspecific indicators, and data samples where these statistical methods can be applied and evaluated. For example, it is instructive and reassuring to note that a normal-mixture model analysis of fish lengths successfully detected taxa for different years of spawning and a similar analysis of another sample of fish detected two sexes and, thereby, correctly refuted a one-sex hypothesis (Titterington, Smith, & Makov, 1985). For example, currently we want to know if for a mixed sample of individuals with and without the HIV virus, the conditional variance and covariance curves for indicators of risky sexual behavior or intravenous drug use have, because of the virus variable, the predicted parabolic shapes that reveal the correct parameter values. Experience with many more examples such as these is obviously required to develop one's intuitions or get a feeling for how well and when Meehl's methodology might work.

Bootstrapsing taxometrics suggests that we think differently about indicators. For example, even though estimated gestational age, birth weight, and head circumference are usually regarded as indicators or even measures of "prematurity," which is regarded as a dimensional construct, we plan to use them as *in-*

dicators of a neonatal brain dysfunction in a large sample of low birth-weight infants. Such a conjectural taxon is based on the fact well known by pediatricians that high-risk infants who are "small for gestational age" have a poor prognosis with regard to brain dysfunction and mental retardation in early childhood (Lubchenco, Delivoria-Papadapoulous, & Searls, 1972; and Lubchenco, Bard, Goldman, Coyer, McIntyre, & Smith, 1974; also see McCarton, Golden, & Vaughan, 1988). Even though we have a dozen or so such indicators to analyze with the taxometric method, we do not expect to find a different "taxon" for every combination; in fact, such a result would merely cast doubt on the validity of the method.

As another example of how we must learn to think differently for bootstrapsing taxometrics, suppose for a sample of older individuals living in the community we attempt to test the existence of a major gene for Alzheimer's disease. Suppose for this population, we believe this gene has a prevalence of about .30 and that there is no other dichotomous causal factor for psychiatric disorders with such a high prevalence. Finally, suppose we first used mental-status and memory tests as indicators to evidently detect a taxon—quite possibly, the Alzheimer gene. If we then used depression scale or rating scores as indicators we should not expect to discover a depression taxon for this population; in fact, if the depression indicators have sufficient validity for the Alzheimer gene (which they well might), we should expect to detect the Alzheimer taxon again. The same can be said if we next used measures of functional disability as indicators or if we used intelligence test scores as indicators or any other variable that has adequate validity for the Alzheimer gene.

It will be necessary to select taxon or species examples from several domains of the biological and social sciences, emphasizing loose clusters that are known to reflect a truly dichotomous causal origin (preferably disease entities where there exists an external criterion provided by pathology and etiology). For each instance the requirements are that we have a syndrome of indicators of only moderate tightness and that we have an independent criterion (such as biopsy) that specifies what it means to carve nature at its joints. Eventually, we hope to employ many such pseudo-real problems ranging over neurology, pediatrics, internal medicine, behavioral genetics, and so forth. These problems are "real" in the sense that there are biological entities being measured and clustered, but "pseudo" in the sense that the taxon and its membership are known to us independently of the taxometric result.

As one example of a pseudo-real trial, we plan to utilize a sample of over 700 intravenous drug users (about half of whom have the HIV virus as determined by a serological test), with self-reports of frequency of injections in different situations such as in shooting galleries, with strangers, and so on as indicator variables. In this example, the presence and absence of the HIV virus is the criterion variable. (It is interesting to note that the HIV virus problem is not totally a pseudo one because there is some doubt, although only among a few investigators, that just a single virus is operating to cause AIDS, and it is suspected by many that the sensitivity and specificity of the serological test are much lower [say .90 each] for previously unhealthy populations such as intravenous drug users than for healthy populations such as homosexual men [believed to be about .98 or higher]. Estimation of these statistical properties might require taxometrics!)

Such empirical trials are important because, no matter how clear the mathematics of a method, it rests ultimately on idealizations or assumptions that are, we believe, always violated to some degree by any example of real data. In the face of these violations, we are always faced with the problem of robustness. How do we know the robustness of a particular method? Do the consistency tests work well enough to detect when a violation is so large that the parameter estimates are highly inaccurate or even meaningless? Do certain indicators fail because they do not discriminate the taxon from the complement well enough, because they do not conform to the auxiliary assumptions of the method and/or because of the existence of causal factors and their associated taxa other than the one of interest? Do the consistency tests tell us how to distinguish these situations?

Second, extensive Monte Carlo runs combining various latent parametric situations and a wide range of sample sizes will be conducted, an important part of that procedure being to study how well the consistency tests detect sample results as untrustworthy, as giving the ''wrong answer.'' Monte Carlo and pseudo-real trials should include situations where (it is known or believed that) there is no taxon, but in which various dimensional relationships produce a pseudo-taxonic situation. The question here is, can the method be fooled into finding a ''taxon'' when there isn't one?

In a live research problem by another investigator who posited a gene for alcoholism, the present method was applied to three psychometric indicators of proneness for alcoholism for a large sample of college students. We were somewhat reassured when each of the present consistency tests was clearly failed not because the etiology of proneness for alcoholism is clearly multifactorial but because there is little prior evidence of a single prominent dichotomous causal factor such as a gene. We believe single prominent dichotomous causal factors are relatively rare and, therefore, we actually expect that attempts to detect a taxon with the present method will meet with failure most of the time.

Finally, it will be deeply appreciated if the reader can help us identify available data bases of 300 or more individuals where suitable indicators of syndromes or diseases are available for live research or pseudo-real trials of the present method.

Summary

The intended purpose of bootstrapsing taxometrics (which is rigorous and convincing *corroboration* of conjectured entities) is quite out of the ordinary and is in stark contrast to that of traditional psychometric *measurement* of personality and psychiatric traits. It is suggested that it should be possible to develop consistency tests that, when passed, allow us to be confident about the existence of a previously conjectured underlying dichotomous causal factor such as a single major gene.

It can be argued that the most important aspect of Meehl's contribution to bootstrapsing taxometrics—beyond the mathematical development of statistical formalism or methods—is the insight he has provided in facing the general problem of statistical inference about a certain kind of causal entity. It is predicted that with bootstrapsing taxometrics, it will be possible to start out with various conjectures about a single major gene and about fallible and causally nonspecific indicators of it and end up, simply on the basis of a statistical analysis of the associations between the indicators, with profound evidence that a gene exists or not, and if it does, what its base rate is and the probability that an individual carries it. The use of "peaked" indicator scales and tests, coupled with the use of the auxiliary assumption of independence within taxonomic class, is suspected as the source of pseudo-taxa of most past analyses with our methods. Requirements of indicators in terms of the causal specificity, level of measurement, and homoscedasticity of measurement precision are discussed. Based on these considerations, a revised taxometric method, which we call the "taxonomic regression method"—an extension of Meehl's MAXCOV-HITMAX method—is proposed and illustrated.

The critical role of pseudo-real trials for the further development and testing of the taxometric method is discussed. It is predicted that such examples will demonstrate that empirical discoveries of dramatic significance are made possible with the present extension of Meehl's methodology.

References

Banks, D. L. (1988). *Exact comparisons of bootstrap methods*. (Report No. 427). Pittsburgh: Carnegie-Mellon University Department of Statistics.

Bartholomew, D. J. (1987). *Latent variable models and factor analysis*. New York: Oxford.

Barnes, D. M. (1988). Schizophrenia genetics: A mixed bag. *Science*, November, 1010.

Blashfield, R. K. (1976). Mixture model tests of cluster analysis: Accuracy of four agglomerative hierarchical methods. *Psychological Bulletin, 83*, 377–388.

Blashfield, R. K. (1984). *The classification of psychopathology: Neo-Kraepelinian and quantitative approaches*. New York: Plenum.

Blashfield, R. K., & Aldenderfer, M. S. (1978). The literature on cluster analysis. *Multivariate Behavioral Research, 13*, 271–295.

Blessed, G., Tomlinson, B. E., & Roth, M. (1968). The association between quantitative measures of dementia and of senile change in the cerebral grey matter of elderly subjects. *British Journal of Psychiatry, 114*, 797–811.

Clogg, C. C. (1977). *Unrestricted and restricted maximum likelihood latent structure analysis: A manual for users*. (Working Paper 1977–04). University Park, Pennsylvania: Population Issues Research Office.

Cronbach, L. J., & Meehl, P. E. (1955). Construct validity in psychological tests. *Psychological Bulletin, 52*, 281–302.

Day, N.E. (1969). Estimating the components of a mixture of normal distributions. *Biometrika, 56*, 463–474.

Diaconis, P., & Efron, B. (1983). Computer-intensive methods in statistics. *Scientific American*, May, 116–130.

Eaves, L. J. (1983). Errors of inference in the detection of major gene effects in psychological test scores. *American Journal of Human Genetics, 35*, 1179–1189.

Efron, B. (1979). Computers and the theory of statistics: Thinking the unthinkable. *Society for Industrial and Applied Mathematics Review, 21*, 460–480.

Efron, B. (1982). *The jacknife, the bootstrap, and other resampling plans*. Philadelphia: Society for Industrial and Applied Mathematics.

Efron, B., & Gong, G. (1983). A leisurely look at the bootstrap, the jacknife, and cross-validation. *American Statistician, 37*, 36–48.

Erlenmeyer-Kimling, L., Cornblatt, B., & Golden, R. R. (1983). Early indicators of vulnerability to schizophrenia in children at high genetic risk. In S. B. Guze, F. J. Earls, & J. E. Barrett (Eds.), *Childhood psychopathology and development*. New York: Raven Press.

Erlenmeyer-Kimling L., Golden, R. R., & Cornblatt B. (1989). A taxometric analysis of cognitive and neuromotor variables in children at risk for schizophrenia. *Journal of Abnormal Psychology, 98*, 203–208.

Everitt, B. S. (1980). *Cluster analysis* (2nd Ed.). New York: Halstead Press.

Everitt, B. S., & Hand, D. F. (1981). *Finite mixture distributions*. London: Chapman and Hall.

Feinstein, A. R. (1963). Boolean algebra and clinical taxonomy: i. analytic synthesis of the general spectrum of a human disease. *The New England Journal of Medicine, 269*, 929–938.

Fleiss, J. L., & Zubin, J. (1969). On the methods and theory of clustering. *Mutivariate Behavioral Research, 4*, 235–250.

Freeman, K. (1981). *Classification of patients with nephrotic syndrome*. Dr.P.H. Thesis. (unpublished). New York: Columbia University.

Gangestad, S., & Snyder, M. (1985). "To carve nature at its joints": on the existence of discrete classes in personality. *Psychological Bulletin, 92*, 317–349.

Gibbons, R. D., Dorus, E., Ostrow, D. G., Pandey, G. N., Davis, J. M., & Levy, D. L. (1984). Mixture distributions in psychiatry research. *Biological Psychiatry, 19*, 939–961.

Golden, R. R. (1982). A taxometric model for detection of a conjectured latent taxon. *Multivariate Behavioral Research, 17*, 389–416.

Golden, R. R., Campbell, M., & Perry, R. (1987). A taxometric method for diagnosis of tardive dyskinesia. *Journal of Psychiatric Research, 21*, 101–109.

Golden, R. R., & Freeman, K. D. (1983). Taxometric diagnosis of a latent disease without use of a criterion variable. (Report No. B-34). *Columbia University Reports*. New York, Division of Biostatistics, School of Public Health, Columbia University.

Golden, R. R., Gallob, H. F., & Watt, N. F. (1983). Bootstrapping conjectural indicators of vulnerability for schizophrenia. *Journal of Consulting and Clinical Psychology, 51*, 937–939.

Golden, R. R., & Golden M. J. (in press). A model of pseudo taxonicity. In R.V. Dawis & D. Lubinski (Eds.), *Assessing individual differences in human behavior: New concepts, methods and findings.*

Golden R. R., Kawas C., & Katzman R. (in preparation). A statistical method using culturally biased indicators to estimate the prevalence rate of clinical dementia without the use of a criterial diagnosis.

Golden, R. R., & Meehl, P. E. (1978). Testing a dominant gene theory without an accepted criterion variable. *Annals of Human Genetics, 41,* 507–514.

Golden, R. R., & Meehl, P. E. (1973a). *Detecting latent clinical taxa, IV: An empirical study of the maximum covariance method and the normal minimum chi-square method, using three MMPI keys to identify the sexes.* (Report PR-73-2). Minneapolis: University of Minnesota Department of Psychiatry.

Golden, R. R., & Meehl, P. E. (1973b). *Detecting latent clinical taxa, V: A Monte Carlo study of the maximum covariance method and associated consistency tests.* (Report PR-73-3). Minneapolis: University of Minnesota Department of Psychiatry.

Golden, R. R., & Meehl, P. E. (1974). *Detecting latent clinical taxa, VIII: A preliminary study in the detection of the schizoid taxon using MMPI items as indicators.* (Report PR-74-6). Minneapolis: University of Minnesota Department of Psychiatry.

Golden, R. R., & Meehl, P. E. (1979). Detection of the schizoid taxon with MMPI indicators. *Journal of Abnormal Psychology, 88,* 217–233.

Golden, R. R., & Meehl, P. E. (1980). Detection of biological sex: An empirical test of six cluster methods. *Multivariate Behavioral Research, 15,* 475–494.

Golden, R. R., Teresi, J. A., & Gurland, B. J. (1984). Development of indicator-scales for the Comprehensive Assessment and Referral Evaluation Interview Schedule. *Journal of Gerontology, 39,* No. 2, 138–146.

Golden, R. R., Tyan, S. H., & Meehl, P. E. (1974a). *Detecting latent clinical taxa, VI: Analytical development and empirical trials of the consistency hurdles theory.* (Report PR-74-4). Minneapolis: University of Minnesota Department of Psychiatry.

Golden, R. R., Tyan, S. H., & Meehl, P. E. (1974b). *Detecting latent clinical taxa, VII: Analytical development and empirical and artificial data trials of the multi-indicator, multitaxonomic class maximum likelihood normal theory.* (Report PR-74-5). Minneapolis: University of Minnesota Department of Psychiatry.

Golden, R. R., Tyan, S. H., & Meehl, P. E. (1974c). *Detecting latent clinical taxa, IX: A Monte Carlo method for testing taxometric theories.* (Report PR-74-7). Minneapolis: University of Minnesota Department of Psychiatry.

Golden, R. R., Vaughan, H. G., Jr., Kurtzberg, D., & McCarton, C. M. (1988). Detection of neonatal brain dysfunction without the use of a criterion variable: Analysis of the statistical problem with an illustrative example. In P. Vietze & H. G. Vaughan, Jr. (Eds.), *Early identification of infants at risk for mental retardation* (pp. 71–95). Orlando: Grune and Stratton, Inc.

Goodman, L. A. (1975). A new model for scaling response patterns: An application of the quasi-independence concept. *Journal of the American Statistical Association, 70,* 755–768.

Grayson, D. A. (1987). Can categorical and dimensional views of psychiatric illness be distinguished? *British Journal of Psychiatry, 151,* 355–361.

Haberman, S. J. (1979). *Analysis of qualitative data,* Vols. 1 and 2. New York: Academic Press.

Hambleton, R. K., & Cook, L. L. (1977). Latent trait models and their use in the analysis of educational test data. *Journal of Educational Measurement, 12,* 75–96.

Hartigan, J. A. (1975). *Clustering algorithms.* New York: Wiley.

Hasselblad, V. (1968). Estimation of parameters for a mixture of normal distributions. *Technometrics, 8,* 431–444.

Holzman, P. S., Kringlen, E., Matthysse, S., Flanagan, S., Lipton, R., Cramer, G., Levin, S., Lange, K., & Levy, D. L. (1988). A single dominant gene can account for eye tracking dysfunctions and schizophrenia in offspring of discordant twins. *Archives of General Psychiatry, 45,* 641–646.

Holzman, P. S., Solomon, C. M., Levin, S., & Waternaux, C. S. (1984). Pursuit eye movement dysfunction in schizophrenia: Family evidence for specificity. *Archives of General Psychiatry, 41,* 136–139.

Iacono, W. G. (1985). Psychophysiologic markers of psychopathology: A review. *Canadian Psychology, 26,* 96–112.

Kolata, G. (1988) Theorist applies computer power to statistics. *New York Times,* November 8, C1.

Lazarsfeld, P. F., & Henry, N. W. (1968). *Latent structure analysis.* Boston: Houghton-Mifflin.

Lipton, R. B., & Golden, R. R. (in preparation). Testing the single dominant gene hypothesis of schizophrenia using eyetracking indicator variables.

Lipton, R. B., Levy, D. L., Holzman, P. S., & Levin, S. (1983). Eye movement dysfunction in schizophrenia: A review. *Schizophrenia Bulletin, 9,* 13–32.

Lord, F. M. (1980). *Application of item response theory to practical testing problems.* Hillside, NJ: Lawrence Erlbaum.

Lord, F. M., & Novick, M. R. (1968). *Statistical theories of mental test scores.* Reading, MA: Addison-Wesley.

Lubchenco, L. O., Bard, H., Goldman, A. L., Coyer, W. E., McIntyre, C., & Smith, D. M. (1974). Newborn intensive care and long-term prognosis. *Developmental Medicine and Child Neurology, 15,* 421–431.

Lubchenco, L. O., Delivoria-Papadapoulos, M., & Searls, D. (1972). Long-term follow-up studies of prematurely born infants. II. Influence of birth weight and gestational age on sequelae. *Journal of Pediatrics, 80,* 509–512.

Lunneborg, C. E. (1985). Estimating the correlation coefficient: The bootstrap approach. *Psychological Bulletin, 98,* 209–215.

Lykken, D. T. (1968). Statistical inference in psychological research. *Psychological Bulletin, 70,* 151–159.

Matthysse, S., Holzman, P., & Lange, K. (1986). The genetic transmission of schizophrenia: Application of Mendelian latent structure analysis to eye tracking dysfunction in schizophrenia and affective disorder. *Journal of Psychiatric Research, 20,* 57–76.

McCarton, C. M., Golden, R. R., & Vaughan, H. G., Jr. (1988). The assessment of perinatal variables in relation to neurological outcome LBW infants. In P. Vietze & H. G. Vaughan, Jr. (Eds.), *Early identification of infants at risk for mental retardation.* Orlando: Grune and Stratton.

Meehl, P. E. (1962). Schizotaxia, schizotypy, schizophrenia. *American Psychologist, 17,* 827–838.

Meehl, P. E. (1965). *Detecting latent clinical taxa by fallible quantitative indicators lacking an accepted criterion.* (Report PR-65-2). Minneapolis: University of Minnesota Department of Psychiatry.

Meehl, P. E. (1968). *Detecting latent clinical taxa, II: A simplified procedure, some additional hitmax cut locators, a single-indicator method, and miscellaneous theorems.* (Report PR-65-2). Minneapolis: University of Minnesota Department of Psychiatry.

Meehl, P. E. (1970). Theory-testing in psychology and physics: A methodological paradox. In D. E. Morrison & R. E. Henkel (Eds.), *The significance test controversy.* Chicago: Aldine.

Meehl, P. E. (1972). Reactions, reflections, projections. In J. N. Butcher (Ed.), *Objective personality assessement.* New York: Academic Press.

Meehl, P. E. (1973a). MAXCOV-HITMAX: A taxonomic search method for loose genetic syndromes. In P. E. Meehl, *Psychodiagnosis: Selected papers.* Minneapolis: University of Minnesota Press.

Meehl, P. E. (1973b). *Psychodiagnosis: Selected papers*. Minneapolis: University of Minnesota Press.

Meehl, P. E. (1978a). Theoretical risks and tabular asterisks: Sir Karl, Sir Ronald, and the slow progress of soft psychology. *Journal of Consulting and Clinical Psychology, 46*, 806–834.

Meehl, P. E. (1978b). Specific etiology and other forms of strong influence: Some quantitative meanings. *Journal of Medicine and Philosophy, 2*, 33–53.

Meehl, P. E. (1979). A funny thing happened to us on the way to the latent entities. *Journal of Personality Assessment, 43*, 563–581.

Meehl, P. E. (1982). *Detecting latent clinical taxa, X: Extension of methods to problem of inductive scanning of multiple taxa*. (Report PR-82-1). Minneapolis: University of Minnesota Department of Psychiatry.

Meehl, P. E. (1986). Diagnostic taxa as open concepts: Metatheoretical and statistical questions about reliability and construct validity in the grand strategy of nosological revision. In T. Millon & G. L. Klerman (Eds.), *Contemporary directions in psychopathology* (pp. 215–231). New York: Guilford.

Meehl, P. E., & Golden, R. R. (1982). Taxometric methods. In J. N. Butcher & D. C. Kendall (Eds.), *The handbook of research methods in clinical psychology* (pp. 127–181). New York: Wiley.

Meehl, P. E., Lykken, D. T., Burdick, M. R., & Schoener, G. R. (1969). *Identifying latent clinical taxa, III: An empirical trial of the normal single-indicator method, using MMPI scale 5 to identify the sexes*. (Report PR-69-1). Minneapolis: University of Minnesota Department of Psychiatry.

Mezzich J. E., & Solomon H. (1980). *Taxonomy and behavioral science*. New York: Academic Press.

Miller, H. R., Streiner, P. L., & Kahgee, S. L. (1982). Use of the Golden-Meehl indicators in the detection of schizoid-taxon membership. *Journal of Abnormal Psychology, 91*, 55–60.

Morrison, D. E., & Henkel, R. E. (Eds.). (1970). *The significance test controversy*. Chicago: Aldine.

Murphy, E. A. (1964). One cause? Many causes? The argument from a bimodal distribution. *Journal of Chronic Diseases, 17*, 301–324.

Murphy, E. A. (1987). A geneticist's approach to psychiatric disease. *Psychological Medicine, 17*, 805–815.

Nichols, D. S., & Jones, R. E. (1985). Identifying schizoid-taxon membership with Golden-Meehl MMPI items. *Journal of Abnormal Psychology, 94*, 191–194.

Popper, K. R. (1962). *Conjectures and refutations*. New York: Basic Books.

Rasch, G. (1960). *Probabilistic models for some intelligence and attainment tests*. Copenhagen: Neilsen and Lydiche.

Reichenbach, H. (1938). *Experience and prediction*. Chicago: University of Chicago Press.

Rindskopf D., & Rindskopf W. (1986). The value of latent class analysis in medical analysis. *Statistics in Medicine, 5*, 21–27.

Rozeboom, W. W. (1960). The fallacy of the null hypothesis significance test. *Psychological Bulletin, 57*, 416–428.

Rozeboom, W. W. (1966). *Foundations of the theory of prediction*. Homewood, IL: Dorsey Press.

Sneath, P. H. A., & Sokal, R. R. (1973). *Numerical taxonomy*. San Francisco: Freeman.

Titterington, D. M., Smith, A. F. M., & Makov, U. E. (1985). *Statistical analysis of finite mixture distributions*. New York: Wiley.

Wright, B. D., & Masters, G. N. (1982). *Rating scale analysis*. Chicago: Mesa Press.

Young, M. A. (1983). Evaluating diagnostic criteria: A latent class paradigm. *Journal of Psychiatric Research, 17*, No. 3, 285–296.

Young, M. A., Tanner, M. A., & Meltzer, H. Y. (1982). Operational definitions of schizophrenia: What do they identify? *The Journal of Nervous and Mental Disease, 170*, 443–447.

Zubin, J., & Steinhauer, S. (1981). How to break the logjam in schizophrenia: A look beyond genetics. *Journal of Nervous and Mental Disease, 169*, 477–492.

Mixed and Mixed-Up Models for the Transmission of Schizophrenia

I. I. Gottesman and M. McGue

*We already realize that you can't make a dominant gene theory
fit the facts without finagling with penetrance (or, saying it a
different way, but one that comes in my view to the same thing,
my not making my theoretical distinction between schizophrenia
and schizoid disease, schizoidia, or schizotypy); and that is
what the pushers of a monogenic theory, such as Slater,
Heston, and myself have regularly done. So we begin by
arguing that the facts require modifiers (in my terminology,
schizophrenic potentiators).*

P. E. Meehl, 1972a, p. 409

Because we currently lack crucial experiments for resolving the ambiguity and
uncertainty surrounding the mode of transmission of schizophrenia or any other
major mental disorder, theoretical arguments that weigh the pros and cons of various alternatives and that have heuristic value for advancing the search for truth
are still needed. In that spirit we present our deliberations as a homage to P. E.
Meehl with respect to a topic that has been one of his major interests during his
brilliant career. His interest in an inferred ''hereditary neurological disorder'' —
schizotaxia — as the base on which schizotypal personality was socially learned
was spelled out in his APA presidential address (Meehl, 1962). Ten years later he
(Meehl, 1972b) called for an integrated theory of schizophrenia, not in the
clichéd sense, but one that would specify the interactions between genetically determined dispositions of the individual and his social learning regime; ''such a
theory will specify *what it is* that is inherited, i.e., what parameters of the nervous system are aberrant as a result close in the causal chain to the gene or genes;
what the *genetic model* (Mendelizing, polygenic?) is; and *how* the combination
of aversive social learnings . . . plus the precipitating stressors . . . results . . .

in the psychodynamics, the phenomenology, and the clinical symptomatology of the disorder'' (1972b, p. 11). Note the encouragement of thinking about more than one gene and of a multifactorial polygenic model.

Further steps on the road we share are marked by the ''underground'' development of the schizotypal checklist (Meehl, 1964) for the detection of schizotypals (equated with the Hoch-Polatin concept of pseudoneurotic schizophrenia) developed after many hours of trying to treat patients resistant to all kinds of psychotherapy. Implicit in the designation of such patients or even nonpatients was a continuum of schizophrenicity compatible with a multifactorial-polygenic model or with (see quote above) a dominant gene and modifiers. We will finesse a lengthy digression about the difficulties of specifying a relevant phenotype for genetic analyses of schizophrenia (Gottesman, McGuffin, & Farmer, 1987) by aligning ourselves with Meehl's insistence upon perceiving schizophrenia as an open concept (Meehl, 1986), one in which operational definitions of the sort found in DSM-III R, for example, may well be pseudo-operational, revering reliability but ignoring validity. Such neo-Popperian flexibility has informed the research of Minnesota graduates under Meehl's influence.

Genetic Epidemiology of Schizophrenia

There are two distinctive features of the genetic epidemiology of schizophrenia. First, the pattern of risk among the relatives of schizophrenics is clearly not consistent with any simple pattern of Mendelian inheritance (i.e., autosomal dominant, autosomal recessive, or X-linked). Second, schizophrenics, as a group, reproduce at about 50% of the rate of nonschizophrenics (e.g., Erlenmeyer-Kimling, 1978; Vogel, 1979; Ødegaard, 1980). Such a high rate of selective disadvantage operating over even a relatively short time span would be expected, absent a high fresh mutation rate, to result in a low rate of disease prevalence. Nonetheless, schizophrenia, conservatively diagnosed, is a relatively common disorder affecting approximately 1% of the population sometime during their lifetime (Gottesman, Shields, & Hanson, 1982; Jablensky, 1986).

Table 1 gives the estimated lifetime risks for developing definite schizophrenia among the relatives of schizophrenics pooled from studies undertaken in Western Europe since 1920 (for a complete description of how the data were compiled see Gottesman et al., 1982; Slater & Cowie, 1971). Values for a broader definition including ''probable schizophrenia'' are about 25% higher than those given in the table. With the exception of the twin data, where a large correlation in age at onset as well as continued follow-up obviates the need, all risks have been adjusted for variable age of onset using the Weinberg method (Gottesman et al., 1982).

There is a strong association between the magnitude of familial risk and the degree of genetic relationship to the proband. Nonetheless, the MZ twin concor-

Table 1. Risks of Definite Schizophrenia among the Relatives of Schizophrenics

Familial Relationship	BZN*	% Affected
Offspring of two schizophrenics	134	36.6
MZ twins	106	44.3
DZ twins	149	12.1
Siblings	7,523	7.3
Offspring of one schizophrenic	1,678	9.4
Half-siblings	442	2.9
Cognate nieces or nephews	3,965	2.7
Grandchildren	739	2.8
First cousins	1,600	1.6
Spouses	399	1.0

*BZN gives the age-adjusted sample size (Gottesman, et al., 1982).

dance rate is substantially less than 100%, and the risk to siblings is significantly less than its expectation under either a simple dominant or simple recessive mode of inheritance. It is clear that environmental factors, be they prenatal, perinatal, sociocultural, or intrafamilial, play a role in the etiology of schizophrenia and thus there can be no simple genetic explanation for the transmission of this disorder (Gottesman, 1991).

Perhaps the most distinctive feature of the pattern of familial risk among the relatives of schizophrenics is the high MZ twin concordance rate relative to the risks among other relatives. The MZ rate is approximately five times the rate among first-degree relatives, which in turn is approximately two and one-half times the rate among second-degree relatives. This rate of exponential decline in familial risk with declining genetic relationship is graphed in Figure 1 where the risk to relatives of an affected proband is plotted as a function of proportion of genetic overlap between the proband and the relative (all first- and second-degree rates given in Table 1 have been pooled).

An imperfect relationship between the inherited genotype and the expressed phenotype, a commonplace in the field of human genetics, is needed to account for the distinctive pattern of familial risk, the influence of environmental factors, and the high prevalence of the disorder despite its selective disadvantage. Quantitative genetic models of disease transmission provide a formal mechanism for specifying alternative hypotheses concerning the relationship between genotype and phenotype. However, these quantitative genetic models do not, by themselves, represent theories about the etiology of schizophrenia in that they fail to specify the mechanisms and processes whereby multiple genetic and environmental factors combine and interact to produce the disorder (Meehl, 1972b).

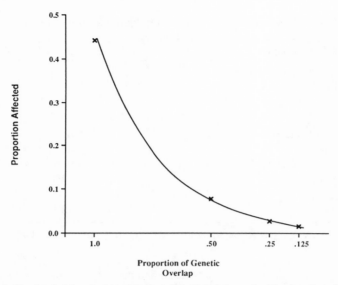

Figure 1. Empirical risks of schizophrenia among the relatives of schizophrenic probands as a function of genetic overlap between the relative and the proband.

Nonetheless, a given theory may be strongly identified with a specific mode of inheritance, or, alternatively, models of inheritance found to be consistent with observed family data may serve to guide future inquiry and/or serve as heuristics to further theory development.

Falconer's (1965) concept of a threshold character for "common" (i.e., a rate greater than 1 in 1000) genetic conditions provides a unifying framework for considering alternative quantitative models of the transmission of schizophrenia. It is assumed that underlying the categorical phenotype of schizophrenia is a continuously distributed quantitative liability for developing the disorder. An individual is affected whenever that individual's total liability exceeds a fixed threshold value along the liability continuum. The inheritance of the categorical phenotype is mediated by the inheritance of the quantitative (combined genetic and environmental) liability. Alternative models of the inheritance of schizophrenia can be characterized by those factors assumed to contribute to this liability.

Quantitative Genetic Models for the Inheritance of Schizophrenia

Single Gene Inheritance

Human geneticists invoke the concept of incomplete penetrance to reconcile single gene inheritance with non-Mendelian familial risks (e.g., sibling risks much less than 50% or 25%). The penetrance of a given genotype with respect to

Table 2. Parameterization of the Generalized Single-Locus Model

Genotype	AA	Aa	aa
Frequency	q^2	$2q(1-q)$	$(1-q)^2$
Penetrance	f_{AA}	f_{Aa}	f_{aa}

a given disease phenotype is defined as the probability that an individual with that genotype becomes affected. Incomplete penetrance corresponds to affection probabilities less than one for at-risk genotypes. It is a statistical entity that represents a statement of ignorance concerning the exact processes that result in phenotypic expression. For example, retinoblastoma is considered the classic example of an incompletely penetrant dominantly inherited disorder (e.g., Vogel & Motulsky, 1986). Nonetheless, the mechanism of gene influence is recessive, the appearance of dominant transmission owing to a high rate of somatic mutation (Knudson, 1971; Cavenee et al., 1983).

All possible single gene models of disease transmission are incorporated into the generalized single locus (GSL) model (James, 1971). Under the GSL model two types of factors are assumed to contribute toward disease liability: a major gene effect and nonfamilial environmental effects. All familial resemblance is assumed to be due to the segregation of two alleles at a single locus in Hardy-Weinberg equilibrium. In its most general form, the GSL model places no restriction on the penetrances of each of the three genotypes (Table 2). Consequently, the model includes as special cases Mendelian patterns of inheritance (e.g., Mendelian dominant would correspond to a penetrance vector of $f_{AA} = f_{Aa} = 1.0$ and $f_{aa} = 0.0$), complex patterns of inheritance that allow for environmental influence through reduced penetrance (e.g., reduced penetrance dominant might correspond to a penetrance vector of $f_{AA} = f_{Aa} = p$ and $f_{aa} = 0.0$) and the existence of misdiagnoses or phenocopies (e.g., reduced penetrance dominant transmission with phenocopies might correspond to a penetrance vector of $f_{AA} = f_{Aa} = p_1$, and $f_{aa} = p_2$).

Although the GSL model may appear so Procrustean as to be consistent with any set of family data, it does yield precise predictions of familial risk. James (1971) has shown that the risk to relatives of a given class (K_r) can be expressed as a function of three parameters of the GSL model; the population prevalence of the disorder (K_p), the additive genetic variance (V_a), and the dominance genetic variance (V_d);

$$K_r = K_p + (\mu_1 V_a + \mu_2 V_d)/ K_p \qquad (1)$$

where μ_1 and μ_2 are the probabilities that the proband and the relative share, respectively, one or two alleles at a locus identical by descent.

The GSL model has enjoyed wide popularity among psychiatric geneticists. Böök (1953), working 35 years ago with an inbred North Swedish isolate, was

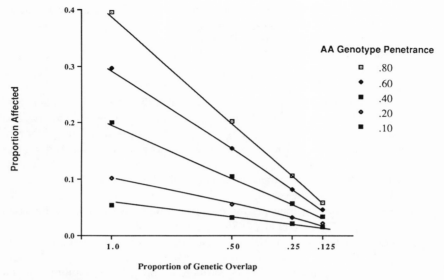

Figure 2. Risks to relatives of schizophrenic probands under a pure GSL model as a function of the penetrance of the most frequently affected genotype. In all cases it was assumed that 2.5% of schizophrenics had the *aa* genotype, that the penetrance of the heterozygote genotype was halfway between the penetrances of the two homozygous genotypes, and that there were no multifactorial influences.

the first to fit a reduced penetrance single-locus model to schizophrenia family data. He hypothesized that the familial aggregation of schizophrenia could be accounted for through an incompletely penetrant dominant mode of transmission (80% of heterozygotes were affected). Similarly, Slater (1958), Slater and Cowie (1971), Heston (1970), and, more recently, Matthysse et al. (1986) and Holzman et al. (1988) have all argued in favor of the GSL model of inheritance. Despite its popularity, the GSL model has repeatedly failed in fitting schizophrenia family data when those data include information on a wide range of genetic relationships (Elston & Campbell, 1970; Kidd & Cavalli-Sforza, 1973; Elston et al., 1978; O'Rourke et al., 1982; Tsuang et al., 1982; McGue et al., 1986; Baron, 1986).

It is informative to consider why the GSL model fails to account for existing schizophrenia family data. In the absence of dominance (as appears to be the case for schizophrenia, where the risk to the siblings is not greater than the risk to the children of schizophrenics) predicted familial risk under the GSL model is given by a linear function of proportion of genetic overlap between the relative and the proband. That is, in the absence of dominance, Equation 1 is reduced to

$$K_r = K_p + (V_a/K_p)\mu_1. \qquad (2)$$

This linear prediction (depicted in Figure 2 for several alternative GSL models) is

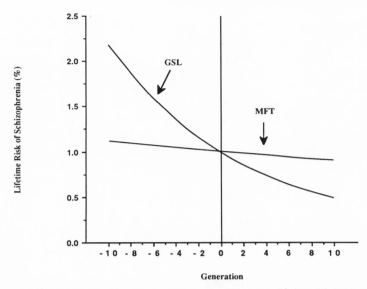

Figure 3. Lifetime risk of schizophrenia assuming that the current lifetime risk is 1% and that the 50% reduction in schizophrenic fertility that exists today existed for the 10 generations prior to today and will continue for the next 10 generations. The GSL model is based upon the parameter estimates reported by Holzman et al. (1988) with a penetrance vector of $f_{AA} = f_{Aa} = .189, f_{aa} = .002$; the MFT model assumes an 80% heritability in liability.

in sharp contrast to the empirically observed exponential relationship (depicted in Figure 1). Specifically, an MZ twin concordance rate that is large relative to the risks among other family members cannot be accounted for through single gene transmission, even if the single gene is assumed to be incompletely penetrant.

It is interesting also to consider how the selective disadvantage associated with schizophrenia (observed during the twentieth century) would be expected to affect the prevalence of the disorder under GSL transmission. Figure 3 gives the expected lifetime risk of schizophrenia under two alternative models of transmission assuming that current selective forces are constant and have existed for 10 generations prior to today (approximately 250 to 300 years) and will continue for another 10 generations. The GSL model given in the figure corresponds to the recently proposed incompletely penetrant single gene model proposed by Holzman et al. (1988) with penetrance vector $(f_{AA} = f_{Aa} = .189, f_{aa} = .002)$. Clearly, schizophrenia under single gene transmission would be subject to severe selection even if the gene penetrance is low. The relatively high prevalence of the disorder despite its twentieth-century selective disadvantage could, of course, be accounted for by assuming that the selective disadvantage is only a recent phenomenon (a realistic possibility given changes in cultural practices surrounding marriage) or that schizophrenia was much more prevalent in previous generations than it is today (an unrealistic possibility given the absence of data supporting changes in the rate of schizophrenic-like psychopathology over the past 100 years; Goldhamer & Marshall, 1949; Ødegaard, 1971; Eaton, 1985). The issue is not that there are no reasonable hypotheses to account for the relatively high prevalence of schizophrenia under GSL transmission; clearly there are. Rather, the issue is that those who argue for single gene transmission must, either explicitly or implicitly, propose some mechanism to account for the prevalence of the disorder. As shown below, sensitivity to the forces of natural selection distinguishes alternative models for the transmission of schizophrenia.

Multiple Gene Inheritance

Although the multifactorial threshold (MFT) model is at the other extreme of the number of genes continuum from the GSL model, it is the model most often considered an alternative to single gene transmission (Faraone & Tsuang, 1985). Under the MFT model, genetic factors are assumed to be polygenic. That is, there is a large number of genes each of small and equal effect that combine additively with the effects of other genes to influence schizophrenic liability. Unlike the GSL model, both familial and nonfamilial environmental influences are allowed. Environmental and genetic effects are assumed to combine additively.

The MFT model predicts that the magnitude of familial risk will decline exponentially as a function of the proportion of genetic overlap between the proband and the relative (Figure 4). The pattern depicted in Figure 4 is clearly consistent with the observed empirical relationship given in Figure 1, and clearly inconsistent with the linear relationship generated under the GSL model (Figure 2). A multifactorial model with a heritability of liability of .80 generates predicted familial risks that are statistically and substantially consistent with the observed risks (Figure 1) (McGue et al., 1983).

Comparison of Figures 2 and 4 will suggest, contrary to platitudes on the issue, the conditions under which the GSL and MFT models can be distinguished. Single gene transmission with *low penetrance* and multiple gene transmission with a *small heritability* generate similar patterns of familial risk, and thus cannot be easily distinguished. Alternatively, single gene transmission with moderate to high penetrance and multiple gene inheritance with moderate to high heritability do predict different patterns of familial risk. In these cases, however, it is primarily the magnitude of the MZ risk (or when available the risk to the offspring of two affected individuals) relative to the risks of the other relatives that differentiates between the two models. Consequently, it will be difficult to distinguish between single gene and multiple gene transmission when observations are made only on first-, second-, and third-degree relatives. For example, there is a nearly linear relationship between familial risk and proportion of ge-

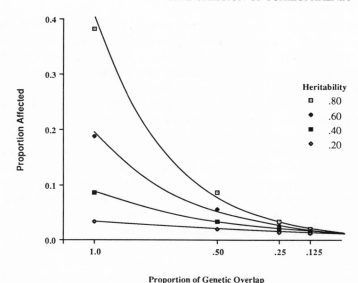

Proportion of Genetic Overlap

Figure 4. Risks to the relatives of schizophrenic probands under a pure multifactorial model as a function of multifactorial heritability.

netic overlap for the first-, second-, and third-degree relatives only in the MFT models given in Figure 4.

Unlike GSL models, MFT models are relatively insensitive to the forces of selection and are consequently consistent with a high disease prevalence despite selective disadvantage. Figure 3 gives the expected lifetime risk of schizophrenia under a MFT model with a multifactorial heritability of .80, assuming a constant 50% selective disadvantage. Under the MFT model, the expected reduction in lifetime risk is less than .5% after 20 generations of such negative selection.

Mixed Single Gene/Multiple Gene Models

Despite its ability to predict the observed familial risks, there has always been a certain reluctance to accepting the MFT model as an explanation for the transmission of schizophrenia. This reluctance stems, perhaps, from the failure to identify the specific genetic and environmental factors that contribute to schizophrenic liability under multifactorial transmission. Alternatively, strict polygenic inheritance (i.e., many genes all of small effect) would seem to preclude the application of recently developed powerful molecular genetic techniques aimed at characterizing single gene effects (Gurling, 1986). There is an understandable desire to use molecular methods (i.e., RFLPs and linkage) in the study of schizophrenia and other human genetic diseases of unknown etiology.

The fit of the MFT model does not, however, preclude the existence of a single, major gene whose effect on schizophrenia risk is large relative to the effects of other (poly)genes, so-called oligogenic effect. Meehl (1972a, 1972b) was one of the first theorists to hypothesize that both a major gene and polygenes might play a role in the etiology of schizophrenia. Under Meehl's theory, inheritance of a single gene gives rise to a neural integrative deficit termed schizotaxia that expresses itself at the personality level as socially learned schizotypy. The single gene characteristic is a necessary but not sufficient condition for the development of schizophrenia. Expression of clinical schizophrenia among individuals who inherit the single gene defect is postulated to be a function of status on a host of polygenically and environmentally influenced potentiators including characteristics like anxiety, anhedonia, and social introversion. Under the present scheme, Meehl's theory of schizophrenic transmission represents a revision of the GSL model that allows penetrance to depend on other genetic factors as well as on environmental factors.

Independently of Meehl's theoretical speculations, the human geneticists Morton and MacLean (1974) introduced a formal analytical procedure for identifying a major gene influence against a polygenic background. Briefly, inference under the mixed model, as it is termed by Morton and MacLean, involves fitting both a pure MFT model and a mixed model that includes both a multifactorial and a major gene component to family data. If the latter model fits the family data significantly better than the former, then the family data are said to support the existence of a major gene influence.

Although, in principle, the mixed model can be applied to identify single gene effects for both quantitative and qualitative phenotypes, applications with categorical data have typically yielded equivocal results in practice. There have been three mixed-model analyses of schizophrenia family data (Carter & Chung, 1980; Risch & Baron, 1984; Vogler et al., 1990). In all three cases, the researchers failed to reject the multifactorial model that included polygenic effects only in favor of a mixed model that included both a single gene and polygenic effects. Failure to reject the multifactorial model in favor of the mixed model may result from a lack of statistical power or from the absence of a single gene effect on schizophrenia. With the given data it is difficult to resolve the choice between these two possibilities, although the repeated failure to support the mixed model statistically would appear to exclude the existence of a single gene that has a large influence on schizophrenic risk. Nonetheless, the identification, through molecular genetic approaches, of a specific genetic mutation associated with schizophrenia risk would represent a major scientific and clinical breakthrough (McGuffin et al., 1990). The search for this breakthrough will not be precluded through mathematical arguments only (Bassett et al., 1988).

A Simulation Experiment

Method

Because attempts to fit the mixed model to schizophrenia family data have resulted in equivocal results, it has been difficult to determine whether there is evidence to support a major gene influence and, if so, what the characteristics of that major gene effect might be. In an attempt to better identify the characteristics of the mixed-single-gene/polygene models that are consistent with observed schizophrenia family data, a simulation experiment was designed and completed. In this simulation, it was assumed that two genetic components contributed to schizophrenic liability: (1) a major gene component with two alleles (A with frequency q and a with frequency $1\text{-}q$) at a single locus in Hardy-Weinberg equilibrium, and (2) a multifactorial component that was assumed to be normally distributed with constant variance for the three major genotypes (AA, Aa, and aa) and was assumed to combine additively with the major gene effect to define overall genetic liability. Environmental effects were assumed not to interact with genetic factors and were assumed to be nonfamilial— assumptions that, although unrealistic when considering course and outcome of schizophrenia, should have little impact upon the present results focusing on familial transmission.

In formulating the major gene effect, it was assumed that possession of the A allele increased schizophrenic risk so that the penetrances for the three genotypes were ordered as $f_{AA} > f_{Aa} > f_{aa}$. Furthermore, given that, among the relatives of schizophrenics, siblings are at no greater risk than offspring, f_{Aa} was constrained to equal $(f_{AA} + f_{aa})/2$ as is expected when there is no dominance variance. In all cases, the cumulative lifetime prevalence (morbid risk) of schizophrenia was fixed at 1.0%

Given these constraints, three parameters suffice to completely specify the mixed model. These three parameters, used as input to the simulation, are (1) f_{AA}, the penetrance of the most frequently affected genotype, (2) s, the percentage of schizophrenics who do not have any copies of the "schizophrenia gene" (i.e., the proportion of schizophrenics with the aa genotype), and (3) h^2, the residual polygenic heritability (i.e., the proportion of liability variance due to polygenic factors after the major gene effect has been partialed out). Given these input parameters, the simulation program computed the remaining parameters of the mixed model under the constraints noted above and then generated expected risks for MZ twin, first-, second-, and third-degree relatives of a schizophrenic proband. A total of 275 different simulations were run as given by all possible combinations of the following values for the input parameters; $f_{AA} = .80, .60, .40, .20,$ or $.10$; $h^2 = .80, .60, .40, .20,$ or $.00$; and $s = 0, .025, .05, .10, .20,$

Table 3. Illustrative Results from the Mixed-Model Simulation of Schizophrenia

	Model									
	Input Parameters			Derived Parameters			Predicted Risks to Relatives of Schizophrenics (%)			
				% Total Variance Due to						
#	f_{AA}	s	h^2	Major Gene	Polygene	Env	MZ	1st °	2nd °	3rd °
Inconsistent Models										
1	.60	.60	.20	4.9	19.0	76.1	17.1	8.1	4.3	2.6
2	.60	.05	.60	18.9	48.7	32.4	59.2	22.0	9.8	5.0
3	.60	.05	.20	18.9	16.2	64.9	37.8	17.2	8.6	4.7
4	.10	.025	.40	32.9	26.8	40.3	24.9	7.6	3.3	2.0
5	.10	.80	.40	2.2	39.1	58.7	10.5	4.0	2.1	1.5
Consistent Models										
6	.60	.80	.80	2.3	78.2	19.5	45.1	11.6	4.7	2.6
7	.10	.025	.60	32.9	40.3	27.8	43.6	10.8	4.1	2.2
8	.10	.80	.80	2.2	78.3	19.5	41.3	9.3	3.6	2.0
9	0.0	1.0	.80	0.0	80.0	20.0	38.3	8.6	3.3	1.9

.30, .40, .50, .60, .70, or .80. The 275 different models were selected to span the range of possible models.

Results

Limitations of space preclude comprehensive reporting of the results from all 275 of the simulation runs. The outcomes from each of the runs were evaluated subjectively to determine whether the predicted family risks were consistent with the observed family risks (i.e., the pattern observed in Figure 1). Clear and consistent patterns emerged from this evaluation allowing summarization of the simulation results through reference to a few illustrative findings (Table 3). Those models found to be either consistent or inconsistent with observed familial risks for schizophrenia can be characterized as follows:

1. When the penetrance of the most frequently affected genotype is high (f_{AA} greater than or equal to .4), but either the percentage of schizophrenics without the major genotype is moderate or low (s less than .60) or the residual heritability is moderate or low (h^2 less than .60), then the predicted familial risks are inconsistent with the observed risks. This failure to account for the observed familial risks is illustrated in Table 3 for three different models all with f_{AA} set at a high value, .60. For Model 1, where s is high (.60) but the residual heritability is low (.20), although the predicted risks to first-,

second-, and third-degree relatives are close to the observed values, the MZ co-twin risk is substantially underpredicted. For Model 2, where h^2 is high (.60) but s is low (.05), all except the MZ risk is grossly overpredicted. Finally for Model 3, where both s ($= .05$) and h^2 ($= .20$) are low, the predicted risk to MZ co-twins is consistent with its observed value, although the risks to other family members are overpredicted.

2. When the penetrance of the most frequently affected genotype is high (f_{AA} greater than .40), and the percentage of schizophrenics without the major genotype is high (s greater than or equal to .60), and the residual heritability is large (h^2 greater than or equal to .60), then the predicted familial risks were consistent with the observed risks. Model 6 in Table 3 illustrates such a consistent model with $f_{AA} = .60$, $s = .80$, and $h^2 = .80$.

3. When the penetrance of the most frequently affected genotype was low (f_{AA} less than or equal to .20), and the residual h^2 was not large (h^2 less than .60), then the model-predicted familial risks were inconsistent with the observed risks no matter what the value of s. This is illustrated for two different cases in Table 3; Model 4 where $s = .025$, and Model 5 where $s = .80$.

4. When the penetrance of the most frequently affected genotype was low (f_{AA} less than or equal to .20), and the residual h^2 was large (h^2 greater than or equal to .60), then the predicted risks were consistent with the observed risks no matter what the value of s. This is illustrated in Table 3 with Model 7, where $s = .025$, and Model 8, where $s = .80$.

The results given here taken together with results published earlier (e.g., Faraone & Tsuang, 1985) suggest that three types of quantitative genetic models are consistent with the schizophrenia family data. (No doubt this is far from a comprehensive list, an issue commented on below.) One, a multifactorial model with large heritability, had been identified in earlier empirical work (e.g., Gottesman & Shields, 1967; Rao et al., 1981; McGue et al., 1983), while the present simulation added two very different types of mixed models as being consistent. The first type of mixed model is, essentially, a heterogeneity model. Although this model allows for the existence of a major gene with a high degree of penetrance, the frequency of the gene is necessarily low (to account for the observed familial risk, derived gene frequency was .003) so that most schizophrenics do not have the gene but are schizophrenic because of a high multifactorial loading.

The second type of mixed model also includes a single gene, although it is best characterized as a gene of modest rather than major effect. In this case the penetrance must be low, and the residual multifactorial component large. Because the genotypic penetrance is low, models with either a very high or a very low percentage of schizophrenics carrying the schizophrenia gene are consistent with the observed family data. It is the second class of mixed model, with a low percentage of schizophrenics without the gene, that Meehl predicted based upon his theory of the transmission of schizophrenia; he is, perhaps, heartened by the present results with its emphasis on consistency tests (cf. Meehl & Golden, 1982).

Discussion and Conclusions

Previous attempts to model the transmission of schizophrenia quantitatively were briefly reviewed and a simulation study completed to identify models consistent with the distinctive pattern of familial risk in schizophrenia. Three types of models were found to be consistent: (1) a multifactorial threshold model with a high degree of heritability, (2) a heterogeneity-like model with a single gene accounting for a small minority of cases while multifactorial factors accounted for the majority of cases, and (3) a mixed-single-gene/polygene model where the single gene had a modest but not a major effect on disease risk (i.e., low penetrance). Clearly there are other models that could account for the transmission of schizophrenia (e.g., a three-gene model). It would appear, however, that for neither of these alternative models nor for the models found here to be consistent with empirical data does a single gene play a prominent role in the etiology of schizophrenia. In short, there is very little evidence to support the existence of a single gene of *large* effect that influences schizophrenic risk for a *large* number of cases. The data do not, of course, preclude the existence of either a single gene of large effect influencing a small number of cases or a single gene of modest effect influencing the majority of cases.

Attempts at linkage analysis using molecular probes (RFLPs) with otherwise unselected schizophrenic families are premised on the assumption that schizophrenia is a homogeneous single-gene disorder unambiguously diagnosed with a moderate or high degree of penetrance. The present results suggest that such a strategy may not be successful. If a single major gene exists, sampling strategies will need to be devised that allow researchers to identify families where the putative gene is segregating. One strategy, widely applied in human genetics, is to sample *multiplex* families. In the case of schizophrenia, however, the likelihood that such a strategy would succeed depends upon the (as yet unknown) mode of transmission of the disorder. In Table 4. we give the expected sample composition for selecting sibships of fixed size three through an affected proband under four alternative models (all consistent with the schizophrenia family data), and three different sampling rules: (1) all sibships are sampled, (2) all sibships with at least one case in addition to the proband are sampled, and (3) only sibships with all three siblings affected are sampled. The table gives the percentage of schizophrenic sibships that would qualify under that sampling regime, a rough measure of the feasibility of ascertaining such a sample, and the percentage of qualifying sibships where the proband is carrying at least one copy of the putative schizophrenia gene, an indicator of the proportion of sampled sibships that will

Table 4. Expected Sample Characteristics under Alternative Sampling Schemes for Models Found to Be Consistent with Schizophrenia Family Data

Model			All Sibships		At Least One Sib Affected		Both Sibs Affected	
f_{AA}	s	h^2	%	% with gene	%	% with gene	%	% with gene
.60	.80	.80	100.0	20.0	21.4	41.0	1.8	69.3
.10	.025	.60	100.0	97.5	20.4	98.7	1.2	99.5
.10	.80	.80	100.0	20.0	17.7	26.4	0.9	35.2
0.0	1.00	.80	100.0	0.0	16.6	0.0	0.7	0.0

Note: Assumes that sampling is through a single proband and that sampling units are all composed of sibships of size three. For each sampling rule, the first % gives the percentage of all schizophrenic sibships that would qualify under the rule, and the second % gives the percentage among those sibships qualifying where the proband has at least one copy of the major gene.

be informative for single-gene inference. Only when the single gene is of modest effect (the second listed model) can a high percentage of affected probands be expected to carry at least one copy of the gene, and, in this case, this is true regardless of the sampling scheme. For the other three models, sampling multiplex sibships does *not* necessarily guarantee that the majority of selected families will be segregating for the gene. For example, the first listed model is a heterogeneity-like model with 20% of schizophrenics carrying the major gene. If we sample affected sib pairs, only 41.0% are expected to be gene carriers; a figure that rises to 69.3% if we sample affected sibships only. In these latter cases, it seems clear that alternative sampling strategies will need to be devised to ensure a high yield of families segregating for the single gene.

There is no doubt that molecular genetics will afford major advances in our knowledge of the etiology of schizophrenia (McGuffin et al., 1990). The nature of these advances would seem to be constrained by the mathematics of genetic transmission and the pattern of familial resemblance for schizophrenia. Consequently, we wonder along what direction these advances will proceed. It is helpful, in this regard, to consider two human genetic disorders where molecular genetics has had significant but vastly different impacts. At one extreme is the fully penetrant dominantly transmitted disorder Huntington Disease (HD). Although, relative to schizophrenia, its genetics are simple, 75 years of research into the pathophysiology of HD has not resulted in the clear identification of the underlying genetic defect (Conneally, 1984). The recent success of tightly linking HD to a restriction fragment length polymorphism (RFLP) on chromosome 4 (Gusella & Conneally, 1983) implies that it is only a matter of time (albeit longer than many would have thought only a few years ago) before geneticists, using molecular techniques, identify the basic biochemical defect. At the other extreme are the multifactorially transmitted (Utermann, 1983) and no doubt genetically heterogeneous disorders collectively termed cardiovascular disease (CVD). For CVD it has been the characterization of the underlying pathophysiological mechanisms related to lipids that has allowed geneticists to move from family studies on the clinical phenotype to the identification, using molelcular methods, of the specific gene loci that contribute to the multifactorial liability (Ordovas et al., 1986).

For schizophrenia, will application of molecular genetic methods result in the identification of the pathophysiological factors (as will eventually occur with HD), or will better characterization of the pathophysiological processes provide phenotypes more amenable to molecular genetic analysis than the clinical diagnosis (as is happening with CVD)? Both approaches will be appropriate at different stages of inquiry. At this stage, however, absent any compelling evidence for a major gene effect, the candidate gene approach used with CVD would appear to be the most promising (Gurling, 1986). To this aim, effort is best directed at identifying both biological and genetic markers of familial risk and then determining whether such markers can be used to resolve the likely heterogeneity of the clinical disorder. It remains a lasting tribute to his influence, and not necessarily a condemnation of lack of progress in the field, that Meehl proposed a similar strategy 28 years ago in his APA presidential address (Meehl, 1962). It would appear that the field is finally catching up with his ideas.

References

Baron, M. (1986). Genetics of schizophrenia: I. Familial patterns and mode of inheritance. *Biological Psychiatry, 21*, 1051–1066.

Bassett, A. S., McGillivray, B. C., Jones, B. D., & Pantzar, J. T. (1988). Partial trisomy chromosome 5 cosegregating with schizophrenia. *The Lancet*, 799–800.

Böök, J. A. (1953). A genetic and neuropsychiatric investigation of a North Swedish population. *Acta Genet Stat Med* (Basel), *4*, 1–100.

Carter, C. L., & Chung, C. S. (1980). Segregation analysis of schizophrenia under a mixed model. *Human Heredity, 30*, 350–356.

Cavanee, W. K., Dryja, T. P., Phillips, R. A., Benedict, W. F., Godbout, R., Gallie, B. L., Murphree, A. L., Strong, L. C., & White, R. L. (1983). Expression of recessive alleles by chromosomal mechanisms in retinoblastoma. *Nature, 305*, 779–784.

Conneally, P. M. (1984). Huntington disease: Genetics and epidemiology. *American Journal of Human Genetics, 36*, 506–526.

Eaton, W. W. (1985). Epidemiology of schizophrenia. *Epidemiological Review, 7*, 105–126.

Elston, R. C., & Campbell, M. A. (1970). Schizophrenia: Evidence for a major gene hypothesis. *Behavior Genetics, 1*, 3–10.

Elston, R. C., Namboodiri, K. K., Spence, M. A., & Rainer, J. D. (1978). A genetic study of schizophrenia pedigrees. II. One-locus hypotheses. *Neuropsychobiology, 4*, 193–206.

Erlenmeyer-Kimling, L. (1978). Fertility of psychotics: Demography. In R. Cancro (Ed.), *Annual Review of the Schizophrenic Syndrome*, Vol. 5 (pp. 298–333). New York: Brunner Mazel.

Falconer, D. S. (1965). The inheritance of liability to certain diseases estimated from the incidence among relatives. *Annals of Human Genetics, 29*, 51–76.

Faraone, S. V., & Tsuang, M. T. (1985). Quantitative models of the genetic transmission of schizophrenia. *Psychological Bulletin, 98*, 41–66.

Goldhamer, H., & Marshall, A. W. (1949). *The frequency of mental disease: Long range trends and present status*. New York: Rand.

Gottesman, I. I. (1991). *Schizophrenia genesis*. New York: W. H. Freeman.

Gottesman, I. I., McGuffin, P., & Farmer, A. E. (1987). Clinical genetics as clues to the "real" genetics of schizophrenia (A decade of modest gains while playing for time). *Schizophrenia Bulletin, 13*, 23–48.

Gottesman, I. I., & Shields, J. (1967). A polygenic theory of schizophrenia. *Proceedings of the National Academy of Sciences, 58*, 199–205.

Gottesman, I. I., & Shields, J. (1972). *Schizophrenia and genetics: A twin study vantage point*. New York: Academic Press.

Gottesman, I. I., Shields, J., & Hanson, D. R. (1982). *Schizophrenia: The epigenetic puzzle*. Cambridge, England: Cambridge University Press.

Gurling, H. (1986). Candidate genes and favoured loci: Strategies for molecular genetic research into schizophrenia, manic depression, autism, alcoholism and Alzheimer's disease. *Psychiatric Developments, 4*, 289–309.

Gusella, J. F., Wexler, N. S., & Conneally, P. M. (1983). A polymorphic DNA marker genetically linked to Huntington's disease. *Nature, 306*, 234–238.

Heston, L. L. (1970). The genetics of schizophrenia and schizoid disease. *Science, 167*, 249–256.

Holzman, P. S., Kringlen, E., Matthysse, S., Flanagan, S. D., Lipton, R. B., Cramer, G., Levin, S., Lange, K., & Levy. D. L. (1988). A single dominant gene can account for eye tracking dysfunctions and schizophrenia in offspring of discordant twins. *Archives of General Psychiatry, 45*, 641–647.

Jablensky, A. (1986). Epidemiology of schizophrenia: A European perspective. *Schizophrenia Bulletin, 12*, 52–73.

James, J. W. (1971). Frequency in relatives for an all-or-none trait. *Annals of Human Genetics, 35*, 47–49.

Kidd, K. K., & Cavalli-Sforza, L. L. (1973). An analysis of the genetics of schizophrenia. *Social Biology, 20*, 254–265.

Knudson, A. G. (1971). Mutation and cancer: Statistical study of retinoblastoma. *Proceedings of the National Academy of Sciences, 68*, 820–823.

Matthysse, S. W., Holzman, P. S., & Lange, K. (1986). The genetic transmission of schizophrenia: Application of Mendelian latent structure analysis to eye tracking dysfunctions in schizophrenia and affective disorder. *Journal of Psychiatric Research, 20*(1), 57–65.

McGue, M., Gottesman, I. I., & Rao, D. C. (1983). The transmission of schizophrenia under a multifactorial threshold model. *American Journal of Human Genetics, 35*, 1161–1178.

McGue, M., Gottesman, I. I., & Rao, D. C. (1986). The analysis of schizophrenia family data. *Behavior Genetics, 16*, 75–87.

McGuffin, P., Sargeant, M., Hett, G., Tidmarsh, S., Whatley, S., & Marchbanks, R. M. (1990). Exclusion of a schizophrenia susceptibility gene from the chromosome 5q11–q13 region; new data and a reanalysis of previous reports. *American Journal of Human Genetics, 47*, 524–535.

Meehl, P. E. (1962). Schizotaxia, schizotypy, schizophrenia. *American Psychologist, 17*, 827–838.

Meehl, P. E. (1964). *Manual for use with checklist of schizotypic signs.* Minneapolis: Psychiatric Research Unit, University of Minnesota Medical School.

Meehl, P. E. (1972a). A critical afterword. In Gottesman, I. I., & Shields, J., *Schizophrenia and genetics: A twin study vantage point* (pp. 367–415). New York: Academic Press.

Meehl, P. E. (1972b) Specific genetic etiology, psychodynamics, and therapeutic nihilism. *International Journal of Mental Health, 1,* 10–27.

Meehl, P. E. (1986) Diagnostic taxa as open concepts: Metatheoretical and statistical questions about reliability and construct validity in the grand strategy of nosological revision. In T. Millon & G. L. Klerman (Eds.), *Contemporary directions in psychopathology* (pp. 215–231). New York: Guilford Press.

Meehl, P. E., & Golden, R. (1982). Taxometric methods. In P. Kendall & J. Butcher (Eds.), *Handbook of research methods in clinical psychology* (pp. 127–181). New York: Wiley.

Morton, N. E., & MacLean, C. J. (1974). Analysis of family resemblance. III. Complex segregation analysis of quantitative traits. *American Journal of Human Genetics, 26,* 489–503.

Ødegaard, Ø. (1971). Hospitalized psychoses in Norway: Time trends 1926–1965. *Social Psychiatry, 6,* 53–58.

Ødegaard, Ø. (1980). Fertility of psychiatric first admissions in Norway 1936–1975. *Acta Psychiatr Scandinavica, 62,* 212–220.

Ordovas, J. M., Schaeffer, E. J., Salem, D., Ward, R. H., Glueck, C. J., Vergani, C., Wilson, P. W. F., & Karathanasis, S. K. (1986). Apolipoprotein A-I gene polymorphism associated with premature coronary artery disease and familial hypoalphalipoproteinemia. *New England Journal of Medicine, 314,* 671–677.

O'Rourke, D. H., Gottesman, I. I., Suarez, B. K., Rice, J., & Reich, T. (1982). Refutation of the general single-locus model for the etiology of schizophrenia. *American Journal of Human Genetics, 34,* 630–649.

Rao, D. C., Morton, N. E., Gottesman, I. I., & Lew, R. (1981). Path analysis of qualitative data on pairs of relatives: Application to schizophrenia. *Human Heredity, 33,* 325–333.

Risch, N., & Baron, M. (1984). Segregation analysis of schizophrenia and related disorders. *American Journal of Human Genetics, 36,* 1039–1059.

Slater, E. (1958). The monogenic theory of schizophrenia. *Acta Genet Stat Med* (Basel) *8,* 50–56.

Slater, E., & Cowie, V. (1971). *The genetics of mental disorders.* London: Oxford University Press.

Tsuang, M. T., Bucher, K. D., & Fleming, J. A. (1982). Testing the monogenic theory of schizophrenia: An application of segregation analysis to blind family data. *British Journal of Psychiatry, 140,* 595–599.

Utermann, G. (1983). Coronary heart disease. In A. E. H. Emery & D. L. Rimoin (Eds.), *Principles and practice of medical genetics* (pp. 956–978). Edinburgh: Churchill Livingstone.

Vogel, F., & Motulsky, A. G. (1986). *Human genetics: Problems and approaches.* (2nd ed.) New York: Springer-Verlag.

Vogel, H. P. (1979). Fertility and sibship size in a psychiatric patient population: A national comparison with census data. *Acta Psychiatr Scand, 60,* 483–503.

Vogler, G. P., Gottesman, I. I., McGue, M. K., & Rao, D. C. (1990). Mixed model segregation analysis in the Lindelius Swedish pedigrees. *Behavior Genetics, 20,* 461–472.

Validity of Taxometric Inferences Based on Cluster Analysis Stopping Rules
William M. Grove

Cluster analysis is often used in an exploratory fashion to generate heuristic groups, or to suggest hypotheses about meaningful partitions of a data set. However, there are numerous occasions when a test of the existence of mixed groups in a sample is needed. An example arose in the author's work, conducted in collaboration with Meehl, Iacono, and Hanson, on the genetics of schizophrenia. It may be that schizophrenia-proneness is transmitted as a dominant or recessive monogenic effect with incomplete expressivity. If this were so, then two populations of individuals would exist: high risk and low risk. Taxometric methods might help discover, in a sample of individuals, who was high risk and who was low risk, by looking at multiple traits related to schizotypy, such as abnormal smooth pursuit eye movements, attentional dysfunctions, and borderline delusional ideas. As is well known, taxometric methods such as hierarchical agglomerative or K-means (partitioning) cluster analyses always yield groups (or dendrograms which can readily be cut to yield groups). The investigator who has placed scientific bets on the existence of a cluster will wish to test whether clusters found are statistically artifactual.

Three approaches to this problem appear in the literature. In the first, one estimates parameters of a multivariate mixture model. The operating characteristics of the χ^2 test for goodness-of-fit have been studied for multivariate normal-mixture models in the non-null case (i.e., distinct taxa do exist) by Everitt (1981). (When the null hypothesis is true, the χ^2 statistic does not have an asymptotic χ^2

The work reported here was supported by the NIMH Clinical Research Branch Collaborative Program on the Psychobiology of Depression—Clinical Studies and a grant from the Minnesota Medical Foundation.

distribution because the parameter set is on a boundary of the space (Bock, 1985). This is statistically perhaps the most elegant approach. Unfortunately, simulations indicate that maximum likelihood estimators of normal-mixture model parameters less accurately recover population partitions than do hierarchical and K-means clustering methods (Bayne, Beauchamp, Begovich, & Kane, 1980).

A less elegant approach is to apply a partitioning type of cluster analysis such as K-means to optimize a test statistic for differentiating groups. One then studies the disturbance of the nominal null distribution of this test statistic, caused by the cluster analysis's capitalizing on chance variations in making group assignments. Originally the $\mathcal{F}$-statistic was studied in this way by Engleman and Hartigan (1969) for the univariate case. Lee (1979) studied the trivariate case by simulation, for a multivariate analysis of variance test statistic (Roy's maximum root). Extensions to higher dimensions commonly used in real cluster analyses apparently have not been made. The fundamental difference between this approach and that of estimating mixture-model parameters is the use of simulations as opposed to reliance on asymptotic distribution theory.

A third approach, studied here, is even less elegant. There are many intuitively appealing stopping rules for hierarchical cluster analysis. One can use such a rule to decide where to cut a dendrogram from cluster analysis, inferring that taxa exist if and only if the clustering stops before all observations are fused into one cluster. The principal advantage offered by this crude method is that it allows use of Ward's method or average linkage clustering as the primary data analytic tool. Simulation studies show these methods are relatively accurate in recovering known population mixtures. Such methods often work even when groups are not very well separated (for review see Milligan and Cooper, 1983). Unfortunately, it is extremely difficult to derive distribution theory under the null hypothesis for such stopping rule statistics. Therefore, studies of such statistics have relied on simulations.

Milligan and Cooper (1983) recently surveyed a large number of proposed hierarchical agglomerative cluster analysis stopping rules for data containing two to five taxa, for just a few variables. Group separation was varied, but data were generated by truncation of multivariate normal distributions so that there was zero group overlap on one dimension. This was done to make sure there was a "correct" solution to recover in the sample, but this strategy restricted the generality of findings. Overlapping clusters are the rule in psychopathology.

The Milligan and Cooper data are useful for choosing between stopping rules if background knowledge assures one that distinct taxa exist. However, often one has no such knowledge. It may be plausible that the population is nearly homogeneous in the sense of lacking distinct taxa, or that subpopulations are separated only by negligible distances. Are the same stopping rules useful for deciding the number of taxa (when the background knowledge specifies that there are at least two taxa) valid for deciding whether there are at least two taxa?

To determine the validity of stopping rules, three different regions of the parameter space should be considered. The first is the case where there are no taxa at all, which under the mixture model of taxa employed here means that data are sampled from a single unmixed distribution. A second region subsumes nonzero intertaxa differences.

A third parametric situation arises in personology and psychopathology, and deserves serious consideration by workers using taxometrics with data consisting of measures of socially relevant behaviors. This situation was suggested by Auke Tellegen (1981) and to my knowledge has not been previously discussed in print or studied numerically. The situation is best explained by detailing circumstances in which it could arise. Cluster analytic studies in psychiatry have frequently taken a sample of identified patients from a clinic, clustering them on symptoms and signs of illness. Suppose that the true state of nature in the population at large is as follows. People are distinguishable on several (for simplicity's sake, we assume normally distributed and independent) personality traits, and each trait is normally distributed. There is no mixture of taxa in the general population, i.e., there do not exist groups of individuals, of distinct genetic or environmental background, scoring higher or lower on any of these traits. Two traits for which such a supposition might be appropriate would be aggressiveness and neuroticism. Further suppose that a selection (or self-selection) on both traits operates in determining who comes to the clinic. For example, subjects might be referred by courts if they are extremely aggressive, while others might decide to come to the clinic if they are very anxious. If samples from clinic populations that are the result of such simultaneous selection were subjected to cluster analysis, apparently aggressive and neurotic taxa might emerge. The figure shows schematically how such selection could produce disparate groups, since each group is just the tail from one of the two trait distributions, with the other distribution for that group being unselected from the other trait distribution.

One may call such clumps "institutional pseudo-taxa" because they result from sampling institutions that have certain implicit or explicit criteria for entry. The possibility of such selection biases complicates formal inferences about the existence of taxa. In one sense such groups are taxa because they occupy distinct regions of the phenotypic space among patients seen in the clinic. However, they are certainly not taxa in the more interesting sense: they are not groups distinguished from one another in the ways that different infectious diseases are, or that different monogenically transmitted disorders are.

One could avoid confusing institutional pseudo-taxa and mixture-model taxa by performing taxometric analyses only in unselected populations, i.e., epidemiological settings. However, many disorders common in the clinic might be difficult or impossible to detect in the general population because they are relatively

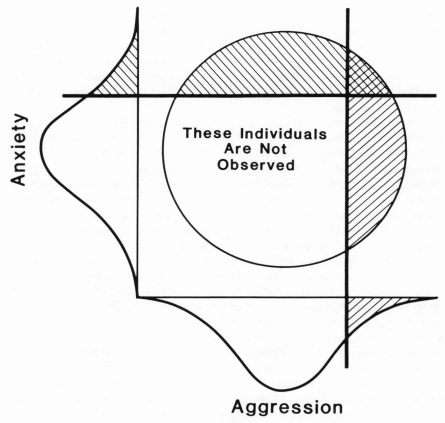

Figure 1. Creation of apparent taxa by institutional selection.

uncommon or because their manifestations in the general population are often mild.

Before giving up taxometric analysis of clinical population data, it would be useful to determine the degree of selection necessary to produce institutional pseudo-taxa indistinguishable from real taxa with distinct means. For psychiatric problems, prevalences of disorders in the general population set fairly narrow bounds on the possible stringency of selection for admission to clinics, hospitals, and prisons. Psychiatric disorders studied taxometrically have mostly been schizophrenia and severe depression. Carefully gathered epidemiological data put the six-month prevalences of these disorders at about 0.9% and 3.2%, respectively (Myers, Weissman, Tischler, Holzer, Leaf, Orvaschel, Anthony, Boyd, Burke, Kramer, & Stoltzman, 1984).

Let us take as convenient approximations of typical prevalences 1% to 5%, and for purposes of illustration assume that patients come to clinical attention if and only if they surpass a sharp selection threshold on the relevant trait. For normal distributions, the threshold for "degree of depression" would be $1.64\ \sigma$ and for "degree of schizophrenia" 2.33σ. If these latent traits were independent, the schizophrenic group would show depression trait scores averaging zero and scores on the schizophrenia trait averaging 2.67σ. Similarly, the depressed group would show average schizophrenia scores of zero and average depressive trait scores of 2.06σ. (Falconer, 1965, gives tables of such figures.) The schizophrenic and depressive groups would be over 2σ apart on each of two latent selection variables. If the manifest traits used to classify patients were correlated strongly enough with these latent selection traits, the schizophrenics and depressed patients might appear as distinct taxa in a taxometric analysis.

Just as plainly, if selection is weak, or if measures used in taxometrics are only weakly related to traits on which selection takes place, institutional taxa are not a threat to the validity of taxometric inferences. However, such truisms are not very useful in conducting real studies.

Over the past several years I have (with colleague Nancy Andreasen and other participants in the NIMH Clinical Research Branch Collaborative Studies on the Psychobiology of Depression—Clinical Studies) conducted cluster analyses of patients with affective syndromes to generate hypotheses about the subtyping of affective disorders (Andreasen, Grove, & Maurer, 1980; Andreasen & Grove, 1982) and to test specific hypotheses about endogenous depression (Grove, Andreasen, Young, Endicott, Keller, Hirschfeld, & Reich, 1987). In the latter investigation, the principal hypothesis was that endogenous depression approximates a distinct disease entity, as inferred from syndromal cohesion and isolation. We found a cluster, comprising about half of the unipolar major depressed patients in the study, which possessed prominent vegetative symptoms and signs. Since it corresponded to a region of overlapping membership in groups defined as endogenous or melancholic by several sets of criteria, we called this subtype "nuclear" depression. Unfortunately, cluster analyses of the kind we used (hierarchical agglomerative methods) always generate clusters, even if random samples from homogeneous distributions are analyzed. Given this fact, we had no particular confidence that our nuclear depressive syndrome was other than a statistical artifact. Before interpreting our results, we needed to know several things. First, how often do cluster analysis stopping rules indicate taxa where there are no taxa at all (institutional or otherwise)? Second, how far apart must indisputable taxa lie in a phenotypic space before cluster analysis stopping rules reliably detect their presence? Third, how stringent must latent trait selection become, and how strong must the correlation between manifest clustering variables and latent selection traits be, before cluster analysis stopping rules indicate the presence of taxa where only institutional pseudo-taxa exist? I investigated these questions by computer simulation.

Table 1. Nontaxonic and Institutional Pseudo-Taxonic Configurations

	Case								
	I			I-A			II		
	Factor			Factor			Factor		
Variable	1	2	Selection	1	2	Selection	1	2	Selection
X_1	.7	0	$F_1 > 2$	.7	0	$F_1 > 2$	.8	0	$F_1 > 3$
X_2	.7	0	or	.7	0	or	.8	0	or
X_3	0	.6	$F_2 > 1.64$	0	.6	$F_2 > 1.64$	0	.7	$F_2 > 2.8$
X_4	0	.6		0	.6		0	.7	
X_5	0	.6		0	.6		0	.7	

Note: No selection (nontaxonic) and selection (institutional pseudo-taxonic, using selection thresholds from table) conditions were examined. In Case I-A with selection. X_1 and X_2 were not used in cluster analyses.

Methods

Artificial Data Generation

All simulations were performed using data generation and analysis procedures of the Statistical Analysis System (SAS; SAS Institute, Inc., 1982) version 82.3 for IBM MVS operating systems, or 6.02 for IBM PC-DOS operating systems. Observations were drawn from a five-variate multivariate normal distribution for all parameter configurations. The standard SAS normal random number generator was used, with independent seeds and independent random number streams for each variable (latent or observed).

A taxon was defined as follows. Taxa exist when there are mixed two (or more) component multivariate normal distributions which differ in centroids but not in within-component covariance matrixes. (This is the situation in which Fisher's linear discriminant analysis is optimal.) Three different structures where investigated: data containing no taxa (centroid difference on each variable identically zero), data containing two taxa, and data containing no mixed-normal taxa but on which selection had taken place, yielding pseudo-taxa.

The nontaxonic and pseudo-taxonic data were generated from a five-variable multivariate normal distribution. The covariance structure of this distribution followed a common factor model with two orthogonal factors (see Table 1). Five variables were used so that there would be multiple measures for each of two selection-relevant latent traits, for the pseudo-taxa configurations. (Psychiatric cluster studies usually use several measures of each of several symptom domains.) For the pseudo-taxa condition, data from the parametric sets in Table 1 were repeatedly sampled until enough "subjects" passed selection for high scores on Factor 1 or Factor 2 (or both) to fill the sample size quota for the cluster analysis. For example, with Case I, if a "subject" had $F_1 > 2$ or $F_2 > 1.64$, the "subject" was included.

For Case I-A, the same conditions were applied, but only variables X_3 to X_5 were used in cluster analyses that followed sample generation. I did this to simulate the procedure used in certain psychiatric studies that have used only variables thought to be typical of one of the groups hypothesized to exist in a clinic population. If the "taxon" mistakenly sought were in fact simply an artifact of institutional selection, only variables relevant to one of the selection traits would be included in the study.

For pseudo-taxa, two sets of selection thresholds were examined to vary selection stringency. For both threshold sets, I placed one at a convenient value, far enough past the other one so that the rarer institutional pseudo-taxon was roughly one-half the size of the commoner. This was done to avoid having pseudo-taxa be equally large. Some authors (e.g., SAS Institute, 1982) have suggested that Ward's method, the clustering method used, is biased toward finding equally sized groups. In our work we have not found this to be true, having seen Ward's method easily identify a psychotically depressed group comprising only 10% of the sample in one study (Andreasen & Grove, 1982). However, I wished to ensure that any such bias, if it occurred, would tend to produce inaccurately sized groups, causing stopping rules to give the wrong answers (giving a maximally stringent test of the rules).

For the taxonic data, I generated observations from a five-variate normal distribution. There were two taxa present, mixed in the ratio 2:1 for the reason stated above. Each of the five observed variables showed equal between-group-centroid differences, to simplify simulations. Within clusters, a one common factor structure was used so that clusters were somewhat hyperelliptical in shape. A combination of factor loadings and between-group mean separations was chosen such that the conditions in Table 2 were satisfied, giving group separations from Mahalanobis $D^2 = 1$ to 5. Smaller separations might with some justice be called taxonic as well, but mixture-model tests of numerous heuristic methods of cluster analysis (Goldstein & Linden, 1969; Cunningham & Ogilvie, 1972; Gross, 1972; Kuiper & Fisher, 1975; Blashfield, 1976; Mojena, 1977; Edelbrock & McLaughlin, 1980; Golden & Meehl, 1980; Bayne et al., 1980; Milligan, 1981; Scheibler & Schneider, 1985) as well as simulations of more formally derived taxometric methods (Golden & Meehl, 1973a, 1973b, 1980; Golden, Tyan, & Meehl, 1974; Golden, 1982) indicate that small group separations are unlikely to be reliably detected.

All variable-pair correlations in the mixed group were held to 0.4, an item intercorrelation size often seen in psychiatric clustering studies. To hold the

Table 2. Taxonic Configurations

	Mahalanobis D^2									
	1		2		3		4		5	
Variable	L	V	L	V	L	V	L	V	L	V
X_i	.69	.58	.53	.93	.49	1.09	.45	1.21	.42	1.30

Note: $X_i = X_1$ to X_5, all having equal common factor loadings (L) and intercluster separations (V), in standard score units. All parameter sets give mixed-group correlations between all pairs of variables of 0.4.

mixed-group correlations fixed, one reduces correlations within taxa as group separation rises. For example, with this five-variable setup having equal group separations on each variable and a mixing proportion of one-third, for $D^2 = 1$ one requires a 0.48 within-group correlation, which is generated with factor loadings of 0.69. For $D^2 = 5$, the corresponding within-group correlation is 0.18, requiring a factor loading of 0.42.

For each parameter set studied, samples of $N = 50$ and 100 observations were drawn so that the effect of sample size could be studied. (Besides ensuring economy in the use of computer time for performing clustering, these sample sizes were chosen to enable comparison to previous studies that have mostly used $N = 50$ or 100.) One hundred replications of each of the sample size x parameter set combinations were generated. In all, 2 (no taxa *versus* institutional pseudo-taxa) x 3 (parameter sets) x 2 ($N = 50$ *versus* 100) x 100 (replications) = 1200 samples were drawn from the cases in Table 1, while 5 ($D^2 = 1$ to 5) x 2 ($N=50$ *versus* 100) x 100 (replications) = 1000 samples were drawn from the Table 2 configurations.

Cluster Analyses and Stopping Rules

After generating artificial data, each replication of each parameter combination was clustered using Ward's method of cluster analysis as implemented in SAS version 82.3. The clustering history for cluster fusions from 10 clusters down to 1 cluster was studied. The behavior of four indices used as stopping rules was examined over these 10 cluster fusions: SAS's Cubic Clustering Criterion (*CCC*; Sarle, 1983); Duda and Hart's (1973) ratio, Beale's (1969) ratio, and Mojena's (1977 statistic. The *CCC* is defined as

$$CCC_k = ln\left[\frac{1 - E[R_k^2]}{1 - R_k^2}\right] \frac{\sqrt{\frac{N_p^*}{2}}}{(0.001 + E[R_k^2])^{1.2}} \tag{1}$$

where R_k^2 is the estimated proportion of multivariate dispersion accounted for by cluster membership at the kth stage of clustering,

$E[R_k^2]$ is the expected value, at the kth stage of clustering, of R^2 under the null hypothesis that data come from a uniform distribution on the hypercube,

N is the total sample size, and

p^* is the dimensionality of between-cluster variation (which may be less than p, the number of dimensions in the phenotypic space).

The Duda and Hart ratio is

$$DH = \frac{SS_{k\ (wp)}}{SS_{k\ (wm)}} \tag{2}$$

while the Beale ratio is

$$B_k = \frac{\dfrac{SS_{k\ (wm)} - SS_{k\ (wp)}}{SS_{k\ (wm)}}}{2^{2/p} \left[\dfrac{n-1}{n-2} \right] - 1} \tag{3}$$

and the Mojena statistic is

$$M_k = SS_{k\ (wm)} \tag{4}$$

where

$SS_{k(wp)}$ is the pooled within-clusters sum of squares at the k-cluster stage, for just those two clusters about to be fused.

$SS_{k(wm)}$ is the within-cluster sum of squares for that cluster formed at the $(k-1)$th stage,

n is the number of observations in the cluster formed at the $(k-1)$th stage, and

p is the dimensionality of the phenotypic space in the mixed population.

The critical value for the Duda and Hart statistic is given by

$$DH_\alpha = 1 - \frac{2}{\pi p} - z_\alpha \frac{\sqrt{2\left[1 - \dfrac{8}{\pi^2 p}\right]}}{N_p} \tag{5}$$

with rejection occurring when $DH < DH_\alpha$. A value for z_α of 3.2 was chosen, based on the simulation results of Milligan and Cooper.

The critical value for the Beale ratio is obtained by assuming that the Beale ratio is distributed as Snedecor's $\mathscr{F}_{p,\ p(n-2)}$. Milligan and Cooper found that rejecting the null hypothesis at a nominal $\alpha = 0.005$ gave best cluster recovery in their simulations, so this value was used.

The critical value for Mojena's statistic is obtained in one of two data-dependent ways, called Rule One and Rule Two; Rule One performed better according to Mojena's simulations as well as those of others, so it was used. Rule One requires consideration of the sequence of values $SS_{k(wm)}$, $k = 1, \ldots$ $N - 1$ as the clustering procedure successively fuses N objects into ever fewer clusters. If $SS_{k(wm)}$ surpasses the mean of all $N–1$ values by at least z_α times the standard deviation of all $N - 1$ values, then one stops fusing clusters and considers the clustering complete at the step just preceding. $z_\alpha = 2.5$ was chosen because Milligan and Cooper found this the best overall value to use, even though the optimal z_α varied with the true number of clusters to be recovered (in a manner which they do not detail).

Sarle (1983) suggests that if $CCC > 2$, strong clusters exist, while if $0 < CCC < 2$ equivocal clusters exist. Therefore, both these critical values were tried.

For each replication in the simulations, the stopping point indicated by each of the stopping rules was tabulated. For non-taxonic data, these are just two outcomes: null hypothesis nonrejection (leading to fusing all observations into one cluster) or stopping fusion short of that point, which is a Type I error in this setting.

For the institutional pseudo-taxa configurations, I considered it a Type I error if a stopping rule terminated clustering before all observations had been fused into one cluster. This corresponds to testing the null hypothesis that the data do not arise from a mixture in the standard multivariate normal-mixture-model sense. The alternative hypothesis in this instance is that the data arose either from a purely nontaxonic situation or from institutional selection effects. From other viewpoints, such a failure to stop fusing clusters might instead be called a Type II error.

Mixture-model taxonic situations are less ambiguous in interpretation. Either the stopping rule, treated as a test for clusters, stops clustering before complete fusion (a correct decision) or it does not (a Type II error). However, even given that a test correctly indicates the presence of taxa in a population, the rule can still indicate the wrong number of taxa. I tabulated such errors.

Results

Table 3 gives the result of submitting nontaxonic data to clustering guided by each of the four stopping rules. Note that Mojena's rule is subject to *universal* Type I errors under all conditions studied. This aberrant behavior is actually hinted at by results of the Milligan and Cooper simulations. They reported that when the true number of clusters was two, Mojena's Rule One often stopped the clustering at three or more clusters. This led Milligan and Cooper to suggest that the optimal critical value for Mojena's statistic is higher for two groups than for three or more. However, this rise in critical value at two clusters is apparently incipient breakdown in the statistic's distribution. The other rules fared better.

Table 3. Probability of Type I Error for Nontaxa

| | Configurations | | | | | |
| | I | | I-A | | II | |
Rule	$N = 50$	$N = 100$	$N = 50$	$N = 100$	$N = 50$	$N = 100$
$CCC > 2$	0	0	0	0	0	0
$CCC > 0$	0	0	0	0	0	1
Duda & Hart	0	0	33	85	1	7
Beale	0	0	13	9	0	0
Mojena	100	100	100	100	100	100

From Table 3, one might conclude that the CCC has excellent protection against Type I error, but one wonders if this has been obtained at the cost of low power to detect real taxa.

Tables 4 and 5 indicate the CCC has low power; these tables give results for taxonic data ($N = 50$ and 100, respectively). Table 4 convincingly demonstrates that the CCC is extremely conservative at either critical value 0 or 2, with power approaching zero for extreme group separations and power indistinguishable from zero for less well separated groups. This behavior is plausible, though surprisingly extreme. The CCC tests the hypothesis that data arise from a uniform distribution on the hypercube. This is a distribution in which extreme values on any one clustering variable are every bit as likely as middling ones. With such data, it is not hard to imagine that clumps that are fairly far apart could occur, even absent the existence of distinct subdistributions. Critical values found to be sufficiently extreme to prevent excessive rejections of the null hypothesis (for the hypercubical null distributions used in Sarle's simulations) are apparently far too high for multivariate normal null distributions. Matters do not improve much for the CCC at $N = 100$ (Table 5).

Duda and Hart's ratio gave poor power (less than .25) at all group separations studied for $N = 50$, improving sharply at $N = 100$ (power .77–.93). It is puzzling that the size of D^2 seems to make little difference. This may indicate that power is a much stronger function of N than of D^2 or that the relevant part of the D^2 parameter region is outside the range studied.

At both values of N, Beale's ratio's power remains low at the pre-set critical value. At $N = 100$, the power of Mojena's rule is indistinguishable from 1, but we have seen that this corresponds to a risk of Type I error estimated at 1 as well.

Table 6 gives results for simulated data sets containing institutional pseudo-taxa. Note that Mojena's test again always indicates two or more groups. The performance of Duda and Hart's statistic at the chosen critical value can be summarized by noting that increasing stringency of institutional selection and in-

Table 4. Results for Taxonic Configurations (N = 50)

Rule	Clusters Found	D^2				
		1	2	3	4	5
CCC > 2	3+	0	0	0	0	0
	2	0	0	0	0	0
	1	100	100	100	100	100
CCC > 0	3+	0	0	0	2	1
	2	0	0	0	0	0
	1	100	100	100	98	99
Duda & Hart	3+	6	8	5	6	3
	2	27	18	22	21	13
	1	67	74	73	73	84
Beale	3+	15	21	15	21	18
	2	0	0	0	0	0
	1	85	79	85	79	82
Mojena	3+	96	99	99	98	97
	2	4	1	1	2	3
	1	0	0	0	0	0

creasing sample size are associated with increased risk of Type I error. This pattern is consistent with a use of Duda and Hart's test for picking out institutional pseudo-taxa and mixture-model taxa, if one considers them both taxonic. The statistic is consistent, since its tendency to reject the null hypothesis grows with rising N. Also, as institutional taxa grow further apart (i.e., as selection grows more stringent), the probability of stopping clustering by Duda's and Hart's test rises.

As a test of a null hypothesis that there are no mixture-model taxa *versus* the studied alternatives, Beale's rule held up best. It did not become very liberal with institutional taxa until extreme selection (Case II) was applied. Recall from Table 1 that Case II involves the equivalent of mixing, in a clinic, the 0.13% most aggressive individuals in the population with the 0.26% most depressed, for example. This is extreme selection. Given the relatively high general population period prevalence of most frequently studied psychiatric disorders (0.5% to 5%), this would not usually be a concern. The CCC at a critical value of 2 retained low rejection rates even under this degree of selection, but a critical value of 0 involved risking false rejection under extreme selection. We surmise from Table 3 that the CCC has essentially nil power at these group separations, whether they are generated from a multivariate normal mixing process or a selection process.

Table 5. Results for Taxonic Configurations ($N = 100$)

Rule	Clusters Found	D^2				
		1	2	3	4	5
$CCC > 2$	3+	0	0	0	0	0
	2	0	0	0	0	0
	1	100	100	100	100	100
$CCC > 0$	3+	0	0	0	0	0
	2	0	0	0	0	0
	1	100	100	100	100	100
Duda & Hart	3+	41	44	29	39	28
	2	45	36	51	54	49
	1	14	20	20	7	23
Beale	3+	20	13	13	16	9
	2	0	0	0	0	0
	1	80	87	87	84	91
Mojena	3+	100	100	100	100	100
	2	0	0	0	0	0
	1	0	0	0	0	0

Table 6. Probability of Type I Error for Institutional Pseudo-Taxa

	Configurations					
	I		I-A		II	
Rule	$N = 50$	$N = 100$	$N = 50$	$N = 100$	$N = 50$	$N = 100$
$CCC > 2$	0	0	0	0	2	7
$CCC > 0$	10	4	0	0	85	86
Duda & Hart	45	88	60	94	100	100
Beale	0	0	19	14	54	54
Mojena	100	100	100	100	100	100

Discussion

The present simulations are a survey of much of the parameter space encountered in psychiatric cluster analyses. If these results were to be extended, one would like to see trials with other forms of cluster analysis that are known to perform reasonably well in recovering normal mixtures (e.g., average linkage), looking at vector similarity coefficients (e.g., correlations) as well as the distance measures used here, higher dimensionality in the phenotypic and common factor spaces, a wider variety of simulated factor structures, a broader range of selection thresholds for institutional pseudo-taxa, larger simulated sample sizes, and more replications at each point in the parameter space. At present, one cannot draw firm or broad conclusions about the risk of errors of inference when using cluster analysis stopping rules. These simulations suggest that larger sample sizes than 100 are required before power to detect mixtures of taxa is acceptably high, if Ward's method, guided by the studied stopping rules at their literature-suggested critical values, is used. At any rate, this seems to be true unless group separation exceeds $D^2 = 5$. This value means that groups are $\sqrt{5}\sigma$ apart in multivariate space, and much larger separations seem to be uncommon in psychopathology research.

The conceptual limitations of this work are also clear. These results may not be generalizable to other definitions of a "real" taxon, such as the graph-theoretic or dissimilarity matrix-reproducing definitions favored by some investigators. As the most troublesome conceptual point, there is the previously noted ambiguity in interpreting the results for the institutional selection cases: are they taxa or not? One may fault my interpretation of the data on the grounds that what I call nontaxonic is really taxonic, so that what I call a Type I error is really a correct rejection of the null hypothesis. After all, institutional pseudo-taxa can be very nearly clusters in the nearest-neighbor sense of the term. For sufficiently stringent selection, in which clustering data are sufficiently tightly correlated with the selection traits, institutional pseudo-taxa overlap very little. In such cases they are almost point-swarms whose nearest neighbors are mutually closer to one another than to any extra-cluster point.

However, there is a straightforward reply to this objection. Every mathematical model involving tests of statistical hypotheses posits some sort of "null" model, against which alternatives are tested. Robustness studies must use data in which the most important aspects of the null model are preserved, but some less central feature is altered. Consider the following analogy. In regression problems, the null hypothesis usually states that no predictor is linearly related to the criterion. One might conduct a study of the robustness of regression procedures under predictor and dependent variable skewness. With sufficiently gross skewing, a quasi-linear relation between predictor and criterion in the skewed data might emerge, even though this relation is absent under skewness-removing transformation. One might further find, from analytic or simulation studies, that the $\mathscr{F}$-test is insensitive to skewness in the data, suggesting that it can still be relied on for correct statements about underlying linear relationships. A critic might point out that the data, as analyzed, no longer manifest lack of linear relationship, and could argue that the results *indict* the sensitivity of the $\mathscr{F}$-test, instead of supporting its robustness.

We can cut this knot by stating that only with a formal, mathematized model can one precisely formulate and debate concepts related to errors of inference. Nonmixture models for taxa could certainly be defended. Absent a compelling example in which institutional selection-produced groups turned out to be disease entities in some useful sense, I consider such groups not to be taxa. I do so because I use taxometric analyses as a first step to try to isolate "loose" monogenically transmitted syndromes (Meehl, 1973). One wants not to be fooled into thinking that institutional selection-induced groups are really distinct, potentially monogenically transmitted diseases, since there is an enormous gulf between the causal mechanisms in these two situations.

I interpret these simulations as showing that cluster analysis, even when guided by stopping rules as good as have been so far developed, has quite limited power to discriminate between competing mechanisms by which multivariate data can arise. Beale's rule appears to perform best of a bad lot. The rules do not strongly discriminate variation arising from subjects' being members of distinct taxa (which might stem from single-gene effects), from graduated differences presumably due to polygenic and (many small) environmental causes, or from pseudo-discontinuities caused by institutional selection.

To discriminate hypotheses about the causal background underlying evidence of taxa, it may be essential to shift from looking at patients' data to family data analyses. Analyses of family data allow further validation of taxa, and they give numerous cross-checks on the validity of one's inferences about the genetic and environmental origins of taxa. A number of such approaches exist. For example, one test for dominant single major locus gene action is to see whether the covariation between parents of patients, on disease-related traits, is close to that predicted from observed covariances between these traits in heterogeneous patient groups (Golden & Meehl, 1978). A similar test for recessive action can be developed based on sib-sib covariances on disease-related traits (Grove, 1982).

It may also be possible to better distinguish taxa created by monogenic action from those due to social selection, by using observations on multiple disease-related traits from various classes of relatives. Approaches using the familial co-aggregation of two traits have been suggested. In one, the first trait is disease status (affected *versus* normal) and the second continuously varies (e.g., serum iron in hemochromatosis; Lalouel, Le Mignon, Simon, Fauchet, Bourel, Rao, & Morton, 1985). Another model, of much current interest in psychiatry, uses two dichotomous traits (e.g., schizophrenia and eye tracking, graded normal *versus* abnormal; Matthysse, Holzman & Lange, 1986) has also been put forth. Meehl (1987) and I (1987) have each been working on multivariate methods related to such bivariate techniques. Such multivariate extensions presumably offer greater power. More important, they should allow more rigorous cross-checks on results than do analyses of only two traits. It is probably with such models that future work should proceed.

Still, even simple heuristic methods like cluster analysis have their place in psychopathology research. If a proposed taxon, hypothesized to have multiple manifestations stemming from a monogenic cause, does not show phenotypic distinctness by cluster analysis (guided by appropriate cautions such as stopping rules), I would have little confidence that formal genetic work using multitrait family data would yield persuasive evidence of monogenic segregation.

References

Andreasen, N. C., & Grove, W. M. (1982). The classification of depression: Traditional *versus* mathematical approaches. *American Journal of Psychiatry, 139,* 45–52.

Andreasen, N. C., Grove, W. M., & Maurer, R. (1980). Cluster analysis and the classification of depression. *British Journal of Psychiatry, 137,* 256–265.

Bayne, C. K., Beauchamp, J. J., Begovich, C. L., & Kane, V. E. (1980). Monte Carlo comparisons of selected clustering procedures. *Pattern Recognition, 12,* 51–62.

Beale, E. M. L. (1969). *Cluster analysis.* London: Scientific Control Systems.

Blashfield, R. K. (1976). Mixture model tests of cluster analysis: Accuracy of four agglomerative hierarchical methods. *Psychological Bulletin, 83,* 377–388.

Bock, H. H. (1985). On some significance tests in cluster analysis. *Journal of Classification, 2,* 77–108.

Cunningham, K. M., & Ogilvie, J. C. (1972). Evaluation of hierarchical grouping techniques—a preliminary study. *Computer Journal, 15,* 209–213.

Duda, R. O., & Hart, P. E. (1973). *Pattern classification and scene analysis.* New York: Wiley.

Edelbrock, C., & McLaughlin, B. (1980). Hierarchical cluster analysis using intraclass correlations: A mixture model study. *Multivariate Behavioral Research, 15,* 299–318.

Engleman, L., & Hartigan, J. A. (1969). Percentage points of a test for clusters. *Journal of the American Statistical Association, 64,* 1647–1648.

Everitt, B. S. (1981). A Monte Carlo investigation of the likelihood ratio test for the number of components in a mixture of normal distributions. *Multivariate Behavioral Research, 16,* 171–180.

Falconer, D. S. (1965). The inheritance of liability to certain diseases, estimated from the incidence among relatives. *Annals of Human Genetics* (London), *29,* 51–76.

Golden, R. R. (1982). A taxometric model for the detection of a conjectured latent taxon. *Multivariate Behavioral Research, 17,* 389–416.

Golden, R. R., & Meehl, P. E. (1973a). *Detecting latent clinical taxa, IV: An empirical study of the maximum covariance method and the normal minimum chi-square method using three MMPI keys to identify the sexes.* Reports from the Research Laboratories No. PR-73-2. Minneapolis, Minnesota: University of Minnesota Department of Psychiatry.

Golden, R. R., & Meehl, P. E. (1973b). *Detecting latent clinical taxa, V: A Monte Carlo study of the maximum covariance method and associated consistency tests.* Reports from the Research Laboratories No. PR-73-3. Minneapolis, Minnesota: University of Minnesota Department of Psychiatry.

Golden, R. R., & Meehl, P. E. (1978). Testing a single dominant gene theory without an accepted criterion variable. *Annals of Human Genetics* (London), *41,* 507–514.

Golden, R. R., & Meehl, P. E. (1980). Detection of biological sex: An empirical test of cluster methods. *Multivariate Behavioral Research, 15,* 475–496.

Golden, R. R., Tyan, S. H., & Meehl, P. E. (1974). *Detecting latent clinical taxa, VII: Maximum likelihood solution and empirical and artificial data trials of the multi-indicator multi-taxonomic class normal theory.* Reports from the Research Laboratories No. PR-74-5. Minneapolis, Minnesota: University of Minnesota Department of Psychiatry.

Goldstein, S. G., & Linden, J. D. (1969). A comparison of multivariate grouping techniques commonly used with profile data. *Multivariate Behavioral Research, 4,* 103–114.

Gross, A. L. (1972). A Monte Carlo study of the accuracy of a hierarchical grouping procedure. *Multivariate Behavioral Research, 7*, 379–389.

Grove, W. M. (June 1982). Unpublished work.

Grove, W. M. (June, 1987). Unpublished research grant application.

Grove, W. M., Andreasen, N. C., Young, M., Endicott, J., Keller, M. B., Hirschfeld, R. M. A., & Reich, T. (1987). Isolation and characterization of a nuclear depressive syndrome. *Psychological Medicine, 17*, 471–484.

Kuiper, F. K., & Fisher, L. (1975). A Monte Carlo comparison of six clustering procedures. *Biometrics, 31*, 777–783.

Lalouel, J. M., Le Mignon, L., Simon, M., Fauchet, R., Bourel, M., Rao, D. C., & Morton, N. E. (1985). Genetic analysis of idiopathic hemochromatosis using both qualitative (disease status) and quantitative (serum iron) information. *American Journal of Human Genetics, 37*, 700–718.

Lee, K. L. (1979). Multivariate tests for clusters. *Journal of the American Statistical Association, 74*, 708–714.

Matthysse, S., Holzman, P. S., & Lange, K. (1986). The genetic transmission of schizophrenia: Application of Mendelian latent structure analysis to eye tracking dysfunctions in schizophrenia and affective disorder. *Journal of Psychiatric Research, 20*, 57–76.

Meehl, P. E. (1973). MAXCOV-HITMAX: A taxonomic search method for loose genetic syndromes. In Meehl, P. E., *Psychodiagnosis: Selected papers*. Minneapolis, Minnesota: University of Minnesota Press.

Meehl, P. E. (May, 1987). Unpublished memorandum.

Meehl, P. E., & Lykken, D. T. (1969). *Identifying latent clinical taxa III: An empirical trial of the normal single-indicator method, using MMPI scale 5 to identify the sexes*. Reports from the Research Laboratories No. PR-69-1. Minneapolis, Minnesota: University of Minnesota Department of Psychiatry.

Milligan, G. W. (1981). A review of Monte Carlo tests of cluster analysis. *Multivariate Behavioral Research, 16*, 379–407.

Milligan, G. W., & Cooper, M. C. (1983). *An examination of procedures for determining the number of clusters in a data set*. College of Administrative Sciences Working Paper Series 83-51. Columbus, Ohio: Ohio State University.

Mojena, R. (1977). Hierarchical grouping methods and stopping rules: An evaluation. *Computer Journal, 20*, 359–363.

Myers, J. K., Weissman, M. M., Tischler, G. L., Holzer, C. E. III, Leaf, P. J., Orvaschel, H., Anthony, J. C., Boyd, J. H., Burke, J. D., Jr., Kramer, M., & Stoltzman, R. (1984). Six-month prevalence of psychiatric disorders in three communities: 1980 to 1982. *Archives of General Psychiatry, 41*, 959–967.

Sarle, W. S. (1983). *Cubic clustering criterion*. SAS Technical Report A-108. Cary, North Carolina: SAS Institute, Inc.

SAS Institute, Inc. (1982). *SAS user's guide: Statistics, 1982 edition*. Cary, North Carolina: Author.

Scheibler, D., & Schneider, W. (1985). Monte Carlo tests of the accuracy of cluster analysis algorithms: A comparison of hierarchical and nonhierarchical methods. *Multivariate Behavioral Research, 20*, 283–304.

Tellegen, A. (March, 1981). Personal communication.

Psychopathology

The Psychodiagnosis of Everyday Conduct: Narcissistic Personality Disorder and Its Components
David M. Buss

An important goal of clinical assessment is to preserve the links between psychodiagnostic classifications and manifestations of psychopathology in everyday conduct (Buss & Craik, 1986). Manifestations of psychopathology are typically first noted in a person's everyday life. The inability to work or play, displays of unusual ideation, expressions of subjective distress, and behaviors injurious to self or others initially come to the attention of the person, family, friends, co-workers, or other members of society. These acts in everyday conduct call attention to the need for some kind of diagnosis, treatment, or intervention from mental health professionals.

The act frequency approach to personality (Buss & Craik, 1983) and psychopathology (Buss & Craik, 1986, 1987) provides a conceptual framework and set of methods for preserving the links between diagnostic classifications and the psychopathology of everyday conduct. This chapter briefly describes the framework and methods, and provides an empirical illustration using the narcissistic personality disorder—a syndrome that has received increasing attention in the past decade (Morrison, 1986; Emmons, 1987; Raskin & Terry, 1988).

Personality Disorders as Syndromes of Clinically Relevant Dispositions

Axis II of the DSM-III (APA, 1980) describes 11 basic personality disorders. A major emphasis in the new DSM-III orientation is on separating descriptions of a particular disorder from explanatory schemes proposed to account for the etiology and proximate mechanisms involved in the disorder. In emphasizing the descriptive component, the DSM-III manual provides behaviorally oriented criteria for each of the 11 personality disorders.

Careful analysis of these diagnostic criteria reveals that they are composed primarily of *dispositional terms* that have been taken from the natural language (see also Widiger & Francis, 1985; Widiger & Kelso, 1983). The act frequency approach to psychopathology takes as a starting point the notion that personality disorders can be analyzed as syndromes of clinically relevant dispositions taken from the natural language.

This lexical approach starts with the basic assumption that dispositional constructs have evolved in the natural language to capture important performance phenomena. As described by Norman (1963), "perceptible differences between persons in their characteristic manner of behaving or changes over time and situations of single individuals in these regards have become codified as a subset of descriptive predicates of the natural language in the course of its development" (p. 574). Features of behavior that have endangered self or others (Maher & Maher, 1985), or that have caused subjective distress to self or others, or that show adaptive inflexibility, the tendency to generate self-defeating cycles, or tenuous stability under stress (Millon, 1981) have become codified as descriptive predicates in the natural language. The natural language provides an important starting point for the act frequency analysis of the psychopathology of everyday conduct.

Indeed, most of the DSM-III personality disorders are contained as trait-descriptive terms within the natural language. Terms such as *dependent, histrionic, narcissistic, antisocial, compulsive, passive, aggressive,* and *avoidant* have been used for centuries by everyday folk, presumably to describe certain classes of behavioral phenomena, cognitive styles, and interpersonal tendencies. The natural language is also replete with clinically relevant terms, only some of which find their way into formal diagnostic classifications. These include anxious, bizarre, insane, perverted, exploitable, licentious, macabre, caustic, chameleonic, hypersensitive, idolatrous, inarticulate, insatiable, intolerant, lachrymose, masochistic, maudlin, mysogynic, and mysterious. Apparently, language users have found these terms useful in describing others, and so terms have been invented and used, and thus evolve within the natural language.

The diagnostic criteria for the narcissistic personality disorder, the focus of this chapter, include both dispositional and non-dispositional descriptors. The dispositional descriptors include: grandiose, exhibitionistic, exploitative, self-centered, and self-aggrandizing. The DSM-III narcissistic personality disorder also includes descriptors that, although not technically trait-descriptive adjectives, can be readily understood in dispositional terms, such as sense of entitlement and lack of empathy. The act frequency approach to psychopathology takes as a starting point the assumption that personality disorders such as narcissism can be understood in part by identifying these dispositionally relevant descriptors, and identifying the classes of everyday acts to which each corresponds (see Fig. 1; see also Livesley, 1984).

Clinically Relevant Dispositions as Classes of Acts

After clinically relevant dispositions have been identified, the next step in the act frequency analysis is to identify the acts subsumed by each syndrome-relevant disposition. Dispositional constructs such as grandiose and exhibitionistic are treated as categories of acts occurring in everyday conduct. For example, "he bragged about his accomplishments" and "she undressed with the curtains opened" were nominated by an undergraduate panel as grandiose and exhibitionistic, respectively. The acts subsumed by each disposition are themselves topographically distinct. They may occur at different points throughout the natural flow of a person's everyday conduct. Dispositions are conceptual units that *summarize general trends*, or act frequencies, in conduct. Because single acts are rarely invariantly diagnostic of dispositions or syndromes (Meehl, 1973), act trends or multiple-act criteria become the units of analysis.

Act trends and their dispositional designations are descriptive rather than explanatory. Stating that *Carol is exploitative*, for example, does not explain *why* she used another's possessions without asking, befriended someone because that person knew the "right" people, borrowed money without repaying, or used someone to make her loved one jealous. Explanatory accounts of act trends must be advanced subsequently. In this sense, the act frequency approach shares with the DSM-III the orientation of separating descriptive from explanatory tasks in the analysis of personality disorders.

Although dispositional constructs are not explanatory, the act trends they subsume have considerable causal impact in affecting observer attributions, reputation, statements about the self, and important life outcomes. Exploitative act trends, for example, may lead to a reputation as manipulative, a self-concept of being interpersonally effective, and life outcomes marked by oscillations of ascendance and social ostracism. In sum, dispositions are not treated as causal or explanatory constructs, but the act trends they subsume can carry considerable causal impact.

Dispositional constructs can be analyzed by their cognitive features. Rosch and her colleagues (Rosch, 1975; Rosch & Mervis, 1975; Rosch, Simpson, & Miller, 1976) have conceptualized the differing cognitive status of category members in terms of the notion of *prototypicality*. Highly prototypical members are the clearest cases, the best examples, the instances par excellence of the category. A robin is a more prototypical member of the category bird than is a penguin or turkey. Similarly, the act "I used my friend for her wealth" may be a more prototypical member of the category of *exploitative* than the act "I left the dishes for someone else to do," although both are clearly within the boundaries of the category.

In sum, dispositional categories, in the act frequency conception, are composed of topographically distinct acts that differ in their within-category status from highly central or prototypical to progressively more peripheral, until the fuzzy boundaries are reached and adjoining categories are entered.

Narcissistic Personality Disorder: Clinical Description

The study of narcissism has received increasing attention in the past decade, both theoretically (Kernberg, 1976, 1980; Kohut, 1976; Millon, 1981) as well as empirically (Emmons, 1987; Raskin & Hall, 1979; Raskin & Terry, 1988). Much of the debate surrounding this personality disorder has focused on matters of etiology and internal dynamics (e.g., parental rejection or abandonment resulting in defensive withdrawal, distrust of love of others, and consequently self-love *versus* failure to idealize parents owing to rejection or indifference).

There is more agreement, however, on the behavioral description of narcissism (Emmons, 1987; Millon, 1981; Raskin & Terry, 1988). Narcissism involves a turning inward for gratification, a reliance on self rather than others for safety and self-esteem. Narcissists tend to be preoccupied with power and prestige, enhancing themselves by believing that they are stronger and more important than others, greater in their abilities, or more beautiful to behold. They often assume personal worth without corresponding objective deeds.

The DSM-III (APA, 1980) descriptive criteria include these clinically relevant features: (1) *grandiose* sense of self-importance and uniqueness, (2) *exhibitionistic* in the sense of requiring attention and admiration from others, (3) *sense of entitlement* in expecting that wishes should automatically be met and special favors granted without reciprocity, (4) *interpersonally exploitative* in using others merely as objects for selfish gains, (5) *self-centered* in their behavior toward others and in their illusions about their talents, (6) *self-aggrandizing* in presenting an inflated self-image to others and exaggerating achievements, and (7) *lacking empathy* for the rights and feelings of others and disregarding social conventions in ways that violate others.

The DSM-III description of the narcissistic personality disorder also contains descriptions that are less readily characterized in dispositional terms, such as the oscillation between overvaluing and devaluating others. Nonetheless, many of the essential features of the disorder can be well described in the above set of trait-descriptive terms, which forms the basis for the following empirical studies of the narcissistic personality disorder.

Narcissistic Acts in Everyday Life

The act frequency approach requires as a first step the generation of a pool of acts relevant to each personality disorder syndrome and to the clinically relevant dispositions subsumed by each syndrome. Act nomination procedures have been developed for this purpose (Buss & Craik, 1984). Act nominations can occur "on line'' from direct observation by peers, family members, or clinicians, or they can occur retrospectively. The instructional set used in this study to generate pools of narcissistically relevant acts is as follows:

"Below are listed *categories* of behavior. In this study, please think of three people you know who typify or exemplify that category. For example, if the category is 'athletic,' you might write down 'played basketball' or 'hit a home-run in baseball.' These events are specific behaviors or acts. Do *not* write down synonyms or adjectives such as 'he is strong.' We are interested in acts or behaviors that reflect each category.

"The first category is *narcissistic* (grandiose, exploitative, exhibitionistic, etc.). Think of the three most narcissistic (grandiose, exploitative, etc.) people you know. With these narcissistic people in mind, write down three acts or behaviors that demonstrate or reflect their narcissism. Do the same for the categories that follow.''

Each of 84 subjects was provided with forms on which they nominated acts subsumed by narcissism, exploitativeness, exhibitionism, entitlement, lack of empathy, self-centeredness, self-aggrandizement, and grandiosity. Sample acts from each of these categories are:

Narcissistic Acts: He looked in the mirror constantly; she baited others for compliments; he asked others how he looked; he bragged about his academics and other accomplishments (e.g., athletics); she asked others questions, insulting their intelligence; he compared himself favorably to others; she put others down (e.g., accomplishments, appearance); he told people he could date anyone.

Exhibitionistic Acts: He became the life of the party; she flaunted money to impress someone; she talked loudly so that others would hear her story; he disagreed for the sake of attention; she became wild at the party; he walked around with no shirt on; she kissed passionately in public; he showed off his possessions.

Grandiose Acts: He expected others to step aside when he walked by; she avoided talking to people she considered to be ''low life''; he said that he was great; she took charge of the meeting; he claimed that he was the best at something; she exaggerated her role in the sporting event; he nominated himself for a position of power.

Self-Centered Acts: He did not ask his partner what she wanted before making the decision for the two of them; she assumed that someone else should pay for dinner when she was low on cash; he insisted that he be heard, but would not listen; she refused to share her food with others; he cut into a long line ahead of his turn; she turned the TV to her channel without asking what the others wanted; he asked others to conform to his schedule.

Acts of Entitlement: He used something without replacing it; she asked a large favor without offering repayment; he showed up at an odd hour and expected to be entertained; she invited herself to a social event; he demanded sexual favors because of love; he made a collect call to a friend; she took the last piece of dessert without asking if anyone else wanted it; he told his parents that they should do things for him because they were his parents.

Self-Aggrandizing Acts: He pulled rank on someone to make a point; she played up her achievements; he discussed how much money he had; she associated only with people of high status; he talked about his good points; she pointed out the faults of others; he appointed himself director when he saw what was needed; she arrived late to make a grand entrance; he talked about his success with the opposite sex.

Lack of Empathy Acts: He did not show much feeling when his friend was upset; she did not get upset over the death of a friend; he did not listen to other people's problems; she did not understand someone because she kept interrupting them; he refused to have pity for people with economic problems because he figured it was their own fault; she threw stones at an animal she didn't like; he ignored a friend who was sad.

Exploitative Acts: He used his friend to gain a better social life; she asked her parents for extra money; he insisted that his friend drop everything to see him; she did the favor only when twice as much was promised in return; he spent time with her only when no one else was around; she used her friend for her wealth; he asked someone else to do his work for him.

In sum, this first stage of research, act nominations, contributes to the identification of a class of acts corresponding to each syndrome and clinically relevant disposition subsumed by each syndrome. These acts shed light on the nature of everyday manifestations of the personality disorder and provide a foundation for further empirical study of it.

Most Prototypical Narcissistic Acts

A second step in identifying the performance phenomena involved in each personality disorder requires specifying which acts are *central* or *prototypical* members of the disorder. Toward this end, three samples were recruited to judge which acts were prototypically narcissistic. The first sample consisted of clinical psychology faculty and advanced clinical graduate students who were familiar with the DSM-III (N = 25). A second sample was composed of undergraduates (N = 39). Both these samples judged each of 60 acts nominated directly for *narcissism* on its centrality to the category. These samples permit a partial examination of the correspondence between experts and laypersons in their views of narcissistic acts in everyday life.

A third sample (N = 60) was composed of undergraduates who judged the centrality of each of 140 acts, initially nominated as exemplars of the seven clinically relevant narcissistic dispositions. Twenty acts from each of these seven dispositions were intermingled, and not identified by the category in which they were initially nominated. This study provides a preliminary evaluation of the rel-

Table 1. Most Prototypical Narcissistic Acts

Expert	Undergraduate	Acts
6.40	5.44	He talked about himself and did not listen to anyone else
6.24	5.72	She cut off a conversation to talk about herself
6.16	5.28	He looked in the mirror while talking to others
5.88	5.77	She had a picture of herself and said she should be in a model magazine
5.76	5.59	He "showed off" his body when others were watching
5.76	5.26	She looked in the mirror constantly
5.68	4.90	He gave everyone pictures of himself
5.64	4.74	She demanded attention when performing any kind of act
5.60	5.85	He told his friend that the best way to pick up women was to be as much like him as possible
5.60	4.74	She always brushed her hair and put on makeup several times in a brief period
5.52	5.82	He said to the girls: "How could anyone not like this body?"
5.52	6.18	He came right out and said that he was beautiful or great

Note: Possible scores range from 7.00 (good example of narcissism) to 1.00 (poor example of narcissism).

ative centrality of each clinically relevant disposition to the syndrome of narcissism, as reflected in conceptions laypersons have of the construct of narcissism.

Table 1 shows the acts judged to be most prototypical of narcissism, as judged by the expert panel. Also shown in Table 1 are the mean ratings for each of the 12 most prototypically narcissistic acts for the expert and undergraduate panels. The correlation between the mean ratings for the expert and undergraduate panels is +.81, suggesting considerable agreement about which acts are central to the narcissism category.

Perusal of these prototypically narcissistic acts suggests themes of *self-*

centeredness (e.g., He talked about himself, but did not listen to anyone else), *self-absorption* (e.g., looking in a mirror while talking with others), *exhibitionism* (e.g., showing off body while others are watching), *self-aggrandizing* (e.g., telling others that the best way to pick up women is to be like him), and *grandiosity* (e.g., coming right out and saying that they are beautiful or great). Thus, many of the components contained in the DSM-III description of this personality disorder are also contained in acts nominated by laypersons as narcissistic and judged by panels of experts and laypersons as narcissistic.

Table 2 shows the 20 acts judged to be most prototypically narcissistic from the set of 140 acts nominated for the clinically relevant narcissistic dispositions. Also shown in the table are the mean prototypicality ratings and the clinically relevant dispositions for which the initial act was nominated.

Grandiose acts make the strongest appearance among the most prototypical narcissistic acts. Indeed, three of the top five narcissistic acts in this study were initially nominated as grandiose: expecting others to step aside, emphasizing one's greatness, and claiming to be the best at something.

Self-centered (e.g., insisting on being heard, but not listening) and self-aggrandizing (e.g., boasting about abilities and intelligence) also show up strongly among the most prototypically narcissistic acts. Three of the top 20 acts were initially nominated as exploitative, including insisting that a friend drop everything, putting others down to make self feel better, and asking a friend to listen to one's troubles, but not reciprocating.

Exhibitionistic acts (e.g., boasting about success with opposite sex) and acts indicating lack of empathy (e.g., interrupting someone who was telling something important) each make two appearances in the top 20 narcissistic acts. Only entitlement has no acts appearing in the top 20. Nonetheless, it is clear that many of these narcissistic acts do involve entitlement in the sense of expectations of special privileges without reciprocity, such as insisting on being heard but not listening, and asking a friend to listen to one's troubles, but not returning the favor.

In sum, it appears that lay conceptions of the syndrome of narcissism capture most or all of the essential components of narcissism as described in the DSM-III. This surprisingly high correspondence between lay conceptions and a professionally crafted description of the syndrome merits further study—a topic to be taken up in the discussion section.

Empirical Covariation among Clinically Relevant Dispositions

Finding the essential clinically relevant components of the DSM-III description of narcissism among the highly prototypical narcissistic acts provides evidence that laypersons believe that these components are central to the concept of nar-

Table 2. 20 Most Narcissistic Acts from 7 Sub-Dispositions

Mean	Category	Act
6.20	Grandiose	I expected others to step aside when I walked by
5.92	Exploitative	I insisted that my friend drop everyone to see me
5.78	Grandiose	I said that I was great
5.75	Self-centered	I insisted on being heard, but would not listen
5.75	Grandiose	I claimed that I was the best at something
5.70	Exhibitionistic	I boasted about my experiences with members of the opposite sex
5.67	Self-aggrandizing	I boasted about my abilities and intelligence
5.63	Lack of Empathy	I interrupted someone who was telling something important in order to convey my own news
5.59	Self-centered	I flirted with someone else and ignored my spouse's feelings
5.54	Self-aggrandizing	I talked about my success with members of the opposite sex
5.54	Self-centered	I demanded attention
5.52	Exhibitionistic	I boasted about my talents
5.50	Self-aggrandizing	I arrived late to make a grand entrance
5.50	Grandiose	I avoided talking to people that I considered to be ''low life''
5.48	Exploitative	I put someone down to make me feel better
5.47	Grandiose	I mentioned that I was sexy
5.45	Lack of Empathy	I laughed at my friend's problems
5.42	Exploitative	I asked my friend to listen to my troubles, but would not return the favor
5.35	Self-aggrandizing	I boasted about my past accomplishments
5.34	Self-centered	I exaggerated my problems to receive attention

Note: Possible scores range from 7.00 (good example of narcissism) to 1.00 (poor example of narcissism)

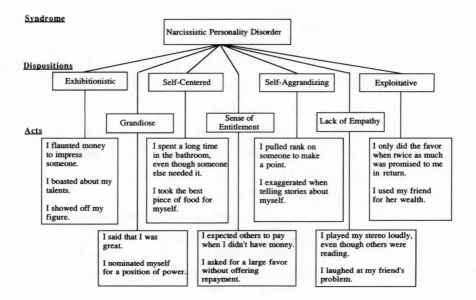

Figure 1. Narcissistic syndrome: Dispositions and acts.

cissism. But it does not provide evidence that these components covary among persons in their actual day-to-day act performance. To address this issue, a study of married couples was conducted (N = 210).

Act reports containing the 140 acts nominated for the narcissistic sub-dispositions were completed by each subject about themselves. Independently, in a separate session, subjects also completed an observer-based act report about their spouse. Thus, two data sources were available about the performance frequencies of each act. Within each data source, the 20 acts comprising each disposition were summed. The correlations among these composites are shown in Table 3.

All correlations are strongly positive, significantly so (p <.001) in each case. This positive manifold occurs for both the self-report and the spouse-observer report data sources. These data suggest that the dispositional components of narcissism covary, providing convergent evidence for the viability of the concept of narcissism as a syndrome subsuming somewhat diverse dispositional components.

Factor Analyses of Seven Dispositions

To further test for the empirical coherence of these seven dispositions, three prin-

Table 3. Correlations among Narcissistic Dispositions

	Exhib.	Aggrand.	Self-center.	Entitle.	Exploit.	Lack Emp.	Gran-diose
Exhibitionistic		.75	.66	.62	.54	.50	.74
Aggrandizing	.76		.73	.67	.59	.55	.82
Self-Centered	.67	.79		.85	.74	.69	.79
Entitlement	.66	.72	.88		.75	.66	.73
Exploitative	.56	.68	.78	.82		.66	.67
Lack of Empathy	.53	.62	.70	.70	.66		.64
Grandiose	.75	.83	.79	.73	.68	.62	

Note: Correlations above the diagonal are between self-reported acts; those below the diagonal are between spouse-reported acts.

cipal components analyses were conducted on the seven composites: one for each data source separately and one for the unit-weighted total scores based on the sum of the self-recorded and observer-recorded acts. Scores were standardized (z-scored) before analysis.

The results of the three principal components analyses were close to identical. In each analysis, one large factor emerged with an eigenvalue greater than 5.00 and accounted for at least 73% of the variance. In no analysis did any other factor exceed or even approach an eigenvalue of 1.00. For the self-report data source, the first principal component had an eigenvalue of 5.11 and accounted for 70% of the variance. The second factor had an eigenvalue of only .66. The communalities for the seven dispositions ranged from .61 to .84.

For the observer-report data source, the first principal component had an eigenvalue of 5.28 and captured 75.4% of the variance. The second component had an eigenvalue of only .61. Communalities ranged from .65 to .87. On the assumption that a composite measure across data sources would reduce error variance, we conducted principal components analysis on the seven unit-weighted composite measures of the seven dispositions. This analysis also produced one large component with an eigenvalue of 5.15, accounting for 73.6% of the variance. The second component had an eigenvalue of only .67. Communalities ranged from a low of .57 (lack of empathy) to a high of .86 (self-centered). These results provide support for the empirical coherence of narcissism in a non-clinical population and suggest that the syndrome designation is appropriate.

Discussion

These empirical studies are limited in several ways that should be enumerated. First, they deal with nonclinical populations and thus may not be generalizable to clinical populations. They deal instead with narcissistic acts in the everyday lives of persons with no known clinical problems. Perhaps clinicians observing the behavior of diagnosed narcissistic persons would identify acts that are more subtle, complex, or deviant than those discovered in the present studies.

A second limitation is that not all features of the DSM-III description of narcissism could be included in the present analysis. Oscillations between extremes of overvaluation and devaluation of others, precarious self-esteem, and sense of humiliation, for example, would be difficult to capture with the present act frequency methods. A third limitation is that these studies do not permit a differentiation between the narcissistic personality disorder and related personality disorders (e.g., histrionic personality disorder) with which it shares clinically relevant dispositional descriptions. These limitations must be addressed by future studies that deal with clinical populations containing persons diagnosed in several of the Axis-II personality disorders.

Given these limitations, several conclusions and future research directions merit note. First, these studies provide a foundation for preserving the links between diagnostic classifications and the psychopathology of everyday conduct. In particular, by identifying clinically relevant dispositions of narcissism and the acts subsumed by each of these dispositions, these studies document the classes of acts to which a diagnosis of narcissism is likely to correspond.

Second, the fact that the major constituents appeared among the most prototypical narcissistic acts lends support for the DSM-III description of the narcissistic personality disorder. The basis for this finding, however, remains unclear. Perhaps these constituents are part of lay conceptions because laypersons have observed over time covariation of these attributes. Alternatively, these results could simply be part of a network of semantically similar dispositions that share features. Future research is needed to identify the basis of these lay conceptions as well as the interesting correspondence between them and the clinical distillation that has emerged in the form of the DSM-III description.

A third conclusion is that empirical support is found for the notion of a narcissistic syndrome that subsumes several distinct constituent dispositions. The strong empirical covariation of these constituents, obtained through two data sources, points to the value of conceptualizing personality disorders at the syndrome level but also analyzing each syndrome into its constituent dispositions and the acts in everyday life subsumed by those dispositions.

This research must be regarded as just the start of an exploration of the links between diagnostic classifications and the psychopathology of everyday conduct. As a general conceptual framework and set of methods, it is not tied to any particular diagnostic scheme such as the DSM-III or psychoanalytic categories. The utility of this framework and these methods with the narcissistic personality disorder lends optimism to the premise that systems of psychodiagnosis can preserve links with manifestations of psychopathology in everyday life.

References

American Psychiatric Association. (1980). *Diagnostic and statistical manual of mental disorders (DSM-III)*. Washington, DC: Author.

Buss, D. M., & Craik, K. H. (1983). The act frequency approach to personality. *Psychology Review, 90*, 105–126.

Buss, D. M., & Craik, K. H. (1984). Acts, dispositions, and personality. In B. A. Maher & W. B. Maher (Eds.), *Progress in experimental personality research: Normal personality processes*, Volume 13, 241–301. New York: Academic Press.

Buss, D. M., & Craik, K. H. (1986). Acts, dispositions, and clinical assessment: The psychopathology of everyday conduct. *Clinical Psychology Review, 6*, 387–406.

Buss, D. M., & Craik, K. H. (1987). Act criteria for the diagnosis of personality disorders. *Journal of Personality Disorders, 1*, 73–81.

Emmons, R. A. (1987). Narcissism: Theory and measurement. *Journal of Personality and Social Psychology, 52*, 11–17.

Kernberg, O. (1976). *Borderline conditions and pathological narcissism*. New York: Jason Aronson.

Kernberg, O. (1980). *Internal world and external reality*. New York: Jason Aronson.

Kohut, H. (1976). *The restoration of the self*. New York: International Universities Press.

Livesley, W. J. (1984). *Criteria for the diagnosis of personality disorder: A comparison of behavioral and dispositional prototypes*. Paper presented to the Canadian Psychiatric Association Annual Meeting, Banff.

Maher, B. A., & Maher, W. B. (1985). Psychopathology: II. From the eighteenth century to modern times. In G. A. Kimble & K. Schlesinger (Eds.), *Topics in the history of psychology, Vol. 2* (pp. 295–329). Hillsdale, NJ: Erlbaum.

Meehl, P. E. (1973). *Psychodiagnosis: Selected papers*. Minneapolis: University of Minnesota Press.

Millon, T. (1981). *Disorders of personality. DSM-III: Axis II*. New York: Wiley.

Morrison, A. P. (Ed.). (1986). *Essential papers on narcissism*. New York: New York University Press.

Norman, W. T. (1963). Toward an adequate taxonomy of personality attributes: Replicated factor structure in peer nomination personality ratings. *Journal of Abnormal and Social Psychology, 66*, 574–583.

Raskin, R. N. & Hall, C. S. (1979). A narcissistic personality inventory. *Psychological Reports, 45*, 590.

Raskin, R. N., & Terry, H. (1988). A principal-components analysis of the Narcissistic Personality Inventory and further evidence of its construct validity. *Journal of Personality and Social Psychology, 54*, 890–902.

Rosch, E. (1975). Cognitive reference points. *Cognitive Psychology, 7*, 532–547.

Rosch, E., & Mervis, C. B. (1975). Family resemblances: Studies in the internal structure of categories. *Cognitive Psychology, 7*, 573–605.

Rosch, E., Simpson, C., & Miller, R. S. (1976). Structural bases of typicality effects. *Journal of Experimental Psychology: Human Perception and Performance, 2*, 491–502.

Widiger, T. A., & Francis, A. (1985). The DSM-III personality disorders: Perspectives from psychology. *Archives of General Psychiatry, 42*, 615–623.

Widiger, T. A., & Kelso, K. (1983). Psychodiagnosis of Axis II. *Clinical Psychology Review, 3*, 491–510.

Toward the Development of a Scientific Nosology of Child Maltreatment

Dante Cicchetti and Douglas Barnett

While history documents that child maltreatment has been in existence since the beginning of civilization (Ariès, 1962; Radbill, 1968; Ross, 1980), the systematic scientific investigation of the etiology, course, intergenerational transmission, and sequelae of this pervasive psychological and social problem is a relatively recent phenomenon. One of the most crucial gaps in our knowledge base is that we do not yet have an adequate taxonomic system for conceptualizing and reliably differentiating between the varying manifestations of maltreatment within the spectrum of maltreatment phenomena. In this chapter, we provide a brief historical account of how the various societal, clinical, and academic conceptions about child maltreatment have evolved. Next we review national studies on the incidence of child maltreatment, illustrating how epidemiological estimates vary as a function of the definitions of child maltreatment that are employed. Subsequently, we delineate reasons why we believe that a nosology of child maltreatment is necessary to advance our knowledge of the causes, consequences, and treatment of child abuse and neglect (Cicchetti, Toth, & Bush, 1988). Finally, we outline a system of operational criteria we have developed for the assessment of child maltreatment from Child Protective Service records.

The writing of this chapter was supported in part by grants from the John D. and Catherine T. MacArthur Foundation Network on Early Childhood, the A. L. Mailman Family Foundation, Inc., the Smith Richardson Foundation, Inc., and the Spunk Fund, Inc., to the first author. We wish to acknowledge the Monroe County Department of Social Services for their assistance on this project. We would like to thank Jody Todd Manly for her thoughtful contributions to this topic and Sheree Toth for her insightful comments. We also would like to thank Victoria Gill for typing this manuscript.

Twentieth-Century Conceptions of Child Maltreatment

The year 1874 marked the establishment of the Society for the Prevention of Cruelty to Children. This widely publicized social institution represents one of the earliest advocates of children's rights, helping to alleviate the trauma of child maltreatment through the arenas of direct intervention, media attention, and legal reform (Williams, 1983). In the 1930s the passing of the Social Security Act officially delegated the monitoring of families and the protection of children to social workers in the then departments of public welfare (Nelson, 1984). During the 1940s and 1950s, several prominent pediatric radiologists suggested that the multiple fractures that infants incurred in association with intracranial bleeding might be the result of parental abuse or neglect (Caffey, 1946; Silverman, 1953). It was apparently not until 1961 that these efforts had a clear impact on the medical community. Alarmed by the increasing number of children with nonaccidental injuries being admitted to pediatric clinics, C. Henry Kempe and his colleagues conducted a symposium on child abuse at the annual national meeting of the American Academy of Pediatrics. In an effort to underscore the pervasiveness and seriousness of the problem, Kempe and his colleagues, in an influential article published in the *Journal of the American Medical Association*, coined the term "battered child syndrome" (Kempe, Silverman, Steele, Droegemueller, & Silver, 1962).

As a direct result of this paper, a dramatic increase in legislative activity ensued, resulting in the establishment of mandated child-abuse reporting laws for all 50 states before the year 1970. These legislative acts of Congress were important because they required all professionals (e.g., psychologists, social workers, teachers, pediatricians, psychiatrists, police officers) working with children and families to report all *suspected* incidents of maltreatment while simultaneously protecting them against legal liability. These mandated reporting laws also made the establishment of public registries of maltreatment a necessity. Centralized record-keeping allowed social workers to keep track of families who had been reported to Child Protective Services (CPS). This was essential for identifying families who were already known to the system and who consequently were receiving protective services (Besharov, 1977). It should be noted here, however, that even before the advent of the legal mandate to develop the central registries which made consolidation of families' records possible, it is highly likely that all agencies dealing with maltreating families kept their own records (see, for example, Young, 1964).

Moreover, at about this same time, a heightened sensitivity to the needs of children emerged in the context of a contemporary ethos that was increasingly concerned about the rights of the disadvantaged sectors of our society. For example, regional centers for retarded children, Project Head Start, and Medicaid all were initiated during this era (Dubowitz & Newberger, 1989). Furthermore, during the past several decades, the legal status of children has changed considerably (Koocher, 1976; Polier, 1975; Rodham, 1973; Wald, 1975); children are now seen as having a right to the fulfillment of their developmental needs (Alvy, 1975; Derdeyn, 1977; Goldstein, Freud, & Solnit, 1973).

Despite the positive consequences of the yeoman efforts of Kempe and his colleagues (Cicchetti & Aber, 1980; Lynch, 1985), a number of unfortunate negative ramifications ensued. The adoption of the term "battered child syndrome" connoted a psychologically disturbed parent-as-perpetrator model of child abuse (Parke & Collmer, 1975). This "narrow" etiological view of helpless infants and children being battered maliciously by psychiatrically ill parents (Spinetta & Rigler, 1972; Steele & Pollock, 1968) virtually absolved society of any responsibility for the occurrence of child abuse (Alvy, 1975). In addition, the treatment prescriptions emanating from this medicalization and legalization of child abuse focused on supplying treatment for the abusing parent without stressing the need to provide concomitant intervention for the abused child (Cicchetti, Taraldson, & Egeland, 1978; Cicchetti & Toth, 1987).

During the 1970s, the laws mandating the reporting of child abuse were changed. The Child Abuse Prevention and Treatment Act of 1974 expanded the definition of child abuse to encompass emotional injury, neglect, parental deprivation of medical services, and factors deleterious to children's moral development (Dubowitz & Newberger, 1989; Giovannoni, 1989). This "broad" definition of child abuse contributed to the belief that not all abusing parents set out to destroy their helpless offspring (Alvy, 1975) and implicated societal factors (e.g., societal attitudes, structures, and stressors) as playing major roles in the etiology of child maltreatment.

David Gil's theory of child abuse highlights the essence of sociological theorizing. Viewing the etiology of child abuse in terms of a sociocultural perspective, Gil (1975) delineated five causal dimensions: (1) the society's basic social philosophy, its dominant value, concept of humans, and the nature of its institutions; (2) the society's definition of childhood (i.e., the rights and expectations of children); (3) the society's acceptance of the use of force in attaining ends; (4) "triggering contexts," which included poverty, overcrowding, inadequate services, large numbers of children, social isolation, and so on; and (5) various forms of psychopathology that Gil considered to be deeply rooted in the social environment of the individual. Furthermore, in a landmark article, Pelton (1978) argued that the "myth of classlessness" surrounding child abuse that had been promulgated by government officials and social scientists supported the "narrow" psychopathological view of the etiology of child abuse. Pelton concluded that poverty, per se, created stresses that could result in the maltreatment of children.

As the etiological models became less focused on parental psychopathology as the cause of child abuse, increased attention was directed to the prevention of child abuse and to the research and treatment of maltreated children (Kempe & Helfer, 1968; Kempe & Kempe, 1978; Martin, 1976). As careful analyses of the foster-care system of the United States demonstrated significant problems (Children's Defense Fund, 1979; Fanshel & Shinn, 1972; Gruber, 1978; Mnookin, 1973), efforts were made to keep children at home whenever possible. The work of Jane Knitzer and her colleagues (Children's Defense Fund, 1979) is exemplary among these studies. Knitzer and her collaborators brilliantly documented and analyzed the dangerous tendency for temporary foster care to become permanent, much to the detriment of the child, who would often develop more soundly and happily living with an abusive parent rather than with a series of foster parents. As a result of such investigations, growing numbers of clinicians advocated that the entire family be treated in maltreatment cases (Cicchetti et al., 1978; Kempe & Kempe, 1978).

Research and intervention directed toward maltreated children and their families has a particular urgency given the numbers of individuals who suffer the consequences of child abuse and neglect. Depending upon the definition employed, recent estimates indicate that between one and one and one-half million children experienced abuse or neglect in 1986 (United States Department of Health and Human Services, 1988; see below for an elaboration and commentary). With increasing awareness of the pervasiveness and gravity of maltreatment phenomena and the development of more stringent reporting laws, the number of reported occurrences of child abuse and neglect has risen dramatically (American Association for Protecting Children, 1986; United States Department of Health and Human Services, 1988; Wakefield & Underwager, 1988). According to the results of a recent national survey of family violence, 10.7% of parents admitted to having perpetrated a "severe violent act" against their child during the previous year (Straus & Gelles, 1986). Prevalence rates for sexual abuse have been estimated to be as high as 62% for girls and 31% for boys (Dubowitz, 1986).

In addition to the large numbers of children and families who are affected by the phenomenon, the economic and human costs of maltreatment in American society are exceedingly high. It is likely that billions of dollars are spent in treatment and social services costs and lost in lessened productivity for a generation of maltreated children (Dubowitz, 1986). The sequelae of maltreatment are a litany of psychological tragedies. Maltreated children suffer from insecure attachment relationships (Carlson, Cicchetti, Barnett, & Braunwald, 1989; Crittenden, 1988; Schneider-Rosen, Braunwald, Carlson, & Cicchetti, 1985), communicative problems (Coster, Gersten, Beeghly, & Cicchetti, 1989), impairments in "self-system" processes (Cicchetti, 1990b; Cicchetti & Beeghly, 1987; Cicchetti et al., 1988; Schneider-Rosen & Cicchetti, 1984; Vondra, Barnett, & Cicchetti, 1989), poor quality peer relations (Kaufman & Cicchetti, 1989; Mueller & Silverman, 1989), and behavior problems and psychopathology

(Aber, Allen, Carlson, & Cicchetti, 1989; Kazdin, Moser, Colbus, & Bell, 1985), among other difficulties. The emotional damage resulting from maltreatment could conceivably last a lifetime.

Historical Perspectives on Defining Child Maltreatment

The lack of precision in conceptualizing the independent variable of child maltreatment has resulted in a blurring of distinctions and a dearth of fine discriminations among maltreatment subtypes. Early clinical investigations and research reports either grouped all maltreated children together or studied only physically abused children (Aber & Cicchetti, 1984). As time went on, researchers began to compare physically abused children to neglected children in an attempt to ascertain the differential impact of these types of maltreatment (Aber & Cicchetti, 1984). Both practical limitations and theoretical considerations have contributed to the paucity of clinical and research investigations that have attended the defining of disparate subtypes of maltreatment.

Giovannoni (1989) discussed a number of factors surrounding definitional considerations in the area of child maltreatment. These issues included specifying how broadly the construct of maltreatment should be defined, delineating the subcategories which should be subsumed under the spectrum of maltreatment phenomena, and noting the role which parental or perpetrator intention plays in given acts of maltreatment. Moreover, Giovannoni argued that it was important: (1) to ascertain whether there were universal definitions that transcend history and culture; (2) to determine the applicability of policy- and practice-oriented definitions for research; (3) to consider how definitions of child maltreatment might be modified as a function of children's varying ages and developmental levels; and (4) to investigate how theory and research on basic child development could improve our existing definitions of the construct of maltreatment. Minimally, Giovannoni believed that an adequate definition of maltreatment must delineate a class or classes of acts that can be distinguished from other related phenomena and events, and specify the operational criteria necessary to assess the appropriateness of including an event within the identified class.

Aber and Zigler (1981) have provided a thoughtful critique of various conceptualizations and definitions of child maltreatment. They review the medical-diagnostic, sociological, legal, and research definitions, including the major determining factors of each. In the *medical-diagnostic definition*, the focus is on the characteristics of the individual abuser. Aber and Zigler (1981) cite the work of Kempe and colleagues (1962) as an attempt to diagnose the underlying pathology that potentiates a parent's infliction of harm upon a child as being exemplary of the medical approach. In keeping with a medical-diagnostic model, efforts in the 1960s and the 1970s were made to predict reliably "risk" for maltreatment based upon parent personality measures. Maltreating phenomena were seen as a subcategory of psychopathology. However, Cicchetti and Aber (1980) have argued that it is unlikely that we will ever reduce our false positive rates to a point where reasonably accurate predictions of families at risk for maltreatment can be made. As Meehl and Rosen (1959/1973) have illustrated, when the population frequency (base rate) of a given phenomenon is quite low (as in the case of child maltreatment), utilization of a test sign possessing slight or moderate validity will result in an *increase* of erroneous clinical decisions. This maxim is especially applicable to child abuse, since not only does it have a low frequency in the population, but it also is caused by many factors, thereby decreasing the likelihood of identifying a particular sign, pattern, or cutting score that would have ample discriminating power.

The medical-diagnostic approach primarily focused on pure physical abuse, though over time it branched out to include nutritional (e.g., nonorganic failure-to-thrive) and emotional abuse as well. Likewise, this approach broadened its etiologic focus, adding symptomatic indicators within the child to its preponderant earlier focus on parents. Medical definitions, by advocating and promoting a "narrow" perspective on child maltreatment, present a compartmentalized approach which ignores the legal and social service systems.

In the *sociological definition*, the focus is on the act of maltreatment. In contrast to the medical-diagnostic approach, the goal is to label and control social deviance, not to cure psychopathology. With its "broad" focus, the aim of the sociological definition is to improve the lives of all children in society by decreasing the hindrances to their optimal development. Aber and Zigler's (1981) major criticism of the sociological approach is that the information gathered via social-service agents may not reflect accurately the severity or scope of maltreatment occurrences. While this criticism has merit, we believe that their concerns can best be addressed empirically. Contrary to their arguments, our work with private and state social-service agencies over the past decade stands in direct opposition to their reservations. Moreover, the system we present herein further demonstrates the utility of social agents' dealings with these matters.

The third perspective Aber and Zigler (1981) describe is the *legal definition*. Like the medical definition, the legal definition of child maltreatment is narrow. However, these conceptualizations differ in important ways. In criteria put forth by Michael Wald and his colleagues in the Juvenile Justice Standards Project (1977), the definitional focus shifts to behaviors or conditions that cause imminent risk or serious harm to the child (e.g., physical harm, emotional damage, severe anxiety, depression, withdrawal, or untoward aggression toward self or others, sexual abuse, parent promotes delinquency). In this framework, the issue of intentionality is addressed as well (e.g., child is suffering from emotional damage, yet his/her parents will not seek services). If the harm to the child can be shown to have been unintentional, then the circumstances are not considered to be maltreatment.

From the legal perspective, different definitions are required to guide decision-making depending on the legal objective at hand. Its most important change is that there must be *evidence* of general harm to the child. This emphasis greatly underscores the need for researchers and clinicians to collaborate with legal and other professionals to provide basic information on the developmental sequelae of maltreatment.

The final scheme elucidated by Aber and Zigler (1981) is the *research definition*. They review two strategies that are common to researchers. One is the use of reports to state departments of social service as the research definition of maltreatment. They argue that this approach suffers from the variability of different reporters' criteria and the likelihood that many cases are unreported, resulting in an atypical sample of reported cases. The second strategy delineated by Aber and Zigler involved a narrow criterion of only physical violence. This definition increases reliability but sacrifices breadth.

We acknowledge the problems inherent in both of these methods. However, given the seriousness of the issue, we feel that the implications of inactivity fostered by excessive caution are far graver than the methodological difficulties they generate. As discussed implicitly and explicitly throughout this chapter, past efforts have demonstrated the merit of social-service reports. Hence we advocate the employment of these data.

As an alternative to the four definitional schemes they critique, Aber and Zigler (1981) proposed three sets of definitions for three different social purposes: (1) legal definitions are needed to inform family courts and lawmakers and caseworkers concerned with coercive state intervention in custody issues; (2) case management definitions are needed to aid in clinical decision-making; and (3) research definitions are needed to allow investigations of causality and specificity of sequelae in various circumstances of maltreatment. This conceptualization of the need for three types of definitions is laudable in that it recognizes the social complexity of maltreatment phenomena. The real world uses of definitions are varied enough so that the clinical case manager and the family court judge may look at the same circumstances from very different perspectives, yet both of them might find the researcher's definitions to be irrelevant to their work. However, this state of affairs does not need to exist. The researcher can do much to inform and to integrate all three fields. As the quality of data on the sequelae of maltreatment evolves sufficiently to allow for stronger causal statements (e.g., about the role of emotional neglect in the development of emotional damage), then the legal thinker, the clinician, and the researcher can begin to speak the same language and the three sets of definitions will begin to converge.

Besharov (1981) stated that the development of better definitions of child abuse and neglect was crucial if continued progress in understanding the causes, consequences, and treatment of child maltreatment was to be made. Specifically, Besharov argued that the lack of specificity in existing definitions failed to meet research needs because they lacked comparability, reliability, and taxonomic delineation.

In the area of comparability, Besharov pointed out that definitions of child maltreatment contain elements of legal, social work, medical, psychological, and/or sociological orientations (see also Aber & Zigler, 1981, Giovannoni, 1989, and Giovannoni & Becerra, 1979). Accordingly, because of this definitional diversity, it is difficult to claim comparability and generalizability of empirical findings across samples and across research laboratories.

Besharov's points about reliability and the need for taxonomic delineation require little commentary other than to underscore two critical points: (1) without precise definitions there can only be poor reliability; and (2) because maltreating parents, maltreated children, and maltreatment acts are not a homogeneous group of phenomena (see below for an in-depth explication), it is essential that a scientifically reliable and valid nosological system be developed.

Zigler (1976) stated this latter point eloquently:

> The nature of child abuse is . . . in need of a more differentiated and concept based classification system. Child abuse is a phenotypic event having a variety of expressions and causes, and we will make little headway so long as we insist on viewing every act of child abuse as the equivalent of every other.

Recent research efforts have come a long way in the specification of a nosology of maltreatment (Cicchetti, Carlson, Braunwald, & Aber, 1987; Egeland and Sroufe, 1981). An important first step has been the development of a series of 10 categories and a 93-item checklist for social-service caseworkers by Giovannoni and Becerra (1979). They surveyed a variety of professionals involved with child maltreatment and derived a list of 10 factors that they considered to be a rough consensual definition of child maltreatment. Based on this work, Giovannoni and Becerra (1979) developed a checklist and validated it on a sample of 949 cases of reported maltreatment. Their subtypes include: physical injury, sexual abuse, drug/alcohol abuse (by the child), emotional mistreatment, moral/legal problems (by the adult), failure to provide, child behavior problems, and inadequate physical environment. They reported that the single best predictor of whether or not a social-service agency or family court will choose to intervene and remove a child from his/her home is the absolute number of different types of maltreatment perpetrated against the child. In fact, most children who have experienced maltreatment have been subjected to more than one subtype (Aber and Allen, 1987; Cicchetti & Rizley, 1981; Egeland & Sroufe, 1981; Pianta, Egeland, & Erickson, 1989). For these reasons among others, researchers and theoreticians have called for the inclusion of subtype definitions in future maltreatment research (Aber & Cicchetti, 1984; Besharov, 1981; Cicchetti & Rizley, 1981).

Variance in Incidence of Estimates as a Function of Definitions of Child Maltreatment

Clearly, depending on how we define child maltreatment, the epidemiological estimates of its incidence rates in America will vary. If the definition is confined only to those cases where observable physical injury has been intentionally inflicted by a caregiver, then the incidence rates will be comparatively small. However, if we utilize a broader definition of child maltreatment, then the incidence rates may be quite high (estimates have ranged to over ten million such children maltreated each year).

In 1975 and again in 1985, Richard Gelles and Murray Straus conducted two nationwide surveys on various aspects of family violence in the United States (see Gelles, 1978; Straus & Gelles, 1986, for representative findings). As part of these two investigations, Gelles and Straus were concerned with documenting the rate of physical child abuse of children between the ages of 3 and 17 years. Our focus here is not on the methodological aspects of these studies (e.g., one could question and/or debate the relative merits of in-person (1975) versus telephone (1985) interviewing, the choice not to include questions about children under three in the interviews, the decision to conduct their inquiry only in families in which children were living with both parents, etc.), but, rather, on how the conceptualization of maltreatment affects the epidemiological findings.

These scientists decided to limit the questions asked of parents in interviews conducted in their surveys to physical abuse. As they put it, "the operationalization of abuse is a source of considerable difficulty and confusion because it covers many types of abuse . . . and because there is no consensus on the severity of violence required for an act to be considered abuse" (Straus & Gelles, 1986, p. 467). In essence, then, Gelles and Straus decided to employ a conservative, narrow definition of maltreatment, and chose to restrict their inquiries to the occurrence of physical child abuse, measured by the Very Severe Violence Index of the Conflict Tactics Scales (CTS) (Straus, 1979). The only modification employed in the operationalization of violence on the CTS was that, to be consistent with existing legal and informal beliefs, hitting or trying to hit a child with an object (such as a belt or a stick) was *not* included.

Utilizing physical abuse as their target, in 1975 Gelles and Straus estimated that 36 of every thousand American children between the ages of 3 and 17 (i.e., approximately 4%) experienced an assault that was rater serious enough to be included in their Very Severe Violence Index. Extrapolating this base rate per thousand to the 46 million children in this age range who were living with both parents in 1975, Gelles and Straus concluded that 1.7 million children were "abused" that year. Furthermore, these investigators found that if one assault occurred on a child, it was very probable that others would follow. Thus, only 6%

of all child abuse cases were isolated incidents; the mean number of assaults each child received per year was over 10.

In 1985, Gelles and Straus conducted a phone interview on a representative national sample of parents to ascertain the incidence rates of physical child abuse compared to the 1975 findings. They concluded that physical child abuse had declined in the past 10 years. In 1985, they found that the rate of very severe physical violence to children had dropped from 36 to 19 per thousand—a decline of nearly 50% since 1975. Even if we disregard the fact that single-parent families, children under three, and phoneless families, three extremely high-risk maltreatment groups (Cicchetti & Carlson, 1989; Cicchetti et al., 1978), were omitted from the interviews (as they had been in 1975), given the current population in the United States, over one million children in this country still had experienced physical assaults serious enough to be labeled abusive.[1]

In addition to the aforementioned studies of family violence, two comprehensive national incidence studies on the broader spectrum of maltreatment have been conducted during the past decade. These investigations provide definitive illustrations of how definitional disputes and problems contribute to the varying epidemiological estimates of child abuse and neglect.

When the Child Abuse Prevention and Treatment Act was passed in 1974, it stipulated that the National Center on Child Abuse and Neglect (NCCAN) be created to support state and local efforts to prevent and treat child abuse and neglect. In addition, it was stated that NCCAN must initiate a complete investigation of the incidence of child abuse and neglect in America.

In 1981, the results of the first National Incidence Study (NIS-I) were published (United States Department of Health and Human Services, 1981). Completed in 1980, the NIS-I developed and utilized explicit operational definitions of maltreatment. These definitions focused on the purposive (nonaccidental) acts or omissions (marked inattentions to the child's basic needs) of the child's parents or other adult caretakers and on the deleterious consequences of those acts/omissions on the child's health or developmental functioning. Moreover, depending on the subtype of maltreatment, the injury or impairment was required to be of at least a "moderate" or "serious" severity level.

The definitions employed in the NIS-I encompassed a range of maltreatment phenomena (e.g., physical assault, sexual exploitation, emotional abuse, physical neglect, educational neglect, emotional neglect). Nonetheless, in some respects, the study definitions were extremely narrow, excluding many situations for which protective services might be suitable (e.g., parental behavior which, though inappropriate, dangerous, or inadequate, did not appear to have caused or exacerbated any injury or impairment to the child; any physical or sexual assault where an in-home parent or other adult caregiver was not implicated directly; institutional abuse or neglect, etc.).

The NIS-I presented national estimates of the incidence and characteristics of maltreated children. It was the first large-scale effort to gather such information using standardized definitions. In the NIS-I, data were collected on cases reported to Child Protective Services and on cases not so reported but identified by other law-enforcement, social-welfare, and health agencies. Unreported cases were included in the investigation to obtain what was thought to be the "true" incidence of child maltreatment. For both the reported and the unreported cases, a distinction was made between those that met the research definitions employed by the study and those that did not.

Among cases reported to the Child Protective Services, the NIS-I estimated the rate of reporting to be 17.8 children per 1,000 per year. Based on an approximate 43% substantiation rate, the aforementioned national estimate drops to around 7.6 per 1,000 per year if one focuses only on the child maltreatment which has been substantiated by protective-service agencies.

The reasons given for not substantiating a case may reflect differences in perceptions about the definitions of maltreatment and about the functions of protective services. The largest category of cases among these unsubstantiated reports was labeled "not serious enough." The notion that a set of cases may be identified as warranting protective services by one group of definers, yet might not be warranted as "serious enough" by the definers empowered to implement that intervention (e.g., protective-service workers) highlights the definitional issues in making relative judgments. All cases were conceived as veridical maltreatment cases; however, the disagreement centered on the relative seriousness of the maltreatment as a criterion for intervention. Clearly, social-service agency resources and treatment capabilities establish the asymptote of cases that an individual agency can assign for intervention. A logical corollary is that substantiation rates are more a reflection of these and other (e.g., resources) constraints than of the actual extent and gravity of child maltreatment.

A second aspect of the data from the NIS-I demonstrates the homogeneity characteristic of the substantiated cases—that is, those considered warranting intervention. When the cases substantiated by the CPS were subjected to the scrutiny of the NIS-I operational criteria for maltreatment, only 44.5% passed the screening. This finding is not surprising given the fact that the NIS-I criteria were stringent. Accordingly, CPS intervention might well have been warranted, even though these cases did not demonstrate evidence of the NIS-I criteria of "injury or impairment." Nonetheless, these data highlight the heterogeneity reflective of CPS cases deemed suitable for intervention.

As a further attempt to ascertain the most accurate incidence rates of maltreatment, cases that had not been reported to CPS were gathered from other investigatory, social, and health agencies (e.g., legal enforcement, hospitals, schools, social agencies, public health, and mental health). When these cases were screened according to the NIS-I operational criteria for maltreatment, 65% adhered to the standards. This increased agreement is expected because the NIS-I criteria were utilized by all non-CPS agencies submitting unreported cases to the study. What is most noteworthy for our purposes is the relatively large portion of cases that were submitted which did not meet the NIS-I criteria, thereby suggesting that certain cases may be difficult to fit into a specific operational definition of maltreatment. Clearly, even with clear-cut definitions, relative judgments must be made and the reliability of those judgments must be examined.

The NIS-I findings do not stipulate why the investigatory, social, and health agencies that submitted cases to the study had not reported them to protective services. However, an examination of the characteristics of the reported and unreported cases reveals two important features — the age of the children and the type of maltreatment experienced. For example, 60% of all children under age six who conformed to the NIS-I criteria had been reported, while only 22% of such children between the ages of 12 and 17 had a similar outcome. Furthermore, fewer than 25% of all cases designated as "emotional abuse," "emotional neglect," or "educational neglect" had been reported to CPS.

The conclusion rendered by the NIS-I investigators concerning the best estimates of the incidence of child maltreatment attests to the wide variability introduced into the definitional process. When only CPS-substantiated cases that met the operational criteria of the NIS-I were employed, then the national incidence was estimated to be approximately 3.4 children per 1,000. If cases submitted by the investigatory agencies are included, then the figure rises to 4.6 per 1,000. Finally, the inclusion of cases from other social and health agencies causes the national estimate to grow to 10.5 cases per 1,000 or approximately 652,000 children per year. Given the very strongest operational criteria as well as the nature of the sampling procedures employed, the NIS-I estimate is most likely quite conservative.

The NIS-II was completed in 1986 and followed essentially the same design as that employed in the NIS-I (United States Department of Health and Human Services, 1988). The goal of the NIS-II was to provide a valid estimate of the current incidence of child maltreatment in the United States and to determine how the frequency, character, and severity of maltreatment phenomena had changed since the NIS-I had been completed.

Because we covered the sampling and definitional aspects of the NIS-I in detail above, we wish here to point out the major difference between the two studies. Each case referred to the NIS-II study was assessed for its conformity to two sets of standardized operational criteria. The first set of definitions were identical to those utilized in the NIS-I and reflected an estimate of the number of children who manifested demonstrable harm as a result of maltreatment. The number of cases generated by these definitions was considered to provide a minimum estimate of the incidence of child maltreatment in America. The second set of operational definitions employed in the NIS-II were broader and more inclusive in scope.

These additional definitions yielded a supplementary estimate of the number of children who were thought to be endangered by maltreatment (i.e., children "at risk" for harm, but not necessarily harmed yet). These standards were added to the NIS-II because it was feared that the NIS-I definitions were not responsive to the broader connotations of child maltreatment presented in the congressional mandate in the Child Abuse Amendments of 1984 (P.L. 98-457). As was the case for the NIS-I, only cases that adhered to the study criteria were deemed to be countable and used to generate the national epidemiological estimates.

The NIS-II results likewise illustrate how the implementation of different definitional criteria results in varying incidence estimates. When the same standards were employed as in the NIS-I, approximately 16.3 children per 1,000 were abused or neglected—a figure exceeding one million cases. If the expanded definition is viewed as the standard, then around 25.2 children per 1,000 experienced maltreatment nationwide—an estimate of over one and one-half million cases.

In addition, if the original set of standards requiring that the demonstrable harm to the child as a result of maltreatment must be apparent, then countable cases of maltreatment increased by nearly 67% over the incidence rate obtained in the NIS-I. Nearly 75% of the increase in countable cases was reflected in a significant rise in the incidence of abuse. In particular, in 1986 physical abuse increased by over 50% and sexual abuse occurred at over 300% of their 1980 rates. Neither emotional abuse nor any of the subtypes of neglect revealed any reliable changes in incidence since the completion of the NIS-I. Most of the changes that occurred in the level of maltreatment-related inquiries were moderate, as opposed to severe, in nature.

Finally, an examination of the expanded definitional criteria reveals that the majority of the cases involved neglect (63%), with less than half (43%) involving abuse. More specifically, the most frequent type of abuse was physical, followed by emotional, and then by sexual, with base rates of 5.7, 3.4, and 2.5 children per 1,000, respectively. The most common type of neglect was physical, followed by educational and then emotional. Their incidence rates were 9.1, 4.6, and 3.5 children per 1,000, respectively. As was the case with the original standards, moderate injuries predominated, occurring in 60% of the countable cases.

The Need for a Nosology of Child Maltreatment

A fundamental difficulty inherent in the investigation of child maltreatment is that the range of phenomena covered by the term is enormously varied. As Cicchetti and Rizley (1981) have argued, child maltreatment is a heterogeneous problem. We believe there are four primary types of heterogeneity that merit our foremost attention: (1) symptom pattern or type of maltreatment; (2) etiology; (3) developmental sequelae; and (4) response to treatment. The first type acknowledges the fact that a spectrum of different problems are subsumed under the term of child maltreatment (Giovannoni & Becerra, 1979). The second acknowledges that different etiological pathways or causal networks exist, giving rise to the spectrum of different types of maltreatment (known as the *principle of equifinality*— von Bertalanffy, 1968). The third type of heterogeneity is revealed in the existing data on the consequences of maltreatment on child developmental outcome (Cicchetti & Carlson, 1989). Not surprisingly, there is no specific single pattern exhibited by maltreated children that can be described as the profile of abuse or neglect. Children of different ages, at different developmental stages, from diverse environments, and with differing experiences, who are exposed to vastly different forms of maltreatment, are likely to manifest vulnerabilities and disabilities in a wide variety of age-specific ways (known as the *principle of multifinality*—von Bertalanffy, 1968). The fourth type of heterogeneity underscores the observation that there is wide variability in response to treatment interventions among families where there has been maltreatment (Cicchetti et al, 1978; Daro, 1988; Kempe & Kempe, 1978; Wolfe, 1987). We believe that the failure to attend to these four sources of heterogeneity, each of which also is interrelated, has contributed to our less than complete understanding of this important problem.

Perhaps the most obvious type of heterogeneity is revealed by the different manifestations of child maltreatment—that is, the manifold expressions or symptoms of maltreatment. The array of problems for which parents are legally identified as having maltreated their offspring cannot be grouped together if we wish to find meaningful relationships between causal factors and type of maltreatment, between developmental consequences and type of maltreatment, and between treatment response and type of maltreatment. It is imperative that the spectrum of problems subsumed under the rubric of child maltreatment be covered by an explicit nosological system. Without clear operational criteria, including identification of the developmental stage during which each type of maltreatment occurs, the frequency of occurrence of each type of maltreatment, detailed information surrounding the nature of each incident, and the seriousness/severity of each maltreatment experience, some children who require protection will go undetected.

Another reason it is essential to have an explicit classification scheme for maltreatment phenomena is that diverse types of child maltreatment may exert a differential impact on maltreated children. Nonetheless, most scientists fail to describe their samples of maltreated children adequately because of the absence of a nationally agreed-upon taxonomic system. Consequently, families who have maltreated their children in a variety of ways and through different etiological pathways are often grouped together for the purpose of statistical analyses. Accordingly, confusion ensues surrounding how to interpret the findings, thereby obscuring the detection of existing real differences in the causes, course, sequelae, prognosis, intergenerational transmission patterns, and treatment response for the different types of maltreatment (Kaufman & Zigler, 1987; King & Cicchetti, unpublished manuscript, 1989). The time has now come for researchers to begin to specify the inclusion and exclusion criteria characterizing their respective samples.

An additional rationale that some investigators give for failing to address the issue of symptom pattern heterogeneity in child maltreatment may stem from the implicit or explicit assumption that different types of maltreatment do not exist and that any classification or nosology represents a rather futile effort to divide into discrete categories something that is, in reality, on a continuum. Our response to this issue is that we will not be able to discover whether or not it makes sense to pay attention to type of maltreatment until we begin to examine the issue empirically. Failure to attend to this major source of heterogeneity runs the real risk of ignoring a source of variation that is critical to an appreciation of the differing pathways, sequelae, cross-generational transmission patterns, and treatment responses to the various subtypes of maltreatment. We believe that the time has come to examine this issue carefully. Child maltreatment is a multi-factorial problem, and we must acknowledge its complexity before we can make progress in understanding it. We think that the development of a practical, reliable, and valid scientific nosology of maltreatment is a crucial step in this direction.

Perhaps investigators in the field of child maltreatment can learn a valuable lesson from research in the area of psychopathology (Akiskal & Webb, 1978; Eaton & Kessler, 1985; Goodwin & Guze, 1984; Meehl, 1959/1973, 1973). Reliability in the diagnosis of mental disorders for research purposes has been greatly enhanced by two improvements: (1) the establishment of more operational, explicit, hence reliable criteria for each "type" of mental disorder; and (2) the development of standardized, structured diagnostic interviews. The first advance reduces the criterion or nosological variance in diagnosis, while the second significantly lowers the diagnostician variation-variance owing to different diagnosticians who may employ different clinical interviewing styles, disparate assumptions about signs and symptoms of disorders, and so on.

Research on child maltreatment would benefit greatly from the utilization of structured classification schemes. The development of a structured, clinically sensitive procedure useful to researchers investigating all subtypes of maltreatment would have the advantage of making more standardized and uniform the means used to assess the particular form or forms of maltreatment experienced. Likewise, the establishment of a set of operational criteria would have the effect of maximizing the precision in the definition and description of different types of maltreatment. With the development and validation of such a precise nosology and a standardized set of assessment procedures, clarity of communication and language across investigators will be facilitated. Consequently, epidemiological estimates and the generalizability of research on the developmental sequelae and on the efficacy of treatment interventions will be improved. Next, we describe our ongoing work on the development and validation of such a nosological system.

The Usefulness of Child Protective-Service Records for Classifying Child Maltreatment

The concerns we have raised surrounding the definitional aspects of the construct of child maltreatment underscore the importance of initiating empirical investigations in this area. A necessary task will be to demonstrate that, by assessing the type(s), severity, frequency/chronicity, and developmental period during which maltreatment occurs, we can account for a greater proportion of the variance when investigating the etiology, sequelae, prevention, and intervention outcomes of child maltreatment than would be possible simply by making dichotomous (maltreated vs. nonmaltreated) comparisons. As one solution addressing these issues, we have developed a comprehensive nosological system for rating and classifying official maltreatment incidents reported to child protective-service units that are kept as permanent records.

Forty-nine of the 50 states, as well as the District of Columbia, have state registries for logging child abuse and neglect reports (United States Department of Health and Human Services, 1988). Although there is some variation from state to state, all include names, dates, and descriptions of the maltreatment incidents and have standard time-frames in which a case must be judged as either founded or unfounded. Our nosological system has been developed on the New York State record-keeping system, and we are now beginning to validate it in the analysis of our longitudinal data on the developmental sequelae of child maltreatment. Unfortunately, at this point we do not know how applicable this system will be to other state record-keeping procedures; however, based on our inquiry into other state systems (United States Department of Health and Human Services, 1988), we are confident that much will be generalizable with minor adjustments.

There are several advantages to utilizing only legally identified protective-service cases of abuse and neglect. First, the field of social work has a longer and more extensive history of documenting occurrences of child maltreatment than the psychological or medical professions (Nelson, 1984). Second, all maltreatment filings in the state registry are legally substantiated. By having the abuse and neglect reports verified by an outside party and not by individuals conducting the research, investigators avoid the risk of alienating families who otherwise might have participated in the research program (Cicchetti & Todd Manly, 1990). In addition, studies of legally identified occurrences of child maltreatment are more representative of cases in protective services and therefore more directly applicable to this broad segment of the population.

Laboratory analogue studies of maltreatment (Vasta & Copitch, 1981) and studies of unreported cases, although useful and quite informative (Besharov, 1981; Giovannoni, 1989), raise questions about their generalizability and relevance to actual clinical incidents of maltreatment. This criticism is similar to those that have been raised in the study of symptom manifestations of psychopathology that do not report the appropriate caveats regarding generalizability (e.g., studies of undergraduates who score above depression cut-offs on self-report measures and then are treated as if they are clinically depressed in the absence of additional substantiating data).

The use of protective-service families for research has not gone uncriticized. Gelles (1982) argued that researchers' reliance on official reports of maltreatment results in the study of the factors that lead to being "caught" as much as, if not more than, the study of maltreatment per se. We acknowledge this criticism but also believe that it is the best currently available approach, and again emphasize that it contributes to our understanding of the families that social-service agencies, clinicians, and the courts deal with most frequently. In addition, it is likely that the reports that are brought to the attention of CPS are among the more severe instances of maltreatment. This is especially true as limited community resources force only the most severe instances of maltreatment to warrant attention and treatment. More broadly, the problem is that protective-service records under-represent the true incidence of child maltreatment (Giovannoni & Becerra, 1979; United States Department of Health and Human Services, 1988). In addition to the unspecifiable number of maltreated children who go unreported, many incidents of maltreatment are difficult to substantiate and thus go unproven. To reduce some of these problems, we strongly advocate gathering data reflecting the types, severity, and frequency of maltreatment from multiple sources both within CPS and within the family. Thus we recommend interviewing the family's social worker and various family members, and making observations of the family during home interviews, in addition to reviewing the family's records. Our system also permits the compositing of different pieces of confirmatory data from within a family's permanent case record.

Toward the Development of an Operational System for Classifying Child Maltreatment

One of the purposes of this nosological system is to extend the empirical sophistication of past and current conceptualizations about child maltreatment. An important step in this direction is the operationalization and quantification of the five dimensions of maltreatment contained in our nosology: (1) type; (2) severity; (3) frequency/chronicity; (4) developmental period or stage at which the maltreatment occurred; and (5) type, length, and number of placements outside the home for the child, resulting from either parent or state initiation. These dimensions are described below.

Type of Maltreatment

Of the five dimensions covered by our system, the issue of documenting the different subtypes of maltreatment and of ascertaining their developmental sequelae has received the greatest empirical attention (Aber & Cicchetti, 1984). While the notion of different types of maltreatment has been implicitly obvious since the earliest recognition of this social problem, this idea explicitly reached its present culmination when Giovannoni and Becerra (1979) proposed their typology of child maltreatment. Now that a more general foundation has been delineated, the next phase of theory and research must address the issues of whether these subtypes have meaning above and beyond mere morphological dissimilarities. That is, do the different subtypes have distinct ties to etiology, sequelae, and treatment responses?

In addition, it is important that investigators attend to the fact that these various subtypes more often than not occur in various combinations (Cicchetti & Rizley, 1981). This state of affairs has been ignored or downplayed by many researchers who report findings on one or more of the subtypes. We believe that they have neglected to address this issue in part owing to methodological concerns and in part to the failure to recognize the importance of this overlap. By not acknowledging the co-occurrence, researchers confound their results and cannot tease apart whether findings are due to the target subtype of maltreatment they are studying or to some unmeasured maltreatment occurrences or to a combination of these factors.

Two related pragmatic problems have precluded a more sophisticated attempt at understanding the meaning of different subtypes of maltreatment. The first is the heavy reliance on "between groups" thinking through the use of analyses of variance or t-test approaches to data analysis. This also has been due to the small sample sizes which are so often found in child maltreatment research. As an alternative, we advocate a multiple regression approach which would then allow the researcher to obtain a better estimate of how much each of the different subtypes are contributing independently to the observed outcomes as well as various combinations of these subtypes of maltreatment and other associated risk factors (e.g., maternal depression, see Walker, Downey, & Bergman, 1989). Moreover, regression procedures can help researchers develop causal models, testing out hypothesized complex pathways leading to the studied outcomes. To carry out this type of investigation would require large numbers of maltreated children and a comprehensive system for coding maltreatment, such as the one we are proposing.

Our current system distinguishes five major subtypes of maltreatment: Physical Abuse (PA), Physical Neglect (PN), Sexual Abuse (SA), Emotional Maltreatment (EM), and Moral/Legal/Educational Maltreatment (MLE). In addition there are two subtypes of Physical Neglect: Failure to Provide (FTP), and Lack of Supervision (LOS). All five subtypes are universally recognized in the literature as distinct phenomena (Giovannoni & Becerra, 1979). Emotional maltreatment has received the least amount of focused empirical study, is the most difficult of the subtypes to identify reliably, and hence is singled out and discussed below.

Emotional Maltreatment

In the present system, EM incorporates the concepts of psychological abuse and psychological neglect. Until relatively recently, EM has received comparatively less attention in the literature (Garbarino, Guttman, & Seeley, 1986). However, in the last decade both theorists and clinicians have become increasingly interested in this phenomenon. EM also is the least developed of the subtypes. Part of the reason for this state of affairs is that it overlaps with each of the other subtypes of maltreatment. This is because all incidents of maltreatment exert strong psychological effects on the victims and witnesses. In fact, much of what the field is concerned with are the psychological consequences more than the physical consequences of abuse and neglect (Garbarino & Vondra, 1987). To avoid overlap, this system includes only parental acts that: (1) unambiguously constitute maltreatment, and (2) do not fit into any of the other four subtypes. The majority of incidents falling into this category involve the thwarting of children's basic emotional needs. These needs include *safety* (i.e., the need for an environment free of excessive hostility and violence, along with the need for physically and emotionally available and stable attachment figures) and *self-esteem* (i.e., the need for positive regard, the feeling that one may have an effect on one's environment, and the absence of excessively negative or unrealistic evaluations). Thus far we have categorized the occurrences of maltreatment from the files of 200 unique families and have successfully fit all incidents into one of the five subtypes.

Severity

While patently obvious, the dimension of severity of maltreatment has received almost no attention in the empirical literature. Leontine Young in her book *Wednesday's Children*, published in 1964, distinguished between moderate and severe abuse and neglect. It is important that her study was based on families' case records in public and private social-service agency files. Based solely on the material present within the families' records, she distinguished between these four types, and then demonstrated external validity among them based on case workers' reports on a forced-choice questionnaire she developed for her study. Severe neglect was defined as "inadequate feeding." Moderate neglect encompassed the "lack of cleanliness or lack of adequate clothing for the children or failure to provide medical care . . . either singly or in combination, but the children were usually fed." She further argued this distinction, claiming that a mother may still care for her children while not keeping them or their environment clean, but not if she fails to feed them. Her distinction between moderate and severe abuse, on the other hand, was based, in part, on criteria reflecting what we refer to in our system as chronicity. Her operational definition of abuse was when "the parents beat the children violently and consistently, so that time after time the results of the beatings were visible, . . . when parents beat their children only now and then, that is when they are drunk or under stress, and the beatings tended to be less violent, the classification moderate abuse was used." If both abuse and neglect occurred, then the family was placed in the abuse category.

Young's study was primarily descriptive because at that time there was very little systematically collected information available on maltreating families. Although her study did not contain a comparison group of more adequately parenting families, she was able to point out similarities and differences among these subtypes and severity distinctions, many of which have been replicated by later investigations. Unfortunately, many of Young's foresightful procedures have been ignored by later researchers—namely, the use of the rich material found in the families' case records and the notion that even within subtypes there are different degrees of severity.

Other researchers have implicitly made efforts at rating the severity of subtypes of maltreatment through the development of checklists or scales. One scale of parental neglect was designed to be filled out by daycare workers (Polansky, Chalmers, Buttenweiser, & Williams, 1977). Straus (1979) has designed the "Conflict Tactics Scales" to assess physical child abuse, based on parental report. Taylor, Underwood, Thomas, and Franklin (1988) have developed a parental self-report scale that assesses the degree of psychological maltreatment of infants and toddlers. With the exception of the Conflict Tactics Scales, none have been adopted into popular use. Moreover, even Straus cautioned that his scale was only valid in a qualitative sense and was not psychometrically valid as an interval or ordinal scale. This is likely to be the case for the others as well. Much research with large populations, collected in multiple laboratories, is needed to validate measures of severity.

In our system, we have developed ordinal scales of severity for each of the five subtypes. For each documented occurrence of a subtype, ratings of the severity of that incident are made. With the exception of moral/legal/educational (MLE) maltreatment, each scale has seven levels. MLE maltreatment has three distinct levels of severity. The reason we have fewer gradations of MLE maltreatment severity is due, in part, to the fact that the sample on which our system was developed was involved in a study focusing mainly on the other four subtypes. Expansion of this scale, based on actual occurrences of MLE maltreatment, needs to be planned and carried out with populations who are likely to have had greater exposure to this type of maltreatment (e.g., researchers studying conduct disorders and juvenile delinquency).

For each of the graduated levels of harshness on each scale, we have provided one or more examples of what we believe best depicts that severity. These examples were taken from actual cases of maltreatment from the original sample of 200 families receiving protective services. These were families with children ranging in age from infancy through adolescence. The descriptors for each severity level are not meant to be taken literally; rather, they are meant to be anchors or examples from which the coder can make decisions about where on the scale a particular incident fits best. Thus far, reliability of trained coders working with these scales has averaged above 0.75 for individual item agreements.

Frequency/Chronicity

A third dimension in our system is related to severity—that is, how frequently experiences of maltreatment occur. Like severity, this factor has been almost completely ignored by researchers. Frequency refers to the day-to-day occurrences of physical and sexual abuse. Chronicity refers to the extent to which conditions of maltreatment persist over longer periods of time. For example, a family may lapse into periods of physical or emotional neglect for several months or years, but may change and begin to function more adequately. Other families begin under conditions of neglect and/or abuse and remain in that state continuously. In our system, frequency is simply the total number of maltreatment referrals filed and substantiated against the family, while chronicity is the number of months the family's protective-service case remains active. In our work, we have found that the number of months families have active cases with CPS ranges from three months to over 15 years; the number of substantiated referrals ranges from 1 to 25.

Focusing on the concept of "risk factors," Cicchetti and Rizley (1981) extended Sameroff and Chandler's (1975) transactional model to examine the etiology and intergenerational transmission of child maltreatment. Cicchetti and Rizley (1981) classify risk factors into two broad categories— *potentiating factors*, which increase the probability of maltreatment, and *compensatory factors*, which decrease the risk of maltreatment. Under each category, two subgroupings are distinguished—*transient*, fluctuating, "state" factors and more permanent, *enduring* conditions or attributes.

Cicchetti and Rizley (1981) argue that it is necessary to examine both positive and negative "risk factors" in order to understand the occurrence of maltreatment and the specific forms it will take. According to the transactional model, maltreatment is expressed only when potentiating factors override compensatory ones. It is then that an act of abuse is committed or a maltreatment condition is allowed to begin.

Unlike earlier attempts that grouped parents according to theoretically deduced personality clusters, King and Cicchetti made broad distinctions based on the notion that maltreatment is not a static trait construct. King and Cicchetti (unpublished manuscript, 1989) have distinguished between different types of maltreating parents based on the tenets of the transactional model (Cicchetti & Rizley, 1981).

Employing measures of chronic, acute, perceived, and objective stress, along with measures of buffering factors such as social support and esteem support, King and Cicchetti examined differences between mothers who had active "open" protective-service cases and mothers who had received services in the past for issues of child maltreatment, but whose cases had been closed. This second type they labeled "in remission." They also included a third comparison group of families who were matched on all relevant demographic variables (e.g., race, maternal educational background and occupation, marital status, number of adults and children in the home) but who had no reported contacts with protective services. As predicted, the active maltreating mothers reported more chronic stress than the "in remission" group as well as the nonmaltreating comparison group. Surprisingly, the active maltreating group reported significantly more social support, which King and Cicchetti attributed to the fact that all these families were receiving supportive services from the department of social services, as well as the possibility that the support they were endorsing may have been that of the close family who might actually be adding to the tensions rather than reducing them (Smith & Hanson, 1975). Unfortunately, qualitative aspects of these supports were not looked at in this early investigation. Although this was not a prospective or a longitudinal study, King and Cicchetti have demonstrated convincing evidence based on clear and precise theoretical predictions regarding the dynamic nature of maltreatment.

Also in keeping with the transactional model, King and Cicchetti made distinctions within the active group of maltreating parents. Using a temporal dimension, derived from the family's protective-service record, King and Cicchetti separated chronically maltreating families (cases open an average of 8 ½ years) from acutely maltreating families (cases open an average of 4 months). Unfortunately, the sample size of their acutely maltreating families was too small to justify statistical significance testing. However, based on a simple observation of the means of these groups, the data support hypotheses based on the Cicchetti and Rizley (1981) model. Namely, the acutely maltreating group had lower chronic stress, with a mean similar to that of the comparison group, and higher transient stress compared to the chronic group. Moreover, unlike the chronically maltreating families, the acutely maltreating families reported lower social supports than either the chronic or comparison groups.

King and Cicchetti's transactional interpretations are based on operational criteria for distinguishing among these groupings of families. Their findings possess strong implications for understanding the etiology of child maltreatment, integrating several different theoretical perspectives. Important implications for grouping and defining different types of maltreating parents, an area that earlier work failed to substantiate empirically, also are present.

One could argue that the operational criteria employed by King and Cicchetti (i.e., the number of founded reports and the number of months a case is open) are likely to be influenced by a number of factors aside from how frequent and chronic the conditions of maltreatment in the family are. For example, the family's degree of isolation, ability to conceal abusive incidents, socioeconomic status, children's degree of emotional disturbance, the neighborhood, the degree of friends' intrusiveness, the credibility of the source of the maltreatment reports, and the protective worker's skills at investigating a case are but a few of the influencing factors that help determine the number of cases filed and substantiated (Eckenrode, Munsch, Powers, & Doris, 1988; Eckenrode, Powers, Doris, Munsch, & Bolger, 1988; Knudsen, 1988). In addition, the willingness or openness of a family to receive help, as well as the protective worker's personal decisions are likely to have an effect on how long a family's case will remain open. Nonetheless, both of the variables (i.e., active/closed and chronic/acute) are easily quantified and make quick and clean assessments of the degree of family dysfunction. Moreover, as demonstrated in the King and Cicchetti study, empirical support has been obtained for making these distinctions.

Developmental Period

The fourth factor in our system concerns the children's age at the time they were maltreated. One of the important tenets of developmental psychopathology is the idea that similar events may have different outcomes depending on the individual's point in the life-span (Cicchetti, 1990a; Cicchetti & Rizley, 1981). This premise grew out of organismic theories of development that view the ontogenetic process as a series of unfolding tasks which emerge as new cognitive, biological, socioemotional, and representational capacities evolve and greater external demands are placed on the organism (Cicchetti, 1990b; Erikson, 1950; Sroufe, 1979). According to this organizational viewpoint, normal development is considered to be the successful integration of these expanding capacities in a fashion that allows for resiliency and future adaptation. It follows then that early adaptation tends to promote later adaptation and integration.

In contrast, pathological development is conceived as a lack of integration of these aforementioned developmental domains. Because early structures often are incorporated into later structures, an early disturbance in functioning may ultimately cause much larger disturbances to appear later on.

In addition, agreement has coalesced regarding the presence of a series of stage-salient issues that are characteristic of child development (Erikson, 1950; Sroufe 1979). Rather than construing the ontogenetic process as a series of unfolding tasks that need to be accomplished and then decrease in importance, we perceive development as consisting of a number of important age and stage-appropriate tasks which, upon emergence, remain critical to the child's continual adaptation, although decreasing somewhat in salience relative to other newly emerging tasks.

For example, we do not consider attachment to be a developmental issue of the first year of life alone; rather, once an attachment relationship develops, it continues to undergo transformations and reintegrations with subsequent accomplishments such as emerging autonomy and entrance into the peer world. Children who experience inconsistent care early in life, such as conditions of physical abuse and physical and emotional neglect, tend to form insecure attachments to their caregivers (Cicchetti, 1990b). Their patterns of behavior may be adaptive with that particular caregiver, allowing the child to meet his/her needs for safety and security, but may be maladaptive with other individuals in other environments such as with teachers in the classroom. Experiencing maltreatment later in development should have different developmental implications, in that earlier more basic competencies will have been better consolidated.

While widely accepted theoretically, these ideas have received scant empirical study in a systematic longitudinal manner (see Erickson, Egeland, & Pianta, 1989, for a notable exception). Cicchetti (1990b) has demonstrated that by studying the sequelae of child maltreatment from an organismic developmental, stage-salient issues perspective, we can increase our understanding of the socioemotional consequences of child maltreatment.

While this work is an exciting first step, further work must be conducted with children who have experienced maltreatment at various points in development as a further test of this developmental theory. Data relating the timing of maltreatment to theory-guided predictions of outcome are greatly needed and have been ignored by the vast majority of investigators. The current nosological system represents a step in that direction.

In our system, we have included a component that allows us to keep careful track of the developmental periods in which the child was subject to maltreatment. This is accomplished by the fact that all maltreatment filings to CPS are dated. Whenever we assign ratings of the severity and type of maltreatment, we also record the developmental period during which it occurred. We have discriminated between nine separate periods that correspond to agreed-upon developmental issues (Cicchetti, 1990b). We acknowledge that information regarding the timing of maltreatment is subject to inaccuracy, in that there is often an unknown amount of maltreatment which occurs but is not reported. Nonetheless, these ratings will allow us to begin to study this phenomenon, and we believe that it will at least prove useful as a gross index of this issue.

Separations/Placement

Removal of maltreated children from their home environment has been a commonly accepted attempt at eliminating the possibility of future abuse and neglect. Beginning with the clinical observations of institutionalized children reported by Bowlby (1969/1982) and others (Rutter, 1972/1981), concern has arisen about the efficacy of interventions such as foster care.

Since the advent of Bowlby's (1969/1982) theoretical formulation on the salience of the child's attachment to the caregiver for the promotion of psychological well-being, psychologists have begun to question removal of the child as an intervention strategy. Despite the vast implications of this issue, surprisingly little research has been conducted looking at the effect out-of-home placements have on maltreated children (see Wald, Carlsmith, & Leiderman, 1988, for an exception).

The effects of out-of-home placement are made even more complex by the current state of the foster-care system. Frequently, a child who has been maltreated and who is therefore likely to be experiencing emotional problems is removed from the home and placed in a situation where the caregivers are not equipped to deal with problems that may occur. It is as if placement alone is expected to alleviate all problems associated with maltreatment. When the child begins to evidence behavioral problems while in care, rejection, serial placements, and, in some cases, additional maltreatment occurs. To reduce these detrimental outcomes, it is critical that alternate caregivers be provided with necessary support and preventive intervention.

Almost all investigations of maltreated children must have contained some percentage of children who had been placed outside the home. Although sometimes alluded to in the subjects section, these data are not incorporated into the analysis. By acknowledging this issue, and by making a system available for recording information about separations, researchers may begin to clarify some of these problems. In our system we record information concerning the developmental period(s) in which the separation or placement occurred, the number of separations the child has experienced, the length of each separation, and finally the type of separation (e.g., placement with a relative, foster care, community group home, residential treatment).

Perpetrator

Carefully kept records on perpetration also will add to our understanding of child maltreatment. This information is especially important in studies on the etiology of child maltreatment. By knowing the acts committed by specific individuals within the family, we can relate these more directly to data on their history, personality, psychopathology, and perceived stress and supports. For example, a child may have been subjected to several types of maltreatment (e.g., abuse and neglect). When interpreting data collected on the parents, however, it is important to separate out which acts each parent was directly responsible for committing. This information should add clarity to the understanding of the dynamics underlying these specific acts. Moreover, information about the relationship of the perpetrator to the child may be important for understanding the psychological significance of certain acts to the child.

Another issue surrounding the establishment of the responsible perpetrator of a given maltreatment act is the documentation of intentionality. Most definitions of child maltreatment include stipulations such as "nonaccidental," "willfully," and "preventable," each of which requires proof of intentionality. Obviously, the inclusion of these conditional statements makes the substantiation of certain ambiguous events extremely difficult. As a result, an unknown percentage of cases undoubtedly is not substantiated because sufficient evidence of perpetrator intentionality cannot be provided. Because our system is utilized on documented protective-service cases, intentionality already has been investigated and demonstrated. Nonetheless, researchers must pursue the investigation of intentionality issues more broadly in future empirical work to continue to make progress in our scientific understanding of this important problem.

Conclusion and Future Directions

While many have articulated the problems surrounding the conceptualization and demarcation of child maltreatment, few have made efforts to alleviate these definitional concerns. In this chapter we have outlined an operationalized system for classifying the subtypes, severity, frequency/chronicity, and developmental period during which child maltreatment occurs. We believe this system to be an important first step toward countering the widely accepted criticisms of the past relating to the difficulties associated with reliability, generalizability, and taxonomic delineation (e.g., Besharov, 1981; Cicchetti & Rizley, 1981).

The next logical steps would be the further validation of this system through its incorporation into studies on child maltreatment nationally. Past efforts attempting to develop operational criteria of maltreatment have relied heavily on survey methodology. Studies in this vein typically polled various professionals and lay people who work in the field of child maltreatment, asking them to rate vignettes, deciding whether or not they constitute maltreatment (Billingsley, 1964; Gelles, 1982; Giovannoni & Becerra, 1979). Overall, these studies have found that professionals are in reasonably good agreement regarding what constitutes maltreatment and about the relative seriousness of the maltreatment subtypes. We strongly believe that future efforts need to move away from vali-dation through the consensus of opinion and toward a system that is validated through the documented harm these acts cause to children. Ultimately there has to be more direct communication between researchers and professionals in the social work, psychological, medical, educational, and legal disciplines. The work of all these groups must be more tightly linked. One important step in this direction would be a single common operationalized system of definitions to meet these ends. Of course, this definition must necessarily reflect the expertise of individuals in a variety of disciplines and must meet the individual needs of the professionals who will be using the definition to guide their decision-making (Aber & Zigler, 1981). For example, drawing upon the psychodiagnostic skills of psychologists and psychiatrists and the sociological perspective of social workers are two mechanisms by which we can enhance the comprehensiveness of our conceptions of child maltreatment. It is this need for incorporation of ideas from diverse disciplines which may ultimately hold the greatest promise for a single language in which to communicate in the best interest of maltreated children.

Through the attainment of this goal, the courts could have access to more ac-curate empirical data concerning the long-term sequelae of various parental acts, while protective workers and other clinicians working with these parents could base their efforts on a more precise knowledge base. It is critical that investiga-tors increase their efforts to conduct research that is more directly policy relevant (Aber et al., 1989; Wald et al., 1988). Direct collaborations between social-service agencies and academic researchers would greatly facilitate these advancements. The similar recording and maintenance of state records of maltreatment with re-search needs in mind will greatly facilitate validation of a system such as we are describing. The costs of failing to pursue this end are far greater than the effort that must be expended before this system becomes a reality.

Note

1. Subsequent to completing this chapter, we became aware of a more recent analysis of the 1985 telephone survey data (Straus and Gelles, 1986). In this study, Gelles (1989) conducted a separate analysis on single-parent households. Not surprisingly, he found that single parents report more "se-vere" and "very severe" violence toward their children than do dual-parent families.

References

Aber, J. L., & Allen, J. P. (1987). The effects of maltreatment on young children's socio-emotional development: An attachment theory perspective. *Developmental Psychology, 23*, 406–414.

Aber, J. L., Allen, J., Carlson, V., & Cicchetti, D. (1989). The effects of maltreatment on develop-ment during early childhood: Recent studies and their theoretical, clinical, and policy implica-tions. In D. Cicchetti and V. Carlson (Eds.), *Child Maltreatment: Theory and research on the causes and consequences of child abuse and neglect*. New York: Cambridge University Press.

Aber, J. L., & Cicchetti, D. (1984). Socioemotional development in maltreated children: An empirical and theoretical analysis. In H. Fitzgerald, B. Lester, and M. Yogman (Eds.), *Theory and research in behavioral pediatrics*, Vol. II. New York: Plenum.

Aber, J. L., & Zigler, E. (1981). Developmental considerations in the definition of child maltreatment. *New Directions for Child Development, 11*, 1–29.

Akiskal, H., & Webb, W. (Eds.). (1978). *Psychiatric Diagnosis*. New York: Spectrum.

Alvy, K. T. (1975). Preventing child abuse. *American Psychologist, 30*, 921–928.

American Association for Protecting Children (AAPC). (1986). Highlights of official child neglect and abuse reporting 1984. Denver: The American Humane Association.

Ariès, P. (1962). *Centuries of childhood*. New York: Vintage Books.

Belsky, J. (1980). Child maltreatment: An ecological integration. *American Psychologist, 35*, 320–335.

Bertalanffy, L. von (1968). *General systems theory: Foundations, development, applications*. New York: Braziller.

Besharov, D. (1977). Putting central registers to work. *Children Today, September–October*, pp. 9–13.

Besharov, D. (1981). Toward better research on child abuse and neglect: Making definitional issues an explicit methodological concern. *Child Abuse and Neglect, 5*, 383–389.

Billingsley, A. (1964). The role of the social worker in a child protective agency. *Child Welfare, 43*, 472–92, 497.

Bowlby, J. (1969/1982). *Attachment and loss*, Vol. I: *Attachment*. New York: Basic Books.

Caffey, J. (1946). Multiple fractures in the long bones of infants suffering from chronic subdural hematoma. *American Journal of Roentgenology, 56*, 163–173.

Carlson, V., Cicchetti, D., Barnett, D., & Braunwald, K. (1989). Disorganized/disoriented attachment relationships in maltreated infants. *Developmental Psychology, 25*, 525–531.

Children's Defense Fund. (1979). *Children without homes: An examination of public responsibility to children in out-of-home care*. Washington, D.C.: Children's Defense Fund.

Cicchetti, D. (1990a). An historical perspective on the discipline of developmental psychopathology. In J. Rolf, A. Masten, D. Cicchetti, K. Neuchterlein, and S. Weintraub (Eds.), *Risk and protective factors in the development of psychopathology*. New York: Cambridge University Press.

Cicchetti, D. (1990b). The organization and coherence of socio-emotional, cognitive, and representational development: Illustrations through a developmental psychopathology perspective on Down syndrome and child maltreatment. In R. Thompson (Ed.), *Nebraska symposium on motivation*. Vol. 36. *Socioemotional development*. Lincoln, NE: University of Nebraska Press.

Cicchetti, D., & Aber, J. L. (1980). Abused children — abusive parents: An overstated case? *Harvard Educational Review, 50*, 244–255.

Cicchetti, D., & Beeghly, M. (1987). Symbolic development in maltreated youngsters: An organizational perspective. *New Directions for Child Development, 36*, 5–29.

Cicchetti, D., & Carlson, V. (Eds.). (1989). *Child maltreatment: Theory and research on the causes and consequences of child abuse and neglect*. New York: Cambridge University Press.

Cicchetti, D., Carlson, V., Braunwald, K., & Aber, J. L. (1987). The Harvard Child Maltreatment Project: A context for research on the sequelae of child maltreatment. In R. Gelles and J. Lancaster (Eds.), *Research in child abuse: Biosocial perspectives*. New York: Aldine DeGruyter.

Cicchetti, D., & Rizley, R. (1981). Developmental perspectives on the etiology, intergenerational transmission, and sequelae of child maltreatment. *New Directions for Child Development, 11*, 31–55.

Cicchetti, D., Taraldson, B., & Egeland, B. (1978). Perspectives in the treatment and understanding of child abuse. In A. Goldstein (Ed.), *Perspectives for child mental health and education*. New York: Pergamon.

Cicchetti, D., & Todd Manly, J. (1990). Problems and solutions to conducting research in maltreating families: An autobiographical perspective. In G. Brody and I. Sigel (Eds.), *Family research journeys*, Vol. 2. Hillsdale, NJ: Erlbaum.

Cicchetti, D., & Toth, S. (1987). The application of a transactional risk model to intervention with multi-risk maltreating families. *Zero to Three*, Vol. VII, 1–8.

Cicchetti, D., Toth, S. & Bush, M. (1988). Developmental psychopathology and incompetence in childhood: Suggestions for intervention. In B. Lahey and A. Kazdin (Eds.), *Advances in Clinical Child Psychology*. New York: Plenum Press.

Coster, W. J., Gersten, M. S., Beeghly, M., & Cicchetti, D. (1989). Communicative functioning in maltreated toddlers. *Developmental Psychology, 25*, 1020–1029.

Crittenden, P. M. (1988). Relationships at risk. In J. Belsky and T. Nezworski (Eds.), *Clinical implications of attachment theory*. Hillsdale, NJ: Erlbaum Associates.

Daro, D. (1988). *Confronting child abuse*. New York: Free Press.

Derdeyn, A. (1977). Child abuse and neglect: The rights of parents and the needs of their children. *American Journal of Orthopsychiatry, 47*, 377–387.

Dubowitz, H. (1986). *Child maltreatment in the United States: Etiology, impact and prevention*. Background paper prepared for the Congress of the United States, Office of Technology Assessment, Washington, D.C.

Dubowitz, H., & Newberger, E. (1989). Pediatrics and child abuse. In D. Cicchetti and V. Carlson (Eds.), *Child maltreatment: Theory and research on the causes and consequences of child abuse and neglect*. New York: Cambridge University Press.

Eaton, W., & Kessler, L. (Eds.). (1985). Epidemiologic field methods in psychiatry. Orlando, FL: Academic Press.

Eckenrode, J., Munsch, J., Powers, J., & Doris, J. (1988). The nature and substantiation of official sexual abuse reports. *Child Abuse and Neglect, 12*, 311–319.

Eckenrode, J., Powers, J., Doris, J., Munsch, J., & Bolger, N. (1988). Substantiation of child abuse and neglect reports. *Journal of Consulting and Clinical Psychology, 56*, 9–16.

Egeland, B., & Sroufe, L. A. (1981). Developmental sequelae of maltreatment in infancy. *New Directions for Child Development, 11*, 77–92.

Erickson, M., Egeland, B., & Pianta, R. (1989). The effects of maltreatment on the development of young children. In D. Cicchetti and V. Carlson (Eds.), *Child maltreatment: Theory and research on the causes and consequences of child abuse and neglect*. New York: Cambridge University Press.

Erikson, E. (1950). *Childhood and society*. New York: Norton.

Fanshel, D., & Shinn, E. G. (1972). *Dollars and sense in the foster care of children: A look at cost factors*. New York: Child Welfare League of America.

Garbarino, J., Guttman, E., & Seeley, J. (1986). *The psychologically battered child: Strategies for identification, assessment and intervention. San Francisco: Jossey-Bass*.

Garbarino, J., & Vondra, J. (1987). Psychological maltreatment: Issues and perspectives. In M. R. Brassard, R. Germain, and S. N. Hart (Eds.), *Psychological maltreatment of children and youth* (pp. 24–44). New York: Pergamon Press.

Gelles, R. J. (1973). Child abuse as psychopathology: A sociological critique and reformulation. *American Journal of Orthopsychiatry, 43*, 611–621.

Gelles, R. J. (1978). Violence toward children in the United States. *American Journal of Orthopsychiatry, 48*, 580–592.

Gelles, R. J. (1982). Problems in defining and labeling child abuse. In R. H. Starr (Ed.), *Child abuse prediction: Policy implications* (pp. 1–30). Cambridge, MA: Ballinger Publishing Co.

Gelles, R. J. (1989). Child abuse and violence in single-parent families: Parent absence and economic deprivation. *American Journal of Orthopsychiatry, 59*, 492–501.

Gil, D. B. (1975). Unraveling child abuse. *American Journal of Orthopsychiatry, 45*, 346–356.

Giovannoni, J. (1989). Definitional issues in child maltreatment. In D. Cicchetti and V. Carlson (Eds.), *Child maltreatment: Theory and research on the causes and consequences of child abuse and neglect.* New York: Cambridge University Press.

Giovannoni, J., & Becerra, R. M. (1979). *Defining child abuse.* New York: Free Press.

Goldstein, J., Freud, A., & Solnit, A. (1973). *Beyond the best interests of the child.* New York: Free Press.

Goodwin, D., & Guze, S. (1984). *Psychiatric diagnosis,* Third Edition. New York: Oxford University Press.

Gruber, A. R. (1978). *Children in foster care.* New York: Human Science Press.

Juvenile Justice Standards Project. (1977). *Standards relating to abuse and neglect.* Cambridge, MA: Ballinger.

Kaufman, J., & Cicchetti, D. (1989). The effects of maltreatment on school-aged children's socioemotional development: Assessments in a day camp setting. *Developmental Psychology, 25,* 516–524.

Kaufman, J., & Zigler, E. (1987). Do abused children become abusive parents? *American Journal of Orthopsychiatry, 57,* 186–192.

Kazdin, A. E., Moser, J., Colbus, D., & Bell, R. (1985). Depressive symptoms among physically abused and psychiatrically disturbed children. *Journal of Abnormal Psychology, 94,* 298–307.

Kempe, C. H., & Helfer, R. E. (Eds.). (1968). *The battered child syndrome,* First Edition. Chicago: University of Chicago Press.

Kempe, C. H., Silverman, F. N., Steele, B. B., Droegemueller, W., & Silver, H. K. (1962). The battered child syndrome. *Journal of the American Medical Association, 181,* 17–24.

Kempe, R., & Kempe, C. H. (1978). *Child abuse.* London: Fontana/Open Books.

King, K., & Cicchetti, D. (Unpublished manuscript, 1989). *Nosological distinction between chronic and acute, active and nonactive, maltreating parents: The role of stress, supports, and perceptions of child rearing hassles.*

Knudsen, D. D. (1988). *Child protective services: Discretion, decisions, dilemmas.* Springfield, IL: Charles C Thomas.

Koocher, G. P. (Ed.). (1976). *Children's rights and the mental health professions.* NY: Wiley-Interscience.

Lynch, M. (1985). Child abuse before Kempe: An historical literature review. *Child Abuse and Neglect, 9,* 7–15.

Martin, H. (Ed.). (1976). *The abused child.* Cambridge: Ballinger Press.

Meehl, P. E. (1959/1973). Some ruminations on the validation of clinical procedures. Reprinted in P. Meehl, *Psychodiagnosis.* Minneapolis: University of Minnesota Press.

Meehl, P. E. (1973). *Psychodiagnosis.* Minneapolis: University of Minnesota Press.

Meehl, P. E., & Rosen, A. (1959). Antecedent probability and the efficiency of psychometric signs, patterns or cutting scores. *Psychological Bulletin, 52,* 194–216. Reprinted in P. Meehl, *Psychodiagnosis.* Minneapolis: University of Minnesota Press.

Mnookin, R. (1973). Foster care: In whose best interest? *Harvard Educational Review, 43,* 599–638.

Mueller, N., & Silverman, N. (1989). Peer relations in maltreated children. In D. Cicchetti & V. Carlson (Eds.), *Child maltreatment: Theory and research on the causes and consequences of child abuse and neglect.* New York: Cambridge University Press.

Nelson, B. (1984). *Making an issue of child abuse.* Chicago: University of Chicago Press.

Parke, R. D., & Collmer, C. W. (1975). Child abuse: An interdisciplinary analysis. In E. Mavis Hetherington (Ed.), *Review of Child Development Research,* Vol. V. Chicago: University of Chicago Press.

Pelton, L. (1978). Child abuse and neglect: The myth of classlessness. *American Journal of Orthopsychiatry, 48,* 608–617.

Pianta, R., Egeland, B., & Erickson, M. (1989). The antecedents of child maltreatment: The results of the mother-child interaction research project. In D. Cicchetti & V. Carlson (Eds.), *Child maltreatment: Theory and research on the causes and consequences of child abuse and neglect*. New York: Cambridge University Press.

Polansky, N., Chalmers, M., Buttenweiser, E., & Williams, D. (1977). *Assessing adequacy of child care: An urban scale*. University of Georgia, Athens. Mimeographed.

Radbill, S. X. (1968). A history of child abuse and infanticide. In R. E. Helfer and C. H. Kempe (Eds.), *The battered child*. Chicago: University of Chicago Press.

Polier, J. W. (1975). Professional abuse of children: Responsibility for the delivery of services. *American Journal of Orthopsychiatry, 45*, 357–362.

Rodham, H. (1973). Children under the law. *Harvard Educational Review, 43*, 487–514.

Ross, C. (1980). The lessons of the past: Defining and controlling child abuse in the United States. In G. Gerbner, C. Ross, and E. Zigler (Eds.), *Child abuse: An agenda for action*. New York/Oxford: Oxford University Press.

Rutter, M. (1972/1981). *Maternal deprivation reassessed*. Harmondsworth, Middlesex: Penguin Books.

Sameroff, A., & Chandler, M. (1975). Reproductive risk and the continuum of caretaking casualty. In F. Horowitz, M. Hetherington, S. Scarr-Salapatek, & G. Siegel (Eds.), *Review of child development research* (Vol. 4). Chicago: University of Chicago Press.

Schneider-Rosen, K., Braunwald, K., Carlson, V., & Cicchetti, D. (1985). Current perspectives in attachment theory: Illustration from the study of maltreated infants. In I. Bretherton and E. Waters (Eds.), *Monographs of the Society for Research in Child Development, 50* (Serial No. 209), 194–210.

Schneider-Rosen, K., & Cicchetti, D. (1984). The relationship between affect and cognition in maltreated infants: Quality of attachment and the development of visual self-recognition. *Child Development, 55*, 648–658.

Silverman, F. N. (1953). The roentgen manifestations of unrecognized skeletal trauma in infants. *American Journal of Roentgenol Radium Therapy Nuclear Medicine, 69*, 413–427.

Smith, S. M., & Hanson, R. (1975). Interpersonal relationships and child-rearing practices in 214 parents of battered children. *British Journal of Psychiatry, 127*, 513–525.

Spinetta, J. J., & Rigler, D. (1972). The child-abusing parent: A psychological review. *Psychological Bulletin, 77*, 296–304.

Sroufe, L. A. (1979). The coherence of individual development. *American Psychologist, 34*, 834–841.

Steele, D. F., & Pollock, C. (1968). A psychiatric study of parents who abuse infants and small children. In R. Helfer and C. Kempe (Eds.), *The battered child* (pp. 89–133). Chicago: University of Chicago Press.

Straus, M. A. (1979). Measuring intrafamily conflict and violence: The Conflict Tactics (CT) Scales. *Journal of Marriage and the Family, 41*, 75–88.

Straus, M. A., & Gelles, R. J. (1986). Change in family violence from 1975-1985. *Journal of Marriage and the Family, 48*, 465–479.

Taylor, J., Underwood, C., Thomas, L., & Franklin, A. (1988). Measuring psychological maltreatment of infants and toddlers. In R. L. Jones (Ed.), *Tests and measures for Black populations*. Berkeley, CA: Cobb and Henry Publishers

United States Department of Health and Human Services. (1981). *Study findings: National study of the incidence and severity of child abuse and neglect*. DHHS Publication No. (OHDS) 81-30325, Washington, D.C.

United States Department of Health and Human Services (1988). *Study findings: Study of national incidence and prevalence of child abuse and neglect*. DHHS Publication No. (OHDS) 20-01099, Washington, D.C.

Vasta, R., & Copitch, P. (1981). Simulating conditions of child abuse in the laboratory. *Child De-velopment, 52,* 164–170.

Vondra, J., Barnett, D., & Cicchetti, D. (1989). *Perceived and actual competence among maltreated and comparison school children, Development and Psychopathology 1,* 237–255.

Wakefield, H., & Underwager, R. (1988). *Accusations of child sexual abuse.* Springfield, IL: Charles C Thomas.

Wald, M. S. (1975). State intervention on behalf of neglected children: A search for realistic stan-dards. *Stanford Law Review, 28,* 625–706.

Wald, M., Carlsmith, J., & Leiderman, P. (1988). *Protecting abused and neglected children.* Stan-ford, CA: Stanford University Press.

Walker, E., Downey, G., & Bergman, A. (1989). The effects of parental psychopathology and mal-treatment on child behavior. A test of the diathesis-stress model. *Child Development, 60,* 15–24.

Williams, G. J. R. (1983). Child protection: A journey into history. *Journal of Clinical Child Psy-chology, 22,* 236–243.

Wolfe, D. A. (1985). Child abusive parents: An empirical review and analysis. *Psychological Bul-letin, 97,* 462–482.

Wolfe, D. A. (1987). *Child abuse.* Newbury Park, CA: Sage Publications.

Young, L. R. (1964). *Wednesday's children: A study of child neglect and abuse.* New York: McGraw-Hill.

Zigler, E. (1976). Controlling child abuse: An effort doomed to failure? In W. A. Collins (Ed.), *Newsletter of the Division on Developmental Psychology, American Psychological Association,* February, 17–30.

Depression and Extreme Violence in Adolescence

Carl P. Malmquist

A persistent problem is that violent behavior can be connected to diverse diagnoses or no diagnosis. In a court population, there is the additional problem of the chronological age that comes before a juvenile court. Which definition of violence to employ, and the sensitivity and specificity of measures used for the diagnosis of depression in an adolescent population, also need clarification (American Psychiatric Association, 1987; Feigner, Robins, Guze, Woodroof, Winokur, & Munoz, 1984; Nelson & Charney, 1981; Spitzer, Endicott, & Robins, 1978). Behavior can also be partly defined by a legal standard. The adolescent subjects selected for investigation were those for whom certification to an adult court had been proposed. If such a proposal was successful, they would be tried as adult defendants with all the consequences that could entail. The behaviors that had gotten them into legal difficulties were of a variety where there would be no debate about whether they were violent. Such acts were either of a homicidal type or those in which a brutal sexual assault had occurred; a few met legal criteria for three or more felonious property offenses in the preceding two years.

Given this group who had committed violent acts, a clinical goal was to understand the diverse manifestations of depression in such a sample of violent adolescents. Their genetic histories, family dispositions, and personality traits might all contribute to the clinical manifestations. There was also the problem of mixed clinical pictures in which depressive symptoms are admixed with other behavior patterns, and whether this is a coincidence or confluence of disparate diagnoses. While meeting criteria for a Major Affective Disorder, many of the signs and symptoms of a Conduct Disorder were present in some of the group; others overlapped with Attention Deficit Disorder, as well as some meeting criteria prior to age 15 that would be consistent with an Antisocial Personality Disorder on reaching the age of 18. Given a sample of violent juveniles selected from a court setting, this type of diagnostic overlap could be expected. Yet, was this all it indicated, or did it reflect some problems in the validity of those diagnoses used in an adolescent population? A specific focus was to assess for the presence of a clinical depression in these adolescents, as well as to take cognizance of overlapping diagnoses. The general approach was that of a descriptive study which would allow hypotheses to be raised about such a group of violent adolescents.

Clinical impressions have often noted the possibility of delinquent or acting-out behavior having a correlation with clinical depression. The problem was often a methodological one of how to study such cases and under what conditions. Few of the studies focused primarily on the adolescent age group in any systematic manner. An unresolved question was whether specific approaches were needed for adolescents who committed violent acts, in contrast to studies focused on adults. With such a caveat, the diagnostic criteria formulated for adults was used with adolescents for assessing the descriptive presence or absence of depressive symptoms. If anything, diagnostic errors for depression occurring with an adolescent-age group would more likely be in the direction of an underassessment or a low sensitivity because of the possibility that more subtle indicators of depression are not being detected by measures developed for use with adults. However, in an adolescent population, utilizing criteria developed with adults for diagnosing an affective disorder, the expectation would be for a higher incidence of depressions than in investigations of younger children because of the closer diagnostic similarity to adults. When the subject group is composed of adolescents who have committed a serious act of violence, the ambiguity of dealing with minor acts of aggression in terms of deciding whether, and to what extent, they were aggressive has been eliminated.

Methodology and Some Problems

In this study, 44 juvenile subjects were screened from an original court population of 6,500 alleged juvenile delinquents. By way of intake processes, dispositional judgments, and prosecutorial discretion, the initial group was sequentially narrowed on the basis of the seriousness of the alleged offense. The types of offenses in the narrowed-down group usually comprised some type of homicide, aggravated sexual assault, or the presence of two or three prior felony offenses (such as aggravated robbery or burglary) having been adjudicated in the juvenile court system in the preceding three years. The resultant subjects were 30 males and 14 females, aged 14–17 years, who were selected by a series of screening procedures. The original sample was from an aggregate population of juveniles awaiting processing and disposition in a juvenile court. The policy was to administer the Minnesota Multiphasic Personality Inventory (MMPI) to those juveniles with a serious charge pending against them, as part of an evaluation screening process. From the initial population, 1,241 were referred for some type of clinical assessment, and 213 of them were in the category of being charged with a serious offense and having had an MMPI administered to them as part of the larger group. A score of "60" or greater on the "D" scale (Depression) screened an initial group of 54 potentially depressed adolescents who had committed a violent act and who were, in turn, given further assessment measures before being in the final group for study.

From the group of 6,500 juveniles seen on an initial intake level, 3,200 juveniles were subsequently processed to the county attorney's office for a decision on whether a juvenile petition should be filed or not. Filing a petition required that some type of court action would ultimately be needed. Once such a petition has been filed, it leads to the requirement for a formal court disposition. It is from this group of juvenile offenders coming to the attention of the county attorney that a legal motion can be made to certify a juvenile to adult court for disposition as an adult accused of a similar felony. Over the three-year period of investigation, 213 juveniles had such motions filed against them. A formal hearing was then required in which the juvenile court would render a decision on whether they would remain in the juvenile court or be certified to be tried as adults with the consequences that could follow if a person was convicted of a major felony. Diverse issues pertaining to the certification process have been discussed elsewhere (Malmquist, 1979). It was from this group of 213 juveniles, with motions pending to certify them to adult court, that a subgroup of 54 subjects was initially selected on the basis of their MMPI "D" scale scores. Ten of them did not meet other criteria (discussed below), so that an eventual group of 44 comprised the study group. Other specific diagnostic criteria for congruency with a Major Affective Disorder were then applied.

Diverse efforts have been made to examine the interrelationships of antisocial behavior and depression. They present an unusual number of problems in methodology and questions about comparability and applicability. In part, this is because we are still at the hypothesis-building stage of understanding personality functioning and its relationship to affective disturbances. Akiskal, Hirschfeld, and Yerevanian offered four possible types of interactions between personality functioning and affective disturbances (1983). The relationship could be in terms of predisposing, modifying, complicating, or attenuating the expression of the depressive components. When dealing with a group of depressed adolescents who exhibit violent behavior, all of these interrelationships are possibilities. Predisposing features of dependency, histrionic tendencies, attentional deficits, and obsessionality can all contribute to depression and acting-out behavior. In turn, the expression of the depressive features may be modified, making diagnosis more difficult and complicating treatment as well.

The formulation of personality disturbances as an attenuation of affective disturbances has had a long history, extending back to Kraepelin, who saw personality defects giving rise to episodes of illness similar to the interpersonal difficulties that are interwoven with depressive features (Frank, Kupfer, Jacob, & Jarret, 1987). Certain behavioral symptoms might then be a direct expression of an affective disorder. If so, we would expect to find other diagnoses longitudinally in this group; hence, one study investigating cyclothymics found 66% had previously been diagnosed as hysterics or sociopaths (Akiskal, Djendered-jaan, Rosenthal, et al., 1977). Symptom overlapping was also present, such as aggressive or explosive outbursts, unstable work histories, unexplained promiscuous behavior, irritable behavior, buying sprees, joining movements, and becoming disillusioned— all of which are seen in affective disturbances and antisocial personalities. Difficulties in encompassing these overlapping symptom pictures of antisocial behavior in depressions give rise to formulations such as "characterological depressions" or "atypical depressions" (Akiskal, Rosenthal, Haykal, et al., 1980; Pies, 1988). Another approach has been the idea of Depressive Spectrum Disease in which first-degree relatives of depressives manifest a loading of alcoholism or antisocial personalities (Winokur, 1979). This hypothesis will be explored further in this chapter. The situation is suggestive of the similar chaos prevailing in studies of Borderline Personality Disorders in adult populations in which there is high comorbidity with affective disorders, organic disorders, histrionic and antisocial personality disorders. In this case, the question has been raised whether the overlap is simply reflecting base rates of pathology in a particular population on the effect of sample selections (Fyer et al., 1988).

Only a few studies have specifically focused on depression and extreme types of violence in juveniles. Offer et al. (1979) looked at the problem in the context of delinquents who were hospitalized. Another study used a group of 13- to 15-year-olds who were in a correctional setting for delinquents where 23% were given a diagnosis of Major Affective Disorder (Chiles, Miller, & Cox, 1980). Kashani et al. (1980) looked at delinquents already incarcerated and found 18% depressed. One variation was to look at self-reported depressed moods. However, such self-reports were found to be significantly related only to minor acts of delinquency and not to major acts of violence (Kandel & Davies, 1982).

One report dealt with 19 males who were condemned to death for acts done while they were juveniles. They ranged in age from 17 to 29 years at the time of the evaluation. While the purpose of the comprehensive examinations was not to look for depression at the time of the acts, it was noted that four of the subjects had histories consistent with severe mood disorders (Lewis et al., 1988). As in so many of these investigations, a multitude of other problems were conjointly present, such as neurological findings, an undiagnosed seizure disorder, a sodomization by adult relatives, and backgrounds of physical abuse and family violence. The absence of looking for depression was also present in a study of 72 adolescents charged with homicide and evaluated at a forensic psychiatric center over a nine-year period (Cornell, Benedek, & Benedek, 1987). Although a diagnostic breakdown was not done, the authors noted that only 5 of the subjects had been diagnosed as psychotic. A study, in a psychiatric hospital setting, of 10 adolescent murderers, had 6 diagnosed as schizophrenic (Sendi & Blomgren, 1975). Nor did Solway et al. (1981) discover any significance regarding depression in a group of 18 cases.

Problems in investigative methodology abound in such selected studies. The following problems that arise are basic in such studies, and, unless addressed, cast serious questions on any conclusions:

1. What definition of ''violence'' should be used? If the criterion is simply to select those juveniles charged with a delinquent act, it would obviously be too inclusive; if the criterion is narrowed to those charged with a major offense against a person, there is a more appropriate group. However, this would still cover a multitude of behaviors varying from grabbing the purse of a woman on the street to attacking a person with a weapon in the course of a property crime, and to homicidal acts and aggravated rapes. It is the latter group of extreme violence with which this study was concerned. Investigations that did not focus on a similar subject group would not be comparable in assessing the significance of the presence or absence of an accompanying major depressive episode.

2. The location of the subjects in such studies may be diverse. Some studies looked at violent youths in hospitals, others in correctional settings, yet others in diverse types of community settings such as while on probation or in group living arrangements.

3. Related to the problem of where they are located is the duration of their stay in a particular setting. Assessing a group of institutionalized adolescents a year or more after a violent episode might give quite different results from those obtained shortly after the offense or while the adolescent is awaiting trial; mixing groups and durations of institutionalized stays skews the results.

4. There is also an old problem that prosecuting attorneys frequently raise about the contaminant effect of being depressed because of the very fact of being charged with a serious offense, or being incapacitated while awaiting trial. It is the clinical problem of the background prevalence of a predisposing trait versus a situational reaction.

5. In reviewing studies, there is also the difficulty that certain treatments may have been carried out, which raises questions about what kind, by whom, for what length of time, etc. These may have been along psychotherapeutic or pharmacological lines, or both. In some studies, this contaminating variable is not even noted.

6. Finally, the criteria used for diagnoses of depression vary in studies. Besides the direct clinical interview, one of many instruments or symptom checklists may have been employed. The validity of different diagnostic approaches used with children is a subject in its own right (Achenbach & Edelbrook, 1984). Since all diagnosis is at least part narrative in the sense of constructing some type of clinical picture, the issue is looking at the time frame of depressive symptoms

as well. For the data reported in this chapter, the adolescents were seen within 60 days of committing the charged offense, with one exception that was extended on the basis of legal questions which delayed proceedings. Hence, we are not looking at depressive symptoms some time subsequent to the act of violence. Whether the total symptom picture could be accounted for by a legal apprehension and detention would seem unlikely since the majority of the juveniles initially screened in the study were not seen as depressed.

7. For adolescent girls there is also the problem of the increased incidence of mood disturbances as a possible independent variable whose etiology remains unsettled (Weissman & Klerman, 1977). The issue of the relationship between depression in adolescent girls and antisociality also remains unresolved.

Results

The goal was to assess a group of adolescents who had committed a seriously violent act and who were being processed through a juvenile court system in terms of whether they would also meet criteria for a clinical depression. To gain initial entry into the study, the following criteria had to be met: (a) Being a juvenile and originally not in an adult court; (b) Being charged either with a serious crime of violence or repetitive crimes of burglary or robbery within a three-year period which would be viewed as acts displaying a high degree of aggression; (c) Finding an elevated "D" score on the MMPI as part of the screening process that would then trigger further screening. Since the MMPI tests were administered and scored "blindly" by psychologists without a clinical history, the high scorers for depression qualified for further assessment as to the presence of other signs and symptoms consistent with a diagnosis of a Major Affective Disorder.

Further assessments were then carried out on the group selected in this manner. The Beck Depressive Inventory (BDI) was administered as well as a clinical psychiatric assessment by the author to determine whether the criteria for a *DSM-III* Major Depressive Episode were also present. Unless a score of 18 or higher on the BDI was achieved, the individual was excluded despite the MMPI score. A score of 18 or over on the BDI would encompass mild, moderate, and severe degrees of depression. Beck's data have mean scores of mild, moderate, and severe depression of 18.7, 25.4, and 30.0, respectively. The correlation between the BDI and the MMPI "D" scale is noted as .75 (Beck, 1972). If both of these psychometric devices for depression met the criteria indicated, the investigation to meet *DSM-III* symptoms was pursued. Inclusion in the final group of 44 subjects then meant that the adolescent had met not only the initial three criteria, but two additional ones: a score above 18 on the Beck and diagnostic criteria for a Major Depressive Episode from *DSM-III*. Table 1 presents the differences in mean scores between the males and females on the MMPI and the BDI.

Table 1. Ratings on Depressed Delinquent Adolescents

Test	Male Probands (N = 30)	Female Probands (N = 14)
MMPI (Mean scores for D scale)	65.6	72.4
BDI	22.3	25.5

Once the diagnostic criteria for the group of adolescents with a Major Depression had been met, diversities within the final subject group of 44 were examined. Some significant differences emerged between the specific symptom pictures in the males and females. These differences in symptom pictures could be compared to an adult population who met criteria for a Major Depressive Episode. All of the adolescents reported some symptoms connected with a dysphoric mood. Irritability was a symptom present in half the males, but in 80% of the females. Vegetative signs revealed interesting contrasts. None of the adolescents reported a poor appetite and weight loss, but some had a history of weight gain. Since *DSM-III* did not specify when a weight gain or loss is to be considered significant, the study used 10 pounds as achieving significance, and also added a requirement that the gain or loss should have taken place over the period of the three months before the offense. While 4 of the 30 boys gained over 10 pounds, half the girls (7 of 14) had such a weight gain. Such a finding raised questions about different character structures or defenses when a depressive episode occurs in adolescent boys and girls prone to violence.

In terms of psychomotor agitation, 15 of the 30 boys reported feeling a greater restlessness and agitation in the month before the violent act; only 1 boy felt grossly slowed down in his movements, but 3 girls did. Perhaps this picture of greater agitation correlates with the "agitated subtype" of Affective Disorder found by Alessi et al. (1984) in their incarcerated sample of depressed adolescents compared to a hospitalized group.

Descriptive correlates were matched with another item of "problems in thinking." There were 16 boys with psychomotor symptoms (15 agitated and 1 retarded) and 3 girls with "problems in thinking." One interpretation of these symptoms is that part of the picture of depression in adolescence reflects a good deal of agitation, turmoil, and restlessness in contrast to the more withdrawn and inhibited variety of depressive manifestations. While 3 girls did seem to present an inhibited model, 5 others were agitated, but only 1 boy was inhibited. The impact on their capacity to think, concentrate, and make decisions would consequently be impaired. These deficiencies could also be classified as problems with attention so that their difficulties in focusing and organizing their thoughts are part of the picture, along with impulsivity. Such findings illustrate the recurrent problem of a mixture of symptom pictures and, depending on which group of symptoms is emphasized, overlapping diagnostic pictures.

One perspective would be to see the behavior of those juveniles as some variety of a Conduct Disorder, either of a Group Type or a Solitary Aggressive Type with depressive affect occasionally being part of the picture. Certainly, some of their overt behaviors would fit this diagnosis. However, there are problems connected with the reliability and validity of these diagnoses as well. There is also the problem that manifestations which seem like an Attention Deficit Disorder may simply be part of a Conduct Disorder. These questions will not be pursued here but are noted as part of the continuing problem of overlapping symptom pictures often present in disturbed adolescents. Similarly, Conduct Disorders may overlap with Affective Disorders in this age group and are difficult to differentiate (Marriage, Fine, Moretti, & Halog, 1986). Medical criteria in terms of biological or etiological precursors for a valid syndrome do not appear to exist to differentiate hyperactivity connected with attention deficits from the aggression connected with conduct problems (Hinshaw, 1987). However, behavioral dimensions may emerge in factor-analytic studies. These problems exist independent of assessing for depression. For the 44 adolescents studied, the symptom picture of a Major Affective Disorder was present that often included some of the attentional, motoric, impulsive, and conduct disturbances seen with these other two diagnoses.

An interesting question is why the diagnosis of depression with its accompanying symptoms was not considered earlier in their lives despite the frequent contacts with community agencies by these adolescents. All of them had contacts with schools, counseling agencies, courts, or independent mental-health services. In fact, almost the entire group (all of the males and 10 of the females) had had previous involvement with some court system for delinquent behavior. A question is whether an emphasis on their antisocial conduct, such as delinquent behavior in a legal setting, contributed to focusing on this to the exclusion of other significant variables, such as their difficulties with attention and focusing or episodes of dysphoria. A possibility is that once they have been classified as delinquents, they are assumed to fit a personality or conduct-type of disturbance without the need for further inquiry. It is the problem in reverse from initially presenting with depressive symptoms and then missing the characterological manifestations. Questions from work with adult patients emphasizing the frequency of personality disturbances (48%) in recurrent depressions become suggestive with respect to this adolescent group (Pilkonis & Frank, 1988).

The subjects did not present themselves as generally inhibited. Even though clinically depressed on clinical and psychometric assessment, they were customarily not perceived as depressed by those who had ongoing contact with them. Although having a dysphoric mood, and feeling "down" a good deal of the time, they had not resorted to verbalizations about how sad and unhappy they were as

Table 2. DSM-III Symptoms of Depression in Violent Delinquents

Symptoms	Male (N = 30)		Female (N = 14)	
	No.	%	No.	%
Dysphoric mood				
Depressed	27	90	14	100
Feeling sad, blue, or in the dumps	27	90	14	100
Hopeless about future	18	60	7	50
Irritable	15	50	11	80
General symptoms				
Poor appetite	0	0	0	0
Weight loss (10 lbs.)	0	0	0	0
Weight gain (10 lbs.)	4	13	7	50
Insomnia	0	0	0	0
Hypersomnia	8	25	6	45
Psychomotor agitation	15	50	5	35
Psychomotor retardation	1	3	3	21
Loss of interest or pleasure in usual activities	15	30	11	80
Decrease in sexual drive	8	25	11	80
Loss of energy; fatigue	1	3	3	21
Feelings of worthlessness; self-reproach, or excessive or inappropriate guilt	18	60	6	40
Problems in thinking (slowed thinking, indecisiveness, or difficulty in concentrating)	8	25	3	21
Suicidal ideation	8	25	6	40
Attempted overdose	4	13	1	7
Wrist-slashing	0	0	1	7
Presence of psychotic features				
Gross impairment in reality testing	3	10	1	7
Hallucinations	0	0	0	0
Delusions	3	10	1	7
Depressive stupor	0	0	0	0

some depressed adults complain. Many of these adolescents did not know what being depressed was although, when asked, they used phrases such as "being down" or "not feelin' like doin' much."

Similarly, inferences can be drawn from the category of "Feelings of worth lessness'' (see Table 2) as part of *DSM-III* criteria for a depressive episode. A good number of these adolescents had low self-esteem (60% of the males and 40% of the females). Yet, it is an item that can easily be missed by those in daily contact with them. First, the adolescents do not present themselves with overt complaints of feeling guilty. Nor, if asked directly whether they feel guilty much of the time, do many respond affirmatively. A similar void exists for those who associate with them on a peer level or for adults who are in contact with them, such as teachers. Yet, when inquiry was directed to their self-concept, such as how they felt about themselves, and their believed failures and lack of accomplishments, phrases were heard such as ''I don't seem to come through,'' or ''I don't know why I haven't been able to get my act together,'' or ''When I think about it, I guess I'm a prize asshole.'' What seems to have happened is a subtle distortion in assessing them, once we know about their delinquent conduct. It is as if deficits in self-esteem are assumed and follow from their behaving in antisocial ways. It is a confluence of the legal category they are presumed to be in with a subsequent clinical impression that would seemingly go together with their antisocial behavior, so that an affective disorder is not considered a primary possibility.

Even in clinical settings, if these adolescents were previously seen as having psychological difficulties, the focus was often on a specific behavior. The problem of substance abuse will be commented on below, but most often complaints made about them (often pre-empting their own complaints) were seen as suggesting other diagnostic possibilities. For example, summaries and reports from preceding contacts frequently interpreted their disinterest in learning or learning problems as a primary problem. For three of the males, there were indications that a contemporary diagnosis of Attention Deficit Disorder would have been appropriate. Nor was it presumptuous to see this as one of their main problems since associations of extreme reading disabilities and symptomatology usually associated with psychosis in a group of incarcerated delinquent boys have been reported (Lewis, Shanok, Balla, & Bard, 1980).

Components of agitation and irritability frequently led to diagnostic confusion reflecting the overlap with personality disorders. Before the major violent episode, the most frequent diagnosis encountered was Adjustment Reaction of Adolescence. There were several reasons for this. First, it allowed a setting to avoid a more ominous diagnosis. The social benefits of minimizing the psychopathology thus kept the clinical profile low. The skills and training necessary for assessing the diverse and complex aspects of personality functioning in adolescence may have been lacking in community settings, making more subtle diagnostic differentiations, such as depression, difficult. The situation is one in which the patient has a set of ambiguous signs and symptoms presented to an assessor who finds it difficult to resolve ambiguity. Finally, in many of the cases, before the violent act, assessing these juveniles may have been quite difficult. It is analogous to the surprise expression when an adolescent commits suicide and associates wonder how it could have happened.

Suicidal Ideation

While suicidal ideation always suggests the possibility of depression, its absence cannot rule out depression. A significant minority of these adolescents had recurrent thoughts of suicide in the preceding 60 days before the offense. Four of the males had drug overdoses in the past two years, but they qualified the episodes by stating they had not intended to kill themselves. The events were described with phrases such as wanting to "get away from the scene," and "wanting my parents to get off my back." Only one of the four males who made an attempt came close to succeeding. While his conscious intent was to kill himself, the act possessed the high degree of ambivalence often seen in suicides; an overdose of tranquilizer medication was taken and he then went to his bedroom. When he did not appear for dinner, his parents checked his room and discovered him in a stupor and rushed him to an emergency room. The risk and time involved could have gone either way given the probabilities. He was admitted to a psychiatric unit but left in three days, with a diagnosis of Passive Aggressive Personality, when his mother acceded to his wishes to leave against medical advice. One of the girls took an overdose of six diazepam tablets after an angry confrontation with her boyfriend. A second girl slashed her wrists when feeling lonely and neglected. The pattern of suicidal thoughts or attempts that are later ignored after the eruption of some violent act against others is not infrequent and deserves further research.

Drug Usage

Another complicating factor diagnostically in these juveniles is the drug abuse-chemical dependency axis that can mask or contribute to the depressive picture. Use of some drugs is so common among a general delinquent population that the problems may be ignored in the context of chronic usage. In part it depends on the drug in question, such as marijuana or alcohol, compared to other chemicals. The amount of use, circumstances, and duration are all significant. Inquiry sought to elicit not simply whether any of the drugs listed in Table 3 had ever been used, but whether they were used in a consistent pattern over time. For example, a girl who said she had drunk alcohol to excess on three occasions over the past two years was not included as a "user." A boy who said he smoked marijuana only once a week, such as on weekends, but did so in a pattern of two to three times per month, was included.

The suggestive conclusion from the pattern of drug use in these depressed, violent delinquents may be little different from the usage pattern among a non-depressed group of delinquent adolescents. Hence, of the 20 males who used

Table 3. Drug Usage in Depressed Adolescent Delinquents

Drug	Male (N = 30)		Female (N = 14)	
	No.	%	No.	%
Marijuana	18	60	7	50
Stimulant types of drugs (amphetamine type)	8	26	3	21
LSD (Lysergic Acid Diethylamide)	3	10	0	0
PCP (Phencyclidine, Angel Dust)	1	3	0	0
Opiates	0	0	0	0
Sedative hypnotics (barbiturates and benzodiazepines)	8	26	6	43
Alcohol	27	90	8	57

drugs out of the sample of 30, 50% were classified as alcohol users and 60% as marijuana users. For girls, the comparable figures were 57 and 50%, respectively. Cultural and demographic variables would have to be considered that were not controlled in this investigation. The conclusion is not to ignore the pattern of drug use in these adolescents in legal trouble, but perhaps to see some types of drug usage as so endemic in some of them as to make it difficult to assess other aspects of personality functioning.

Even more impressive than the past history connected with their drug usage was the finding that only one of the 44 subjects was ever diagnosed as depressed before getting into serious antisocial behavior of the type that led to his being included in this study. The difficulty is partly explained by where they happened to make contact, such as in a court probation system, a chemical-dependency referral, a clinic, or an in-patient hospital unit. The few times depression was considered, it was viewed as secondary to the primary problem of chemical dependency. The resultant approach then adopted was that if the drug usage could be controlled, accompanying phenomena, such as a dysphoric mood, would disappear. A related finding was that 10 of the males and 3 of the females had previously been through chemical-dependency treatment programs.

Child Abuse History

The child-abuse background was interesting. Clinical history produced a history of child abuse in 7 of the 14 girls, and 8 of the 30 boys. Caution is needed in interpreting these types of histories. First, sexual abuse must be distinguished from physical abuse. For the latter, gradations of physical discipline that were used can confuse the issue further. There is always a question about the validity of a history of child abuse, given its current popularity as an explanation for diverse types of psychopathological development. The elusiveness of what is to be included as child abuse raises difficult legal questions when the juvenile has not admitted such a history before the current legal charges. Hence, if these reports of abuse were antecedent to the current episode of violence, the abuse was counted as a positive inclusion. A girl who simply reported that her stepfather had made unsuccessful sexual advances to her that were rebuffed was not included. Conflicts of a covert, neurotic nature involving power struggles and accusations in a family, without confirmation, were not included. Only a full picture of repeated, physically assaultive acts by a parental figure, or overt sexually coerced behavior, were included. A history of being slapped or the use of physical discipline per se by the parents was not viewed as sufficient to establish child abuse by these strict criteria.

Four girls reported sexual abuse involving three stepfathers, one stepbrother, and grandfather (one girl was involved with two of her relatives). Five girls reported a pattern of regular physical beatings by their mothers or fathers when younger (including two who also reported sexual abuse). The pattern in the eight boys was that of repeated strappings or beatings when younger by one or both of their parents. The history of child abuse related to delinquent, and even violent, behavior has begun to receive increased attention (Hunner & Walker, 1981). How much significance should be attached to this background variable in a group who later emerged with overt conduct disturbance of a violent type and who were also depressed? This leads to a broader question regarding what the incidences of different types of child abuse would be in different delinquent juvenile populations. Careful assessment would be required to determine whether the incidence of abuse would be significantly different from other delinquent samples of different types of major and minor antisocial behaviors. What is encompassed under behaviors called "abuse" needs careful definition, as does the frequency and the impact on specific areas of development (Finkelhor, 1986). If the abuse is carefully documented, it may be related to the hostility, anger, and irritability seen as part of the clinical picture.

Discussion

What does such a complex clinical picture of one subtype of a group of violent adolescents signify? One is the difficulty in discriminating diagnostic subtleties through the diverse community and legal contacts of assistance and intervention to which these delinquents were exposed. There is also the possibility that the adolescents may not have been depressed when seen earlier in their communities and had only become so after the event. Such a hypothesis would be in the direction of changing diagnoses over time, or the existence of disparate diagnoses. While the latter is a possibility, it is contradicted by the overlap in time of the symptom picture presented by these juveniles. The problems that Meehl (1954; Meehl & Rosen, 1955) pointed out some time ago in his classic regarding difficulties in prediction of rare events has applicability for the difficulties in being sensitive to the occurrence of extreme violence in adolescence.

A suggestive question arises about whether the group of depressed adolescents might fulfill the criteria for a Depressive Spectrum Disease entity as originally proposed by Winokur (1979) in his work with adults. In this framework, the patients are those who are depressed, and it is their first-degree family members who have had problems with alcoholism and/or Antisocial Personalities. The relatives meet the spectrum criteria whereas the patient is depressed. Yet, in the current study the adolescents presented with clinical pictures over time which are suggestive that they should not be ruled out as depressives. The sample juvenile group, eventually diagnosed as depressed, was selected from a far larger group who had all exhibited antisocial behavior of a serious type. Is the group of depressed adolescents, in fact, the offspring of parents who fulfill the criteria of first-degree relatives either with Antisocial Personalities or alcoholic problems, but in addition do the adolescents themselves manifest antisocial behavior along with their depression?

To further examine this hypothesis, inquiry was made about the relatives. The results are shown in Table 4. The criteria used were stringent since the data on relatives were obtained directly from the juvenile subjects themselves and from their court files which often contained data on the parents. In all cases the family history was supplemented by outside information from at least one parental person in accord with a family history approach to diagnosis (Andreasen, Rice, Endicott, Reich, & Coryell, 1986). When the cases of alcoholism or antisocial personality were only suggestive in family members, they were not included as positives. The result became a minimally positive detectable group; if the findings were then positive in this restricted group, greater significance would prevail.

A higher degree of validity was attained in obtaining a history of alcoholism than with Antisocial Personality. To attain a high degree of validity for a diagnosis of Antisocial Personality in family members, prominent symptoms and signs over a period of time were required; if not, the family members were excluded. If a history of alcoholism in terms of a family member receiving treatment for a drinking problem and/or a history of overt bouts of intoxication was obtained from the adolescent along with outside documentation, the diagnosis in a family member was confirmed.

One finding was the degree of confirmation with respect to family alcoholism for the 14 females. Seven of the fathers, four of the mothers, and two brothers

Table 4. Comparison of Alcoholism and Antisocial Personality in
First-Degree Relatives of Depressed Delinquents

Family Member	Male (N = 30)			Female (N = 14)		
	Depression	Antisocial Personality	Alcoholism	Depression	Antisocial Personality	Alcoholism
Father	4	12^a	6^b	0	4^a	7^b
Mother	1	3^a	2^b	3^c	0^a	4^b
Brothers	1	1	2	1	0	2
Sisters	1	0	0	0	1	2

^{a}p<.05 in comparing both parents of boys and girls.
^{b}p<.001 in comparing both parents of boys and girls.
^{c}p<.05 in comparing mothers with depression for boys and girls.

and sisters had a history of alcoholism. Hence, 15 first-degree relatives had problems with alcoholism in a cohort of 14 depressed adolescent females who had participated in violent, antisocial behavior to a degree sufficient to raise the issue of their being certified for trial in adult criminal court. In addition, four of their fathers appeared to qualify for a diagnosis of Antisocial Personality. Note should be taken of the fact that none of the subjects was yet beyond the age of 18. In time, further diagnoses of alcoholism or Antisocial Personalities would be likely to occur in other family members. The overlap of these diagnoses in first-degree relatives and the pattern of child abuse correlated for the biological fathers and stepfathers as well. These findings are impressive given the small sample size, but it should be recalled that the 44 subjects (20%) came from a larger sample of 213 considered for special legal processing. The sample was too small to base any definitive conclusions on the question of some variation of Depressive Spectrum Disease, but it remains suggestive.

Significance was also found when the boys and girls were compared. When Antisocial Personality in both parents was considered, it attained significance with half of the boys coming from such families (p<.05). For alcoholism in both parents, 26% of the boys, but 79% of the girls (p<.001) had such a finding—a striking finding in the opposite direction. There is also significance (p<.05) if the girl, in contrast to a boy, had a depressed mother.

Critical questions can be raised beyond the suggestiveness possible from a small sample. For example, is the incidence of alcoholism in the first-degree relatives of the girls, despite using stringent criteria, no different from what might be found in a general population of delinquent adolescent girls? Any possible answer is complex. First, this study did not simply compare a group of girls involved in serious violence to some type of control group, such as that of female status offenders. Comparability would also require both groups of females to be diagnosed as depressed. Although it is difficult to obtain valid data on the incidence of depression in relatives, data are beginning to emerge for specific subtypes with large samples of adults (Weissman et al., 1984). What did seem apparent in the current study is that depression was underdiagnosed in a subgroup of delinquents who had committed violent acts.

If we keep these caveats in mind, we can offer some hypotheses with respect to alcoholism in families that have a depressed adolescent who has committed an act of serious violence. We would be seeking to distinguish the differential pattern of alcohol use in the families of two female adolescent delinquent groups— one depressed and the other not. Our theory would postulate parental alcoholism as an accompaniment of a pattern of violence deviation in the adolescents. This would be congruent with a social learning theory of modeling that would encompass observing and internalizing parental behavior conducive to a potential for violence as well as the diverse factors contributing to depression. A combination of alcoholism and depression in parents, in comparison to groups of offspring whose parents were either rated as "normal" or "nonalcoholic depressed," found a higher incidence of conduct disorder and deviant drinking behavior (Merikangas et al., 1985). This does not resolve the problem of primacy, but would argue for a loading effect.

The methodological problem of evaluation is similar to assessing the incidence of alcoholism in families where child abuse has occurred. The difficulties in determining whether abuse is present have been noted. Similar problems attend efforts to determine alcoholism in families with violent adolescents, given the enormous variety of delinquent behavior. Many studies do not define how they are using alcoholism—be it by such qualitative judgments as drinking to excess, "out of control" drinking, a reported number of incidents, or only when social or legal problems arise. Given such problems, it is not surprising that in families of abused children there are inconsistent findings regarding the prevalence of alcohol problems. Despite the small sample used in this study, it is difficult to ignore the findings on alcoholism in the parents of the depressed girls and Antisocial Personalities in the parents of the depressed boys.

What creates difficulties in assessing such empirical variables in a group of depressed adolescents who have committed such acts of violence are the endless number of factors that may be relevant. Even in a descriptive diagnostic sense, as noted above, the nosology for an adolescent group has low validity owing to the overlap of several diagnostic categories. Beyond this problem, there is the difficulty with a seemingly endless list of developmental and environmental variables that can affect a child and take an eventual toll in the course of adolescence. In considering the variable of parental alcoholism, its significance might lie in: prenatal exposure to excess maternal alcohol consumption, the age at which the effects of the parents' alcoholism became manifest to the child, how severe or persistent it was over the years, whether there was any treatment or hospitalization of the parents, family reactions to the problems that emerged, assessment of the efficacy of diverse treatment modalities that were tried, etc. Any one of these variables could account for differences not owing just to the alcoholism. A similar set of strictures could be given for assessing the significance of Antisocial Personality in a family member. There is also the pervasive problem of diverse outcomes being possible for any given adolescent, even though a similar set of environmental antecedents is documented.

There is also overlap between symptom patterns of hyperactivity and conduct disorder that complicates assessment of the impact of parental alcoholism. Results are often confused in assessing the significance of symptoms of agitation or hyperactivity from that of aggressive behavior (West & Prinz, 1987). There is also the problem of attributing emerging delinquent behavior in adolescents to having an alcoholic parent when they are studied in a juvenile court population (Offer et al., 1978). Yet, when a comparison was made, using families with nondelinquent sons, parental alcoholism did not increase the risk for delinquency beyond what could be attributed to the presence of divorce. Similar caution emerges from a long-range study over 20 years of children from lower-class families with diverse problems ranging from being on welfare, mental illness in the family, to criminal behavior (Miller & Jung, 1977). Among the results, parental alcoholism was only one stressor present. Others were living on welfare, divorce being twice as prevalent as with children of nonalcoholics, and almost the same differential for parental arrest, imprisonment, absence, or hospitalization. The complexity of interacting variables in such a milieu is more often the normative pattern for these adolescents, which means that causal attribution to alcoholism or psychopathy, or any one variable, is not satisfactory. Nor can we ignore the impact of possible genetic predispositions toward alcoholism or psychopathy, although it would appear that diverse family environmental factors are crucial in eliciting such behavior. Perhaps what is most significant is that something happens to disrupt the family interaction and equilibrium toward childhood psychopathological development. Yet, this pushes the question back to what does have such a critical impact—mental disorder, disrupted family values, inadequate guidance and nurturance, modeling of maladaptive coping styles, etc.?

Psychodynamic Hypotheses

At such a junction, one shifts from analysis of environmental variables to developmental psychopathology and dynamic factors. Here is where someone such as

Paul Meehl has been among the small number of people who can be not only a hard-nosed empiricist, but also someone open to hypotheses involving dynamic factors within the individual case, and without feeling that one approach need be neglected in favor of another.

Let us take a brief incursion into the world of some of these depressed adolescents who have exhibited homicidal behavior to see what else may be found. Apart from questions of legal responsibility, or whether the legal system should handle these adolescents in a juvenile court setting versus an adult court, there are some striking clinical impressions. If we move beyond a symptom level, we find that developmental processes seem to have gone awry. This is not stated simply because we know that something in the nature of extreme violence has occurred, but, rather, because the defenses these adolescents have been employing up to that point had not been functioning effectively. The emotions and impulses that were supposed to be contained from the defenses have not been. Some of the antecedent states these adolescents were in raise questions about why many other adolescents have not also committed violent acts, although they may go on to other areas of psychopathological development. Hence, although we would argue it is not "normal" for an adolescent to kill someone, in the sense of the defenses against such a degree of aggression usually working better than that, questions are left about what significance to attribute to adolescents who verbalize to friends that they are not only depressed at times but also thinking of killing. If a view is taken that depression is often part of the developmental flux of adolescence (and, perhaps, of human existence), at what point should such cognitions be seen as signs of a major mental disorder? How do we assess whether their defenses will be able to contain the aggression? While some of these later-to-be homicidal adolescents had been suicidal, does that, in itself, indicate a threshold had been crossed? Overt signs of behavioral disturbance might have been treated by psychopharmacological approaches, or by a brief incapacitation if the behaviors seemed sufficiently threatening to society, yet these approaches did not get to the antecedent line of development that had emerged. At least for this group, in retrospect, the idea that dealing with a current crisis was all that was needed was insufficient. The problem of predicting which "solution" the adolescent might use on any given occasion, and which would require more intensive intervention, looms throughout a retrospective examination of these cases.

Certain developmental themes emerge on examining the material. Some of the males, while externally trying to play the "macho" role, were, in fact, blocked in terms of their capacity for any extended gratification which involved comfortable intimate or close relationships. The image the male had of himself was often at variance with how others saw him. One distortion was the dependency on parental figures which they denied and disavowed. At the same time, they tried to identify with aspects of parental figures, but it might be with an aspect that infelicitously raised their anxiety. For example, a boy with difficulties in feeling comfortable with himself as a post-pubertal male selectively identified with his father's aloofness and abstractedness. In turn, this left the boy even more uncomfortable with his own groping for closeness to those outside his family, and angry at his family whose distancing devices left him feeling helpless to move off this conflicted state.

Prominence of denial loomed as one of the most ominous signs. The need not to experience anxiety to a degree that banished it from conscious awareness, was gained at the expense of agitated states, a need to seek physical flight, to escape through drugs or alcohol, or to have periods of gross inhibition and inactivity. They might also deny the degree of their anger or agitation, and finally of depression itself. When in a withdrawn state, events that would ordinarily have elicited an emotional response did not, indicating a progressive withdrawal into their inner world. In some cases, a valiant effort at forced gaiety, or entertaining others, provided the hope of avoiding their own despair.

Viewed over a period of a few years, cycles of such behavioral patterns become more apparent, and can be seen from different perspectives. They do not change much even though adverse consequences have often ensued, and they are frequently coupled with a denial of their own subtle contribution to misery. The misery could take many forms — sometimes overt, and other times more subtle, such as damaging their reputations, low self-esteem, or limiting future options in their lives (such as existed when they were detained in institutions).

While guilt operated in these adolescents, it was often attributed to some overt misdeed. It was rarely connected with their provocative actions that led to a cycle of attack and retaliation. In some cases, the cycle could get out of hand and lead to violence. One perspective could see their capitulation in a final act of violence, such as a group assault on a victim, as a final act of despair — that they would never attain what they needed to relieve their depressed state. Hence a frequent term used to describe these adolescents was "callous" because of their not seeming upset after committing a homicide. This was especially so when they communicated in the course of an evaluation that they felt better than they had before the homicide. The dynamics of relief related to a violent act, which temporarily displaced the depression, was usually missed.

Another model was the peace experienced after "giving up." The giving up by participating in an act of violence meant that the severe demands laid on themselves to measure up to exaggerated expectations through an inflated ego-ideal would now be bypassed. Such giving up seemed incongruous to those involved in evaluating these cases, let alone the public. That an adolescent would feel the event was over, and that it should be put behind them, so their desire to get on with their lives could take place, often evoked strong countertransference feelings. Minimal insight existed as to the unreality of their desire to have the event simply put aside or forgotten. Since their depression was often temporarily alleviated, however, their perception was that there was no need to dwell on the past. As one of them stated, "What's done is done. Let's get on with life."

While in some cases excessive physical punishment had taken place to the point of what could be labeled physical abuse, in a number of cases an opposite phenomenon was observed. These were cases where the youth described being in a state of morbid physical fear of a parental figure, yet, even by their own description, no beatings had occurred. One boy, later charged with murdering several members of his family, made recurrent statements involving his past fears of his father beating him. Not until a detailed psychiatric inquiry was made did it become clear that no such beatings had ever occurred. A similar distortion occurred involving a girl regarding an alleged sexual abuse. Inquiry regarding episodes she described revealed them to have occurred ten years earlier when she was age five, and which involved her getting into bed to cuddle between her parents and remembering it as arousing.

Yet, in these cases the descriptions were not conscious dissimulations, since the patients did not lie about the events. Rather, they were asserted as if such factual events might occur, even though they had not. In some cases, these appeared to be an exaggeration of hysterical trends to portray themselves as victimized, related to repressed components in their personalities. In others, it was related to their anger at realizing how dependent they were, with the accompanying hatred to which this gave rise. The anger was then projected onto parental figures who were seen as persecutors. A third possibility seen was an occasion which arose that triggered homicidal aggression. It was the manifestation of a type of conflict that had commenced with the onset of puberty in which different types of integrations and object choices were necessary but not accomplished. The naïve quality in some of these exaggerations, often at a time when there was a flight into involvement with a peer group, suggests a struggle about autonomy. Yet, at the same time, an adult would be blamed for their states of anxiety and depression. Retrospective evaluation indicated activated sado-masochistic trends.

What seemed clear in these cases was that victims of the homicide were often coincidental victims—being on the receiving end for displaced and projected aggression. The victims were those who happened to be available on the right occasion or the right time. Even if the victims were known to the perpetrator, they were often on the receiving end because of a distorted process of thinking and defensive failure. Questions can be raised about the dynamics of youths who, in circumstances less favorable, did not succumb to a homicide, yet their vulnerabilities were similar.

There is also a need to consider the significance when a depressed adolescent begins to entertain ideas about the possibility of committing a homicide. This is usually not equivalent to tendencies toward general types of aggressive behavior such as committing a robbery, high-risk ventures such as muggings, or addictive drug use, all of which can inadvertently lead to homicide. In some cases, these activities result in homicide. In one of the not atypical cases, a smaller boy was being baited by a physically stronger boy which led to a confrontation in a parking lot. At one point, the stronger boy was pulling the smaller one by his hair to a place where the stronger boy wanted to continue to beat the smaller one. A knife was pulled, and a single stab wound to the heart by the smaller boy ended the fight. In another case, a youth, while drinking quite heavily, became aware of a desire to fight someone. He went to bars looking for an opponent. The victim selected was someone more intoxicated than he, and, after one blow, the actual fight was over. However, the youth became aware of an urge to keep beating the unconscious victim and proceeded to do so, including jumping on his head. Neither of these cases started with a conscious wish to perpetrate a homicide, although presumably the second case became so after the fight began.

What about the depressed adolescent who becomes aware of a conscious desire to kill someone? A question about the impairment of the ability to perceive reality and react correctly to it is relevant. This need not be to the degree of psychotic thinking in the sense of a delusional system whereby a supposed persecutor must be eliminated, but it could signify a distortion in his thinking to a degree that an assessment of the need for the act, its meaning, and its consequences have not been appreciated. The possibility of their own destruction or death is not entertained.

When the depressed adolescent is entertaining cognitive solutions of homicide, many background factors may overlap with those of suicide. A direct similarity is their belief system that the state of despair they are in will continue without relief. A corollary belief is that the act of homicide will relieve their anxiety and tension. Some type of precipitating event, representing a failure, with a resultant loss of self-esteem can often be identified. This stressor has been identified as particularly potent for suicides in substance abusers (Rich, Fowler, Fogarty, & Young, 1988). It would also appear to operate in depressed, homicidal adolescents.

An adolescent girl who had run away from home several times, and then prostituted, only to return home to a strict mother who emphasized sin and guilt in a religious context, made another attempt at leaving. A decision was made to return home again, but, shortly before doing so, she joined a pimp and another girl who had set out to "punish" a girl who had left. While the pimp and the other girl held the victim, she slit the victim's throat. There was then no need to return home, or to stay in the life she had been leading, for her fate was in the hands of others. Just as in a suicide, the depressed adolescent feels trapped in a conflict they cannot extricate themselves from by a decision-making act of their own. The adolescent female had fought against dependence on her mother, but could not deal with the hostility that accompanied such dependency. She was able to recall fears of losing control and killing her mother before she participated in the homicide of her peer. In many of these cases, the transformation of a feeling state of helpless passivity into one of taking charge of themselves was retrospectively clear.

A variation on this theme is the *Götterdämmerung* finale. It is a final conviction that nothing matters. Just as in a suicide when the ideation takes a turn into a belief that the world would be better off without them, in the homicidal state it is a final fatality — that nothing has gone right and the time has come to externalize the hopelessness within them. There is a blocking out in this type of thinking, as an accompaniment, that misery and suffering will result for many from their act, and, hence, their correlative lack of guilt. At that point, even before the act has occurred, it is a theoretical question who is to die, or has already been killed since a decision has been made. A sense of relief or calmness may take over, given that the act is now viewed as inevitable. Within this thinking, a homicide-suicide attempt may occur. A variation is the breakthrough of anxiety that can result from the realization that they are going to commit a killing, which leads to a suicide attempt.

In those adolescents whose homicide attempts have been aborted, or called off, there may be an attempt to minimize their thinking. It may be laughed off as "just a joke." This is an area requiring astute clinical judgment since, at the time of revealing these past thoughts, the homicidal impulse may be transiently gone. Yet, lurking is the sense of control they have from being able to reinstate it. The control is that they can always put the plan into action if need be, and, hence, from the power they have, they need not view their future as being as bleak as they thought it in the past. Unfortunately, their sense of comfort is based on their power to effect a homicide when needed, and is hardly a resolution of their conflicted state. The difficulty, unless the clinician can tap into these fantasies, is that they may look quite intact externally and may "talk a good game."

The practical problems that emerge when the clinician becomes privy to these thought processes are enormous, especially in obtaining the treatment such adolescents need. Their fear of involvement in another relationship that may make them dependent, which is what they see themselves as conquering, provides a tenuous basis for maintaining a treatment relationship. It is easier to see others as the source of their difficulties; this carries the risk of homicidal acts. While not going into therapeutic efforts in this chapter, it can be pointed out that one of the primary goals in treatment with this group is to allow them to appreciate cognitively ways to gain control, other than through the specious and grandiose ways in which they have been operating. The need to regress and test out whether they are still in control always looms. The pressure from many sources will, unfortunately, be to bypass or ignore these more subtle aspects of their personalities which contribute to homicide, leading to the conviction that homicide or suicide is the answer. The adolescent, and many involved in the situation, will push to forget the past or minimize it. When the efforts are meant to persuade the clinician that the homicidal thoughts were just a one-time aberration, and are "out of their system," we can be assured that many sources are collaborating with the adolescent to banish the disharmony, with hopes of keeping the repressed repressed.

References

Achenbach, T. M., & Edelbrook, C. S. (1984). Psychopathology of childhood. In M. R. Rosenzweig & L. W. Porter (Eds.), *Annual review of psychology* (pp. 227–256). Palo Alto: Annual Reviews, Inc.

Akiskal, H. S., Djendered-jaan, A. H., Rosenthal, R. H., et al. (1977). Cyclothymic disorder: Validating criteria for inclusion in the bipolar affective group. *American Journal of Psychiatry, 134,* 1227–1233.

Akiskal, H. S., Hirschfeld, R. M. A., Yerevanian, B. I. (1983). The relationship of personality to affective disorders; A critical review. *Archives of General Psychiatry, 40,* 801–809.

Akiskal, H. S., Rosenthal, T. L., Haykal, et al. (1980). Characterological depressions. *Archives of General Psychiatry, 37,* 777–783.

Alessi, N. E., McManus, M., Grapentine, W. I., & Brickman, A. (1984). The characteristics of depressive disorders in serious juvenile offenders. *Journal of Affective Disorders, 6,* 9–17.

American Psychiatric Association. (1987). *Diagnostic and statistical manual of mental disorders* (3rd ed., rev.). Washington, DC: Author.

Andreasen, N. C., Rice, J., Endicott, J., Reich, T., Coryell, W. (1986). The family history approach to diagnosis. *Archives of General Psychiatry, 43,* 421–429.

Beck, A. T. (1972). *Depression: Causes and treatment.* Philadelphia: University of Pennsylvania Press.

Chiles, J. A., Miller, M. L., & Cox, G. B. (1980). Depression in an adolescent delinquent population. *Archives of General Psychiatry, 37,* 1179–1184.

Cornell, D. G., Benedek, E. P., & Benedek, D. M. (1987). Characteristics of adolescents charged with homicide: Review of 72 cases. *Behavioral Sciences and the Law, 5,* 11–23.

Feigner, J. P., Robins, E., Guze, S. B., Woodruff, R. A., Winokur, G., & Munoz, R. (1984). Diagnostic criteria for use in psychiatric research. *Archives of General Psychiatry, 138,* 1–13.

Finkelhor, D. (1986). *A sourcebook on child sexual abuse.* Beverly Hills: Sage Publications.

Frank, E., Kupfer, D. J., Jacob, M., & Jarret, M. (1987). Personality features and response to acute treatment in recurrent depression. *Journal of Personality Disorders, 1,* 14–26.

Fyer, M. R., Frances, A. J., Sullivan, T., Hurt, S. W., & Clarkin, J. (1988). Comorbidity of borderline personality disorder. *Archives of General Psychiatry, 45,* 348–352.

Hinshaw, S. P. (1987). On the distinction between attentional deficits/hyperactivity and conduct problems/aggression in child psychopathology. *Psychological Bulletin, 101,* 443–463.

Hunner, R. T., & Walker, Y. E. (Eds.). (1981). *Exploring the relationship between child abuse and delinquency.* Monclair, NJ: Allanheld, Osmun.

Kandel, D. B., & Davies, J. (1982). Epidemiology of depressive mood in adolescents. *Archives of General Psychiatry, 39,* 1205–1212.

Kashani, J., Manning, G. W., McKnew, D. H., Cytryn, L., Simonds, J., & Wooderson, P. (1980). Depression among incarcerated delinquents. *Psychiatric Research, 3,* 185–191.

Lewis, D. O., Pincas, J. H., Bard, B., Richardson, E., Prichep, T. S., Feldman, M., & Yeager, C. (1988). Neuropsychiatric, psychoeducational, and family characteristics of 14 juveniles condemned to death in the United States. *American Journal of Psychiatry, 145,* 584–589.

Lewis, D. O., Shanok, S. S., Balla, D. A., & Bard, B. (1980). Psychiatric correlates of severe reading disabilities in an incarcerated delinquent population. *Journal of American Academy of Child Psychiatry, 20*, 611–622.

Malmquist, C. P. (1979). Juveniles in adult courts: Unresolved ambivalence. *Adolescent Psychiatry, 7*, 444–456.

Marriage, K., Fine, S., Moretti, M., & Halog, C. (1986). Relationship between depression and conduct disorder in children and adolescents. *Journal of the American Academy of Child Psychiatry, 25*, 687–691.

Meehl, P. E. (1954). *Clinical vs. statistical prediction*. Minneapolis: University of Minnesota Press.

Meehl, P. E., & Rosen, A. (1955). Antecedent probability and the efficiency of psychometric signs, patterns, and cutting scores. *Psychological Bulletin, 52*, 194–216.

Merikangas, K., Weissman, M., Prusoff, B., Pauls, D., & Leckman, J. (1985). Depressions of secondary alcoholism: Psychiatric disorders in offspring. *Journal of Studies on Alcohol, 46*, 199–204.

Miller, D., & Jung, M. (1977). Children of alcoholics: A 20-year longitudinal study. *Social Work Research and Abstracts, 13*, 23–29.

Nelson, J. D., & Charney, D. S. (1981). The symptoms of major depressive illness. *American Journal of Psychiatry, 138*, 1–13.

Offer, D., Allen, N., & Abrams, N. (1978). Parental psychiatric illness, broken homes, and delinquency. *Journal of the American Academy of Child Psychiatry, 17*, 224–238.

Offer, D., Marohn, R. D., & Ostrov, E. (1979). *The psychological world of the juvenile delinquent*. New York: Basic Books.

Pies, R. (1988). Atypical depression. In J. P. Tupin, R. I. Shador, & D. S. Harnett (Eds.), *Clinical handbook of psychopharmacology*. 2nd ed. Northvale, NJ: Jason Aronson.

Pilkonis, S., Pilkonis, P. A., & Frank, E. (1988). Personality pathology in recurrent depression: Nature, prevalence, and relationship to treatment response. *American Journal of Psychiatry, 145*, 435–441.

Rich, C. J., Fowler, R. C., Fogarty, T. A., & Young, D. (1988). San Diego suicide study (III). Relationship between diagnoses and stressors. *Archives of General Psychiatry, 45*, 589–592.

Sendi, I. B., & Blomgren, P. G. (1975). A comparative study of productive criteria in the predisposition of homicidal adolescents. *American Journal of Psychiatry, 132*, 423–428.

Solway, K. S., Richardson, L., Hays, J. R., & Elion, V. H. (1981). Adolescent murderers: Literature review and preliminary research findings. In J. R. Hays, T. K. Roberts, & K. S. Solway (Eds.), *Violence and the violent individual*. New York: SP Medical and Scientific Books.

Spitzer, R. L., Endicott, J., & Robins, E. (1978). Research diagnostic criteria: Rationale and reliability. *Archives of General Psychiatry, 34*, 136–141.

Weissman, M. M., Gershon, E. S., Kidd, K. K., Prusoff, B. A., Leckman, J. F., Dibble, E., Hamouit, J., Thompson, W. D., & Pauls, D. L. (1984). Psychiatric disorders in the relations of probands with affective disorders. *Archives of General Psychiatry, 41*, 13–21.

Weissman, M. M., & Klerman, G. L. (1977). Sex differences and the epidemiology of depression. *Archives of General Psychiatry, 34*, 98–111.

West, O. W., & Prinz, R. J. (1987). Parental alcoholism and childhood psychopathology. *Psychological Bulletin, 102*, 204–218.

Winokur, G. (1979). Unipolar depression: Is it divisible into autonomous subtypes? *Archives of General Psychiatry, 36*, 47–50.

Environment, Schizophrenia, and Academic Psychology

Leonard L. Heston

Behavioral science cannot specify an environmental contributor to the etiology of major psychopathological disorders excepting only drug-associated states such as alcoholism. Although studies of monozygotic twins regularly discover phenotypic discordances that must be associated with environmental differences, those professionally concerned with behavior have no bases upon which to predict the results of given environments. No one could design an environment that would predictably produce or prevent, as examples, schizophrenia or bipolar illness or obsessional illness. A major test of credibility as a science is thereby failed.

This failure is becoming increasingly visible and important because molecular genetics has been making slow but steady progress in the definition of the molecular basis of memory, and rapid, dramatic progress in elucidating cellular mechanisms which promise to give terms such as "stress" specific physical dimensions. Lack of a rudimentary grasp of environment prevents exploiting these advances made by sister sciences. The further implications of this evolving situation for behavioral science, academic psychology in particular, will be explored in this paper.

The Argument

It now seems hard to believe, but only a few decades ago, most behavioral scientists held that schizophrenia was produced by faulty environment. The "schizophrenogenic mother" and the "double bind" were regarded seriously as bases for etiologic theories. Paul Meehl was then a voice in the wilderness. A famous question that he posed at oral examinations to the intense disquiet of doctoral candidates is worth recalling. "How would you choose a person with the highest probability of developing schizophrenia?" The answer was not "find a child of a schizophrenogenic mother"; it was "find the monozygotic (MZ) co-twin of a schizophrenic.'' Right on, Paul. Of course the logic of that view has since carried the day. One would have to search hard to find a serious student of schizophrenia who would not acknowledge a necessary genetic contribution to the disease.

At the same time, evidence makes it clear that environment has a co-equal etiologic role. Paul's question only maximized the probability of finding an incipient schizophrenic. Not all MZ co-twins of schizophrenics will themselves become schizophrenic. Far from it. About half such twins do not develop schizophrenia, and even though entities such as ''schizoid'' or ''spectrum'' or ''schizotype'' make possible quibbles about the expression of the genotype associated with schizophrenia, there are unquestionably phenotypic nonschizophrenics among MZ co-twins of schizophrenics. Moreover, it is known that children of these phenotypically nonschizophrenic co-twins are as much at risk for schizophrenia as children of schizophrenics generally (Fischer, 1971). It has been demonstrated, then, that carrying DNA compatible with schizophrenia does not compel development of the disease. Events occurring after conception can effect profound modifications in the expression of schizophrenic genotypes, even suppress them entirely. One class of post-conceptual events consists of genetic imprinting or gene inactivation which appear to be stochastic in nature. Luck is an underestimated contributor to outcome. The other class of events is environment. Genes respond to moment-to-moment environmental challenges throughout life. That interaction is the very basis of adaptation, and failure to adapt is a hallmark of disease.

That much has long been known and, indeed, is an implicit expression of psychopathology's basic etiologic theory, formally stated as ''gene-environment interaction.'' A wonderful phrase. Elegantly simple, yet with overtones of enlightened humanism. Moreover, it works perfectly well so long as both ''gene'' and ''environment'' remain abstractions. It encourages research publications based on partitioning variance in ingenious ways, which is good clean fun and which leads to academic advancement. All this will remain true as long as no one can specify exactly what is meant by ''gene'' or ''environment'' much less the mechanics of their interaction. But because ''gene'' is being specifically defined, I shall argue that those happy days of unbridled naïveté are behind us.

Progress in molecular genetics is rapidly undermining ''gene-environment interaction.'' ''Gene'' is no longer an abstraction, but, rather, is becoming a palpable structure with knowable physical and chemical properties. The detailed structure of several human genes is known today, and that structure implies the mechanics of their regulation. Gene regulation, in turn, is the very basis for interaction with environment.

No doubt knowledge of the detailed structure of the human genome will continue to accumulate. In the foreseeable future, the entire genome will be mapped, first by large DNA sequences defined by their length, ''fragment length polymorphisms''; then, starting with sequences thought critical for one reason or another, nucleotide by nucleotide. Already DNA sequences associated with psychopathology have been tentatively assigned to specific areas of specific chromosomes: Alzheimer's disease to chromosome 21 (St. George-Hyslop, 1987); variants of bipolar illness to 11 and the X chromosome respectively (Egeland, 1987; Gershon 1988); Huntington's disease to 4 (Gilliam, 1987); Prader-Willi to 15; and, it now seems likely, schizophrenia to 5 (Ledbetter, 1982). We are now very early in the mapping process, and some of these results will doubtless not be confirmed. But that is not important. The basic technology now in place makes certain that DNA segments associated with disease will be identified. The number of markers precisely mapped to human chromosomes has been increasing at 200% per year compounded since 1977, the year the application of fragment length polymorphisms to mapping began. It is evident that those concerned with schizophrenia must anticipate and prepare for a time when the composition of the DNA of subgroups of schizophrenics will become known exactly and can be directly compared to that of nonschizophrenics.

Because developments such as these in molecular genetics may connote magical powers to nonbiologists, a pause is now needed to provide perspective. The accomplishments have been immense, the prospects awesome. Yet the actual mapping of DNA relevant to psychopathology done thus far is very crude. The DNA sequences linked to psychopathology are on the order of 300 to 400 kilobases in length, while DNA sequences associated with a single protein product are generally on the order of 2 to 4 kilobases. A lot of slogging work remains before mapping gets down to that scale, and only then will it be possible to isolate and precisely characterize chemically the relevant DNA sequences. Even then there will remain many intermediate steps between DNA and pathological behavior which must be understood. DNA studied in isolation will probably not tell us much because in vivo its product will certainly function as one component of a system. Before therapeutic approaches can be devised which may lead to engineering paths bypassing or neutralizing the defective DNA and its product, it will be necessary to comprehend the system. Behavioral science may yet have time to prepare.

Preparation is needed, I believe, because progress in molecular genetics implies responsibilities for behavioral science which our scientific peers have started reminding us about with increasing stridency and which, if not discharged, may well expose us to society's fully warranted revenge. Research has convinced not only behavioral scientists, but also other scientists, patients, their families, and society at large that genes contribute importantly to diseases such as schizophrenia. Yet what would we do with the test tubes containing mutant and normal DNA that cell biologists will one day present to us? Today, nothing. We could not devise logical experiments which, starting from the problematic DNA, would set us on a trail ending with discovering how the aberrant product contributed to schizophrenia. I shall argue that this is largely because we would know nothing about the environment in which the DNA and its product operated.

Let me more concretely define the problem as I think it will increasingly be seen as advances in molecular biology make present formulations of psychopathology ever more irrelevant. Environment has always been claimed as psychology's domain, the subject of its special expertise. But psychology cannot now define environmental factors causal in schizophrenia and, moreover, has no methods available to even approach the job. To illustrate this, let us suppose as a result of prenatal diagnosis, a capacity realizable when the problematic DNA is characterized, we are told that a newborn infant has DNA sequences necessary to develop schizophrenia. Even given this information, there would be no rational basis for predicting the phenotypic outcome. Psychology could neither specify an environment that would predictably produce schizophrenia nor one that would prevent it. There is not even evidence upon which to base plausible guesses. We would have to confess to the parents and to the world at large that any interventions we might devise would be at least as likely to harm as to help. A basic test of science, the ability to predict, would thereby have failed. Further, let us suppose our infant has an identical twin so that there is a potential control for environment. There would be no rational basis for selecting variables to measure in a prospective study of such newborns; virtually every event would have to be recorded in any serious effort to discover disease-producing environments on the known schizophrenic genotypes. And if such an effort were mounted, would anyone be foolish enough to bet that a meaningful result would be obtained?

Given such a challenge or one analogous to it, the disciplines concerned with psychopathology simply could not respond. The public position would be this: psychopathologists proved decades earlier to nearly everyone's satisfaction that DNA is a necessary contributor to schizophrenia but, equally, that post-conceptual events can greatly modify the expression of the DNA, and hence outcome. Then the problematic DNA is received nicely gift-wrapped. Now behavioral science finds that there is no way to take the next steps toward discovering the mechanisms underlying the terrible disease for which it long ago accepted scientific responsibility because doing that would require experiments exploring in concrete detail the mechanisms tying defective DNA to defective behavior. I think this failure will rightly be laid at the door of those branches of psychology that focus on psychopathology. I say this as a friend of psychology, I hope as a constructive critic, and especially as a clinician who needs psychology as an essential ally in his professional life.

What has gone wrong? Not lack of effort or money. I am sure that more energy and resources have been expended on the study of environment with respect to schizophrenia than on any other disease. The problem seems much more profound. At its root is a simple relationship. DNA is a chemical and it interacts with other chemicals, not with abstractions such as "stress" that characterize current formulations of psychopathology. In turn, this overabstraction originates, I think, with epistemological underpinnings, with the "black box" theory of brain. It is now evident that knowing input and output does not permit understanding of brain because as a living tissue, brain changes. It cannot be understood as a black box. But eliminating black box terms such as "reinforcement history" that sneak black box concepts into everyday thought has proven extremely difficult and is far from complete. Yet if we are seriously to explore the interaction of environment with DNA, we must eschew such black box terms and concepts as dimensionless, unmeasurable, and unusably vague. The test of environmental research must become "does the result define an environmental variable as a chemical capable of interacting with DNA?"

A related black box mind-set that may get in the way of productive study of environment warrants brief exposition. I know of no example of gene-environment interaction becoming phenotypically manifest after the long delays often postulated by those interested in psychopathology. Phenotypic effects of an environment are usually apparent a short time after exposure to it. There are possible exceptions. Cancer, as a phenotypic effect of smoking which develops after considerable time has passed, may be associated with a class of genes (the P-450 group). Some immune system interactions may be manifest after a lapse of years. But at this time, molecular genetics offers no wholly satisfactory model of gene-environment interaction as that term is understood and used in psychopathology.

What can be done? While remedial actions can be sketched out, they will certainly be difficult to apply. First, it must be acknowledged that our current tools for studying environment have failed us. Intelligent, dedicated investigators have spent their careers with little result. Continuing along the same tracks would be nonproductive and irresponsible; worse, silly. This conclusion has been made painfully explicit to me through my experience as one of a team of investigators studying MZ twins separated from infancy. Such twins have identical genotypes but different environments through life. Their phenotypic differences must be attributed to their differing environments; indeed there is no more powerful natural experiment available to us for studying the effects of environment on human subjects. So far, 54 pairs of separated MZ twins have come to Minneapolis for six working days during which they were studied by a team of professionals, mainly psychologists and psychiatrists, using what we believe are state-of-the-art methods. The twins have been volunteers, which certainly implies selection for relative health. However, there have been several diagnosable psychopathological conditions, and minor deviations of personality have been common. Within pairs, we find startling phenotypic resemblances in the most surprising places. "Spooky" is a term we frequently use to express our astonishment at the resemblances we discover. Of course, we find phenotypic differences too, including some rather striking differences in the extent of psychopathology; but we have not uncovered a single environmental feature associated with the differences discovered. If our tools were of any use at all, study of this group of twins should have at least yielded a few clues. My conclusion is that using the same old methods to test the same old hypotheses is unworthy of a credible science.

Happily, just when the situation seems darkest, help appears on the horizon. New tools are becoming available that make possible, for the first time, routinely getting past that great barrier to investigation of the living brain, the skull. Positron emitting tomography, spectroscopic magnetic imaging, and measurements of electrical activity make possible study of living brain under experimental conditions. No longer must the brain be treated as a black box. However, using these new technologies to explore relationships between DNA, environment, and psychopathology will require training and equipping different sorts of psychopathologists.

This is so because of the nature of these new technologies. Each one would require a monograph from an expert to explore in any depth, so I shall illustrate the point with an overview of one further example, the "heat shock genes" (Bienzm, 1987). My purpose is to describe one promising lead to the actual mechanism of gene-environment interaction and then to go on to point out the actions needed if, as I hope, academic psychology equips itself to do the research.

The proteins coded for by heat shock genes are often called "stress proteins" or another similar name. They are produced by cells subject to one of several aversive stimuli: heat, which explains the historical origin of the name, but also some dozens of drugs, anoxia, hydrogen peroxide, some endogenous hormones, among many others. Affected cells immediately slow or stop production of proteins appropriate to them under normal conditions and augment production by up to 100-fold of several species of small heat shock proteins, some of which combine directly with DNA. These several proteins are coordinately expressed; that is, their rates of production vary together and the amount of protein produced is generally proportional to the concentration of the aversive stimulus. The genes involved have been highly conserved through evolution from bacteria to man. Evidently, their products serve essential purposes. One purpose is certainly to protect cellular machinery when it is subject to environmental challenge by shutting down routine operations. Another purpose is apparently to mark the place on genomic DNA where routine transcription was stopped to facilitate prompt restarting when conditions again become favorable. The mRNA for these proteins is unusual in that no introns are present; this eliminates the need for splicing, thereby facilitating rapid production of protein product. Production of heat shock proteins and cessation of normal cell metabolism persists for variable periods of time. Once induced, subsequent aversive stimuli augment production of heat shock proteins over previous levels; there is a hint here of "memory" for stressful events.

Now heat shock may or may not have anything to do with what ''stress'' denotes to behavioral scientists. But I think that we must agree that it is a likely candidate for study in this regard and that gets us back to the nub of the problem I have been defining. The biology of heat shock is complex. The experimental techniques used to study it require much more concentration of effort than those actually engaged in clinical practice can possibly supply. Then who should do the indicated experiments? In any branch of medicine or applied science, it would be affiliated basic scientists. Where are psychopathology's basic scientists? I submit that we almost totally lack them. Heat shock provides a likely lead into ''stress,'' into what large branches of psychology purport to be about. But what department of psychology in the nation, or the world for that matter, is prepared to set up the laboratories and credential the scientists needed to study heat shock proteins? (Or positron emitting tomography? Or magnetic imaging?) A few individual psychologists are involved in these or related areas and I have followed the careers of several of them. Those I know work in industry or in departments of psychiatry, neurology, or pharmacology. Most began in academic psychology but were isolated because they found few like-minded colleagues. They also found that there was no career path really open to them in psychology and, in any event, there were no laboratories to support their work.

Of course, it is possible to agree with such arguments and still maintain that the hard ball biology implied by them should remain the province of cell biologists or protein chemists, not psychologists. Clearly, psychology does have a choice. As its increasing irrelevance to the study of psychopathology is recognized, it may opt, perhaps by inaction, to become a minor player or even get out of the field altogether. Psychology encompasses a large and diverse set of disciplines and there would remain a lot for psychologists to do. However, I think opting out would be a profound error. While my subject has been psychopathology, the same arguments apply in principle across a much broader range of psychology's activities. Psychopathology is a great place to start establishing credibility in the biology of behavior generally. Moreover, I have a selfish reason for hoping that psychology stays in the fight. I have found that wet-lab scientists of the sort qualified to do research in areas such as heat shock lack the depth of understanding of behavior, the immersion in it, which is needed for intimate participation with clinicians in the development of experimental approaches. We need psychologists who are cell biologists and protein chemists. Then they must be provided an academic home where exchanges with each other and with colleagues knowledgeable at all levels of behavior are an integral part of professional life.

The price for developing such psychologists will be high, no less than a major reorientation of departments of psychology and the training of psychologists. Substantial knowledge of molecular biology would have to be required of all graduate students in psychology. Resources on a wet-lab scale would have to be made available to academic psychologists. A daunting challenge, but I believe that there is no better way to systematically set out to solve the riddles of psychopathology, including, in particular, schizophrenia. Further, I think that if psychology does not soon address and meet that explicit challenge, its contribution to psychopathology will come to be seen as a continuing search for phlogiston, entertainingly quixotic perhaps, but irrelevant to the real world.

References

Bienzm, M. et al. (1987). Mechanisms of heat-shock gene actuation in higher eukaryotes. *Advances in Genetics 24,* 31–72.

Egeland, J. A., Gerhard, D. S., Pauls, D. L., et al. (1987). Bipolar affective disorders linked to DNA markers on chromosome 11. *Nature, 325,* 783–787.

Fischer, M. (1971). Psychoses in the offspring of schizophrenic monozygotic twins and their normal co-twins. *British Journal of Psychiatry 118,* 43–52.

Gershon, E. S. (1988). Genetics. In F. K. Goodwin & K. R. Jamison (Eds.) *Manic-depressive illness.* New York: Oxford University Press.

Gilliam, T. C., Bucan, M., MacDonald, M. E., et al. (1987). A DNA segment encoding two genes very tightly linked to Huntington's disease. *Science, 238,* 950–952.

Gurling, H. Personal communication. Paper in press in *Nature.*

Ledbetter, D. H., Mascarello, J. T., Riccardi, V. D., et al. (1982). Chromosome 15 abnormalities and the Prader-Willi syndrome: A follow-up report of 40 cases. *American Journal of Human Genetics 34,* 278–285.

St. George-Hyslop, P. H., Tanzi, R. E., Polinsky, R. J., et al. (1987). The genetic defect causing familial Alzheimer's disease maps on chromosome 21. *Science, 216,* 885–890.

A Developmental Model for the Etiology of Schizophrenia

Joseph Zubin, Richard S. Feldman, and Suzanne Salzinger

Although we have made some progress in describing, diagnosing, and even treating schizophrenia, we are abysmally ignorant of its etiology. However, a variety of scientific etiological models have been postulated, and Zubin (1972; Zubin & Steinhauer, 1981) has proposed seven—genetic, anatomical, internal environmental, neurophysiological, developmental, learning, and ecological—and a superordinate model for integrating them into a vulnerability paradigm (Zubin & Spring, 1977). One of these, the developmental model, is the subject of this essay.

Historically, the developmental approach to schizophrenia has given rise to etiological hypotheses based on the effect of disturbed interaction between mother and child, and especially hypotheses about schizophrenogenic mothers, family structure, pseudomutuality, double bind, communication deviance, and several others. While these proved heuristic to varying degrees, none comes close to having the scope or power needed to address the wide range of issues now represented in developmental thinking in general and in the burgeoning field of developmental psychopathology in particular (Cicchetti, 1990; Goldberg & Kearsley, 1983; Goldstein & Tuma, 1987). Therefore, we will leave these hypotheses to history and deal only with a transactional model based on current developmental theory.

In contrast to the other etiological models cited above, each of which is defined in terms of substantive areas of biological or behavioral functioning, the developmental model is in an important sense a temporal model, dealing at least

An earlier version of this paper was presented at the 12th Lauretta Bender Symposium, Queens Children's Psychiatric Center, Bellerose, NY, October 1987.

The presentation of this paper was supported by the Medical Research Service of the Veterans Administration.

as much with the "when" as with the "what" of behavior and its biological, social, and environmental concomitants. The other etiological models have rather clear substantive domains, albeit with varying degrees of overlap and interaction between them, but the special characteristic of the developmental model is that it represents the outcome of all etiological forces arranged in time. In that sense it, like vulnerability, is superordinate to the other models. There is no unique domain for development itself except as it is expressed in the changes in behavior brought about by the phenomena addressed by the other models and the interactions between them. Time, so crucial in the physical sciences, has played an unimportant role in the theories and models proposed thus far for psychopathology. Two considerations are important here: the time or period or age when *etiological factors* begin to operate and the time when their *behavioral expression* occurs.

In its most basic form, the developmental model we propose is transactive in that it explicitly recognizes that any early insult or predisposing factor—whatever its nature (genetic, neurophysiological, behavioral, etc.) and however arrived at (inherited or acquired)—exists in a changing organism developing in a changing environment. This provides a general mechanism or context for either the mitigation or the exacerbation of deviant biological or behavioral phenomena which at their initial stages might not in themselves be remarkable or even detectable.

We suggest that a developmental model of schizophrenia include four components: (1) evidence of early preschizophrenic, possibly even prenatal, deviance at some level, which could range all the way from internal biological processes to social behavior; (2) specificity of signs or markers, so that even if not everyone who has them becomes overtly schizophrenic—there could be protective or other operative contextual factors—the individuals who have them are more likely to develop schizophrenia than some other condition; (3) increasing deviance with age, into the period of greatest risk for schizophrenia or until an actual episode develops; and (4) an account of the interaction between the preschizophrenic or schizophrenic behavior and longitudinal developmental variables that include internal biological changes, such as the growth of the central nervous system, changes in age-related social, emotional, and cognitive behavior, and changes in the child's environment, both proximal and distal, with age.

These four components seem to us reasonable, if not in all cases absolutely essential. To begin with, deviance, in principle, need not appear early, since "development" is, after all, a lifelong process and is not to be taken as synonymous with "child development." It is true that the period of greatest risk for the first actual episode of schizophrenia is not before adolescence or young adulthood. Nevertheless, there are young children who appear to meet all or most of the criteria for schizophrenia (e.g., Cantor, Evans, Pearce, & Pezzot-Pearce, 1982) and, in addition, there is evidence, particularly from studies of high-risk infants and children, of deviance of various kinds very early in life (e.g., Erlenmeyer-Kimling & Cornblatt, 1987b; Fish, 1987; Massie & Rosenthal, 1984; Weintraub, 1987), although it is by no means established that these deviations are uniquely associated with schizophrenia. As for onset, it could, in principle, be sudden and not preceded by a period of increasing deviance, and it could occur at almost any point in the life span. Again, however, with the period of greatest risk for morbidity being well before middle age and with the data we have on deviance of various kinds in infancy and childhood, the evidence would appear to support the search for an early and extended expression of deviance before the first episode. Of course, the definition of "sudden" is open to some interpretation.

The definition or diagnosis of schizophrenia remains problematic, and it is possible that there are multiple "schizophrenias," some fitting a developmental model better than others. This has also been suggested, for example, by Walker and Emory (1983) for models based on genetic data and by Woods, Kinney, and Yurgelun-Todd (1986) for neurologic models. And Konner (1987), commenting on possible analogies with both manic depressive illness and cancer, points out that in the former case, genes associated with different forms of what is usually considered the same disease have been found on different chromosomes, while in the latter case, different forms of the disease appear to have very different etiologies even though all cancers have some important common features. Thus, neither a single type of etiological factor (e.g., genetic) nor a given set of clinical manifestations can be taken as sufficient evidence for a unitary condition. If, as seems increasingly likely, there are indeed various "schizophrenias" and not one "schizophrenia," then it becomes clear that any model, but particularly a developmental model, if it aims for maximum usefulness, will need to be both wide-ranging and flexible.

As for the interactive or transactive component, it may be the most fundamental and least equivocal aspect of the model. Given the doubtfulness of the proposition that any single endogenous or exogenous factor, not excepting genetic loading, will independently and inevitably lead to schizophrenia, a transactive perspective seems indispensable.

Overall, then, we feel that the four components we have listed are, at least for now, the most heuristic.

Early Deviance

There are a variety of possible candidates for the early insult or predisposition to schizophrenia. The most likely appear to be genetic, biochemical, and neurological, although it is not *necessarily* the case that the prime etiological factors are biological (e.g., Cicchetti & Schneider-Rosen, 1986). The familial evidence is well known; it is the foundation of most high-risk research designs and it is a principal argument against a developmental model based entirely on external environmental factors, however much these might be critical to the actual behavioral expression of the condition. The existence of genetic risk—even it it turns out to occur in only a subset of schizophrenics—adds to the plausibility of the search for early premorbid expressions of deviance, and evidence from genetic high-risk studies will be included in the present discussion.

However, there are other data, as well as other models, that point in the same direction. In neurology, Weinberger's (1987) model, speculative as it is at this stage, is a true developmental model in that, while an early brain lesion is postulated, neither its cause nor its location is as important as its influence on brain maturation. Thus, according to this model, the primary etiological agent is the lesion, yet its effects on maturation of the brain areas related to symptom development are the proximate cause of the anomalies associated with schizophrenia. The presumed presence of the originally "silent" lesion postulated by Weinberger will no doubt lead to attempts to detect it as a marker as well as to track its effects in the developing child for signs of early deviance.

Murray and his colleagues have proposed a neurodevelopmental model according to which fetal or neonatal neuronal abnormalities are associated with early deviance and negative symptoms of schizophrenia, while the subsequent maturation of the anomalous brain throughout childhood, adolescence, and early adulthood eventually leads to positive symptoms and overt schizophrenia (Murray, Lewis, Owen, & Foerster, 1988; Murray, Owen, Goodman, & Lewis, 1990). Murray and his colleagues, like many others, view schizophrenia as a heterogeneous condition, and they state that their hypothesis applies to the subtype closest to the Kraepelinian concept. They base their hypothesis on a review of evidence from studies of pregnancy and birth complications, brain abnormalities as revealed by CT and histological data, soft signs, and other work.

Murray's model is of particular interest here because it addresses two considerations that we have suggested should characterize a developmental model: it explicitly predicts childhood deviance, and it acknowledges a probable interactive component in determining the extent to which fetal or neonatal abnormalities will become expressed functionally. In this regard, one could also consider the hypothesis, discussed by Woods et al. (1986), that any neurological deficit has to exceed some threshold of severity, perhaps pushed there by other, secondary factors, before it will be expressed clinically.

Massie and Rosenthal (1984), in a study quite different from other work in the literature, have provided some interesting evidence of very early behavioral deviance in children later diagnosed as psychotic or autistic. Home movies which had been taken by fond parents of their offspring from birth to two years of age were collected from across the country and divided into two groups, those who were subsequently referred for evaluation and treatment because of deviant behavior and those who were not, with the latter serving as normal controls. These home movies were blind-coded for various aspects of behavior. All five of the control children, but only one of the five children eventually diagnosed as psychotic, and none of the four children diagnosed as autistic, had reached Piaget's stage 6 of sensorimotor development by age two. Observational measures of sensorimotor behavior (interaction with the environment) and age-appropriate behavior in general showed the control children to exceed the others. The study is problematic particularly in regard to the small sample size and the degree of diagnostic precision; it is hard to be certain that the nonautistic psychotic children were, or would become, true schizophrenics. Furthermore, on only some measures were the psychotic children different from the autistic children or from the controls. Nevertheless, the study is of interest for providing contemporary recorded evidence of very early premorbid behavioral deviance of the sort for which, before prospective high-risk infancy studies, we usually had only retrospective reports to go on.

Prospective studies of high-risk infants and children have, for obvious reasons, provided some of the best evidence of early deviance. Fish (1987), summarizing some of her longitudinal data beginning in infancy for children born to chronic schizophrenic and control mothers, found a relationship between schizophrenia in the mother and what she terms "pandysmaturation" or degree of neurointegrative disorder as assessed by testing from birth to two years of age, which in turn was related to blind ratings of psychopathology at age 10. The high-risk subjects who eventually developed schizophrenia or other serious psychopathology showed social, perceptual, or other types of impairment before age six and already needed treatment by that age. The Jerusalem Infant Development Study and the NIMH Israeli Kibbutz-City Study (Marcus et al., 1987) report similar findings: The former finds sensorimotor dysfunction before age one in a subgroup of high-risk infants, which is followed by attentional and other dysfunction in childhood, and the latter study, which did not recruit subjects younger than 8 years, confirms the childhood findings.

The New York (Erlenmeyer-Kimling & Cornblatt, 1987b) and the Stony Brook (Weintraub, 1987) high-risk projects both report deviance of various kinds in middle childhood. The Stony Brook project reports deviance on a variety of speech measures (Harvey, Weintraub, & Neale, 1982); on cognitive-attentional measures (Winters, Stone, Weintraub, & Neale, 1981), although children of unipolars sometimes perform as poorly as children of schizophrenics; and on peer ratings of competence (Weintraub, Prinz, & Neale, 1978), although again some comparisons show little difference between children of schizophrenics and children of depressives. With regard to their finding that the older daughters of schizophrenic mothers (children in grades 6-9) were different from the daughters of depressed mothers on the ratings given by their classroom peers, Weintraub and his colleagues commented that this was "the first clear differentiation, in the realm of competence, of the offspring of schizophrenics from the offspring of a psychiatric control group" (1978, p. 417). The differential response by peers to children at risk for schizophrenia, if it were to hold up as a widespread phenomenon, would not only bolster the social validity of behavioral differences detected by other measures (such as language, attention, etc.) but would have enormous developmental implications because of the significance of peer relationships for child development generally. Also, it is interesting to speculate that this might mark the initial stage of the process resulting in Kreisman's (1970) finding that adult schizophrenics had lacked intimate adolescent friendships. The New York project also finds poor performance on attentional tasks for the high-risk children, and some deviance, although less than the Stony Brook project reports, for the psychiatric controls. Cornblatt and Erlenmeyer-Kimling (1985) attribute this difference between studies to what they say is the Stony Brook group's more "liberal" criterion for deviance and its use of tests that tap more complex cognitive functioning, not as likely to show deficits specific to any one kind of psychopathology.

Overall, then, dysfunction or deviance of many kinds has been reported from infancy on for individuals at risk for, or who in some cases have eventually developed, schizophrenia. Of course, not all individuals who show such deviance actually become schizophrenic. In some cases, the measures do not distinguish the offspring of schizophrenics from the offspring in psychiatric (usually affectively disordered) control groups and not all studies actually include such controls. Unsettled diagnostic criteria, differing conceptual orientations and measures across studies, and lack of replication are only some of the many fundamental problems complicating interpretation of the findings. Nevertheless, the data already available give ample encouragement for continuing the search for early premorbid dysfunction.

Specificity of Signs and Markers

Weinberger's (1987) model, mentioned previously, fits in the general category of the search for "markers" that identify individuals at high risk. The deviation indicated by the marker may not reach behavioral expression immediately or may never do so. If we ever detect the DNA segment containing the allele or alleles for schizophrenia, this would be another silent marker of high risk even though it might never express itself. Numerous studies in this literature indicate that as early as the perinatal period, certain anomalies in development are already apparent in those individuals who develop schizophrenia in their late teens or 20s, including reports of minor physical anomalies, abnormal dermatoglyphics, more frequent pregnancy and birth complications (Lewis & Murray, 1987), neuropathological findings (Kovelman & Scheibel, 1984), and a seasonality of births (Torrey & Kaufmann, 1986). The birth seasonality is especially noteworthy, with a late-winter or spring excess of schizophrenic births of between 5 and 15% having been demonstrated in every northern hemisphere country studied (England,

Wales, Ireland, Denmark, Norway, Sweden, Japan, the Philippines, and the United States) (Torrey, Rawlings, & Waldman, 1988). It is clear that exposure to certain diseases during the prenatal period also increases the risks of schizophrenia. Thus, Mednick, Parnas, and Schulsinger (1987) report an increase in the rate of schizophrenia for individuals whose mothers were exposed to the 1957 influenza epidemic in Finland during their second trimester of pregnancy. It should be added that Murray et al. (unpublished manuscript) note exceptions to the birth seasonality effect in some samples of schizophrenics, and they also remark on a general decline in seasonality for other disorders. Murray suggests that this decline may be due to better ante- and perinatal care. If such were the case for any of the conditions sometimes found associated with increased risk for schizophrenia (e.g., some viral infections), then the seasonality effect might become increasingly attenuated or eventually disappear altogether.

Some psychosocial variables that would have an early effect on the infant and might raise the risk are given in the study by Huttunen and Niskanen (1978), who found an increase in the rate of schizophrenia in the offspring of mothers whose husbands died during their pregnancy. Still another early marker has been reported by Venables et al. (1978) in the area of attention. Using the electrophysiological measure of skin conductance, Venables studied habituation to various stimuli in an unselected group of 3-year-old children in Mauritius. On the basis of the psychophysiological data, subgroups of these children were identified as responders or nonresponders and then observed in a play-group setting at age six. By that time, there were behavioral differences among the groups, and, in particular, the children who had been psychophysiological nonresponders at age three displayed less interaction and less constructive play than did their responder peers. Venables argues that the nonresponders are at particularly high risk, and he draws an analogy between these children and a subgroup of adult schizophrenics with similar psychophysiological responses, although of course the children's ultimate outcome is not known. For the children at least, the relationship between psychophysiological data and later observed behavior cannot be accounted for by hospitalization, medication, or labeling, though whether it is related to any lack of optimal parenting or experiential reinforcement remains an issue. Regardless, the habituation response appears to be a high-risk indicator that may eventually prove to be a marker of vulnerability identifying at least a portion of the vulnerable population, although Erlenmeyer-Kimling and Cornblatt (1987a) point out that the response pattern in question has not been demonstrated in offspring of schizophrenics and there is no solid evidence that it is a marker for schizophrenia.

The evidence for specificity at this stage must come almost entirely from differences between preschizophrenic high-risk children and comparison groups. Some of the most interesting behavioral evidence with regard to specificity comes from the New York project. Not only are more high-risk children than psychiatric or normal controls deviant on the attentional measures, but the attentionally deviant high-risk children become increasingly deviant in their social and other behavior as they get older, while children in the other groups do not (Cornblatt & Erlenmeyer-Kimling, 1985). Thus, Erlenmeyer-Kimling and her colleagues believe that they may well be tapping a specific predictor for schizophrenia or closely related disorders.

Other candidates for possible markers, covering the spectrum from fundamental biological processes to various aspects of social behavior, are discussed elsewhere in this paper. Erlenmeyer-Kimling and Cornblatt (1987a) conclude that while some biological or psychological variables look very promising as specific markers, no background variables do at this point. In any case, we are a long way from conclusively identifying any unambiguous and universal markers for schizophrenia, even biological ones (DeLisi, Goldin, & Gershon, 1987). The search is complicated by many factors; in the context of high-risk studies, Walker and Emory (1983) cite limitations of measurement, diagnostic imprecision, and possible etiological heterogeneity, among others. Nevertheless, the high-risk studies in particular, and a variety of neurodevelopmental and other hypotheses, have produced enough suggestions of possible specific markers, or types of specific markers, that researchers have plenty of clues to track down.

Increasing Deviance with Age

The concept of increasing deviance with age can refer to (1) deviance due to a static defect: an increasing number of areas in which the individual becomes dysfunctional, even though the degree of dysfunction in each area does not increase beyond its initial level (e.g., the child's social skills fail to develop appropriately and therefore over time deviate increasingly from those of normally developing peers, even though the behavior itself does not deteriorate), or (2) deviance due to deterioration: an actual deterioration of functioning such that the child is doing measurably worse than previously in any given area (e.g., the child no longer exhibits certain social skills that had once been achieved). Not all functions can be assessed, or assessed in the same way, at all ages. Expressive language, self-care, peer relations, and academic achievement are good examples — no less significant for being obvious — of areas that cannot be assessed before certain developmental stages and events have taken place or, according to the relevant norms, should have taken place. Therefore, it is not always certain which of the two types of increasing deviance is occurring as individuals are followed from infancy through childhood and adolescence.

The clinical importance of the distinction made above is not altogether clear, but empirical data suggest that both types of increasing deviance occur. Some of the data already cited as evidence of early deviance (e.g., Fish's work [1987] and the Jerusalem Infant Study [Marcus et al., 1987] also demonstrate that high-risk children who showed sensorimotor dysfunction in infancy have deficits in social competence later on—an example of more areas of functioning appearing as deviant without implying that sensorimotor functioning itself has deteriorated. On the other hand, once deviant behavior or psychopathology appears in these children, it has been reported to worsen over time (e.g., Fish, 1987; Cornblatt & Erlenmeyer-Kimling, 1985)— apparently not simply because the children's peers grow increasingly different from them as time goes by, but because they themselves become behaviorally more dysfunctional and look "sicker."

Cicchetti and Schneider-Rosen (1986) have discussed a process or mechanism whereby increasing deviance could come about. In essence, they suggest that to the extent that earlier developmental achievements are a necessary foundation for later ones, cumulative dysfunction will result whenever these essential precursors are deviant or absent. Whatever the process, the longitudinal high-risk studies, as well as other work, support the hypothesis of increasing deviance with age before any actual schizophrenic episode.

Transactive Nature of the Model

As we have said, a developmental model is essentially transactive (Sameroff & Chandler, 1975; Sroufe & Rutter, 1984), one in which a maturing organism, or subsystem within the organism, interacts with a changing internal or external environment, resulting in recursive effects that modify the characteristics of both the organism or subsystem and the environment. We will attempt to describe some of the transactions within and between variables comprising the individual's internal environment, behavior, and external environment which are consistent with an account of the etiology of schizophrenia within a developmental framework.

At the present time, none of these transactions characterizes all cases of schizophrenia. As has been mentioned earlier, there is increasing evidence that schizophrenia is a heterogeneous condition; therefore, examples we cite of the association with schizophrenia of particular interactions do not necessarily account for all the psychotic cases that are currently categorized under the rubric of schizophrenia. Until we have a better classification or nosology for schizophrenia, these accounts will have to stand side by side, each representing a different path to pathological outcome. Nonetheless, to account for the occurrence of any "schizophrenia" within a developmental model, we need to understand (1) the developmental progression of the child, (2) the mediating effect of the child's dysfunction, whether it stems from a genetic vulnerability or an early insult, and (3) the environment, both social and physical, both internal and external.

In normal development, a transactive model implies that both the organism and the environment are engaged in mutual adaptation to each other's requirements (Bell, 1974), resulting in growth and normal functioning appropriate for increasing age. The processes by which this takes place in normal development have been characterized in similar ways by various investigators, and although the processes themselves are not the primary subject of this essay, it might be helpful to refer to some of them here to better understand the transactions we will describe that influence the emergence of pathological behavior.

Cicchetti and Schneider-Rosen (1986), using an organismic model (Werner, 1957; see also Wapner, Kaplan, & Cohen, 1973) describe development as "qualitative reorganizations" among and between behavioral systems (cognitive, affective, and social) which take place by means of "differentiation" and "hierarchical integration." The variables comprising the entire system are comprehensive—genetic, constitutional, neurobiological, biochemical, behavioral, psychological, environmental, and sociological—and, with time, are in "dynamic transaction" with one another. Piaget's model for the development of cognitive behavior uses the concepts of "assimilation" and "accommodation" to describe the transitions from one stage of behavioral development to the next; the two processes are ones in which the individual is actively engaged and they depend upon the child's developing capabilities in interaction with the environment. A third system has been put forth by Bronfenbrenner (1979), who describes a nested or hierarchical ecological system in which individual development is mediated through the interactive effects of ever-widening social contexts on the child's behavior. Within each of these models, despite their differences, what happens in one part of the system affects what happens in the other parts of the system, a developmental lag in one subsystem influences development in another, and what occurs at one point in time affects what occurs later on.

Throughout the course of development, there are life-stage transitions, developmental milestones to be met, that are of major significance. These periods of transition may be considered analogous to the concept of critical, or sensitive, periods, which has been a part of the developmental literature for a long time. At this stage of theory-building in developmental psychopathology, their importance stems as much from the fact that they direct our attention to processes within the course of development for scrutiny and study as from the fact that they may be more important than other periods in the course of development. Despite the continuing reconceptualization that exists regarding the concept of critical periods (see Greenbough, Black, & Wallace, 1987), there are periods in which certain processes appear to be of exceptional significance for the development of psychopathology, in this case schizophrenia, and which are truly indigenous to development. Some of these are primarily concerned with changes in internal processes and some with changes in the external environment.

With respect to internal processes, among the most promising phases to examine in this regard is the migration of the neural cells from their development in the ventricular area to the superficial cortical layer (Edelman, 1987; Rakic, 1972). The transition between the pre- and neonatal periods, as well as the perinatal period itself, when neurological processes are in rapid growth and proliferation and differentiation (Weinberger, 1987), should be considered as heuristic points to search for some early insult or markers for the condition. And finally, one should consider the reduction in cortical synaptic density around the time of adolescence (Feinberg, 1982/83) and its possible relationship to normal cognitive development (Goldman-Rakic, 1987); this is particularly suggestive because adolescence, of course, marks the beginning of the period when people are most at risk for the actual overt onset of schizophrenia.

Other periods of transition, more concerned with external events and having to do with life-cycle changes, can equally well be considered as critical for the development of psychopathology. One can imagine that the increased stress associated with adapting to ever-widening environments and with becoming more independent causes individuals to become temporarily more unstable or more susceptible to pathology. These periods, paradoxically, can produce either the greatest developmental spurts or the onset of pathological symptomatology. Among these periods one would consider, for example: (1) the development of sensorimotor competence before the age of two years, which corresponds to important neurological changes and which is fundamental for the infant's mastery of the environment; (2) the early development of language as the basis for communicative competence; (3) the transition from home to school with its demands for separation from parents and for increased intellectual and social competence; (4) early adolescence with its increased demands for adaptation to peers as well as to internal pubertal changes; and (5) late adolescence and early adulthood, with its increased demands for independent behavior and responsibility in all areas and the most likely occasion for the onset of schizophrenic symptomatology.

In considering transactional accounts involving the internal environment, new brain imaging techniques (e.g., CT scans) and histological studies have given rise to better measures of both the adult brain and the early neurological effects of pregnancy and obstetrical complications. This in turn has enabled investigators to examine the relationship between the adult neurological status of schizophrenics and the neurological status of younger patients and infants (Folkai & Bogerts, 1986; Kovelman & Scheibel, 1984). Such studies have revealed the same enlarged ventricles and cortical sulcal widening in adult chronic schizophrenics as in younger patients in the early stages of the illness and in infants who have been subject to obstetrical complications. This would suggest that neural dysfunction, at least for some schizophrenics, either occurs as a result of an acute insult at the beginning of the illness or actually antedates it (Murray et al., 1988). The finding by Weinberger, Cannon-Spoor, Potkin, and Wyatt (1980) that chronic schizophrenics with abnormalities in their CT scans showed poor premorbid adjustment would be consistent with such an account. However, it is not consistent with the earlier idea that schizophrenia is a deteriorating condition; rather, it suggests that some neuronal dysfunction is present early on which can develop into schizophrenic symptoms at a later stage when other neural developmental processes, such as myelination and synaptic pruning, take place (Feinberg, 1982/1983; Goldman-Rakic, 1987). Insofar as normal developmental outcomes depend upon early intact neuronal circuitry, reactions to early insult caused by birth injury may undermine the orderly developmental neural outcomes at later stages (Nowakowski, 1987). For example, early brain injury resulting from periventricular hemorrhage in premature babies or from asphyxia can impair neuronal proliferation and cell migration or can interrupt axon retraction which, beginning in the last month of gestation and continuing into early childhood, rationalizes axonal connections. As a result, early immature and anomalous patterns may tend to persist. Feinberg (1982/1983) suggests that the synaptic eliminations which take place in adolescence may "lay open" previously "faulty wiring." And Goldman-Rakic (1987) suggests similarly, based on her studies of primates, that the delay in the effect on behavior of prenatal experimental lesions in the dorsolateral prefrontal cortex (DPFC) is due to the maturation of the DPFC which takes over functions from other frontal areas, resulting in the display of previously unnoticed behavioral abnormalities.

Specifically, Murray, Lewis, Owen, and Foerster (1988) hypothesize that the establishment of deviant neural end-pathways or other neural aberrations, resulting from the interaction of pre- and perinatal brain injury with normal neurological developmental processes, may make for the misinterpretation of internal and external stimuli, resulting in such symptoms as delusions and hallucinations. A behavioral counterpart which can be mapped onto this maturational interactive sequence has been suggested by these investigators to consist of neural dysplasia, showing up in CT abnormalities which in turn are revealed in childhood deviance, presenting as abnormal personality, cognitive deficits, and negative symptoms, the sequence eventually leading to pathological outcome in late adolescence when the above-mentioned neural processes take place.

Another transactional account involves the interaction between early dysfunctional behavior, brought about by a genetic predisposition for schizophrenia, and the child's social environment. Such behavior can produce aggravated responses in the child's caretakers, which in turn can affect the already vulnerable child in such a way as to exacerbate the dysfunctional behavior. It is not difficult to see that the result of such a recurring sequence would be to increase dysfunctional behavior not only in the preschizophrenic or high-risk child, for which we have already cited some evidence, but in the parents as well. A review of the literature by Brodsky and Brodsky (1981) relevant to such an account has provided evidence, based on replicated research findings, which is consistent with such a model. They propose specifically that schizophrenia results from a "continuing malforming transaction," which begins at birth, between a genotype for a temperamentally easily aroused infant and an "unempathic/insensitive, physically rejecting, noncontingent mother." The aversive interaction between parent and child results, through a classical conditioning paradigm, in an anxious avoidant response to people which, the authors suggest, may have permanent biochemical and structural effects. The authors take their account even further by proposing a more general model for the prediction of psychopathological and normal behavior which is based on the interaction between the entire range of infant temperamental genotypes and the whole spectrum of mothering styles, taking into account differences in neonatal status of the infant (either normal or having suffered perinatal complications) and the mental-health status of the mother (either normal or schizophrenic). With this expanded model, they suggest that they can predict outcomes ranging from "superphrenic" through normal, through spectrum disorders, to acute and chronic schizophrenia.

Although the Brodsky and Brodsky review was concerned primarily with an interactive sequence based in part on a genetic vulnerability to schizophrenia, there may be other routes to schizophrenia involving a similar interactive sequence between early behavioral dysfunction and the child's caretaking environment but in which the early behavioral dysfunction is not a function of genetic predisposition. Unfortunately, except for the high-risk studies, which include only a small proportion of preschizophrenic children, there is really little prospective behavioral observation of children who later actually become schizophrenic. Of related interest here is the Massie and Rosenthal study, cited earlier, which examined the home movies of babies before they, still as young children, were referred for treatment for psychotic illness. Systematic blind observations, utilizing a Piagetian framework, of the babies' interaction with objects in their environment before the age of two showed that these children did not demonstrate the same sensorimotor competence as control babies of the same age. Analysis of the interactive behavior of the mothers with their babies revealed that these mothers showed fewer proximal interactive behaviors, such as touching, holding, eye gaze, and affect, than control mothers. Unfortunately, although the study was a controlled study utilizing systematic assessment, it was based on a very small sample of only five psychotic children.

The evidence suggesting that early dysfunction and poor caretaking interact in increasing the risk for schizophrenic outcome seems to be accumulating as more studies find both early behavioral deviance in high-risk and prepsychotic children and poorer parenting. There does seem to be increasing evidence that the mothers of psychotic babies and high-risk children behave differently from other mothers, more of them providing a poorer environment, i.e., less play stimulation, fewer learning experiences, and less emotional and verbal involvement (Goodman, 1987)—even aside from the fact that there are more schizophrenic mothers among this group of parents. Unfortunately, most of our information about the interaction of early behavioral disturbance and parenting of preschizophrenic children comes from the genetic high-risk studies, where risk is defined as being the child of either one or two schizophrenic parents; thus the evidence remains inconclusive, confounded by the difficulty of separating the effects of poor parenting from genetic vulnerability. The significance of the early interaction between infant deviance and poor parenting lies in the fact that normal development in all areas is aided enormously by the early establishment of mutually reinforcing patterns of interaction of infants with their parents (or parent surrogates). It should be noted, of course, that given the likelihood of early behavioral deviance, whatever the cause, it is not necessarily a case of mothers causing deviance in their children. It needs to be stressed that the studies incriminating parenting behavior in the development of episodes of illness do not necessarily claim that deviant parenting is the cause. The issue is no doubt best viewed as another reminder of the transactive nature of the developmental process, where the child's behavior and the parent's behavior interact to produce any given outcome.

As children grow older, they must adapt to increasingly more demanding extrafamilial contexts. The best prospective information we have about preschizophrenic adaptive behavior comes from the high-risk studies. It should be noted here that although differences are often found between high-risk children and normal control children, it has been less often possible to document differences between the children of parents with different types of mental illness. In fact, the severity of parental mental disorder has generally been a better predictor of childhood behavioral deviance than the type of parental disorder (Sameroff & Seifer, 1983). Nonetheless, using the data from the high-risk studies, one can begin to test some specific predictions about the probable success with which preschizophrenic children and adolescents will master the important developmental tasks they face as they get older. These predictions are based on the idea that within an organismic developmental model (Cicchetti & Schneider-Rosen, 1986), maladaptive behavior, or deviance, tends to be associated with later deviance.

First, with respect to social development, the peer group becomes an increasingly important part of the child's social environment with age. Given the likely fact that mentally ill parents may be less able than nonmentally ill parents to provide a conducive environment for the development of social competence in their children, one would expect that high-risk children would find extrafamilial social adjustment more difficult than other children. There is some evidence of this in the study by Weintraub et al. (1978), which reported that, already in elementary school, their peers rate high-risk children as more deviant than other children on at least some of the measures used.

Possibly contributing to the children's difficulties with peers may be deviance in the children's speech patterns reported by Harvey et al. (1982) for the same group of high-risk children. Evidence for speech dysfunction similar to that found among adult schizophrenics was found in the Stony Brook high-risk sample when the children's speech was examined using the Rochester and Martin technique (1979) for the analysis. Although not as dysfunctional as adult schizophrenics, these children's deficiency in communicative competence could contribute to making interaction with both peers and adults more problematic.

School itself, a challenge to most children, might be expected to prove even more difficult for the high-risk children for a number of reasons—poorer supportive peer relations, less competent parental support, less communicative competence, impairments of attention which increase with age (Cornblatt & Erlenmeyer-Kimling, 1985) and the exacerbation, given the stress of school demands, of earlier constitutional or externally caused behavioral or neurological deviance.

In adolescence, coping with the social environment, when the requirements for friendship change and intimacy becomes more important, may be a problem. Kreisman (1970) reported that schizophrenics had had difficulty forming intimate friendships at that age, although the study does not seem to have been replicated. And finally one might expect that environmental stress should be greatest in late adolescence when the structured settings of home and school give way to the responsibilities entailed in living more independently, holding a job, and establishing a family. One might even speculate that the earlier onset for male schizophrenics might in part be accounted for by the increased stress of having to become financially independent at an earlier age than females. If this were the case, we might expect to see a downward trend in the age of onset for women as they become less dependent upon men for their living and enter the workforce in increasing numbers. The concatenation of environmental stresses at this stage, cumulated behavioral and biological deviance, and neurological changes during adolescence, might serve as a sufficient trigger for the overall increased onset of schizophrenia at this age.

The transactive nature of the model enables us to examine protective as well as risk factors for schizophrenic outcome. Thus far we have concentrated primarily on the risk factors for poor outcome. However, not all persons with a vulnerability for schizophrenia, even a genetic vulnerability, develop episodes of illness. We agree with Cicchetti and Schneider-Rosen (1986), at least in principle, that it need not be the case that only genetic or biological factors are "permissive" (predisposing) and that psychological or environmental factors are "efficient" (either contributory or protective). However, at the present time, there is more evidence available to entertain the hypothesis as it is usually stated, namely, that biological factors are predisposing, while environmental and psychological factors act to protect against or exacerbate biological vulnerability.

All of the evidence relevant to moderating effects has come from the high-risk studies, which have included in their prospective designs measures of a number of physical and social environmental and psychological factors along with the primary measure of risk, namely the mental illness of a parent. The Rochester Longitudinal Study (Sameroff & Seifer, 1983; Sameroff, Seifer, Zax, & Barocas, 1987) of children born to chronically ill schizophrenic mothers, in its search for early markers of later psychopathology, utilized an interactive model in predicting the social, emotional, and intellectual functioning of high-risk children from birth to four years of age. In addition to the presence and severity of mental illness, the social status of the families, the parental perspectives on child development and parenting, and family stress were measured. Even after the effect of parental mental illness was partialed out, a significant residual effect of all three other variables remained in accounting for children's mental functioning. Social-emotional functioning was nonetheless best predicted by the severity, not the type, of parental mental illness. The study also found that the best predictor of childhood competence was the total number of risk factors. Further examination of which risk factors were associated with competence for children with moderate risk showed that all types of risk were implicated. The study has also consistently shown, as in Werner and Smith's Kauai studies (1982), that the children of poor and minority-group families are at least as much at risk for developmental problems as children whose parents are mentally ill.

Other studies have concurred in their identification of protective factors in high-risk children. Structured regularity of early infant and childhood settings, having mothers who are somewhat older and better educated, having mothers who work and at the same time have help with child care (Goodman, 1987), all seem to mitigate the occurrence of symptomatology among high-risk children. And in a dramatic example of the potentially ameliorating effect of childrearing context, the Finnish study (Tienari et al., 1987) of high-risk children removed from their biological parents reported that the children adopted into better functioning homes fared better than the children adopted into poorer functioning homes.

Thus, there appears to be good evidence to support a transactive model that looks to the interplay between biological, psychological, social, and environmental factors to account for the development of childhood competence in high-risk children and focuses our attention specifically on those factors that may play a mitigating as well as an aggravating role in the onset of schizophrenia.

Concluding Comments

We have indicated that a transactive developmental model, like the vulnerability model, can serve as a superordinate model and that it can provide the temporal framework for the development of both normal and deviant individuals. It was further pointed out that in searching for indicators to identify vulnerable individuals, we have two broad classes — one more heavily dependent on biological (including genetic) factors, and one more heavily dependent on environmental factors. Given the widely acknowledged probable heterogeneity of what is now usually referred to simply as schizophrenia, neither one of these classes of indicators alone can reasonably be expected to account for all cases. Furthermore, there may well be interactions among factors such that, for example, individuals at demonstrable genetic risk nevertheless do not develop schizophrenia because they live in environments that protect against it through optimal parenting or absence of key types or degrees of stress. Perhaps, just as the acquisition as well as the inheritance of vulnerability has come to be considered a possibility (e.g., Zubin & Spring, 1977), we should consider that *in*vulnerability or stress-resistance (e.g., Garmezy, 1987) can likewise be acquired.

The goal of the identification of vulnerable individuals is to try for prevention. It is clear that neither the inheritance of a vulnerability to schizophrenia nor its acquisition through the environment necessarily and inevitably leads to the development of the disorder. If we could more effectively identify the vulnerable, it would become possible to apply educational strategies and prophylactic techniques for prevention of both the initial episode and recidivism, perhaps through reduction of exposure to stress or through stress inoculation procedures, as suggested by Walker and Emory (1983).

There are now two reigning types of models: the disease model and the vulnerability model. To varying degrees, both types of models recognize an interactive component and the role of endogenous and exogenous factors; therefore the developmental model we propose can be encompassed by either type or by both. But how do they differ? The conventional view of the disease model regards the patient as essentially a sick person with intermittent periods of remission but with a high risk of eventual chronicity and deterioration. The vulnerability model regards the patient as essentially a healthy person with intermittent episodes of illness but with a high probability of eventual return to a premorbid state of health. The essential difference between these two points of view is *hope*, and what a difference this can make to the treating clinician.*

References

Bell, R. Q. (1974). Contributions of human infants to caregiving and social interaction. In M. Lewis & L. A. Rosenblum (Eds.), *The effect of the infant on its caregiver*. New York: Wiley.

Brodsky, P., & Brodsky, M. (1981). A model integrating risk variables involved in the development of the schizophrenia spectrum. *Journal of Nervous and Mental Disease, 169*, 741–750.

Bronfenbrenner, U. (1979). *The ecology of human development: Experiments by nature and design*. Cambridge, MA: Harvard University Press.

Cantor, S., Evans, J., Pearce, J., & Pezzot-Pearce, T. (1982). Childhood schizophrenia: Present but not accounted for. *American Journal of Psychiatry, 139*, 758–762.

Cicchetti, D. (in press). An historical perspective on the discipline of developmental psychopathology. In J. Rolf, A. Masten, D. Cicchetti, K. Neuchterlein, & S. Weintraub (Eds.), *Risk and protective factors in the development of psychopathology*. New York: Cambridge University Press.

*Joseph Zubin died on December 18, 1990, before publication of this book. His coauthors, Richard S. Feldman and Suzanne Salzinger, longtime students and colleagues of his, would like to acknowledge his inspiration and generous contribution to the content of this article, and to express their pleasure in having had the opportunity of working closely with him on this recent venture.

Cicchetti, D., & Schneider-Rosen, K. (1986). An organizational approach to childhood depression. In M. Rutter, C. Izard, & P. Read (Eds.), *Depression in children: Developmental perspectives*, New York: Guilford.

Cornblatt, B. A., & Erlenmeyer-Kimling, L. (1985). Global attentional deviance as a marker of risk for schizophrenia: Specific and predictive validity. *Journal of Abnormal Psychology, 94*, 470–486.

DeLisi, L. E., Goldin, L. R., & Gershon, E. S. (1987). Studies of biological factors associated with the inheritance of schizophrenia: A selective review. *Journal of Psychiatric Research, 21*, 507–513.

Edelman, G. M. (1987). *Neural Darwinism: The theory of neuronal group selection*. New York: Basic Books.

Erlenmeyer-Kimling, L., & Cornblatt, B. (1987a). High-risk research in schizophrenia: A summary of what has been learned. *Journal of Psychiatric Research, 21*, 401–411.

Erlenmeyer-Kimling, L., & Cornblatt, B. (1987b). The New York High-Risk Project: A follow-up report. *Schizophrenia Bulletin, 13*, 451–461.

Feinberg, I. (1982/83). Schizophrenia: Caused by a fault in programmed synaptic elimination during adolescence. *Journal of Psychiatric Research, 17*, 319–333.

Fish, B. (1987). Infant predictors of the longitudinal course of schizophrenic development. *Schizophrenia Bulletin, 13*, 395–410.

Folkai, P., & Bogerts, B. (1986). Cell loss in the hippocampus of schizophrenics. *European Archives of Psychiatry and Neurological Science, 336*, 154–161.

Garmezy, N. (1987). Stress, competence, and development: Continuities in the study of schizophrenic adults, children vulnerable to psychopathology, and the search for stress-resistant children. *American Journal of Orthopsychiatry, 57*, 159–174.

Goldberg, S., & Kearsley, R. B. (Eds.). (1983). Infants at risk. *Child Development (special issue), 54*.

Goldman-Rakic, P. S. (1987). Development of cortical circuitry and cognitive function. *Child Development, 58*, 601–622.

Goldstein, M. J., & Tuma, A. (Eds.). (1987). High-risk research. *Schizophrenia Bulletin, 13*, 369–536.

Goodman, S. H. (1987). Emory University Project on children of disturbed parents. *Schizophrenia Bulletin, 13*, 411–423.

Greenbough, W. T., Black, J. E., & Wallace, C. S. (1987). Experience and brain development. *Child Development, 58*, 539–559.

Harvey, P. D., Weintraub, S., & Neale, J. M. (1982). Speech competence of children vulnerable to psychopathology. *Journal of Abnormal Child Psychology, 10*, 373–388.

Huttunen, M. O., & Niskanen, P. (1978). Prenatal loss of father and psychiatric disorders. *Archives of General Psychiatry, 35*, 429–431.

Konner, M. (1987). The many faces of madness. *The Sciences*, July/August, 6–8.

Kovelman, J. A., & Scheibel, A. B. (1984). A neurohistological correlate of schizophrenia. *Biological Psychiatry, 19*, 1601–1621.

Kreisman, D. (1970). Social interaction and intimacy in preschizophrenic adolescence. In J. Zubin & A. Freedman (Eds.), *Psychopathology of adolescence*. New York: Grune & Stratton.

Lewis, S. W., & Murray, R. M. (1987). Obstetric complications, neurodevelopmental deviance and risk of schizophrenia. *Journal of Psychiatric Research, 21*, 413–421.

Marcus, J., Hans, S. L., Nagler, S., Auerbach, J. G., Mirsky, A. F., & Aubrey, A. (1987). Review of the NIMH Israeli Kibbutz-City Study and the Jerusalem Infant Development Study. *Schizophrenia Bulletin, 13*, 425–438.

Massie, H. N., & Rosenthal, J. (1984). *Childhood psychosis in the first four years of life*. New York: McGraw-Hill.

Mednick, S. A., Parnas, J., & Schulsinger, F. (1987). The Copenhagen High-Risk Project, 1962–86. *Schizophrenia Bulletin, 13*, 485–495.

Murray, R. M., Lewis, S. W., Owen, M. J., & Foerster, A. (1988). The neurodevelopmental origins of dementia praecox. In P. McGuffin & P. Bebbington (Eds.), *Schizophrenia: The major issues*. London: Heinemann.

Murray, R. M., Owen, M. J., Goodman, R., & Lewis, S. W. (1990). A neurodevelopmental perspective on some epiphenomena of schizophrenia.. In C. Cazullo, G. Invernizzi, E. Sacchetti, & A. Vita (Eds.), *Plasticity and Morphology of the Central Nervous System*. Lancaster: MTP Press Limited.

Nowakowski, R. S. (1987). Basic concepts of CNS development. *Child Development, 58*, 568–595.

Rakic, P. (1972). Mode of cell migration to the superficial layers of fetal monkey neocortex. *The Journal of Comparative Neurology, 145*, 61–84.

Rochester, S. R., & Martin, J. R. (1979). *Crazy talk: A study of the discourse of schizophrenic speakers*. New York: Plenum.

Sameroff, A., & Chandler, M. (1975). Reproductive risk and the continuum of caretaking casualty. In F. Horowitz, M. Hetherington, S. Scarr-Salapatek, & G. Sigel (Eds.), *Review of child development research, Vol. 4*. Chicago: University of Chicago Press.

Sameroff, A. J., & Seifer, R. (1983). Family risk and child competence. *Child Development, 54*, 1254–1268.

Sameroff, A., Seifer, R., Zax, M., & Barocas, R. (1987). Early indicators of developmental risk: Rochester Longitudinal Study. *Schizophrenia Bulletin, 13*, 383–394.

Sroufe, L. A., & Rutter, M. (1984). The domain of developmental psychopathology. *Child Development, 55*, 17–29.

Tienari, P., Sorri, A., Lahti, I., Naarala, M., Wahlberg, K.-E., Moring, J., Pohjola, J., & Wynne, L. C. (1987). Genetic and psychosocial factors in schizophrenia: The Finnish Adoptive Study. *Schizophrenia Bulletin, 13*, 477–484.

Torrey, E., & Kaufmann, C. (1986). Schizophrenia and neuroviruses. In H. Nasrallah & D. Weinberger (Eds.), *The neurology of schizophrenia* (pp. 361–376). Amsterdam: Elsevier.

Torrey, E. F., Rawlings, R., & Waldman, I. (1988). Schizophrenic births and viral disease in two states. *Schizophrenia Research, 1*, 73–77.

Venables, P. H., Mednick, S. A., Schulsinger, F., Raman, A. C., Bell, B., Dalais, J. C., & Fletcher, R. P. (1978). Screening for risk of mental illness. In G. Serban (Ed.), *Cognitive deficits in the development of mental illness*. New York: Brunner/Mazel.

Walker, E., & Emory, E. (1983). Infants at risk for psychopathology: Offspring of schizophrenic parents. *Child Development, 54*, 1269–1285.

Wapner, S., Kaplan, B., & Cohen, S. (1973). An organismic-developmental perspective for understanding transactions of men and environments. *Environment & Behavior, 5*, 255–289.

Weinberger, D. R. (1987). Implications of normal brain development for the pathogenesis of schizophrenia. *Archives of General Psychiatry, 44*, 660–669.

Weinberger, D. R., Cannon-Spoor, E., Potkin, S. G., & Wyatt, R. J. (1980). Poor premorbid adjustment and CT scan abnormalities in chronic schizophrenia. *American Journal of Psychiatry, 137*, 1410–1413.

Weintraub, S. (1987). Risk factors in schizophrenia: The Stony Brook High-Risk Project. *Schizophrenia Bulletin, 13*, 439–450.

Weintraub, S., Prinz, R. J., & Neale, J. M. (1978). Peer evaluations of the competence of children vulnerable to psychopathology. *Journal of Abnormal Child Psychology, 6*, 461–473.

Werner, E. E., & Smith, R. S. (1982). *Vulnerable but invincible: A longitudinal study of resilient children and youth*. New York: McGraw-Hill.

Werner, H. (1957). The concept of development from a comparative and organismic point of view. In D. B. Harris (Ed.), *The concept of development*. Minneapolis: University of Minnesota Press.

Winters, K. C., Stone, A. A., Weintraub, S., & Neale, J. M. (1981). Cognitive and attentional deficits in children vulnerable to psychopathology. *Journal of Abnormal Child Psychology, 9,* 435–453.

Woods, B. T., Kinney, D. K., & Yurgelun-Todd, D. (1986). Neurologic abnormalities in schizophrenic patients and their families. *Archives of General Psychiatry, 43,* 657–663.

Zubin, J. (1972). Scientific models of psychopathology in the 1970's. *Seminars in Psychiatry, 4,* 283–296.

Zubin, J., & Spring, B. (1977). Vulnerability—A new view of schizophrenia. *Journal of Abnormal Psychology, 96,* 103– 126.

Zubin, J., & Steinhauer, S. (1981). How to break the logjam in schizophrenia: A look beyond genetics. *Journal of Nervous and Mental Disease, 169,* 477–492.

Control Groups in Schizophrenia Research: A Neglected Source of Variability

William G. Iacono

Some years ago, Meehl (1973) characterized the research literature on schizophrenia as "vast and dismal," and added that most of it "does not tend appreciably to confirm anything" (p. 203). Although currently research interest in schizophrenia is experiencing something of a renaissance and we have made positive strides since the early 70s, most psychopathologists would still be hard pressed to formulate a list of a half-dozen statements about this disorder that they would be willing to defend a decade hence. The task would be more difficult still if they were asked to confine their list to new findings uncovered in the last 10 years, and virtually impossible were the instructions to focus on results that have been consistently replicated.

The reasons why it is so difficult to generate reproducible research findings in investigations of schizophrenia are legion; an entire volume could easily be devoted to the topic. In addition to the unsettled questions that plague psychological research in general, such as how to operationalize variables and quantify them, there are many problems unique to psychopathology research that contribute to failures to replicate. A number of these have to do with the characteristics of the subjects chosen for study. Because the schizophrenics selected in one study usually differ from those examined in other settings, when two research reports obtain contradictory results, the different qualities of the patients are often suspected as the source of the discrepancy.

There are many ways in which patients may vary from study to study. They might differ in age, sex, social class, years of schooling, age of onset, family history, the operational criteria used to define schizophrenia, subtype diagnosis,

The writing of this chapter was supported by a Faculty Summer Research Fellowship to the author from the Graduate School of the University of Minnesota.

presence of an axis II disorder, level of acute symptomatology, presence of specific symptoms (e.g., positive vs. negative, first-rank), medication regimen, illicit drug use, cumulative effect of prior treatments, chronicity, length of time in hospital, and premorbid status. These factors, to the extent they can be determined or were of interest to the investigator, tend to be reported from one study to another, and I believe this occurs more so now than it has in the past.

Consider, for example, the criteria used to define schizophrenia. Not too long ago, there were no operational definitions of schizophrenia; investigators had to rely on the vague descriptions found in the DSM and ICD manuals. All too frequently, the hospital chart diagnosis was used to identify schizophrenic patients. Investigators intent on adding some rigor to their diagnostic approach would focus on chronic patients whose schizophrenic diagnoses were less likely to be questioned, or tell us that two diagnosticians agreed on the classification of each patient. Under these circumstances, we knew the diagnosis was reliable, but did not know how it was made. Now, the operational criteria used to define schizophrenia are specified in almost all research reports (however, it is my impression that the reliability with which the diagnosis is made is less commonly reported than before [see Grove et al., 1981, for further comments on this point]). I reviewed 92 recently published studies of schizophrenia (this review is described below) and found only four that did not specify the operational definition for the diagnosis.

I believe that differences in the characteristics of schizophrenic patients from study to study do contribute appreciably to inconsistency in the literature. I also believe that increasingly investigators are describing clinical samples with sufficient detail to allow the consumer to evaluate how differences in patient characteristics might account for variable findings across studies. However, I would like to focus this chapter on another, largely ignored way in which subjects differ across studies, one that could also account for inconsistent findings, but in a manner that often cannot be determined because essential information is usually lacking.

Control Groups and Electrodermal Nonresponding

Ten years ago, I carried out two studies of electrodermal habituation in psychiatric outpatients with schizophrenia or a major affective disorder (Iacono, 1982; Iacono et al., 1983). Because I wanted those involved with the treatment of the patients to encourage them to participate in the study, I offered to run members of the hospital staff through the experimental protocol. In all, nine people took advantage of this opportunity. All of these subjects appeared to be interested in the study, asked appropriate questions, and wanted to know if their results revealed anything interesting about themselves.

A major dependent variable in this investigation, as in other studies of habituation in schizophrenia, concerned whether or not subjects responded to the stimuli. About half of various schizophrenic samples have been described as nonresponders—individuals who never produce an electrodermal response to one of the stimuli. Normal subjects display nonresponding infrequently, about 10% of the time or less often in most studies, so I was not surprised when none of the hospital staff subjects was nonresponsive.

The psychiatric outpatients in these studies were being seen in a clinic that was part of a public hospital. I decided that the normal control subjects, with whom the patients would be compared, should also be individuals served by an outpatient clinic of this same hospital. The comparison group would thus come from the same geographical area, have similar socioeconomic status, and probably have many of the same reasons for choosing to receive care at this particular medical facility. Like the patients, one of their primary reasons for participating in the study was the subject payment they received.

It was important that the health of the control subjects not be compromised because the psychophysiological measurements could be affected, a consideration that led me to choose the family practice clinic as the source of control subjects. Patients with chronic medical disorders or acute medical conditions that were not resolved quickly were excluded from the sample. So were individuals with abnormal MMPI test results. The selected subjects were treated at the clinic for infections and other minor ailments, had routine physical exams, wanted pregnancy tests, etc., or were the parents of children seen at the clinic.

These subjects had a laboratory demeanor that was noticeably different from that observed among the hospital staff I tested earlier and from what I was familiar with when I used undergraduate volunteers as research subjects. As was the case with the schizophrenic patients, they seemed uninterested; their concerns were directed toward issues such as when the session would be over or when they could smoke a cigarette. Several characterized the whole affair as boring or expressed the sentiment that they could not see how such investigation could be of any value. Only a few appeared to be genuinely interested in their physiological recordings.

The family practice subjects were also far less responsive to the stimuli than were the hospital staff I tested earlier. Although the schizophrenic patients were about as nonresponsive (46% failed to respond) as those studied by other investigators, my normal control group had a much larger proportion of nonresponders than had ever been reported in any other study. Of 46 family practice volunteers, 11 or 24% failed to respond. This nonresponsive rate differed significantly from the expected rate of 10%, chi square $= 8.41, p<.01$.

Why was the rate of nonresponding in my control subjects higher than that observed by others? The answer to this question lies in the many ways in which the other studies of electrodermal nonresponding in schizophrenia differ from my work. Indeed, because there is more than just a single procedural difference among these studies, it is not possible to provide an unequivocal response to this query. However, because the schizophrenics were just as nonresponsive as in other studies, the different experimental methods used may not be a primary determinant of the discrepant results. I was intrigued by the fact that had I used the hospital staff as the control group, a lower (in fact zero) rate of nonresponding would have been obtained. Could the nature of the control sample used in these studies account for the different rates of nonresponding?

In the six studies that examined nonresponding in schizophrenics and normal controls (Bernstein et al., 1981; Gruzelier et al., 1981; Gruzelier & Venables, 1972; Patterson, 1976; Patterson & Venables, 1978; Straube, 1979), 13 of 143 (9%) of the normal subjects were nonresponders. For all but one of these reports (Gruzelier & Venables, 1972), the source of the normal controls was specified. Leaving out this one paper, the overall rate of nonresponding was 10%, and all of these investigations used hospital staff for the comparison group.

Reflecting on my personal experience with these two types of control subjects led me to suspect that differences in the source of subjects used in comparison groups could account for the reported difference in the rate of electrodermal nonresponding. My review of prior research yielded findings consistent with my suspicion. Members of the hospital staff undoubtedly approach their participation with expectations and concerns that are different from nonstaff volunteers (and psychiatric patients). They are more likely than others to know the investigators, be familiar with their research, and view it as important and interesting. Participation in an experiment may be perceived as a learning opportunity, one that is intellectually stimulating. For these same reasons, it may also be emotionally arousing. The same cannot be said for the family practice volunteers. They were frequently on welfare, poorly educated, ignorant about research participation, trusting, and uninterested. As a group (and like the psychiatric patients), they were probably less engaged by this enterprise. All these factors could have contributed to their being less reactive as well.

While these arguments are certainly speculative, the above illustration was not developed to argue that the control subjects used in my research were more appropriate than those used by others. Rather, I wish to make a point that is generally ignored in psychopathology research: the source of the subjects that compose normal control groups may affect the outcome of a study. Of course all psychopathology researchers know that the control group is an important part of the research design, but I do not believe enough weight has been given to the possible influence of this factor on the outcome of experimental psychopathology research, either by the investigators who conduct the studies or by those who review this work for publication.

Qualities of Control Groups

What are the qualities of the ideal contrast group in a study of schizophrenia? The answer to this question depends, of course, on the purposes of the study. At the very least, the control group should not have schizophrenia. In many cases, nonschizophrenic psychiatric patients will be appropriate. Schizophrenic subjects differ from normal individuals not only because they have schizophrenia, but also because they are institutionalized, medicated, and possess other characteristics that are common to those with mental disorders. Unlike normal controls, other psychiatric patients may be similar to schizophrenics on these dimensions. Their use as a comparison group can serve as a control for these factors.

Because those with nonschizophrenic psychiatric disorders may also be deviant on the variable of interest, it is useful to include a nonpsychiatric control group. Indeed, such a group is fundamental in the assessment of schizophrenic differences. If these individuals generate values on the dependent measures that are equivalent to those of the schizophrenics, it matters little that the patients also differ in treatment and hospital status (unless these factors are viewed as having ameliorative effects). In most studies, the nonpsychiatric subjects are selected because the investigators believe that they are representative of the "normal" population or, as is probably more common, that they do not differ in important ways from "normal" people. Exactly what qualifies a person as "normal" is unclear, but, as a minimum requirement, these individuals presumably should not have schizophrenia or another psychiatric disorder.

As Meehl (1970, 1971) has noted, a serious hazard may exist when control and psychopathological groups differ on variables other than those of interest to the investigator (e.g., social class, educational attainment) but which may influence the relationship between the dependent measures and diagnosis. Typical strategies for dealing with these "nuisance" variables are matching and analysis of covariance which are alternative means of achieving the same end. The aim is to remove the influence of the nuisance variables so that the hypothesized relationship between psychiatric classification and the dependent variable can be evaluated uncontaminated by its effects. Consider the following example: Suppose an investigator wishes to determine if schizophrenics have a neuropsychological impairment. Schizophrenic patients are compared to those with major affective disorder and normal subjects. The investigator notes that the schizophrenics have a lower level of educational attainment. Because this factor may determine how an individual subsequently performs on neuropsychological tests, the groups are matched for the number of school grades completed. Meehl (1970, 1971) has described three problems with this procedure.

1) *Unrepresentative subpopulations.* Because the populations from which samples are drawn may differ on a nuisance variable, matching on this variable will lead to unrepresentative subpopulations. In this case, since schizophrenics as a group tend to be more poorly educated than people who are normal or who have affective disorders, matching will lead to a sample of schizophrenics that is better educated and samples of normal and affective subjects that are more poorly ed-

ucated than the respective populations from which they were drawn. The obvious result will be biased, unrepresentative samples.

2) *Systematic unmatching.* Matching on the nuisance variable may lead to unmatching on some other variable. In the example, matching on educational attainment may produce groups that are mismatched for social class. The impairment in role functioning experienced by schizophrenics is such that they tend to be in the lowest social class regardless of how well educated they are. For the affective patients and even more so for the normal subjects, the correlation between social class and progress in school may be much stronger, with the result that proportionately far fewer well-educated subjects in these groups will be in the lowest class. Under the circumstances, matching for educational level will lead to groups unmatched for social class.

3) *Causal arrow ambiguity.* Meehl argues that the decision to control a nuisance variable must be based on a model of how it operates. Although too often they assume they do, investigators usually do not know how the nuisance factor operates. Hence, they run the risk of eliminating the opportunity to uncover the hypothesized relationship. In the example, it is possible that a poor education will lead to poor performance on neuropsychological tests and that the lack of adaptive skills that results from poor schooling predisposes individuals to develop schizophrenia. As a result, both the neuropsychological deficit and schizophrenia are partly derived from poor education. Not removing the effect of educational attainment would produce a misleading understanding of the relationship between schizophrenia and neuropsychological performance. On the other hand, it is possible that a subtle, nonspecific, neurological impairment predisposes individuals to schizophrenia and interferes with their ability to function well in school. In this case, correcting for educational level may eliminate the opportunity to uncover the hypothesized schizophrenic deficit in neuropsychological performance.

While these problems have been identified, there are no straightforward solutions available to deal with them. It is important for investigators to be thoughtful in dealing with these issues and to approach their data analysis and interpretation using different perspectives to understand how nuisance variables may affect the results.

The Normal Control Group in Psychopathology Research

The characteristics of both nonschizophrenic patients and normal control subjects may influence the outcome of an investigation. However, the qualities of nonschizophrenic patients are usually not crucial to the interpretation of results. In part, this is true because, unlike normal controls, nonschizophrenic subjects are infrequently used as the sole control group; most studies that include these patients also include normal subjects. It is the latter group that is critical to data interpretation because the experimental hypotheses usually deal with how schizophrenia may differ from normal. Moreover, when nonschizophrenic patients are included in a study, the characteristics of this group are typically specified with as much detail as are those of the schizophrenics, thus providing some insight into how the use of this group might affect the results.

It is my thesis that nonpsychiatric control subjects are an underrecognized source of variability in schizophrenia research. One of the reasons why they are seldom considered as such is that in most reports they are not described in sufficient detail to allow conclusions to be drawn about how the results may have been affected.

To evaluate the extent to which deficient reporting is associated with the description of nonpsychiatric controls, four prominent journals that publish articles on schizophrenia were surveyed. The papers in each journal that examined schizophrenia and included a nonpsychiatric control group were read to determine the nature of the group. In all, 92 reports were located. Two of the journals (*Journal of Abnormal Psychology, American Journal of Psychiatry*) were surveyed over the five-year period 1982–1986; the others (*Archives of General Psychiatry, Biological Psychiatry*) were reviewed for two years, 1985–1986.

Table 1 summarizes the information regarding the source from which the control subjects were recruited. The column totals in the table add up to more than 100% because in some studies subjects were recruited from two or more sources. The percentage of studies following this approach is indicated in the bottom row of the table. As the summary statistics indicate, the most common practice is not to reveal any information about the source of these subjects. Otherwise, control subjects are most frequently recruited from hospital staff. Considering how unlike they are to schizophrenics, it is somewhat surprising that a substantial fraction of studies continue to use university students as the normal group.

The most obvious conclusion to draw from this survey is that little is known about the character of the control groups. In 40% of the studies, there is no way of discerning from what population these subjects were drawn. While identifying the source as institutional staff may be viewed as an improvement over the providing of no information, it is only a minor improvement. The staff includes both professional employees, such as physicians, psychologists, and nurses, and nonprofessional personnel, such as receptionists, psychiatric aides, janitors, and tradespeople. Whether one or the other or both of these sources are used could be an important aspect of a study. Unfortunately, of the 32 studies that used professional staff, less than one-third distinguished between these two sources. Of the 19 reports drawing subjects from more than one population, only 2 indicated how many came from each source, a factor of potential interest when the control group has a diverse composition such as "hospitalized patients with orthopedic disorders, secretaries, and undergraduate students." Of the 92 studies examined, only 30 (33%) described the source of the control subjects with enough detail to

Table 1. Source of Normal Control Subjects Used in Schizophrenia Studies

Control Group Source	Percentage of Studies from[a]				
	JAP (N = 15)	AJP (N = 29)	AGP (N = 19)	BP (N = 30)	Combined (N = 92)
Unknown	7	36	47	57	40
Institutional staff[b]	40	29	47	30	35
Medical patients	27	25	16	10	18
Students	33	7	11	10	14
Community volunteers[c]	13	21	16	7	14
More than one of above	20	18	32	17	21

[a]JAP = *Journal of Abnormal Psychology*, AJP = *American Journal of Psychiatry*, AGP = *Archives of General Psychiatry*, BP = *Biological Psychiatry*.

[b]Includes studies in which subjects were solicited by in-house advertising.

[c]Includes studies in which subjects were recruited by advertising in the community.

allow the interested investigator to draw from a similar source and duplicate the composition of the group.

Already alluded to is the fact that the definition of "normal control" is elusive. Upon reading the studies included in this survey, one is left with the impression that as long as the control subjects were unlikely to include formally diagnosed schizophrenics, they can be considered normal. The extent to which the control participants in the surveyed studies were actually screened to determine if they were psychiatrically normal is indicated in Table 2. A large percentage (45%) received at least some type of evaluation to rule out those with possible mental disorders. This is probably a worthwhile practice because recent evidence indicates that psychiatric disorders are relatively commonplace. For example, in an epidemiological survey of the lifetime prevalence of 15 DSM-III psychiatric disorders that can be diagnosed from the administration of the NIMH Diagnostic Interview Schedule, Robins et al. (1984) found that 32% of the community participants interviewed in three metropolitan areas met the criteria for at least one of these diagnoses.

Table 2. Extent to Which Control Subjects Are Qualified as Normal

Subjects Screened for	Percentage of Studies from[a]				
	JAP (N = 15)	AJP (N = 29)	AGP (N = 19)	BP (N = 30)	Combined (N = 92)
Psychopathology	60	46	47	33	45
Family history of psychopathology	27	7	11	10	12
Neurological disorders	0	7	32	20	15
Medical disorders	13	11	11	7	10
Medication use	0	7	11	13	9

[a]JAP = *Journal of Abnormal Psychology*, AJP = *American Journal of Psychiatry*, AGP = *Archives of General Psychiatry*, BP = *Biological Psychiatry*.

Table 2 also lists the extent to which nonpsychiatric control subjects are evaluated for the presence of other factors that could influence the dependent measures. Screening for these factors may be especially important if the dependent variables could be influenced by genes and/or biology.

One conclusion that follows from this review is that investigators have not worried about the nuisance variable problems raised by Meehl. Matching subjects on variables like educational attainment is not a common practice. Indeed, few reports provided enough descriptive information about their control subjects to allow the reader to estimate how nuisance factors may or may not have influenced the results.

Ventricular Enlargement in Schizophrenia: The Influence of Control Groups

Although the discussion to date has laid the foundation for the concern that psychopathologists are not paying enough attention to control groups, I have not as yet shown how choice of nonpsychiatric controls may lead to inconsistencies in schizophrenia research. This is difficult to do, in part because there are only a few areas of the schizophrenia literature where there have been many attempts at replication using similarly defined dependent measures. Most studies are one-shot affairs; when they are followed up by other investigators, usually the methodology is so substantially changed that it is difficult to determine the role control groups played in the outcomes. One area of schizophrenia research where this may not be the case involves the use of computerized tomography (CT) scanning to examine the size of the lateral ventricles in schizophrenia. Together with Geoffrey Smith and other colleagues of mine at the University of British Columbia, I have been using CT scanning to investigate brain morphology in schizophrenia, paying special attention to the role control groups may play in determining the outcome (Iacono, Smith, Moreau, Beiser, Fleming, Lin, & Flak, 1988; Smith, Iacono, Moreau, Tallman, Beiser, & Flak, 1988; see also Depue & Iacono, 1989).

The common index of lateral ventricular size is derived from the ventricular brain ratio or VBR (Synek & Reuben, 1976). To compute the VBR, the serial scan that depicts the lateral ventricles at their largest is identified and the area of the ventricles is determined using a planimeter or other technique. This figure is then divided by the area of the brain evident in the same scan. The resulting proportion is multiplied by 100 to express ventricle size as a percentage of brain size. The VBR has been shown to correlate well with estimates of ventricular volume (Penn, Belanger, & Yasnoff, 1978).

An Analysis of Published Studies

Beginning with the work of Johnstone et al. (1976), there are now over two dozen CT studies of schizophrenia in which this operational definition of ventricle size was used and that also used a nonpsychiatric control group. About two-thirds of these investigations have found lateral ventricular enlargement in schizophrenia; in one-third of the reports, the ventricle size of schizophrenics did not differ from that of the control group. In those studies that reported positive findings, the prevalence of ventricular enlargement in schizophrenia ranged from 7% (Andreasen et al., 1982) to 94% (Johnstone et al., 1976). What could account for these variable findings?

A number of different procedural factors could explain, in part, these discrepant results. Variations in CT scanning techniques (e.g., thickness of slice, resolution of scanner) and in ventricular measurement (e.g., determining boundaries between ventricular space and brain tissue) can affect the size of the computed VBR (Jernigan et al., 1982; Maser & Keith, 1983). Because this type of variability should affect schizophrenic and control groups equally if uniform procedures are applied to all subjects in a study, it should not have a substantial influence on the likelihood of obtaining group differences. It does make it unwise to compare values between two studies. However, if a large number of investigations have been carried out, variability in VBRs resulting from methodological idiosyncrasies should be randomly distributed across reports, thereby making it possible to compare the results of groups of studies.

In the analysis that follows, the studies by Johnstone et al. (1976, 1978) are not included because these investigators did not employ the standard definition of

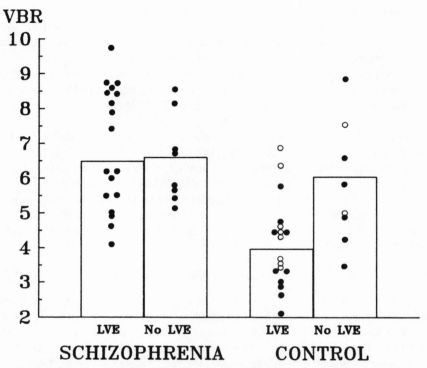

Figure 1. Mean (or median) ventricular brain ratios (VBR) for schizophrenic and control groups in investigations that reported lateral ventricular enlargement (LVE) and those that did not find enlargement (No LVE). For the control group plots, open and closed circles indicate normal and medical patient control groups, respectively.

VBR. Instead of using the single scan that displayed the lateral ventricles at their largest, they used two scans, one showing the anterior and posterior horns of the ventricles and the third ventricle, and the other the body of the ventricles. Apparently, the total area of these ventricular spaces was summed and divided by the brain area. Hence, the VBRs recorded by this research team are considerably larger than those reported by other investigators.

Figure 1 and Tables 3a and 3b expand on and update an earlier report by Smith and Iacono (1986) by summarizing the results of the CT studies of schizophrenia that used the VBR and a control group. The figure separates these studies into those that reported lateral ventricular enlargement in schizophrenia and those that did not. Portrayed in this fashion, it is obvious that the average VBR of schizophrenic patients across all these investigations is about the same. The mean VBR for schizophrenics in those studies that found and did not find enlargement is,

Table 3a. Nonpsychiatric Control Groups in Studies That Reported Lateral Ventricle Enlargement and Used the Ventricular Brain Ratio

Type of Control	Study	Description of Control Subjects
Medical	Andreasen et al. (1982)*	Patients referred "usually for headache" complaints
	Cazzullo et al. (1985)	Patients with "minor accidental head trauma"
	Kling et al. (1983)*	Patients with "reported head injury or vague complaints of headache or dizziness"
	Luchins et al. (1984)*	Patients with "complaints of tension or migraine headaches"
	Luchins & Meltzer (1986)*	Same as Luchins et al. (1984)
	Nasrallah et al. (1982)*	Patients evaluated for head trauma following a motor vehicle accident
	Obiols Llandrich et al. (1986)	Patients with a "history of nonspecific headaches, seizures, and other miscellaneous medical conditions"
	Schulz et al. (1983)	Patients with "nonspecific headaches, questionable seizures, or minor head trauma"
	Weinberger et al. (1982)	"Consecutive admissions to the neurology unit," mostly seizure patients and those with peripheral nervous system disorders
	Williams et al. (1985)*	Mostly headache, epilepsy, and head injury patients
Normal	DeLisi et al. (1986)	"Normal volunteers"
	Losonczy et al. (1986)	Subjects recruited by newspaper advertisements

*Indicates a study in which the CT scans from control subjects were described as being "normal."

Table 3a. Continued

Nonpsychiatric Control Groups in Studies That Reported Lateral Ventricle Enlargement and Used the Ventricular Brain Ratio

Type of Control	Study	Description of Control Subjects
Normal	Kemali et al. (1985)	Apparently normal, source of subjects not specified
	Pearlson et al. (1984)	Hospital employees and their relatives
	Reveley et al. (1982)	"Volunteer twins"
	Turner et al. (1986)	Hospital staff, "usually porters, secretaries, and nurses, but also some doctors and psychologists"
	Weinberger et al. (1979)	First-degree relatives of Huntington's disease patients who were asymptomatic plus normal volunteers

*Indicates a study in which the CT scans from control subjects were described as being "normal."

respectively, 6.7 (N = 662) and 6.6 (N = 213). However, the mean VBRs for the respective control groups is 4.0 (N = 539) and 6.0 (N = 205). One can use the means, standard deviations, and numbers of subjects reported in these studies to calculate t-statistics comparing values across studies. For two studies (Largen et al., 1984; Turner et al., 1986) that did not report standard deviations, these were estimated. The two schizophrenic means do not differ significantly from each other. This finding, although it does not rule out variability in ventricle size resulting from patient characteristics, does indicate that ventricle size in schizophrenics does not determine whether or not ventricular enlargement is detected. The mean values for control subjects, on the other hand, differ significantly from those reporting enlargement and those failing to find it ($p<.001$). The apparent conclusion that follows from this analysis is that the interpretation of obtained CT results depends on the size of the ventricles in control subjects but not in schizophrenic patients.

Are there features of the control subjects used in these studies that could explain why the control groups vary in ventricle size? Tables 3a and 3b briefly summarize the characteristics of the control subjects. The tables divide subjects into those drawn from medical populations and those that can be characterized as "normal" because they do not have any identified medical or psychiatric pathol-

Table 3b. Nonpsychiatric Control Groups in Studies That Did Not Report Lateral Ventricle Enlargement and Used the Ventricular Brain Ratio

Type of Control	Study	Description of Control Subjects
Medical	Benes et al. (1982)	Patients referred for headache and dizziness
	Boronow et al. (1985)*	Mostly cancer and headache patients
	DeMeyer et al. (1984)	"Chiefly headache" patients
	Largen et al. (1984)	Patients with headache complaints
	Smith et al. (1983)	Headache patients
Normal	Jernigan et al. (1982)	Mostly hospital staff and professional trainees
	Shima et al. (1985)	"38 healthy asymptomatic volunteers" and 8 headache patients

*Indicates a study in which the CT scans from control subjects were described as being "normal."

ogy. As can be seen in Figure 1, whether controls come from one or the other of these sources cannot explain the major finding of the preceding analysis. Medical patients in studies reporting ventricular enlargement had smaller VBRs (M = 3.8, N = 329) than the same subjects in studies with negative findings (M = 5.7, N = 126), $p<.001$. The same VBR pattern held for normal subjects in studies with positive (M = 4.4, N = 210) vs. negative (M = 6.5, N = 79) results, $p<.001$. Interestingly, medical patients across all studies combined generated smaller VBRs (M = 4.3, N=455) than did normal subjects (M = 5.3, N = 289), $p<.001$, a point to be considered further later.

As can be seen from Tables 3a and 3b, it is very difficult to uncover any other qualities of control groups that could account for the association between the size of the control group VBR and study outcome. This is in part because the control groups were not described in the published report in enough detail to provide the opportunity for a thorough analysis. One difference between studies with positive versus negative results is that for the medical patient groups, 6 out of 10 (60%) of the studies with positive outcomes reported that the CT scans of their medical patients were "normal." This same procedure was followed for only one of five (20%) of the medical patient groups in the reports that failed to uncover ventricular enlargement. This procedure could have the effect of removing from these samples medical patients with normal but unusually large ventricles, a practice that, because it was not followed with the schizophrenics, would tend to exaggerate group differences.

Another difference between the medical patient groups is that in those studies with negative outcomes, all the medical subjects are characterized primarily as headache sufferers. Although it is unclear what types of headaches these individuals had, vascular headaches have been associated with ventricular dilation, a factor that could cause these subjects to have larger than normal ventricles, thus minimizing schizophrenia–medical patient group differences. For the 10 studies with positive results, the same is true in at least four reports, with an additional three also using headache patients. However, five of these studies used accident victims. Because the edema following head trauma may decrease ventricular size, the use of accident victims may result in the inclusion of patients with atypically small ventricles, thus also exaggerating schizophrenic–control group differences. Unfortunately, in those studies with positive results, there is no indication from the mean VBRs reported for the medical patients that suspected head trauma cases have smaller VBRs than do headache patients. Both types of control group yield virtually identical VBRs on average.

The above explanations are obviously speculative, in part because the characteristics of medical patients included in each study are too often not specified in detail and in part because the procedures for selecting and reviewing CT scans for these groups are not described fully. For example, the proportions of different types of medical patients included in a control group are seldom given and authors that did not specifically state that they used only ''normal'' scans also did not state in their sparse subject descriptions that they did not follow this procedure. Moreover, these conjectures do not explain how using normal control subjects leads to the same result regarding the evaluation of studies with positive and negative outcomes. The fact remains, however, that the outcome of these studies seems to depend on qualities of the control groups, qualities that unfortunately cannot be identified from the inadequate characterizations investigators have provided for these subjects.

A CT Scan Study of Schizophrenia

The preceding section, although illustrating that control groups may influence the outcome of a CT scan study, is somewhat unsatisfactory because a convincing explanation of what it was about the control group that led to the calculation of an average VBR that was similar to or different from that of schizophrenic patients was lacking. Also absent was a direct demonstration that in a single study using two different control groups, the outcome of the study may differ depending upon which group the schizophrenic patients were compared to.

To address these issues, Geoffrey Smith, Margaret Moreau, Karen Tallman, Morton Beiser, Borys Flak, and I have conducted a preliminary analysis of lateral ventricular size in chronic schizophrenic patients, normal volunteers, and medical patients. Earlier I noted that our survey of the literature revealed that medical patients tend to have slightly smaller lateral ventricles than do normal subjects. Exactly why this may be so is not entirely clear, but medical patients are susceptible to pathological changes in ventricle size and to selection bias. Various physical disorders may result in increased (e.g., migraine headache, hydrocephalus) or decreased (e.g., edema, head trauma, vasospasms) ventricle size (Schneider et al., 1982). In addition, individual differences in normal brain morphology have not received systematic study, so precisely what falls within the bounds of normal variability may not be clear to radiologists who normally examine CT scans to detect neuropathology. Thus, an individual with normal but large ventricles who is suspected of having a physical condition, (e.g., migraine) associated with ventricular enlargement will be excluded from a medical patient control group. In addition, selection of only CT scans that are "normal" could lead to the systematic elimination of the individuals with normal but unusually large ventricles and the overinclusion of those with ventricles that are small because of their neuropathology.

Fourteen chronic schizophrenic male patients who were consenting consecutive admissions to a large chronic-care mental institution were examined. Subjects were diagnosed according to DSM-III criteria following a structured interview with the Present State Exam (Wing, Cooper, & Sartorius, 1974) and a thorough review of hospital charts. Ages ranged from 22 to 34 years (M = 28.3, SD = 4.0) and time spent in this institution ranged from 2 to 55 months (M = 30.9, SD = 19.0). None of the participants had a history of head trauma or a known neurological condition.

A normal control group of 27 healthy volunteer males was recruited from family practice clinics, employment centers, community centers, and a vocational institute. Ages ranged from 16 to 30 (M = 22.9, SD = 3.5 years). Individuals with psychiatric disorder, drug or alcohol abuse, or chronic medical illness in themselves were excluded as were those with first-degree relatives who had been treated for psychopathology.

The medical patients were 13 males who received a CT scan as part of a medical examination (ages ranged from 15 to 32, M = 22.9, SD = 5.5 years). All age-appropriate male medical patients who received a CT scan during a three-month period in which the schizophrenic and normal individuals were scanned were included. Reasons for referral for the CT scan were to investigate headaches (N = 5), rule out space occupying lesions (N = 5), rule out multiple sclerosis (N = 1), investigate intracerebral calcification (N = 1), and assess post-injury head trauma (N = 1). To be selected, the radiologist's report had to indicate no pathology. Interpretative comments indicating that the ventricles were unusually large for the subject's age did not disqualify a patient from inclusion in this group.

All scans were obtained using a third-generation, high resolution, total body scanner (Siemens Somatom DR2) that yielded cross-sections of the brain that were 8mm thick. VBRs were calculated without knowledge of the subjects' identity or group membership. The VBR was determined from the scan that showed the lateral ventricles at their largest using a precision polar compensating planimeter.

Pearson correlations between two independent raters indicated high interrater reliability for VBR computations ($r = .93$). As predicted, the VBR was greatest in the schizophrenic patients (M = 7.21, SD = 1.93), second greatest in the normal control subjects, (M = 6.32, SD = 2.36), with the medical patients having the smallest ventricles (M = 5.44, SD = 2.00). The difference between the schizophrenics and medical patients was significant, t(24) = 2.34, $p<.05$. However, there was no significant difference between the schizophrenic patients and normal controls, t(39) = 1.22.

These results support the contention that the choice of comparison group can influence the outcome of a CT scan study. They also suggest that the use of medical patients as control subjects is likely to exaggerate the estimated prevalence of ventricular enlargement in schizophrenia. Because only a small sample of schizophrenics was included in this preliminary study, it would be unfair to conclude from this one analysis that lateral ventricular enlargement does not exist in chronic schizophrenia because the schizophrenia-normal control comparison was not significant. However, the mean VBR that we found for our chronic schizophrenics (7.2) is similar to that reported in all CT scan studies of schizophrenia reported to date (M = 6.7, N = 875). Because this value is only slightly larger than the mean VBRs reported for either control group, the present results suggest that ventricular dilation is minimal in schizophrenia and likely to go unnoticed unless large patient and control samples are used.

Conclusions and Recommendations

To a certain extent, I have felt very awkward writing this chapter because every psychopathology researcher knows that control group selection is an integral aspect of the research enterprise. Thus, my thesis seems both obvious and trivial. However, I have endeavored to show that the selection of comparison subjects is not always executed thoughtfully (or if it is, this is not apparent in most research reports). If current publication practices tell us anything, control group selection is not viewed as important by many authors and journal editors. We now have very specific operational criteria to define schizophrenia and they were employed in 94% of recently surveyed studies of schizophrenia in four of our best journals. It is ironic that we can now define schizophrenia with some precision but that we cannot describe our control groups with comparable precision. This same survey also revealed that the source of control subjects is unknown in 40% of these reports and that in only a third is the source of the controls described well enough to provide the reader with the information needed to create a comparable group.

I have also attempted to demonstrate, by drawing on the CT scan literature, that the choice of comparison subjects can be a primary determinant of the outcome of psychopathology research. It is my belief that in many other types of psychopathology research the role of the control group is equally critical. The CT scan literature was chosen only to illustrate a point, and because the number of studies using similar procedures was substantial enough to justify the type of analysis presented.

Journal editors, reviewers, and authors must give more attention to control subject selection and description. These research participants should be characterized with the same attention to detail devoted to the psychopathology groups. The source from which nonpsychiatric subjects are drawn should be specified and the rationale for using the source should be given. To the extent that the source was simply one of convenience (which is probably why university students and professional staff are so frequently used), authors should consider in their papers what the consequences of using such a group might be to the interpretation of their results. If control subjects are to be characterized as *normal*, authors should be required to document that they have been screened for psychopathology in some way.

My only innovative recommendation is that investigators be encouraged to use more than one control group source in their studies. These multiple groups can then be compared to each other as well as to the psychiatric patients. If the various groups generate similar values on the dependent measures, the generality of the study's results will be greatly strengthened. If they do not generate similar values, then the ways in which the controls differ from each other (and are like the patients) will provide insight into how various factors affect the dependent variable and which control source is most appropriate. If having multiple comparison groups seems too radical a departure from currently accepted practices, then a single control group can be divided into subgroups (e.g., high vs. low SES, professional vs. nonprofessional staff) and the same procedures followed. Following this recommendation also provides a partial solution to the nuisance variable problems raised by Meehl. With the use of at least two control groups, the nuisance variable question becomes not whether patients and controls should be matched, but how to sensibly interpret data from control groups that are similar to and different from the patients in various ways.

References

Andreasen, N. C., Olsen, S. A., Dennert, J. V., & Smith, M. R. (1982). Ventricular enlargement in schizophrenia: Relationship to positive and negative symptoms. *American Journal of Psychiatry, 139*, 297–302.

Andreasen, N. C., Smith, M. R., Jacoby, C. G. Dennert, J. V., & Olson, S. A. (1982). Ventricular enlargement in schizophrenia: Definition and prevalence. *American Journal of Psychiatry, 139*, 292–296.

Benes, F., Pearson, S., Jones, B. D., LeMay, M., Cohen, B. M., & Lipinski, J. F. (1982). Normal ventricles in young schizophrenics. *British Journal of Psychiatry, 141*, 90–93.

Bernstein, A. S., et al. (1981). Bilateral skin conductance, finger pulse volume, and EEG orienting response to tones of differing intensities in chronic schizophrenics and controls. *Journal of Nervous and Mental Disease, 169*, 513–528.

Boronow, J., Pikar, D., Ninan, P. T., Roy, A., Hommer, D., Linnoila, M., & Paul, S. M. (1985). Atrophy limited to the third ventricle in chronic schizophrenic patients: Report of a controlled series. *Archives of General Psychiatry, 42*, 266–270.

Cazzullo, C. L., Sacchetti, E., Vita, A., Illeni, M. T., Bellodi, L., Maffei, C., Alciati, A., Bertrando, P., Calzeroni, A., Ciussani, S., Conte, G., Pennati, A., & Invernizzi, G. (1985). Cerebral ventricular size in schizophrenic spectrum disorders: Relationship to clinical neuropsychological, and immunogenetic variables. In C. Shaggass, R. C., Josiassen, W. H. Bridger, K. J. Weis, D. Stuff, & G. M. Simpson, (Eds.), *Biological Psychiatry*. New York: Elsevier Science Publishing.

DeLisi, L. E., Goldin, L. R., Hamovet, J. R., Maxwell, M. E., Kurtz, D., & Gershon, E. S. (1986). A family study of the association of increased ventricular size with schizophrenia. *Archives of General Psychiatry, 43*, 148–153.

DeMeyer, M. K., Gilmor, R., DeMeyer, W. E., Hendrie, H., Edwards, M., & Franco, J. N. (1984). Third ventricle size and ventricular brain ratio in treatment-resistant psychiatric patients. *Journal of Operational Psychiatry, 15*, 2–8.

Depue, R. A., & Iacono, W. G. Neurobehavioral aspects of affective disorders. *Annual Reivew of Psychology, 40*, 457–492.

Grove, W. M., Andreasen, N. C., McDonald-Scott, P., Keller, M., & Shapiro, R. W. (1981). Reliability studies of psychiatric diagnosis: Theory and practice. *Archives of General Psychiatry, 38*, 408–416.

Gruzelier, J., Eves, F., Connolly, J., & Hirsch, S. (1981). Orienting, habituation, sensitization, and dishabituation in the electrodermal system of consecutive, drug free, admissions for schizophrenia. *Biological Psychology, 12*, 187–209.

Gruzelier, J. H., & Venables, P. H. (1972). Skin conductance orienting activity in a heterogeneous sample of schizophrenics: Possible evidence of limbic dysfunction. *Journal of Nervous and Mental Disease, 155*, 277–287.

Iacono, W. G. (1982). Bilateral electrodermal habituation-dishabituation and resting EEG in remitted schizophrenics. *Journal of Nervous and Mental Disease, 170*, 91–101.

Iacono, W. G., et al. (1983). Electrodermal activity in euthymic unipolar and bipolar affective disorder: A possible marker for depression. *Archives of General Psychiatry, 40*, 557–565.

Iacono, W. G., Smith, G. N., Moreau, M., Beiser, M., Fleming, J. A. E., Lin, T-Y., & Flak, B. (1988). Ventricular and sulcal size at the onset of psychosis. *American Journal of Psychiatry, 145*, 820–824.

Jernigan, T. L., Zatz, L. M., Moses, J. A., & Berger, P. A. (1982). Computed tomography in schizophrenics and normal volunteers: Fluid volume. *Archives of General Psychiatry, 39*, 765–770.

Johnstone, E. C., Crow, T. J., Frith, C.D., Husband, J., & Kreel, L. (1976). Cerebral ventricular size and cognitive impairment in chronic schizophrenia, *Lancet, 2*, 924–926.

Johnstone, E. C., Crow, T. J., Frith, C.D., Stevens, M., Kreel, L., & Husband, J. (1978). The dementia of dementia praecox. *Acta Psychiatrica Scandinavica, 57*, 305–324.

Kemali, D., Maj, M., Galderisi, S., Ariano, M. G., Cesarelli, M., Milici, N., Salvati, A., Valente, A., & Volpe, M. (1985). Clinical and neuropsychological correlates of cerebral ventricular enlargement in schizophrenia. *Journal of Psychiatric Research, 19,* 587–596.

Kling, A. S., Kurtz, N. K., Tachiki, K., & Orzeck, A. (1982–83). CT scans in subgroups of chronic schizophrenics. *Journal of Psychiatric Research, 17,* 375–384.

Largen, J. W., Smith, R. C., Calderon, M., Baumgartner, R., Lu, R., Schoolar, J. C., & Ravichandran, G. K. (1984). Abnormalities of brain structure and density in schizophrenia. *Biological Psychiatry, 19,* 991–1013.

Losonczy, M. F., Song, I. S., Mohs, R. C., Small, N. A., Davidson, M., Johns, C. A., & Davis, K. L. (1986). Correlates of lateral ventricular size in chronic schizophrenia. I: Behavioral and treatment response measures. *American Journal of Psychiatry, 143,* 976–981.

Luchins, D. J., Lewine, R. R. J., & Meltzer, H. Y. (1984). Lateral ventricular size, psychopathology and medication response in the psychoses. *Biological Psychiatry, 19,* 29–44.

Luchins, D. J., & Meltzer, H. Y. (1986). A comparison of CT findings in acute and chronic ward schizophrenics. *Psychiatry Research, 17,* 7–14.

Maser, J. D., & Keith, S. J. (1983). CT scans and schizophrenia: Report on a workshop. *Schizophrenia Bulletin, 9,* 265–283.

Meehl, P. E. (1970). Nuisance variables and the ex post facto design. In M. Radner & S. Winokur (Eds.), *Minnesota studies in the philosophy of science,* IV (pp. 373–402). Minneapolis: University of Minnesota Press.

Meehl, P. E. (1971). High school yearbooks: A reply to Schwarz. *Journal of Abnormal Psychology, 77,* 143–148.

Meehl, P. E. (1973). MAXCOV-HITMAX: A taxonomic search method for loose genetic syndromes. In P. E. Meehl, *Psychodiagnosis: Selected papers.* Minneapolis: University of Minnesota Press.

Nasrallah, H. A., Jacoby, C. G., McCalley-Whitters, M., & Kuperman, S. (1982). Cerebral ventricular enlargement in subtypes of chronic schizophrenia. *Archives of General Psychiatry, 39,* 774–777.

Obiols Llandrich, J. E., Ruscalleda, J., & Masferrer, M. (1986). Ventricular enlargement in young chronic schizophrenics. *Acta Psychiatrica Scandinavica, 73,* 42–44.

Pandurangi, A. K., Dewan, M. J., Lee, S. H., Ramachandran, T., Levy, B. F., Boucher, M., Yozawitz, A., & Major, L. (1984). The ventricular system in chronic schizophrenic patients: A controlled computed tomography study. *British Journal of Psychiatry, 144,* 172–176.

Patterson, T. (1976). Skin conductance responding/nonresponding and pupillometries in chronic schizophrenia: A confirmation of Gruzelier and Venables. *Journal of Nervous and Mental Disease, 163,* 200–209.

Patterson, T., & Venables, P. H. (1978). Bilateral skin conductance and skin potential in schizophrenic and normal subjects: The identification of the fast habituator group of schizophrenics. *Psychophysiology, 15,* 556–560.

Pearlson, G. D., Garbacz, D. J., Breakey, W. R., Ahn, H. S., & DePaulo, J. R. (1984). Lateral ventricular enlargement associated with persistent unemployment and negative symptoms in both schizophrenia and bipolar disorder. *Psychiatry Research, 12,* 1–9.

Penn, R. D., Belanger, M. G., & Yasnoff, W. A. (1978). Ventricular volume in man computed from CAT scans. *Annals of Neurology, 3,* 216–223.

Reveley, A. M., Reveley, M. A., Clifford, C. A., & Murray, R. M. (1982). Cerebral ventricular size in twins discordant of schizophrenia, *Lancet, i,* 540–541.

Robins, L. N., et al. (1984). Lifetime prevalence of specific psychiatric disorders in three sites. *Archives of General Psychiatry, 41,* 949–958.

Schneider, R. C., Kahn, E. A., Crosby, E. C., & Taren, J. A. (Eds.). (1982). *Correlative neurosurgery* (3rd Ed.). Springfield, IL: Charles C Thomas.

Schulsinger, F., Parnas, J., Petersen, E. T., Schulsinger, H., Teasdale, T. W., Mednick, S. A., Moller, L., & Silverton, L. (1984). Cerebral ventricular size in the offspring of schizophrenic mothers: A preliminary study. *Archives of General Psychiatry, 41*, 602–606.

Schulz, S. C., Koller, M. M., Kishore, P. R., Hamer, R. M., Gehl, J. J., & Friedel, R. O. (1983). Ventricular enlargement in teenage patients with schizophrenia spectrum disorder. *American Journal of Psychiatry, 140*, 1592–1595.

Shima, S., Kanba, S., Masuda, Y., Tsukumo, T., Kitamura, T., & Asai, M. (1985). Normal ventricles in chronic schizophrenics. *Acta Psychiatrica Scandinavica, 71*, 25–29.

Smith, G. N., & Iacono, W. G. (1986). Lateral ventricular size in schizophrenia and choice of control group. *Lancet, i*, 1450.

Smith, G. N., & Iacono, W. G. (1988). Ventricular size in schizophrenia: Importance of choice of control subjects. *Psychiatry Research, 26*, 241–243.

Smith, G. N., Iacono, W. G., Moreau, M., Tallman, K., Beiser, M., & Flak, B. (1988). Choice of comparison group and computerized tomography findings in schizophrenia. *British Journal of Psychiatry, 153*, 667–674.

Smith, R. C., Largen, J., Calderon, M., Schoolar, J., Shvartsburd, M. S., & Ravichandran, G. K. (1983). CT scans and neuropsychological tests as predictors of clinical response in schizophrenics. *Psychopharmacology Bulletin, 19*, 505–509.

Straube, E. R. (1979). On the meaning of electrodermal nonresponding in schizophrenia. *Journal of Nervous and Mental Disease, 167*, 601–611.

Synek, V., & Reuben, J. R. (1976). The ventricular-brain ratio using planimetric measurement of EMI scans. *British Journal of Radiology, 49*, 233–237.

Turner, S. W., Toone, B. K., & Brett-Jones, J. R. (1986). Computerized tomographic scan changes in early schizophrenia—preliminary findings. *Psychological Medicine, 16*, 219–225.

Weinberger, D. R., DeLisi, L. E., Perman, G. P., Targum, S., & Wyatt, R. J. (1982). Computed tomography in schizophreniform disorder and other acute psychiatric disorders. *Archives of General Psychiatry, 39*, 778–783.

Weinberger, D. R., Torrey, E. F., Neophytides, A. N., & Wyatt, R. J. (1979). Lateral cerebral new enlargement in chronic schizophrenia. *Archives of General Psychiatry, 36*, 736–739(a).

Williams, A. O., Reveley, M. A., Kolakovska, T., Arden, M., & Mandelbrote, B. M. (1985). Schizophrenia with good and poor outcome. II. Cerebral ventricular size and its clinical significance. *British Journal of Psychiatry, 146*, 239–246.

Wing, J. K., Cooper, J. E., & Sartorius, N. (1974). *The measurement and classification of psychiatric symptoms*. London: Cambridge University Press.

Zatz, L. M. & Jernigan, T. L. (1983). The ventricular brain ratio on computed tomography scans: Validity and proper use. *Psychiatry Research, 8*, 207–214.

Contributors

Douglas Barnett, psychologist, Mt. Hope Family Center, University of Rochester.

Paul H. Blaney, professor, Department of Psychology, University of Miami, Coral Gables.

Thomas J. Bouchard, Jr., director, Minnesota Center for Twin and Adoption Research; chairman, Department of Psychology, University of Minnesota.

David M. Buss, associate professor, Department of Psychology, University of Michigan, Ann Arbor.

Dante Cicchetti, professor, Departments of Psychology and Psychiatry; director, Mt. Hope Family Center, University of Rochester.

Richard S. Feldman, research scientist, Department of Psychiatry, New York State Psychiatric Institute and Columbia University.

Judy Garber, assistant professor, Department of Psychology and Human Development, Vanderbilt University.

Robert R. Golden, director, Division of Neurostatistics and Neuroepidemiology, Department of Neurology and Rose F. Kennedy Center for Research in Human Development and Mental Retardation, Albert Einstein College of Medicine.

I. I. Gottesman, professor, Department of Psychology, University of Virginia.

Harrison G. Gough, professor emeritus, Department of Psychology, University of California at Berkeley.

William M. Grove, assistant professor, Department of Psychology, University of Minnesota.

Leonard L. Heston, M.D., director, The Washington Institute for Mental Illness Research and Training; professor, Department of Psychiatry, University of Washington.

Lloyd G. Humphreys, professor, Department of Psychology, University of Illinois.

William G. Iacono, professor, Department of Psychology, University of Minnesota.

Jane Loevinger, Stuckenberg Professor of Human Values, Emerita, Department of Psychology, Washington University, St. Louis.

Brendan A. Maher, Edward C. Henderson Professor of the Psychology of Personality, Department of Psychology; dean, Graduate School of Arts and Sciences, Harvard University.

Carl P. Malmquist, professor of social psychiatry, Department of Sociology, University of Minnesota.

M. McGue, associate professor, Department of Psychology, University of Minnesota.

Suzanne Salzinger, research scientist, Department of Psychiatry, New York State Psychiatric Institute and Columbia University.

B. F. Skinner, formerly professor emeritus, Department of Psychology, Harvard University. Now deceased.

Zvi Strassberg, graduate fellow, Department of Psychology and Human Development, Vanderbilt University.

Auke Tellegen, professor, Department of Psychology, University of Minnesota.

George S. Welsh, professor emeritus, Department of Psychology, University of North Carolina at Chapel Hill.

Jerry S. Wiggins, professor, Department of Psychology, University of British Columbia.

Joseph Zubin, Distinguished Research Professor of Psychiatry, School of Medicine, University of Pittsburgh; professor emeritus of psychology and special lecturer in psychiatry, Department of Psychology and College of Physicians and Surgeons, Columbia University. Research Career Scientist, VA Medical Center, Highland Drive, Pittsburgh.

Index

Dr. William M. Grove is assistant professor in the Department of Psychology at the University of Minnesota and was previously a researcher at the University of Iowa. He obtained his doctoral degree under Paul Meehl. Grove is the author of publications on the diagnosis, classification, and genetics of mental illness.

Dr. Dante Cicchetti is professor in the departments of Psychology and Psychiatry at the University of Rochester and director of the Mt. Hope Family Center, University of Rochester. He obtained his doctoral degree in clinical and developmental psychology under Paul Meehl. Currently, Cicchetti's theoretical and research interests are focused on the area of developmental psychopathology. He is the author of numerous articles and books on normal and abnormal development.